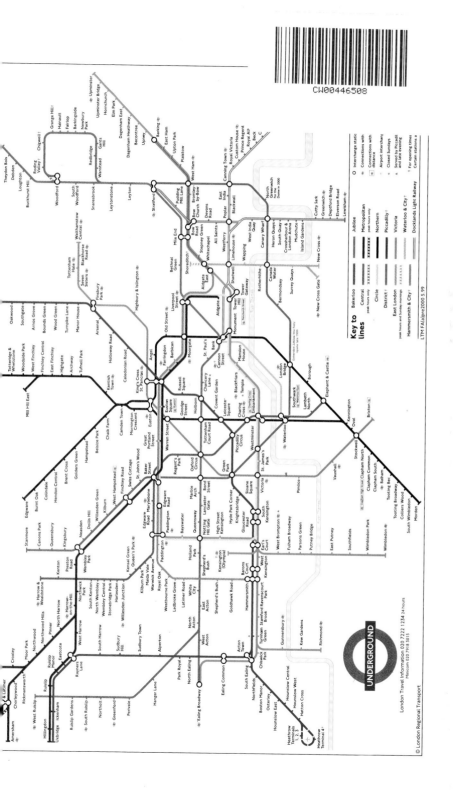

London
Regent's Park
Inner Circle
Outer Circle
Chester Rd.
Albany St.
Hampstead Rd.
Euston Rd.
Park Rd.
Marylebone Rd.
Devonshire St.
Cleveland St.
Portland Pl.
Gt. Portland St.
Harley St.
Marylebone High St.
Baker St.
Gloucester Pl.
Upper Montague St.
Seymour Pl.
Crawford St.
Edgware Rd.
Lisson Grove
St. John's Wood Rd.
Wellington Rd.
Prince Albert Rd.
Circus Rd.
Grove End Rd.
Abbey Rd.
Abercorn Pl.
Maida Vale
Hall Rd.
Clifton Rd.
Bloomfield Rd.
Harrow Rd.
Marylebone Flyover
Bishop's Bridge Rd.
Paddington Station
Praed St.
Sussex Gdns.
Queensway
Craven Hill
Bayswater Rd.
N. Carriage Dr.
Marble Arch
Oxford St.
Manchester Square
Wigmore St.
Duke St.
Oxford Circus
Oxford
Berners St.
Bond St.
Brook St.
Grosvenor Square
Grosvenor St.
Regent St.
Speaker's Corner
U.S. Embassy
Berkeley Square
Park Lane
Sth. Audley St.
Curzon St.
Jermyn St.
Hyde Park
Kensington Gardens
Dr.
The Serpentine
W. Carriage
Kensington Palace
Piccadilly
St. James's Palace
Green Park
Hyde Park Corner
St. James Park
Constitution Hill
S. Carriage Rd.
Knightsbridge
Kensington Rd.
Kensington Gore
Royal Albert Hall
Prince Consort Rd.
Exhibition Rd.
Victoria & Albert Museum
Palace Gate
Gloucester Rd.
Queen's Gate
Sloane St.
Basil St.
Brompton Rd.
Pavilion Rd.
Cadogan Pl.
Pont St.
Grosvenor Pl.
Belgrave Square
Eaton Square
Buckingham Palace Rd.
Victoria Station
Wilton Rd.
Coach Station
Warwick Way
Cromwell Rd.
Natural History Museum
Walton St.
Draycott Ave.
Sloane Ave.
Ixworth Pl.
Sloane Sq.
Old Brompton Rd.
Cale St.
Pimlico Rd.
Chelsea Br. Rd.
Ebury Br. Rd.
Sutherland St.
Lupus St.
Sydney St.
Old Church St.
King's Rd.
Flood St.
Royal Hospital Rd.
Royal Hospital
Grosvenor Rd.
Redcliffe Gdns.
Finborough Rd.
Fulham Rd.
Oakley St.
Carlyle's House
Cheyne Walk
Chelsea Embankment
Chelsea Br.
Beaufort St.
Albert Br.
River Thames
Battersea Park

King's Cross Station

Pentonville Rd.

City Rd.

t. Pancras Station

King's Cross Rd.

Gray's Inn Rd.

Judd St.

Rosebery Ave.

St. John's St.

Goswell Rd.

Lever St.

Bath St.

East Road

Hoxton St.

Old St.

Kingsland Rd.

Gt. Eastern St.

Shoreditch High St.

Commercial St.

Coram's Fields

Woburn Pl.

Southampton Row

Guilford St.

Theobalds Rd.

Farringdon Rd.

Clerkenwell Rd.

Aldersgate

City Rd.

Barbican Centre

Moorgate

Liverpool St. Station

Bishopsgate

Houndsditch

sh m

Charterhouse St.

Smithfield Market

London Wall

New xford St.

Holborn

High

Kingsway

Chancery La.

Fetter La.

Holborn Viaduct

Old Bailey

Newgate St.

St. Paul's

Cheapside

Bank of England

Cornhill

Leadenhall St.

Gracechurch St.

Fenchurch St.

Drury La.

Aldwych

Law Courts

Fleet St.

Queen Victoria St.

Cannon St.

Eastcheap

The Tower

Tower Hill

Cross Rd.

Strand

Victoria Embankment

Blackfriars Br.

Blackfriars Station

Southwark Br.

Cannon St. Station

London Br.

Upper Thames St.

National Gallery

Charing Cross Stn.

ar re

Whitehall

Waterloo Br.

National Theatre

Stamford St.

Royal Festival Hall

York Rd.

The Cut

Blackfriars Rd.

Southwark St.

Union St.

River Thames

Tooley St.

St. Thomas St.

London Bridge Station

Tower Bridge Rd.

Abbey St.

Westminster Br.

Houses of Parliament

Millbank

Lambeth Palace Rd.

Waterloo Station

Westminster Br. Rd.

Lambeth Rd.

London Rd.

Borough Rd.

Borough High St.

Long La.

Great Dover St.

Harper Rd.

Tabard St.

Tower Bridge Rd.

ferry Rd.

Lambeth Br.

Imperial War Museum

Kennington Rd.

Crampton St.

New Kent Rd.

Willow Walk

ate llery

Albert Embankment

Black Prince Rd.

Kennington Park Rd.

Manor Pl.

Walworth Rd.

Rodney Pl.

Flint St.

East St.

Portland St.

Thurlow St.

Old Kent Rd.

Vauxhall Br.

Kennington La.

Braganza St.

Albany Rd.

Vauxhall Station

Kennington Oval

N

0   1/2 mile

0   1/2 kilometer

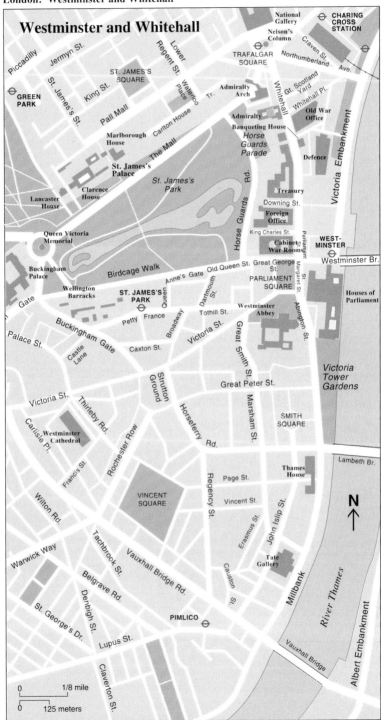

Westminster and Whitehall

National Gallery
CHARING CROSS STATION
Nelson's Column
Craven St.
TRAFALGAR SQUARE
Northumberland Ave.
Piccadilly
Jermyn St.
Lower Regent St.
St. James's St.
King St.
ST. JAMES'S SQUARE
Waterloo Place
Tr.
Admiralty Arch
Whitehall
Gt. Scotland Yard
Whitehall Pl.
GREEN PARK
Pall Mall
Carlton House
Admiralty
Banqueting House
Old War Office
Marlborough House
The Mall
Horse Guards Parade
Defence
St. James's Palace
St. James's Park
Horse Guards Rd.
Treasury
Lancaster House
Clarence House
Downing St.
Foreign Office
King Charles St.
Victoria Embankment
Queen Victoria Memorial
Cabinet War Rooms
Parliament St.
WEST-MINSTER
Westminster Br.
Buckingham Palace
Birdcage Walk
Anne's Gate
Old Queen St.
Great George St.
Margaret St.
Gate
Wellington Barracks
ST. JAMES'S PARK
Queen
Dartmouth St.
Broadway
PARLIAMENT SQUARE
Houses of Parliament
Palace St.
Buckingham Gate
Petty France
Caxton St.
Tothill St.
Victoria St.
Westminster Abbey
Abingdon St.
Castle Lane
Strutton Ground
Great Smith St.
Great Peter St.
Victoria Tower Gardens
Victoria St.
Thirleby Rd.
Horseferry Rd.
Marsham St.
SMITH SQUARE
Carlisle Pl.
Westminster Cathedral
Rochester Row
Lambeth Br.
Francis St.
Page St.
Thames House
Wilton Rd.
VINCENT SQUARE
Regency St.
Vincent St.
Erasmus St.
John Islip St.
Warwick Way
Tachbrook St.
Vauxhall Bridge Rd.
Causton St.
Tate Gallery
Millbank
River Thames
St. George's Dr.
Belgrave Rd.
Denbigh St.
PIMLICO
Lupus St.
Vauxhall Bridge
Albert Embankment
Claverton St.

N

0   1/8 mile
0   125 meters

London: Soho and Covent Garden

Soho and Covent Garden

N

Scale: 0 — 1/8 mile; 0 — 125 meters

HOLBORN
Lincoln's Inn Fields
Kingsway
Southampton Row
Newton St.
BLOOMSBURY SQUARE
Bloomsbury Way
High Holborn
Parker St.
Great Queen St.
Drury Lane
Bow St.
Russell St.
ALDWYCH
Aldwych
Lancaster Pl.
Waterloo Br.
Catherine St.
Wellington St.
Theatre Museum
London Transport Museum
Savoy St.
Cleopatra's Needle
Savoy Hotel
Embankment
Victoria
Floral Hall
COVENT GARDEN
Royal Opera
Floral Pl.
Southampton St.
The Strand
Charing Cross Station
Charing Cross
Bloomsbury St.
Great Russell St.
New Oxford St.
Short's Gardens
Endell St.
Shelton St.
Long Acre
Neal St.
Earlham St.
Langley St.
King St.
St. Paul's Covent Garden
Henrietta St.
Maiden La.
Chandos Pl.
William IV St.
St. Martin-in-the-Fields
St.Martins La.
Bedfordbury
New Row
Garrick St.
National Jazz Center
Monmouth St.
LEICESTER SQUARE
St. Giles St.
High St.
Shaftesbury Ave.
CAMBRIDGE CIRCUS
Charing Cross Rd.
Cranbourne St.
Irving St.
Orange St.
National Gallery
TOTTENHAM COURT RD.
Tottenham Court Rd.
Sutton Row
St. Barnabas in Soho
SOHO SQUARE
Manette St.
Greek St.
Frith St.
Old Compton St.
Shaftesbury Ave.
CHINATOWN
Gerrard St.
Lisle St.
LEICESTER SQUARE
St. Martin's St.
Whitcomb St.
Rathbone Pl.
Charles II Statue
Bateman St.
Dean St.
St. Anne's
Windmill St.
Coventry St.
Haymarket
Newman St.
Great Chapel St.
Carlisle St.
Wardour St.
Berwick St.
Noel St.
Lexington St.
Glasshouse St.
PICCADILLY CIRCUS
Regent St.
Jermyn St.
Berners St.
Oxford St.
Poland St.
SOHO
Marshall St.
Broadwick St.
Brewer St.
Beak St.
GOLDEN SQUARE
Piccadilly
Eastcastle St.
Great Marlborough St.
Carnaby St.
Albemarle St.
Dover St.
Burlington Gardens
Royal Academy
Margaret St.
Argyll St.
OXFORD CIRCUS
Regent St.
Savile Row
Clifford St.
Old Bond St.
Berkeley St.
CAVENDISH SQUARE
HANOVER SQUARE
St. George St.
New Bond St.
BERKELEY SQUARE

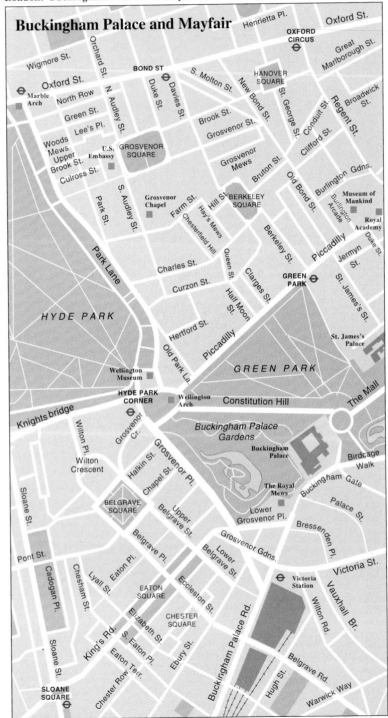

Buckingham Palace and Mayfair

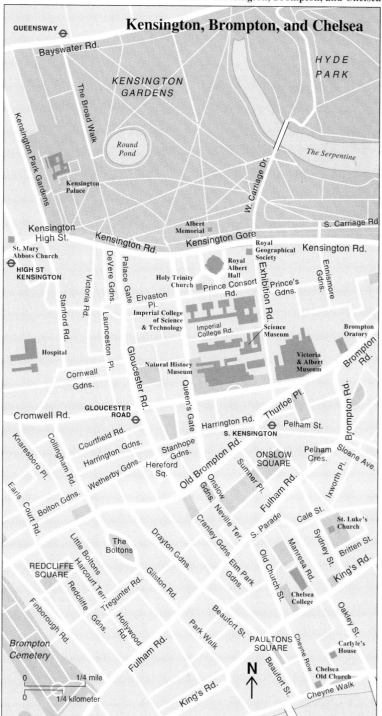

Kensington, Brompton, and Chelsea

QUEENSWAY

Bayswater Rd.

KENSINGTON GARDENS

HYDE PARK

The Broad Walk

Kensington Park Gardens

Round Pond

The Serpentine

W. Carriage Dr.

Kensington Palace

S. Carriage Rd.

Kensington High St.

Albert Memorial

Kensington Gore

Kensington Rd.

St. Mary Abbots Church

Kensington Rd.

HIGH ST KENSINGTON

Royal Geographical Society

DeVere Gdns.

Palace Gate

Royal Albert Hall

Exhibition Rd.

Prince's Gdns.

Ennismore Gdns.

Stanford Rd.

Victoria Rd.

Holy Trinity Church

Prince Consort Rd.

Elvaston Pl.

Imperial College of Science & Technology

Imperial College Rd.

Science Museum

Brompton Oratory

Launceston Pl.

Hospital

Gloucester Rd.

Natural History Museum

Victoria & Albert Museum

Brompton Rd.

Cornwall Gdns.

Queen's Gate

Thurloe Pl.

Cromwell Rd.

GLOUCESTER ROAD

Harrington Rd.

Pelham St.

Brompton Rd.

Collingham Rd.

Courtfield Rd.

S. KENSINGTON

Pelham Cres.

Knaresboro Pl.

Harrington Gdns.

Stanhope Gdns.

ONSLOW SQUARE

Sloane Ave.

Earls Court Rd.

Wetherby Gdns.

Hereford Sq.

Old Brompton Rd.

Onslow Gdns.

Sumner Pl.

Fulham Rd.

Ixworth Pl.

Bolton Gdns.

Cranley Gdns.

Neville Ter.

Elm Park Gdns.

S. Parade

Cale St.

Pelham

St. Luke's Church

Little Boltons

Drayton Gdns.

The Boltons

Marresa Rd.

Sydney St.

Britten St.

REDCLIFFE SQUARE

Harcourt Terr.

Tregunter Rd.

Gilston Rd.

Old Church St.

King's Rd.

Finborough Rd.

Redcliffe Gdns.

Hollywood Rd.

Fulham Rd.

Beaufort St.

Park Walk

Chelsea College

Oakley St.

Brompton Cemetery

PAULTONS SQUARE

Cheyne Row

Carlyle's House

0   1/4 mile

N

Beaufort St.

Chelsea Old Church

0   1/4 kilometer

King's Rd.

Cheyne Walk

The City

Leman St.

Commercial St.

ALDGATE EAST

Mansell St.

Royal Mint St.

E. Smithfield

St. Katharine's Way

Tower Br. Approach

Tower Br.

Middlesex St.

Widegate St.

Minories

ALDGATE

Aldgate

Fenchurch St. Station

Pepys St.

TOWER HILL

TRINITY SQUARE

Tower Hill

The Tower

All Hallows

Tower Pier

Houndsditch

Liverpool St. Station

St. Mary Axe

Leadenhall St.

Fenchurch St.

Lloyd's

St. Olave's

Seething La.

Mark La.

Mincing La.

St. Dunstan's

Gt. Tower St.

Lower Thames St.

HMS Belfast

Bishopsgate

Old Broad St.

London Stock Exchange

Threadneedle St.

Leadenhall St.

Leadenhall Market

Lime St.

Gracechurch St.

St. Mary at Hill

Billingsgate Market

Sun St.

South Pl.

MOORGATE

FINSBURY CIRCUS

London Wall

Moorgate

Throgmorton Ave.

St. Margaret's

Lothbury St.

Bank of England

BANK

Cornhill

Lombard St.

King William St.

Eastcheap

The Monument

Monument St.

St. Magnus Martyr

MONUMENT

London Br.

Ropemaker St.

Chiswell St.

Moorfields

Coleman St.

Basinghall Ave.

Princes St.

St. Mary Abchurch

St. Mary Woolbrook

Southwark Br.

Silk St.

Fore St.

Basinghall St.

Guildhall

King St.

Mansion House

Poultry

St. Stephen Walbrook

Temple of Mithras

Cloak La.

CANNON

Cannon St. Station

Beech St.

London Wall

Wood St.

Gresham St.

Milk St.

St. Mary le Bow

Watling St.

St. Mary Aldermary

MANSION HOUSE

Queen St.

Cannon St.

Upper Thames St.

Barbican Centre

St. Giles without Cripplegate

Museum of London

Cheapside

Bread St.

New Chance

Cannon St.

Queen Victoria St.

River Thames

Aldersgate St.

St. Bartholomew the Great

Little Britain

St. Martin's-Le-Grand

Newgate St.

ST. PAUL'S

St. Paul's Cathedral

St. Andrew-by-the-Wardrobe

St. Benet's

St. Mary

Puddle Dock

Blackfriars Station

BARBICAN

Long Lane

West Smithfield

Giltspur St.

Old Bailey

Warwick La.

Ludgate Hill

St. John St.

Smithfield Market

Snow Hill

Holborn Viaduct Station

Fleet La.

Holborn Viaduct

LUDGATE CIRCUS

New Bridge St.

BLACKFRIARS

Blackfriars Br.

FARRINGDON

Cowcross St.

Farringdon Rd.

Shoe Lane

St. Bride St.

GOUGH SQ.

Fleet St.

Tudor St.

Temple Ave.

Blackfriars Br.

Clerkenwell Rd.

Farringdon Rd.

Ely Pl.

Greville St.

Hatton Garden

New Fetter La.

Fetter La.

Temple Church

Middle Temple La.

The Temple

Victoria Embankment

1/4 mile

1/4 km

N

0

◤ Let's Go writers travel on your budget.

"Guides that penetrate the veneer of the holiday brochures and mine the grit of real life."

—*The Economist*

"The writers seem to have experienced every rooster-packed bus and lunar-surfaced mattress about which they write."

—*The New York Times*

"All the dirt, dirt cheap."

—*People*

◤ Great for independent travelers.

"The guides are aimed not only at young budget travelers but at the independent traveler; a sort of streetwise cookbook for traveling alone."

—*The New York Times*

"Flush with candor and irreverence, chock full of budget travel advice."

—*The Des Moines Register*

"An indispensible resource, *Let's Go*'s practical information can be used by every traveler."

—*The Chattanooga Free Press*

◤ Let's Go is completely revised each year.

"Only *Let's Go* has the zeal to annually update every title on its list."

—*The Boston Globe*

"Unbeatable: good sightseeing advice; up-to-date info on restaurants, hotels, and inns; a commitment to money-saving travel; and a wry style that brightens nearly every page."

—*The Washington Post*

◤ All the important information you need.

"*Let's Go* authors provide a comedic element while still providing concise information and thorough coverage of the country. Anything you need to know about budget traveling is detailed in this book."

—*The Chicago Sun-Times*

"Value-packed, unbeatable, accurate, and comprehensive."

—*Los Angeles Times*

Let's Go Publications

Let's Go: Alaska & the Pacific Northwest 2001
Let's Go: Australia 2001
Let's Go: Austria & Switzerland 2001
Let's Go: Boston 2001 **New Title!**
Let's Go: Britain & Ireland 2001
Let's Go: California 2001
Let's Go: Central America 2001
Let's Go: China 2001
Let's Go: Eastern Europe 2001
Let's Go: Europe 2001
Let's Go: France 2001
Let's Go: Germany 2001
Let's Go: Greece 2001
Let's Go: India & Nepal 2001
Let's Go: Ireland 2001
Let's Go: Israel 2001
Let's Go: Italy 2001
Let's Go: London 2001
Let's Go: Mexico 2001
Let's Go: Middle East 2001
Let's Go: New York City 2001
Let's Go: New Zealand 2001
Let's Go: Paris 2001
Let's Go: Peru, Bolivia & Ecuador 2001 **New Title!**
Let's Go: Rome 2001
Let's Go: San Francisco 2001 **New Title!**
Let's Go: South Africa 2001
Let's Go: Southeast Asia 2001
Let's Go: Spain & Portugal 2001
Let's Go: Turkey 2001
Let's Go: USA 2001
Let's Go: Washington, D.C. 2001
Let's Go: Western Europe 2001 **New Title!**

Let's Go *Map Guides*

Amsterdam	New Orleans
Berlin	New York City
Boston	Paris
Chicago	Prague
Florence	Rome
Hong Kong	San Francisco
London	Seattle
Los Angeles	Sydney
Madrid	Washington, D.C.

Coming Soon: *Dublin* and *Venice*

Let's Go

London

2001

John T. Reuland editor

researcher-writers
Whitney K. Bryant
Daryl Sng
Tobie E. Whitman

Mike Durcak map editor
Luke Marion photographer

Macmillan

HELPING LET'S GO

If you want to share your discoveries, suggestions, or corrections, please drop us a line. We read every piece of correspondence, whether a postcard, a 10-page email, or a coconut. Please note that mail received after May 2001 may be too late for the 2002 book, but will be kept for future editions. **Address mail to:**

Let's Go: London
67 Mount Auburn Street
Cambridge, MA 02138
USA

Visit Let's Go at **http://www.letsgo.com,** or send email to:

feedback@letsgo.com
Subject: "Let's Go: London"

In addition to the invaluable travel advice our readers share with us, many are kind enough to offer their services as researchers or editors. Unfortunately, our charter enables us to employ only currently enrolled Harvard students.

Published in Great Britain 2001 by Macmillan, an imprint of Macmillan Publishers Ltd, 25 Eccleston Place, London, SW1W 9NF, Basingstoke and Oxford.
Associated companies throughout the world
www.macmillan.com

Maps by David Lindroth copyright © 2001, 2000, 1999, 1998, 1997, 1996, 1995, 1994, 1993, 1992, 1991, 1990, 1989, 1988 by St. Martin's Press.

Published in the United States of America by St. Martin's Press.

ISBN: 0-333-90145-2
First edition
10 9 8 7 6 5 4 3 2 1

Let's Go: London is written by Let's Go Publications, 67 Mount Auburn Street, Cambridge, MA 02138, USA.

HOW TO USE THIS BOOK

How to use this book? Ideally, you should read it cover to cover and memorize everything. This **brand-new, redesigned** (complete with **photos**) guide to is just too irresistible to put down. So go ahead, bring it with you and join in-the-know tourists exploring the mesmerizing, never-ending streets and sights of London. Know, however, that you are carrying the savviest guide available to all that is hip, cutting-edge, and not-to-be-missed in London.

So you're going to London. Overwhelmed? It's part of the deal. Check out our **Discover** chapter, in which we lay out the best London has to offer. When you get there, **Once in London** will be your best friend, dishing the dirt on the city's neighborhoods, public transport, and other practical information. The neighborhood breakdown here mirrors that of the rest of the book. **Life and Times,** your Cliff's Notes-style history of London, makes great reading for the plane or the Tube. **Sights, Museums & Galleries, Shopping, Food,** and **Accommodations** are all organized in the same geographical order. If you don't know exactly where that trendy Japanese place or super-budget hostel is, these chapters all feature break downs of listings by type and by price. All neighborhoods—complete with their hotels, museums, monuments, restaurants, bars, and subway stops—are plotted in the **map appendix** at the end of the book. **Gay and Lesbian** listings are indicated throughout the book. Finally, the **Service Directory** is a quick reference to phone numbers you might need; if you want to visit an embassy or learn where to check your email, find that info here. Should you, for some reason, want you leave the city, the **Daytrips** chapter will guide you around the greater metropolitan area.

Scattered throughout this guide are tips on how best to explore London. Entries with a 🖾 are our favorite favorites. Look for **On the Cheap,** the sidebars that highlight everything from finding the best deal on apartments to getting dressed best for less. If you want to live large, seek out **The Big Splurge** sidebars. Plain old **black sidebars** give the low-down on London's many curious quirks; whether you want to know about the apparently strange names of pubs or the phenomenon of football hooliganism you'll find the details here. Our *ultimate* insider's scoop, however, is detailed in one of our many **walking tours.** Let us plan out an entire day for you, including which museums to visit to where to chow and drink; you'll find these tours on map spreads in the Sights chapter.

And remember, anything you can't find is probably in the **index.**

A NOTE TO OUR READERS The information for this book was gathered by *Let's Go* researchers from May through August of 2000. Each listing is based on one researcher's opinion, formed during his or her visit at a particular time. Those traveling at other times may have different experiences since prices, dates, hours, and conditions are always subject to change. You are urged to check the facts presented in this book beforehand to avoid inconvenience and surprises.

Contents

✈ planning your trip 213

▲ accommodations 241

☕ living in london 261

☎ service directory 271

🔢 index 277

maps 288

✚ Hospital	✈ Airport	🏛 Museum	▲ Mountain
🛡 Police	🚌 Bus Station	🏠 Hotel/Hostel	Park
✉ Post Office	🚂 Train Station	⛺ Camping	
ⓘ Tourist Office	Ⓜ METRO STATION	🍎 Food & Drink	Beach
💲 Bank	⚓ Ferry Landing	🛍 Shopping	
⚑ Embassy/Consulate	✝ Church	♪ Arts & Entertainment	Water
▪ Site or Point of Interest	✡ Synagogue	🍸 Nightlife	
☎ Telephone Office	☪ Mosque	💻 Internet Café	🖐 N
🎭 Theater	♜ Castle	⋯ Pedestrian Zone	The Let's Go thumb always points NORTH.

ACKNOWLEDGMENTS

Shoutouts, props, and plaudits due to the many friends who saw this book through to completion. The artistry of Wesley Willis has provided constant inspiration. City podmates—Lucy, Brady, Melissa, Val, Terry, Olivia—you've leavened the summer with cheer. Sarah, thanks for the delicious meals. Keja, you've been a source of calm in a sometimes chaotic office; your cheerful composure has helped keep us sane. Mike, your mapping and spinning abilities are unmatched. Thanks for all the effort you put into the book. Melissa G., thanks for answering so many questions; Melissa R., thanks for your technical competence. Nora, thanks for the coffee: I'm glad to know someone who parties with rock stars but has far more scruples. Thanks to everyone who helped proofread. Special thanks to Jonathan, whose punctiliousness has been remarkable and whose suggestions regarding coverage and format have been invaluable. This book is largely a product of your efforts. I'm grateful for all your hard work. Friendships as much as anything have made this experience meaningful. Thanks to Ian, Jess, and Christina for so many tremendous experiences and memories; thanks to Pete and Clare, our hospitable Leytonstone neighbors. To Jamin DeProto, Jack Hight, Hooman Kamel, Fiona McKinnon, Nora Morrison, Neil Rosenberg, Brian Smith, and Chris Soto— thank you for all your support this summer. You're good people I'm proud to call friends. You've made a real difference in my life. I value your friendship and all the ball games, movies, Persian meals, and tasteless jokes that have come with it. Chris, you've been a great roommate. Thanks especially to family, extended and immediate, for your kindness and boundless love. Ruth Owens, may all your travels be happy. This book is dedicated to my family with love: To Dad, Mom, Meg, and Tom.

Editor
John T. Reuland
Managing Editor
Daryush Jonathan Dawid
Map Editor
Michael Durcak

Publishing Director
Kaya Stone
Editor-in-Chief
Kate McCarthy
Production Manager
Melissa Rudolph
Cartography Manager
John Fiore
Editorial Managers
Alice Farmer, Ankur Ghosh, Aarup Kubal, Anup Kubal
Financial Manager
Bede Sheppard
Low-Season Manager
Melissa Gibson
Marketing & Publicity Managers
Olivia L. Cowley, Esti Iturralde
New Media Manager
Daryush Jonathan Dawid
Personnel Manager
Nicholas Grossman
Photo Editor
Dara Cho
Production Associates
Sanjay Mavinkurve, Nicholas Murphy, Rosa Rosalez, Matthew Daniels, Rachel Mason, Daniel Visel
(re)Designer
Matthew Daniels
Office Coordinators
Sarah Jacoby, Chris Russell

Director of Advertising Sales
Cindy Rodriguez
Senior Advertising Associates
Adam Grant, Rebecca Rendell
Advertising Artwork Editor
Palmer Truelson

President
Andrew M. Murphy
General Manager
Robert B. Rombauer
Assistant General Manager
Anne E. Chisholm

RESEARCHER-WRITERS

Whitney K. Bryant   *Bloomsbury, Hampstead and Highgate, The South Bank, Earl's Court, Covent Garden, Notting Hill and Bayswater, Chelsea and Belgravia, Docklands, Greenwich*

Attacking London with three years of Let's Go experience, Whitney suffused her dispatches with her dry, perceptive wit. Her nightlife explorations knew no limits as she hopped from club to pub to club, even while an injury sustained in the line of duty temporarily hobbled her boogie. With sober eyes and an acid pen Whitney covered Greenwich with precision, honesty, and courage. A lone American among antipodean hordes, she braved the hostels and pubs of Earl's Court to bring readers the solid, just-the-facts-ma'am coverage that's become this valued veteran's hallmark.

Daryl Sng   *Mayfair, City of London, Marylebone and Regent's Park, Kensington, Knightsbridge, Hyde Park, Islington, Soho, Camden, Shepherd's Bush, Brixton*

An editor can only sing the praises of this meticulous researcher, whose outstanding copybatches missed nary a vowel. A third-time Let's Go vet, Daryl used his vast musical knowledge (he's an amateur DJ) both to sort out the bewildering variety of music currently shaking London and to point Let's Go readers to the city's top clubs. He explored Tate Modern with a careful eye and a cultivated sensibility. Daryl's sense of style and adventure did justice to London's fashion scene while his acute sensitivity gave all his write-ups balance and accuracy. Daryl's meticulousness and unflagging enthusiasm for hard facts have improved this guide at every turn.

Tobie E. Whitman   *Holborn, Clerkenwell, Westminster, South Bank*

This three-time Let's Go veteran brought a wide knowledge of London and the UK to bear on her research. Her coverage of restaurants reflected her willingness to ferret out London's finest budget restaurants. She covered crucial sights with lucid prose and a dutiful devotion to accuracy. At night, Tobie trekked tirelessly to bars and clubs, returning compelling copy every time. Assigned some of the toughest coverage in the guide, Tobie discovered fascinating aspects of London's less-touristed neighborhoods. Tobie researched with the confidence and competence of a true international traveler.

Johs Pierce	*Editor, Britain and Ireland*
Lisa Herman	*Associate Editor, Britain and Ireland*
Teresa Crockett	*Oxford, Stratford*
Kate D. Nesin	*Cambridge, Liverpool*
Jason Schwartz	*Bath, Brighton, Canterbury, Stonehenge*

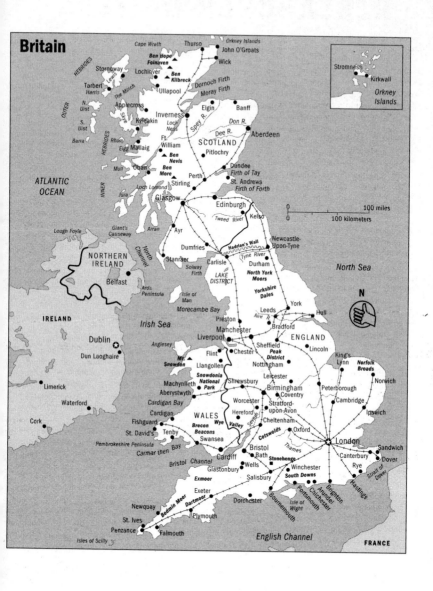

Discover London

Today, visitors come to London for its energy. Pubs may close early, but London is truly an around-the-clock city, with 24-hour cafes and clubbing that runs through mid-morning. London never stops, and you don't have to either. You can begin the day at 5am (or continue the previous night) at Smithfield Market, sightsee and shop all day, then drink and dance all night. London, manic but never schizophrenic, has integrated a fascinating past into a dynamic present. The two seem to coexist seamlessly, and it's up to you how intensely you want to experience each of them. History buffs can imagine London in centuries past, while a trip to one of Soho's futuristic boutiques will eclipse any impression, culled from bobbies and Big Ben, that London is chained to bygone days.

You can do and buy almost anything in London. Nightlife includes everything from jazz to dancing, the classical music is unparalleled, and the theater is perhaps the finest in the world. Trends bloom and die in here; buy something in London and six months later you'll see it on the catwalks. Despite the stereotypes about British food, London has steadily gained status as a culinary hotspot. Its multinational population has spiced British cuisine with an array of flavors and now, Indian food is just as common as bangers and mash. If you expected a city full of Queen-loving, tea-drinking, tweed-wearing gardeners with bad teeth, you'll be surprised at London's vibrance (and at how well Londoners care for their teeth).

WHEN TO GO

London swells with tourists during the summer months. Be sure to book accommodations early, because lodging can be hard to secure. Traveling during the off-season—November through March—will save you money and give you more room to yourself in the city. The exception to this is the period from mid-December to mid-January, when crowds return and fares increase again.

CLIMATE

Summers tend to be mild though hot days visit London occasionally. It's just as rainy during the summer as it is the rest of the year. On a positive note, London doesn't get terribly cold in the winter; prepare for blustery wind and rain, not snow. London, by the way, isn't very foggy—its pea-soupers became infamous during the Industrial Revolution but thanks to cleaner industry, it's not as bad today as it was a century ago.

AVG. TEMP. (LO/HI), PRECIPITATION											
	JANUARY			APRIL			JULY			OCTOBER	
	°C	°F	mm	°C	°F	mm	°C	°F	mm	°C	°F	mm
London	6/2	43/36	54	13/6	55/43	37	22/14	72/57	59	14/8	57/46	57

To convert from °C to °F multiply by 9/5 and add 32. To convert from °F to °C subtract 32 and multiply by 5/9.

LET'S GO'S LONDON 15

Whatever the duration of your visit, Let's Go thinks you should experience the following 15 things, as they best capture the character of London.

British Museum (p. 113). No trip to London would be complete without visiting the giant British Museum, but seeing all of it is impossible in a day. The immense structure stores plunder from around the world in its acres of exhibits, themselves testament to Britain's past greatness.

Regent's Park (p. 82). Strolling through Regent's park at dusk is an unmatched experience. London, poised on nighttime, pauses.

The South Bank (p. 100). An evening walk along the South Bank's quays offers an excellent view of the north bank lit at night. Sit outside and watch the lights reflected on the river.

The Tube (p. 26). London's public transportation is among the best in the world, despite what the locals think. You can usually get where you're going quickly and reliably. The Tube offers excellent people-watching opportunities, and the politeness of the "Mind the Gap" woman is uncanny.

Shopping (p. 127). From high end custom shops to trendy boutiques to the thriftware street markets, you'll find almost anything you need or want in fashion's most avant-garde city.

Westminster Abbey (p. 67). The magnificent royal Abbey is the final resting place of most of England's kings, as well as many of her civic and cultural heros.

Clubbing (p. 181). London affords any kind of clubbing experience you want: Loud and sweaty, eclectic and small, expensive and super glamorous, cheap and chill.

Tate Modern (p. 118). This new modern art museum has opened to an abundance of well-deserved praise. London is undergoing an artistic revival, and the Tate captures its spirit.

Brixton (p. 103). Have a great night out at this south London neighborhood's many clubs and bars, or visit during the day, when street markets and multicultural flair make for an experience unique even in London.

Wagamama (p. 162). Everyone's talking about this Soho noodle bar, where the quality of the food matches the novelty of the experience. Waiters radio your order into the kitchen in a restaurant that's straight out of AD 2045.

Pub Crawling (p. 170). There's nothing like a pub crawl for a wild night out with friends. This British institution will help you get good and pissed—maybe you'll even pick a local.

Harrods (p. 128). This venerable department store has everything under the sun. It lives up to its motto, *Omnia Omnibus Ubique* (All things for everyone everywhere). During sales, a police detail manages the excited crowds.

Institute of Contemporary Arts (p. 124). The ICA hosts a superb exhibitions of the most cutting-edge contemporary art. With a cinema, theater, and snazzy cafe-bar, it's a favorite hang-out for London's artsy crowd.

St. Paul's (p. 53). Sir Christopher Wren gave St. Paul's the second-highest dome in the world (the Vatican's is higher). Wren's churches pepper London, and this is the greatest.

Lloyd's Building (p. 60). Richard Rogers' inside-out structure (perhaps the most arresting of London's modern buildings) is hard to miss—the ventilation ducts are on the outside.

AYLESBURY

LEEDS, BIRMINGHAM

LUTON, BEDFORD

PETERBOROUGH

Potters Bar

Chesham

A416

AYLESBURY

A41

20

21

21A

A405

22

M25

23

24

A1(M)

A1

19

5

A6183

Amersham

A404

Watford

Bushey

18

A411

17

M1

Barnet

Beaconsfield

A413

M25

A404

A412

A40

A410

A410

Edgware

A5

A1

A411

A1000

A1000

Highgate

Hampstead

A40

A404

A4006

Harrow

Camden Town

2

M40

A355

16

1

A40

A312

A409

Brent

A406 North Circular Rd.

Kilburn

Marylebone

Paddington

East

Slough

A412

A4007

A4020

A312

Wembley

Ealing

A4020

Acton

A40

Notting Hill

CENTRAL LONDON

Victoria

Chels

A4

6

M4

A4

5

15

M4

4

3

M4

2

Hammersmith

Earl's Court

Fulham

Batter sea

Windsor & Eton

A332

14

13

Heathrow Airport

4a

A4

Hounslow

A316

Richmond-upon-Thames

A3

Wandsw

A308

13

Staines

A30

A214

Egham

A308

A329

A30

2-12

M3

1

M3

A308

A3050

Hampton Court Palace

Kingston-upon-Thames

Wimbledon

A3

A308

A24

Morden

Mitcha

A3

Sutto

11

A319

M25

A3050

A309

Esher

A240

A217

A232

A319

A3046

A320

A245

Weybridge

A245

A245

A307

A3

Epsom

A243

A24

Banstead

A322

A324

Woking

A3

10

M25

9

A24

A217

B2032

A247

Leatherhead

A246

M25

8

East Horsley

A246

A24

A25

A31

A323

Guildford

Dorking

Reigate

A3

A3100

A281

A248

A25

A24

A217

PORTSMOUTH

WORTHING, ARUNDEL, CHICHESTER

BRIGHTON, CRAWLEY, GATWICK AIRPORT

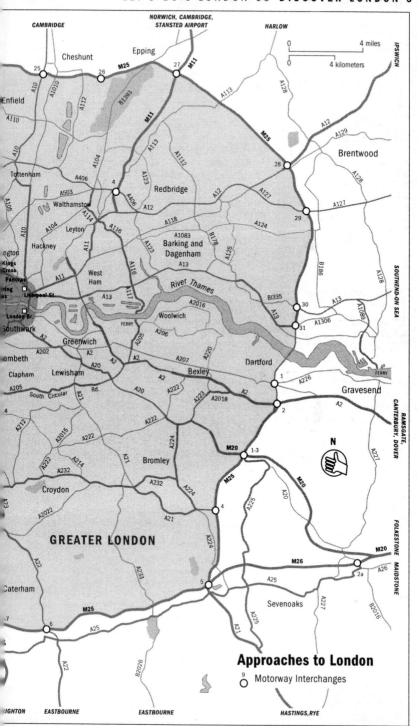

Approaches to London

Motorway Interchanges

FACTS AND FIGURES

1. London is the largest city in Europe, with a population of 7 million.

2. The oldest financial center in the world, London has over 500 foreign banks and more headquarters of banks than any other city.

3. Over 30% of the population is made up of first, second, or third generation immigrants.

4. London's maze of streets has 20 with "Shakespeare" in their name.

5. London draws up to 7 million visitors a year.

6. London has a population density of 10,500 per mile.

LET'S GO PICKS

BEST MUSEUM DESIGNED BY A CRAZY MAN. It's a close call: **Sir John Soane,** architect extraordinaire, has his hallucinatory house in Holborn (see p. 122), complete with Seti II's sarcophagus and stacked walls covered in Hogarth paintings. Frederick **Horniman** also has his own museum (see p. 121) complete with a stuffed walrus, 2,000 musical instruments, and an authentic voodoo altar. Thankfully, both are free.

BEST MUSEUM DEDICATED TO SOMEONE WHO CURED CRAZY MEN. The **Freud Museum** (p. 120) in Hampstead, displays the couch and personal artifacts of noted psychologist and self-help guru Sigmund Freud. Stop repressing your desire and light another cigar.

MEATIEST MEAT MARKET. Smithfield Market (p. 58) opens before dawn, selling vast quantities of wholesale meat. Smithfield is one of the best places to get an early, hearty, and heart-stopping English breakfast—pubs open at 7:30am.

THINGS TO DO

ROYAL LONDON

Those seeking the London of kings and queens will be busy indeed. If visions of stiff guards, flashy heraldry, burnished armor, and the like make your engine race, see the **Changing of the Guard** at Buckingham Palace (see p. 74), **Hampton Court Palace** (p. 110), and the **Tower of London** (p. 61). Visit Prince Charles at **St. James's Palace** and pop next door to see his grandma, the Queen Mum. Visit **Windsor Castle** (see p. 189) to see where the latest royal supercouple, Edward and Sophie, tied the knot, then stalk His Royal Sighness, Prince William, at **Eton** (p. 189). Finally, make a pilgrimage to **Althorp** (p. 211), the childhood home and final resting place of Princess Diana.

MULTICULTURAL LONDON

Today's Londoner is as likely to hail from Pakistan as Piccadilly. Colorful textile shops line Brick Lane, heart of London's **Bangladeshi** community (see p. 98). Grab an authentic Turkish coffee in parts of Hackney and east of the Essex Road junction, where a large **Turkish Kurd** community thrives, or peruse an Arabic language newspaper in one of the **Lebanese** cafes of the Edgeware Road. Golders Green (see p. 96) is the center of London's **Jewish** community, and is the perfect place to head on a Sunday afternoon, when shops and restaurants are bustling. Shop for exotic vegetables in the markets of **Chinatown** (see p. 85), or visit the market stalls of Brixton (see p. 103), home to much of London's **African** and **Caribbean** community.

ANGLICAN LONDON

England is remarkable for its homegrown religion and remarkable churches—architecture buffs will not want to miss the glorious places of worship that make up

Anglican London. The oldest district, the City, is dotted with a number of churches open to visitors. A lovely day may be spent walking from church to Wren church (see **The City of London,** p. 52). The two most famous houses of worship—gargantuan **St. Paul's** (see p. 53) and ancient **Westminster Abbey** (p. 67)—showcase two completely different eras of English Christianity.

LITERARY LONDON

Spend a day searching for the down and out in the Inns of Court (see p. 63), setting of **Charles Dickens's** *Bleak House.* **Keats** buffs will want to visit the museums which occupy their idol's former domicile (see p. 94). Explore the meticulously recreated lodgings of **Sir Arthur Conan Doyle's** detective character at the Sherlock Holmes Museum (see p. 123). Visit Greenwich Observatory (see p. 104), inspiration for **Joseph Conrad's** *Secret Agent,* or trek to Senate House at the University of London (see p. 83), which served as the base of the Ministry of Truth in **George Orwell's** classic *1984.* Fans of **Colin MacInnes'** *Absolute Beginners* will want to visit Soho (see p. 84) and **Notting Hill** (p. 79), the locations of his novel set in the 1950's.

Tralfalgar Square

SWINGIN' LONDON

In the 1960s, *Time* magazine dubbed "Swingin' London" the nexus of a raucous new youth movement. See what started it all on **Carnaby Street** (see p. 86), the center of the hippest fashions of that debaucherous decade. Snap a picture for posterity at the crosswalk on **Abbey Road** (see p. 94), site of the Beatle's album cover of the same name. Today the city guards this hedonistic flame—rave culture began here and London's clubs are second to none. **Soho** (see p. 84) is center of the night scene—cafes and nightclubs swing all night and all day, attracting night owls and early risers.

NOCTURNAL LONDON

London seems to come alive at night—the city of money, politics, and history becomes the nexus of European nightlife: every night, office workers exchange collars for club wear and the streets fill with giddy clubbers. Begin a night with a stroll around **Piccadilly Circus** (see p. 87), under the landmark neon signs. Stroll around Piccadilly, taking in the numerous street performers and the hordes of tourists. Dinner in **Chinatown** (see p. 85) is a wonderful way to commence a night out. If you've never experienced London clubbing, **Ministry of Sound** (see p. 183), the Capital's internationally renowned über-club, makes a superb first night out.

Bobbies

SUGGESTED ITINERARIES
THREE DAYS

DAY ONE. Cheesy as it may seem, a bus tour is the best way to get to know the city and see its major sights at the same time. Taking a bus tour on your first day in London will be richly rewarding. Leaving the bus at **Trafalgar Square** (see p. 75), commune with the pigeons before checking out the **National Gallery** (p. 115). Eat at **Belgo Centraal** (p. 162) and spend the evening amid the bustle and street performers of **Covent Garden** (p. 84).

DAY TWO. If your arteries can stand it, begin your morning with a traditional **English breakfast** and spend the day wander-

Tower Hill

ing through the **British Museum** (see p. 113). If you start to suffer from museum fatigue, take our literary walking tour through **Bloomsbury's** (see below) intellectual-nourishing streets. Cap off the day with dinner at **Wagamama** (p. 162), and round it out with a drink in one of Bloomsbury's student-oriented pubs.

DAY THREE. Get up early and make your way to **Buckingham Palace** to watch the **Changing of the Guard** (see p. 74). Then walk down the Mall to see the latest art at the **ICA** (p. 124), and strike out across **St. James's Park** (p. 88) for **Westminster.** Pay homage to England's great and good in **Westminster Abbey** (p. 67), then take in a debate at the **Houses of Parliament** (p. 71). Head to **Soho** for dinner at **Yo!Sushi** (p. 163), and take the night from there.

FIVE DAYS

DAY FOUR. Spend the first part of the day at the **Tate Modern** (see p. 118), then cross the **Millennium Bridge** (assuming it's fixed by now) to **St. Paul's Cathedral** (p. 53). From here, the City of London is at your feet; see 900 years of history in action at the **Tower of London** (p. 61) and 2000 years behind glass at the **Museum of London** (p. 121), in the **Barbican Centre** (p. 57). From the City, it's only a short swing north to **Islington** (p. 90) for dinner—try to get a reservation at **Tartuf** (p. 166).

DAY FIVE. How could you go to London and not go shopping? **Oxford Street** (see p. 127) has most of London's department stores; from here walk past the swanky boutiques of **Bond Street** (see p. 89) to **Piccadilly** (p. 87), home of the Ritz and Fortnum and Mason. Then take a bus around Hyde Park to **Knightsbridge** (p. 128) and take high tea at **Harrods** (p. 128) before heading for the unbeatable collections of **Harvey Nichols** (p. 128). If you're looking for something more affordable, **Camden Market** (see p. 139) has seen more trends born than anywhere else. Now you've got the gear, it's time to flaunt it and hit the clubs (p. 181).

SEVEN DAYS

DAY SIX. By now the city must be taking its toll, so take the train out of town—it takes less than an hour to reach **Oxford** or **Cambridge** (see **Daytrips**). Amble your way around the ancient colleges and try your skill on the river.

DAY SEVEN. London's not all grey stone and red brick, you know—it's got more green space than almost any other major city. Take your pick of **Hyde Park** (p. 78), **Regents Park** (p. 82), **Kew Gardens** (p. 107), or **Hampstead Heath** (p. 93) for a relaxing day wandering in the open air. Complete a stress-free day with a meal at **Mandalay** (p. 161) in Marylebone.

WALKING TOURS
EMERALD LONDON

No visit would be complete without time spent luxuriating in London's glorious parks and gardens. To start, head to Charing Cross station and exit towards **Trafalgar Square** (see p. 75). The Mall, off Trafalgar Square, leads to **St. James's Park** (p. 88); the lake is a good place to play duck-spotting. On Sundays, the Mall is closed to traffic, which makes for a lovely walk (a quick detour off Marlborough Rd. leads to **St. James' Palace** (p. 88). At the other end of the Mall is **Buckingham Palace**, SW1 1AA, home to some German family who moved in couple of centuries ago (see p. 74). Near Buckingham Palace is **Green Park** (p. 88), which may not be the most spectacular of London's parks (it doesn't even have a lake), but is often more peaceful because of it.

To get from Green Park to the enormous **Hyde Park** (see p. 78) and **Kensington Gardens** (p. 78), you'll have to go under the giant roundabout that is Hyde Park Corner. Still, the subways here can be interesting: they're decorated with a history of Arthur Wellesley, Duke of Wellington, whose former residence, **Apsley House**, stands on the corner itself. The **Wellington Monument** sits in the middle of the roundabout. From Apsley House, a variety of routes take you to different parts of Hyde Park and Kensington Gardens.

From Hyde Park Corner, you can take one of two routes. If you're heading for the **Serpentine Gallery** (see **p. 125**), go straight across Rotten Row, a route which passes the **Holocaust Memorial** along the way. Alternatively, going down Serpentine Rd. allows you to see the beautiful **Serpentine Lake** (see p. 79). From Serpentine Rd., turning left onto the Ring (also known as the West Carriage Dr.) leads to the [...] From here, a walk down the Ring and a right leads to the [...] **Memorial**; further west is **Kensington Palace** (see p. 79).

On the other hand, If you're heading for **Speaker's Corner** (see p. 79) and **Marble Arch** (p. 79) from Hyde Park Corner, go up Broad Walk. Speaker's Corner is the paved section in the northeast corner of Hyde Park—you'll recognize it from the sounds of proselyting. **Marble Arch**, opposite, is really just a large arch abandoned on a traffic island.

If you still have the legs for it, **Regent's Park** (p. 82) is central London's last major park. Take the Tube to Baker St., and exit on to Baker St. Turn right (you'll pass the **Sherlock Holmes Museum**, p. 123, on the way) and keep going. A walk around Regent's Park Outer Circle passes by the gold minaret of the **London Central Mosque** and finally, near Camden Town, the **London Zoo**.

INTELLECTUAL LONDON

Although now more a place for the interchange of commuters than literary ideas, **St. Pancras** station (see p. 83) is the best place to start a walking tour of Bloomsbury. The **British Library** (p. 82), next door to St. Pancras, is full of contemporary scholars laboring hidden from public view, as well as excellent exhibits, including one on the history of British literature. Continuing down Euston Rd. and taking a left on Gower St., will bring you to the beating heart of academic London, **University College London** (see p. 83). Apart from the mummified body of philosopher Jeremy Bentham, there are some decent bookstores and students wandering around pontificating, as they are wont to do. Bloomsbury paydirt, however, is to be found at 46 Gordon Sq., off Tavistock Place from Gower St. It is here that the children of Sir Leslie Stephen, renowned biographer, created a latter-day salon, filling it with some of the great minds in the humanities and social sciences, commonly known as the **Bloomsbury Group** (see p. 42). Most famous amongst the Stephen children was **Virginia**, who married **Leonard Woolf** and moved to 52 Tavistock Square (two blocks down from Gordon Sq., on the left). Here, she wrote some of her most famous works, including *Orlando*, *Mrs. Dalloway*, and *To The Lighthouse*. Diagonally across from the northern end of Tavistock Square is Woburn Walk. Here, **WB Yeats** lived from 1895-1919, and entertained the likes of Eliot, Pound, and Tagore. Continuing south on Woburn Place brings you to **Russell Square**. This large quadrangle, now full of roses and lunch-eating office workers, squares off as central London's second-largest, after Lincoln's Inn Fields. **T.S. Eliot,** the "Pope of Russell Square," hid from his ailing first wife at no. 24 while he worked as an editor and later director of Faber and Faber, the famed publishing house, from 1925 until his death. From Russell Square, Montague St. leads south to Great Russell St, and the front entrance of the **British Museum** (see p. 113), the uber-tourist draw, and cultural powerhouse. In its former reading room, Marx labored away at *Das Kapital*, and relaxed with a pint at the **Museum Tavern** (p. 173) across the street. From the tavern take Museum St. away from the museum to Bloomsbury Way. At **St. George's** (see p. 83), you can have a peak at the baptismal font that watered the head of a tiny **Anthony Trollope**, before continuing east, where Bloomsbury Way becomes Theobald's Rd. Take a left on John St., and follow it until it

St. Paul's

Thames at Night

Buckingham

...ughty St. from 1837 to 1839, scribbling ..., *Barnaby Rudge*, and *Oliver Twist*. ...ickens paraphernalia, the house holds ..., and personal effects. What it lacks in ...ative. The rusty iron grill mounted on a ...e Marshalsea Jail, a notorious debtor's ...n labored in a shoeblack factory.

...especially at night) and are home to a **of London** (see p. 61), cross **Tower Bridge** ...footpath along the river. You'll pass the ...Normandy during WWII. Continue along ...Southwark Bridge. Turn onto Bankside, ...Walk. The **Globe Theatre** (p. 102), where Shakespeare performed many of his plays, is on this small street at 21 New Globe Walk. After the Globe, proceed to 1 Sumner St., where you can finish your walk at the **Tate Modern** (p. 117). Make your way across the river on the new **Millennium Bridge** and head for **St. Paul's Cathedral** (see p. 53). Just out of sight of the Thames, walk parallel to the river on **Fleet Street** (see p. 64) and the **Strand** (p. 65), stopping by the **Inns of Court** (p. 63), then cross again over **Waterloo Bridge** to take in the riverside panorama and rest at the **South Bank Center** (SEE p. 100). Continuing west will take you past the **Millennium Wheel** (p. 100) to **Westminster Bridge** and the **Houses of Parliament** (p. 71).

KIDS IN LONDON

Here are some suggested thematic itineraries. Remember, though, that even with children's prices and family tickets, extensive sight-seeing can be expensive. Most of the sights listed below are covered in greater detail elsewhere.

CASTLES AND KINGS. The **Tower of London** (p. 61) offers endless entertainment for the entire family, including the informative Beefeater tours—kids are sure to be intrigued by the sight of the Crown Jewels. The **Tower Bridge Experience** (p. 59) offers an interactive tour of the engineering and history of the Bridge. Let your kids run through **Buckingham Palace** (p. 74). Otherwise, you'll have to make do with seeing the **Changing of the Guard** (p. 74) that takes place outside daily.

AHOY. There's something about being on deck. **HMS Belfast** and the **Golden Hinde** (see p. 103) are moored on Bankside near London Bridge station. Both give children the chance to run around and explore. Farther west in Greenwich, the kids can swab the deck of the **Cutty Sark,** one of the last great clippers (see p. 106). If their taste of the seafaring life whets an appetite for a real boat ride, you can take advantage of the **boat tours** that operate along the Thames (see p. 29).

BRIGHT LIGHTS, BIG CITY. In **Trafalgar Square,** children never seem to tire of feeding the pigeons, playing in the fountains, scaling the lions, and watching red double-deckers swirl around the square (see p. 75). When they (or you) have had enough, venture toward **Piccadilly Circus,** where the **Trocadero** (p. 87) offers older kids video games and bumper cars. Next door, **Madame Tussaud's Rock Circus** (p. 87) features waxwork incarnations of popular music artists with an accompanying sound tour.

MUSEUM. The **Science Museum** (see p. 122) is full of interactive exhibits and now boasts an IMAX cinema in the all-new Wellcome Wing. Perhaps best of all for wallet-weary parents, it's free for children. Next door, the **Natural History Museum** (p. 122) gets the kids gaping with its numerous dinosaur fossils. The "Creepy Crawlies" and "Earthquake" rooms are also popular with children. Both museums are free after 4:30pm.

PARKS. Some London parks cater specifically to children. **Coram's Fields,** a children's park with petting animals, an aviary, and a pool for children under five (see p. 83). In general, most of the major London parks are great fun for children. **Regent's Park** (p. 82) and

Kensington Gardens (p. 78) both have boat rentals for children, while **Holland Park** has a popular playground. Signs help children identify the different varieties of ducks in **St. James's Park's** menagerie.

ANIMAL HOUSE. The biggest menagerie of the lot, of course, is the **London Zoo** (p. 82). The **Mudchute City Farm,** near Canary Wharf, offers petting animals and horseback-riding (see p. 99). The wild deer of **Greenwich Park,** not far south, provide another animal-spotting opportunity.

TOYS. Along with a number of inexpensive children's clothing stores, the East End holds the **Bethnal Green Museum of Childhood,** devoted to displaying children's books, dolls, & more. You'll be having more fun than the kiddies (p. 120). And while mega-toystore **Hamley's** (p. 134) may not be a church, it's a religious experience for children.

THEATER. It's not just Punch and Judy, you know: the **Little Angel Theatre** (p. 91) in Islington is a popular children's puppet theater. They don't allow infants, and some shows may have minimum age restrictions, so make sure you phone the theatre ahead to check. The **Open Air Theatre** in Regent's Park (p. 144) always puts on one children's show, a great way to give little ones the experience of outdoor theater. As for the long-running **West End** plays, most of the musicals have enough spectacle to entertain, although shows like *Les Misérables* may be too serious or too long for younger children to enjoy.

FILM. Most London cinemas have children's prices for tickets, and those in the UGC chain offer family tickets. The **National Film Theatre** (p. 147) runs children's matinees on Saturday around 3pm and Sunday around 4pm. The **Ritzy** (p. 147) also has a special kids' screening. At the **Prince Charles,** the Sunday 3pm matinee screening of *Sing-a-Long-a-Sound-of-Music* lets you introduce your children to the joys of solving a problem like Maria. Note that the British rating system groups movies into the following categories: **U** (suitable for all ages), **PG** (open to all, but parental guidance advised), **12** (no one admitted under 12), **15** (no one admitted under 15), and **18** (no one admitted under 18).

SPORT. London's **Premiership football clubs** (Arsenal, Charlton, Chelsea, Tottenham Hotspur, and West Ham) are lots of fun for soccer-crazy kids. While the clubs have made great steps towards drawing families, vulgar chants are still common. Tickets to the Premiership games are expensive and difficult to get without buying in advance (although you might have some luck with Charlton). The **Henley Royal Regatta,** at Henley-on-Thames (☎ (01491) 572153; get a train from Paddington) takes place between the last week of June and first week of July. Children under 14 enter the enclosure free.

BON VOYAGE!

This brief introduction is merely that—there's no way any travel guide could cover all of London. It's impossible to contain a city as dynamic and fluid as London in a single book. To really know London, you must explore it yourself. Wander its streets and parks, become anonymous on the Tube, make a pub your own. Your sense of adventure will be richly rewarded.

Big Ben

St. Margaret's

Queen Anne Statue

Kensington Palace was home to the late Princess Diana, but centuries before it housed William and Mary. In 1689, they comissioned Sir Christopher Wren to renovate it.

Tucked in the middle of the Hyde Park, **Serpentine Gallery** contains an outstanding collection, a dose of man-made beauty in the midst of natural beauty.

Speaker's Corner

Bayswater Rd.

N. Carriage Dr.

Hyde Park

Kensington Gardens

Kensington Palace

The Serpentine

8

7

6

Kensington Palace

W. Carriage

finish

Kensington Rd.

Kensington Gore

Kensington Rd.

Royal Albert Hall

Prince Consort Rd.

KNIGHTSBRIDGE

Victoria & Albert Museum

Natural History Museum

SOUTH KENSINGTON

SOUTH KENSINGTON

Cromwell Rd.

Hyde Park is more spectacular and more crowded than Green Park. Don't miss the boaters in the Serpentine Lake. Other noteworthy sights include Marble Arch and Speaker's Corner.

CHELSEA

EMERALD LONDON
Glorious parks and gardens

Walkintour1

After you exit Charing Cross Station, head to **Trafalgar Square,** home to pigeons, the National Gallery, the statue of Admiral Nelson, and New Year's celebrations. The Mall, off Trafalgar Square, leads you to St. James's Park.

The lake in St. James's Park is a great place to feed ducks.

Green Park is one of London's less busy parks, and as such it's a great place to meditate.

start

1

TRAFALGAR SQUARE

CHARING CROSS

5 Green Park

3 St. James's Park

The Mall

2

Constitution Hill

Birdcage Walk

4

At the other end of the Mall you'll find **Buckingham Palace.** No one really knows what's interesting about this big house, but if you ask the tourists congregated outside, one of them could probably tell you.

Prince Charles resides in **St. James Palace,** where Charles I slept for four hours in the palace's guardroom before crossing St. James's Park to be executed. When the other Stuarts regained power they called it home until 1668.

start 1

Begin your tour at **St. Pancras Stantion,** a neo-gothic structure that once housed the Midland Grand Hotel.

9 finish

Charles Dickens dwelled at **48 Doughty St.** from 1837-1839; now the building is the Dickens Museum. Not such a bleak house after all, eh?

2

University College London contains the body of Jeremy Bentham, who along with other religious dissenters founded the college as a religiously and intellectually progressive instituition.

Cross the street to the immense **British Library,** where you'll find a trove of manuscripts and fascinating exhibits.

4

At **46 Gordon Sq.,** Virginia Woolf, T.S. Eliot, Clive and Vanessa Bell, John Maynard Keynes, and others met to discuss matters of the mind. Now commonly known as the Bloomsbury group, those who passed through

3

INTELLECTUAL LONDON
The Great Brains of Great Britain

Walkintour2

5 T.S. Eliot lived at **24 Russell Sq.**, while he composed verse and managed Faber and Faber, the famous publishing House.

6 The **British Museum**, housed in a building that seems like it could contain everything there is to know, houses the collections of a once vast empire.

7 Compelled by laws of materialism and the dialectic of work and play, Marx sipped a pint at the **Museum Tavern** each day after working in the reading room of the British Museum.

8 The baptismal font of **St. George's** has sprinkled the heads of numerous Bloomsbury babies, Anthony Trollope among them. Like many London churches, it was damaged during WWII.

century's brightest.

The Millennium Bridge will take you back into history to **St. Paul's Cathedral,** Sir Christopher Wren's famous masterwork.

mbling around **Fleet Street and the Strand,** you'll find that London is business-as-usual. The Strand is home to the Inns of Court, where the Supreme Court of the Judicature hears important cases.

St. Bartholomew the Great

Samuel Johnson's House

Inns of Court

St. Paul's Cathedral

Royal Courts of Justice

Fleet St. **7**

Ludgate Hill

6

St. Bride's

St. Clement Danes

The Temple

nd London Economics

mersey House

Upper Thames St.

Victoria Embankment

Thames River

Blackfriars Br.

Millennium Bri.

Southwark Rd

Waterloo Br.

8

Cross the **Waterloo Bridge** to the South Bank Centre and relax. Take in the riverside panorama.

Rose Thea

5

4 Globe Thea

Stamford St.

Southwark St.

Once you've had enough history, immerse yourself in modernity at **Tate Modern,** housed in a converted power station. Tate Modern opened in May 2000 to rave reviews.

York Rd.

9 finish

ster Br.

If you feel like continuing west, you'll encounter the Millennium Wheel, **Westminster Bridge,** and the Houses of Parliament.

Shakespeare put on a number of his plays at the **Globe Theatre.** The original theater burnt down in 1613, but the current structure is an operational replica.

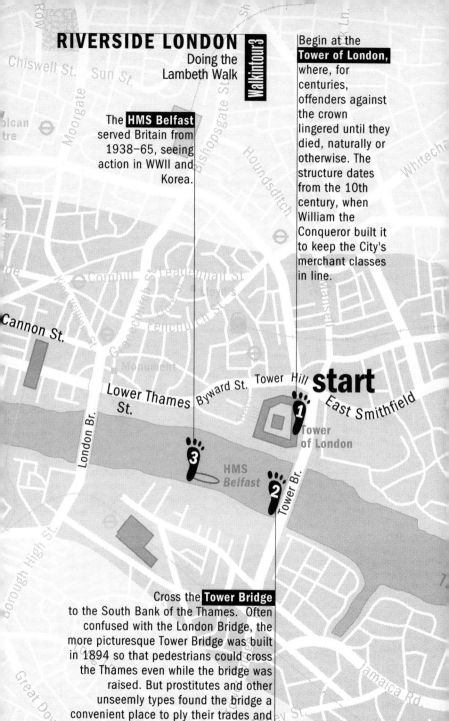

RIVERSIDE LONDON
Doing the Lambeth Walk

Walkintour 3

Begin at the **Tower of London,** where, for centuries, offenders against the crown lingered until they died, naturally or otherwise. The structure dates from the 10th century, when William the Conqueror built it to keep the City's merchant classes in line.

The **HMS Belfast** served Britain from 1938–65, seeing action in WWII and Korea.

Cross the **Tower Bridge** to the South Bank of the Thames. Often confused with the London Bridge, the more picturesque Tower Bridge was built in 1894 so that pedestrians could cross the Thames even while the bridge was raised. But prostitutes and other unseemly types found the bridge a convenient place to ply their trades and so the walkways were closed from 1909–82.

start

Once in London

ORIENTATION

Thanks to its fabulous public transportation, London is one of the world's easiest cities to navigate—save for the fact that its labyrinthine streets baffle even lifetime residents. Familiarizing yourself with an Underground map and picking up an *A-Z*, the indispensable street finder used by cabbies and American college kids alike ($4), will help you get your bearings. London is divided into six concentric zones, of which Zone 1 is most central. Most of London's sights, nightlife, restaurants, and accommodations fall into Zones 1-2; Zones 3-6, largely suburbs incorporated into London over the years, tend to be more residential. While the Thames clearly divides north London from south London, the boundaries between neighborhoods can be a little murky; places sometimes take their names from important landmarks but just as often a name's origin has been obscured by time. Soho, for example, took its name from an early modern hunting cry. What follows should give you some idea of London's layout and the major features of each neighborhood. London, however, is a walking city; it enjoyed its imperial heyday well before cars were invented. The best way to understand London's geography is to stretch your legs a bit—taking the Tube everywhere will only give you a subway sense of the city.

CENTRAL LONDON

see map pp. 288-289

THE CITY OF LONDON AND CLERKENWELL. The City and Clerkenwell encompass the east central part of London. **St. Paul's Cathedral** (p. 53) is the area's major attraction. Also known as **the square mile**, the City of London is the financial center of London and has been for centuries. A few nightlife spots liven up the otherwise empty evenings, when the office workers who cram the area head for home or the pub. These neighborhoods also have an ample share of budget

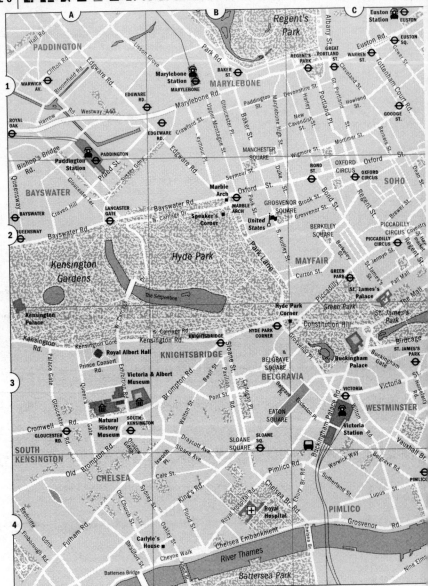

Central London: Major Street Finder

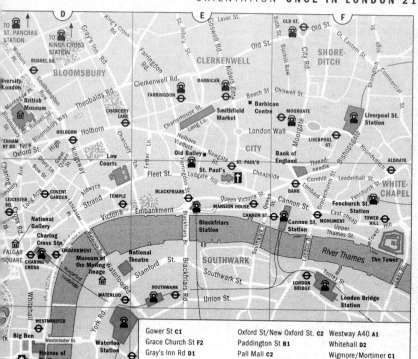

Gower St **C1**
Grace Church St **F2**
Gray's Inn Rd **D1**
Gt Portland St **C1**
Gt Russell St **D1**
Grosvenor Pl **C3**
Grosvenor Rd **C4**
Grosvenor St (Upr) **C2**
Haymarket **C2**
Holborn/High/Viaduct **D1**
Horseferry Rd **C3**
Jermyn St **C2**
Kensington High St/Rd **A3**
King's Cross Rd **D1**
King's Rd **B4**
Kingsway **D2**
Knightsbridge **B3**
Lambeth Palace Rd **D3**
Lisson Grove **A1**
Lombard St **F2**
London Wall **E1**
Long Acre/Grt Queen **D2**
Long Ln **E1**
Ludgate Hill **E2**
Marylebone High St **B1**
Marylebone Rd **B1**
Millbank **D4**
Montague Pl **D1**
Moorgate **F1**
New Bridge St **E2**
New Cavendish **C1**
Newgate St **E1**
Nine Elms Ln **C4**
Oakley St **B4**
Old St **F1**
Old Brompton Rd **A4**
Onslow Sq/St **A3**

Oxford St/New Oxford St. **C2**
Paddington St **B1**
Pall Mall **C2**
Park Ln **B2**
Park Rd **B1**
Park St **B2**
Piccadilly **C2**
Pont St **B3**
Portland Pl **C1**
Queen St **E2**
Queen Victoria St **E1**
Queen's Gate **A3**
Queensway **A2**
Redcliffe Gdns **A4**
Regent St **C2**
Royal Hospital Rd **B4**
St. James's St **C2**
Seymour Pl **A1**
Seymour St **A2**
Shaftesbury Ave **C2**
Sloane/Lwr Sloane **B3**
Southampton Row **D1**
Southwark Bridge Rd **E2**
Southwark Rd **E2**
Stamford St **E2**
Strand **D2**
Sydney St **A4**
Thames St(Upr&Lwr) **F2**
The Mall **C2**
Theobald's Rd **D1**
Threadneedle St **F2**
Tottenham Ct Rd **C1**
Vauxhall Br. Rd **C4**
Victoria Embankment **D2**
Victoria St **C3**
Warwick Way **C4**
Waterloo Rd **E1**

Westway A40 **A1**
Whitehall **D2**
Wigmore/Mortimer **C1**
Woburn Pl **D1**
York Rd **D3**

RAILWAY STATIONS

Barbican **E1**
Blackfriars **E2**
Cannon St **F2**
City Thameslink **E2**
Charing Cross **D2**
Euston **C1**
Farringdon **E1**
King's Cross **D1**
Liverpool St **F1**
London Bridge **F2**
Marylebone **B1**
Moorgate **F1**
Old St. **F1**
Paddington **A2**
St Pancras **D1**
Victoria **C3**
Waterloo East **E2**
Waterloo **D3**

BRIDGES

Albert **B4**
Battersea **A4**
Blackfriars **E2**
Chelsea **C4**
Hungerford Footbridge **D2**
Lambeth **D3**
London Bridge **F2**
Southwark **E2**
Tower Bridge **F2**
Waterloo **D2**
Westminster **D3**

Edgware Rd **A1**
Euston Rd **C1**
Exhibition Rd **A3**
Farringdon Rd **E1**
Fenchurch/Aldgate **F2**
Fleet St **E2**
Fulham Rd **A4**
Gloucester Pl **B1**
Gloucester Rd **A3**
Goswell Rd **E1**

TUBE TIPS

...on traipsing through the Underground's numerous connections. Here's the best of our travel tips.

1. Remember the Tube map is only an approximation of geography: it is sometimes quicker to get off on the line you're at and just walk. Stations that are particularly close without any connecting lines are: Bayswater and Queensway; Regent's Park and Great Portland Street; Warren Street and Euston Square.

2. Conversely, some transfers between lines at large stations are especially long. Don't change from the Central to the Circle at Bank/Monument; use Liverpool St. instead.

3. Some stations share the same name: there are two Shepherd's Bush stations, two Edgware Roads, two Paddingtons, and (despite what the Tube map seems to indicate) two Hammersmiths. **Don't arrange to meet friends "in front of the station exit" without clarifying which one you mean.**

4. Changing at Oxford Circus between Bakerloo and Victoria trains going in the same direction is a breeze.

accommodations. *Tube: Farringdon, Old Street, Liverpool Street, Barbican, Moorgate, Bank, and Cannon Street.*

HOLBORN. Holborn lies up the Thames (west) from the City. The center of London's legal profession, Holborn is home to more than suits. Under Holborn's business-as-usual façade lie fascinating leftovers of London's history, including the **Temple** (p. 64) and the **Inns of Court** (p. 63) *Tube: Temple, Holborn.*

WESTMINSTER. Westminster (p. 67) is the religious and political center of England. The majesty of Anglican churches and the dignity of governmental buildings together present an imposing picture of England's essential institutions. Upriver from Holborn, the Houses of Parliament dominate the cityscape, and **Westminster Abbey, 10 Downing Street,** and **St. Margaret's Cathedral** are some of the brightest stars in firmament of England's religious and political culture. *Tube: Pimlico, Westminster, St. James's Park, Victoria, Charing Cross.*

CHELSEA AND BELGRAVIA. The tastefulness of their shops guard these tony residential areas southwest of Westminster against rank philistinism. The boutiques lining **Kings Road** (p. 128) may break a budget traveler's bank, but the people watching is priceless. *Tube: South Kensington, Sloane Square.*

KENSINGTON, KNIGHTSBRIDGE, AND HYDE PARK. North of Chelsea, Kensington delights visitors with its **museums** and bourgeois charm. Mick Jagger once warned a Knightsbridge woman about the danger of playing with fire in the famous Stones tune and its reputation for opulence hasn't changed since those halcyon days. Most notably, Knightsbridge is home to the massive **Harrods** (p. 128) department store. If you want satisfaction money can't buy, head to **Hyde Park** (p. 78), the biggest green space in central London. *Tube: Hyde Park Corner, Knightsbridge, South Kensington, High Street Kensington, Lancaster Gate, Marble Arch, Gloucester Road.*

NOTTING HILL AND BAYSWATER. Perhaps no neighborhoods encompass West End cool like these. Tons of mod restaurants and chic wine bars have helped Bayswater stay consistently cool; Notting Hill's artsy bent and multicultural flavor make it a worthwhile destination day or night. However, you might find more than a few "Trustafarians" out here—namely slumming trust fund poseurs basking in the area's bohemian reputation. *Tube: Bayswater, Queensway, Notting Hill Gate.*

MARYLEBONE AND REGENT'S PARK. Just North of London's busiest parts, Marylebone's main attractions are its museums and accommodations. **Regent's Park** (p. 82) is always full of Londoners at play; the **London Zoo** in Regent's Park may interest kids. *Tube: Paddington, Edgware Road, Marylebone, Regent's Park, Great Portland Street.*

BLOOMSBURY. East of Regent's Park and north of Holborn, Bloomsbury has historically been London's intellectual center. Virginia Wolfe, E.M. Forester, and John Maynard Keynes called this area home at one point in their lives. The **British Library** (p. 82) and the colossal **British Museum** (p. 113) rank among the area's most famous sights. Budget accommodations are plentiful here and their location close to major sights makes them a solid value. *Tube: Goodge Street, Russell Square, King's Cross St. Pancras, Tottenham Court Road, Warren Street.*

COVENT GARDEN. Covent Garden was once a monastery's vegetable garden; however, there's nothing monastic about the neighborhood's crazy nightlife. Come closing time Aussies, Kiwis, Canadians, and the Americans who love them stumble out of the many nationally themed pubs, wandering the streets in search of more kicks. By day, Covent Garden's shopping is its biggest draw. *Tube: Covent Garden, Charing Cross.*

Double Decker

SOHO. Though its once-famous seediness has become a little quaint (the 60s sex industry has given way to the sex shop industry of the Internet age), Soho still promises a good time. Restaurants, pubs, and clubs abound in the area where London began to swing. Soho is also home to London's Chinatown, where a number of excellent restaurants are found. *Tube: Leicester Square, Tottenham Court Road.*

MAYFAIR, ST. JAMES'S, AND PICADILLY. Mayfair addresses have ranked among London's most coveted since...well, since Londoners began using addresses. Mayfair and St. James's put aristocracy on display; among the area's most famous residences is Buckingham Palace. The aristocratic shops around the Pall Mall are fit to grace the backs of royalty, and have outfitted generations of aristocrats. If you need a custom suit and have thousands of pounds to spare, this is the place to go. If you don't need a tailored suit, enjoy the window shopping. *Tube: Green Park, Picadilly Circus.*

NORTH LONDON

see map p. 306

ISLINGTON. Once London's socialist center, an influx of capital has turned Islington into one of London's hippest neighborhoods. Islington's restaurants, pubs, and clubs are more remarkable than its sights. *Tube: Angel, Highbury & Islington.*

British Museum

CAMDEN. Camden has survived the gentrification of northern London, now only slightly less dirty than it was a decade ago. The enormous **Camden Market** (p. 139) is its distinguishing feature, but fun pubs and restaurants line the high road. Tube: *Camden Town, Chalk Farm.*

HAMSTEAD AND HIGHGATE. "Ham and High" were once the leafy getaways of London's elite. Now connected to central London by Underground, the area's bucolic beauty is available to all. Literature buffs won't want to miss **Keats's** house (see p. 94). *Tube: Belsize Park, Hampstead, Gihgate, Archway, East Finchley Rail: Hampstead Heath, Gospel Oak.*

London at Night

TRAINSPOT-TING

The Underground trains aren't the only trains in London, and those travelling outside central London (Zone 1) or through South London may sometimes find that rail services are quicker or involve fewer station changes, although they may not run as frequently as Tube trains. The *London Connections* map, available at some rail stations, is a handy map of all train connections within Greater London. **National Rail Enquiries** (☎ (08457) 484 950) answers questions regarding train routes and schedules. These train lines may be of particular interest to travellers:

NORTHERN LINE, PART 3. The Thameslink connects **Elephant & Castle, London Bridge, Blackfriars, City Thameslink** rail station, **Farringdon, King's Cross,** and **Kentish Town** along with other stations and **Luton airport.**

SOUTHWEST LONDON. South West Trains runs trains from **Waterloo** to **Vauxhall, Wimbledon, Richmond,** and **Hampton Court.**

NORTH LONDON. WAGN runs a line connecting **Moorgate, Old Street, Essex Road** rail station, **Highbury & Islington,** and **Finsbury Park.** Unfortunately, it doesn't run on weekends.

IN THE MEAN TIME. Connext South Eastern runs trains from **Charing Cross** and **Cannon Street** to **Greenwich** rail/DLR station (near the observatory, not the Dome, although a bus runs from Greenwich station to the Dome).

EAST LONDON

see map p. 320

WHITECHAPEL. Whitechapel has gradually traded its gangland rep for a more arty one. The **Whitechapel Gallery** (p. 125) consistently features some of the finest modern art in London. Whitechapel is widely considered the epicenter of London's **Bangladeshi** community. *Tube: Bethnal Green, Whitechapel, Stepney, Mile End.*

DOCKLANDS. During the 80s, the Docklands underwent a regeneration that has had mixed results. Office buildings sprang up and the Docklands Light Railway was built to connect the out-of-the-way area to central London. The effort has yielded mixed results. Many offices in the shiny new buildings remain empty, though **Canary Wharf** (p. 98), at 500m the UK's tallest structure, is considered an architectural triumph by many. *DLR: West India Quay, Canary Wharf, Heron Quays, South Quay, Crossharbour & London Arena, Mudchute, Island Gardens.*

SOUTH LONDON

see map p. 319

SOUTH BANK & SOUTHWARK. The new **Tate Modern** (p. 117) is this area's gem. In the short time it's been open the new Tate has been a hit with critics and museum-goers alike. Southwark, home to the Elizabethan Period's more sordid entertainments, including the **Globe Theatre** (p. 102), is now a quaint tourist area. *Tube: Waterloo, Embankment, Southwark.*

BRIXTON. Brixton was once associated with London's racial strife. While memories of early-80s riots are a reminder of a grim past, Brixton's future looks bright. The neighborhood has some of London's most cutting-edge nightlife. *Tube: Brixton.*

GREENWICH. This is the place where it all begins—a day in the Western Hemisphere that is! Greenwich is accross the Thames from the Docklands and packed with sights, many of which pertain to navigation and astronomy. The **Millennium Dome** (p. 106) has been the talk of London for the past year or so and attracts many visitors. *DLR: Cutty Sark, Greenwich, Deptford Bridge, Elverson Road, Lewisham.*

WEST LONDON

see map pp. 310-311

EARL'S COURT. Earl's Court is a little South Africa west of Kensington. It truly is backpackers' London, and here you'll find great budget accommodations, populated with an international crowd, and few sights. *Tube: Earl's Court.*

SHEPHERD'S BUSH, HAMMERSMITH, & HOLLAND PARK.
There's not much this far west—a few well-priced accommodations and some pubs. The yard of what once was Holland House is now Holland Park—little remains of this mansion, badly damaged during WWII. The **Shepherd's Bush Empire** (p. 186) is a major rock venue. *Tube: Shepherd's Bush, Godlike Road, Hammersmith.*

GETTING INTO LONDON FROM THE AIRPORTS

HEATHROW

With planes landing every 47 seconds, Heathrow Airport (☎ (020) 8759 4321) in Hounslow, Middlesex, is the world's busiest international airport. The bureaux de change in each terminal are open daily; cash machines are also located in each terminal.

The cheapest way to reach London from Heathrow is by Underground. (Piccadilly line; about 50-60min. to central London, Zone 6, with one stop for terminals 1, 2, and 3, and another for terminal 4.) The **Heathrow Express** (www.heathrowexpress.co.uk) is the fastest way to reach Heathrow from central London and travels between Heathrow and Paddington Station every 15 minutes. (15min. 5:10am-11:40pm. Single £12, return £22, up to four children under 12 go free with an adult. The express train departs from Heathrow terminals 1, 2, 3, and 4. Tickets can be bought at Heathrow Express ticket counters, on board, or at self-service machines that accept pounds (coins and bills), credit and debit cards, and most foreign currencies (if you buy your ticket from the ticket window) Wheelchair accessible.)

London Regional Transport's **Airbus** (☎ (08705) 757 747) makes the one-hour trip from Heathrow to central points in the city approximately every 20 minutes. Travelers over 50 and under 25 qualify for discounts. (Adult single £7, return £12; discount single £3 or £5; children under 16 free) **Airbus Direct** is a faster bus service (same prices as Airbus) running only from Victoria. **Hotelink** runs from Heathrow and Gatwick to various hotels around the city (☎ (0) 1293 552 251); www.hotelink.co.uk; to Heathrow: single £14, return £24; to Gatwick: single £20, return £24.

GATWICK

Gatwick Airport in West Sussex (☎ (01293) 535 353) is farther from the city than Heathrow, but many budget flights arrive here. A number of 24-hour restaurants, cash machines, and bureaux de change are located in both the North and South Terminals. From Gatwick, the **BR Gatwick Express** (☎ (0990) 301530) zooms to Victoria Station (30-40 min; every 30 min., daily 5am to midnight, midnight to 5am approx. every 30min.; children half-price) gives the same discount for travel in the Network Southeast area. Ask at any mainline station. Schedules for all lines can be found on www.railtrack.co.uk.

STANSTEAD, LUTON, AND CITY

A number of international flights arrive at Stanstead, Luton, and City Airports. Stanstead Airport, in Stanstead, Essex

(☎ (01279) 680 500), is served by British Rail's **Stanstead Skytrain** (☎ (08457) 484 950) to Liverpool Street station (40min.; every 30min.; M-Sa 5am-11pm; £12, under 15, £6).

Many discount airlines use Luton (www.london-luton.com). Thameslink runs to Luton from Kings Cross, Farington, and Blackfriars (35min., approximately every hour on the hour; £9.60 single, £16.80 return; under-16 half price.)

London City Airport (☎ 7646 0888, www.londoncityairport.com, call 0800 834 163 for reservations on any airline) can be reached on the Underground via shuttle at Liverpool st. or Canning Town stations, or by bus routes 473, 69, or 474.

FROM THE BUS STATIONS

Victoria Coach Station (Tube: Victoria), located on Buckingham Palace Rd., is the hub of Britain's coach network. **National Express coaches** (☎ (0990) 80 80 80, www.nationalex-press.co.uk) service an expansive network. Coaches are considerably less expensive than trains but also take longer. National Express offers a **Discount Coach Card** (one year £8, three year £19) to passengers 16 to 25, and seniors (over 50).

Much of the commuting area around London is served by **Green Line** coaches, which leave frequently from Eccleston Bridge behind Victoria Station. (☎ (0870) 608 7261; open daily 9am-5pm; www.greenline.co.uk) Purchase tickets from the driver. Prices for day returns are higher before 9am Monday through Friday. Discounts include the one-day **Rover** ticket. (£7.50, children half price, and seniors £4. Valid on almost every Green Line coach and London Country bus M-F after 9am, Sa-Su all day.)

GETTING AROUND LONDON
BY UNDERGROUND

The color-coded Underground railway system, or Tube, is the easiest way to get around London, with over 260 stations on 11 lines. Call the 24-hour Tube info line for help (☎ 7222 1234). Small but invaluable "Journey Planner" maps are available at all stations and inside the front and back cover of *Let's Go: London*.

Fares depend on the number of zones passed through—a journey within Zone 1 will cost much less than a trip to a distant suburb. On Sundays and Bank Holidays, trains run less frequently. All transfers are free. A single adult ticket will cost between £1.50 and £3.50, with most central London trips costing £1.50 to £1.80. Return tickets cost exactly double the price of a single ticket. If you plan to make multiple trips in a day, a **Travelcard** will save you money. Travelcards also let you ride buses within the zones it covers. Most travellers won't venture out of Zones 1 and 2, making a pass beyond that superfluous. You may also consider buying a **Carnet** (£11), which is a booklet entitling you to 10 trips within Zone 1, if you'll be using the Tube sporadically.

You can buy your ticket either from the ticket window or from a machine. The ticket allows you to go through the automatic gates; **keep your ticket** until you reach your final destination, where the exit gates will collect it. Inspectors are rather strict about enforcing the Tube's on-the-spot £10 fine for travel without a valid ticket. Be aware that **"Ticket touts"** sometimes try to harass passengers into buying or selling used Travelcards. Not only is this illegal, it's also the new mayor's pet peeve; remember that entrepreneurship of this kind is a bad idea.

Most tube lines' last trains leave Central London between midnight and 12:30am M-Sa and between 11 and 11:30pm Su. Service resumes around 6am. **Night buses** (see **By Bus**, below) bridge the gap in service. The tube, packed during rush hour (M-F roughly 7-10am and 4:30-7:30pm) and high season (July-Aug.), earns its share of flack due to delays, dirt, and diverted trains; the Northern line has been nicknamed "the misery line" because of rush-hour bedlam, though the Central line rivals it in congestion.

Many stations feature labyrinthine tunnels and steep staircases. If you have **mobility problems,** are pushing a **stroller,** or are carrying a lot of **luggage,** you may fare better on a longer route that requires fewer transfers. Unfortunately, elevator access to platforms is still abysmal. The best bet is to call the information number (see above) and ask which stations are accessible. Remember to stand to the right and walk on the left on escalators, or risk a rude tumbling from commuters in full stride.

BY BUS

If you're in a hurry, don't take a bus. The Tube is faster and just as convenient to central London locations. But gliding through subway tunnels can hardly match the majesty of rolling along London streets on top of a double-decker. Not only is a bus ride a great way to orient yourself to the city's layout, but it also provides a fantastic opportunity to soak up London's atmosphere and sights. Route #11, beginning at Liverpool Street station, rides past St. Paul's, Fleet St., the Strand, Trafalgar Sq., Westminster, Sloane Sq., and all of King's Rd. #14 originates in Riverside-Putney and coasts down Fulham Rd., past the South Kensington museums, Knightsbridge, Hyde Park Corner, Piccadilly Circus and Leicester Sq., and terminates on Tottenham Court Rd. in Soho.

North Greenwich Station

Unfortunately, double-decker Routemaster buses, with their conductors and open rear platforms, are being replaced to save money. On modern double-deckers and single-deck "hoppa" buses, you pay your fare to the driver as you board. These newer buses, **while not strictly wheelchair accessible**, do have a lower platform that makes it possible to board, and are definitely more **stroller-friendly.** On Routemasters, take a seat and wait for the conductor, who can tell you the fare and let you know when to get off. Bus stops are marked with route information; at busy intersections or complicated one-way systems, maps tell where to board each bus. Each stop is marked with route numbers and only those buses stop there. The signs saying which route stops there also say which zone the stop is in, and in which direction the bus is headed. On stops marked "request," buses stop only if you flag them down to get on or pull the bell cord to get off. Service is notoriously sporadic during the daytime; waiting 20 minutes only to be greeted by a succession of three identical buses is not uncommon. Regular buses run from about 6am to midnight.

Charing Cross Station

The bus network is divided into four zones. Trips to, from, or within Zone 1 cost £1; any trip within outer London (not traveling in Zone 1) costs 70p. Be sure you have change to pay your fare because drivers will not accept bills. **Travelcards** purchased for the Underground are valid on buses; with a Travelcard, you may hop on or off as often as you like.

Night buses (routes preceded by "N") cater to late night transportation needs while the Underground is out of service. All night buses originate at Trafalgar Sq., with many also making a stop at Victoria station. Night buses (the "N" routes) start at 11:30pm and run until the first day buses get going. London Transport's information offices put out a free brochure about Night buses, which includes times of the last British Rail and Underground trains. Call London Transport's 24-hour information line (☎ 7222 1234) for fares and schedules. During New Year's celebrations, all night bus routes are diverted away from Trafalgar Square. Travelcards valid for more than 7 days are valid on night buses; the fare otherwise is £1.50 in Zone 1, £1 outside.

Victoria Station

If you're planning on utilizing the bus network, London Transport issues a **free bus map** for London called the *All-London Bus Guide*, available at most tube stations and LRT information offices. The *Central Bus Guide* is a more manageable pamphlet, describing only bus routes in Zone 1. If you require more detailed info about bus routes, there are 35 different local bus guides which will help you navigate specific neighborhoods. The *Visiting London* pamphlet is aimed directly at tourists and may be downloaded (in Adobe format) from www.londontransport.co.uk. To find out whether buses are running on schedule or whether routes have changed call 7222 1200. To acquire free local guides, call 7371 0247.

Wheelchair accessible Mobility Bus routes, numbered in the 800s and 900s, service most of outer London. Stationlink, a **wheelchair accessible bus** (numbered SL1 and SL2), travels hourly between the major train stations (9am-7pm; £1). For information on either service, call 7918 3312. For more information, see Travelers with Disabilities, p. 235.

BY DOCKLANDS LIGHT RAILWAY

The Docklands Light Railway (DLR), London's newest transport system, connects the flashy developments of the old docks with the City of London (from Bank in the City or from Tower Gateway). Call the railway's **customer service line** (☎7363 9700; open M-F 8:30am-5:15pm) for information. DLR's driverless trains run on an elevated track—having an underground here would require scuba gear. The Tube's zone system applies to the DLR; DLR lines appear on all tube maps. Fares are the same as for the tube and Travelcards apply. Alternatively, you can purchase a Docklander ticket ($3.10) which entitles you to unlimited travel after 9:30am. There are four lines: one running north-south (connecting with the tube at Bow Church and Stratford); the green line running west-east to merge with the north-south line (connecting with the tube at Bank, Shadwell, and Tower Hill/Gateway), and the Beckton line, which starts at Poplar Station (on the red line) and extends 5 mi. to the east. Another line from Island Gardens to Lewisham via Greenwich is scheduled to open sometime during 2000. (The rail cars run M-F 5:30am-12:30am, Sa 6am-12:30am, Su 7:30am-11:30pm.; bicycles not allowed on the DLR.)

BY TRAIN

Most of London is fully served by buses and the Tube. Some districts, however, notably southeast London, are most easily reached by train. Local surface trains are speedy and runs frequently to suburbs and daytrip areas around London, functioning as a commuter rail that is often cheaper than the tube. The North London Link, stretching across north London from North Woolwich to Richmond, often deposits travelers closer to sights (such as Keats's house) than the Tube. Trains (every 20min.) scoot from Hampstead Heath to Kew in 25 minutes.

BY TAXICAB

To earn a license, London taxicab drivers pass a rigorous exam called "The Knowledge," proving that they know the city's streets by heart; the route taken by a cabbie is virtually certain to be the shortest and quickest. Most of the distinctively shaped cabs are black, although many are plastered bumper to bumper in ads of all colors.

You are most likely to find cabs at large hotels or at major intersections, but cabs abound throughout Central London and are easy to hail except in rain. A taxi is available if the taxi sign on the roof or blue light in its window is lit. You can catch a cab yourself or call a radio dispatcher for one (☎7272 0272; 7253 5000); beware that you may be charged extra for ordering a cab by phone. Drivers are required to charge according to the meter for trips within London. A 10% tip is expected, with a surplus charge for extra baggage or passengers. Taxis in London are notoriously expensive, but may be worth the cost if you have a party of three or more who are splitting the tab. Apart from the licensed cabs, there are many "minicab" companies listed in the Yellow Pages. Ask the price when you order a minicab because most are not metered. **Freedom Cars**, 52 Wardour St., W1 (☎7734 1313; Tube: Piccadilly Circus) is a gay and lesbian minicab company.

Ladycabs (☎7254 3501) has only female cabbies and accepts only female passengers. (Open M-F 8am-12am, Sa 9am-2am, Su 10am-5pm.)You can reclaim **lost property** left in a licensed taxicab at 15 Penton St., N1. (☎833 0996. Tube: Angel; open M-F 9am-4pm.)

BY FOOT

Walking is the best way to get to know London. Major landmarks and tube stops may be closer than you think—the tube map, of course, is not to scale. If you choose to tackle London by foot, use caution when exploring; while you're unlikely to encounter violence anywhere in central London during the day, you should be on guard against pickpockets. At night, walk in groups and make sure where you go is safe; use common sense and stay in well lit, busy areas. Day or night, carry a reliable map, but duck into a shop or a cafe if you need to check it. Bear in mind, however, that even Londoners refer to their *A-Z London* to navigate their city's labyrinthine streets. Even if you plan on staying in London only a short time you may find this comprehensive and unbeatable atlas of London indispensible. London's many green spaces afford travelers ample walking space, but don't take that tempting short cut across the park at night; it's too dangerous, even in upscale neighborhoods.

For most visitors to London, though, the single biggest danger comes from the fact that UK drivers drive on the left—**look right when crossing the street** (except, of course, on certain one-way roads). Mindful of this, zebra crossings (crosswalks) in central London often have reminders of which way to look. **Jaywalking** is legal and ubiquitous among Londoners, but those unused to local driving habits are best off waiting for the lights.

Finally, a **walking tour** helps you see sights in an organized fashion while getting a bit of exercise. *Let's Go* suggests some walking tours itineraries on p. 8, but you should feel free to draw up your own. It's truly possible to walk across London in a day—try it!

BY BOAT

River boats provide excellent views of many of London's major sights, with a number of services ploughing up and down the Thames. **Thames Leisure** offers an hour long circular cruise leaving from Tower Pier and going west as far as the Houses of Parliament. (☎7623 1805; www.thamesleisure.co.uk. Boats run daily 11am-6pm every 30min. £5.80, ages 5-15 £3.20, family £16.50.) **Westminster Passenger Services Association** offers cruises from Westminster Pier (Tube: Westminster) upriver to Richmond, Kew, and Hampton Court Palace; schedules and journey times vary according to the tides. (☎7930 2062; www.wpsa.co.uk. To Kew £7, day return £11, children £3, day return £5; to Richmond £8, £12, £3.50, £6; to Hampton Court £10, £14, £4, £7.) You can also glide down the **Regent's Canal** between Camden Town and Little Venice through Regent's Park; call the **London Waterbus Company** for details. (☎7482 2660. Daily service in summer; low season Sa-Su only.)

Life & Times

LONDON THEN

History will be kind to me, for I intend to write it.
— Winston Churchill

ROMAN TIMES

In AD 43, the Roman Emperor Claudius successfully invaded Britain with an army of 40,000. He wasn't the first Italian to visit Britain (and as a visit to London will attest, he certainly wouldn't be the last)—Julius Caesar had invaded in 55 BC, but the British, who apparently developed their reputation for hospitality in later centuries, dealt him a rare defeat. **Londinium** became a thriving commercial outpost with a population of 15,000. Despite London's prosperity, establishing authority proved difficult, and during the first years of Roman rule a number of small rebellions shook England. In AD 60 the rebel forces of **Queen Boudicca**, whose husband and daughters were slain by the Romans, burned London and massacred the Roman garrison. But by 200 the Romans had established firm control and London was a flourishing, fortified city of 50,000.

CHRISTIANITY AND THE NORMANS

With Italy in the clutches of barbarians, Roman forces withdrew from Britain in 410 and chaos ensued as imperial legal institutions disintegrated. Marauding Germanic tribes established settlements around the island, which was not yet united by a central government. When in 597 Pope Gregory sent **Augustine of Canterbury** to convert England, Christianity arrived. Reigning Saxon King Ethelbert welcomed conversion, and by the end of the 7th century Christianity had become England's established religion. Augustine appointed Mellitus (who founded St. Paul's Cathedral in 604) as the first Bishop of London.

The 9th century saw the beginning of London's tumultuous relationship with the Vikings. In 841 and 851, Vikings reduced London to rubble and it was over 30 years before the English retook London under **King Alfred the Great** of Wessex. But by 1013 the Danes managed to seize the city from Alfred's successor, the aptly-named **Ethelred the Unready.** In response, Ethelred enlisted the help of his better-prepared friend Olaf (later a saint), who led a fleet up the Thames to London Bridge in 1014. Olaf tied ropes to the bridge supports and rowed away, the Danes fell into the Thames, and the nursery rhyme "London Bridge is Falling Down" was born. Despite Olaf's prodigious bridge-wrecking capacities, the Vikings triumphed.

In 1042, the English again regained the throne under **Edward the Confessor.** He built Westminster Abbey, which became the center of government while the City, two miles east, developed into the center of English commerce. But Edward failed to leave a clear line of succession. When he died, his brother-in-law Harold and Duke William of Normandy both claimed the throne; in 1066 William invaded from France and defeated Harold's army at the Battle of Hastings. On Christmas Day, he was crowned in Westminster Abbey.

THE MIDDLE AGES

During the 12th and 13th centuries, Londoners steadily gained rights against the king. **Henry I** first chartered the City of London in 1130, thus allowing it to self-govern, but obstacles still remained. **Henry II** revoked London's new autonomy and **Richard I** (better known as the Lionheart) increased taxes on London so he could finance a crusade to Jerusalem. Soon after that expansion of power, noblemen, tired of royal abuses of authority, forced Richard's brother King John to sign the **Magna Carta** in 1215. The document is often credited with laying the groundwork for modern democracy.

History took a sad turn in 1290 when **Edward I** expelled the entire Jewish population of England. In London, Lombard Italians replaced the substantial Jewish community which had flourished through money-lending and finance. The **Black Plague** ravaged the city during the 14th century, killing over a third of the population. In 1399, the throne fell to the Lancaster house when **Henry Bolingbroke** seized the throne while **Richard II** was in Ireland. In 1415, **Henry V** defeated the French in the Battle of Agincourt, a victory for the British underdogs that soon became legendary. But **Henry VI** proved to be an incompetent ruler, squandering the advantage his predecessor had gained, and was executed in the Tower of London, allowing Richard III to take over the crown.

REFORMATION AND RENAISSANCE

The second king of the Tudor family, **Henry VIII** was at first such a devout Catholic that Pope Clement VII named him "Defender of the Faith." However, his political ambition soon overrode religious obligations. Convinced that his first wife Catharine of Aragon would not give birth to a son, he asked the Pope to grant him a separation. When the Pope refused, he called Parliament and requested that England break with the papacy. In 1534, he formed the **Church of England** and married Anne Boleyn. Four more marriages later, Henry had produced only one male heir, the sickly **Edward VI**, whose early death brought Henry's daughter **Bloody Mary** to the throne, so named for her relentless persecution of Protestants. Luckily for the Church of England, Mary also died soon; her (Anglican) half-sister **Elizabeth** became the most powerful of the Tudor monarchs. Queen Elizabeth I became a symbol for the **English Renaissance:** she spoke French, Italian, and Spanish fluently, played the lute, wrote poetry, and was a domineering diplomat. During her rule, the British fleet defeated the Spanish Armada, establishing Britannia's dominion over the seas; joint-stock ventures such as the Virginia Company sent the British flag fluttering across the seas; and the **Royal Exchange** was established, securing London's status as a financial center. In 1581, writer John Lyly declared that London "may be called the storehouse and mart of all Europe." Coffeehouses cropped up, brewing business deals alongside literary and political discussions. Playwrights and poets amused commoners in the outdoor theaters of Southwark, including Shakespeare's **Globe Theatre.**

THE PROTECTORATE AND THE RESTORATION

In the 17th century, political and religious turmoil climaxed in a clash between **Oliver Cromwell's** Puritan forces and **King Charles I's** Anglican army. On January 4, 1642, Charles I entered Parliament and tried to arrest five MPs. Charles mobilized an army and fought Cromwell's Roundheads until 1649. Royalists attempted to attack the capital, but the city stood firmly on the side of Parliament: on January 30, 1649 Charles was tried for treason and became the first and only English king to be publicly executed. Cromwell was named Lord Protector of the Commonwealth in 1653, but died of malaria five years later. His short reign had a profound effect on the country; he sent troops to Ireland, starting a conflict that still exists today, but ended three centuries of expulsion by allowing Jews to return to England. In London his Puritanism resulted in the end of all music and theater in the capital; Parliament even abolished Christmas Day in 1652.

The monarchy was restored when Cromwell's son Richard proved unable to sustain the government; **Charles II** returned to an enthusiastic London, where he restored the lost merriment of the city. Disasters visited the early years of Charles's reign—the **Plague** in 1665 and the **Great Fire** which ravaged the city in 1666 caused economic collapse. Under the guidance of Sir Christopher Wren, the city was rebuilt.

The **Restoration** did not, however, signal the end of Parliamentary troubles: although Charles II was pliant enough to suit Parliament, there was heated debate about whether to exclude Charles II's fervently Catholic brother James from the succession. Debate during the **Exclusion Crisis** spawned the establishment of two political parties, the **Whigs** (who were firmly Protestant) and the **Tories** (who likened their opponents to the lately discredited Puritans). The bloodless **Glorious Revolution** of 1688 settled the question when, to prevent James II from achieving a Catholic monarchical dynasty, Protestant William of Orange and his wife Mary invaded from Holland. After assenting to the **Bill of Rights,** they took over the monarchy, ending a century of violent upheaval, although the Jacobites (supporters of James II) remained a distant threat. The Bill of Rights did far more than end debate about who would hold the Crown; it permanently aligned the balance of power between Crown and Parliament in the latter's favor. Over the 18th century, the office of Prime Minister, held at the beginning of the century by Robert Walpole, gradually eclipsed the monarch as the head of government. As Parliament's power grew, the Whigs and Tories became full-fledged political parties; the Tories became more generally conservative and loyal to the monarch, while the Whigs became a group of reformers and progressives. In the 19th century, the **Conservative** and **Liberal** Parties formed along these ideological lines. Today, "Tory" is still used to indicate a Conservative Party supporter.

The 18th century was one of transition for London. The German-speaking Hanoverian dynasty took over and did very little to lead England, a task left more and more to Parliament. However, it was during this time that London became a truly modern city. Massive portions of the rural

HISTORY TIMELINE

AD 43 Invading Romans cross the Thames to establish Londinium.

836 Vikings invade London.

1066 Norman Invasion; William I crowned; Charter granted to London.

1100 Henry I assumes the throne.

1189 Henry FitzAilwyn appointed first mayor of London.

1240 First Parliament held at Westminster.

1272 Edward I becomes king.

1290 Jews expelled from London.

1348 Black Death ravages the city.

1377 Richard II crowned.

1461 House of York comes to power with coronation of Edward IV.

1509 Henry VIII assumes throne.

1558 Queen Elizabeth crowned.

1599 Construction of Globe Theatre.

1649 Commonwealth established under Cromwell after execution of Charles I.

1660 Stuart dynasty restored.

1665 Plague ravages the city leaving over 100,000 dead.

1666 Great Fire destroys medieval city.

1688-9 Glorious Revolution. William and Mary crowned.

LONDON UN-DERGROUND

While today, most give little thought to the Underground public transit system, aside from bemoaning its rush hour delays, those who survived World War II probably know the Tube system far more intimately than anyone could ever ask for. During the war, over 150,000 people found shelter on the platforms of London's Tube stations. The government originally forbade the camping out of London residents in spaces designed for people to momentarily stand upon. During the German air raids, however, it soon became apparent that many of the city's inhabitants intended to avoid falling bombs by getting as far away from them as possible—namely, by burrowing underground. Once the government realized that the platform squatters were there to stay, fear that an epidemic would result from the squalid conditions prompted the emergence of British hospitality. Bathrooms were provided, refreshments and tea were served, lights were dimmed in the evenings, and bunks were provided for added comfort. A spirit of community began to evolve among the Underground inhabitants beneath London's surface. Over 50 lending libraries were created to provide entertainment. Recorded music was played. Mini-schools and day-care centers were arranged. Ever obsessed by the news, some of the tube stations began their own newspapers. For instance, the Swiss Cottage tube station published the *Swiss Cottager*, perhaps one of the few real examples of an underground press. (See **London Transport Museum**, p. 121).

populace migrated to London, pushed off the land by the agricultural revolution and the **Enclosure Acts** and lured by rapidly growing opportunities in industrial employment. Over the next hundred years, industrialization irreversibly altered the texture of British and global society as Britain expanded into Empire. The gulf between workers and owners that began as early as the 11th century was replaced by a wider gap between factory owners and their laborers. Riots and crime were common. The 1780 **Gordon Riots,** ostensibly fueled by anti-Catholicism, left hundreds dead.

THE 19TH CENTURY

As Britannia's rule expanded under **Queen Victoria,** London enthusiastically took up its position at the center of the Empire. **The Great Exhibition,** a fair celebrating and displaying British and imperial products, along with Queen Victoria's Golden and Diamond Jubilees and Prince Albert's South Kensington Museums, would long stand as symbols of the pinnacle of Britain's technological and imperial prowess.

By the 1830s, the combined forces of class division and frightening workplace conditions spurred the beginnings of domestic industrial regulation. A century of reform was inaugurated by moderate franchise reform in 1832. At the same time, some morally stringent Victorian Liberals such as **William Gladstone** picked up where free-traders like **Robert Peel** left off, extending the economic notion of a free market to encompass a more open attitude toward different religions. The **Chartist movement** of the mid-19th century dramatically pressed for universal manhood suffrage regardless of class, but modest reforms during the 1840s effectively curbed more radical reform until later in the century.

As the Empire burgeoned, the city became increasingly crowded. Rampant growth in the 18th and 19th centuries worsened structural problems that the government was unable to address. Increasing pollution of the Thames led to the "Big Stink" of 1858. Private enterprise stepped into the gap; the first **Underground** line was financed by private backers. The **London County Council,** created in 1889, provided a more substantial public transit solution. It developed public motor-buses to reduce congestion and eventually passed clean air legislation. The grimy, foggy streets of Jack the Ripper and Sherlock Holmes would never be the same again.

By the end of the century, trade-unions grew more powerful, assuming their modern form during the 1889 strike of the East London dockers and eventually finding a political voice in the **Labour Party,** founded in 1906. Despite the gains of organized labor, the quality of urban life declined alarmingly. In the capital, three out of four children did not live beyond the age of five, and an outbreak of cholera struck many of the city's poor. The Victorian elite took up aid to the poor as its pet project, paving the way for a slew of welfare programs established by the Liberal government in 1910. Meanwhile, pressures to alter the position of different marginalized groups just before the war proved largely futile. The **Suffragettes,** led by **Emmeline Pankhurst,** attempted to win women the right to vote by disrupting Parliament and staging hunger strikes; their methods only alienated political support for their cause.

Britain was at the height of its economic and political power in the second half of the 19th century. By Victoria's death in 1901, the UK controlled the largest Empire the world had yet seen and most of the world's finance. However, the death of the Queen, whose reign lasted over 60 years ,for many marked the beginning of the end of Empire.

THE 20TH CENTURY

WWI AND DEPRESSION

The Great War, Britain's first continental military action in a century, scarred the British with the loss of a generation and dashed Victorian dreams of a peaceful, progressive society. Though women gained the vote after the war, a sense of aimlessness overtook the nation's politics. One major change was the newly-found strength of the Labour party; which rode to power in 1918 on the votes of decommissioned soldiers, pushing the Liberal party into a political backwater from which it has yet to emerge. The 1930s brought the **depression** and mass unemployment during Stanley Baldwin's prime ministry. In 1936, **Edward VIII** shocked the world with the announcement of his abdication from the throne to marry Wallace Simpson, a twice-divorced Baltimore socialite. The decade came to a close with the appeasement of Hitler, led by Neville "peace in our time" Chamberlain, followed soon after by Britain's entry into the war.

WORLD WAR II AND AFTER

"We would rather see London laid in ruins and ashes than that it should be tamely and abjectly enslaved," declared **Winston Churchill** in 1940. During the Battle of Britain, the city endured bombing every night except one for three straight months. Even when Hitler transferred the Luftwaffe to the Russian front, and London emerged from the Blitz, the city still faced periodic bombings. Beginning in September, 1944, Hitler's V2 missiles brought terror to London for six months.

The war's end left England with vast imperial holdings, but the second empire immediately lost its power. Queen **Elizabeth II,** who continues to reign today, was crowned in 1953. Postwar affluence propelled Britain to the center stage of international popular culture and gave rise and fall to countless subcultures clustered around pop music and fashion. **Harold Wilson's** Labour government introduced a number of crucial social liberalizations, including reform of divorce and homosexuality laws and the abolition of capital punishment. Wilson also sought to drive the nation forward with the "white heat" of technological advance, but toward the end of the 60s became mired in the government's decreasingly reciprocal

1707 Act of Union unites England and Scotland under one government.

1776 American colonies declare independence.

1815 Wellington defeats Napoleon at Waterloo.

1837 Victoria becomes Queen.

1851 Great Exhibition sees thousands flock to London.

1888 Serial murderer Jack the Ripper's reign of terror.

1901 House of Saxe-Coburg (later called Windsor) comes to power with coronation of Edward VII.

1914-18 World War I.

1918 Women allowed to vote.

1939-1945 World War II.

1940 London devastated by German bombs during the Blitz.

1952 Queen Elizabeth crowned.

1982 Falklands War.

1996 Tony Blair elected Prime Minister.

2000 Ken Livingstone becomes first elected Mayor of London.

SEX SCANDALS, A QUICKIE HISTORY

British attitudes towards sexuality can be baffling: while tabloids sport topless girls, they're also willing to act totally shocked when a Member of Parliament is caught *in flagrante delicto*. Perhaps the most famous of British sex scandals was the **Profumo Affair,** when John Profumo, then Secretary of State for War, had to leave government after he lied about having sex with Christine Keeler, a society girl who was also having an affair with a Soviet naval attaché. Scandal also shook John Major's Conservative government: David Mellor, Heritage Secretary, had to resign in 1992 after his affair with actress Antonia de Sancha was disclosed, while the revelation of Piers Merchant's affair with teenager Anna Cox added to voter discontent with the Major government in 1997. Merchant was quoted as saying "My male instinct was far stronger than any immediate thoughts I had for John Major." But if voters thought they'd finally managed to "throw the bums out," the current Labour government proved them wrong.

relationship with organized labor, which now represented middle-class clerical workers as much as railwaymen and miners. The London County Council became the **Greater London Council** in 1965, and its authority over the city was gradually diminished.

Britain gradually relinquished the majority of its colonial holdings in Africa, the Middle East, and South Asia. Visionary Conservative **Harold Macmillan** heard "the winds of change" blowing and paved the way for the denouement of the Empire. He hoped to win Britain its place in the **European Community** (EC), a task completed in 1974.

Increasing economic problems that stemmed from Britain's colonial retreat led to increased belief in the 70s of the theorization of "decline." Would Britain be able to prosper without the income from her former empire? Conservative and Labour governments alike floundered in their attempts to curtail unemployment while maintaining a base level of social welfare. The discovery of oil in the North Sea lifted hopes prematurely, but plummeting prices hobbled its market value. Government after government wrangled with labor unions, culminating in a series of public-service strikes in early 1979, the **"Winter of Discontent."**

It was against this backdrop that Britain grasped at what looked like a chance for change: the admonishing "Victorian values" and nationalism of Prime Minister **Margaret "The Iron Lady" Thatcher.** Her first term seemed doomed by a painful economic recession, but by 1983 the victory following the invasion of the **Falkland Islands** (a UK territory) by Argentina and embarrassing disarray in the Labour Party clinched her second term. Thatcher turned from the war in the islands to "the enemy within," referring to the bitter miners' strike of 1983-84, while denationalizing industries and dismantling the welfare state. Unlike her Tory and Labour predecessors, Thatcher neither believed nor succumbed to the long-standing view that the government should focus its economic policies on reducing unemployment. The first Prime Minister to break with the postwar consensus, she advocated privatization and preferred to control inflation by cutting taxes and welfare programs.

Thatcher prided herself on "politics of conviction," but her stubbornness was her undoing, as she clung to the unpopular poll tax and resisted European integration. Conflicts with London's Ken Livingstone led her to completely abolish the Greater London Council. A 1990 leadership challenge led to her resignation and replacement by **John Major** as Prime Minister. Major quietly jettisoned the poll tax and stepped more carefully around Europe. His "Citizens' Charter" continued the reform of public services, though less radically, by gently speaking of Health Service "customers" and promising refunds to delayed rail passengers. But Major's cabinet became more occupied with predicting the end to a deep recession resulting partly from the credit-fueled 80s boom. In 1993, the British pound toppled out of the EC's monetary regulation system, embarrassing Major's government and casting doubt on Britain's place in the Community. Finally, in August of the same year, after severe division between Major and anti-treaty rebels within the Conservative Party, Britain became the last member of the EC to ratify the **Maastricht Treaty** on a closer **European Union (EU).**

Even with these Conservative debacles, Labour failed again to shed the image gained during 70s recessions, and the Tories under John Major won another five years in April 1992. Labour's defeat spurred the election of a new leader, Scotsman **John Smith,** and the pursuit of reform, but the beloved Smith's untimely death in May 1994 dashed Labour hopes once more. From 1992-97, Major struggled with constant unpopularity; the aftermath of the 1991-92 recession, the 1993 tax increases, and continuing strife within the Conservative Party over relations with Europe all accounted for drops in support.

By 1995, Major's ratings were so low that he resigned as leader of the Conservative Party to force a leadership election. Major won, restoring some semblance of authority, but as the Conservatives lost parliamentary seats in by-elections and continued to languish in the polls, the Labour Party, under the leadership of charismatic **Tony Blair,** refashioned itself into the alternative for discontented voters.

LONDON NOW

POLITICS

As the UK enters the new millennium, **Tony Blair** leads the Labour Party and Britain under the aegis of **"New Labour,"** a reincarnation of the party that has tried to shed its old socialist affiliations. Blair has supported schemes for privatizing public transport that would have done his Tory predecessors proud, and shortly after entering office made the historic decision to give the Bank of England independence in setting interest rates. He has also made significant progress in bringing peace to Northern Ireland. Blair's most lasting achievement may well be the constitutional changes wrought by his government; since taking power Scotland and Wales have been given their own elected legislatures and London a directly-elected mayor; the changes run to the heart of Westminster following the expulsion of the hereditary Lords from the House in 1999. His government, however, is criticized being more spin than substance, and Conservative Party leader **William Hague** is pursuing a populist manifesto aimed at upsetting the pundits in the next election, which will most probably take place some time in 2001.

It is impossible to understand London without some recognition of the city as a truly political animal. As home to the **Houses of Parliament** and all of the royal palaces but Balmoral (in Scotland), London has always been at the fore of British politics. Since Henry I first chartered the city in 1130, it has struggled to maintain its autonomy within England, a struggle which culminated with the election of a maverick Ken Livingstone as mayor in May 2000. **Parliament** is divided into two houses, the **House of Lords** and the **House of Commons.** The Members of Parliament (MPs) convene in the House of Commons and are elected to their positions; Life Peers, who are appointed for life by the Queen on the recommendation of the Prime Minister, sit in the House of Lords. In a nod to tradition, an election was held among hereditary Lords in 1999 to select a few born aristocrats who would continue to sit in the House; since Lords may not vote in parliamentary elections.

The **Prime Minister** is not elected directly, although he or she must be an MP; following a general election, the Queen formally invites the leader of the largest party in the House of Commons to form a government (and hence become Prime Minister). There are no set dates for **parliamentary elections;** while the Prime Minister must request that the monarch dissolve Parliament and hold an election at least every five years, he or she can call an election at any time at three weeks notice, a rule which keeps elections short and inexpensive. The second-largest party moves into **Opposition;** "Leader

RED KEN AND THE RACE TO RUN LONDON

Unlike most major cities in the world, London had not had a mayor before 2000. Thanks to the crusading zeal of Britain's Labour government, however, a directly elected, American-style mayor has been introduced to Britain's capital city. There's just one small problem: Mr. Blair can't stand the man who won the election, Ken Livingstone. Christened "Red Ken" by the tabloid newspapers, Livingstone is just the kind of traditional socialist that Blair has tried to eradicate from the Labour party. When it became clear that Ken had overwhelming support among Londoners (and especially Labour Party members), Blair supporters changed the rules to stop him becoming the official Labour Party candidate. Rather than giving each person an equal vote, they set up three equally-weighted electoral colleges: MPs, trades unions (which did not have to poll their members), and party members. In this skewed system Frank Dobson, Blair's preferred candidate, was selected, even though Livingstone won a vast majority of member's votes. Unperturbed, Ken stood as an independent—and won easily. While from the outside it's all smiles between Ken and Tony, rumor has it the government is planning to sabotage Ken's transportation ideas.

of the Opposition" is an officially paid post, as are various "shadow ministers," who lambast the policies of their government counterparts and prepare for an eventual election victory. Though such a system is ostensibly a two-party one, **"third parties"** persist. The **Liberal Democrats** were formed from the old Liberal Party and the Social Democratic Party, a moderate Labour splinter group. Other parties include the Social Democratic and Labour Party (SDLP), the Greens, Sinn Fein, the Scottish Nationalist Party, Plaid Cymru (the Welsh nationalist party), and the Ulster Unionists.

RECENT NEWS

The story of 2000 was the election of Ken Livingstone as the first-ever elected Mayor of London (see **Red Ken and the Race to London**), on a platform promising to solve the capital's perennial transport and pollution problems (see **London Fog**, p. 42). At the dawn of the 21st century, London's millennium celebrations captivated the world as the city unveiled the **Millennium Dome.** Tony Blair has expressed hopes that the structure will galvanize national pride, but £758 million later, no one's really sure what the dome has accomplished. Visitor levels have plummeted since its opening, and when the millennium exhibition shuts down at the start of 2001, a Japanese developer will convert this pride of Britain into an indoor amusement park. Linking the Dome to the rest of London, the **Jubilee line extension** was completed, finally integrating Greenwich and Docklands into the Tube network; the Northern line is also undergoing long-needed improvements.

Far more potent a symbol of Britain's cultural regeneration than the posturing of the Dome, **Tate Modern** (see p. 102) opened in May 2000 to rave reviews. A converted power plant, the museum contains an expansive collection of 20th-century art that had long since outgrown its original Millbank home. Trouble dogs the new **Millennium Bridge** though; linking the Tate Modern to St. Paul's, the first new bridge over the Thames in a century was closed soon after opening when it began swaying under the tread of thousands of feet. It is planned to re-open by 2001. Luckily, the 443 ft. **Millennium Wheel** (see p. 100) shows no sign of falling over.

On a more somber note, the **Euro 2000** tournament brought football hooliganism back to the headlines, as English fans caused trouble in Holland and Belgium. The offenders were sent back to England, embarrassing the country and ruining England's chances of hosting the 2006 World Cup. The incidents prompted a national discussion of England's "drinking culture" (see **Football Fans are Coming Home,** p. 150).

ARTS AND CULTURE

ARCHITECTURE

The Angles and the Saxons began the story of London architecture with a style that combined the severe Roman and simple Celtic approaches. In the 11th century, the **Normans** brought the first distinctive national style in churches that combined long naves with rectangular wings. These Romanesque elements survive in the 12th-century church of St. Bartholomew the Great (see p. 57). Ribbed vaulting, pointed arches, and flying buttresses marked Gothic architecture. The predecessor to today's St. Paul's Cathedral (see p. 53) was one of Europe's largest Gothic churches.

In the early 17th century, court architect **Inigo Jones** introduced Palladian architecture (a style that adhered rigidly to classical models) to London. He coated James I's Banqueting House in Whitehall with gleaming Portland stone, constructed the airy Covent Garden Piazza, and built the first Neoclassical church in England for Charles I's Spanish fiancée.

King George II

The Great Fire of 1666 provided the next opportunity for large-scale construction. In its aftermath, as most of London lay an ashy wasteland, ambitious young architect **Christopher Wren** presented Charles II his blueprints for a new city. Wren envisioned broad avenues and spacious plazas but the pragmatic king was well aware that the plan, which took no account of existing property lines, would anger landowners. So he vetoed Wren's design and the city was rebuilt in the same piecemeal way that it had risen. Nevertheless, Wren built 51 new churches, flooding the skyline with a sea of spires leading up to St. Paul's, his masterwork and final church.

The lyrical styles begun by Jones and Wren continued to shape London's architecture for much of the next century. Other designers, like **James Gibbs, Colin Campbell,** and **William Kent** blended their styles with the Baroque trend sweeping the Continent. The tower and steeple plan of St. Martin's-in-the-Fields proved a popular model for Gibbs's colonial churches, particularly in the USA. Campbell built early mansions such as Burlington House, now home of the Royal Academy (see p. 124). Kent designed the walls and pseudo-Pompeiian ceiling of Kensington Palace and the interior of the Palladian Chiswick House (see p. 111). Kent's landscaping truly distinguished him from his contemporaries. In contrast to the rigid severity of his buildings, he designed his gardens to reflect the formless beauty of nature.

On the Street

By the late 1700s, patrons and builders sought relief from ponderousness but continued to build in Neoclassical modes. **Robert Adam** broke with Palladian strictness and combined different modes of classical design, as in the graceful **Kenwood House** (see p. 94). The romantic pediments, triumphal arches, and sweeping pavilions of Regent's Park bear witness to **John Nash's** rich vision for London's cityscape.

Victoria's reign dampened enthusiasm for Neoclassicism and ushered in a spirited Gothic revival. Completed in 1860, the Houses of Parliament (see p. 71) occupied architect **Sir Charles Barry** for most of his life. Barry led London's

Tower Hill

THE MANY FACES OF LONDON

It's difficult not to notice the many ethnic groups and communities from around the globe that inhabit the city—today's Londoners are just as likely to worship at a Hindu mandir as at a Gothic Wren church, and newsstands feature dailies in Chinese alongside the *Times* and the *Daily Telegraph*. The diversity began with the vast British Empire, which once stretched across the globe, and was intensified in London as the government encouraged the immigration of Commonwealth citizens to compensate for the labor shortage caused by World War II. The expansion of the British Empire paved the way for the immigration of West Indians, Hong Kong Chinese, and South Asians, who arrived via the South Asian sub-continent and sub-Saharan Africa. During World War II, European Jews fled to the city to escape Fascist persecution and immediately after the war, Eastern Europeans anticipating a dismal future beneath the Iron Curtain migrated to London in large numbers. The wide variety of cultures and backgrounds is evident in vibrant ethnic areas such as Brixton; home to a large Caribbean community; the East End, a thriving Southeast Asian neighborhood; and Golders Green, center of the Jewish community.

Gothic Revival, and **The Reform Club** on Pall Mall bears his name. While many architects insisted on bringing back Gothic, others worked in Italian Renaissance, French, and Dutch forms; still others latched onto Tudor, and some lonely pioneers discovered new building possibilities in iron and glass. **Sir Joseph Paxton** created the splendid Crystal Palace for the World's Fair of 1851. The inspirational 1600-foot-long building burned down at the time of Edward's abdication.

After WWII, the face of building in London, perhaps exhausted by the demolition of the war, took a harsher turn. The 1951 Festival of Britain, a centennial celebration of the Great Exhibition and postwar "Tonic to the Nation," created such buildings as the Royal Festival Hall (see p. 149). The hopes of postwar utopian planning, and their varying degrees of fulfillment, are embodied in the vast and interplanetary Barbican Centre (see p. 149). Then came the early 60s and a building boom in which the post-Blitz face of the City was established. Hulking monoliths now neighbor Victorian door pillars and spiraling chimneys. London's most recent architectural triumph is Lloyd's of London, remarkable for being decked on the *outside* with elevators and ducts. Designed by **Richard Rogers** and completed in 1986, the Lloyd's building embraces a technological future. Beginning in 1981, the London Docklands Development Corporation was given free reign to develop eight miles of wasteland, causing a frenetic race to create offices and luxury apartments on the Thames. At the center of this showcase of modern architecture is the dazzling Canary Wharf, the tallest building in Britain at 800 ft.

ART

Aside from woodcuts, tapestries, and illuminated manuscripts, England produced little visual art until the Renaissance. In contrast to its Catholic neighbors, Sixteenth century Protestant England turned to an aesthetic that rejected religious themes in favor of secular ones. Despite these distinguishing marks, many of England's early stars were imported. In the 16th century, the German **Hans Holbein** (1497-1543) worked in London as the official painter to the king. A century later, **Sir Anthony Van Dyck** (1599-1641) played the same role, painting dramatic royal portraits of Charles I. Partly in reaction to these foreign artists who had helped shape the conventions of British painting, Londoner **William Hogarth** (1697-1764) prided himself on his distinctly English sense of style. *A Harlot's Progress* and *A Rake's Progress*, two series of morally instructive engravings, established his reputation and broadened the audience for British art. He brought an appreciation of folk culture to his work; *Southwark Fair* expresses the exuberance of lowbrow London.

From the mid-18th to mid-19th century, portraiture continued to thrive under the influence of painters **Thomas Gainsborough** (1727-1788) and **Joshua Reynolds** (1723-1792). Reynolds founded the **Royal Academy,** which since its creation has trained generations of artists. Londoner **J.M.W. Turner** (1775-1851) painted mythic light-filled landscapes in both watercolor and oil paint. He is famed for the visual records of his travels, including a set of engravings entitled *Picturesque Views of England and Wales.* The Tate displays a magnificent collection of Turner's work (see **Tate Britain,** p. 117).

The mid- to late-19th century infused British painting with an unbridled spirit. **William Blake** (1757-1827) captured the Romantic spirit in fantastical paintings, while the Pre-Raphaelites, **John Everett Millais** (1829-1896), **Dante Gabriel Rossetti** (1828-1882), and **Edward Burne-Jones** (1833-1898), lamented that painting had become too academic and tried to restore sincerity to the medium. Poet, architect and painter **William Morris,** profoundly influenced by Rossetti, set up shop in Bloomsbury in the last half of the century and created some of the most recognizable design patterns associated with the **Arts and Crafts Movement,** which sought to reassert the priority of beauty and craftsmanship in design, thought to have been perverted by the Industrial Revolution.

Beginning in the 1930s, **Henry Moore's** (1898-1986) rounded and abstracted human forms and **Barbara Hepworth's** (1903-1975) carved elemental materials thrusted modern British sculpture into international fame. London-born photographer **Bill Brandt** (1904-1983) illuminated English life with his visual essays of industrial workers and the terror of WWII. His haunting photograph "St. Paul's Cathedral in the Moonlight" (1942) captures the deserted war-time streets of London.

The mid-20th century brought about the transformation of English portraiture. **Francis Bacon** (1909-1992) shocked the crusty whitebreads with his "Screaming Popes," a take on Velazquez's portrait of Pope Innocent X, and the oddly unrealistic "realism" of **Lucien Freud** (b.1922), Sigmund's youngest, had more than one stuffy patron headed for the couch. **David Hockney** (b. 1937) is perhaps one of the most recognizable names in 20th century British art. Trained at the Royal Academy in London, Hockney works in a variety of mediums from prints to photography.

Each year, the **Turner Prize** recognizes Britain's best young artists. Recent honorees have included such controversial luminaries as **Damien Hirst** (b. 1965), whose most well-known work may be his "Mother and Child Divided," featuring a cow and its calf cut in half and suspended in formaldehyde. Advertising mogul Charles Saatchi has remained a loyal patron of the artist and is the proud owner many of Hirst's works, including "A Thousand Years," a piece made of a rotting cow's head, maggots, flies, and a bug zapper. Rumor has it Hirst cooks a great burger.

LITERARY LONDON

Since the pilgrims in Chaucer's *Canterbury Tales* (c. 1387) set off from the Tabard Inn, London has cast a long shadow over the English literary imagination. **William Shakespeare** catered to aristocracy and groundlings alike in the Rose and Globe theaters across the Thames, the heart of the red-light district. Second in reputation only to Shakespeare, rowdy dramatist **Ben Jonson** held sway in the English court of the early 17th century as an actor, author, and literary critic. **John Donne** set his first and fourth satires in London, drawing attention to urban evils, and **Alexander Pope** wrote in the epilogue to his satires that in London, "nothing is sacred…but villainy." Pope drank away his gloom with professional genius and renowned conversationalist **Samuel Johnson** in the Cheshire Cheese Pub, while **James Boswell** scurried around collecting crumbs for his grand biography, the *Life of Johnson.* Poets of the Age of Reason fantasized about a city different from the crime-filled one that they inhabited. London remained a haven for publishing and literary cliques wrestling with ideas of social justice. In the early 18th century, **Joseph Addison** and **Richard Steele** attacked urban ills in a new way: the *Tatler* and *Spectator* delivered moral and political essays to subscribers, while **Jonathan Swift** suggested in his *Modest Proposal* (1729) that to curb urban poverty the poor should eat children. **Daniel Defoe** and **Henry Fielding** explored themes of urban injustice, using journalism, satire, and sermons as their tools. Most famous as the author of *Robinson Crusoe*, Defoe was deeply embroiled in the political and religious controversies of his day. He opposed the reign of the Hanoverian dynasty and

LONDON FOG

The little-known fact that the oft-romanticized London fog was in fact the result of pollution from the Industrial Revolution would be just a historical curiosity if it weren't for the bleak condition of present-day air quality. Many first-time visitors to London are shocked by the constant smell of diesel fumes, haze, and the very sexy phenomenon of "grey nose." The sad truth is that air quality in London is very poor, only underscored by prominent signs at clogged intersections informing asphyxiated pedestrians that "this is an air quality improvement area." This has been a political hot button for some time, and a big part of newly-elected mayor Ken Livingstone's campaign. Here are a few of the pedestrianization schemes hoping to keep us all from choking, or at least prove contentious discussion topics in the news:

Most likely to be implemented, if only after a lengthy fight with the Westminster City Council, is the pedestrianization of **Trafalgar Square**, making its northern and eastern sides impassable to cars.

Soho, on weekend nights, is already essentially pedestrianized, apart from the odd idiot who decides speeding through is the best way to their destination. The proposed changes would close Frith and Old Compton Streets to cars during part of the day.

A bigger ban for the already walker-friendly **Covent Garden** would encompass the area around Seven Dials, and penalize polluting cars entering the area.

viciously attacked the Anglican Church's intolerance of Dissenters, among whom he numbered. Fielding, author of *Tom Jones*, penned a satirical play so irksome to Robert Walpole that he urged a law requiring plays to be approved by the government. **Jane Austen** brought the novel to new heights, slyly criticizing self-importance in such works as *Pride and Prejudice* (1813) and *Emma* (1815).

As a gray haze settled over the city's houses and the beggars on the streets swelled into what Marx referred to as the capitalists' "reserve army," the wretchedness attracted the empathy and creative interest of a number of writers, most famously **Charles Dickens.** Dickens described his characters' windings through the 19th century's filthy back allies, poorhouses, and orphanages. Some Romantic poets had the same idea. They abandoned the classical idealization of the city and some even London itself: **John Keats** lived in Hampstead, a distant suburb at the time, while Percy Bysshe Shelley wrote that "Hell is a city much like London."

By the close of the century, when reforms began to mitigate the effects of industrialization, some writers turned to purely aesthetic issues. The relentlessly quotable Irish playwright **Oscar Wilde** proclaimed that art could only be useless, **W.B. Yeats** cofounded the London Rhymers' Club, a group of poets that included London's most promising literary talent, and **Lewis Caroll** sent Alice through the looking glass.

After World War I destroyed 19th-century confidence in a progressive civilization, European high culture spun into a crisis of meaning. No one was better equipped to address Europe's problems than St. Louis's own **T.S. Eliot,** who in 1921 turned London into an angst-ridden *Wasteland*. Between the wars Bloomsbury became a hub of London intellectual life. The **Bloomsbury Group** included Yeats and Eliot, as well as **Virginia Woolf, Clive** and **Vanessa Bell, John Maynard Keynes, Lytton Strachey,** and **E.M. Forster.** They met at the Bell house to discuss the true, the good, and the beautiful. **Evelyn Waugh** turned a satirical eye on society in *Vile Bodies* (1930), while **Graham Greene** studied moral ambiguity in *Brighton Rock* (1938). Meanwhile, a concerned **George Orwell** was meeting street people and weaving yarns of urban poverty in his ultimate tale of budget travel, *Down and Out in Paris and London* (1933). Orwell put forth his disturbing and compelling critique of the direction of modern life in *1984* (1949) while living in Notting Hill; much of it is a reflection of Orwell's somewhat sordid surroundings and consequent misgivings about city life.

Aside from Orwell's haunting account and **Anthony Burgess's** description of the "ultra-violence" of future life in *A Clockwork Orange* (1962), much of London's modern literature is witty and bright. **P.G. Wodehouse** wrote a clever and light novel for each of the

70-some years of his long life. While questions about London's future European and world status in the emerging order may be open for discussion, a survey of recent titles—such as **Doris Lessing's** *London Observed* (1993) and **Julian Barnes's** 1999 novel *England, England* (in which the most visited sites in London are transported to an isle created solely for tourists)—tells us that it retains a distinguished place in the world's intellectual and literary life. **Kingsley Amis** and his now famous son **Martin** write well-loved satirical novels. **Sue Townsend's** multi-book *The Diary of Adrian Mole* brilliantly sets adolescence in Thatcherite England, while **Stephen Fry's** *The Liar* (1992) exploits that bastion of Britain education, the elitist boarding school. For more contemporary reading suggestions, see **Books For the Road** below.

For a taste of what Londoners are reading, it's always worthwhile to pay attention to the annual **Booker Prize** (more correctly, the Booker McConnell Prize) winner. The most prestigious literary award given in the UK, the Booker is given for the best full-length novel written in English by a citizen of the UK, Commonwealth, Republic of Ireland, Pakistan or South Africa. 1999's winner was J.M. Coetzee, who took the prize for *Disgrace*. The winner for 1998 was Ian McEwan's *Amsterdam*, while the previous year Arundhati Roy became the first Indian to claim the honor for *The God of Small Things*.

Kensington Gardens

FURTHER READING: BOOKS FOR THE ROAD

Besides the works listed above, these books are our picks for further glimpses into London life—and for sheer light-reading entertainment.

Martin Amis, *London Fields*. Witty observations of low-life London. Satire at its best. The fields themselves, deep in east London, are worth a visit for those interested in the lives of Eastenders, crazed Amis enthusiasts, and those seeking some peace and quiet.

Helen Fielding, *Bridget Jones's Diary*. This amusing chronicle of single womanhood in 1990s London was a cult sensation, making Notting Hill resident Fielding very popular.

St John's College

Nick Hornby, *Fever Pitch*. If you've ever been a fan of any sport, you'll appreciate Hornby's fine novel about the Arsenal Football Club and obsessive fanship.

MUSIC

Long called "a land without music," England hardly deserves the tag. During the 16th century **Thomas Morley, Thomas Weelkes,** and **John Wilbye** developed **madrigals,** polyphonic vocal pieces with stanzas of two or three lines each; **John Dowland** wrote lachrymose works for lute. **Henry Purcell** was England's best-known composer for centuries; his opera *Dido and Aeneas* is still performed. He set *A Midsummer Night's Dream* to music, and served in the court of Charles II as a composer. London welcomed Handel, Mozart (who wrote his first symphony in Chelsea), and Haydn (whose last cluster of symphonies was named "London"). Although they

Buckingham Palace

SOAPS AND SUDS

Addiction to the soaps broadcast over the airwaves could almost be a marker of British identity. Britain pioneered the soap opera on radio with *The Archers*, the longest-running soap in the world. Set in the fictional village of Ambridge, *The Archers* chronicles the escapades of a farming family in its weekday broadcasts at on Radio 4. It is television, however, that has become the preferred purveyor of soaps. The most popular TV soaps, with almost 20 million viewers a week each, are *Eastenders* on BBC1 (M, Tu, and Th nights at 7pm) and *Coronation Street* on ITV (M, W, F, and Su evenings), which chronicle the lives of rough-and-tumble working-class neighborhoods in London and Manchester respectively. Public enthusiasm for these TV soaps has infected even the once-pastoral *Archers*, who now boast their own share of disasters and illicit love-affairs.

allegedly hated each other, Gilbert and Sullivan collaborated on such 19th-century operettas as The Mikado, H.M.S. Pinafore, and The Pirates of Penzance, loved for their puns, social satire, farce, and pomp. Serious music began a "second renaissance" under **Edward Elgar** *(Enigma Variations)*, whose occasional bombast is balanced by moments of quiet eloquence. Elgar was the first internationally renowned English composer since Purcell. **Frederick Delius** redid Impressionism, while **Gustav Holst** *(The Planets)* adapted Neoclassical methods and folk materials to his Romantic moods.

William Walton and **Ralph Vaughan Williams** brought musical modernism to England in the 20th century. **Benjamin Britten's** *Peter Grimes* turned a broader audience on to opera, and his book *The Young Person's Guide to the Orchestra* continues to introduce classical music to young and old alike. **Michael Tippett** wrote operas, four symphonies, and the oratorio *A Child of Our Time*, for which he asked T.S. Eliot to write the words; Eliot told Tippett he could do better himself. Today, a crop of younger composers, including **Brian Ferneyhough**, maintains Britain's reputation in serious music.

After World War II, American blues provided musical inspiration for the first wave of "British Invasion" rock groups. From Liverpool and then London's Abbey Road, the **Beatles** spun out the classic songs that became part of the international cultural vocabulary and stood at the fore of every musical and cultural trend. **The Rolling Stones**, London's enduring, hard-edged answer to the Fab Four, celebrated vice and welcomed the media attention their antics drew. **The Kinks** spurned psychedelia and voiced horror at the American vulgarity that seemed, to them, to have crushed Little England. **The Who** began as Kinks-like popsters and then expanded into "rock operas" like *Quadrophenia*, which chronicled the fights between "rockers" (who liked leather jackets and America) and "mods" (who liked speed, androgyny, and the Who).

Psychedelic drugs and high hopes produced a flurry of great tunes by adapters of the blues. **The Yardbirds** hatched heroes such as **Eric Clapton** (of the group Cream) and **Jimmy Page**, whose ax powered **Led Zeppelin** into dominance of 70s rock. The same period's **"art-rock"** (Pink Floyd, Yes, Roxy Music) was at times exciting, at times dreadful.

While glam rockers flitted through personae, "pub rock" groups tried to return rock to the people, leading to the punk movement. In London, Malcolm McLaren organized the **Sex Pistols** to get publicity for his King's Road boutique, "Sex." With the Pistol's clothes and Johnny Rotten's snarl, the Pistols changed popular music forever. **The Clash** made political punk with an idealistic leftist slant, while the sloppy sounds of **The Damned** degenerated into goth posturing. Perhaps the most popular of punk's first-wave bands among the British was **The Jam,** led by Paul Weller's resolutely British lyrics. Long before Girl Power sloganeering, the all-female **Slits** mixed their punk with reggae, while Birmingham's **Au Pairs** asked feminist questions over a driving backbeat.

Inspired by punk's DIY ethos, but adding synthesizers, **Joy Division** and Factory Records made Manchester echo with gloomily poetic rock, and **The Cure** shook English-speaking teens everywhere. **Elvis Costello** and **Squeeze** found that punk had cleared the ground for a pop music that could stay bitingly British even as it took over world charts.

However, punk's popularity could not destroy the heavy metal beast spawned by Zepplin and their followers. **Ozzy Osbourne,** who took art to a new level the night he bit the head off a bat, and **Iron Maiden,** best known for their operatic vocal stylings, social criticism, and use of classical mythology, rokked on long after John Bonham's untimely death stopped the Swan Song juggernaut.

The melancholy stylishness of groups like **Felt** and **Eyeless in Gaza** passed sadly unnoticed through the 80s, but **The Smiths** of Manchester took up the slack and rocked the house. **The Police** exploded onto the international music scene with the ska-punk hit "Don't Stand So Close to Me." **Human League** and **Cabaret Voltaire** shook up clubbers with their heavily synthed sound, and **Yaz, Depeche Mode,** and **New Order** soon joined them. A decade later, unemployed kids and easy access to the drug ecstasy created rave culture's all-night, all-day, sweaty, anaesthetic gatherings and the faceless electronic music that accompanied them.

National trends are made and unmade by London-based music weeklies. An unknown band can make "single of the week," graduate to the papers' covers, sell 600,000 CDs, and then vanish. "Indie" bands like **Pulp, Blur,** and **The Verve** continue to wrestle with the same credibility problems as their American "alternative" counterparts. Though not as well known outside the UK, **The Beautiful South** (who along with **Fatboy Slim** represents the remains of the former **Housemartins**) combined pleasant pop sounds and wickedly smart lyrics to send their last album triple platinum in Britain. The star of the studio-manufactured **Spice Girls** is fading now that Ginger has left to pursue her higher calling of UN Goodwill Ambassador, but all-girl pop phenoms **All Saints** (a fave of the young princes) are carrying on with their own brand of pre-fab cuteness.

Electronic music enjoys a large following in the London music scene with bands like **Prodigy** and the **Chemical Brothers.** Hip-hop's burgeoning popularity is reflected by British trip-hop bands like **Massive Attack, Portishead,** and **Tricky.** Despite this, London's sole momentous contribution to rap remains the fact that it's the birthplace and childhood home of Ricky Walters, a.k.a. **Slick Rick (the Ruler).** Swingin' London was recently resurrected by lounge star/satirist extraordinaire **Mike Flowers Pops.**

GET YOUR ROCKS OFF

If you're looking for road tunes, you could do worse than to pick something from this selection of albums.

British Invasion: The Beatles, *Sergeant Pepper's Lonely Hearts Club Band; Something Else by the Kinks;* and The Rolling Stones, *Beggar's Banquet.*

Progressive rock: Genesis, *Selling England by the Pound;* Pink Floyd, *Dark Side of the Moon;* and Yes, *Fragile.*

Punk/post-punk: The Clash, *London Calling;* Joy Division, *Permanent;* and The Sex Pistols, *Never Mind the Bollocks, Here's the Sex Pistols.*

Synth-pop: Depeche Mode, *101;* Duran Duran, *Decade; (The Best of) New Order;* The Pet Shop Boys, *Discography;* and Spandau Ballet, *True.*

Indie: The Smiths, *The Queen is Dead,* The Stone Roses; Blur, *Parklife;* Oasis, *What's the Story (Morning Glory);* and Pulp, *Different Class.*

Dance: Basement Jaxx, *Remedy;* Fatboy Slim, *On the Floor at the Boutique;* Massive Attack, *Blue Lines;* and Roni Size vs. Reprazent, *New Forms.*

FILM

British film, most produced by the large London-based studios, has endured an uneven history marked by cycles of relative independence from Hollywood followed by increasing drains of talent stateside. Some of America's biggest stars pre-World War II were British by birth, including vaudeville star **Charlie Chaplin** (*The Kid*, *The Gold Rush*) and *Gone With the Wind* vixen **Vivien Leigh.** During WWII the government commissioned and funded a series of propaganda films, including **Sir Lawrence Olivier's** glorious *Henry V* (1944). Subsidies continued until the late 70s, when conservative cut-backs triggered another stream of talent to America. In recent years collaborations between British artists and American money has contributed to a thriving British film scene.

Early British film was heavily influenced by two trend-setting directors and one incomparable actor. Master of suspense **Alfred Hitchcock** snared audiences with films made on both sides of the Atlantic, including *Dial M for Murder* (1954), *Psycho* (1960) and 1971's *Frenzy*, filmed on location in the old Covent Garden market. **David Lean's** *Brief Encounter* (1945) made him the preeminent British director of the 40s. He went on to further successes, employing the brilliant **Peter O'Toole** as his lead in *Lawrence of Arabia* (1962). The late **Sir Alec Guiness,** famous as Obi-Wan Kenobi, started his career with a string of wickedly funny films such as *The Man in the White Suit* (1951), and *The Lavender Hill Mob* (1951), from London-based **Ealing Studios.**

The 60s phenomenon of "swingin' London" created new momentum for the British film industry, and jump-started an international interest in British culture. American director Richard Lester made rock stars into film stars in the **Beatles's** *A Hard Day's Night* (1963), and guitarist **George Harrison** later became a driving force in the production of another British cultural icon—the Monty Python movies. As the hopes and promises of the decade began to look a little tarnished, elements of British cinema took on a darker edge.

Sweeping epics and elaborate costume dramas have come to represent British film in the last twenty years. The heroic sagas of **Hugh Hudson's** *Chariots of Fire* (1981) and **Richard Attenborough's** *Gandhi* (1982) swept the Oscars in successive years, and British film was again thrust to the forefront of international cinema. Attenborough directed and appeared in many more films of epic scale, including the anti-apartheid *Cry Freedom* (1982). Director-producer team **Merchant-Ivory** have led the way in adaptations of British novels, ranging from Forster films *A Room With A View* (1986) and *Howard's End* (1992) to Ishiguro's *The Remains*

A VERY, VERY FINE HOUSE

The UK's music has played a distinctive role in world DJ culture, but many people have no idea what distinguishes one genre of music from another. **House music** is a modern adaptation of disco music, with 4 beats to the measure (at around 120 beats per min.—the heartrate of the dancer) and a disco clap at 2 and 4. Popular music is frequently overlaid to make **commercial house.** Soul is added to house to make **garage.** Disco classics (or influences of) make **disco house.** Other types of house include hard house, handbag, happy house, popcorn, funky house, and combinations of the above (i.e. disco funky hard house). **Techno** has the same beat, but brings it to the forefront and speeds it up a bit.

of the Day (1993). Continuing the nostalgic pursuit of all things starched and petticoated, the devastatingly witty *Shakespeare in Love* (1998) premiered to both commercial and Academy recognition as the cumulative combination of costume drama and sweeping epic. The most recent period release, an adaptation of Oscar Wilde's *An Ideal Husband* (1999), features the ubiquitous Ozzy Cate Blanchett with randy Brit **Rupert Everett**.

Offbeat, independent films represent the best and brightest of the current British film scene. *The Full Monty* (1997) bared the comedic underbelly of the Sheffield unemployed and, along with *Lock, Stock and Two Smoking Barrels* (1998), tapped into earlier cinematic conventions established in the 1960s. East End boy **Peter Greenaway** produced less commercially viable but more esoteric independent films: both *The Cook, the Thief, his Wife and her Lover* (1990) and his Tempest adaptation *Prospero's Books* (1991) are cutting edge and definitely not family fare. **Mike Leigh's** work is equally disturbing, with his *Secrets and Lies* (1995) making a sizable impression on an international audience. During 1999 the visually stylish *Bedrooms and Hallways* (1998) about the sexual adventures of some young Londoners, and *Human Traffic* (1999), a psychedelic romp with five post-teen ravers were both released. London's status as the hub of the UK film scene ensures that the best of British and North American film is found in its theaters.

FURTHER VIEWING: CELLULOID LONDON

London has been the setting for many a technicolor tribute. Here's our pick of a few favorites to get you started.

The Day the Earth Caught Fire (Val Guest, 1961). Sci-fi flick depicts London heading toward the sun after a nuclear test goes very, very wrong. Do not try this at home.

A Clockwork Orange (Stanley Kubrick, 1971). So scary they don't even screen it officially in Britain anymore. You will never want to hear "Singin' in the Rain" again.

The Elephant Man (David Lynch, 1980). I am not an animal! I am a black and white film about Victorian London!

Sliding Doors (Peter Howitt, 1997). See Gwyneth with short hair. See Gwyneth with long hair. Think twice about closing Tube doors.

Lock, Stock and Two Smoking Barrels (Guy Ritchie, 1998). London lads lose their shirts after a high-stakes card game and have a week to pay up. Pure fun.

THE PRESS

NEWSPAPERS

In a culture not yet completely addicted to the telly, the influence of papers is enormous. The UK's plethora of London-based national newspapers provides a range of political points of view. **The Times,** for long a model of thoughtful discretion and mild infallibility, has turned Tory under the leadership of Rupert Murdoch. The **Daily Telegraph** (dubbed "Torygraph") is fairly conservative and old-fashioned; the **Guardian** leans leftist, while **The Independent** lives up to its name. Of the infamous tabloids, **The Sun,** a daily Rupert Murdoch-owned tabloid known for its page-three topless pin-up, is probably the most influential. Among the other tabloids, **The Daily Mail, The Daily Express,** and **The Evening Standard** (an evening paper) make serious attempts at popular journalism, although the first two tend to position themselves as the conservative voice of Middle England. The **Daily Mirror, News of the World,** and the **Star** are as shrill and lewd as the Sun. The best international news is in the Times, the Guardian, and the Independent, while **The Financial Times,** printed on pink paper, does more elegantly for the City what the *Wall Street Journal* does for Wall Street.

Although they share close association with their sister dailies, the **Sunday newspapers** are actually separate newspapers, with a distinctive look and style. **The Sunday**

Times, The Sunday Telegraph, The Independent on Sunday, and the highly polished **Observer** (sister to the Guardian) publish multi-section papers with glossy magazines. Sunday editions offer detailed arts, sports, and news coverage, together with a few more "soft bits" than their daily counterparts.

MAGAZINES

Joining a plethora of papers is a wide-ranging list of magazines published in the capital city. World affairs are covered with candor and surreptitious wit by **The Economist. The New Statesman** on the left and **The Spectator** on the right cover politics and the arts with verve and sense and the satirical **Private Eye** delivers politically subversive hilarity.

Time Out features fascinating pieces on London living and is the most comprehensive listings guide available, while **The Face** remains the ultimate scene mag. Some of the best music mags in the world hail from London: **Melody Maker** and **New Musical Express** (NME for short) trace the latest trends with wit; check these for concert news. **Q** covers a broader spectrum of rock music in excellent detail. Club kids should check out **Mixmag** and **Jockey Slut** for listings and dance music reviews. Aesthetes will appreciate glossy style-mags **i-D** and **Wallpaper.**

RADIO AND TELLY

The **BBC** (officially the British Broadcasting Corporation, and sometimes known as the "Beeb" or "Auntie") established its reputation for fairness and wit with its radio services, and for innovation with the world's first regular TV service, launched in 1936. Foreigners are often astounded that BBC radio and television is uninterrupted by advertising; instead the BBC is funded by a license fee that all TV owners in the UK must pay. Once home of *Monty Python's Flying Circus* and *Absolutely Fabulous,* and still a repository for wit and innovation, BBC TV broadcasts on two national channels. **BBC1** carries news at 1, 6, and 9pm as well as various Britcoms and popular soaps like *Neighbours*. Less popular and more highbrow shows are telecast on **BBC2,** which often acts as an incubator for ground breaking shows which then transfer to BBC 1 when they hit the mainstream; *Ab Fab* and *Blackadder* followed this well-trodden path, though the ubiquitous and subversive Teletubbies have bucked the trend, staying on BBC2. **ITV,** Britain's first and most established commercial network carries drama and comedy, along with its own news. **Channel 4** has the hilarious *Big Breakfast* morning show, highly respected arts programming and a fine news broadcast at 7pm on weeknights; it also broadcasts popular American shows (including *Friends* and *ER*). **Channel 5,** the newest channel, features late-night sports shows. National TV listings are slightly modified to fit the region. Cable TV has low penetration in the UK; instead those limited by broadcast stations generally turn to **Satellite TV,** dominated by Rupert Murdoch's **Sky TV.** You'll find football, *futbol,* soccer, and any other incarnations of the global game that it can find on its Sky Sports channel; its Sky One features a selection of American shows and some British ones like *Dream Team,* a football-based drama.

To expand your listening pleasure, turn your dial to one of these stations:

BBC RADIO STATIONS

BBC Radio 1 (98.8FM): Features rock institution John Peel as well as current pop-rock with radio personalities like Zoë Bal.

BBC Radio 2 (89.1FM): Easy listening and non-rock forms of music such as folk and jazz.

BBC Radio 3 (91.3FM): classical music, radio plays, and highbrow culture.

BBC Radio 4 (93.5FM and 128LW/AM): The news arm of the BBC radio staple.

BBC Radio 5 live (909MW/AM): Carries mainly sports broadcasts.

BBC London Live (94.9FM): London-oriented programming.

COMMERCIAL STATIONS

Capital FM (95.8FM), **Heart** (106.2FM), **Virgin** (15.8FM and 1215MW/AM): The latest pop.

Classic FM (100.9FM), and **Jazz FM** (102.2FM) have self-explanatory names.

Capital Gold (1548MW/AM): Classic rock and pop tunes plus live sports coverage.

LBC (1152MW/AM): London's original talk station; mostly phone-in shows.

XFM (104.9) Semi-mainstream indie station.

Kiss (100.0FM) Super-trendy dance station.

Spectrum (558MW/AM). A station run by various London ethnic communities; foreign-language broadcasts from French to Farsi, often locally produced.

Sights

TOURING

*The characteristic of London is that you never go where you wish nor do what you wish,
and that you always wish to be somewhere else than where you are.*
—Sydney Smith, 1818

You can begin to familiarize yourself with the eclectic wonders of London through a
good city tour. Most tour buses stop at Marble Arch and do not require reservations. The
Original London Sightseeing Tour provides a convenient overview of London's attractions
from a double-decker bus. (☎8877 1722. Tours daily in summer 9am-7pm, rest of year
9:30am-5:30pm; £12, under 16 £6.) Two-hour tours depart from Baker St., Haymarket
(near Piccadilly Circus), Marble Arch, Embankment, and Victoria. A ticket allows you to
ride the buses for a 24-hour period, permitting visitors to hop off at major sights and hop
on a later bus to finish the tour. **Walking tours** can fill in the specifics of London that bus
tours run right over. Among the best are **The Original London Walks** (☎7624 3978) which
cover a specific topic such as Legal London, Jack the Ripper, or Spies and Spycatchers.
The two-hour tours are led by well regarded guides. **Historical Tours of London** also leads
popular tours. (☎8668 4019. £5, concessions £4.) If glancing at London from the top of a
bus is unsatisfactory and hoofing it seems daunting, a tour led by **The London Bicycle Tour
Company** may be the happy medium. (☎7928 6838. Tours £11.90.)

A cheaper way to see the city is from the top of an ordinary double-decker bus; you'll
miss the commentary, but gain authentic London experience. Bus #11 cruises between
the city's main sights, passing Chelsea, Sloane Sq., Victoria, Westminster Abbey, the
Houses of Parliament, Whitehall, Trafalgar Sq., St. Paul's, and various stops in the City.

CENTRAL LONDON

LIFE AFTER DEATH

Oliver Cromwell's job as Lord Protectorate ended when he died of tuberculosis. His body was secretly embalmed and interred in Westminster Abbey on November 10, 1658, two weeks before his official funeral which was to cost £60,000 (an enormous sum both then and now). His eternal rest, however, did not last long. When the monarchy ousted Cromwell's son, King Charles II was unhappy with Cromwell's body lying next to the kings and queens of England. On January 30, 1661, the anniversary of the execution of Charles I, Cromwell's body was exhumed and taken to Tyburn. The procession was greeted by the "the universal outcry and curses of the people." The corpse was hanged from the gallows for a day, the body drawn and quartered, and the head taken to Westminster Hall, where it was exhibited on a pole for 25 years, until it was blown off in a storm and someone ran off with it. Never fear, though—he hasn't been forgotten. A stone in Westminster Abbey still marks his preliminary, if temporary, resting place.

see map p. 300

THE CITY OF LONDON AND CLERKENWELL

🚩 *The City of London information center, St. Paul's Churchyard* (☎ 7332 1456; Tube: St. Paul's) *provides information on a host of traditional municipal events. One of the largest is the Lord Mayor's Show, held each year on the second Saturday of November. Information and street plans are available from mid-Oct. Open Apr.-Sept. daily 9:30am-5pm; Oct.-Mar. M-F 9:30am-5pm, Sa 9:30am-12:30pm.*

God and Mammon coexist in the one square mile of the City of London (known simply as "the City"), both the financial center of Europe and the historical center of London. Until the 18th century, the City of London was London; all other boroughs (now swallowed up by "London") were merely neighboring towns or outlying villages. Each weekday morning, 270,000 people surge into the City, only to rush out again at night, leaving behind a resident population of just 7900. The City thus has a reputation for being dead on Saturdays and downright ghostly on Sundays. Bordered roughly by Old St., Commercial St., the Tower of London, Chancery Lane, and the Thames, the City's unofficial center is the convergence of streets near the Bank Tube station. Here, the massive Bank of England controls the country's finances, and the Stock Exchange makes or breaks the nation's fortune. International banks proliferate around them, bowing in homage to these great temples of Mammon. But the names of streets (Poultry, Bread St., etc.) and the original layout are reminders that the City has always been a trading center. Interspersed among this array of modern chaos rest pieces of another city: old London. Aged churches and pubs dwell behind small alleys and among steel office buildings. St. Paul's Cathedral (p. 53), the most glorious of these structures, anchors London to its religious past. The City owes much of its graceful appearance to Sir Christopher Wren, who was the chief architect working after the Great Fire of almost completely razed the area. The 3-day fire that started in a bakery on Pudding Lane on September 2, 1666, leaping between the overhanging houses to bring destruction upon the City. Wren's studio designed 52 churches to replace the 89 destroyed in the fire, and the surviving 24 are some of the only buildings in the City from the period immediately following the Great Fire. A host of variations on a theme, they gave Wren a valuable chance to work out design problems that would come up as he rebuilt St. Paul's. The original effect of a forest of steeples surrounding the great dome of St. Paul's is perhaps his greatest contribution to London's cityscape; unfortunately, modern skyscrapers now obscure that effect.

Here's your ticket to freedom, baby!

**Wherever you want to go...
priceline.com can get you there for less.**

- Save up to 40% or more off the lowest published airfares every day!

- Major airlines serving virtually every corner of the globe.

- Special fares to Europe!

If you haven't already tried priceline.com, you're missing out on the best way to save. **Visit us online today at www.priceline.com.**

priceline.com℠
Name Your Own Price℠

THE LIVERY COMPANIES

⚑ *Goldsmiths', Foster Ln. Tube: St. Paul's; Wax Chandlers', Gresham St. Tube: St. Paul's; Fishmongers', London Bridge. Tube: Monument.*

Perhaps the most powerful secular structures of the City are the buildings of the Livery Companies, which promote charitable works and control a significant amount of the City's land and trading activities. Dating from before the 12th century, their names reflect long-lost crafts (a Fletcher, for instance, refers to an arrow maker). Many Companies have expanded the scope of their functions. Fanmakers now represent the air-conditioning industry and new industries have generated new guilds: the 23 emerging since World War II fix the current total at 102. Numbers 101 and 102 are the World Traders and the Water Conservators, respectively. Thirty-seven Companies own **livery halls,** which are scattered around the square mile; most halls do not open to the public and those that do often require tickets. In early February, The City of London Information Centre (see above) receives a batch of tickets that sells out quickly. If you're lucky, one of the halls may open its doors for an exhibition (the marble-floored **Goldsmiths' Hall** often does so), allowing you to peek at the grandeur, or you can look from the outside at the **Wax Chandlers'** or **Fishmongers' Hall.**

St. Paul's Cathedral

ST. PAUL'S CATHEDRAL

⚑ *Tube: St. Paul's. Open M-Sa 8:30am-4pm. Dome open M-Sa 9:30am-4pm. Ground floor and crypt wheelchair accessible. Admission to cathedral, galleries, and crypt £5, students and seniors £4, children £2.50. "Supertours" depart at 11am, 11:30am, 1:30pm, and 2pm; 90min.; £2.50, students and seniors £2, children £1. Audio tours available 8:45am-3:30pm; 45min.; £3.50, concessions £3.*

St. Paul's, topped by its beautiful neoclassical dome, is arguably the most stunning architectural sight in London, a physical and spiritual symbol of the city. Sir Christopher Wren's enormous (157m by 76m) creation dominates its surroundings, even as modern usurpers sneak up around it. The current edifice is the 5th cathedral dedicated to St. Paul to stand on the site; the first was founded in AD 604 and destroyed by fire. The 4th and most massive cathedral, now referred to as "Old St. Paul's," was a medieval structure built by the Normans. It is one of the largest in Europe, topped by a spire ascending 150m, a structure taller than the current one, which tops out at 111m. Falling into almost complete neglect in the 16th century, the cathedral became more of a marketplace than a church. Wren had already started drawing up his grand scheme in 1666 when the Great Fire demolished the cathedral, giving him the opportunity to build from scratch.

Tower Bridge

However, controversy dogged the cathedral's design. Like his Renaissance predecessors, Wren preferred an equal-armed Greek Cross plan while ecclesiastical authorities insisted on a design with a long nave and choir for services. Wren's 2nd model received the king's warrant of approval (and is thus known as the "Warrant Model"), but still differed from today's St. Paul's. The shrewd architect won permission to make necessary alterations as building proceeded and, behind the scaffolding, Wren had his way. Work began in 1675, and in 1710 St. Paul's was finally topped off; at 111m above the ground, the huge classical dome is the second larg-

Lloyd's

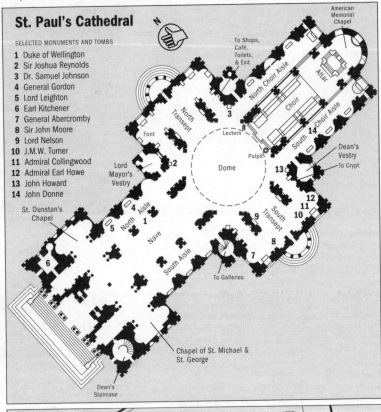

St. Paul's Cathedral

SELECTED MONUMENTS AND TOMBS

1 Duke of Wellington
2 Sir Joshua Reynolds
3 Dr. Samuel Johnson
4 General Gordon
5 Lord Leighton
6 Earl Kitchener
7 General Abercromby
8 Sir John Moore
9 Lord Nelson
10 J.M.W. Turner
11 Admiral Collingwood
12 Admiral Earl Howe
13 John Howard
14 John Donne

American Memorial Chapel

To Shops, Café, Toilets, & Exit

North Choir Aisle
Altar
Choir
South Choir Aisle

North Transept
Font
Lectern
Pulpit
Dome

Dean's Vestry
To Crypt

Lord Mayor's Vestry

St. Dunstan's Chapel

North Aisle
Nave
South Aisle

South Transept

To Galleries

Chapel of St. Michael & St. George

Dean's Staircase

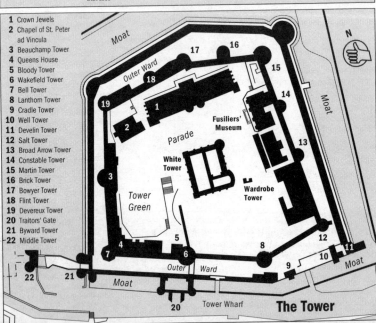

1 Crown Jewels
2 Chapel of St. Peter ad Vincula
3 Beauchamp Tower
4 Queens House
5 Bloody Tower
6 Wakefield Tower
7 Bell Tower
8 Lanthorn Tower
9 Cradle Tower
10 Well Tower
11 Develin Tower
12 Salt Tower
13 Broad Arrow Tower
14 Constable Tower
15 Martin Tower
16 Brick Tower
17 Bowyer Tower
18 Flint Tower
19 Devereux Tower
20 Traitors' Gate
21 Byward Tower
22 Middle Tower

Moat
Outer Ward
Fusiliers' Museum
Parade
White Tower
Wardrobe Tower
Tower Green
Outer Ward
Moat
Tower Wharf
The Tower

est free-standing dome in Europe, after St. Peter's in the Vatican. On December 29, 1940 St. Paul's was once again in flames but this time the cathedral survived. Fifty-one firebombs landed on the cathedral, all swiftly put out by the heroic volunteer St. Paul's Fire Watch; a small plaque in the floor at the end of the nave honors them.

QUIRE. The stalls in the Quire narrowly escaped a bomb, but the old altar did not. It was replaced with the current marble **High Altar,** above which looms the crowning glory, the ceiling mosaic of Christ Seated in Majesty. William Holman Hunt's third version of *The Light of the World* hangs in the north transept. Farther into the church, **the north quire aisle** holds *Mother and Child,* a modern sculpture of the Virgin Mary and Baby Jesus by Henry Moore. One month after the sculpture's arrival, guides insisted a name plaque be affixed to the base because no one knew what it was meant to represent. The south aisle contains a statue of John Donne (Dean of the Cathedral 1621-31) in shrouds, one of the few monuments to survive from Old St. Paul's. The graceful, intricate gates were created by Jean Tijou early in the 18th century. Behind the altar you'll find the **American Memorial Chapel,** dedicated to the 28,000 US soldiers based in Britain who died during WWII.

London Bridge

WHISPERING GALLERY. Climbing to any of the three levels within the dome rewards the stout of heart, leg, and soul. 259 steps lead to the Whispering Gallery, on the inside base of the dome. It's a perfect resounding chamber: whisper into the wall, and your friend on the other side should be able to hear you. Well, they could if everyone else wasn't trying the same thing. The dome displays scenes from the life of St. Paul. A further 119 steps up, the first external view beckons from the **Stone Gallery,** only to be eclipsed 152 steps up by the incomparable panorama from the **Golden Gallery** atop the dome.

THE CRYPT. In the other vertical direction, the crypt (supposedly the largest in Europe) is saturated with tombs and of monuments to great Britons Florence Nightingale, Lawrence of Arabia, and Alexander Fleming, the discoverer of penicillin. The massive tombs of the Duke of Wellington and Horatio Nelson command attention; Nelson was the first national hero to be buried in the crypt (predecessors had their tombs moved here), and his black coffin lies directly beneath the dome. To the right of the crypt entrance, a black slab in the floor marks Wren's grave, with his son's famous epitaph close by: *Lector, si monumentum requiris circumspice* (roughly, "If you seek his monument, just look around you"). Near Wren lie tombs and memorials to various artists, including J.M.W. Turner, William Blake, and Henry Moore. The crypt also houses **models** of St. Paul's in all of its incarnations. The star exhibit is the great model of 1674. In the treasury is a glittering collection of plates, cups, and the magnificent Jubilee cope, a silk robe with 73 churches and St. Paul's Cathedral embroidered upon it with gold silk.

Stock Exchange

EVENSONG. Evensong is performed Monday through Saturday at 5pm. This lovely Anglican ceremony celebrates Christ's assumption of mortal form, and gives visitors a chance to hear the Cathedral's superb choir. Five minutes before the singing begins, worshippers will be allowed to sit in the choir, a few feet from the singers, though this means that you must stay for the duration (about 45min.).

Museum of London

CITY (WESTERN SECTION): ST. PAUL'S TO BANK

GUILDHALL

🚩 *Guildhall Yard, off Gresham St. Library entrance on Aldermanbury.* ☎ *7606 3030. Tube: St. Paul's or Bank. Wheelchair access. Guildhall open May-Sept. daily 10am-5pm; Oct.-Apr. M-Sa 10am-5pm. Library open M-Sa 9:30am-5pm.*

The cavernous, Gothic-looking Guildhall, built between 1411 and 1430, is the headquarters of the Corporation of London, the City's all-powerful governing authority. Its gigantic **Great Hall** hosts monthly city council meetings and banquets. On the balcony stand the nine-foot gilded statues of the ancient Celtic giants Gog and Magog. Visitors are welcome every third Thursday to watch the Lord Mayor, bedecked in traditional robes and followed by a sword-wielding entourage, preside over council meetings. He ranks above the Queen when she enters the City. Under the Guildhall is the largest medieval crypt in London. To one side of the Guildhall stand Corporation offices, the **Guildhall Clock Museum** (see **Museums,** p. 121), and the **Guildhall Library,** which specializes in the history of London. You're free to browse through the collection of books and maps but may not take books out. To the other side of the hall is the **Guildhall Art Gallery.**

ST. SEPULCHRE-WITHOUT-NEWGATE

🚩 *Holborn Viaduct.* ☎ *7248 3826. Open Tu and Th 12am-2pm, W 11am-3pm, and often for lunchtime concerts.*

"Without" meaning "outside," of course. St. Sepulchre's (not a real saint: the church's original name was St. Edmund and the Holy Sepulchre) is the City's largest parish church. Captain John Smith, of *Pocahontas* fame, worshipped here before and after his stay in Virginia, and his grave is marked by a slab in the aisle. The church has a strong association with music, containing a Musicians' Chapel and a huge pipe organ once played by Handel and Mendelssohn. The church also sounds a sadder note; the execution bell of Newgate Prison, rung outside the cells of the condemned on the eve of their execution.

OTHER CITY (WESTERN SECTION) SIGHTS

TEMPLE OF MITHRAS. The few remaining stones of this 3rd-century Roman temple, dedicated to a god popular among the Roman military, dwell incongruously in the shadow of the Temple Court building. The 2ft. tall walls outlining the original temple were discovered during construction work and shifted a few yards from its original location. A reconstruction of the temple, and artifacts unearthed during the excavation may be seen at the Museum of London (see p. 121). *(11 Queen Victoria St., near Budge Row. Tube: Bank or Mansion House.)*

ST. MARY-LE-BOW CHEAPSIDE. This Wren creation is home to the famous bells mentioned in the medieval nursery rhyme, Oranges and Lemons: "I do not know says the Great Bell of Bow." Traditionally, true-blue Cockneys are those born within the range of the bells' toll. **The Place Below** (p. 158) occupies the medieval crypt. *(Cheapside, by Bow Ln. Tube: St. Paul's or Mansion House.* ☎ *7246 5139. Open M-F 6:30am-6pm.)*

ST. JAMES GARLICKHYTHE. The parish name of St. James refers to the garlic once sold nearby. Its famous steeple gave it the nickname "Wren's Lantern." *(Garlick Hill, near Upper Thames St.* ☎ *7236 1719. Tube: Mansion House. Open M-F 10am-4pm.)*

ST. MARTIN LUDGATE. A peaceful haven is offered by St. Martin's, a Wren church on Ludgate Hill untouched by the Blitz. The interior boasts some fine Gibbons woodwork, and the spire still pierces the dome of St. Paul's when seen from Ludgate, as Wren intended. *(*☎ *7248 6054. Open M-F 11am-3pm.)*

POSTMAN'S PARK. A wonderful, hidden space for a quick snooze or picnic. Once the churchyard of St. Leonard's Foster Ln. and the graveyard for Christ Church Newgate St., crumbling gravestones line the park's southern edge. At the back of the park rests a 19th-century memorial to firefighters, police officers, and good samaritans killed in the line of duty. *(Between Aldersgate and King Edward St. Tube: St. Paul's.)*

ST. LAWRENCE JEWRY. The seemingly absurd title of the official church of the Corporation of London reflects the fact that the church was, in days of yore, the sole Christian house in a predominantly Jewish area. It was rebuilt after the war, after damage from what the sign outside formally refers to as "action by the King's Enemies," namely, a German bomb. *(Gresham St., next to the Guildhall. ☎ 7600 9478. Open M-F 7:30am-2pm.)*

OTHER NOTABLES. The College of Arms regulates the granting and recognition of family coats of arms. Visitors can enter and see the Earl Marshal's Court, lined with paintings of famous people. The Officer in Waiting can assess your claim to a British family coat of arms for a fee. Acting pretentious won't help. *(Queen Victoria St. ☎ 7248 2762; www.college-of-arms.gov.uk. Tube: Blackfriars. Open M-F 10am-4pm. Free.)* **St. Andrew-by-the-Wardrobe.** This church was built next to the site of Edward III's Great Wardrobe, where the royal ceremonial clothes were kept. Now the church cowers beneath the Faraday building, the first building allowed to exceed the City's previously strict height limit. *(146 Queen Victoria St. Tube: Blackfriars. ☎ 7248 7546. Open M-F 9am-5pm.)* At one point in its career, the **London Stone** was significant enough that a parish (St. Swithun London Stone) was named after it. Now, this uninspiring fragment of limestone is indistinguishable from the other stones near it. Life's like that sometimes. *(In the side of the Overseas-Chinese Banking Corporation building on Cannon St. Tube: Cannon St.)*

Tower Hill

CITY: THE BARBICAN AND NORTHERN SECTION

THE BARBICAN

🏛 *Between London Wall and Beech St. Tube: Barbican or Moorgate. Box office ☎ 7638 8891; www.barbican.org.uk. Box office open daily 9am-8pm. Library open M and W-F 9:30am-5:30pm, Tu 9:30am-7:30pm, Sa 9:30am-12:30pm.*

The vast, 35-acre Barbican holds restaurants, gardens, most of the City's apartments, and the **Barbican Centre,** home to some of England's greatest cultural treasures. Most of the "streets" are off ground level (as are many of the complexes) and the layout is so labrinthine the City had to put up color-coded signs everywhere to direct confused visitors—a pity, really, since the quality of culture at the Centre, described at its 1982 opening as "the City's gift to the nation," is often spectacular. The Royal Shakespeare Company, the London Symphony Orchestra, the Barbican Art Gallery, the Museum of London (see p. 121), and the Guildhall School for Music and Drama call this complex home. Artificial lakes and planned gardens temper the relentless urbanity. The courtyard also holds the church of **St. Giles Cripplegate,** where John Milton is buried; it was the only building to survive the bombings of the area in 1940. The main entrance to the Centre is on Silk St., where statues of nine golden Muses exemplify the Barbican's dazzling elegance. If you're entering through any of the other 11 gates, don't be too daunted: the Centre can be found by following the yellow stripe on the ground. The main box office on the ground floor sells tickets for all events in the center. Free concerts are held daily in the foyer.

Tower of London

ST. BARTHOLOMEW THE GREAT

🏛 *Off West Smithfield (☎ 7606 5171). Tube: Barbican. Open M-F 8:30am-5pm, Sa 10:30am-1:30pm, Su 8am-1pm and 2-8pm. Closed M in Aug.*

Barbican Theatre

One must enter through a narrow Tudor house to reach this architectural jewel, which has a grand, neck-stretching nave. Founded by an Augustinian monk in 1123, parts of the church are original, although 800 years of alteration have much embellished it. The tomb near the central altar belongs to Rahere, a courtier of Henry I who allegedly founded the church after he was cured of malaria through prayer. The sick are still healed at the neighboring **St. Bartholomew's Hospital,** which was founded at the same time as the church; its history is detailed in the small **museum** (see p. 123).

SMITHFIELD MARKET

🚩 *Between West Smithfield and Charterhouse St. Tube: Barbican or Farringdon. Open daily 4-8am.*

If you want to visit this ancient meat and poultry market, you'd better be up early or up late: it finishes by noon. Smithfield is really more of a wholesalers' market, but individual customers are usually welcome. Smithfield, or "smoothfield," once held the raucous Bartholomew Fair; authorities decided to build the present-day meat market on the site in the mid-19th century. Smithfield's associations with butchery predate the market. Wat Tyler, leader of the Peasants' Revolt of 1381, and Scotsman William Wallace (a.k.a. Mel Gibson in *Braveheart*) rank among those executed here in the Middle Ages.

OTHER CITY (NORTHERN SECTION) SIGHTS

The Charterhouse was first established as a priory and converted in 1611 to a school and hospital for poor gentlemen. The school has moved, but the 15th- to 17th-century buildings still house 40 residents, who are required to be bachelors or widowers over 60. *(Off the north side of Charterhouse Sq. Tube: Barbican. ☎ 7253 3260. Tours Apr.-July W 2:15pm; small donation expected.)* The **London Wall** dates from the days London had to repel invaders. Today, foreign encroachers just take pictures.

CITY (EASTERN SECTION): BANK TO THE TOWER

BANK OF ENGLAND

🚩 *Threadneedle St. Tube: Bank. Museum open M-F 10am-5pm.*

The massive walls and foreboding doors of England's central bank enclose four full acres. The present building dates from 1925, but the 8-foot-thick, windowless outer wall is the same one built by eccentric architect Sir John Soane in 1788. The only part open to the public is the plush **Bank of England Museum** (see p. 120). The Bank's neighbors, the Greek-columned **Royal Exchange,** the **Stock Exchange,** and the **Lloyd's** building, remind of the days when this block was the financial capital of the world. All three are closed to visitors, but there is not much to see in them anyway. The trading pit of the Royal Exchange has been vacated by traders who now use office-based computers. The room is so empty, in fact, that the government considered turning it into a gymnasium. Head to the **Futures Market,** Cannon St., to see frenetic traders in brightly colored jackets continue the bustling tradition.

OLD BAILEY

🚩 *At the corner of Old Bailey and Newgate St.; entrance in Warwick Passage (☎ 7248 3277). Tube: St. Paul's or rail: City Thameslink. Open M-F 10:30am-1pm and 2-4:30pm. No cameras, drinks, food, or large bags.*

Technically the Central Criminal Courts, the Old Bailey crouches under a copper dome and a wide-eyed figure of Justice. Some of the most celebrated cases in Britain's legal history were heard here, including Oscar Wilde's trial for homosexuality in 1895, and trial-watching persists as a favorite diversion; the courts fill up whenever a sensational case is in progress. The Old Bailey stands on the site of the infamous Newgate Prison, in its heyday Britain's grimiest. Enter the public Visitors' Gallery and watch bewigged barristers at work.

ST. STEPHEN WALBROOK

🚩 *39 Walbrook (☎ 7283 4444). Tube: Bank or Cannon St. Open M-Th 9am-4pm; F 9am-3pm.*

Arguably Wren's finest church and his personal favorite, St. Stephen's beautiful, airy hall combines elements of four major styles of church architecture: the old-fashioned English church characterized by nave and chancel; the Puritan hall church (seen in the lack of any formal separation between priest and congregation); the Greek Cross; and the domed church, a study for St. Paul's. The Samaritans, a hotline that advises the suicidal and severely depressed, was founded here in 1953 by current rector Chad Varah. In one corner you can see the phone he used while in another is an honorary phone given to him by British Telecom. The mysterious object ringed by the lime, orange, purple, and pink cushion in the center is the altar, sculpted by Henry Moore in 1985.

ALL HALLOWS BY THE TOWER

🔁 *Byward St. (☎ 7481 2928). Tube: Tower Hill. Open daily 9am-6pm. Audio tours of church and crypt £2.50, crypt only £2.*

SamuelPepys witnessed the spread of the Great Fire from atop this intriguing church. Although much of the structure is postwar reconstruction, many different ages mark it. Near the church's bookshop stands a Saxon arch from 675 AD, discovered when the church was bombed in 1940. To the left, the baptistry has a striking wood font cover by Grinling Gibbons. The church has some connections with American pioneers: William Penn was baptized in the original font, and John Quincy Adams was married here. To the east stands a cross made with wood from the Spanish Armada.

MONUMENT

🔁 *Monument St., off Fish St. (☎ 7626 2717). Hill. Tube: Monument. Open Apr.-Sept. daily 10am-6pm. £1.50, child 50p. Joint ticket with Tower Bridge Experience £6.75, child £4.*

Another one of Sir Christopher Wren's architectural contributions to the City, although this was a collaboration (with his friend Dr. Robert Hooke). This simply-named Doric pillar commemorates the rebuilding of London after the Great Fire. The 202 ft. column was completed in 1677, and supposedly stands exactly that many feet from where the Great Fire broke out in Pudding Lane. As the inscription on the outside says, the fire "rushed devastating through every quarter with astonishing swiftness and worse." In 1681, a small addition was made: "but Popish frenzy, which wrought such horrors, is not yet quenched." This anti-Catholic sentiment was removed in 1830. The column offers an expansive view of London. Bring stern resolution to climb its 311 steps. Upon successfully descending the tower, you'll receive a certificate announcing your feat.

TOWER BRIDGE

🔁 *Over the Thames next to the Tower of London. Tube: Tower Hill or London Bridge. Tower Bridge Experience: ☎ 7403 3761; www.towerbridge.org.uk. Open Apr.-Oct. daily 10am-6:30pm; Nov.-Mar. 9:30am-6pm. Last entry 1¼hr. before closing. £6.25, concessions £4.25, family £18.25.*

A granite-and-steel structure reminiscent of a castle with a drawbridge, Tower Bridge is one of London's most recognizable sights. Folklore has it that when the old London Bridge was sold and moved brick-by-brick to Texas to make way for a replacement, the Americans thought they were getting Tower Bridge. The bridge itself, a major thoroughfare, is open to pedestrians and traffic 24hr. except when the ancient Victorian lifting machinery is put into operation to let ships pass. Bridge openings are rare; your best bet to see it in operation is to charter a large sailing ship and take it upriver. Leaping over the opening bridge is a staple of London movie car-chases; *Let's Go* does not recommend speeding over opening bridges. For those interested in the history and engineering behind the bridge, the **Tower Bridge Experience** explains the bridge's genesis through the eyes of its designers, and ghosts in cute but expensive 75-minute tours. The view from the upper level, hampered by steel bars, is far less panoramic than it seems from below.

OTHER CITY (EASTERN SECTION) SIGHTS

MANSION HOUSE. After Dublin, York, and Doncaster had all built houses for their mayors, London, not wishing to be upstaged, decided to build this lavish home for their own Lord Mayor. Completed in 1752 on an English Palladian plan, Mansion House contains numerous grand rooms for entertaining guests, including the Egyptian Room. *(Between Walbrook and Mansion House Pl. Tube: Bank. Open only for visits by organized groups. Write to the Principal Assistant, The Mansion House, London EC4N 8BH.)*

LOCKED UP

The Tower has functioned as an upper-class prison for much of its history: the last prisoner held here (in the Queen's House) was Rudolph Hess, Deputy Fuhrer of Germany, who was caught after parachuting into Scotland in 1941.

Although more famous for the prisoners who languished and died here, the Tower has seen a handful of spectacular escape attempts. In 1101, the Bishop of Durham, the first recorded prisoner, escaped from Henry I by climbing out of a window and sliding down a rope. The Welsh prince Gruffydd ap Llewelyn, prisoner of Henry III in 1244, had a less successful escape attempt—his rope of knotted sheets broke and he fell to his death.

Prisoners of special privilege sometimes received the honor of a private execution, particularly when their public execution risked escape or riot. The **Scaffold Site**, a block on Tower Green inside the Inner Ward, marks the spot where the axe fell on Catherine Howard, Lady Jane Grey, Anne Boleyn, and the Earl of Essex, Queen Elizabeth's rejected suitor. All these and More (Sir Thomas) were treated to unconsecrated burial in the nearby **Chapel of St. Peter ad Vincula** (St. Peter in Chains). Entrance to the chapel is by Yeoman tour only.

LLOYD'S. Not so much a building as a vertical street, as one commentator put it. Richard Rogers designed perhaps the most visually arresting structure in the City in 1986 for insurance giants Lloyd's. With metal ducts, lifts, and chutes on the outside, it wears its heart (or at least its internal organs) on its sleeve. Part of the older building, dating from 1925, is attached for traditionalists. (Off Leadenhall St. Tube: Bank. No admission.)

ST. MARY WOOLNOTH. The church of St. Mary Woolnoth may look odd without a spire, but the interior proportions confirm the talents of Wren's pupil Nicholas Hawksmoor. The upper reaches are light and airy; lower portions are filled with dark wood. It's the only City church untouched by the Blitz. (At King William and Lombard St. ☎ 7626 7901. Open M-F 7:45am-5pm.)

LONDON BRIDGE. The current, rather bland incarnation of London Bridge succeeds a slew of ancestors. The famed version crowded with houses stood from 1176 until it burned down in 1758, but the most recent predecessor didn't fall down; in 1973 it was sold to an American millionaire for £1.03 million and shipped, block by block, to Lake Havasu City, Arizona. The story goes that the Americans thought they were getting the far more impressive Tower Bridge.

ST. MAGNUS-THE-MARTYR. St. Magnus stands next to the old path to London Bridge, and proudly displays a chunk of wood from a Roman jetty. According to T.S. Eliot, the walls of the church "hold inexplicable splendor of Ionian white and gold," a soothing contrast to the former Billingsgate fish market next door. (At the bottom of Fish Street Hill at Lower Thames St. Tube: Monument. ☎ 7626 4481. Open Tu-F 10am-4pm, Su 10am-1pm.)

ST. OLAVE HART STREET. At this tiny church, built in 1450, an annual memorial service is held for Samuel Pepys, who lived in nearby Seething Ln. and is buried here with his wife. According to a 1586 entry in the church's burial register, Mother Goose is also interred here. (8 Hart St. Tube: Tower Hill. ☎ 7488 4318. Open M-F 9am-5pm.)

OTHER NOTABLES. St. Margaret Louthbury, Wren's penultimate church, was built in 1689 and contains a sumptuous carved-wood screen. Most of the furnishings have been conglomerated from demolished City churches. (Lothbury. Tube: Bank. ☎ 7606 8330. Open M-F 8am-4:30 pm.) A couple of blocks north, the **National Westminster Tower** hovers at over 600 ft. and was Britain's tallest building until Canary Wharf (p. 98) was built. From the air, it looks like the bank's logo. **Leadenhall market** is not particularly market for shoppers, unless you're looking for gourmet fish or meat. But if you're an architectural buff, Horace Jones' intricate Victorian design definitely merits a peek. (Off Gracechurch St. Tube: Bank or Monument. Open 7am-4pm.) Another Wren church, **St. Mary-at-Hill** had its interior reconstructed in Victorian and modern times. The lack of pews and high dome give it an expansive feel. *(6-7 St. Mary at Hill. Tube: Monument.* ☎ *7626 4184. Open M-F 11am-4pm.)* Only Wren's amazing spire remains from **St. Dunstan-in-the-East,** which suffered severe damage in the Blitz. The ruins, covered in green, have been converted into a gorgeous little garden that makes a fine picnic spot. *(St. Dunstans Hill. Tube: Monument or Tower Hill.)*

THE TOWER OF LONDON

◪ *Tube: Tower Hil or DLR: Tower Gateway.* ☎ *7709 0765; www.hrp.org.uk/tol/indextol.htm. Yeoman Warders ("Beefeaters") lead tours every 30min. starting 9:30am M-Sa, Su 10am. Frequent daily themed tours: "Prisoners and Punishment" 9:30, 11:30am, 2:15, 4:30pm; "Life as a Yeoman Warder" 10:15am, 5:15pm; "Attack the Tower" 12:15, 3pm. All free. Audio tours available in 7 languages; £2. Frequent special exhibitions, traditional ceremonies, and re-enactments of historical events; call for details. For tickets to the Ceremony of the Keys, the ritual locking of the gates that has taken place every night for 700 years, write 6 weeks in advance to the Ceremony of the Keys, Waterloo Block, HM Tower of London, EC3N 4AB, with the full name of those attending and a choice of dates, enclosing a stamped addressed envelope or international response coupon; free. Open Mar.-Oct. M-Sa 9am-5pm, Su 10am-5pm; Nov.-Feb. closes 4pm; tower closes 1hr. after last admission. Last ticket sold at 4pm. £11, students and seniors £8.30, ages 5-15 £7.30, families £33. Entrance queues are looong; avoid them by calling for tickets in advance, or buying tickets from the Tube stations.*

British Museum

The Tower of London, palace and prison of English monarchs for over 900 years, is soaked in blood and history. Its intriguing past and striking buildings attract over two million visitors per year. The oldest continuously occupied fortress in Europe, "The Tower" was founded by William the Conqueror in 1066 to provide protection for and from his subjects. Richard the Lionheart, began the construction of additional defenses around William's original White Tower in 1189, and further work by Henry III and Edward I brought the Tower close to its present condition. Now 20 towers stand behind its walls, all connected by massive walls and gateways, forming fortifications disheartening to visitors even today. The whole castle used to be surrounded by a broad moat, but cholera epidemics led to its draining in 1843. The filled land became a vegetable garden during World War II but has since sprouted a tennis court for the Yeomen of the Guard Extraordinary. These "Beefeaters"—whose nickname is supposedly a reference to their daily allowance of beef in former times—still guard the fortress. To be eligible for Beefeaterhood, a candidate must have at least 22 years of service in the armed forces, as well as a strong appetite for flash photography.

Russell Square

BYWARD TOWER. Visitors enter the Tower through this tower on the southwest of the **Outer Ward,** which sports a precariously hung portcullis. The password, required for entry here after hours, has been changed every day since 1327. German spies were executed in the Outer Ward during WWII. Along the outer wall, **St. Thomas's Tower** (named after Thomas à Becket) tops the evocative **Traitors' Gate,** through which boats once brought the condemned to the Tower.

WHITE TOWER. Many associate the White Tower with the Tower of London. Completed in 1097, it overpowers all the

University of London

RAVENS MISBEHAVIN'

No one's quite sure how, why, or when ravens took to living in the Tower, but these large black birds have become an integral part of London folklore. According to legend, when the ravens leave, the Tower will crumble and the monarchy will fall. To prevent such calamitous occurrences, Charles II ordered that ravens be kept at the Tower, if not exactly under lock and key, then at least under a very close watch; even today the superstition is strong enough that the current incumbents have their wings clipped.

There's not much reason for the birds to wander far, though—they rival the Beefeaters in popularity and are treated suitably regally, being fed each day on 6oz. of raw meat and bird formula biscuits soaked in blood. Even so, some birds seem to prefer life outside; Grog escaped to the Rose and Punchbowl pub in the East End in 1981.

Naturally, with all the tourist attention they get, the ravens have to be on best behavior all the time; cantakerous fowl have been given the sack. George was dismissed in 1986 after becoming obsessed with eating TV aerials. The dispatch read "On Saturday 13 Sept 1986, Raven George, enlisted 1975, was posted to the Welsh Mountain Zoo. Conduct unsatisfactory, services therefore no longer required."

fortifications that were built around it in the following centuries. Originally a royal residence, the last monarch it housed was James I. It has since served as a wardrobe, storehouse, records office, mint, armory, and prison. On the first floor of the White Tower nests the 11th century **Chapel of St. John,** considered the finest Norman chapel in London. Stark and pristine, it is the only chapel in the world with an aisled nave and encircling ambulatory, a balcony where women were allowed to join the otherwise men-only chapel services. The White Tower also houses an expansive display from the **Royal Armouries** and a display of **Instruments of Torture.** Don't expect an extensive collection; there are only a couple of instruments of torture on display, the scariest of which is the long queue.

BELL TOWER. The Bell Tower squats in the southwest corner of the **Inner Ward.** Since the 1190s, this tower has sounded the curfew bell each night. Sir Thomas More, "the king's good servant but God's first," spent time here, courtesy of Henry VIII, before he was executed on **Tower Hill,** the scaffold site just northwest of the fortress where thousands gathered to watch the axe fall.

BLOODY TOWER. Along the curtain wall hovers the most infamous part of the fortress. Once pleasantly named the Garden Tower, the Bloody Tower supposedly saw the murder of the Little Princes, the uncrowned King Edward V and his brother (aged 13 and 10), by agents of Richard III. The truth remains a mystery; some believe that Richard was innocent and that Henry VII arranged the murders. All that is confirmed is that the princes were taken to the Tower in 1483, shortly before Richard's ascension to the throne, and never seen again. Two children's remains found in the grounds in 1674 have never been conclusively identified as those of the princes.

WAKEFIELD TOWER. Henry III lived in this adjacent tower, the 2nd-largest in the complex. The crown kept its public records and its jewels here until 1856 and 1967 respectively, although Wakefield also has its own gruesome past. Lancastrian Henry VI was imprisoned by Yorkist Edward IV during the Wars of the Roses and was murdered on May 21, 1471, while praying here. Students from Eton and King's College, Cambridge—both founded by Henry—annually place lilies on the spot of the murder.

WALL WALK. Counterclockwise around the inner Wall Walk come the **Lanthorn, Salt, Broad Arrow, Constable,** and **Martin** towers. In 1671, the self-styled "Colonel" Thomas Blood nearly pulled off the heist of the millennium. Blood befriended the ward of Martin tower, where the crown jewels were kept, and visited him late at night with some "friends." They subdued the guard and stuffed their trousers with booty, only to be caught at the nearby docks. Surprisingly, Blood wasn't executed, and was later awarded a privileged spot in the court of Charles II, the moral being, of course, that crime does pay (*Let's Go* does not endorse the theft of state treasures). The inner ring comes full circle, completed by the **Brick, Bowyer, Flint, Devereux,** and **Beauchamp** towers.

QUEENS HOUSE. The Tudor Queen's House (which will become the King's House when Prince Charles ascends to the throne) once served as a prison for some of the Tower's most notable guests (see **Locked Up,** p. 60). The only prisoners remaining today are the clipped **ravens** hopping around on the grass outside the White Tower.

JEWEL HOUSE. For many, a visit to the Tower climaxes with a glimpse of the **Crown Jewels.** The queue at the Jewel House is a miracle of crowd management. Tourists file past room after room of rope barriers while video projections on the walls show larger-than-life depictions of the jewels in action, including footage of Elizabeth II's coronation. Finally, the crowd is ushered into the vault and onto moving walkways that whisk them past the dazzling crowns and insure no awestruck gazers hold up the queue. Cromwell melted down much of the original booty; most now dates from after Charles II's restoration in 1660. The **Imperial State Crown** and the **Sceptre with the Cross** feature the Stars of Africa, cut from the Cullinan Diamond. Scotland Yard mailed the stone third class from the Transvaal in an unmarked brown paper parcel, a scheme they believed was the safest way of getting it to London. **St. Edward's Crown,** made for Charles II in 1661, is only worn during coronation. Look for the **Queen Mother's Crown,** which contains the Koh-I-Noor diamond. Legend claims the diamond will only bring luck to women.

HOLBORN

see map pp. 296-297

Home to grey buildings and grey flannel, the Holborn area has traditionally been the stomping ground of the legal profession. The historical center of English law lies in an area straddling the precincts of Westminster and the City and surrounding long and litigious precincts of **High Holborn, Chancery Lane,** and **Fleet Street.** From the imposing spires of the Royal Court of Justice to the secret gardens of the Temple Bar, tourists get a sense that more goes on than meets their eyes.

ROYAL COURTS OF JUSTICE

🚇 *Tube: Temple.* ☎ *7947 6000. Courts and galleries open to the public M-F 9am-6pm last entrance 4:30pm. Court cases start at 10-10:30am, but they break for lunch 1-2pm.*

The Strand and Fleet St. meet at this wonderfully elaborate Gothic structure designed in 1874 by architect G.E. Street for the Supreme Court of Judicature. At the Strand entrance there are a helpful set of displays explaining the court system. Security is tight, and the metal detectors are highly sensitive. The biggest draw for tourists who sit in on proceedings are the wigs the justices and barristers wear. On hot days the judge may allow everyone to remove their wigs, but newer weaves make this allowance rare. You can trace the history of the wig in the legal costume exhibit on the first floor. In the Great Hall, you stand upon the largest mosaic floor in Europe.

THE INNS OF COURT

🚇 *Most inns are closed to visitors; take the "Legal London" walking tour (☎ 7624 3978), or spend 4 years in law school. Tours, 2hr., leave M 2pm, W 11am, and F 2pm from Holborn tube. Students £3.50.*

Barristers in the City are affiliated with one of the famous Inns of Court (Middle Temple, Inner Temple, Lincoln's Inn, and Gray's Inn), four ancient legal institutions that provide lectures and apprenticeships for law students and regulate admission to the bar. The tiny gates and narrow alleyways that lead to the Inns are invisible to most passersby. Inside, the inns are organized like colleges at Oxford, each with its own gardens (great for sunbathing or picnicking), chapel, library, dining hall, common rooms, and chambers. Most were founded in the 13th century when a royal decree barred the clergy from the courts of justice, giving rise to a new class of professional legal advocates. Today, students may seek their legal training outside of the inns, but to be considered for membership they must "keep term" by dining regularly in one of the halls.

TEMPLE. South of Fleet St., this labyrinthine structure encloses the prestigious and stately Middle and Inner Temple Inns. Temple is comprised of two of the four Inns of Court and provides barristers with dining facilities, residences, gardens, and a church. They derive their name from the clandestine, crusading Order of the Knights Templar, who embraced this site as their English seat in the 12th century. The secretive order dissolved in 1312 (although some claim it still exists in the form of the Masons and Skull and Bones) and this property was eventually passed on to the Knights Hospitallers of St. John, who leased it to a community of common law scholars in 1338. Virtually leveled by the Germans in the early 1940s, only the church, crypt, and buttery of the Inner Temple survive intact from the Middle Ages. *(Tube: Temple.)*

TEMPLE CHURCH. Held in common by both the Middle and Inner Temples, the Temple Church is formed from an older round church (AD 1185) and a newer addition of a rectangular nave (AD 1240). The older portion is the finest of the few round churches left in England, with stained-glass windows, a handsome 12th-century Norman doorway, an altar screen by Wren (1682), and 10 arresting, armor-clad stone effigies of sinister Knights Templar dating from the 12th-14th centuries.

MIDDLE TEMPLE. According to Shakespeare's *Henry VI*, the red and white roses that served as emblems throughout the War of the Roses were plucked from the Middle Temple Garden. On Groundhog Day, 1601, Shakespeare himself starred in a performance of *Twelfth Night* in Middle Temple Hall, an Elizabethan dining room on Middle Temple Lane, just past Brick Ct. *(Closed to the public.)* A large wooden dining table is said to be made from the hatch of Sir Francis Drake's *Golden Hinde.* Nearby, London's last functioning gas lamps illuminate the lane. *(Gardens open May-Sept. M-F noon-3pm.)*

LINCOLN'S INN FIELDS AND ENVIRONS. London's largest square stands to the north of the Law Courts. On its north side is found **Sir John Soane's Museum;** it's the house bedecked with sculptures amidst a row of plain buildings (see p. 122). **New Square** and its cloistered churchyard (to the right as you enter from Lincoln's Inn Fields) appear today much as they did in the 1680s. The **Old Hall**, east of New Sq., dates from 1492; here the Lord High Chancellor presided over the High Court of Chancery from 1733 to 1873. The best-known chancery case is that of Jarndyce and Jarndyce, whose life-sapping machinations are played out in the many pages of *Bleak House.* Dickens knew well what he described, having worked as a lawyer's clerk in New Court just across the yard. **Lincoln's Inn**, back across Fleet St., on the other side of the Royal Courts, was the only inn to emerge unscathed from the Blitz. The lawyers of Lincoln's Inn were mocked by John Donne's couplets in *Satire: On Lawyers.* *(Tube: Holborn.)*

NEW HALL. To the west of Lincoln's Field, this Tudor-style hall houses a 19th-century mural by G.F. Watts and a collection of lugubrious, legal portraits. Built in 1497, the adjacent library is London's oldest. John Donne, William Pitt, and Benjamin Disraeli number among the many luminaries associated with Lincoln's Inn. Only the grassy quadrangle and the New Chapel are open to visitors. *(Open M-F noon-2:30pm.)*

GRAY'S INN. Dubbed "that stronghold of melancholy" by Dickens, this inn stands at the northern end of Fulwood Pl., off High Holborn. Reduced to ashes by German bombers in 1941, Gray's Inn was restored during the 1950s. The Hall, to your right as you pass through the archway, retains its original stained glass (1580) and most of its ornate screen. Francis Bacon maintained chambers here from 1577 until his death in 1626, and is the purported designer of the gardens. *(Tube: Chancery Ln. Open M-F noon-2:30pm.)*

FLEET STREET

🏴 *Tube: Temple, Blackfriars, Holborn, or Chancery Lane.*

Named for the one-time river (now a sewer) that flows from Hampstead to the Thames, **Fleet Street** was until recently the hub of British journalism. Nowadays, Fleet St. is just a celebrated name and a few (vacated) famous buildings. Following a standoff with the printing unions in 1986, *The Times*, under the command of infamous media mogul Rupert Murdoch, moved to cheaper land at Wapping, Docklands, initiating a mass exodus from the street. The *Daily Telegraph* soon abandoned its startling Greek and Egyptian Revival building, in favor of the delights of Canary Wharf. The

Daily Express, once the occupant of an Art Deco manse of chrome and black glass on Fleet St., now resides in Blackfriars. *The Sun*, also under the command of Murdoch, followed its sister paper to Wapping. When looking for addresses of the following sights, beware that Fleet St. is numbered up one side and down the other. *(Tube: Blackfriars or St. Paul's.)*

ST. BRIDE'S. The tiered spire of Wren's 1675 church, near 89 Fleet St., became the inspiration for countless wedding cakes thanks to an ingenious local baker. Dubbed "the printers' cathedral" because the first printing press with moveable type was housed here in 1500, it has long had a connection with newspapermen. In fact, church officials seem to have taken a lesson from the tabloids in creating their sign board, covered with catchy (and somewhat misleading) "Did you know?" facts about the church. One listing asks (paraphrasing): Did you know that a German bomb falling in 1940 caused the discovery of ancient ruins below the church? The full story is that in 1952, 12 years after the bomb fell, during foundation inspections made before rebuilding the church, a set of skeletons were found below the church. The bodies had been buried in a sealed-off crypt during a 19th-century cholera epidemic. The current church is sparklingly clean and quite beautiful inside. Next to St. Bride's stands **Reuters,** one of the last remaining media powerhouses left on Fleet St. *(Open M-F 8am-6pm, Sa 9am-5pm.)*

Dickens House

SAMUEL JOHNSON'S HOUSE. Samuel Johnson, a self-described "shrine to the English language," lived in this abode from 1748 to 1759. Here he completed his Dictionary, the first definitive English lexicon, even though rumor falsely insists that he omitted "sausage." He compiled this amazing document by reading all the great books of the age and marking the words he wanted included in the dictionary with black pen. The books he used were unreadable by the project's end. *(17 Gough Sq.; an alley leads to the square from opposite #54 Fleet St. ☎ 7353 3745. Open May-Sept. M-Sa 11am-5:30pm; Oct.-Apr. M-Sa 11am-5pm. Guided tours available for groups by reservation; day tours £2 per person; evening tours (after closing) £3, with coffee £5, with wine £6. House also available for private functions; call for details. Admission £4, concessions £3, children £1, family £9. Audio tour 50p.)*

University College

ST. DUNSTAN-IN-THE-WEST. A few more blocks down Fleet St., this neo-Gothic church holds its magnificent lantern tower high above the banks surrounding it. The chimes of its 17th-century clock are sounded on the quarter hour by a pair of hammer-wielding mechanical giants. A statue of Elizabeth I rises above the vestry door. The three 16th-century effigies leaning against the porch may represent King Lud, mythical founder of London. *(☎ 7405 1929. Open Tu and F 9:30am-3pm, Su 10am-4pm.)*

THE STRAND

🚇 *Tube: Charing Cross or Temple.*

Hugging the embankment of the Thames river, The Strand connects the City with Westminster Palace and Parliament. Today, as host to two major London universities, it is a center of education in London, as well as being home to the original **Twining's Tea Shop** (see **Shopping,** p. 133)—it's not only the oldest business in the UK on its original preimises, it's also London's narrowest shop.

St. George the Martyr Church

STONED

On Christmas Day, 1950, daring Scottish patriot Ian Hamilton—posing as a visitor—hid himself in Westminster Abbey until it closed. He meant to steal the 200kg Stone of Scone and return it to Scotland. As he approached the door near Poet's Corner to let in his three accomplices, he was detected by a watchman. Hamilton (now a prominent Scottish MP) talked fast enough to convince the watchman that he had been locked in involuntarily.

That same night the foursome forcibly entered the Abbey and pulled the stone out of its wooden container, in the process inadvertently breaking the famed rock into two uneven pieces. Hamilton sent his girlfriend driving off to Scotland with the smaller piece, while he returned to deal with the larger piece. The remaining two accomplices had been instructed to drag the larger piece toward the cars, but when he returned Hamilton found only the stone. He lugged the piece to his car, and, while driving out of London, happened across his wayward accomplices. The stone was repaired in a Glasgow workyard, but the patriots were frustrated that they could not display it in a public place. On April 11, 1951, Hamilton and Company carried the stone to the altar at Arbroath Abbey where it was discovered and returned to England.

The final chapter of the story is that now-deceased Glasgow councilor Bertie Gray claimed, before he died, that the stone was copied and that the stone that resided in the Abbey was a fake. The British authorities dispute his claim.

SOMERSET HOUSE. A magnificent Palladian structure built by Sir William Chambers in 1776, Somerset House stands on the former site of the palace where Elizabeth I resided during the reign of her sister Mary. Formerly the administrative center of the Royal Navy, the building now houses the exquisite **Courtauld Collection** of Impressionist paintings (see **Galleries**, p. 124) and provides impressive views of the Thames.

ST. CLEMENT DANES. Further down the Strand stands this handsome church, whose melodious bells get their 15 seconds of fame in the nursery rhyme "Oranges and lemons, say the bells of St. Clement's." Children get their 15 minutes of fruit when oranges and lemons are distributed in a ceremony near the end of March. Designed by Wren in 1682, the church was built over the ruins of an older Norman structure reputed to be the tomb of Harold Harefoot, leader of a colony of Danes who settled the area in the 9th century. In 1720, Gibbs replaced Wren's truncated tower with a slimmer spire. Although firebombs gutted the church in 1941, the ornate white stucco and gilt interior has been restored. Today it is the official church of the Royal Air Force. A crypt-cum-prayer chapel houses an eerie collection of 17th-century funerary monuments. (☎ 7242 8282. Tube: Charing Cross. Open daily 8am-5pm.)

ST. MARY-LE-STRAND'S. The slender steeple and elegant portico of this church rise above an island of decaying steps and bright flower pots in the middle of lanes of traffic. Designed by James Gibbs and consecrated in 1724, the church overlooks the site of the original Maypole, where London's first cabs assembled in 1634. Parishioner Isaac Newton claimed the pole for a telescope stand. Inside, the Baroque barrel vault and altar walls reflect not only the glory of God but also Gibbs' Roman architectural training. The mesmerizing windows are a reminder of things more temporal; they replace those blown out in World War II. (☎ 7836 3205. Open M-F 11am-4pm. £1 recommended donation.)

STRAND UNIVERSITIES. As you stroll away from the Courts of Justice on Houghton St., two of London's top educational institutions come into view. The first, **King's College,** is an unremarkable concrete building. Straight across the road stands the prestigious **London School of Economics and Political Science** (LSE), the setting for feisty student radicalism in the 1960s and now Tony Blair's favorite source of political ideas.

WIG AND PEN CLUB. The only Strand building to survive the Great Fire stands at 229-230 The Strand. Constructed over Roman ruins in 1625, the club is frequented by the best-known barristers and journalists in London. The club is open to members only, though an overseas traveler dressed in a coat and tie may be able to peek upstairs. If you have the nerve, walk up the ancient, crooked staircase—the only remnant of the original 17th-century house—and take note of the photo of Prince Charles dining at the club, as well as signed photos of US Presidents Nixon, Reagan, and Bush. Beware—the doorman will reject underdressed travelers. *(Members only upstairs, pricy restaurant open to the public. Open M-Sa 11am-11pm.)*

EMBANKMENT. To the south of the Temple Bar Monument Embankment runs along the Thames, parallel to The Strand. The first person to suggest a river embankment green was Christopher Wren after the fire of 1666. The **Victoria Embankment Gardens** sit next to the Embankment tube station. *(☎ 7641 5264. Open 7:30am-dusk.)* Between the Hungerford and Waterloo Bridges stands London's oldest (though not indigenous) landmark, **Cleopatra's Needle**, an Egyptian obelisk from 1450 BC, stolen by the Viceroy of Egypt in 1878. A sister stone stands in Central Park in New York. *(Tube: Charing Cross or Embankment.)*

ST. ETHELREDA'S ELY PLACE. St. Ethelreda is Britain's oldest Catholic church thanks to Bishop Luda of Ely's decision to build his palace there in the early 1200s. The original sprawling compound of chapels and cloisters was abbreviated in 1576 when Elizabeth I forced the Bishop of Ely to rent some of the gardens and buildings to Sir Christopher Hatton. An intimate church high above ground level, Henry VIII and his Queen Katherine held a debaucherous five-day banquet in the main hall in 1531. The Bard was also versed in the bounty of the church as Gloucester in Richard III says "My Lord of Ely, when I was last in Holborn, I saw good strawberries in your garden there. I do beseech you, send for some of them." Should you be beseeched, the Strawberry Fayre is held in June. The Upper Church boasts two colorful stained glass windows, one of whch is the largest in London with a glazed area of over 500 square feet. *(Ely Place. Tube: Chancery Lane. ☎ 405 1061. Open M-F 8am-6pm, Sa-Su 9:30am-6pm.)*

WESTMINSTER

WESTMINSTER ABBEY

🚩 *Parliament Sq. (☎ 7222 5152; www.westminster-abbey.org). Tube: West-minster or St.James's Park. "Supertours" include admission to Abbey and all sights inside (bookings ☎ 7222 7110), offered M-F 10, 11am, and 2pm, M-Th also 3pm, Sa 10am, 11am, and 12:30pm; Apr.-Oct. also M-F 10:30am and 2:30pm. £10. Audio tour £3. Open M-F 9am-4:45pm, Sa 9am-2:45pm; last admission 1hr. before close. Closed for special events. £5, students and UK seniors £3, ages 11-16 £2, family £10.*

see map p. 68

The site of every royal coronation since 1066, Westminster Abbey's significance is secular as well as sacred. The Abbey, controlled by the Crown and not the Church of England, is the temple of England's civic religion. Only the Pyx Chamber and the Norman Undercroft (now the Westminster Abbey Undercroft Museum) survive from the original structure, which was consecrated by King Edward the Confessor on December 28, 1065. Most of the present Abbey was erected under Henry III in the 13th century. The North Entrance, completed after 1850, is the youngest part of the Abbey.

STATESMEN'S AISLE. The north transept is full of memorials to important figures. Prime Ministers Disraeli and Gladstone could not stand each other in life, but in death their figures sit close together. On the left is the tomb of Sir Francis Vere, a 16th century army commander. In front of his tomb is the imposing monument to James Wolfe, who won British supremacy in Canada.

SHRINE OF ST. EDWARD AND LADY CHAPEL. The plain tomb of Edward I (1239-1307) is the first of the kings' tombs that surround the **Shrine of St. Edward.** Following these tombs leads to the **Lady Chapel.** The exquisite ceiling was hand-carved in chunks of stone and set in place after the chapel was erected. Every one of its magnificently carved stalls, reserved for the Knights of the Order of the Bath, features a colorful headpiece bearing the chosen personal statement of its occupant. The chapel walls display representations of 95 saints. Henry VII and his wife Elizabeth lie at the end of the chapel. Nearby is the stone that once marked Cromwell's grave (see **Life after death,** p. 52). Protestant Queen Elizabeth I and the Catholic cousin she had beheaded, Mary Queen of Scots, are buried on opposite sides of the Henry VII chapel (in the north and south aisles, respectively).

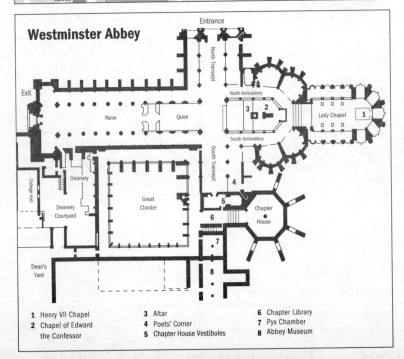

Houses of Parliament and Westminster Abbey

Westminster Abbey

1 Henry VII Chapel
2 Chapel of Edward the Confessor
3 Altar
4 Poets' Corner
5 Chapter House Vestibules
6 Chapter Library
7 Pyx Chamber
8 Abbey Museum

CORONATION CHAIR. At the exit of the Lady Chapel stands the Coronation Chair. The chair used to rest on the ancient Stone of Scone (see **Stoned,** p. 66) which was used in the coronation of ancient Scottish kings; James I took it to London to represent the Union. During WWII, it was hidden from possible capture by Hitler—rumor has it that only Churchill, Roosevelt, the Prime Minister of Canada, and the two workers who moved it knew its whereabouts. The chair sits by the 7-ft State Sword and the shield of Edward III.

CHAPEL. A number of monarchs are interred here, from Henry III (d. 1272) to George II (d. 1760). Edward I saw himself as a secret weapon—dead or alive. He had himself placed in an unsealed crypt, in case he was needed again to fight the Scots; his mummy was used as a standard by the English army in Scotland. An engraving by William Blake commemorates the moment in 1774 when the Royal Society of Antiquaries opened the coffin to assess the body's state of preservation.

Kensington Gardens

POETS' CORNER. The Poets' Corner celebrates those who have died and been anthologized; note that most of the poets are not actually buried here. It begins with Geoffrey Chaucer, who was originally buried in the Abbey in 1400—the short Gothic tomb you see today in the east wall of the transept was not erected until 1556. A modern stained-glass window includes the name of Oscar Wilde, who was honored in 1995, the centenary of his conviction for sodomy. Floor panels commemorate Tennyson, T.S. Eliot, Henry James, Lewis Carroll, Lord Byron, and W.H. Auden, all at Chaucer's feet. Each bears a description or image for puzzle solvers: D.H. Lawrence's publishing mark (a phoenix) and T.S. Eliot's symbol of death.

SOUTH WALL. The south transept is graced with the graves of Samuel Johnson and actor David Garrick, as well as busts of William Wordsworth, Samuel Taylor Coleridge, and Robert Burns. A full-length representation of Shakespeare overshadows the tiny plaques memorializing the Brontë sisters and the ashes of Sir Lawrence Olivier. On the west wall of the transept, Handel's massive memorial looms over his grave next to the resting place of Charles Dickens. On this side of the wall, you'll also find the grave of Rudyard Kipling and a memorial to Thomas Hardy. Among the writers and poets lie two outsiders: Old Parr, who reportedly lived to the age of 152, and "Spot" Ward, who healed George II of a thumb injury.

Harrod's

HIGH ALTAR. The High Altar, between the North and South transepts, has long been the scene of coronations, royal weddings, and funerals. The quire contains elaborately decorated stalls and a 1268 mosaic floor. The Queen's stall is just to the left of the High Altar Screen, marked by the royal coat of arms.

SCIENTISTS' CORNER. Scientists' Corner holds a memorial to Sir Isaac Newton, which sits next to the grave of Lord Kelvin. Visitors may be surprised to see Charles Darwin here; thanks to his friends in the clergy and his affirmation of faith before his death, his body is interred in a place of worship.

MUSICIANS' AISLE. Just before the gate to the north aisle of the nave, this' aisle contains the Abbey's most accomplished organists, John Blow and Henry Purcell, as well as memorials to Elgar, Britten, Vaughan Williams, and William Walton.

Hyde Park

THE LORD MAYOR

The Lord Mayor's position has not always been entirely ceremonial, nor has it always been lordly. The job originally consisted of running the affairs of the City 900 years ago. The wily merchants of the City used their financial leverage to win increasing amounts of autonomy from the monarchy throughout the years, culminating in the construction of Guildhall—the Lord Mayor's official worshipping site—and the move from just plain Mayorship to Lord Mayorship. While the position today is ceremonial, it retains its pomp and grandeur. The Lord Mayor is the Chief Magistrate, Chairman of the Court of Aldermen and the Court of Common Council. In the City, he is second only to the Queen, although the Queen—and only the Queen—has to ask his permission before entering the city gates.

CHAPTER HOUSE AND PYX CHAMBER. The Chapter House, east down a passageway off the cloister, has one of the best-preserved medieval tile floors in Europe. The windows in the ceiling depict scenes from the Abbey's history. The King's Great Council used the room as its chamber in 1257 and the House of Commons used it as a meeting place in the 16th century. Even today, the government, and not the Abbey, administers the Chapter House and the adjacent Pyx Chamber, once the Royal Treasury and now a plate museum. (*Chapter House open Apr.-Oct. 10am-5:30pm, Nov.-Mar. 10am-4pm; last admission 30min. before closing. Pyx Chamber and Abbey Museum open daily 10:30am-4pm; last admission 3:45pm. Hours often depend on the light. Admission to all three £2.50, concessions £1.30; with Abbey admission £1.*)

LIBRARY. The library of Westminster Abbey holds a collection of 14,000 books, most dating from before 1801. Among the exquisite books and manuscripts on display is a house lease dated 1399 and granted to Geoffrey Chaucer by the Abbey. (*Open May-Sept, W only 11am-3pm. Admission with Chapter House ticket.*)

GRAVE OF THE UNKNOWN WARRIOR. Past the cloisters, in the Abbey's narrow nave, the highest in all of England, a slab of black Belgian marble marks the Grave of the Unknown Warrior. Here the body of a World War I soldier is buried in soil from the battlefields of France, with an oration written in letters made from melted bullets. A piece of green marble engraved with "Remember Winston Churchill" sits nearby, rather than among fellow prime ministers in Statesmen's Aisle. Parliament placed it here 25 years after the Battle of Britain.

EVENSONG. Music lovers can catch Evensong and Organ recitals. Evensong is sung at 5pm M-Tu and Th-F and at 3pm Sa-Su. Organ recitals are given on Tuesday during the summer at 6:30pm. (*Reserve on ☎222 5152 or write to the Concert Secretary, 20 Dean's Yard, SW1P 3PA. £6, concessions £4.*)

ST. MARGARET'S WESTMINSTER

🏛 Parliament Sq. (☎7222 6382). Tube: Westminster. Open daily 9:30am-4:30pm when services are not being held. Free.

Literally in Westminster Abbey's shadow, St. Margaret's is the church that tourists point to and ask "Is that the Abbey?" St. Margaret's has served as the parish church of the House of Commons since 1614, when Protestant MPs feared Westminster Abbey was about to become Catholic. John Milton, Samuel Pepys, and Winston Churchill were married here. The stained-glass window above the main entrance depicts a blind Milton dictating Paradise Lost to one of his dutiful daughters, while the stunning east window, made in Holland in 1501, honors the marriage of Catherine of Aragon to Prince Arthur. The modern windows on the south side provide a marked contrast; entitled "Spring in London," they are appropriately composed in shades of gray. Beside the high altar lies the headless body of Sir Walter Raleigh, who was executed across the street in 1618. The inscription on his memorial asks readers not to "reflect on his errors." Reflect on the four modernist sundials that grace the tower and guess the hour.

THE HOUSES OF PARLIAMENT

🏛 *Parliament Sq. Tube: Westminster. Public tours offered early Aug. to mid-Sept. M-Sa 9:30am-4:15pm. Tickets, £3.50, go on sale in mid-June and must be booked in advance from Ticketmaster (☎ 7344 9966; www.ticketmaster.co.uk). For foreign-language tours book 4 weeks ahead. At other times of the year, UK residents should contact their MP or a friendly Lord; tours normally available M-Th 9:30am-noon and F 3:30-5:30pm. Overseas visitors can request tours through the Parliamentary Education Unit, Norman Shaw Building (North), London SW1A 2TT (☎ 7219 3000; edunit@parliament.uk); tours, limited to 16 people, offered only F 3:30-5:30pm, so book faaaaaaaar ahead. Government business may lead to cancellation of tours at any time.*

For the classic view of The Houses of Parliament, captured by Claude Monet, walk about halfway over Westminster Bridge, preferably at dusk. Like the government offices along Whitehall, the Houses of Parliament occupy the former site of a royal palace. Only Jewel Tower (see below) and Westminster Hall (to the left of St. Stephen's entrance on St. Margaret St.) survive from the original building, which was destroyed by a fire in 1834. Sir Charles Barry and A.W.N. Pugin won a competition for the design of the new houses. The immense complex blankets eight acres and includes more than 1000 rooms and 100 staircases. Space is nevertheless so scarce that Members of Parliament (MPs) do have neither private offices nor staff, and the archives—the originals of every Act of Parliament passed since 1497—are stuffed into **Victoria Tower,** the large tower to the south. A flag flown from the tower indicates that Parliament is in session.

Access to Westminster Hall and the Houses of Parliament has been restricted since a bomb killed an MP in 1979. However, if you didn't manage to secure a tour place, don't despair of—you might still be able to watch the business of government being done from the visitors' galleries in both the House of Commons and the House of Lords (see below for details).

BIG BEN. Big Ben is not the famous northernmost clocktower but rather the 14-ton bell that tolls the hours. Ben is most likely named after the robustly proportioned Sir Benjamin Hall, who served as Commissioner of Works when the bell was cast and hung in 1858. The familiar 16-note tune that precedes the top-of-the-hour toll is a selection from Handel's *Messiah*. On the clock, still wound manually, 14ft. minute hands point to Roman numerals 2ft. long.

HOUSE OF COMMONS' GALLERY. After you sign a form promising not to read, use cameras or opera glasses, or otherwise cause disturbances, the guards will show you to the Chambers of the House of Commons. Destroyed during the Blitz, most traditional features of the chamber still remain, like the two red lines fixed two sword-lengths apart, which (for safety's sake) debating members may not cross. The Government party (the party with the most MPs in the House) sits to the Speaker's right, and the Opposition sits to her left. There are not enough benches in the chamber to seat all 650 members, which adds a sense of huddled drama to the occasions when all are present. MPs vote by filing into **division lobbies** parallel to the chamber: ayes to the west, nays to the east.

You can watch MPs at work from the House of Commons Gallery for "Distinguished and Ordinary Strangers". If you don't have an advance booking (see below), arrive early and wait at the public entrance at St. Stephen's gate; keep left (the right-hand queue is for the Lords) Weekdays after 6pm and Fridays are the least crowded; afternoon waits can be as long as two hours. MPs set their own hours, so don't be surprised if everyone's packed up and gone home earlier than expected. Places in the gallery during Prime Minister's Question Time (W 3-3:30pm), when the Prime Minister answer questions from MPs, are particularly hard to obtain. *(☎ 7219 4272. Gallery open M-W 2:30-10:30pm, Th 11:30am-7:30pm, F normally 9:30am to around 3pm. For advance tickets, UK residents should contact their MP; overseas visitors must apply for a Card of Introduction from their Embassy or High Commission in London. Book at least a month in advance. Free.)*

POMP AND CIRCUM- STANCE

For folks who can't get enough of mounted, betassled guards, another battery of the Queen's Life Guard mark time on the west side of Whitehall north of Downing St. Monday to Saturday at 11am and Sunday at 10am. The arrival of more mounted troops and lots of barking in incoherent English mark **Whitehall's Changing of the Guard,** a less crowded and impressive version of the Buckingham Palace spectacle (see **Buckingham Palace,** p. 74). The barking occurs again daily at 4pm, this time accompanied by dismounting and strutting, and is called the **Inspection of the Guard.** Note that many of the guards now wear UN medals after having served in Bosnia in 1995; the Queen's Cavalry serve six-month tours of duty with UN peace-keeping forces.

The Armistice Day Parade (closest Sunday to Nov. 11) and the Belgian Army Veteran's Parade (closest Sunday to July 15) are launched annually from the Horse Guards' Palace, a large court opening onto St. James's Park. In addition, Beating the Retreat, a must for lovers of pomp and circumstance, takes place here at the beginning of June (call 7414 2271 for dates and ticket information). Beating the Retreat is merely a warm-up for Trooping the Colour, in which the Queen gives the royal salute to the Root Guards. The ceremony takes place in the middle of June and is preceded by two rehearsals open to the public (without the Queen).

HOUSE OF LORDS' GALLERY. To enter the Lords' Gallery, go through the Central Lobby and pass through the Peers' corridor where the MPs have bedecked the passage with scenes of Charles I's downfall. The ostentation of the **House of Lords,** dominated by the sovereign's Throne of State under a gilt canopy, contrasts with the sober, green-upholstered Commons'. The Lord Chancellor presides over the House from his seat on the **Woolsack,** stuffed with wool from all nations of the Kingdom and Commonwealth. At first glance, the woolsack appears to be a small white pillow on the throne where no one sits, but actually it's a red behemoth the size of a VW Beatle. Next to him rests the almost 6ft. **Mace,** which is brought in to open the House each morning. The Lords is generally far easier to get into than the Commons, since the Lords do less important parliamentary business. (☎ 7219 3107. *Keep right in the queue at St. Stephen's entrance. Open M-W from 2:30pm-rise, Th from 3pm, occasionally F 11am. Free.*)

ST. STEPHEN'S HALL. After entering St. Stephen's Gate and submitting to an elaborate security check, you will be led into St. Stephen's Hall. This chapel is where the House of Commons used to sit. In the floor are four brass markers where the Speaker's Chair stood. Charles I, in his ill-fated attempt to arrest five MPs, sat here in the place of the Speaker in 1641. No sovereign has entered the Commons since.

OUTSIDE THE HOUSES. Old Palace Yard hosted the executions of Sir Walter Raleigh and the Gunpowder Plot conspirator Guy Fawkes (the palace's cellars are still ceremonially searched before every opening of Parliament). To the north squats **Westminster Hall** (rebuilt around 1400), where high treason trials, including those of Thomas More, Fawkes, and Charles I, were held until 1825. **New Palace Yard** is a good place to spy your favorite MPs as they enter the complex wait-free through the Members' entrance.

JEWEL TOWER. The 14th-century tower, built for Edward III to store personal treasures, stands by the southeastern end of the Abbey, across from the Houses of Parliament. Formerly Parliament's outsized filing cabinet and later the Weights and Measures office, it now contains eclectic exhibits ranging from bits of the original Westminster Hall to a Norman sword dredged from the moat. The moat, as it happens, was built not only for protection in less stable days, but also to provide fish for the king's table. (☎ 7222 219. *Open daily Apr.-Sept. 9:30am-6pm, last admission 5:30pm; Oct.-Mar. 9:30am- 5pm, last admission 4:40pm. £1.50, concessions £1.10.*)

ST. JOHN OF SMITH SQUARE

◪ *Smith Sq. Tube: Westminster (☎ 7222 1061; www.sjss.org.uk). For concert info, see Music, p. 149.*

Four assertive corner towers distinguish this former church, now a chamber music concert hall. Queen

Anne, whose imagination was taxed by her leading role in the design of 50 new churches, supposedly upended a footstool and told Thomas Archer to build the church in its image. Dickens likened Archer's effort to a "petrified monster." Chamber music, choral, and orchestral concerts take place most evenings; tickets cost £6-£20.

WESTMINSTER CATHEDRAL

🚩 *Cathedral Piazza, off Victoria St. (☎ 7798 9055; www.westminster-cathedral.org.uk). Tube: Victoria. Open daily 7am-7pm. Suggested donation £2. Lift open daily Apr.-Nov. 9am-5pm; Dec.-Mar. Th-Su 9am-5pm. £2, concessions £1, families £5.*

Not to be confused with the Anglican abbey, the Cathedral is the headquarters of the Roman Catholic church in Britain. The architecture is Christian Byzantine, in pointed contrast to the Gothic abbey. The structure, completed in 1903, rests on the former site of a 19th century prison complex. It has an as-yet-unfinished interior, and the blackened brick of the domes contrasts dramatically with the swirling marble of the lower walls. A lift carries visitors to the top of the rocket-like, striped 273ft. tall brick bell tower for a decent view of the Houses of Parliament, the river, and Kensington.

Trafalgar Square

WHITEHALL

🚩 *Tube: Westminster.*

"Whitehall," which stretches from Parliament to Trafalgar Sq., has become the home and a synonym for the British civil service. Whitehall was originally a residence for the Archbishops of York. Henry VIII later took up residence there in 1530.

10 DOWNING STREET. Conveniently enough, the Prime Minister's headquarters lies just steps up Parliament St. from the Houses of Parliament. Sir George Downing, ex-Ambassador to the Hague, built this house in 1681. Prime Minister Sir Robert Walpole made it his official residence in 1732. The Chancellor of the Exchequer traditionally resides at #11, and the Chief Whip at #12. However, Tony Blair's family is too big for 10 Downing St., so he's moved next door to #11. Visitors have long been barred from entering Downing St. by gates and a wall of bobbies.

Big Ben

NEW SCOTLAND YARD. The headquarters of the Metropolitan Police will probably fall short of crime-hounds' expectations. The second of three incarnations of the lair of those unimaginative detectives (humbled by Sherlock Holmes and Hercule Poirot) is no more than two buildings, connected by an arch, that currently contain government offices. The original Yard was at the top of Whitehall, on Great Scotland Yard, and the current New Scotland Yard is on Victoria St. *(6 Derby Gate, just off Whitehall.)*

MINISTRY OF DEFENSE BUILDING. In 1953, the government erected this massive structure (the largest office building in London when it was built) on Whitehall over Henry's VIII's wine cellar. The late-17th-century cellar had to be relocated deeper into the ground to accommodate the new structure. Technically, visitors may view the cellar, but permission is dauntingly difficult to obtain (apply in writing to the Department of the Environment or the Ministry of Defense with a compelling story). Near the statue of General Gordon in the gardens behind the Ministry of Defense Building, you'll find

Trafalgar Square

the remnants of **Queen Mary's terrace,** built for Queen Mary II. The bottom of the steps leading from the terrace mark the 17th-century water level, a reminder of the extent to which river transport determined the locations of 16th- and 17th-century buildings.

BANQUETING HOUSE. This 1622 house is one of the few intact masterpieces of Inigo Jones. Charles I and James I held feasts and staged elaborate masques (thinly-disguised pieces of theatrical propaganda) in the main hall. Charles commissioned the 18m ceiling; the scenes Rubens painted are allegorical representations of the divine strength of James I. The party ended on January 27, 1649, when Charles, draped in black velvet, stepped out of a ground-floor window to the scaffold where he was beheaded. The weather vane on the roof tells another tale of Stuart misfortune—James II placed it there to see if the wind was favorable for his rival-to-the-throne William of Orange's voyage from the Netherlands. From 1724 to 1890, the Banqueting House served as a Chapel Royal. These days the hall serves state dinners and the occasional concert, not death warrants. *(At the corner of Horse Guards Ave and Whitehall, opposite Horse Guards Hall.* ☎ *7930 4179. Open M-Sa 10am-5pm, last admission 4:30pm. Closed for government functions. £3.80, concessions £3, children £2.30.)*

CABINET WAR ROOMS. A protected Winston Churchill directed operations at the end of World War II from the Cabinet War Rooms (p. 120). The formal **Cenotaph,** which honors the war dead stands where Parliament St. turns into Whitehall. *(At the end of King Charles St.)*

BUCKINGHAM PALACE

I must say, notwithstanding the expense which has been incurred in building the palace, no sovereign in Europe, I may even add, perhaps no private gentleman, is so ill-lodged as the king of this country.
—Duke of Wellington, 1828

🖪 *Buckingham Palace Rd. (Recorded info* ☎ *7799 2331, info office* ☎ *7839 1377; www.royal.gov.uk). Tube: Victoria, Green Park or St. James's Park. Open daily Aug.-Sept. 9:30am-4:30pm. £10.50, seniors £8, under 17 £5. Tickets before the opening dates at* ☎ *7321 2233.*

When a freshly-crowned Victoria moved from St. James's Palace in 1837, Buckingham Palace, built in 1825 by John Nash, had faulty drains and a host of other difficulties. Improvements were made, and now the monarch calls it home. The 20th-century facade on the Mall is only big, not beautiful—the Palace's best side, the garden front, is seldom seen by ordinary visitors as it is protected by the 40-acre spread where the Queen holds garden parties.

Visitors are allowed in the **Blue Drawing Room,** the **Throne Room,** the **Picture Gallery** (filled with pictures by Rubens, Rembrandt, and Van Dyck), and the **Music Room** (where Mendelssohn played for Queen Victoria), as well as other stately rooms. In the opulent **White Room,** the large mirror fireplace conceals a door used by the Royal Family at formal dinners.

CHANGING OF THE GUARD. Though public support for the royal family has waned considerably in the past years, tourist enthusiasm for the fur-capped Buckingham guards has not. From April to June, the ceremony takes place daily; during the rest of the year, it occurs on odd-numbered dates. The "Old Guard" marches from St. James's Palace down the Mall to Buckingham Palace, leaving at approximately 11:10am. The "New Guard" begins marching as early as 10:20am. When they meet at the central gates of the palace, the officers of the regiments then touch hands, symbolically exchanging keys, *et voilà,* the guard is officially changed. The soldiers gradually split up to relieve the guards currently protecting the palace. The ceremony moves to the beat of royal band music and the menacing clicks of thousands of cameras. In wet weather or on pressing state holidays, the Changing of the Guard does not occur. To witness the spectacle, show up well before 11:30am and stand directly in front of the palace. You can also watch along the routes of the troops prior to their arrival at the palace (10:40-11:25am) between the Victoria Memorial and St. James's Palace or along Birdcage Walk.

OTHER SIGHTS. The **Royal Mews Museum** houses the royal coaches and other historic royal riding implements. A combined pass for the Gallery and Mews may be purchased. *(Off Buckingham Gate. Open Oct.-Jul. M-W and Th noon-4pm, last admission 3:30pm; Aug.-Sept. M-Th*

10:30am-4:30pm, last admission 4 pm. £4.30, seniors £3.30, under 17 £2.10, family £10.70.) The **Guards Museum** features, among other things, over 350 years of red coat history. Go around 10:30am and you might see them hanging around for the Changing of the Guard. *(Near the Royal Mews at Wellington Barracks on Birdcage Walk, off Buckingham Gate. Open M-Th and Sa-Su 10am-4pm. £2, concessions £1, family £4.)*

TRAFALGAR SQUARE AND CHARING CROSS

🚇 *Tube: Charing Cross or Leicester Sq.*

Unlike many squares in London, Trafalgar Square (Tube: Charing Cross), which slopes down from the **National Gallery** (see **Museums,** p. 115) into the center of a vicious traffic roundabout, has been public land ever since the razing of several hundred houses made way for its construction in the 1830s. Now, streams of tourists mingle amongst the legions of pigeons that sit upon the most unwilling of shoulders. Floodlights bathe the square after dark, when it fills up with eager tourists and club kids trying to catch the right night bus home. Enthusiastic, rambunctious New Year's celebrations take place here, featuring universal indiscriminate kissing.

NELSON'S COLUMN. This fluted granite pillar commands the square, with four majestic, beloved lions guarding the base. The monument and square commemorate Admiral Horatio Nelson, killed during his triumph over Napoleon's navy at Trafalgar; the monument's reliefs were cast from French cannons.

ST. MARTIN-IN-THE-FIELDS. This church on the northeastern corner of the square dates from the 1720s. Designer James Gibbs topped its templar classicism with a Gothic steeple. The interior, despite the gilded and chubby cherubim, is simple, its walls relatively uncluttered with monuments. The church is also home to the acclaimed **Academy of St. Martin-in-the-fields** and has an active concert schedule incorporating performers from around the world; in addition to regular free lunchtime concerts, there are normally three candlelit evening concerts per week as well as a summer festival in mid-July. The **crypt** has been cleared of all those dreary coffins to make room for a gallery, a book shop, a brass rubbing center, and a surprisingly good cafe. *(Trafalgar Sq. ☎ 7930 0089; www.stmartin-in-the-fields.org.uk. Free concerts M-Tu and F 1:05pm. Reserve seats for evening concerts online; by phone M-F 10am-4pm at ☎ 7839 8362; or in the crypt bookstore, open M-W 10am-6pm and Th-Sa 10am-7:30pm. Cafe open M-Sa 10am-8pm, Su noon-6pm.)*

CHARING CROSS. The original Charing Cross, the last of 13 crosses set up to mark the stages of Queen Eleanor's royal funeral procession in 1291 ("charing" is a corruption of *chère reine,* French for "beloved queen"), was actually located at the top of Whitehall, immediately south of Trafalgar Square. Like many things, it was destroyed by Cromwell, and a replica now stands outside Charing Cross Station. "Fleet Street has a very animated appearance," Samuel Johnson once remarked, "but I think the full tide of human existence is at Charing Cross." An overfull tide of traffic now engulfs the place, and the bronze statue of King Charles drowns in the ebb and flow of automobiles. The statue escaped the cross's fate with the aid of one wily John Rivett. He bought the statue "for scrap" and did a roaring trade in brass souvenirs supposedly made from the melted-down figure; it was in fact hidden and later sold, at a tidy profit, to Charles II.

CHELSEA AND BELGRAVIA

see map pp. 316

Now quiet and expensive, **Chelsea** has historically been one of London's flashiest districts—Thomas More, Oscar Wilde, and the Sex Pistols have all been residents here at one time or another, and for a brief period, all at once. On Chelsea's famed **King's Road,** mohawked UB40s (a reference to the unemployed: it's the form they fill out to get benefits) and pearl-necklaced Sloane Rangers (the London equivalent of US preppies) gazed at trendy window displays and at each other. Today the hordes still flock here on Saturday afternoons to see and be seen, but the ambience is muted; most current scenesters look like they are desperately trying to recapture a past they have only read about.

Previously an open field popular for duels, **Belgravia** was first constructed to billet servants after the building of Buckingham Palace in the 1820s, but it soon (as with many other parts of London) became the bastion of wealth and privilege. Belgravia lies south of Hyde Park, ringed by Sloane St. to the west, Victoria Station to the south, and Buckingham Palace Gardens to the east. The spacious avenues and crescents of the district surround **Belgrave Square,** 10 acres of park surrounded by late-Georgian buildings that were the setting for *My Fair Lady*, and now populated by a zany, singing cast of characters employed in the innumerable embassies and consulates in Belgravia. Nearby **Eaton Square** was one of Henry James's favorites. The 8-year-old Mozart composed his first symphony at no. 180.

WORLD'S END

☎7352 6551. Tube: Sloane Square then bus #11 or #22.

The number one sight in these parts is probably the edge of land and the beginning of the abyss that is deep space. In the 70s, impresario Malcolm McLaren and designer **Vivienne Westwood** masterminded a series of trendy boutiques here, at 430 King's Road, that capitalized on the subcultural fashions then in vogue, like the Teddy Boy look. Let it Rock, Too Young To Live Too Fast To Die, and Seditionaries were some of the shop's various inventions; its most important incarnation was Sex, the punk clothing store in which the **Sex Pistols** (and, some would argue, punk rock) were born. Ripped clothing and bondage gear as fashion originated here. While Westwood still displays her designs in a boutique at this address, she now sells fabulously expensive couture. Ironically, the boutique's current neighbor is the Chelsea Conservative Club.

CHEYNE WALK, CHEYNE ROW, AND TITE STREET

Tube: Sloane Sq.

These three thoroughfares formed the heart of Chelsea's artist colony at the turn of the century. J.M.W. Turner moved into a house in Cheyne Walk, and Edgar Allan Poe lived nearby. Mary Ann Evans (a.k.a. George Eliot) moved into #4 just before her death. Dante Gabriel Rossetti kept his disreputable *ménage* (which included peacocks and a kangaroo) in #16, where he doused himself with chloral hydrate. #19-26 cover the ground that used to be Chelsea Manor, where Elizabeth I once lived. The area's arbiter of the aesthetic, Oscar Wilde, reposed stylishly at 34 Tite St. from 1884-1895 and was arrested for homosexual activity at Chelsea's best-known hotel, the **Cadogan,** at 75 Sloane St. John Singer Sargent, James MacNeill Whistler, Radclyffe Hall, and Bertrand Russell also lived on Tite St. Today, fashionable artists' and designers' homes line the street, though the area is too expensive to remain a true bastion of bohemian culture.

CARLYLE'S HOUSE

24 Cheyne Row (☎7352 7087). Tube: Sloane Sq. Open Apr.-Oct. W-Su 11am-5pm. Last admission 4:30pm. £3.50, children £1.75.

Just beyond Cheyne Walk stands the former home of historian Thomas Carlyle, where he hung out with Dickens, Thackeray, Geoge Eliot, and Ruskin. The house has remained virtually unchanged since the "Sage of Chelsea" expired in his armchair. Family portraits and sketches ornament the walls—which he had doubled in thickness, vainly hoping to keep out noise. Be sure to read the letters between Disraeli and Carlyle that are displayed in the upstairs study.

ROYAL HOSPITAL

Royal Hospital Rd. Tube: Sloane Sq. or buses # 11, 19, 22, 137. ☎7730 5282. Grounds open daily Apr.-Sept., 10am-8pm. Museum open Apr.-Sept. M-Sa 10am-noon and 2-4pm, Su 2-4pm. Free.

Totally immune to the ever-changing world of King's Rd. are the commandingly militaresque buildings of Wren's Royal Hospital, founded in 1691 by Charles II for retired soldiers and still inhabited by 400 ex-army "Chelsea pensioners". Former soldiers in Royal Hospital uniform welcome visitors to the spacious, well-groomed grounds and splendid buildings. The museum features war medals of deceased veterans. The north wing has borne war's scars quite directly in the last century. In 1918 a 500 lb. German bomb destroyed the wing, killing 5 residents. After the war it was rebuilt only to be destroyed toward the end of WWII by a German V2 rocket, again killing 5 retired soldiers.

SLOANE SQUARE

Tube: Sloane Sq.

Mostly just a square, with four sides at 90° angles, Sloane Square takes its name from Sir Hans Sloane (1660-1753), who founded the British Museum. The nearby **Royal Court Theatre** (see **Theaters**, p. 144) debuted many of George Bernard Shaw's plays. Until 1829, King's Rd., stretching southwest from Sloane Sq., served as a private royal thoroughfare from Hampton Court to Whitehall. Today the street is a commercial thoroughfare where overpriced restaurants, historic pubs, and antique stores lurk amid über-trendy boutiques. The recent presence of three supermodeling agencies in the square fills many of the boutiques with London's most fashionable/thinnest women.

Queen Anne

OTHER CHELSEA SIGHTS

CHELSEA OLD CHURCH. At the west end of Cheyne Walk lies this church, known as All Saints, and partially designed by Sir Thomas More. Isn't irony a laugh: the old church, flattened in the wars, has been rebuilt so as to look mostly new. Henry VIII is reported to have married Jane Seymour here before the official wedding took place. The friendly verger will point out **Crosby Hall** down the street, a 15th-century hall that was More's residence in Bishopsgate before it was moved, stone by stone, to its present position in 1910. *(Church open M-F noon-4pm, Su 8am-1pm and 2-7pm.)*

CHELSEA PHYSIC GARDEN. The oldest botanical garden in England, the Physic Garden was first established in 1676 by the Apothecaries' Company. Even plant-haters will be interested in the range of useful botanicals on show, from dyes to medicinal, on show within its walls. Today the gardens are used mostly for educational purposes, although sampling the plants by eating each one might be particularly enlightening. *(66 Royal Hospital Rd., next to the Royal Hospital. ☎ 7352 5646. Open Apr. 2-Oct. 29 W noon-5pm, Su 2-6pm. Admission £4, concessions and children £2. Wheelchair accessible.)*

Westminster Abbey

RANELAGH GARDENS. East of the Royal Hospital lie these gardens, where 18th-century pleasure-seekers spent their evenings watching pageants and fireworks and imbibing to excess. Feel free to follow their lead. The **Chelsea Flower Show** (www.rhs.co.uk) blooms here during the 3rd week in May, but even Royal Horticultural Society members have trouble procuring tickets for the first two days. *(Tube: Sloane Sq. Usually open until dusk; free.)*

KENSINGTON, KNIGHTSBRIDGE, AND HYDE PARK

see map p. 313

KENSINGTON

Two years are significant for Kensington's development: 1689, when William III decided digs in Kensington Palace suited his humors better and high society tagged along; and 1851, when the Great Exhibition brought in enough profit to finance the museums and colleges of South Kensington. These days, Kensington is a well-off, cosmopolitan area. Kensington High St. has become a locus for shopping and scoping.

Sir Walter Raleigh

SOUTH KENSINGTON MUSEUMS

🚩 *V&A, Natural History Museums on Cromwell Rd.; Science Museum on Exhibition Rd. Tube: South Kensington.*

It's tempting to try to "do" South Kensington's trio of museums in as quick a time as possible. Tempting, but probably not advisable. Not only are they each enormous, making any such endeavour physically daunting, they're also individually fascinating, and it would be a pity to rush things. The **Victoria and Albert Museum** (p. 119), the **Natural History Museum** (p. 122), and the **Science Museum** (p. 122) all testify on a grand scale to the Victorian mania for collecting, codifying, and cataloging.

BROMPTON ORATORY

🚩 ☎ *7589 4811. Open daily 6:30am-8pm. Solemn Mass Su 11am.*

The architecture of this grand Catholic Church, which is properly known as the Oratory of St. Philip Neri, balances Baroque stylings with Victorian influences. H. Gribble oversaw the building of the edifice, which was started in 1874 and completed in 1884, designing a nave wider than St. Paul's Cathedral. It features many stunning side altars; the enormous Renaissance altar in the Lady Chapel came from Brescia. One of the altars was considered by the KGB to be the best dead drop in London—until 1985, agents left microfilm and other documents behind a statue for other agents to retrieve. The church lives up to its reputation for music during its **Solemn Masses,** sung in Latin.

OTHER KENSINGTON SIGHTS

HOLLAND PARK. A pasture of small pleasures. **Holland House,** a Jacobean mansion built in 1607, lies on the park's grounds. Destroyed in WWII, the house has been restored and turned into a youth hostel (see **Accommodations,** p. 258). The park also contains the open-air **Holland Park Theatre** (see p. 146), an ecology center, and the traditional Japanese **Kyoto Gardens**. The flag-ridden **Commonwealth Institute** stands by the park's southern entrance on the High St. *(Between Holland Park Ave and Kensington High St. Tube: High St. Kensington or Holland Park. Park police ☎ 7471 9811. Park open daily 7:30am-half hour after dusk.)*

LEIGHTON HOUSE. Sumptuous or merely presumptuous? Either way, Leighton House's pastiche of various styles of Oriental art, devised by Lord Leighton in the 19th century, remains intriguing. The thoroughly blue Arab Hall, with ornate inlaid tiles and a pool, was an attempt to recreate the wonders of the "exotic" Orient in thoroughly Occidental Kensington. Other rooms contain paintings by Leighton. Now a center for the arts, Leighton House features frequent art exhibitions, as well as the occasional concert *(12 Holland Park Rd. ☎ 7602 3316. Open W-M 11am-5:30pm. Free. Tours W-Th noon.)*

OTHER INSTITUTIONS. Also in the area, north of Cromwell Rd., are various institutions of learning and culture, including the Imperial College of Science, the Royal College of Music, the Royal College of Art, the Royal Albert Hall, the Royal School of Needlepoint, and the Royal Geographical Society.

HYDE PARK AND KENSINGTON GARDENS

🚩 *Framed by Kensington Rd., Knightsbridge, Park Lane, and Bayswater Rd. Constabulary ☎ 7298 2076. Tube: Bayswater, High St. Kensington, Hyde Park Corner, Knightsbridge, Marble Arch, or Queensway. "Liberty Drives" for people with disabilities ☎ (0407) 498 096; available May-Oct. Tu-F 10am-5pm. Hyde Park open daily 5am-midnight; Kensington Gardens open daily dawn-dusk.*

Totalling 630 acres, Hyde Park and the contiguous Kensington Gardens constitute the largest open area in the center of the city, thus earning their reputation as the "lungs of London." Henry VIII used to hunt deer here, but nowadays picnic baskets and suntan lotion are far more common than bows.

ALBERT MEMORIAL

🚩 *In Kensington Gardens on Kensington Gore. ☎ 7495 0916. Tours Su 2pm and 3pm; 45min.; £3, concessions £2.50.*

It's hard to imagine that this gleaming statue of Prince Albert was once painted completely black to avoid German detection during World War II. But an £11.2 million restoration program has restored the gigantic golden statue and its base (with representations of Africa, America, Asia, and Europe) to their full glory. The tour gets you past the railings to see the Parnassus Frieze, featuring various artists of the past.

KENSINGTON PALACE

▶ In Kensington Gardens (☎ 7937 9561; www.hrp.org.uk). Tube: High St. Kensington. Open Mar.-Oct. daily 10am-6pm, Nov.-Dec. daily 10am-5pm; last admission 1hr. before closing. Audio tour included. £8.50, concessions £6.70, under 16 £6.10, families £26.10.

It was once plain old Nottingham House in 1689, but William III and Mary II bought it, enrolled Sir Christopher Wren to overhaul it, and turned it into a royal palace. While George II was the last monarch to actually rule from Kensington, Queen Victoria was born here, and the building was home to the late Princess Diana. The uninhabited **State Apartments** are now home to the stunning **Royal Ceremonial Dress Collection,** which contains royal clothing from the 18th century to the present. Princess Diana's wedding gown has since been removed to Althorp, her ancestral home (see **Daytrips,** p. 211), but some of her dresses are set to return in April 2001. The **King's Gallery** contains art from the Royal Collection and an amazing ceiling by William Kent. **Orangery Gardens,** an exquisite flower display studded by young couples getting mushy, lines the eastern side of the palace. Also on the palace grounds, the **Orangery,** built for Queen Anne, is a sumptuous white tea room that offers a variety of set teas from £7.75.

OTHER HYDE PARK AND KENSINGTON GARDEN SIGHTS

SERPENTINE. This 41-acre lake, carved in 1730, runs from the Fountains in the north, near Bayswater Rd., southeast toward Knightsbridge. From the number of people who pay to row in the pond, you'd think it was the fountain of youth. Perhaps not—Harriet Westbrook, Percy Bysshe Shelley's first wife, numbers among the people who drowned in this human-made "pond." A bone-white arch derived from a Henry Moore sculpture stands on the northwest bank, but the best view is from across the water. A statue of **Peter Pan,** actually modeled from a girl, stands near the **Italian Fountains** on the west bank. *(Between Hyde Park and Kensington Gardens. Boat rental ☎ 7262 1440; £3.50 for 30min., £5 for 1hr.; child £1 for 30min, £2 for 1hr.; deposit may be required; no credit cards.)*

MARBLE ARCH. Poor Marble Arch, constantly abandoned throughout its history. It was built in 1828 as the front entrance to Buckingham Palace, but extensions to the palace meant it became too small, so it was moved to the present site as an entrance into Hyde Park. Then new roads cut the arch off, leaving it stranded forlornly on a traffic roundabout. Marble Arch stands where the public gallows of Tyburn rested until 1759. The gathered would jeer and throw rotting food at the unfortunate criminals as they rolled in carts to the "Tyburn Tree," which stood at the present corner of Bayswater Rd. and the Edgware Road. *(Where Bayswater Rd. meets Oxford St. Tube: Marble Arch.)*

OTHER NOTABLES. In the northeast corner of Hyde Park, near Marble arch, proselytizers, politicos, and flat-out crazies dispense the fruits of their knowledge to whoever's biting at **Speaker's Corner** on summer evenings and Sundays from late morning to dusk. *(Tube: Marble Arch.)* At the southern end of Hyde Park clusters a group of statues: a **Diana fountain** (the goddess, not the princess), the "family of man," a likeness of **Lord Byron,** and a fig-leafed **Achilles** dedicated to Wellington. **Rotten Row,** whose name is a corruption of *Route du Roi* or "King's Road," was the first English thoroughfare lit at night to prevent crime. However, this east-west path through southern Hyde Park, like the rest of the park, is dangerous at night.

NOTTING HILL AND BAYSWATER

see map p. 312

Contrary to what Hollywood and children's characters would have you believe, Notting Hill is not a white yuppieville infested with yellow bears looking for marmalade. In the days after World War II Notting Hill was an undesirable area where waves of poor immigrants (mostly West Indian) lived in dirt-cheap flats. Today, Notting Hill is thoroughly mixed—the media whores party alongside blue-collar Londoners. Genteel streets with private garden squares intersect with noisy avenues of bargain hunters and wafting incense; Joseph Fiennes, Elvis Costello, and large Portuguese, West Indian and Moroccan communities all share the W11 and W2 postal codes.

BEEFCAKE WELLINGTON

Before television, film, and Hugh Grant, British women culled their sex symbols from the military, and few soldiers set pulses racing faster than Arthur Wellesley, Duke of Wellington. Charlotte Brontë fancied the victor at Waterloo so much as a child that she modeled Jane Eyre's Rochester after him. Countess Lavinia Spencer showed her affection in another way, by launching a women-only public subscription to raise funds for a memorial statue. The result was the "Ladies' Trophy," Hyde Park's nude statue of Achilles, cheekily referred to as the ladies' fancy. The statue, London's first nude, was embroiled in controversy from its creation. Lady Holland wrote saucily: "A difficulty has arisen, and the artist had submitted to the female subscribers whether this colossal figure should preserve its antique nudity or should be garnished with a fig leaf. It was carried for the leaf by a majority...The names of the *minority* have not transpired." Those eager to accuse women of prudery should be advised that it was in fact the gentleman head of the statue committee who insisted on the fig leaf.

The scenery that surrounded the village of Notting Hill in the mid-19th century (a few cornfields, a meadow, an occasional lane) changed drastically when the Great Western Railway opened up North Kensington to development in 1838. The Ladbroke family commissioned high-society architects to develop the area, whereupon upper-middle-class families took up residence in spacious Neoclassical townhouses. Today those homes are inhabited by Notting Hill's fast-growing population of "Trustafarians." These young and inherited come looking for a more "bohemian" (but not "cheaper") lifestyle.

The area has a checkered past of racial conflict that it is gradually being put to rest. Irish and Jewish immigrants were the first to occupy the poor areas of "Notting Dale" in the late 19th century, but the 1930s saw the arrival of Fascist demonstrations against Jews and local immigrant groups. Inter-ethnic tension re-emerged in the 1950s when Teddy-Boy gangs engaged in open warfare against Afro-Caribbean immigrants—the devastating riots that ensued are depicted in Colin MacInnes's novel *Absolute Beginners* (later made into a movie musical starring David Bowie). Amy Garvey (widow of Marcus Garvey, the famed black separatist) helped the black community on Notting Hill survive various onslaughts. Today the multi-ethnic area sees little racial animosity, a fact London's novelists have not overlooked. The area's most recent literary resident—dartsman Keith Talent of Martin Amis's *London Fields*—does not engage in bigotry. He cheats and swindles everyone, regardless of color or creed.

The neighborhood explodes with exuberant festivity every summer during the **Notting Hill Carnival,** Europe's biggest outdoor festival, which is held over the last weekend in August. Around 2 million people line Portobello Rd. to watch and walk in a parade of steel drummers, fantastic costumes, entranced followers, and dancing policemen while Caribbean music reverberates through the streets. A bit of warning: the Notting Hill Carnival attracts huge crowds to come and drink in a small area.

PORTOBELLO ROAD. This commercial road is the heart of Notting Hill's bustling activity. The name "Portobello" may evoke childhood memories, even if you've never been to London—one of the market's patrons is **Paddington Bear,** whose purchases at the famous **Portobello market** (see p. 139) always landed his paws in a pot of trouble. Antique stores and galleries line the quiet southern end of Portobello near the Notting Hill Gate tube station. As the idler meanders north, antiquarians give way to fresh produce and baked goods stalls, as summer gives way to autumn, youth to old age. Near Lancaster Rd. and the Westway (the overhead highway), stalls vend secondhand clothing, collector's vinyl, and desirable trinkets. Just ahead, upscale restaurants and bars have recently staked their claim. Finally, Golborne Rd. offers its own lively street scene, marked by dirt-cheap and delicious Portuguese and Morrocan patisseries. Fans of architect Ernö Goldfinger will also be pleased to see another of his creations, **Trellick Tower.** This characteristically ultra-modern apartment block is reviled by many, and loved by men named Ernö.

MARYLEBONE AND REGENT'S PARK

St. Margaret's Church

see map p. 303

MARYLEBONE

Located between Regent's Park and Oxford St., the grid-like district of Marylebone (MAR-lee-bun) is dotted with elegant late-Georgian town houses. The name derives from "St. Mary-by-the-bourne," the "bourne" referring to the Tyburn or the Westbourne stream, both now underground. The eternally dammed Westbourne now forms the Serpentine in Hyde Park. There's little to see in this well-kept region of residences and office buildings, but Marylebone has had its share of notable denizens. **Wimpole Street** saw the reclusive poet Elizabeth Barrett write the fabulous *Sonnets from the Portuguese* before she eloped and moved in with Robert Browning. At different times, **19 York Street** has been the home of John Milton, John Stuart Mill, and William Hazlitt. **Marylebone High Street** is hardly your average British high street, as the presence of a Conran Shop (from upscale designer Terence Conran) indicates. **Harley Street** is the address for Britain's pre-eminent medical specialists. Among Marylebone's most popular sights are **Madame Tussaud's** waxwork museum (see **Museums,** p. 121) and the art- and armor-crammed **Wallace Collection** (see **Galleries,** p. 125). Disraeli said of Hertford House, which houses the collection, that it was a "palace of genius, fancy and taste."

Nelson's Column

221B BAKER STREET. Marylebone's most fondly remembered resident is Sherlock Holmes, who, although fictitious, still receives about 50 letters per week addressed to his Baker St. residence. The **Abbey National Building Society** currently occupies the site and employs a full-time secretary to answer requests for assistance in solving mysteries around the world. The official line is that Holmes has retired from detective work and is keeping bees in the country. Nearby, the **Sherlock Holmes Museum** (at #239 but marked "221b Baker St."; see p. 123) will thrill enthusiasts with the meticulous re-creation of the detective's lodgings. *(221b Baker St. Tube: Baker St.)*

THE BBC EXPERIENCE. In Broadcasting House (still used for radio broadcasts) stands this exhibition on the history of Auntie, from its beginnings as a radio broadcaster in 1922 to its present-day status as TV-radio-Internet media conglomerate. While the exhibit is largely geared towards fans of British radio and TV, most people will find the playback of radio broadcasts from World War II moving. Interactive displays let you commentate on sports using real BBC footage, or listen to rare recordings, including, of all things, a William Shatner and Leonard Nimoy version of "Proud Mary". *(Portland Pl. ☎(0870) 603 0304. Tube: Oxford Circus or Great Portland St. Open M 11am-6pm, Tu-Su 10am-6pm. Last admission 4:30pm.)*

Cabinet War Rooms

REGENT'S PARK

500 acres of gardens, promenades, and Londoners between Marylebone Rd. and Camden Town. ☎ 7486 7905; constabulary 7935 1259. Tube: Regent's Park, Great Portland St., Baker St., or Camden Town. Open 6am-dusk.

During the weekend, the vast spaces of Regent's Park sing with the cheers of a hundred games of football. It wasn't always meant to be this popular with the public. Formerly Marylebone Park, a royal hunting ground, the area was cleared in 1650 when Cromwell felled 16,000 trees to raise cash for his cavalry's payroll. In 1812 scrappy architect **John Nash** drew up plans for the Prince Regent (the future George IV) for a park dotted with 40 luxury villas. It was to be a project for "the wealthy and the good" which would separate the fine districts from the less fashionable ones to the east. Parliament became concerned that too much of London would become the province of the wealthy, and the park was opened to the public in stages. Of the eight villas that were actually built, only two remain. The **Regency terraces** on the outskirts of the park present a magnificent facade. The cream-colored, porticoed, and pillared buildings of Hanover Terrace have been home to the likes of H.G. Wells (#17) and Wallis Simpson (#7).

At the heart of the park are 30 or so beautiful acres of well-groomed lawns and gardens, circumscribed by a drive given the exclusive-sounding title of the **"Inner Circle."** Within the Circle are the **Queen Mary's Gardens,** a stunning, heady display of roses and **St. John's Lodge,** one of a pair of remaining Nash villas. The public is free to stroll through the villa's sumptuous formal beds. Near Queen Mary's Gardens stands the **Open Air Theatre,** which has hosted performances every summer since 1932 (see **Theaters,** p. 144). Just outside the Inner Circle, is the large **Boating Lake.** If you're feeling hale, rowboats are available for any landlubber willing to take on the flocks of swans, geese, and ducks. Children may toot around in small rowboats or pedalboats in the smaller, calmer lake next to the full-sized one. *(Rowboats £3 per person for 30min., £4 per hr., plus £5 deposit. Wheelchair boat £3.50 per person for 30 min. Children's pedalboats £3 for 30 min. Available daily 10am-dusk.)*

The enormous golden minaret visible from the lake is the **London Central Mosque,** on Park Rd. After the mosque had been completed, it was discovered that the builders had neglected to build it facing Mecca. Visitors can enter the Islamic Cultural Centre, but should be modestly dressed (i.e. no miniskirts, shorts, or sleeveless clothing).

BLOOMSBURY

see map pp. 296-297

During the first half of the 20th century, Bloomsbury gained a reputation as an intellectual and artistic center because of the presence of the renowned **Bloomsbury Group** (see **Literature,** p. 42), a coterie including Lytton Strachey, E.M. Forster, T.S. Eliot, and John Maynard Keynes that met periodically to discuss art and philosophy. Even after the Bloomsbury Group's disintegration, the area continued to be a center of intellectual life. Young artists and radicals populated the area, giving rise to the term "Bloomsbury Bluestockings," which described young women who smoked, drank, and defied restrictive mid-century gender conventions. Although very little intellectual gossip or high modernist argot emanates from Bloomsbury anymore, the area maintains a cerebral atmosphere. The **British Museum** (see p. 113), the **British Library,** and **University College London** balance tourism and intellectualism.

BRITISH LIBRARY

96 Euston Rd. ☎ 7412 7332. Tube: King's Cross or Euston. Open M 9:30am-6pm, Tu 9:30am-8pm, W-F 9:30am-6pm, Sa 9:30am-5pm, Su 11am-5pm. Free. Special exhibitions £3, concessions £2. Reading rooms are open for research purposes only; students may be able to get in with a letter from their university explaining why they need access.

Next door to St. Pancras station, this sprawling new library, home to millions of books and manuscripts of the past millennium, is Bloomsbury's latest addition and the most expensive public building in England. The treasures of the British Library include beautiful manuscripts and some cool Beatles memorabilia (aural as well as visual). Along the hallway to the cafeteria is a kick-ass stamp display (don't lick). In 2001, the library will feature exhibitions on Oscar Wilde, Armenia, and Black History.

UNIVERSITY COLLEGE LONDON

◪ *Tube: Russell Square or Goode St.*

Excluded from the Anglican-dominated universities at Oxford and Cambridge, Jeremy Bentham and a group of dissenters founded University College on Gower St. in 1828. They banned the teaching of theology and admitted Catholics and Jews. University College was chartered (along with King's College in The Strand) as the University of London in 1836, making London the last major European capital to acquire a university. In 1878, the university became the first in the UK to admit women to its degree courses. From the main quadrangle, climb the steps to the impressive collonade and head right in the building to reach the eerie preserved **body of Jeremy Bentham**—the wax head is the only non-original part, the original having been lost during a morbid game of student football. Jeremy is occasionally wheeled out to preside over university board meetings, as the college statutes demand. The university's **library** resides in Senate House, the white concrete tower dominating Malet St. *(Open M-F 8:30am–5pm.)*

OTHER BLOOMSBURY SIGHTS

ST. PANCRAS OLD CHURCH. London's first parish church sits serenely in its leafy garden. Parts of the church date from the 11th century. Satanists attacked the church in 1985, so it's difficult to get a peek inside. The accompanying graveyard was a public garden in the 1870s, though it has fallen into disrepair. Mary Godwin met Percy Bysshe Shelley here in 1813 by the grave of her mother, Mary Wollstonecraft. Rumor has it that Godwin insisted Shelley make love to her on the grave. Soon after, they eloped to Italy. *(On St. Pancras Rd. Tube: Kings Cross-St. Pancras or Euston Sq.)*

ST. GEORGE'S, BLOOMSBURY. To the south of the British museum, the shrapnel-scarred Corinthian portico of St. George's looms on Bloomsbury Way. A statue of George I crowns the heavy steeple, modeled on the tomb of King Mausolus (origin of the term "mausoleum") in Turkey. The gilded mahogany altar of this church, before which novelist Anthony Trollope was baptized by Nicholas Hawksmoor, was the setting of Dickens's "Bloomsbury Christening." *(Tube: Russell Square. Open M-Sa 9:30am-5:30pm.)*

THOMAS CORAM FOUNDATION. In 1747, retired sea captain Thomas Coram established the Foundling Hospital for abandoned children. In order to raise funds, he sought the help of prominent artists, including William Hogarth, who, in addition to serving as a governor of the hospital, donated paintings and persuaded his friends to do the same. The composer Handel also lent a hand, giving the hospital an organ and performing in a number of benefit concerts. Although the hospital was torn down in 1926, its art treasures remain, displayed in a suite of splendidly restored 18th-century rooms. *(40 Brunswick Sq. ☎ 7841 3600. Tube: Russell Square. Open only for tours; call to book.)*

CORAM'S FIELDS. Across from the Foundation lie seven acres of old Foundling Hospital grounds that have been preserved as a children's park. A menagerie of petting animals and a paddling pool for tykes under five are free to kids and accompanying adults. The adjacent parks are open to the public, with or without little ones, although there are no sheep to pet. *(93 Guilford St. ☎ 7837 6138. Open daily Easter-Oct. 9am-dusk; Nov.-Mar. 9am-5pm. Free. No adults admitted without children.)*

OTHER BLOOMSBURY NOTABLES. Along Euston Rd. to the northeast of Bloomsbury is **St. Pancras Station,** a monument to Victorian prosperity, which now rises over a rather shabby neighborhood. The rear of the building still houses a busy main-line railway station, while the red-brick Neo-Gothic fantasy opening onto Euston Rd. opened in 1874 as the Midland Grand Hotel. After serving as an office building from 1935 until the early 1980s, the abandoned building may soon become reincarnated as a Marriott. *(Tube: King's Cross/St. Pancras.)* West of the British Museum, **Bedford Square** is one of London's best-preserved 18th-century squares. Several community centers provide venues and resources for alternative cultural activity, while numerous galleries display art from around the world. Particularly noteworthy are the **Drill Hall** (see p. 144), **The Place** (see p. 150), the **October Gallery** (see p. 124), **The Percival David Foundation of Chinese Art** (see p. 124), and the **Brunei Gallery** (see p. 123).

COVENT GARDEN

The outdoor cafes, upscale shops, and slick crowds animating Covent Garden today belie its medieval beginnings as a literal "convent garden" where the monks of Westminster Abbey grew their vegetables. When Henry VIII abolished the monasteries in 1536, he granted the land to he Earl of Bedford, whose descendants developed it into a fashionable *piazza* (designed by Inigo Jones) in the 1630s. The

see map pp. 292-293   piazza has gone through many reincarnations, from aristocratic enclave to brothel/ale house central, and back again. Today Covent Garden is filled with street performers. The area has two fab museums: on the piazza's southeast corner is the truly excellent **London Transport Museum** (see p. 120), and just off the piazza east side is the **Theatre Museum** (see p. 123). The streets are constantly bustling—Friday and Saturday nights, when theater crowds and pub crawlers converge, are downright hectic.

THE THEATRE ROYAL AND THE ROYAL OPERA HOUSE

⊓ *Tube: Covent Garden.*

These venerable venues represent a long tradition of theater in the Covent Garden area. The **Theatre Royal** was first built in 1663 as one of two legal theatrical venues in London. Four previous incarnations burnt down; the present building dates from 1812. It now offers "Through the Stage Door," tours of the theater, led by an actor, which take visitors backstage, and then some. For ticketing info, see **Theater,** p. 143. *(Drury Lane. ☎ 7494 5091. Box office open M-Sa 10am-8pm. Tours offered M-Tu, Th, F, and Su 12:30pm, 2:15pm, 4:45pm; W and Sa 11am and 1pm. £7.50, Children £5.50.)* The **Royal Opera House** began as a theater for concerts and plays in 1732 and currently houses the Royal Opera and Royal Ballet. For performance details, see **Music,** p. 151. *(Bow St. ☎ 7304 4000. Open M-Sa 10am-3pm, box office open M-Sa 10am-8pm. Guided tours £3.)*

ST. PAUL'S CHURCH

⊓ *Covent Garden Piazza. Tube: Covent Garden. Open M 10am-2:30pm, Tu 9am-4pm, W 9:30am-4pm, Th 8:30am-4pm, F 9:30am-4pm, Su 9am-12:30pm. Frequent weekday concerts 1:30pm. Evensong 2nd Su of the month, 4pm.*

Not to be confused with St. Paul's Cathedral, this Inigo Jones church now stands as the sole remnant of the original square, although the interior had to be rebuilt after a 1795 fire. Known as "the actor's church," St. Paul's is filled with plaques commemorating the achievements of Boris Karloff, Vivien Leigh, Noel Coward, and Tony Simpson ("inspired player of small parts"), among others. The connection to the theater dates back to the mid-17th century when this was the center of London's theatrical culture.

OTHER COVENT GARDEN SIGHTS

Curious stage design shops cluster near the Opera House, and moss-covered artisans' studios, interspersed with an odd assortment of theater-related businesses, stud the surrounding streets. Rose St. leads to the notorious **Lamb and Flag** (see **Pubs,** p. 174), supposedly the only timber building left in the West End. It was here that Dryden was attacked by an angry mob hired by the Duchess of Portsmouth, who held him responsible for "certain scurrilous verses and lampoons then published concerning her behavior." The attempted murder is commemorated on December 19th (Dryden Night). Further along, Neal St. leads to **Neal's Yard,** where the adventurous can come face to face with wild vegetarians and peruse stores and restaurants selling wholesome foods and homeopathic remedies. At the northern end of St. Martin's Lane, six streets converge at the **Seven Dials** monument; the 7th dial is the monument itself, a sundial.

SOHO

Soho takes its name from a 17th-century hunting cry, although it's hard to fathom, considering the narrow streets and distinct lack of open space that make up the area today, that this was ever hunting grounds. Loosely bounded by Oxford St. to the north, Shaftesbury Ave. to the south, Charing Cross Rd. to the east, and Regent St. to the west, Soho was London's red-light district for centuries. Though most

see map pp. 292-293   of the prostitutes were forced off the streets by legislation in 1959,

Hmm, call home or eat lunch?
With YOU℠
you can do both.

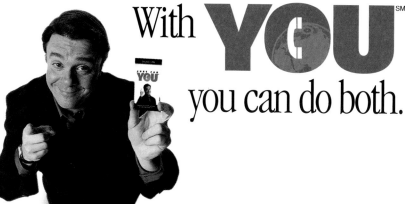

Nathan Lane for YOU℠.

No doubt, traveling on a budget is tough. So tear out this wallet guide and keep it with you during your travels. With YOU, calling home from overseas is affordable and easy.

If the wallet guide is missing, call collect 913-624-5336 or visit www.youcallhome.com for YOU country numbers.

Dialing instructions:
Need help with access numbers while overseas? Call collect, 913-624-5336.

Dial the access number for the country you're in.
Dial 04 or follow the English prompts.
Enter your credit card information to place your call.

Country	Access Number	Country	Access Number	Country	Access Number
Australia ∨	1-800-551-110	Israel ∨	1-800-949-4102	Spain ∨	900-99-0013
Bahamas ✚	1-800-389-2111	Italy ✚ ∨	172-1877	Switzerland ∨	0800-899-777
Brazil ∨	000-8016	Japan ✚ ∨	00539-131	Taiwan ∨	0080-14-0877
China ✚ ▲ ∨	108-13	Mexico ∪ ∨	001-800-877-8000	United Kingdom ∨	0800-890-877
France ∨	0800-99-0087	Netherlands ✚ ∨	0800-022-9119		
Germany ✚ ∨	0800-888-0013	New Zealand ▲ ∨	000-999		
Hong Kong ∨	800-96-1877	Philippines T ∨	105-16		
India ∨	000-137	Singapore ∨	8000-177-177		
Ireland ∨	1-800-552-001	South Korea ✚ ∨	00729-16		

YOU℠
Service provided by Sprint

∨ Call answered by automated Voice Response Unit.   ✚ Public phones may require coin or card.
▲ May not be available from all payphones.   ∪ Use phones marked with "LADATEL" and no coin or card is required.
T If talk button is available, push it before talking.

Pack the Wallet Guide
and save 25% or more* on calls home to the U.S.

It's lightweight and carries heavy savings of 25% or more*
over AT&T USA Direct and MCI WorldPhone rates. So take this
YOU wallet guide and carry it wherever you go.

To save with YOU:
- Dial the access number of the country you're in (see reverse)
- Dial 04 or follow the English voice prompts
- Enter your credit card info for easy billing

Service provided by Sprint

the peep shows and porn shops along **Brewer Street** and **Greek Street** honor this wanton tradition. Far from defining its flavor, however, the sex industry adds merely one small ingredient to the cosmopolitan stew. It's a vibrant, cheerfully dirty area with streets lined by cafes and classic pubs. Many Londoners agree that some of the city's best eats (especially for budgeteers) are to be found here, not to mention joyfully cheap and plentiful offerings sold at **Berwick Street Market** (see p. 138).

Soho has a history of welcoming all colors and creeds to its streets. The district was first settled by French Huguenots fleeing religious persecution after the revocation of the Edict of Nantes in 1685, and the area maintained a French connection for a long time: although the last French grocer, Roche, shut down in the 1980s, a French Protestant church remains off Soho Sq. In more recent years, the area has acquired a significant and visible gay presence; a concentration of gay-owned restaurants and bars has turned **Old Compton Street** into the heart of gay London.

Soho also has a rich literary past: William Blake and Daniel Defoe lived on **Broadwick Street,** and Thomas de Quincey (*Confessions of an English Opium Eater*) did dope in his houses on **Greek Street** and **Tavistock Street.** To the north, a blue plaque above the Quo Vadis restaurant at **28 Dean Street** locates the austere two-room flat where the impoverished Karl Marx lived with his wife, maid, and five children while writing *Das Kapital. Kapital*, however, has almost made Soho too stylish for its own good. Sanitized chains threaten to destroy the area's distinct character and turn it into another Covent Garden. Nevertheless, today's Soho manages to skillfully tread the line between sleazy grit and boring corporate sanitization.

LEICESTER SQUARE

🚇 *Tube: Leicester Sq.*

Amusements at this entertainment nexus range from mammoth cinemas, including London's two largest, the **Odeon Leicester Square** and the **Empire** (see **Film**, p. 147) to free performances provided by street entertainers, to the glockenspiel of the **Swiss Centre.** Its 25 bells ring M-F at noon, 6, 7, and 8pm, Sa-Su at noon, 2, 4, 5, 6, 7, and 8pm; the ringing is accompanied by an animated model of herdsmen leading their cattle through the Alps. A more interesting Alpine experience can be had at Sing-a-Long-a-Sound-of-Music, at the neabry **Prince Charles** cinema (see p. 147). Portraitists crowd around the Swiss Centre offering to sketch pictures for around £15. On the south side, a long queue marks the **Half-Price Ticket Booth** (see **Theater,** p. 142).

CHINATOWN

🚇 *Gerrard St. and Lisle St. form the main heart of Chinatown. Tube: Leicester Sq.*

Cantonese immigrants first arrived in Britain as cooks on British ships, and London's first Chinese community formed around the docks near Limehouse, in the East End. The area around **Gerrard Street** swelled with immigrants from Hong Kong in the 1950s, becoming the heart of Chinatown. There's not really much to see here except the scroll-worked dragon gates that frame Gerrard St., the Chinese language street signs, and the pagoda-capped phone booths. Still, there's plenty to

St. James Park

Buckingham Palace

Royal Academy of Arts

OLD BOYS

Pall Mall and St. James's St., together with **Jermyn Street,** parallel to Pall Mall to the north, flank the traditional stomping grounds of the upper-class English clubman. At 70-72 Jermyn he will buy his shirts from **Turnbull and Asser** (one of Churchill's custom-made "siren suits" is on display). His bowler will be from **Lock & Co. Hatters** (ask politely to see their sinister-looking head measuring device), and his bespoke shoes will be the craft of **John Lobb. Berry & Co.** Wine merchants supply the madeira, and Cuban cigars should really be purchased at **Robert Lewis,** where Churchill indulged his habit for 60 years. "I am the sort of man easily pleased by the best of everything," claimed Sir Winston. Revel in the patrician solemnity of the area at the quintessential men's store **Alfred Dunhill,** 30 Duke Street (entrance on Jermyn)—lurking upstairs above the staid merchandise is a riotously sublime collection of smoking vessels from the world over.

eat. Chinatown is most vibrant during the year's two major festivals: the Mid-Autumn Festival at the end of September, and the raucous Chinese New Year Festival in February.

OTHER SOHO SIGHTS

SOHO SQUARE. Soho first emerged as a discrete area in 1681 with the laying out of this square. It remains one of Soho's only spots of green. *Time Out* said one of the 10 most interesting places to have sex in public in London was up against the mock-Tudor hut in the middle of the square. *Let's Go* does not recommend sex in public. *(Soho Sq., off Soho St. Tube: Tottenham Court Rd. Open daily 10am-dusk.)*

ST. ANNE'S CHURCH. For a long time, the ruins of this church provided an eerie backdrop to Wardour St. Only Wren's 1685 tower and the ungainly steeple added by Cockerell in 1803 emerged unscathed from the Blitz; a new building was constructed around it in 1991. *(Wardour St. ☎7437 5006. Church gardens open M-Sa 8am-dusk, Su 9am-dusk.)*

CARNABY STREET. In the 1960s, Carnaby St. was at the heart of Swingin' London. The street witnessed the rise of youth culture, becoming a hotbed of sex, fashion, and Mods. Many of the chic boutiques and parading celebrities have long since left the street, which has lapsed into a lurid tourist trap. However, a few denizens (like **Luderwicks,** the oldest pipe-makers in London), have weathered storms of fads and tourists alike, and some newer labels have opened branches. Fashionistas will probably find more interesting diversions in nearby **Foubert's Place.** *(Parallel to Regent St. Tube: Oxford Circus.)*

MAYFAIR, PICCADILLY, AND ST. JAMES

see map p. 302

Mayfair takes its name from the 17th-century May Fair held on Shepherd's Market near Green Park. While the fair was famously raucous, modern Mayfair is blue-blooded to the core. After all, how many other parts of central London have proper mansions? In the 18th and 19th centuries, the aristocracy kept houses in Mayfair where they lived during "The Season" (winter was the time for opera and balls in the city), retiring to their country estates in the summer. The reigning queen was born in a house at 17 Bruton St., although that has since been demolished. Novelist Laurence Sterne ended his life on haughty Bond St. (#39). Back in the 60s, Vidal Sassoon revolutionized hair styles at his first salon, on Davies Mews (now the Vidal Sassoon School; see **Entertainment,** p. 151).

PICCADILLY

◪ *Tube: Piccadilly Circus or Green Park*

PICCADILLY CIRCUS. Five of the West End's major arteries (Piccadilly, Regent St., Shaftesbury Ave, and the Haymarket) merge and swirl around Piccadilly Circus, and at times it seems as though the entire tourist population of London has decided to bask in the lurid neon signs. The central focus of the Circus is the **statue of Eros,** by Lord Shaftesbury; Eros originally pointed his bow and arrow down Shaftesbury Avenue, but recent restoration work has put his aim significantly off. Once ground zero for Victorian popular entertainment, today only the **Criterion Theatre** survives (see p. 143), along with the grand facades of former music halls.

MADAME TUSSAUD'S ROCK CIRCUS. Wax versions of rock stars through the ages, from Elvis to the Beatles to Robbie Williams, plus their handprints, other rock memorabilia, and a creepy "cemetery" commemorating rock's dearly departed. Apparently some people don't like their rock stars live. *(London Pavilion, 1 Piccadilly Circus.* ☎*(0870) 400 3030 Open Mar.-Aug. Su-M and W-Th 10am-8pm, Tu 11am-8pm, F-Sa 10am-9pm; Sept.-Feb. Su-M and W-Th 10am-5:30pm, Tu 11am-5:30pm, F-Sa 10am-9pm £8.25, students and seniors £7.25, children £6.25)*

TROCADERO. Electronic diversions ahoy! The Trocadero contains souvenir stores, a cineplex, and **Funland,** a video arcade (games 50p-£2) that is devilishly hard to get out of. *(13 Coventry St. ☎7439 1791. Open Su-Th 10am-midnight, F-Sa 10am-1am.)*

BURLINGTON HOUSE. One of the remnants of Piccadilly's stately past is this showy mansion, built in 1665 for the Earls of Burlington and redesigned in the 18th century by Colin Campbell to accommodate the burgeoning **Royal Academy of Arts** (see **Galleries,** p. 124). Founded in 1768, the Academy comprises 50 academicians and 30 associates who administer exhibitions galleries, and a massive annual summer show. *(Piccadilly, opposite Fortnum and Mason. ☎7300 5959.)*

THE ALBANY. Built in 1771 and remodeled in 1812, the Albany evolved into an exclusive enclave of literary repute. Lord Byron wrote his epic "Childe Harold" here. Other past residents include Macaulay, Gladstone, Canning, "Monk" Lewis, and J.B. Priestley. *(The easily-overlooked Albany Court Yard, off Piccadilly next to the Royal Academy.)*

REGENT STREET. Running north from Piccadilly Circus and leading to Oxford Circus are the grand facades of (upper) Regent Street. John Nash designed the street and its buildings in the early 19th century as part of a processional route for the Prince Regent to his house in Regent's Park. Regent St. has evolved since Nash's time, although **Liberty's** (see **Shopping,** p. 128) makes a false claim to age with a mock-Tudor facade. Today the street has everything from the crisp cuts of Burberry raincoats to the Continental slickness of Zara trousers; those with kids will find it hard to resist the Pied Piper of **Hamley's,** London's largest toystore (see p. 134).

ST. JAMES'S

◪ *Tube: Green Park, St. James's Park, or Charing Cross.*

Roughly bounded by St. James's Park, Green Park, Piccadilly, and the Haymarket, St. James's is London's aristocratic quarter, as you might expect from an area inhabited by Prince Charles, the Queen Mum, and various lesser royals. To the north stands **Jermyn St.,** province of men's tailors (see p. 128). Most of the areas of interest for visitors are to the south, around The Mall and Pall Mall (both parts rhyme with "pal"). The Mall itself is lined with trees and the imposing facades of grand houses, beginning at an equestrian statue of notorious madman George III on Cockspur St. off Trafalgar Sq. and grandly reaching across to Buckingham Palace. Two monuments to Queen Victoria contribute to the grandeur: the golden horses of the **Queen Victoria Memorial,** near Buckingham Palace, and the massive **Admiralty Arch** opening onto Trafalgar Square.

ST. JAMES'S PALACE

North of the Mall, up Stable Yard or Marlborough Rd. Tube: Green Park.

The residence of the monarchy just after the Restoration (1660-68) and again from 1715 to 1837, St. James's has hosted tens of thousands of the young girls whose families "presented" them at Court. Ambassadors and the elite set of barristers known as Queen's Counsels are still received "into the Court of St. James." Of Henry VIII's original palace, only the gate and clocktower remain; the rest of what you see comes courtesy of John Nash's 19th-century reworking. Today **Prince Charles** inhabits St. James's, and the **Queen mum** bunks next door at **Clarence House,** where she can keep a grandmotherly eye on the future king. Sadly for royal watchers, the palace is closed to the public, except for the **Chapel Royal,** open for Sunday services at 8:30 and 11am (Oct.-Good Friday). Charles I slept for four hours in the palace's guardroom before crossing St. James's Park to be executed at Banqueting House (see **Whitehall,** p. 74).

ST. JAMES'S PARK AND GREEN PARK

Tube: Green Park. Deck chair rentals Apr.-May and Sept. 10am-6pm, June-Aug. 10am-10pm. £1 for 4hr.—don't find the attendants, just sit and they'll find you.

Henry VIII declared St. James's Park to be London's first royal park in 1531. The fenced-off peninsula at the east end of the park's pond **Duck Island** is the mating ground for thousands of waterfowl, including the odd pelican. St. James's is also a good place to discover that lawn chairs in England are not free—chairs have been hired out here since the 18th century. For a nice view of the **changing of the guard** at Buckingham Palace, wait between the Victoria Memorial and St. James's Palace from about 10:40 to 11:25am. You might miss the band (it usually travels down Birdcage walk from Wellington Barracks), but you will also avoid the swarm of tourists. **Green Park,** another of Henry VIII's acquisitions, may not hold the attractions of St. James's Park or its other neighbor Hyde Park, but it is the more idyllic for it.

OTHER ST. JAMES'S SIGHTS

GENTLEMEN'S CLUBS. The coffeehouses of the early 18th century were transformed into exclusive clubs for political and literary men of a particular social station (and particular political leanings). The chief Tory club is the **Carlton,** at 69 St. James's St. The chief Liberal club, the **Reform,** at 104 Pall Mall, served as a social center of Parliamentary power. In 1823, a prime minister and the presidents of the Royal Academy and the Royal Society founded the **Athenaeum,** on Waterloo Pl., for scientific, literary, and artistic men.

QUEEN'S CHAPEL. Inigo Jones's chapel was begun in 1623 for Charles I's intended bride, the Infanta of Castile, and completed in 1627 for his eventual wife, Henrietta Maria. *(In Marlborough House, on the corner of Marlborough Rd. and Pall Mall. Tube: Green Park. Open Easter-July for Sunday services at 8:30 and 11am.)*

CARLTON HOUSE. In the 1820s John Nash designed Carlton House as a replacement for George IV's old house (which stood on the same place). The building became the office of the Free French Forces from 1940-45 under the leadership of General Charles de Gaulle. It now contains the Royal Society and the avant-garde **Institute of Contemporary Arts** (see **Museums,** p. 124 and **Film,** p. 147). The column on Carlton House Terrace commemorates "The Grand Old Duke of York", he of the 10,000 men. *(The Mall. Tube: Charing Cross or Green Park.)*

CHRISTIE'S. The full name is Christie, Manson, and Wodds Fine Art Auctioneers, but even they call themselves Christie's. The galleries display furniture, historical documents, and artwork being auctioned. Auctions, open to the public, are held at 10:30am or 2:30pm. Don't cough. *(8 King St., off St. James's St. Tube: Green Park. ☎ 7839 9060; www.christies.com. Open M-F 9am-4:30pm; during sales also open Tu 4:30-8pm and Su 2-5pm.)*

ST. JAMES'S CHURCH PICCADILLY. A postwar reconstruction by Albert Richardson of what Wren considered his best parish church. The flowers, garlands, and cherubs display the work of Grinling Gibbons, Wren's master carver. Blake was baptized here, which will delight fans of innocence and experience alike. *(197 Piccadilly; enter on Jermyn St. Tube: Green Park or Piccadilly Circus. Market open Th-Sa 10am-6pm.)*

MAYFAIR

Trodden by London's well-heeled, these streets retain the cachet they have enjoyed since the 17th century.

BOND STREET

🚇 *Tube: Bond St. or Green Park.*

The traditional address for the oldest and most prestigious shops, art dealers, and auction houses in the city. There's no real "Bond Street"; rather, the street is divided into **Old Bond St.** (nearer Piccadilly) and New Bond St. (nearer Oxford St.). Old Bond Street is the locale of choice for the area's most expensive shops, with Cartier, Armani, and Prada exhibiting their wares in elaborate window displays. Alongside these Continental extravagances stand long-established homegrown shops such as the imposing emporium Asprey and Garrard, often displaying crests indicating royal patronage. Art dealers and auctioneers with public galleries frequently offer shows of exceptional quality.

Piccadilly

SOTHEBY'S

🚇 *34-35 New Bond St. (☎ 7293 5000; www.sothebys.com). Tube: Bond St. Open for viewing M-F 9am-4:30pm, and some Su noon-4pm.*

This world-famous auction house displays everything in its honeycomb of galleries from Dutch masters to the world's oldest condom before they're put on the auction block. While the 257-year-old institution may seem daunting, they're really quite welcoming, and you can spend a delightful hour perusing the collections that you can't afford (bids for some rare items may start at £1 million). Still, even though there's no official dress code, you might want to dress smartly to avoid feeling self-conscious. Catalogs with pictures of current offerings cost £5-20; some old catalogs are half-price.

GROSVENOR SQUARE

🚇 *Tube: Bond St. or Marble Arch.*

Running west off Bond St., Grosvenor St. ends at Grosvenor Square, one of the largest in central London. The square has gradually evolved into a US military and political enclave. Before his Presidential stint, John Adams lived at no. 9 while serving as the first American ambassador to England in 1785. Almost two centuries later, General Eisenhower established his wartime headquarters at no. 20, and memory of his stay persists in the area's postwar nickname, "Eisenhowerplatz." The humorless and top-heavy **US Embassy** rises to the west. The metal eagle atop it is as long as a double-decker bus.

The Mall

OTHER MAYFAIR SIGHTS

SAVILE ROW. This street's name has become synonymous with the elegant and expensive bespoke (made-to-measure) tailoring that has prospered here for centuries. Hardy Amies and Gieves & Hawkes number among the renowned denizens of Savile Row, but the currently hip name is Ozwald Boateng, even if his store isn't technically on the street (it's on 9 Vigo St.). For £2500 you can take home a suit by London's haberdasher to the stars. *(Tube: Piccadilly Circus. Most stores open M-Sa 10am-6pm.)*

Fortnum and Mason

CHARBONNEL ET WALKER. The oldest chocolate shop in London, opened in 1875 by request of Edward VII (then Prince of Wales). He encouraged Mme Charbonnel to leave her Parisian chocolate house and join Mrs. Walker in opening a shop on Bond St. Chocolate lovers swoon at the delicious smell of truffles crafted of fresh cream, based on the same recipe Mme Charbonnel once used. An assortment of these delectable treats is expensive, as you might expect from chocolate that the Queen herself nibbles on, but if you just want one, help yourself (politely) to a free sample. *(28 Old Bond St., in the Royal Arcade.* ☎ *7491 0939. Open M-Sa 10am-6pm.)*

OTHER MAYFAIR NOTABLES. The venerable **Claridge's Hotel** was where Handel wrote the *Messiah*. Their afternoon tea features liveried footmen in an amazing Art Deco setting. *(Brook St. Tube: Bond St.* ☎ *7629 8860. Singles £295; 2-bedroom penthouse £3500.)* Near Hanover Sq. stands **St. George's Hanover Church**, where the *crème de la crème* of London society have been married. Shelley, George Eliot, Benjamin Disraeli, and Teddy Roosevelt came here to tie the bonds of matrimony beneath the radiant barrel vault. *(On the corner of Maddox St. and Mill St. Tube: Oxford Circus.)* Housed in Michael Faraday's lab in the basement of what is now the Royal Institution, the **Faraday Museum** contains the great scientist's original equipment. For electromagnetism buffs only. *(Royal Institution, 21 Albemarle St.* ☎ *7409 2992. Open M-F 9am-6pm, last admission 5pm.)* The sign at the beginning of the **Burlington Arcade** sets the tone for this Regency-period group of stores: "no whistling, singing, or hurrying." This seems to be the place for buying supplies before setting off to the Empire, including the ever-useful "town" and "country" twin address books. *(Beside Burlington House. Tube: Green Park.)* Named not for agriculturalists but for 17th-century architect Edward Shepherd, **Shepherd Market** was the site of the Mayfair, before snooty neighbors had the fair shut down in 1708. Pedestrianised streets, pubs, and tiny restaurants give this southwestern part of Mayfair a village-like charm. *(Tube: Hyde Park Corner.)*

NORTH LONDON

ISLINGTON

🇫 *Tube: Angel or Highbury and Islington.*

Lying in the low hills just north of the City, Islington began as a royal hunting ground. The village was first absorbed into the city by fugitives from the Great Fire of 1666, and later by industrialization and trade along Regent's Canal. Islington became "trendy" during the late 17th century, when its ale houses and cream teas made it popular for wealthy scene-makers. In more recent times, Islington, home to

see map pp. 308-309

George Orwell, Evelyn Waugh, Douglas Adams, and Salman Rushdie, has established a reputation as an academic and artistic haven. Indeed, a clutch of wonderful theatres—the **Almeida**, the **King's Head**, the **Little Angel**, and nearby **Sadler's Well**—continue to serve Islington's increasingly upmarket populace. Previously known as The People's Republic of Islington for its reputation as a socialist hotbed, the area's politics step in time with the Labour Party. The borough is today considered the home territory of New Labour. When former resident Tony Blair's promotion required a move to No. 10 Downing St. he didn't want to leave the area, but attempts to provide his Richmond Crescent house with adequate security proved too difficult. As the gay pubs in the area attest, Islington is also home to a large gay community—Chris Smith, one of the few voluntarily out MPs, was elected from this area. Islington doesn't hold many tourist attractions, but travelers willing to walk around the area near the **Angel** tube station (home to London's highest escalators, incidentally) and along **Upper Street** will find it rewarding. Since 1995 Islington has put on a summer display of its artistic resources in the annual **Islington International Festival** on Upper St. during the last week of June. *(☎ 7689 9891; www.islington-festival.co.uk.)*

SADLER'S WELLS THEATRE. Sadler's Wells has played a role in London's theatrical history since 1684, when Richard Sadler, not content with selling "therapeutic" water from his eponymous well, added musical entertainment to the house. The well still stands inside the theater building. Joe Grimaldi, the father of clowns, performed here in the early 19th century. Following a £20 million renovation in the 1990s, Sadler's Wells remains London's premiere venue for dance. *(Rosebery Ave. For info on tickets, see p. 151.)*

REGENT'S CANAL. The banks of the canal, a short stretch of the 300-mile Grand Union Canal linking London to the north of England, are a lovely spot for a walk. Inhabited houseboats line the canal. The mile-long **Islington Tunnel** runs between here and Caledonian Road; in the past, people had to get through the tunnel by "legging it," i.e. sticking their legs out and pushing against the walls of the tunnel to propel the boat. *(Steps lead down to the canal banks from Vincent Terr. and Noel Rd. Watch out—the steps can get icy in winter.)*

THE HOUSE OF DETENTION. An appropriately damp underground dungeon of a former Victorian prison, now converted into a museum of sorts. The site housed criminals and debtors from 1616, when Bridewell Prison was founded, until 1886. Displays largely focus on the hard prison life of Victorian times. Instruments of torture shown include a branding iron, thumbscrews, and a spiked throat-catcher, while the medical instruments, if anything, are scarier still: rusty retractors and trephine saws (for cutting at the cranium) seem to have been par for the course. There's also a fair amount on Jack Sheppard, the prison's most famous inmate—he was the only person to ever escape Bridewell and became the basis for John Grays' *Beggars Opera*. People were shipped off to the colonies from this jail, and the office keeps lists of former inmates for those interested in ancestor-seeking. *(Clerkenwell Close. ☎ 7253 9494. Tube: Farringdon. Open daily 10am-6pm; last admission 5:15pm. £4, students and seniors £3, children £2.50, families £10.)*

OTHER ISLINGTON NOTABLES. Social worker Caroline Chisholm is commemorated on a blue plaque on **Charlton Place**, where she lived after returning from Down Under; Aussies will recognize her as the figure on the Australian $5 note. Near the Angel, all manner of food and trinkets can be bought at **Chapel Market** (see **Markets**, p. 139); Penton St., at the end of the market, is where London cabbies take their exams in the Knowledge (see **Taxicabs**, p. 28). Like many of the smaller streets that run off Upper St., Cross St. is home to many quirky shops, as well as the **Little Angel Theatre**, a world-renowned center for puppetry that puts on shows, as well as workshops, for children. The **Estorick Collection**, housed in Northampton Lodge, is a remarkable collection of modern Italian art (see **Galleries**, p. 124). Another artistic resource is the **Crafts' Council**, which hosts exhibitions of contemporary pottery, textiles, and printing (see p. 124).

CAMDEN TOWN

◪ Camden tourist information center, Camden Town Hall, Argyle St., WC1 (☎ 7974 5974; www.camden.gov.uk; Tube: King's Cross), has information the entire borough of Camden, which includes Camden Town, as well as Bloomsbury, King's Cross (hence its location), and other parts of north London. The Where to Stay in Camden booklet lists accommodations throughout the borough. Open M-F 9am-5pm.

see map pp. 308-309 Famously bohemian, **Camden Town** is a stomping ground for all subcultural affiliations. At the raucous **Camden Market** (see **Markets**, p. 139), hundreds of merchants set up stands that draw swarms of bargain-seekers every weekend. Almost anything can be found here, from vintage pornography to antique sewing machines. When the Regent's Canal (which passes through Camden Town) was constructed in the 19th century, Camden was a solid working-class district ribbed with railways and clothed in soot. **Charles Dickens** spent his childhood here, crowded in a four-room tenement with his extended family at 141 Bayham St; the experience served as the model for the Cratchits in *A Christmas Carol*. Waves of Irish, Cypriot, Greek, Italian, and Portuguese immigrants brought a diversity to the area that persists to this day. Although many parts of Camden Town have turned into upmarket residential enclaves, the area hasn't completely given itself over to gentrification, as the scruffy storefronts on **Camden High Street** and dilapidated warehouses along **Regent's Canal** will attest. While trendy establishments have moved in, Camden Town retains some attractively dingy restaurants and pubs, gathering places for rising indie stars and rock sensations. Sweat-laden band members and drunk fans stumble into local hangouts after gigs for a last taste of Saturday night fever;

CANON-BURY RUN

Away from Upper Street's bars and restaurants you can see the reason people are prepared to pay so much to live in Islington. For a pleasant walk in Islington, try this: from Upper St. head down Canonbury Ln. through Canonbury Sq. (site of the **Estorick Collection,** p. 124) and turn right onto Canonbury Rd. Turn left onto Canonbury Grove, at the top of which you'll find Canonbury St. and **The Marquess,** a good spot for a pint. Next door is one of London's strangest pieces of modern architecture, the **glass house** (40 Douglas Rd.). In a rather risky move, the owners chose to surround the property with a lawn of tiny stones. Canonbury Grove runs alongside the **New River Walk,** a slender waterside public garden full of wild herbs, irises and willows. The park is build around an early 17th-century aqueduct that brought fresh water to the growing population of London from the springs of Hertfordshire (a feat accomplished by engineer Myddelton, who is commemorated by a statue on Islington Green).

even in the grungiest places you can still find stars like Morrissey and Björk mellowing out. If all the bohemia gets to you, browse through Camden's numerous specialist bookstores, or walk around the 110 acres of nearby **Primrose Hill,** which offers some of the grandest views in all of London. No wonder property here is so desirable. *(Off Prince Albert Rd., Regent's Park Rd., and Primrose Hill Rd. Tube: Chalk Farm.)*

CAMDEN MARKET. Opened in 1974 with only four stall holders, **Camden Market** (technically a few separate markets, although it's often hard to tell where one ends and the next one begins) now crams in hundreds of bohemian vendors. You don't need to be looking for anything specific to buy to enjoy the markets: people-watching is half the fun. Small dogs drag hirsute neo-hippies around, black-clad goths bake stoically in the afternoon sunshine, and sixth-form Lolitas hunt out improbably chunky sneakers and impossibly skimpy T-shirts. Meanwhile, renouncing centuries of sartorial and gastronomic superiority, pierced Italian punks feed on burgers and fried onions. The sprawling market's predominant trade is clothes (some new, others second-hand), but records, books, crafts, and various other gewgaws can all be found. The most popular section is the Camden Lock Market, near the canal. Closer to Chalk Farm, **The Stables** market is a wonderful array of must-have antiques, lamps, rugs, and retro furniture. The popularity of the markets (they're among London's top five attractions) means Camden Town tube is a nightmare to negotiate on weekends; indeed, on Sundays, it's exit-only. Avoid the crush either by coming early, or by taking the tube to Chalk Farm and walking back towards the market. (☎ 7284 2084. Stables Market ☎ 7485 5511. Off and along Camden High St. and Chalk Farm Rd. Tube: Camden Town or Chalk Farm. Open Sa-Su 10am-5pm.)

OTHER SHOPS. On weekdays, you can avoid the elbows and boots of your fellow shoppers (though also the atmosphere that defines the place). Although most of the market's stalls will be closed (the indoor stalls in **Camden Lock Market** being the exception), the area's restaurants, cafes, and specialty shops remain open. The shops, mostly on **Camden High Street,** include one of London's best left-wing bookstores, a gay sex and fetish-wear shop, and a few independent record stores. The high street is otherwise dominated by a series of almost identical shops: each offers a few flavors of Dr. Martens, a few cheap leather jackets, and a selection of cutting-edge sneakers and courier bags. In front of the shop will invariably stand several bored salesmen. After visiting a few of these shops you may find yourself wearing a similar expression.

CAMDEN LOCKS AND CANALS. A walk along the **Regent's Canal,** which connects Camden to Regent's Park and Little Venice, is a fine antidote to the market's craziness. Camden High St. crosses over the main canal. The occasional barge being lowered or raised in the Lock is visible from here; a 10min. jaunt westwards will bring you to the middle of London Zoo, which sprawls on either side. Don't expect to see much wildlife, though—it's well hidden from canal walkers. The **London Waterbus Company** offers rides on the canal. *(Camden Lock.* ☎ *7482 2550. Tube: Camden Town. Single £4, children £2.60; return £5.50, £3.20. Trips run Apr.-Oct. daily 10am-5pm, Nov.-Mar.)*

HAMPSTEAD, HIGHGATE, & GOLDERS GREEN

see map p. 318

The "villages" of Hampstead and Highgate have captivated London's elite for centuries. Precipitous hills prevented them from being swallowed by urban sprawl, and the villages have remained lush. The tidy streets lined with Mercedes, boutiques, and Georgian houses offer insights into the theory and practice of being unnecessarily rich, which may explain why Karl Marx chose to live here. Such affluence gives rise to curiosities that make the area worth a visit, though none is particularly earth-shattering on its own. Keats, Dickens, and Freud all worked here, and the villages claim more writers per capita that any other London postcodes.

HAMPSTEAD

HAMPSTEAD HEATH

🚩 *Train: Hampstead Heath, Tube: Hampstead, or Tube: Kentish Town and then C2 or 214 bus to Parliament Hill. Ponds* ☎ *7485 4491, Lido* ☎ *7485 3873. Open summer 7-9:30am and 10am-7pm, rest of the year 7-10am. Lido only: Adults £3, concessions £1, free before 10am. Heath open 24hr.; be extremely careful in the park after dark.*

London's largest green space has been common ground since the Middle Ages, when peasants would use it to graze their flocks. Today, it serves to separate Hampstead from Highgate, and its green acres go some way towards explaining the area's desirability. The Heath is far more rural than the central parks, the perfect place to get lost in acres of meadow and woodland and forget the "Air Quality Improvement Area" that is London amongst care-free picnickers, kite-flyers, and dozing anglers.

The southeastern tip of the heath, grazing Highgate, is called **Parliament Hill;** its name derives from the fact that it was toward this hill that Guy Fawkes and his accomplices fled after planting explosives under the House of Commons in 1605, hoping for a good view of the explosion. Today the hill itself is more normally referred to as Kite Hill after park-goers favorite activity there. At the summit, a plaque points out the major sights of the London skyline. According to legend, a copse of pine trees on the neighboring hill holds that the bones of Boudicca—the mighty Celtic warrior queen who sacked Roman London. Wandering along the crest of the hills will bring you into the heart of the Heath, while on the northern side of Kite Hill a series of ponds lead up to Kenwood House (see below). On a hot day, you can take a dip in the murky waters of the strictly single-sex **Kenwood Ladies' Pond** and **Highgate Men's Pond,** or in the **Mixed Bathing Pond.** If the weeds put you off, and

Chinatown Gate

Chinese Lantern

Chinatown Streets

THE LONG AND WIND- ING ROAD

Liverpool may be **Beatles** memorabilia central, but who could pass up a photographic foray into music history with a visit to Abbey Road? NW8's musical treasure (unless you count resident Liam Gallagher) is definitely the EMI **Abbey Road Studio** (at No. 3), where the eponymous album was made, and the cover photograph shot on the zebra crossing in front. These days, it's a tourist draw, with graffitists permitted to leave their "immortal" messages to Ringo and the boys on the studio's white fence, while other are just content to stop traffic for the perfect photo— shoes are optional.

concrete and weak-bladdered children seem preferable, there's also the outdoor pool of the **Parliament Hill Lido,** at the southwestern edge of the Heath.

KENWOOD HOUSE

◪ *Hampstead Lane; ☎8348 1286; Tube: Archway or Golders Green, then bus #210 to Kenwood. Grounds open daily 10am-8:30pm or dusk. Free.*

This gracious home, a picture-perfect example of an 18th-century country estate, presides over Kenwood, a piece of forest contiguous with the Heath, though technically separate. The airy mansion now houses the **Iveagh Bequest** (see **Museums,** p. 124), as well as temporary exhibits (the most recent being on English feasts). Chief Justice Lord Mansfield, the original owner of Kenwood, decreed an end to slavery on English soil. Mansfield's progressive policies did not win him universal popularity: the Gordon Rioters, angered by his support for the 1780 Catholic Relief Act, destroyed his townhouse in Bloomsbury and pursued him north to Hampstead. Luckily for him (and for Kenwood House), his pursuers stopped for a drink at the **Spaniards Inn** on Spaniards Rd., where the publican plied them with drink until the militia could seize them. In summer, Kenwood hosts a hugely popular series of **outdoor concerts** (see **Music,** p. 150) in which top-flight orchestras play from a bandshell across the lake. If it's a sunny day, Kenwood is a pleasant walk from central Hampstead; from the tube station, head up the hill along Heath Street and then strike northwards across the Heath from the pond.

KEATS HOUSE

◪ *Keats Grove (☎7435 2062). Tube: Hampstead; Rail: Hampstead Heath rail station is much closer. Phone ahead as hours are erratic, but generally Apr.-Oct. M-F 10am-1pm and 2-6pm, Sa 10am-1pm and 2-5pm, Su 2-5pm; Nov.-Mar. M-F 1-5pm, Sa 10am-1pm and 2-5pm, Su 2-5pm. Free.*

One of London's finest literary shrines is the restored house of writer John Keats. Before dashing off to Italy to breathe his last in true Romantic style, Keats pined here for his next-door fiancée, Fanny Brawne. Not only did he cough up his first consumptive drop of blood in the house, he also coughed up "Ode to a Nightingale" under a plum tree here. The decor and furnishings stay true to the Regency style of the early 19th century, providing an evocative showcase for manuscripts, letters, and contemporary pans of Keats' works by critics dead and forgotten. The **Keats Memorial Library** next door contains 8,500 books on the poet's life, family, and friends. (☎7794 6829. Open by appointment for research only.)

FREUD MUSEUM

◪ *20 Maresfield Gdns (☎7435 2002; www.freud.org.uk). Tube: Hampstead. Open W-Su noon-5pm; £4, concessions £2, under 12 free.*

Hampstead was home to at least one celebrity shrink, noted psychoanalyst Sigmund Freud. In this home, his last, Freud completed *Moses and Monotheism* and began the unfinished *Outline of Psychoanalysis*. Both he and daughter Anna practiced here, and the museum preserves his study, which includes the infamous analytic couch he had brought over from Vienna, and his "old and dirty gods" (Freud's description of his collection of antiquities), including the Gradiva frieze. Among the permanent articles on display is Dali's portrait of Freud; the museum also hosts temporary exhibitions.

FENTON HOUSE

🛅 ☎ 7435 3471. Open Mar. Sa-Su 2-5pm, Apr.-Oct. W-F 2-5pm, Sa-Su 11am-5pm. £4.20, children £2.10, concessions £4. Gardens free.

Among the delicate china, furniture, and early keyboard instruments exhibited in this National Trust house sits a prototype 18th-century "double guitar," proving that Britain's fascination with excessively stringed instruments predates Jimmy Page. Area musicians can occasionally be found strumming, plucking, and tickling as you stroll through. Concerts on some of the instruments rip up the drawing room on sporadic Wednesday eves in the summer. Note the boarded windows of Fenton House—the revenue man tried to levy a tax upon the number of windows in people's homes, leading people like the Fentons to board up their glass and setting a fine example of tax evasion for the area's prosperous denizens to emulate.

OTHER HAMPSTEAD SIGHTS

TWO WILLOW ROAD. Fans (or enemies) of modern architecture will want to hot foot it to this 1939 house that is a showcase for renegade Ernö Goldfinger's philosophy of design. *James Bond* author Ian Fleming loathed Goldfinger's work so much he named the infamous villain after him. (Address unknown—just kidding. From Hampstead tube, take Hampstead High St. down the hill, turn left on Gayton Rd., and right onto Willow Rd. ☎ 7435 6166; Open Apr.-Oct. Th-Sa noon-5pm; tours 12:15-4pm every 45min. £4.20, children 5-15 £2.10.)

BURGH HOUSE. A tour of the Queen Anne-style Burgh House in New End Square is infinitely more satisfying than the exhibitions of mainly local interest at the "museum" housed within. The main draw, even locals will concede, is the cream tea ($2.50) at **The Buttery** in the cellar. (☎ 7431 0144. Open W-Su noon-5pm. Free.)

CHURCH ROW AND THE VALE OF HEALTH. Just off of the southern end of Heath St., **Church Row** assiduously guards its 18th-century style and dignified terraces. The narrow alleyways off of the Row transport visitors to the land of Mary Poppins, complete with small, overflowing secret gardens. The painter John Constable lies buried in **St. John's Churchyard** at the end of the row. At the border of the village and the Heath is a small enclave of Victorian houses known as the **Vale of Health.** An exquisite cluster of rose-rambled cottages and studios, these terraces hosted meetings between Byron and other Romantics, and were later home to William Blake, D.H. Lawrence, and Stanley Spencer.

HIGHGATE

🛅 Tube to Archway (not Highgate), then Bus #210 to Highgate Village. From Hampstead, it's about a 45min. walk across the Heath, staying more or less parallel to Spaniard's Rd.

To the northeast of Hampstead lies Highgate. While not the home of glittering literati like neighboring Hampstead, it does contain one of London's most well-known cemeteries, home to the bones of everyone's favorite socialist. A good way to get a feel for Highgate (and a good glimpse of London) is to climb Highgate Hill, London's highest at 424 ft. above the Thames.

HIGHGATE CEMETERY. Highgate's most famous resident is Karl Marx, buried in the Eastern Cemetery in 1883, and the larger-than-life bust placed above his grave in 1956 is hard to miss. But the cemetery has ignored poiltical allegiances—Herbert Spencer, who vehemently opposed socialism, also lies in here. Spencer's bones rest near those of his lover George Eliot (Mary Ann Evans), buried in the Western Cemetery. Michael Faraday and the Dickens family also RIP here among the ornate tombs and mausolea filled with now anonymous occupants; the spooky graves also served as the backdrop to numerous horror movies. The cemetery closes its gates to visitors during funerals. *(Swains Lane. ☎ 8340 1834. East cemetery open Apr.-Nov. M-F 10am-5pm, Sa-Su 11am-5pm; Dec.-Mar. daily 10am-4pm. £2, children free. Western Cemetery accessible by guided tour only. Tours M-F noon, 2, and 4pm (3pm in Nov.), Sa-Su every hr. 11am-5pm. £3, no children under 8. Cameras £1 per section.)*

THE GROVE. Behind Highgate Cemetery heading away from Archway station hides **The Grove,** an avenue of late 17th-century houses secluded behind magnificent elms. Poet and critic Samuel Taylor Coleridge lived at #3 for the last 11 years of his life, entertaining Carlyle, Emerson, and other literary luminaries. *(South Grove off Highgate High St.)*

GOLDERS GREEN

🚇 *Tube: Golders Green, or Bus #13 from Oxford Circus, #268 from Hampstead, #28 from Kensington, or #210 from Archway. All buses drop off at the intersection of North End Way and Golders Green Rd.*

At first glance, Golders Green, located north of Hampstead, is in many ways an archetypal London suburb, but a brief walk reveals a richer texture. WIgged women, *kippah*-bedecked youths, and Kosher restaurants reveal this to be the center of London's Jewish community. Along Golders Green Rd. and Finchley Rd. Jewish eateries and Hebrew signs start appearing several blocks from the station.

GOLDERS GREEN CREMATORIUM. Spanning several acres of pastoral land, Golders Green was the first legal crematorium in England, cremating such luminaries as T.S. Eliot (every day is "Ash Wednesday" now!), Enid Blyton, Peter Sellers, and Bram Stoker, and is still the busiest in the country. The ashes of Freud, in his favorite Greek vase, rest near those of ballerina Anna Pavlova. Other celeb memorials include five prime ministers, Marks and Spencer founder Lord Sieff, Marc Bolan of T-Rex and "Get It On" fame, composer Gustav Holst, and writer H.G. Wells. To prevent disgruntled psychology students' vandalism, Freud's ashes are locked away in the **Ernest George Columbarium**—ask an attendant to let you in on weekdays. *(Hoop Ln. Walk under the Golders Green Tube's bridge and up Finchley Rd., then turn right at the first traffic light. ☎ 8455 2374; open daily 9am-5pm. Free.)*

GOLDERS HILL PARK. This grassy collection of fields, intricate gardens (including a Japanese display), and a small zoo rests on the other side of the Golders Green tube station. This horticultural utopia attracts plant lovers and kite-flyers alike. During the summer there is free music every Sunday. The cafeteria, with outdoor terrace, is a great place to sit and watch the world slowly pass. *(Off North End Rd. Tube: Golders Green or Hampstead, then the #210 bus. Open daily 8am-dusk.)*

EAST LONDON
THE EAST END

see map p. 305

Marked today by an invisible line across Bishop's Gate St., today's East End eludes the simple characterization that earlier times would have allowed. Once it was the Jewish center of London, then the Huguenot center, and later the center for a number of more recent immigrant groups—Irish, Somalis, Chinese, and Muslim Bangladeshi. Though its traditional working-class character is being slowly eroded by corporate culture oozing in from the City, you still get a "neighborhood" feel walking through this area.

London's East End nonetheless continues to serve as a refuge for both those who aren't welcome in the City and for those who don't want to be subject to the City's jurisdiction. During the 17th century, this included political dissenters, religious orders, and the French Huguenots (Protestants fleeing religious persecution in France). By 1687, 13,000 Huguenots had settled in Spitalfields, the area northeast of the City of London. A large working-class population moved into the district during the Industrial Revolution, followed by a wave of Jewish immigrants fleeing persecution in Eastern Europe, who settled around **Whitechapel.** Jewish success in the rag trade drew the attention of the British Union of Fascists, who instigated anti-Semitic violence that culminated in the "Battle of Cable Street" in 1936. A mural on St. George's Town Hall, 236 Cable St., commemorates the victory won in the streets that day. Today, the East End is home to another group of immigrants; Bangladeshis who arrived in the late 1970s now dominate the area around **Brick Lane.** In addition to the cockneys and colorfully dressed South Asians, the East End is home to an increasing number of artists, drawn by cheap studio rents, and some of London (and the world's) best and most cutting-edge contemporary art can be seen in **Whitechapel Art Gallery** (see **Galleries,** p. 125).

PETTICOAT LANE. On Sundays, vibrant stalls selling books, bric-a-brac, leather jackets, and salt beef sandwiches flank Brick Lane and "Petticoat Lane" (known officially as Middlesex St.). Its name is drawn from the street's historical role as a center of the clothing trade. The market runs throughout the week, but is best on Sundays. *(Tube: Aldgate East.)*

Wharf Building

EAST LONDON MOSQUE. This was London's first mosque to have its own building, which was financed by the Saudi community. Its towering minarets, grand scale, and large congregation testify to the size of London's Muslim community. *(82-92 Whitechapel Rd. Tube: Aldgate East. ☎ 7247 1357.)*

CHRIST CHURCH. In any other London neighborhood this church on Commercial St. would be just another ancient building; here it is an island of Anglicanism amid a spectrum of other traditions. The church was begun by Hawksmoor in 1714. The church sponsors the **Spitalfields Festival** of classical music during June. *(Tube: Aldgate East. Spitalfields box office ☎ 7377 1362; tickets free-£25. Open M-F noon-2:30pm.)*

BEVIS MARKS SYNAGOGUE. The city's oldest standing synagogue sits at Bevis Marks and Heneage Ln. The congregation traces its roots back to Spanish and Portuguese Jews who inhabited the area as early as 1657. Rabbi Menashe Ben Israel founded the synagogue in 1701, 435 years after the Jews were first expelled from England. Its distinguished congregation has included Rothschilds, Montefiores, and Disraelis. *(Tube: Aldgate; from Aldgate High St. turn right onto Houndsditch; Creechurch Ln. on the left leads to Bevis Marks. ☎ 7626 1274. Organized tours Su-W and F noon; call in advance. Open Su-M, W, and F 11:30am-1pm, Tu 10:30am-4pm. Entrance donation £1.)*

Pontoon Bridge

SPITALFIELDS FARM. Buy produce, plants, manure, and other goodies at this genuine working farm in the middle of the city, located on Weaver/Pedley St. Seasonal activities are offered during the summer, including a play scheme. *(Tube: Shoreditch or Whitechapel. ☎ 7247 8762. Open Tu-Su 10:30am-5pm. Free.)*

MARKETS. Brick Lane is the center of the East End's South Asian community, with a vibrant and well-known street market (see p. 138) and numerous Indian and Bangladeshi restaurants and grocers (see p. 167). The East End is also home to **Spitalfields Market** (see p. 139), whose site has hosted stalls since the 13th century. Formerly the site of East London's main trade market for fresh produce (now relocated to the suburbs), there's still a thriving local market in the soaring iron-and-glass Victorian hall.

Docklands

DOCKLANDS

see map p. 319

London Docklands, the largest commercial development in Europe, is the only section of London built wholly anew—a total break from the city's typically slow architectural evolution. Developers have poured tons of steel, reflective glass, and money onto the banks of the Thames east of London Bridge. The crazy architecture and water-lined streets make it worth a visit to those interested in London's future.

ORIENTATION

Docklands proper covers a huge expanse (55 mi. of waterfront to be exact), from the Tower of London to Greenwich. The center of the new 8.5 sq. mi. development is on the **Isle of Dogs,** the spit of land defined by a sharp U-shaped bend in the Thames. To the east lie the **Royal Docks,** once the center of one of history's proudest trading empires. A new Fleet St. and a heavyweight financial center have risen from the desiccated East London docks. But the areas surrounding the glass and steel monuments to commercialism remain some of London's poorest, testifying to the inorganic nature of the project, causing some to label it "the architectural embodiment of Thatcherism."

The best way to see the area is via the **Docklands Light Railway** (DLR), a driverless automatic elevated railway. The DLR's smooth ride affords a panoramic view that helps you put the huge expanse of the Docklands into perspective and is a hit with the ladies. Travelcards are valid on the DLR, provided they cover the correct zones. The closest tourist information center is across the river in **Greenwich.**

HISTORY

London has a long history as a maritime gateway—Londoner was already a prominent port in Roman times—and by the Middle Ages the city's wharfs and quays had crept east from the City. As London grew in importance, the docks grew with it, stretching miles down the Thames, until they had become the powerful trading center of the British Empire. During World War II, the Blitz obliterated much of the dock area. Though the sun had set on the empire, the docks continued to do brisk business until the early 1960s, when the advent of container transport, modern shipping methods, and the move of the Port of London to Tilbury rendered them obsolete. By 1982, all had closed, leaving the Docklands barren.

As part of the Thatcher government's privatization program, redevelopment of the area was handed over to the private sector in the form of the **London Docklands Development Corporation (LDDC)**—which in 1981 took helm of what it called "the most significant urban regeneration program in the world." The LDDC's first mission was to convince Londoners that this blossoming area was an organic part of the city and not a distant, capitalistic wasteland. To do this, these genii sloganeers came up with the catchphrase "Looks like Venice, works like New York."

Since then, building has taken place on a phenomenal scale, but the task of populating new office space with businesses initially lagged behind. Hesitantly at first but now more steadily, big businesses have begun to take up residence in the area, filling in the previously empty floors of shiny new skyscrapers. After a disastrous recession slump, the Docklands are experiencing a housing boom, with communities springing up all over the southern bank, especially on the Isle of Dogs. Whatever recent successes they may have had, however, Docklands and the LDDC remain a sort of Disneyland Paris of urban renewal, resented by some, disregarded by most.

CANARY WHARF

⁊ DLR: Canary Wharf.

At a towering 800 ft., this is Britain's tallest edifice and the jewel of Docklands, visible from almost anywhere in London. The pyramid-topped structure, officially known as **One Canada Square,** contains shops, restaurants, and a concert hall. Below the towering building sprouts a huge fountain, which, during the lunch hour, is carpeted by an expanse of conservative colors, starched fabrics, power ties, and tightly pulled-back hair.

MUDCHUTE PARK

🚇 *DLR: Mudchute.* ☎ *7515 5901. Open daily 8am-5pm. Free.*

On the southern end of the Isle of Dogs, the pastoral expanses of this park come as a relief after the modernity of Canary Wharf. The round stone pathways leading into the park from West Ferry St run parallel to the prime meridian, which is defined by the green-domed observatory across the river (see **Royal Greenwich Observatory,** p. 104). Also, note the cement walls and ditches at the entrance to the park. These were anti-aircraft gun sites installed just before the Battle of Britain. At **Mudchute City Farm,** Pier St., E14 there are 32 acres of grassy heath, plus horses to ride and farm animals to pet.

OTHER DOCKLANDS SIGHTS

LIMEHOUSE AREA. The Limehouse and Westferry stops cover the historic Limehouse area, where dock and factory workers once lived. The legacy of Limehouse's 19th-century Chinese community can be seen in the Chinese restaurants along West India Dock Rd. The famous **Narrow Street** along the Thames is an official conservation area, with many early Georgian houses and ancient pubs, as well as expensive new condos. At 76 Narrow St., **The Grapes,** the pub Dickens described in *Our Mutual Friend,* maintains its original ambience.

ST. GEORGE-IN-THE-EAST. Getting off at Shadwell station, you'll see an old, working-class community—drab housing, dusty streets, traditional pubs, cafes, and pie-and-mash shops—in the throes of a major transformation brought on by an infusion of Bengali immigrants. Amid this scene (down Cable Rd., and left onto Cannon St.) are the four towers of St. George's, built between 1714-26. Designed by Wren's disciple Nicholas Hawksmoor, it was bombed in WWII and, in 1964, restored with a modern interior. *(☎ 7481 1345. Open daily 9am-5pm.)*

ST. ANNE'S. From the Westferry DLR, turn left onto West India Dock Rd., then left onto Three Colt St. for another, now sadly grafitti-ridden, Hawksmoor church. St. Anne's, built between 1712 and 1724, presides over a leafy churchyard and barely legible Victorian headstones. Along with St. George-in-the-East, its clock face comes from same workshop as Big Ben's. The Victorian organ won the organ prize at the Great Exhibition of 1851. In the cemetery, the architect also built a pyramid covered in masonic messages, now more worn than creepy. *(☎ 7987 1502. Open M-F 2-4pm, Sa 2-5pm, Su 2:30-5:30pm.)*

BECKTON ALPS SKI CENTRE. Many of the ancient Docklands' wharfs have now been turned into major leisure spots. Six sailing centers, three pools, a go-carting racetrack, and an artificial ski mountain, the year-round Beckton Alps, currently stand where ships and toxic waste used to rest. The one-run hillock rises 45m above the surrounding superstores and is covered with a specially designed carpet sprayed with water to make it slippery. The center is billed it as "London's Premiere Ski Centre," which, by force of logic, it is. The slope is open most days, but call to check on conditions—cold rainy days are the best. Trousers, long sleeves, and gloves required. *(DLR: Beckton Park. ☎ 7511 0351. Open W 1-10pm, Sa-Su 10am-10pm. £1 per 2hr., including equipment.)*

SOUTH LONDON

Hot tip for London visitors: South London is fast becoming the "it" destination, combining a rich history of bawdy fun with a slightly more austere, contemporary one, all fueled by millennial money and the pedestrian friendly **Millennium Mile.** All this Y2K hype would be tiresome if it weren't for the substance underneath the hullabaloo. The **Millennium Wheel,** sponsored prominently by British Airways, looms large over the Thames, providing what is probably the best view of London. The **Millennium Bridge,** though experiencing a stuttered start due to too much sway (which caused fears of a millennium drop into the millennium river), is the first bridge over the Thames in a century, and links the South Bank to the City, symbolically enabling the continued flow of development money. Last, but certainly not least, is the new **Tate Modern,** the power-station-turned-art-gallery that has drawn millions of visitors since its spring 2000 opening.

THE SOUTH BANK

see map p. 299

This region south of the Thames has long been home to entertainment, much of it rather bawdy—until the English Civil Wars, when most of this area fell under the legal jurisdiction of the Bishop of Winchester, and was thus protected from London censors. The region stayed almost entirely rural until the 18th-century Westminster and Blackfriars bridges were built. Until German bombs flattened the area in World War II, it was a den of working-class neighborhoods, dark breweries, and murky wharves through which suburbanites passed on their way into the city. Regeneration has been ongoing since the end of the war; additions to the South Bank landscape include the **Jubilee Gardens,** planted in 1977 to celebrate the first 25 years of Elizabeth II's reign.

SOUTH BANK CENTRE

Tube: Waterloo, or Embankment and cross the Thames.

Behind the Brutalist concrete facade of this massive performing arts center lies London's most concentrated campus of artistic and cultural activity. The South Bank Centre is comprised of a series of concrete buildings, among them the National Film Theatre, the Hayward Gallery, the Queen Elizabeth Hall complex, and the Royal National Theatre. Recent calls for the demolition and replacement of the Queen Elizabeth Hall and the Hayward Gallery have prompted many to declare their fondness for the complex. The **Royal National Theatre** (see p. 142), opened in 1978 with 3 auditoriums, promotes "art for the people" through convivial bargain platform performances, foyer concerts, lectures, tours, and workshops. The **Hayward Gallery** (see p. 124), on Belvedere Rd., houses imaginative contemporary art exhibitions. Multicolored posters displaying Russian titles and Asian warriors distinguish the entrance to the **National Film Theatre** (see p. 147), directly on the South Bank. The 3000-seat Royal **Festival Hall** (see p. 149), together with the smaller **Queen Elizabeth Hall** and **Purcell Room,** is London's preeminent classical music complex; in addition, the Festival Hall's enormous foyer hosts exhibitions of contemporary art, free jazz concerts on W-Su lunchtimes and F evenings, and a very, very long bar. Around the corner from the center rests another South Bank development project, Gabriel's Wharf, home to some snack-worthy restaurants and cafes and a weekend craft market.

MILLENNIUM WHEEL

On the river (☎ 0870 500 0600; www.ba-londoneye.com). Tube: Waterloo. £7.45, children 5-15 £4.95, under 5 free. Open Apr.-Oct. daily 9am-dusk; Nov.-Mar. daily 10am-6pm.

The Millennium Wheel, or more officially the **British Airways London Eye,** has been billed as "the biggest observational wheel in the world." Initially, engineers were unable to put the wheel upright—after months of head-scratching and confusion, and a Virgin Atlantic Airlines balloon flying overhead with "BA can't get it up" emblazoned on it, they finally figured out how to hoist this 443ft. behemoth. Located between Jubilee Gardens and the London Aquarium, the wheel offers spectacular views over the city during its 30min. revolution; London fog permitting, riders can even spot Windsor.

LONDON AQUARIUM

County Hall, Westminster Bridge Rd. (☎ 7967 8000; www.londonaquarium.co.uk). Tube: Westminster or Waterloo. Open 10am-6pm daily, last admission 5pm. £8.50, concessions £6.50, under 14 £5, families £24, disabled free.

The basement of the former County Hall, one of the capital's disused administrative buildings, has been reincarnated as the London Aquarium. Entertaining enough on a rainy afternoon, the aquarium houses a variety of aquatic life. The main attractions are two 3-story tanks; the Atlantic tank's biggest inhabitants are some whopping conger eels, while the Pacific tank hosts the ever-popular sharks. There is also a beach area where jello-fleshed rays seem happy enough to be stroked and petted, and a seaside display where parents can bully terrified children into picking up crabs and starfish.

OXO TOWER

🔊 *Riverside Walk. Tube: Blackfriars or Waterloo.*

The most colorful recent changes in the South Bank result from the unflagging efforts of a non-profit development company, Coin Street Community Builders (CSCB). Their grandest project, the OXO Tower, rises between Waterloo and Blackfriars bridges on Barge House St. Formerly the headquarters of meat-extract producing company, the Art Deco building is notable for its clever subversion of rules prohibiting large advertising on buildings—architects built the tower's distinct windows in the shape of the company's logo. CSCB boasts that the meticulously planned potpourri of rooftop cafes, retail outlets, designer work-shops, performance spaces, and flats that opened three sum-mers ago at the OXO Tower Wharf will make it a hub of London activity. The rooftop restaurants and cafes are in fact some of London's most expensive, but the nearby **Museum Of...** and **gallery@oxo** succeed in providing a democratic artistic forum.

Docklands

OTHER SOUTH BANK SIGHTS

WATERLOO STATION. Built in 1848, Waterloo Station now houses the British terminus of the "Chunnel" and one of the longest railway platforms in the world. The spectacular blue and silver **International Terminal,** designed by Nicholas Grimshaw and built in 1993, has become many visitors' introduction to Britain. Next to the station, the dodecagonal, £20 million **BFI London Imax Cinema** contains the largest screen in Europe. (For details on how to bring on cinematic nausea, see **Entertainment,** p. 147.)

THE OLD VIC. On the corner of Waterloo Road and what is quite possibly the best-named London street, The Cut, looms a big white building, the magnificently restored Old Vic. This elder statewoman of London theater is the former home of Sir Lawrence Olivier's National Repertory Theatre, which later became the Royal National Theatre (see above). The Vic cur-rently hosts popular seasons of lesser-known classics and worthy revivals in one of the most beautiful performance spaces in London. The smaller, quirkier **Young Vic** is just across from its older sibling. *(Tube: Waterloo. See **Theater,** p. 144.)*

Fisherman's Walk

LAMBETH PALACE. On the Embankment opposite the Lam-beth Bridge in Archbishop's Park stands what has been the Archbishop of Canterbury's London residence since 1207. Although Archbishop Langton founded it in the early 13th cen-tury, most of the palace dates from the 19th century. The pal-ace's exterior includes the entrance at the 15th-century brick Morton's Tower, and Lollard's Tower, where John Wyclif's fol-lowers were imprisoned. *(Tube: Lambeth North. Visits by prior arrangement only; contact Lambeth Palace, Lambeth Palace Rd., SE1.)*

MUSEUM OF GARDEN HISTORY. Housed in the former church of St. Mary-at-Lambeth, this museum for the green-thumbed gives a bit of insight into the English obsession with gardening, and the accompanying drunken hooliganism. The extensive collection of gardening plans, tools, and photos is probably only of passing interest to city slickers, but out back is a replica 17th-century knot garden, where Captain Bligh, commander of the mutinously ill-fated Bounty, lies buried. *(Lambeth Palace Road, by Lambeth Palace's southernmost entrance. Tube: Westminster, Waterloo, or Vauxhall. ☎ 7401 8865. Open Feb. to mid-Dec. M-F 10:30am-4pm, Su 10:30am-5pm. Free.)*

Docklands Streets

SOUTHWARK

🔲 *Southwark Tourist Information Centre, Tooley St., Hay's Galleria Lower Level (☎ 7403 8299), provides information on the area's sights. It also books rooms and gives out a list of conveniently located accommodations. Open M-Sa 10am-5pm, Su 11am-5pm.*

see map p. 299

Historically a hotbed of prostitution, incarceration, and bear-baiting, Southwark (across London Bridge from the city) seems an unlikely location for a revival of bear-baiting of any of these vices. Now, the area's main attractions are its sights, not its amusements.

The area around the Borough High Street, **"the Borough,"** has survived—with a few minor changes—for nearly 2000 years. Until 1750, London Bridge was the only bridge over the Thames in London, and the inns along the highway leading to it hosted many travelers (6-10 bed dorms 15 shillings, key deposit a peck of a potatoes. Cited by Marlowe for their clean showers and friendly staff). The neighborhood has also been associated with entertainment from the days of the frost fairs (when the Thames froze over during the late Middle Ages) to the more vicious pleasures depicted in Defoe's *Moll Flanders*. Located along the Thames's bank, **Bear Gardens** received its name from the arena that stood there in Elizabethan times, when bears and bulls were pitted against mastiffs for sport. If you're looking to pick up an original souvenir, try the **Bermondsey antique market** (see p. 138)—though you'll have to be up early.

SHAKESPEARE'S GLOBE THEATRE

🔲 *21 New Globe Walk (☎ 7902 1400; www.shakespeares-globe.org). Tube: Mansion House, Southwark, or London Bridge. Open May-Sept. daily 9am-12:30pm, Oct.-Apr. daily 10am-5pm. No tours May-Sept. due to performances. £7.50, students £6, under 15 £5, family £23. See also **Theater**, p. 143.*

Not far from where the remains of the original Globe Theatre, burnt down in 1613, were discovered is a historically accurate and now fully operational replica of the Elizabethan Globe. The theater held its first full season in 1997. Admission includes a tour on par with those given by the crazy Beefeaters across the river. The replica is also part of the **International Shakespeare Globe Centre**, which houses an exhibit on the history of Shakespeare, as well as the theater itself, and will ultimately contain a second theater for winter performances, an archival library, an auditorium, and various shops, hopefully by early 2001. Nearby lie the remains of the Elizabethan **Rose Theatre**, built in 1587. Shakespeare's and Marlowe's plays were performed on this stage, which was rediscovered during construction in 1989. The remnants will be preserved and displayed under a new office block on the corner of Park St. and Rose Alley.

TATE MODERN AND THE MILLENNIUM BRIDGE

🔲 *Tate Modern: Bankside. Tube: Southwark, Blackfriars, or St. Paul. See **Museums**, p. 117.*

An awesome architectural monolith looms menacingly over the Globe. The huge, windowless tower that formerly served as a power station opened as the **Tate Modern** in early 2000 to rave reviews from modern art fans. The new museum is linked by the **Millennium Bridge** to St. Paul's Cathedral across the river. Originally opened in June 2000, the bridge was closed at going to press after a literally shaky debut. Though a suspension bridge, with some sway anticipated, it was found to be verging on unsafe in its 3-4ft. side to side keels. London's first new bridge over the Thames in over a century also has the distinction of being the only one just for pedestrians. It is anticipated that it will reopen in fall 2000.

SOUTHWARK CATHEDRAL

🔲 *Montague Close (☎ 7367 6712; www.dswark.org). Tube: London Bridge. Open M-F 8am-6pm. Evensong Su 3pm. Free. Photo permit £1, video permit £5.*

The cathedral, an endearing remnant of ecclesiastical power, is probably the most striking Gothic church in the city after Westminster Abbey. It is certainly the oldest, having been the site of a nunnery as early as 606AD. Mostly rebuilt in the 1890s, only the church's 1207 choir and retro-choir survive. The glorious altar screen is Tudor, with 20th-century statues. The cathedral is dotted with interesting stone and wood effigies, which have explanatory notes. Ed Shakespeare, brother of Will, was buried in the church in 1607 and lies beneath a stained-glass window depicting many of his talented sibling's characters. More millennial money is flowing into these walls, creating an exhibit on the cathedral's history and a library. Expect it to be completed in early 2001.

OTHER SOUTHWARK SIGHTS

LIBERTY OF THE CLINK. Before the "hoose-gow," the "big house," and "Club Fed," there was "the Clink," testament to Southwark's less than rosy past. The Liberty comprised 70 acres of bankside land, under the jurisdiction of the Bishop of Winchester's Court. "The Clink" itself, which was in operation for more than six centuries, was the Bishop's private prison for London's criminals. Henry Barrowe and John Greenwood, early Separatists, were imprisoned here before being hanged. The **Clink Prison Museum,** 1 Clink St., recreates the "glory days" of the prison with an eerie choral soundtrack and hands-on restraining and torture devices, all contributing to a not altogether tasteful display. *(1 Clink St. Do not pass Go, do not collect £200. Tube: Southwark.* ☎ *7378 1558; www.clink.co.uk. Open daily 10am-6pm. £4, concessions £3, families £9.)*

HMS BELFAST. Moored on the south bank of the Thames, just upstream from Tower Bridge, this World War II warship once led the bombardment of the French coast during D-Day landings. Today it is used when London goes to war with other cities over tourist supremacy. Take that, you Parisian dogs! The labyrinth of the engine house and the whopping great guns make it a fun place to play sailor, but swabbing the deck in a silly hat sort of detracts. *(Morgan's Lane, Tooley St. Tube: London Bridge.* ☎ *7940 6300. Open daily Mar.-Oct. 10am-6pm, last admission 5:15pm; Nov.-Feb. 10am-5pm, last admission 4:15pm. £5, students £3.90, children under 16 free.)*

GOLDEN HINDE. Around the corner from the Globe, landlubbers are given the chance to board a rebuilt 16th-century galleon. Yarrrrrrr. Attendants clad as pirates lead tours through the five levels of the vessel geared especially toward the kiddies. Families with children aged 6-12 can spend a night on board learning seafaring skills, eating Tudor meals, and wearing period clothes. No one will be asked to walk the plank. *(Cathedral St. Tube: London Bridge.* ☎ *7403 0123. www.goldenhinde.co.uk. Open daily 10am-6pm. £2.50, children under 13 £1.75, concessions £2.10, families £6. 50.)*

OLD OPERATING THEATRE & HERB GARRET. Your hair will rise and your spine will chill at this museum, a carefully preserved 19th-century surgical hospital. Rediscovered in 1956, it is the only known example of a pre-Victorian operating theater. See the wooden table where fully conscious unanesthetized patients endured surgery, or travel through the herb garret and museum to learn the properties of mugwort and why John Keats never finished his medical training. On the first Sunday of every month, the museum offers special lectures at 2:30pm. *(Located at 9a St. Thomas St. Tube: London Bridge.* ☎ *7955 4791. Open daily Tu-Su 10am-4pm and "frequent Mondays." £2.90, concessions £2, families—and what a family affair it is—£7.25.)*

BRIXTON

see map p. 318

While Brixton began as a classic Victorian railway suburb, it now stands out in South London as particularly urban. Architecturally it is still dominated by the initial period of building, witnessed by the shops, restaurants, and clubs found in the railway arches, the church of St. Matthew (now the site of the **Mass** club and the **Bug Bar;** see p. 183), and the terraces such as **Electric Avenue,** the first in London with electric street lighting.

In the 1950s, Brixton's earliest black residents came to Britain on the ship "Empire Windrush," the first ship that carried immigrants to the country from the Caribbean. Brixton is now associated with the West Indian community that was established here in the 50s and 60s and with the memory of the fierce riots between locals and police that took place in the early 1980s. Headlines screamed about "The Battle of Brixton," and alarmist copy spoke of "Bloody Saturday"—simmering fires, charred buildings, Molotov cocktails, and widespread looting. The desperation of those times was captured in The Clash's anthem "The Guns of Brixton," as well as Hanif Kureishi's film *Sammie and Rosie Get Laid*. During the 1990s the look of the place changed, partly as a result of government investment. With it there was a change of character—perversely perhaps as a result of the reputation it once had—and it is now a desirable area for young people to live in. An ample supply of bars and clubs, as well as the beautiful **Ritzy** cinema and the **Brixton Academy** music venue, keeps residents around on evenings and weekends.

Brixton remains a major center of Afro-Caribbean culture. The West Indian influence is most evident in: the **market** (see p. 139) where you can buy all the ingredients for Caribbean cooking; the record shops on Coldharbour Lane selling reggae, ragga, and rap; and in the Caribbean eating houses on Atlantic Rd. and Acre Lane.

BROCKWELL PARK. Brockwell has such civic amenities as a playground, wildlife reserve, walled garden and tennis courts, as well as the **Brockwell Lido,** a popular outdoor pool that has become a summer institution. The park is a wonderful place from which to view London landmarks, among them the Houses of Parliament and Battersea Power Station. *(Between Tulse Hill and Dulwich Rd. Tube: Brixton. Park open daily 7:30am-dusk. Lido ☎7274 3088. Open mid-May to mid-Sept. M-F 6:45-10am and noon-7pm, Sa and Su noon-7pm. £2.50.)*

GREENWICH

🛈 *Greenwich Tourist Information Centre arranges a variety of afternoon tours. The building also contains a decent caff and a slick exhibit on the history of Greenwich. Opposite the Cutty Sark. DLR: Cutty Sark. ☎0870 608 2000 or 8858 6376; tic@greenwich.gov.uk; www.greenwich.gov.uk. Open daily 10am-5pm. 1-1½hr. tours at 12:15pm and 2:15pm; £4, concessions £3, under 14 free.*

see map p. 321 A real sea town in its own right, Greenwich (GREN-itch) seems a world away from London and, ironically, timeless. London's long-forgotten love affair with the Thames and Britain's love affair with the sea culminate in the place where these two watery bodies meet. Many of England's best loved heroes, among them Drake, Cook and Raleigh, set sail from these docks. In modern-day minds, Greenwich is synonymous with time. After Charles II authorized the establishment of a small observatory here in 1675 "for perfecting navigation and astronomy," successive Astronomer Royals perfected their craft to such a degree that an international convention held in Washington, D.C. blessed the village with the **Prime Meridian** in 1884. Today, the area retains two local markets, the bric-a-brac bargains of **Greenwich Market** and the serious stuff of the **Antique Market** (see **Markets,** p. 139). Local residents fight to maintain local character; a recent victory was the listing of the Greenwich Street **Ye Old Pie Shop,** established in 1890, as a landmark. In the past year, Greenwich has been on the ascent, economically and on the tourist scene, as it was chosen to be millennium central, sight of the highly controversial Millennium Dome (see **Are You Experienced,** p. 106).

GETTING TO GREENWICH. The **Docklands Light Railway** brings seafarers and wannabe pirates directly into town (DLR: Cutty Sark or Greenwich). The spanking new **Jubilee line** extension runs to North Greenwich and the Dome. Alternatively, take the DLR to Island Gardens—from there, Greenwich is just a seven-minute walk through a **foot tunnel** under the Thames. 33ft. below the river, and 53 ft. below at high tide, the 1217 ft. white-tiled Victorian tunnel was the first under the river, and tends, rather ominously, to drip. The most picturesque (and appropriate) passage to Greenwich is by **boat.** Cruises to Greenwich pier depart from the Westminster (☎7930 4097), Charing Cross, and Tower piers (☎7987 1185 for both). Make sure you choose a boat with running commentary on the river's major sights.

ROYAL OBSERVATORY GREENWICH AND FLAMSTEED HOUSE

🛈 ☎8312 6565. Open daily 10am-5pm; last admission 4:30pm. Old Royal Observatory, National Maritime Museum, and the Queen's House £10.50, concessions £8.40, family £15, under 16 and *seniors who can make it up the hill free. Observatory alone £6, concessions £4.80, children free. 45min. observatory audio guide £2. Planetarium shows usually M-Sa afternoon. £2.50, concessions £1.50.*

At the top of the hill in the middle of the park stands a Christopher Wren designed **observatory,** cunningly disguised as a freakishly large onion. Wren also designed **Flamsteed House,** remarkable for its octagonal top room. Inside its walls are Britain's largest refracting telescope and an excellent collection of early astronomical instruments displayed with nearly comprehensible explanations. The Prime Meridian is marked by a brass strip in the observatory courtyard and a laser beam inside; play the "now I'm west, now I'm east" game for as long as you're amused. Greenwich Mean Time is displayed on a clock over 120 years old. The red **time ball,** used since 1833 to indicate time to ships on the Thames, drops unspectacularly each day at 1pm. Just outside the house and observatory glares a statue of **General Wolfe** (conqueror of French Canada) generously donated by the Canadian government. Next to the Planetarium is a picturesque Victorian building housing a reasonably priced cafeteria.

Tate

GREENWICH PARK

🚹 *DLR: Cutty Sark or Greenwich. Open May-Sept. daily 7am-dusk.*

This splendid park, used as a burial ground during the 1353 plague (and you wondered why the flowers bloomed so well here), is a spot of green in which to spend some time. The royal park rolls up and down a series of gentle hills, giving each area a feeling of seclusion. On the east side of the park is the **Queen Elizabeth Oak,** a rather grand title for a big dead log. For centuries the tree marked the spot where Henry VIII frolicked with an 11-fingered Anne Boleyn, and so the remains remain, protectively fenced off from would-be stump vandals. The garden in the southeast corner of the park combines English garden and fairy tale, with a wild deer park thrown in for good measure. In summer, bands perform at Greenwich Park as a part of the Royal Park Band performance series. *(Free shows at 3 and 6pm June-Aug. every Sunday in the bandstand north of the gardens, weather permitting.)* The **Children's Boating Pool** next to the playground gives kids a chance to unleash pent-up seafaring energy accumulated in the nearby museums. All this, plus pirate puppet shows—Greenwich truly does have it all. *(Adults £2 for 20 min., children £1.)*

HMS Belfast

NATIONAL MARITIME MUSEUM AND QUEEN'S HOUSE

🚹 ☎ *8858 4422. DLR: Cutty Sark or Greenwich. Open daily 10am-5pm. National Maritime Museum £7.50, concessions £6, seniors and children free. Free maps are available, and a display in the basement guides you through the house's muddled jumble of commissioners, architects, and occupants.*

At the foot of the hill is the so-called "Queen's House," a 17th-century home that was started for James I's wife, Anne of Denmark, who unfortunately died before construction was completed. The house was finished for Henrietta Maria, the wife of Charles I. Designed by the age's master architect, Inigo Jones, it is England's first Palladian villa, known to the Queen as her "house of delights," and celebrated by architects and art historians for its purity and strictness. The renovated

OXO Tower

ARE YOU EX-PERIENCED?

Perhaps Greenwich's most famous (or was that infamous?) sight is "**The Millennium Experience**," more commonly known as "**The Dome**," or "That Damn Dome." This enormous white structure received at least £700 million pounds in Lottery money, its own stop on the Jubilee line (North Greenwich), and more than its share of bad press. With visitor numbers clocking in well below those expected, and numerous snags along the way resulting in financial chaos, the Dome quickly became synonymous with the trip-ups of the Blair government, and policy gone horribly wrong. At the time this book went to press, it was unclear if the Millennium Experience would be able to remain open for the duration of 2000 without further money to bail it out. Thankfully, it was always expected it would be sold off at the end of the year, and the winner this round seems to have been Nomowura, the Japanese investing firm that bought the monolith and plans to reopen it as a high-minded theme park. Despite claims of "Sold Down the River" by the press, it seems clear that Labour will be very happy to have this "experience" done with and over.

house's 17th-century furnishings and rich silk hangings are as sumptuously swank as the featured art is stolidly stately. Queen's Park will be cleaning up from its millennial exhibit on "Time," and therefore closed in the early months of 2001. The western addition to the house is the highly-informative **National Maritime Museum** (see p. 122), which will not be closed for clean-up. Instead, 2001 will see a special exhibit called "South: The Race To The Pole."

ROYAL NAVAL COLLEGE

🛪 *King William Walk* (☎ 8269 4744; www.greenwichfoundation.org.uk). *DLR: Cutty Sark. Open M-Sa 10am-5pm, Su 12:30-5pm. £5, students £3, children under 16 free.*

Charles II commissioned Wren to tear down the Royal Palace of Placentia, a favorite home of Henry VIII and his daughter Elizabeth, and to construct the College in its place. Because it was situated directly between the Queen's House and the river, the College was constructed in two halves in order to leave the Queen's view unobstructed. James Thornhill's elaborate ceiling in the Painted Hall, which took 19 years to complete, and Benjamin West's painting of a shipwrecked St. Paul in the chapel provide an excellent opportunity to view breathtaking art in its original location. The navy packed its bags and took the next boat out of town in 1998, and the University of Greenwich blew in.

CUTTY SARK

🛪 *On the waterfront by Greenwich Pier* (☎ 8858 3445). *DLR: Cutty Sark. Open daily 10am-5pm, last entry 4:30pm. £3.50, concessions £2.50, families £8.50.*

The Cutty Sark is one of the last great tea clippers, anchored in dry dock. The ship carried 1.3 million pounds of tea on each 120-day return trip from China. In the prime of its sea-going days, between 1869 and 1938, it set new records for speed. The ship's cannon is fired at 1pm every day; but as the large sign informs you, it is very loud indeed. Don't say you haven't been warned.

OTHER GREENWICH SIGHTS

GIPSY MOTH IV. Resting nearby the Cutty Sark is this cozy 54ft. long craft. The 66-year-old Sir Francis Chichester spent 226 days sailing solo around the globe in the Gipsy in 1966, covering a grand total of nearly 30,000 miles. The ship is not open to the public, so you will have to make do by looking at its sleek exterior.

BLACKHEATH. Just south of Greenwich Park, these sloping fields offer a checkered history of rebellion, love, rugby, and golf. Wat Tyler and his fellow peasants, revolting over a poll tax, congregated on the heath in 1381. Henry VII fought Cornish rebels here, while Henry VIII had a similarly unfortunate experience—it was here that he met his betrothed

Ann, the "mare of Cleves." Henry chose his bride, sight unseen, based on a flattering portrait by Holbein, but repeatedly commented on her equine features when life failed to imitate art. The **Royal Blackheath Golf Club** was founded on the common—James I was known to take a bash here with his nine iron. Another sporting milestone took place in the **Princess of Wales** pub, where the world's first rugby union club, Blackheath FC, was founded. A traditional site for celebrations, Blackheath still holds fairs on Bank Holidays, and serves as the starting point for the **London Marathon.**

THAMES BARRIER. A bit farther down the river than Blackheath stands the world's largest movable flood barrier, the reason that London no longer enjoys the exciting high tides of yesteryear. Constructed during the 1970s, the barrier spans 520m and consists of 10 separate movable steel gates; when raised, the main gates stand as high as a five-story building and are able to protect London from the flood of a thousand years, the worst case scenario. Now there's a sobering thought. A suprisingly developed and intriguing visitors' center has a working model of the barrier, in addition to exhibits explaining its history. *(Tube: North Greenwich to the Dome, then an interesting 45min. walk along the Thames, or take bus 161 from the Dome and ask the driver to let you off near the barrier. ☎8305 4188. Open M-F 10am-5pm, Sa-Su 10:30am-5:30pm. £3.40, concessions £2, families £7.50.)*

GREATER LONDON

Lo, where huge London, huger day by day,
O'er six fair counties spreads its hideous sway.
        —Jane Austen, The Golden Age

KEW GARDENS

🛈 *On the south bank of the Thames near Richmond, 6 mi. southwest of London. Main Gate is on Kew Green, near the boat pier; Victoria Gate, Kew Road, is nearest to Kew Gardens station (☎8332 5622; email info@rbgkew.org.uk; www.rbgkew.org.uk). Tube and train: Kew Gardens (Zone 3). Westminster Passenger Association (☎7930 4721; www.wpsa.co.uk) boats travel daily between Kew and Westminster pier (Tube: Westminster). £7, day return £11; ages 5-15 £3, £5: schedules and trip times vary according to the tide. 1hr. walking Tours offered daily 11am and 2pm, leaving from Victoria Gate visitor center. Free. "Discovery" bus tour for mobility-impaired visitors M-F 11am and 2pm, leaves from the Main Gate; reserve ahead at ☎ 8332 5642 for bookings. "Kew Explorer" hop-on hop-off garden shuttle stops at most sights in the gardens; £2.50 per day, ages 5-16 £1.50; buy tickets from the driver, visitor centers, or ticket offices. Gardens open approx. Apr.-Aug. M-F 9:30am-6pm, Sa-Su 9:30am-7pm; Sept.-Oct. daily 9:30am-6pm; Nov.-Mar. daily 9:30am-4:15pm. Last admission 30min. before closing. Glasshouses close Apr.-Oct. 5:30pm, Nov.-Mar. 3:45pm. £5, concessions £3.50, ages 5-16 £2.50; family £13; under 5, blind, and partially-sighted free. Late admission £3.50. Season ticket (valid 1yr.) £19, concessions £12, family £38, family concession £28.*

Founded in 1759 by Princess Augusta, the 300-acre Royal Botanic Gardens at Kew provide a breath of fresh air. Originally intended to recreate Eden by bringing together plants from all over the world, today the park is home to the living bank of a research collection that contains millions of DNA and seeds, displaying thousands of flowers, fruits, trees, and vegetables from throughout the globe. To cope with the needs of plants from different climate zones and environment, large parts of the collection are housed in giant conservatories, which for many people form the highlight of the gardens.

PALM HOUSE. The steamy, tropical Palm House, a unique masterpiece of Victorian engineering built in 1848 (its unusual hull-like shape stems from the fact that the architect was a shipbuilder), will stun you with the revelation that bananas are in fact giant herbs. Still reeling from this blow, one may then visit Encephalartos Altensteinii, "The Oldest Pot Plant In The World," which is not at all what it sounds like, but interesting nonetheless. Downstairs, the beautifully lit aquariums of the Marine Display let you watch batfish and porcupine puffer fish interact with colorful sea kelp. Ask one of the "roving guides," identifiable by their sashes, about the plants for informative titbits such as the a role the Madagascan periwinkle plays in the treatment of leukemia.

PRINCESS OF WALES CONSERVATORY. Opened by Diana, but named for Augusta, the 1980s building is the newest of the glasshouses and is home to a much-envied collection of orchids. Here you can browse through 10 different tropical climates; it's just a few steps from a rainforest to an arid desert. Its award-winning pyramidal design allows it to both remain innocuous among the foliage and conserve energy.

TEMPERATE HOUSE. The other buildings in Kew are dwarfed by the Temperate House, which has reigned as the world's largest ornamental glasshouse since its completion in 1862. The cooler climate here nurtures 3000 species, arranged over 50,000 square feet according to geographical origins; most of them come from the southern hemisphere, though there is also a Mediterranean section.

EVOLUTION AND ALPINE HOUSES. Across from the Temperate House, the **Evolution House** leads you through 3.5 billion years of floracentric history, from the primordial ooze (recreated with relish) to the exciting moment when flowering plants appeared. Its misty waterfalls and dinosaur footprints play like a cross between *Land of the Lost* and Biosphere II. The fascinating **Alpine House** contains specimens from both the poles, as well as mountaintops; although the smallest of the Kew conservatories, over the course of a year it actually displays a greater range of species than any other house.

KEW PALACE. In the northeastern section of the gardens stands scarlet Kew Palace. Built in 1631, it was leased as a royal stop-over residence in 1730 and later served as a permanent home for part of George III's mighty brood of children when they outgrew his home. Hundreds of 17th-century medicinal plants flourish in the **Queen's Garden,** and small placards boast their uses: from the plant that "cures bites of mad dogs" to those that "stirreth up bodily lust," or "be most effectual for burstings or ruptures." **Queen Charlotte's Cottage,** a small, picturesque structure given by George to his wife as a picnic site, is also worth a visit. The cottage's distinctly Bavarian feel recall the couple's shared Teutonic roots. *(Cottage open Sa-Su and holidays 10:30am-4pm).*

OTHER SITES. Outside the controlled environment of the houses, the Gardens proper are home to a wide variety of cloud-and-rain loving fauna from around the world. The **Japanese Gateway and Landscape** bring eastern formalism to this international collection that also includes more local specialities, like the **Rose Garden,** the **Lilacs,** and the **Azaleas.** Kew's appeal extends beyond the horticultural. Aside from the glass houses, other architectural curiosities litter the garden. Three temples, an Italianate campanile and a ruined arch lie on the edge of the park farthest from the river. The **Pagoda,** a 10-story oriental sensation in the southern corner of the park, was apparently even more impressive when fire-breathing dragons appeared from each floor. Their disappearance is attributed to George IV's attempt to pay off his debts. Other points of interest in Kew include the **Marianne North Gallery,** a small but well-displayed collection of 19th-century paintings by a Victorian woman who painted her way around the globe, the **Rhododendron Dell** (built by Capability Brown), and the **Waterlily House.**

RICHMOND AND TWICKENHAM

Except in the Elysium shades of Richmond, there is no such thing as love and pleasure
   -Lady Mary Wortley Montagu, 1723.

Tube: Richmond, or take a Westminster Passenger Association (☎ 7930 4721; www.wpsa.co.uk) boat from Westminster Pier (Tube: Westminster). Boat fares: £8, day return £12, ages 5-15 £3.50, £6; times and trip lengths depend on the tide. The Tourist Information Centre, Whittaker Ave (☎ 8940 9125; www.richmond.gov.uk), in the old Victorian Town Hall, has information on Richmond and surrounding areas, including lots of accommodation listings. Open May-Sept. M-Sa 10am-5pm, Su 10:30am-1:30pm; Oct.-Apr. M-Sa 10am-5pm.

Here, the banks along the Thames become rural, with trendy shops giving way to luscious fields and forests along the river. Richmond is easy to get around, especially given its proliferation of signposts. A left turn from the Tube/train station exit leads onto **The Quadrant,** which becomes **George Street** (you'll recognize it by the high-class chains) and then **Hill Street.** Off Hill St. is **Whittaker Avenue,** where the tourist office and the Museum

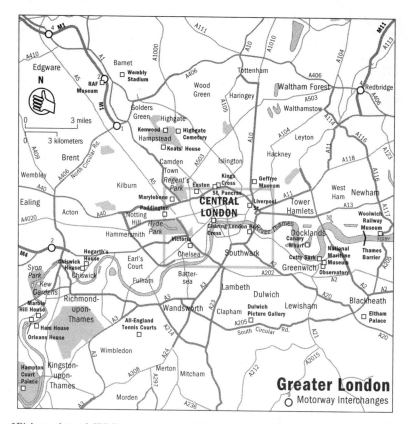

N

0 _____ 3 miles

0 _____ 3 kilometers

Greater London

○ Motorway Interchanges

of Richmond stand. Hill St. continues onto **Hill Rise,** which forks into **Petersham Road** and **Richmond Hill.** A right turn off Hill St. leads to **Richmond Bridge,** which has some spectacular views of the Thames. Across the bridge is **Twickenham,** home of English rugby and of various mansions.

THE MUSEUM OF RICHMOND. An excellent local museum with exhibits on the history of the town, including a model of the now-demolished Richmond Palace, and on famous inhabitants, from actor Edmund Kean to writers George Eliot and Virginia Woolf. In 2001, the museum will celebrate the 500-year anniversary of the naming of Richmond by Henry VII—it had previously been known as Shene. *(Whittaker Ave., in the same building as the information centre. ☎8332 1141; www.museumofrichmond.com. Open Sept.-Apr. Tu-Sa 11am-5pm and Su 1-4pm; May-Oct. Tu-Sa 11am-5pm. £2, students and seniors £1, children free.)*

RICHMOND HILL AND RICHMOND PARK. Richmond Hill provides an extraordinary view of the Thames and its bankside mansions. So many English paintings have copied this view that Parliament declared it a protected site. Richmond Park, atop Richmond Hill, is Europe's largest city park. A former royal hunting ground, its 2500 acres are still home to several hundred deer. **The Isabella Plantation** garden, deep inside the park, bursts with color in the spring, when its azaleas and rhododendrons bloom. **Note: tick-borne Lyme disease is a danger in the park. Wear long trousers and take adequate precautions.** *(From the tourist office, follow Hill St. onto Hill Rise, which becomes Richmond Hill.)*

ORLEANS HOUSE. This Georgian house holds a gallery of art and artifacts of local history. Only the geometrically interesting Octagon Room survives from the original building. The grounds surrounding the house remain untrimmed wildland. *(Riverside,*

Twickenham. Tube: Richmond or Rail: Twickenham. Buses #33, 90, H22, R68, R70, and 290 from Richmond Tube stop just before Sion Rd., which leads to Riverside. ☎8892 0221; www.guidetorichmond.co.uk/orleans.html. Wheelchair accessible. Open Apr.-Sept. Tu-Sa 1-5:30pm, Su 2-5:30pm; Oct.-Mar. Tu-Sa 1-4:30pm, Su 2-4:30pm. Grounds open daily 9am-dusk. Free.)

HAM HOUSE. A small passenger ferry runs between Marble Hill Park (next to Orleans House) and this home on Ham Street. Built in 1610, this house boasts artwork and room designs that are almost as beautiful as the grounds outside. The Duke of Lauderdale inherited the house from his father-in-law, Charles I's "whipping boy." (As part of his "reward" for taking all the future king's punishments whenever he misbehaved, he received the lease to the Ham estate.) Rooms filled with family portraits of royalty, including Charles II and his loyal servants, overlook the recently restored gardens and sprawling fields. Don't be too surprised to see some recent touch-ups; the house was "modernized" during the 1960s. *(Bus #65 or 371 from Richmond station. Ferry runs Feb.-Oct. Sa-Su 10am-6:30pm, M-F 10am-6pm; 40p, kids 20p.; ☎8892 9620. Ham House ☎8940 1950. Open Apr.-Oct. M-W 1-5pm, Sa-Su noon-5:30pm; Nov. to mid-Dec. Sa-Su 1-4pm. £5, children £3. Gardens open M-W and Sa-Su 10:30am-dusk. Free.)*

HAMPTON COURT PALACE

🚩 *Take the train to Hampton Court from Waterloo (32min.; every 30min.; day return £4, £3.50 with zone 2-6 Travelcard) and walk the 2min. to the palace, take the tube to Richmond and take the R68 bus (70p), or take a Westminster Passenger Association (☎7930 4721; www.wpsa.co.uk) boat from Westminster Pier (Tube: Westminster). Boat fares £10, day return £14; ages 5-15 £4, £7; times and trip length depend on the tide. ☎8781 9500; www.hrp.org.uk. Free audio guides and tours. Wheelchairs and electric buggies available from West Gate; just ask a warder. Palace and privy gardens open mid-Mar. to mid-Oct. M 10:15am-6pm, Tu-Su 9:30am-6pm; mid-Oct. to mid-Mar. closes 4:30pm. Last admission 45min. before close. Gardens open daily 7am-dusk. Palace, privy gardens, and maze £10.15, students and seniors £8, ages 5-15 £7, families £31.40; maze only £2.50, ages 5-15 £1.60; Gardens free.*

Although a monarch hasn't lived here since George II packed it in over 200 years ago, **Hampton Court Palace** continues to exude regal charm. Located 6 mi. down the Thames from Richmond, the palace housed over 1500 court members at its height. Cardinal Wolsey built it in 1514, showing Henry VIII by his example how to act the part of a splendid and all-powerful ruler. Henry learned the lesson well, confiscating the Court in 1525 when Wolsey fell out of favor, and added new lodgings for each of his numerous wives.

To help tourists make sense of the chaotic and schizophrenic arrangement of the palace, it is divided into six "routes" through which visitors may meander. Seeing all six plus the gardens and maze could easily take up the whole day; if you've got less time, the staff at the impressive **information centre,** off the **Clock Court,** can help you.

Fans of Henry have myriad options for discovering how the king lived, reigned, and ate his way to a 54-inch waist. **Henry VIII's State Apartments,** including the spectacular **Great Hall,** allow would-be sycophants a chance to reenact some Tudor brown-nosing. For those curious as to how Henry acquired his massive girth in the days before deep-fat fryers, the **Tudor Kitchens** provide the answer. Sir Christopher Wren's work can be seen in the opulent **King's and Queen's Apartments,** built for William III and meticulously restored after a catastrophic fire in 1986. In **King's Guard Chamber,** almost 3000 guns and weapons remind visitors that the monarch they were about to see was not to be trifled with. The **Wolsey Rooms,** which housed Cardinal Wolsey before he fell from favor, now house some of the finest treasures of the Royal Collection, including **tapestries** woven from the Raphael cartoons in the Victoria and Albert Museum (see p. 119), and a roomful of *grisaille* work originally by Mantegna but poorly repainted in the 18th century.

The exterior of the palace holds nearly as many delights. Sixty marvelous acres of Palace gardens are open and contain some celebrated amusements, including the **maze,** a hedgerow labyrinth first planted in 1714 that inspired the hedges in Stanley Kubrick's *The Shining.* "Solve" the maze by getting to the benches in the middle and back.

CHISWICK

🚇 *Tube: Turnham Green or Rail: Chiswick.*

CHISWICK HOUSE. Built for Lord Burlington, a grand patron of the arts and supporter of Pope, Swift, and Handel, the Chiswick House that stands today was originally an Italianate villa. The villa was William Kent, "dear old Kentino," and housed the collection of paintings and antiquities culled *en route*. The interior of the villa, hugely influential in its day, is not yet fully restored. (☎ 8995 0508. *House open daily 10am-6pm; closed 1pm-2pm; Oct.-Apr. W-Su 10am-4pm. Grounds open daily 8am-dusk. £3, concessions £2.30, children £1.50.*)

HOGARTH HOUSE. Just northeast of the Chiswick House grounds on Hogarth Ln., the modest abode of artist and social critic William Hogarth stands as a subtle jab to Lord Burlington's extravagance. Rumor has it that the two hated each other; Hogarth, the great moralist, saw Lord Burlington as a sycophant who imported foreign trends to England. Hogarth spent his time at the home, with Henry Fielding, author of *Tom Jones*, and other fellow Freemasons. His work and life lives on in this small museum, which focuses on the historical and biographical detail of Hogarth's prints. Die-hard fans can avenge Hogarth by skipping the ornate Chiswick House and enjoying this house's simple subtlety. (☎ 8994 6757. *Open Apr.-Oct. Tu-F 1-5pm, Sa-Su 1-6pm; Nov.-Mar. closes 1hr. earlier. Free.*)

FULLER, SMITH & TURNER'S BREWERY. The remains of Alexander Pope's summer house reside near to Hogarth's House on the site of London's oldest brewery. Beer connoisseurs will recognize Fuller's London Ale, Chiswick Bitter, London Pride, and ESB, all four of which are popular in the city's pubs. Tours end with a tasting. But be warned—you may hear the ghostly meowing of the Brewery cat who, in the 19th century, fell into the boiling sugar-dissolver. Unfortunately, Cat Ale was not as successful as the consultants predicted. (☎ 8996 2048. *1½hr. tours M,W,F at 11am, noon, 1pm, and 2pm. £5; must be over 14. Call to book in advance.*)

Tate Modern

Hay's Galleria

Southwark Bridge

Museums

Centuries as the capital of an empire upon which the sun never set, together with a decidedly English penchant for collecting, have endowed London with a spectacular set of museums. Art lovers, history buffs, and amateur ethnologists will not know which way to turn when they arrive.

Avoiding crowds at major museums is a field of study in itself; they tend to be most peaceful on weekday mornings and during weekly evening openings, if applicable. Admission to major collections is usually free, but many museums, no longer heavily subsidized by the government, now charge admission or request a £1-5 donation; students, seniors, and children are normally entitled to a reduced rate (often listed as "concessions"). In addition, many of the larger museums offer free entry a few hours a week. Almost all charge extra for temporary exhibitions.

The **London Go See Card** is a discount card that allows unlimited access to 13 participating museums for a period of three or seven days. The card can be purchased at any of the participating museums, but will afford you substantial discounts only if you plan to visit *many* museums, or if you plan to visit a particularly expensive museum more than once. Participating museums are: the V&A, the Science Museum, the Natural History Museum, the Royal Academy of Arts, the Hayward Gallery, the Design Museum, the London Transport Museum, the Museum of London, the Museum of the Moving Image, and the Courtauld Institute. (3-day card 16, families 32; 7-day card 26, 50.)

BRITISH MUSEUM

◪*Great Russell St., WC1; Rear entrance on Montague St. ☎ 7323 8299; www.british-museum.ac.uk. Tube: Tottenham Court Rd., Goodge St., Russell Sq., or Holborn. 1½hr. highlights tour M-Sa 10:30, 11am, 1:30, 2:30pm; Su 12:30, 1:30, 2:30, and 4pm; £7, students and under 16 £4. 1hr. focus tours*

THE TOP TEN LIST

The British Museum can be daunting, and wandering through nearly 3 miles of galleries is frustrating for even the most die-hard museum-goer. To catch the main attractions, buy the £5 souvenir guide, take a "highlights" tour (see above), or do-it-yourself with our guide to the must-sees, in order by room number.

Nereid Monument
Room 7

Elgin Marbles
Room 8

Ninevah Reliefs
Rooms 17, 19, & 21

Rosetta Stone
Room 25

Lindow Man
Room 37

Mildenhall Treasure
Room 40

Sutton Hoo Ship Burial
Room 41

Lewis Chessmen
Room 42

Egyptian Mummies
Rooms 60 & 61

Portland Vase
Room 70

depart M-Sa 1pm from upstairs, 3:30pm downstairs, Su 4:30pm; £5, students and under 16 £3. Visually-impaired should enquire about tactile exhibits and touch tours of Roman and Egyptian sculpture. Open M-Sa 10am-5pm, Su 12pm-6pm. Free; suggested donation £2; special exhibits £4, concessions £3.

Founded in 1753, the museum began with the personal collection of the physician Sir Hans Sloane. In the following decades, it became so swollen with gifts, purchases, and imperialist spoils that a new building had to be commissioned. Robert Smirke drew up the design of the current Neoclassical building in 1824; construction took 30 years.

In addition to their prodigious permanent collections, the most outstanding of which are listed below, the British Museum puts on a number of temporary exhibits. Those for 2000 included "A Noble Art: Amateur Artists and Drawing Masters 1600-1800" and "The Salcome Cannon Site Treasure."

EGYPTIAN GALLERIES. This outstanding collection contains imposing statues of Amenophis III as well as the Rosetta Stone. The head of Ramses II dominates the northern section of Room 25. The black granite Sesostris III remains more noteworthy for its ears than its warmth. The central gallery is filled with tributes to the animal world, including a tiny blue hippo. The Egyptian gallery contains papyri such as the *Book of the Dead of Ani*, a comprehensive exhibit on Egyptian funerary archaeology, and a how-to guide on mummification.

THE ASSYRIAN GALLERIES. These galleries contain enormous reliefs from Nineveh (704-668 BC). Room 16's entrance is guarded by the giant five-legged, human-headed bulls, made to look stationary from the front, mobile from the side.

GREEK ANTIQUITIES. These exhibits are dominated by the **Elgin Marbles,** 5th-century BC reliefs from the Parthenon, now residing in the spacious Duveen Gallery. In 1810, Lord Elgin procured the statues and pieces of the Parthenon frieze while serving as ambassador to Constantinople. The museum claims that Elgin's "agents removed many sculptures from the Parthenon with the approval" of unnamed "authorities" for £75,000. When he needed the money, he sold them to Britain for £35,000. Every so often, the Greeks renew their efforts to convince the British government to return the marbles. Carved under the direction of classical Athens' greatest sculptor, Phidias, the marbles comprise three main groups: the frieze, which portrays the most important Athenian civic festivals; the metopes, which depict incidents from the battle of the Lapiths and Centaurs (symbolizing the triumph of "civilization" over "barbarism"); and the remains of large statues that stood in the east and west pediments of the building. Recently opened are two new galleries devoted to the Elgin marbles, complete with a miniature model of the Acropolis. Other Hellenic highlights include the complete Ionic facade of the **Nereid Monument,** one of the female caryatid columns from the Acropolis. Frieze slabs and some freestanding sculpture commemorate the second wonder—the **Temple of Artemis,** built to replace the one buried by Herostratus in 356 BC to perpetuate his name.

ROMAN ANTIQUITIES. Among the many sculptures of the **Roman antiquities,** the dark blue glass of the **Portland Vase** stands out. The inspiration for ceramic designer Josiah Wedgwood, the vase has tenaciously survived mishaps and reconstructive operations that first took place even before being dug up in 1582. When it was discovered, the base had already been broken and replaced. In 1845, it was shattered by a drunken museum-goer; when it was put back together, 37 small chips were left over. Since then, the vase has been beautifully reconstructed twice, with more left-over chips being reincorporated each time—don't touch! The scene depicted is an enigma; controversy still rages about what it means.

ROMAN-BRITAIN COLLECTION. The Roman-Britain section includes the **Mindenhall Treasure,** a magnificent collection of 4th-century silver tableware. With a diameter of almost two feet and weighing over 18 lb., the aptly named Great Dish impresses with its size and elaborate decorations. Nearby lies **Lindow Man,** an Iron Age Celt apparently sacrificed in a gruesome ritual and preserved in a peat bog. The **Money Gallery** is next door, tracing finance from cowrie shells to credit cards.

MEDIEVAL GALLERIES. The **Sutton Hoo Ship Burial,** an Anglo-Saxon ship buried (and subsequently dug up) in Suffolk complete with an unknown king, is the centerpiece of the Medieval galleries. Other fascinating highlights of these allegedly dark ages include a display of clocks and the elaborately carved 800-year-old ivory **Lewis Chessmen.**

ORIENTAL COLLECTIONS. The majority of the museum's Oriental Collections resides in Gallery 33. The gallery's eastern half is dedicated to the Chinese collection, renowned for its ancient Shang bronzes and fine porcelains, and the western half is filled by Indian and Southeast Asian exhibits, which include the largest collection of Indian religious sculpture outside of India. Upstairs, the collection continues with a series of three galleries displaying Japanese and Korean artifacts, paintings, and calligraphy. Downstairs by the Montague St. entrance, don't miss the **Islamic art gallery** with its tiles, ceramics and other treasures from all over the Muslim world.

NATIONAL GALLERY

🚪*Trafalgar Sq., WC2. ☎ 7747 2885; www.nationalgallery.org.uk. Tube: Charing Cross, Leicester Sq., or Piccadilly Circus. Mid-May to Sept., a free Art Bus shuttles between the National Gallery, the Tate Britain, and the Tate Modern (every 30min. 10am-6pm). Tours start from the Sainsbury Wing info desk daily at 11:30am and 2:30pm and W 6:30pm; tours for the visually impaired 3rd Sa of month 11:30am; British sign language tour 1st Sa of month 11:30am. Audio guides covering almost every work available at main entrance and Sainsbury Wing foyer; voluntary donation requested. Orange St. and Sainsbury Wing entrances are wheelchair accessible. Open Th-Tu 10am-6pm, W 10am-9pm. Main galleries free; additional charge for some exhibitions.*

The National Gallery maintains one of the world's finest collections of Western art from the Middle Ages to the end of the 19th century, divvied up chronologically among four distinct wings. You could spend days ambling through the maze of galleries; if you're pressed for time and know what you want to see, the high-tech **Micro Gallery,** in the Sainsbury wing, will guide you through the collection on-line and print out a personalized tour of the paintings you want to see.

SAINSBURY WING. The newest part of the National Gallery holds the oldest part of the collection. Designed by postmodernist Philadelphian Robert Venturi, the new wing attracted the wrath of Prince Charles, who famously described it as a "monstrous carbuncle on the face of a much-loved and elegant friend." Whatever your opinion of its external appearance, inside the spotlight is on the art; arches and columns are used to emphasize paintings such as Botticelli's *Venus and Mars*, Raphael's *Crucifixion*, and da Vinci's famous *Virgin of the Rocks*, just some of the gallery's mostly devotional works created between 1260 and 1510. Although Van Eyck's *Arnolfini Marriage* appears to be a depiction of a medieval "shotgun wedding," the bride is merely holding up the hem of her dress as per the style of the day. More mystery surrounds the mysterious figures reflected in the mirror—many believe one of them to be Van Eyck himself.

WEST AND NORTH WINGS. Paintings from 1510 to 1600 are found in the **West Wing** left of the Trafalgar Sq. entrance. Here you can admire the mastery of contrast in Titian's *Bacchus and Ariadne* and El Greco's stormy *Adoration of the Name of Jesus.* Hans Holbein's *The Ambassadors* contains a cunning blob that resolves itself into a skull when viewed from the right. The **North Wing** contains 17th-century Italian, Spanish, Dutch, Flemish and French paintings, among them Caravaggio's *Christ Appearing to St. Peter* and Rubens' *Le Chapeau de paille.* The North Wing is also home to no less than 12 Rembrandts; the *Self portrait at the age of 34* and famous *Self portrait at the age of 63* make a fascinating contrast. Elsewhere, placid Poussin landscapes are routed by the unabashed romanticism of Caravaggio and Velázquez. Van Dyck's *Equestrian Portrait of Charles I* headlines the State Portrait room.

EAST WING. The East Wing, to the right of the main entrance, is devoted to painting from 1700 to 1900, including a strong English collection. In summer, the curtains are drawn and lights dimmed to allow the works to be viewed in natural sunlight. Many of the paintings seem to acquire a special luminosity, such as Turner's *Rain, Steam, and Speed* (note the tiny jackrabbit running alongside the train). Gainsborough's tight *Mr. and Mrs. Andrews* and Constable's rustic *The Hay Wain* whet the appetite before the Impressionists clamor for attention. Famous works by the world's favorite movement include a number of Monet's near-abstract water lilies, Cézanne's *Old Woman with Roses,* and Rousseau's rainswept *Tropical Storm with a Tiger.*

EXHIBITIONS AND SPECIAL EVENTS. The National Gallery holds frequent special exhibitions in the basement galleries of the Sainsbury Wing, for which there is generally an admission charge. Wondering how the Gallery supports free entry and audio guides? Just come and see the masses paying to see *Impression: Painting quickly in France 1860-1890* from Nov. 1, 2000, to Jan. 28, 2001. Other exhibitions in 2001 include: *Berlin's National Gallery: Paintings for Germany, 1812-1914,* Mar.7-May 13; *Vermeer and the Delft School,* June 20-Sept. 16; and *Pisanello,* Oct. 24-Jan. 13, 2001. The Gallery also screens free films about art and holds afternoon lecture series; call for schedules and details, or check the website. Should hunger pangs strike amid the masterpieces, you can choose between splashing out at **Crivelli's** (☎ 77472869), a fancy Mediterranean-inspired restaurant in the Sainsbury wing, or the more egalitarian **Prêt-à-Manger,** in the basement of the same building; both are open during gallery hours until about 30min. before closing.

NATIONAL PORTRAIT GALLERY

⚐ *St. Martin's Pl., WC2, just opposite St.-Martin's-in-the-Fields.* ☎ *7306 0055, recorded info* ☎ *7312 2463; www.npg.org.uk. Tube: Charing Cross or Leicester Sq. Frequent free daytime lectures. Evening lectures Th 7pm (£3, concessions £2); concerts F 7pm (mostly free). Most events take place in the Ondaatke lecture theatre. Orange St. entrance is wheelchair accessible. Audioguide, including interviews with artists and sitters, available in entrance hall; suggested donation £3, ID or credit card deposit required. Open M-W 10am-6pm, Th-F 10am-9pm, Sa-Su 10am-6pm. Free, excluding temporary exhibits.*

This unofficial Who's Who in Britain began in 1856 as "the fulfillment of a patriotic and moral ideal"—namely to showcase Britain's most officially noteworthy citizens. The museum's declared principle of looking "to the celebrity of the person represented, rather than to the merit of the artist" does not seem to have affected the quality of the works displayed. Portraits by Reynolds, Lawrence, Holbein, Sargent, and Gainsborough that have stared up from countless history books segue easily into Warhol's depictions of Queen Elizabeth II and Elizabeth Taylor, Annie Leibovitz's classic photos of John Lennon and Yoko Ono, and Lucien Freud's compellingly tweaked self-portrait.

The sleek new Ondaatje wing opened in May 2000, providing a suite of climate-controlled top-floor rooms for the oldest paintings. The Elizabethan portraits hang in a room modelled after a Tudor long gallery; the dark walls and dramatic fiber-optic backlighting highlight pictures such as William Scrot's astonishing distorted-perspective portrait of Edward VI, designed to be viewed from an extreme angle. Following the chronologically-ordered display down and around is a study in British history, from the War of the Roses (Yorks and Lancasters), to the Civil War (Cromwell and his buddies), to the American Revolution (George Washington), to imperial days (Florence Nightingale). In the twentieth century display the importance of pop culture makes itself felt; in the balcony gallery, dedicated to mid-to-late 20th century, Paul McCartney, Joan Collins, and footballer George Best jostle for space with Princess Diana, Baronness Thatcher, and Philip Larkin. Painters Lucien Freud and Graham Sutherland provide a postmodern twist with their self-portraits. The Gallery normally commissions three new portraits a year; new backs against the wall for 2000 include stage director and physician Jonathan Miller, author Doris Lessing, and tycoon Richard Branson.

Tate

The gallery often mounts temporary displays. Forthcoming exhibitions include the *John Kobal Photographic Portrait Award* show, Sept. 28, 2000 to Jan. 7, 2001 (free), and *Painting the Century.* Oct. 26, 2000 to Feb. 7, 2001 (£5, concessions £4). The annual British Petroleum Portrait Award brings out a selection of works from England's most promising portrait artists (June-Oct.).

TATE BRITAIN

🚩*Millbank, SW1 (☎ 7887 8008, recorded info ☎ 7887 8000; information@tate.org.uk; www.tate.org.uk) Tube: Pimlico. Museum tour M-F 12:30pm, Sa 3pm; Turner collection tour M-F 11:30am. Audio tour £3, concessions £2. Touch tours available for visually impaired visitors; call ☎ 7887 8725. Shop open M-Sa 10:30am-5:40pm, Su 10am-5:40pm. Café open daily 10:30am-5:30pm; Espresso Bar daily 10am-5:30pm. Restaurant, a swanky setting for a pricey lunch, open M-Sa noon-3pm and Su noon-4:30pm; AmEx, MC, V. Museum open daily 10am-5:50pm. Free.*

Tate Modern

The Tate gallery opened in 1897 to display contemporary British art. In time, the museum collection expanded to include modern art from all over the world, and a significant stash of older British paintings. With the opening of the new Tate Modern (see below), the original Tate has now been renamed the Tate Britain, and holds a superb collection of British works from the 16th century to the present day.

The collection starts with a room at the far end of the gallery devoted to 16th- and 17th-century painting. The parade of Constables includes the famous views of Salisbury Cathedral, and a number of Hampstead scenes dotted with red saddle splashes. George Stubbs's landscapes and sporting scenes lead to Gainsborough's landscapes and Reynolds' portraits. Don't miss the visionary works of William Blake, or the haunting images of Sir John Everett Millais, a founder of the Pre-Raphaelite Brotherhood. His *Ophelia* and Waterhouse's *The Lady of Shallot* are infamous women whom crowds admire.

Inside National Gallery

The Tate's chronologically ordered displays have been supplemented by thematic arrangements. "Representing Britain 1500-2000" combines works to explore "Literature & Fantasy," "Public & Private," "Home & Abroad," and "Artists & Models." There are also rooms devoted to individual artists; works by Gainsborough, Hockney, Wright of Derby, Sickert, and Blake are all highlighted. The chronologically grouped part of the collection offers a clear perspective on the development of British art, from early landscapes and portraits through Victorian, Pre-Raphaelite, and Impressionist paintings.

The Tate's 300-work J.M.W. Turner collection, the world's largest, resides in the neighboring **Clore Gallery.** Architect Sir James Stirling designed the annex to allow natural light to illuminate both the serenity of *Peace—Burial at Sea* and the raging brushstrokes of gale-swept ocean scenes. The collection covers all of Turner's career, from early, dreamy landscapes such as Chevening Park to the later visionary works. Also part of the Clore Gallery is a collection of Constable works.

Tate Britain's Centenary Development will increase the size of the gallery by 35% when completed in 2001, providing four new galleries to display the 3470 pieces of British art held by the museum and six new exhibition galleries for temporary displays.

TATE MODERN

🛱*Sumner St., Bankside (☎ 7887 8000; www.tate.org.uk) Tube: Southwark. Mid-May to Sept., a free Art Bus shuttles between the National Gallery, the Tate Britain, and the Tate Modern (every 30min. 10am-6pm). Daily highlights tours: 10:30am "History/Memory/Society" (Level 5); 11:30am "Nude/Body/Action" (Level 5), 2:30pm "Landscape/Matter/Environment" (Level 3), 3:30pm "Still Life/Object/Real Life" (Level 3). Call for schedule of special talks. All tours and talks free. Audioguide £1. Wheelchair access; you can reserve on of 6 wheelchairs at ☎ 7887 8888. Guide dogs welcome. Open Su-Th 10am-6pm, F-Sa 10pm-10pm. Cafe 7 open until 11pm F-Sa. Free; admission charged to some exhibitions.*

Some might call it instant karma. Where other millennium projects struggled to pull in the crowds, the Tate became an instant landmark and the crowning glory of the revitalized South Bank area upon its opening in May 2000. Crowds snaked around London's first large-scale museum dedicated entirely to modern art, housed in a stunning converted power station designed by Giles Gilbert Scott. The Swiss firm Herzog and de Meuron renovated the building and have turned the old turbine room into an immense toplit cavern 155m long and 35m high while preserving the old power station's industrial feel. On seeing the amount of art displayed in the vast expanses of the Bankside space, it's hard to believe all these were once crammed into the Tate Britain.

Despite the fanfare that greeted its opening, Tate Modern has taken some flak for its controversial curatorial method, which groups works thematically instead of chronologically. The permanent collection is divided into four major sections ("Landscape/Matter/Environment," "Still Life/Object/Real Life," "History/Memory/Society," and "Nude/Action/Body"), spread over floors 3 and 5, with floor 4 dedicated to temporary exhibits. For instance, in the "Desire for Order" room in the Still Life/Object/ Real Life section, Cezanne's more conventional *Still Life with Water Jug* shares the room with Carl Andre's 1970s low-form sculpture *Steel Zinc Plain*. And while Auguste Rodin's *The Kiss* sculpture puts on a public display of affection outside Nude/Action/Body section, the room next door contains a series of harsh, flat Nan Goldin photographs.

Whatever you think about the way it's arranged, there's no doubt that the Tate now has the space to put more of its collection on display. The third floor alone has Marcel Duchamps's *Fountain*, Roy Lichtenstein's *Bull Profile Series: Bull I-VI*, and Jackson Pollock's hyperactive *Summertime 9a*, while the fifth holds Andy Warhol's *Marilyn Diptych* and Picasso's *Weeping Woman*. Brit Art is also fairly well represented, with Bridget Riley, Sam Taylor-Wood, and Steve McQueen getting whole rooms to themselves. And of course, there's a plethora of works that will invoke the usual "is that art?" response: the slashed canvas of Fontana's *Spatial Concept*, the pure blue canvas of Yves Klein's *IKB 79*, and Carl Andre's *Equivalent VIII*, an innocuous-looking cuboid grouping of 120 bricks that sparked a major controversy in the 1970s when the Tate spent a few hundred thousand pounds on it.

Perhaps the best rooms are the ones that exploit their height and size. Two of these are in the Landscape/Matter/Environment section. The Mark Rothko room in the center of the section presents the artist's works in a dimly lit and meditative space. Nearby, the Richard Long and Claude Monet room cleverly contrasts Richard Long's *Waterfall Line*, a huge wall covering made in 2000 that captures all the energy and the fury of a waterfall, with Monet's famous *Waterlilies*, painted 84 years ago.

VICTORIA AND ALBERT

◨*Cromwell Rd. (☎ 7942 2000; www.vam.ac.uk). Tube: South Kensington. Wheelchair users should use the side entrance on Exhibition Rd and call ahead (☎ 7942 2000). 1hr. tours meet at the Cromwell St info desk daily 12:30, 1:30, 2:30 and 3:30pm, Tu-Su also 10:30 and 11:30am; free. Open M-Su 10am-5:45pm plus W 6:30-9:30pm. £5, seniors £3; free for students, disabled, and under 15; free for everyone 4:30-5:45pm. Night openings (select galleries only) £3. Season ticket for all 3 South Kensington museums (the V&A, the Science, and the Natural History) £29, two adults £49.50, students £16.*

Museum of London

The V&A is one of the most enchanting museums in London and one of the finest museums of decorative arts and design in the world. Its 5 million square meters of galleries house the best collection of Italian Renaissance sculpture outside Italy, the largest collection of Indian art outside India, and a fashion collection to satisfy any fashion fetish. The V&A supplements its vast collection with numerous temporary exhibitions.

Founded in 1852 to encourage excellence in art and design, the original curators were deluged with objects from around the world. The 150-odd galleries arrange items either by time and place or by material and style. The popular **dress collection** traces clothing fashions, focusing mainly on women's wear, from the 16th-century to the present.

The **Asian collections** are particularly formidable, and the Gallery of Indian Art contains splendid textiles, painting, Mughal jewelry and decor. Persian carpets and Moroccan rugs distinguish the V&A's collection of Islamic Art, the largest and most breathtaking piece of which is the Persian Ardabil carpet. The elegant Gallery of Chinese Art divides its 5000 years of Chinese art into six categories—Eating and Drinking, Living, Worship, Ruling, Collecting, and Burial. Nearby, the Japanese gallery displays elaborate armor and intriguing contemporary sculpture, and the Korean gallery recognizes the depth and longevity of Korean culture.

National Gallery

The **European collections** are just as impressive. The Medieval Treasury, in the center of the ground floor, features vestments, plates, stained glass, and illuminations. Galleries 46A-B appear to be glorious collections of Western art, with Michaelangelo's *David* and a 24m Roman column crammed into the same space. Sadly, these are merely plaster cast reproductions, part of a 19th-century movement to place casts of great Western art in European cities for the benefit of the masses.

Among the upstairs collections you'll find the **silver, stained glass,** and the heavily-protected **jewelry** galleries. Galleries 70-74 exhibit 20th-century **design,** with some emphasis on chairs, typefaces (including Johnston Sans Serif, the omnipresent London Transport font), and packaging. Salvador Dali's luscious *Mae West's Lips* sofa (1936) sits here. The **Frank Lloyd Wright Gallery** shows designs by the architect, including the interior of the Kauffmann Office, originally commissioned for

Antiquities Collection

a Pittsburgh department store. On the same floor, the **Gallery of Photography** traces the history of photography and displays famous snaps.

If you really must look at painting, John Constable's prodigious collection of weather studies resides on the Floor 6 of the **Henry Cole Wing.** For those with smaller tastes, galleries 406 showcases English and Continental portrait **miniatures,** including Holbein's *Anne of Cleves* and *Elizabeth I.*

There are various less conventional ways to see the museum. On Sundays, the New Restaurant hosts a jazz brunch, with live music accompanying either an English breakfast or lunch. Late View, late night openings on most summer Wednesdays and occasional Fridays, feature lectures, live performances, guest DJs, and a bar.

OTHER MUSEUMS

Bank of England Museum, Threadneedle St, EC2 (☎7601 5545). Tube: Bank. Entrance on Bartholomew Ln., left off Threadneedle St. In the Bank of England itself, this museum traces the Bank's history from its 1694 foundation. Includes notes, gold bars, and muskets once used to defend the bank. Open M-F 10am-5pm. Free.

Bethnal Green Museum of Childhood, Cambridge Heath Rd., E2 (☎8980 3204). Tube: Bethnal Green. Colorful toy-store entrance leads into elegant Victorian warehouse full of toys. Pay 20p to activate an automaton that graphically displays "what little boys are made of" and recounts what follows in therapy years later. Open M-Th and Sa 10am-5:50pm, Su 2:30-5:50pm. Free.

Bramah Tea and Coffee Museum, The Clove Building, Maguire St, Butlers Wharf, SE1 (☎7378 0222). Tube: Tower Hill or London Bridge, or DLR: Tower Gateway. A highly educational, refreshingly straightforward collection whose holdings include many tea and coffee plants themselves, some elegant espresso machines, and an engrossing collection of novelty teapots. Open daily 10am-6pm. £4, concessions £3, families £10.

British Library, 96 Euston Rd., NW1 (tel. 412 7332). Tube: King's Cross/St. Pancras or Euston. This red brick building beside St. Pancras station is a modern, airy home to Britain's national books collection of over 180 million works. While the reading rooms are not open to the public, you can still enjoy the excellent exhibits downstairs. In the manuscript area, the English Literature displays contain parchments of *Beowulf* (c. 1000) and the *Canterbury Tales* (1410), as well as works by Jonson, Jane Austen, Elizabeth Barrett Browning, James Joyce, Virginia Woolf, Philip Larkin, and others. Tours M, W, F 3pm, Tu 6:30pm, Sa 10:30am and 3pm, and Su 11:30, 4pm; £5, concessions £4. Book in advance. Open M and W-F 9:30am-6pm, Tu 9:30am-8pm, Sa 9:30am-5pm, Su 11am-5pm. Free.

Cabinet War Rooms, Clive Steps, King Charles St, SW1 (☎7930 6961). Tube: Westminster. Churchill ran a nation at war from these underground rooms. A free audioguide leads you through the room where he made his famous wartime broadcasts and points out the transatlantic hotline disguised as a loo. Open daily Apr.-Sept. 9:30am-6pm; Oct.-Mar. 10am-6pm. Last entrance 5:15pm. £5, concession £3.60, under 16 free, disabled reduced price.

Commonwealth Institute, Kensington High St., W8 (☎7603 4535; www.commonwealth.org.uk). Tube: High St. Kensington. This offering to the end of Empire has a well-regarded gallery celebrating the 53 Commonwealth states' histories and culture. Tu-Su 10am-5pm. Free.

Design Museum, Butlers Wharf, SE1 (☎7403 6933; www.designmuseum.org). Tube: London Bridge. Dedicated to classics of culture and industry, with everything from cars to underwear. Half the space is devoted to excellent changing exhibitions. Open daily 11:30am-6pm, last entry 5:30pm. £5.50, students £4.50, under 16 and over 60 £4, families £15.

Freud Museum, 20 Maresfield Gardens (☎7435 2002; www.freud.org.uk). Tube: Hampstead. The museum preserves his study, which includes the infamous analytic couch he brought from Vienna, and his "old and dirty gods" (Freud's description of his collection of antiquities), including the Gradiva frieze. Among the permanent articles on display is Dalí's portrait of Freud; the museum also hosts temporary exhibitions. Open W-Su noon-5pm. £4, concessions £2, under 12 free. Children over 12 can blame it on their parents.

Geffrye Museum, Kingsland Rd, E2 (☎7739 9893; www.geffrye-museum.org.uk). Tube: Old St. then bus #243, or Tube: Liverpool St, then bus #242 or 149. Set in a large former poorhouse founded by 17th-century Lord Mayor Sir Robert Geffrye, the museum traces the history of English interior design from Elizabethan times to the loft conversions of the 1990s. The items on display, taken from houses all over London (including a whole staircase), are set up in a series of intriguing rooms designed to show what a typical middle-class person's house would have looked like. Excellent temporary exhibits. Wheelchair accessible. Open Tu-Sa 10am-5pm, Su noon-5pm. Free.

Guildhall Clock Museum, Guildhall Yard, off Gresham St; enter through the library entrance on Aldermanbury (☎ 7606 3030). Tube: St. Paul's or Bank. A tiny museum bearing over 500 years of clocks, watches, chronometers, and sundials. Includes a watch that belonged to Mary Queen of Scots, and one worn by Sir Edmund Hillary when he climbed Mt. Everest. Open M-F 9:30am-4:45pm.

Horniman Museum, London Rd, SE23 (☎ 8699 1872). Rail: Forest Hill (12 min. from Victoria) or buses #176, 185, 63. An extraordinary collection, brought together by the kleptomania of 19th-century tea merchant Frederick Horniman. A flood of lottery money made 2000 a year primarily for renovation. A new gallery, African Worlds, brims with anthropological treasures. An aquarium, formal garden, and small zoo are attached. Open M-Sa 10:30am-5:30pm, Su 2-5:30pm. Free.

Imperial War Museum, Lambeth Rd, SE1 (☎ 7416 5000). Tube: Lambeth North or Elephant and Castle. Gripping exhibits illuminate aspects of two world wars. The Blitz and Trench Experiences recreate every detail (even smells); veterans and victims speak through telephone handsets. In 2000, the museum opened a new wing dedicated entirely to the Holocaust. Wheelchair accessible. Open daily 10am-6pm. £5.20, students £4.20, ages 16 and under free. Free 4:30-6pm.

The Jewish Museum, Camden, 129-131 Albert St, NW1 (☎ 7284 1997). Tube: Camden Town. This elegant museum contains a collection of antiques and paintings documenting the history of Britain's Jewish community. It also displays objects relating to Judaism, including a magnificent 16th-century synagogue ark. Wheelchair accessible. Open Su-Th 10am-4pm. £3, seniors £2, students and children £1.50, families £7.50. MC, V.

London Dungeon, 28-34 Tooley St, SE1 (☎ 7403 0606). Tube: London Bridge. Plague, decomposition, and anything else remotely connected to horror and Britain thrown in for effect. New in 2000 is "Firestorm! 1666," a look at the Great Fire of London. Reserve at least 2hr. ahead, not including the queue, to get in. Open daily Apr.-Sept. 10am-5:30pm; Nov.-Feb. 10am-5pm; last entrance 1hr. before close. £9.95; students £8.50; under 14, seniors, and disabled £6.50.

⬛ **London Transport Museum,** Covent Garden, WC2 (☎ 7379 6344, recorded info ☎ 7565 7299). Tube: Covent Garden. Exhibits provide a thought-provoking cultural history: see how the expansion of the transportation system fed the growth of suburbs. You can endanger the lives of scores of cyber-commuters as you take the helm of a virtual subway train. A fabulous place for kids. Wheelchair accessible. Open M-Th and Sa-Su 10am-6pm, F 11am-6pm, last admission 5:15pm. £4.95, concessions £2.95, families £12.85, under 5 free. MC, V.

Madame Tussaud's, Marylebone Rd, NW1 (☎ (0870) 400 3000; www.madame-tussauds.com). Tube: Baker St. The classic waxwork museum, founded by an *emigré* aristocrat who manufactured life-size models of French nobility who met their demise at the guillotine. Figures are disconcertingly lifelike, with a tendency towards being flattering (see Bogart) with some exceptions (see Prince Charles). To avoid the horrific queues, call ahead and book a ticket. Alternatively, form a group with at least 9 fellow sufferers and use the group entrance, or go either when they first open or in the late afternoon. Open summer daily 9am-5:30pm (last admission); rest of year opens 1hr. later. £11.50, seniors £9, children £8; combined entry with Planetarium (see below) £13.95, £10.80, £9.30. 50p credit-card fee for advance bookings.

⬛ **Museum of London,** 150 London Wall, EC2 (☎ 7600 3699, 24hr. info ☎ 7600 0807; info@museum-london.org.uk). Tube: St. Paul's or Barbican. Comprehensive is an understatement: this fabulously engrossing museum tells the story of the metropolis from its origins as Londinium up through the present day. The fast-changing Capital Concerns gallery displays a series of short exhibits looking at what's new in London. Free historical lectures W-F; check for times. Wheelchair accessible. Open Tu-Sa 10am-5:50pm, Su noon-5:50pm, last admission 5:30pm. £5, concessions £3, under 17 free.

National Army Museum, Royal Hospital Rd, SW3 (☎ 7730 0717; www.national-armymuseum.ac.uk). Tube: Sloane Sq. or Bus #239. This 4-story concrete block charts the history of the army in Britain, emphasizing the personal side of soldiering. The displays, while somewhat confusingly laid out, are fairly engrossing. Most are chronological, starting from "Redcoats" and ending at "The Modern Army." The expected assortment of weapons and medals are on display, as are, more interestingly, numerous models (including a WWI trench), and random artifacts like the skeleton of Marengo, Napoleon's favorite horse. Sadly, the skeleton is hoofless—some 19th-century entrepreneur had them made into snuff boxes. Open daily 10am-5:30pm. Free.

National Maritime Museum, Romney Rd., Greenwich, SE10 (☎ 8858 4422). Rail: Greenwich or DLR: Island Gardens and use the pedestrian foot tunnel under the Thames. The museum's loving documentation of the history of British sea power will have even the staunchest land-lubber swearing allegiance to Admiral Nelson. Open daily 10am-5pm, last admission 4:30pm. Admission £7.50, concessions £6, children under 16 free.

Natural History Museum, Cromwell Rd, SW7 (☎ 7942 5000; www.nhm.ac.uk). Tube: South Kensington. As the gaping and pointing indicate, there's something about huge dinosaur fossils that awakens your sense of wonder, whatever your age. The Natural History Museum, displays such awe-inspiring fossils in its **Life Galleries.** The superb Mammals section contains models of pygmy antelopes, pink fairy armadillos, and other lesser-spotted mammals, as well as a gasp-inducing blue whale. The **Earth Galleries,** near the Exhibition Rd entrance, focus on the history of the planet. "The Power Within" simulates being in an earthquake or a volcanic eruption. Wheelchair accessible. Open M-Sa 10am-5:50pm, Su 11am-5:50pm. £7.50, students £4.50, seniors and under 17 free; free for everyone M-F 4:30-5:50pm, Sa-Su 5-5:50pm. Season ticket for all 3 South Kensington museums (the V&A, the Science, and the Natural History) £29, two adults £49.50, students £16. AmEx, MC, V.

London Planetarium, Marylebone Rd, NW1 (☎ (0870) 400 3000). Tube: Baker St. Next to Madame Tussaud's, under a distinctive green dome. Ride the Space Trail through a model universe and watch a Star Show. £6.30, seniors £4.85 children £4.20; combined with Madame Tussaud's £13.95, £10.80, £9.30.

Pollock's Toy Museum, 1 Scala St. (entrance on Whitfield St.), W1 (☎ 7636 3452). Tube: Goodge St. Housed above a modern toy shop in a maze of tiny, 18th-century rooms congested with antique playthings. Highlights include Eric, the oldest known teddy bear (b. 1905), and German "saucy Frauliens," who expose their britches at the tug of a string. Open M-Sa 10am-5pm, last admission 4:30pm. £3, under 18 £1.50.

Prince Henry's Room, 17 Fleet St, EC4 (☎ 7936 2710) Tube: Temple. Tiny upstairs museum with interesting collection of photos, letters and memorabilia from the likes of Samuel Pepys. Open M-Sa 11am-2pm. Free.

Royal Air Force Museum, Grahame Park Way, NW9 (☎ 8205 2266 or 8205 9191 for 24hr. information; www.rafmuseum.org.uk). Tube: Colindale. The RAF has converted this former WWI airbase into a hangarful of the country's aeronautic greatest hits. WWI Bristols, Korean War submarine hunters, Falkland War Tornados, and Gulf War footage display the dignified history of the RAF. Wheelchair accessible. Open daily 10am-6pm, last admission 5:30pm. £6.50, students and under 16 £3.25, family £16.60. MC, V.

Science Museum, Exhibition Rd, SW7 (☎ (0870) 870 4868; IMAX bookings ☎ (0870) 870 4771; disabled info ☎ 7942 4446; www.sciencemuseum.org.uk). Tube: South Kensington. A wonderland of planes, trains, and automobiles, with a few spaceships thrown in for good measure. "The Making of the Modern World" gallery displays numerous objects that have shaped modern life, from Stephenson's Rocket to the Pill. The original displays—covering areas of science as diverse as papermaking and nuclear physics—are fairly impressive, too. The huge space rockets and the hands-on Flight Lab, in particular, hold their own against the new additions. The perfect place for children to run free, with numerous exhibits geared toward the under 12 sector. Trekkers will flock to the *Star Trek: Federation Science* exhibition, running until April 22, 2001. Wheelchair accessible. Open daily 10am-6pm. £6.95, including IMAX £12, including IMAX and "virtual voyages" £15; students £3.50, £8, £10; under 16 free, seniors £5.75, disabled £7.75; family pass (including IMAX, "virtual voyages," and guidebook) £43. Free for everyone 4:30-6pm. Season ticket for all 3 South Kensington museums (the V&A, the Science, and the Natural History) £29, two adults £49.50, students £16.

Sir John Soane's Museum, 13 Lincoln's Inn Fields, WC2 (☎ 7405 2107). Tube: Holborn. A must-see: Soane was an architect's architect, but the idiosyncratic home he designed for himself will intrigue even laypersons. His use of perspective and the narrow, labyrinthine hallways, coupled with strategically placed mirrors, are delightfully disorienting. Artifacts on display include fold-out walls covered with Hogarth paintings, the massive Egyptian sarcophagus of Seti I, and casts of famous buildings and sculptures from around the world. Open Tu-Sa 10am-5pm. Tours (£3; restricted to 22 people) leave Sa 2:30pm; tickets sold from 2pm on day of tour. Free.

Sherlock Holmes Museum, 239 Baker St (marked "221b"), W1 (☎7738 1269). Tube: Baker St. Students of Holmes's deductive method will be intrigued by the museum's meticulous recreation of his storied lodgings. Upstairs is a display of "artifacts" from the stories, and wax replicas of key plot moments. Open daily 9:30am-6pm. £6, children £4.

Museum of St. Bartholomew's Hospital, through the main hospital entrance on West Smithfield (☎7601 8033). Tube: Barbican or St. Paul's. Bart's, as the hospital is affectionately known, has existed in some form since 1123, when an Augustinian monk built both the hospital and the nearby church of St. Bartholomew the Great (see p. 57). The tiny museum details the history of the hospital, including material on William Harvey, who discovered the circulation of the blood while serving as a physician there in the 17th century. On the Grand Staircase to the Great Hall hang two huge, impressive Hogarth paintings (the artist was born in nearby Bartholomew Close); for a close up of the paintings and the hall, you'll have to go on the tour. Also in the hospital grounds is the church of **St. Bartholomew-the-Less,** mostly an 1820s restoration. Tours, which also take in the Smithfield area, meet at the hospital entrance; F 2pm; £4, concessions £3. Open Tu-F 10am-4pm. Free.

British Museum

Theatre Museum, 1E Tavistock St, WC2 (☎7836 7891, box office ☎7836 2330). Tube: Covent Garden. This branch of the V&A contains Britain's richest holding of theatrical memorabilia, although that makes it sound much stuffier than it really is. Theater models are exhibited, and other stage-related arts such as ballet, opera, puppetry, the circus and rock music play supporting roles. Plenty of interactive puppet-fun—kids dig it! Wheelchair accessible. Open Tu-Su 11am-6pm, last admission 5:30pm. £4.50, concessions £2.50, under 16 and over 60 free. AmEx, MC, V.

Winston Churchill's Britain at War, 64-66 Tooley St, SE1 (☎7403 3171; www.britain-at-war-co.uk). Tube: London Bridge. Macabre and sometimes mawkish reconstruction of underground life in London during the Blitz. Open Apr.-Sept. 10am-5:30pm, last entry 5pm; Oct.-Mar. daily 10am-4:30pm, last entry 4pm. £5.95, concessions £3.95, under 16 £2.95, families £14.

Royal Academy of Art

OTHER GALLERIES

Bankside Gallery, 48 Hopton St, SE1. Tube: Blackfriars. Across the river from St. Paul's is the home of the Royal Watercolour Society and the Royal Society of Printmakers. Both run rotating exhibits of contemporary and not-so-contemporary members' work. Surprisingly, not a denizen of gauzy paintings of wildlife, but a melange of landscapes, London scenes, and not-quite-heavy hitters. Open Tu 10am-8pm, W-F 10am-5pm, Sa-Su 1-5pm. £3.50, concessions £2.

Brunei Gallery, Thorhaugh St (☎7898 4915; www.soas.ac.uk/brunei). Tube: Russell Sq. Administered by the University of London's School of Oriental and African Studies, the Brunei showcases exhibitions of Asian and African art. Open M-F 10:30am-5pm. Free.

Inside National Gallery

The Courtauld Gallery, Somerset House, the Strand, WC2 (☎7848 2526), Tube: Temple, Embankment, Charing Cross. This intimate 11-room gallery in Somerset House is an ideal place to see some world-famous masterpieces, mostly Impressionist and post-Impressionist works. Holds periodic free lectures; call for info. Wheelchair accessible. Open M-Sa 10am-6pm, Su 2pm-6pm. £4, concessions £2; M half-price.

Crafts Council, 44a Pentonville Rd (☎7278 7700; www.craftscouncil.org.uk). Tube: Angel. The refurbished 19th-century Claremont Chapel now houses Britain's national organization for the promotion of contemporary pottery, textiles, and printing. The council sponsors fantastic temporary exhibitions in the Gallery. Wheelchair accessible. Open Tu-Sa 11am-6pm, Su 2-6pm. Free.

Dulwich Picture Gallery, Gallery Rd, SE21 (☎8693 5254 or 8693 8000 for recorded information; www.dulwichpictuegalery.org.uk). Tube: Brixton and take bus P4 to the door. This eccentric gallery, designed by Sir John Soane, is definitely worth the trip. English Portraiture and Dutch landscapes, including Gainsborough, Reynolds, and Rembrandt. Open Tu-F 10am-5pm, Sa-Su 11am-5pm. £4, seniors £3, children and students free; free for everyone F.

The Estorick, 39a Canonbury Sq.; entrance on Canonbury Rd (☎7704 9522; www.estorickcollection.com). Tube: Highbury and Islington. The Esoterick, housed in Northampton Lodge, is a remarkable collection of modern Italian art. Particularly strong on Italian Futurists, with several paintings by Giacomo Balla and Gino Severini. Among the non-Futurist paintings are a number of Amadeo Modiglianis. Also exhibits long-term loans from other private collections, including an exhibit on Futurism and photography from Jan.-Apr. 2001. Limited wheelchair access. Open W-Sa 11am-6pm.

Hayward Gallery, at Royal Festival Hall, Belvedere Rd, SE1 (☎7960 4242, or recorded info ☎7261 0127; www.sbc.org.uk). Tube: Waterloo. High-powered exhibitions of 20th-century art. Open daily 10am-6pm, Tu-W until 8pm. Around £6, concessions £4, under 12 free with adult.

Institute of Contemporary Arts (ICA), the Mall, SW1 (☎7930 3647, recorded info 7930 6393). Tube: Charing Cross. Vigorous outpost of avant-garde visual and performance art. 3 temporary galleries, a cinema featuring first-run independent films (£6.50, concessions £5), experimental space for film and video, and a theater. Annual membership (£25, concessions £15), gives free entry, invitations to gallery openings, and prebooking for films and events. The sleek cafe/bar is often host to live music from up-and-coming bands. Box office open daily noon-8:30pm. Bar open Tu-Sa noon-1am, 5:30-10:30pm M-Su. Galleries open Su-Th noon-7:30pm, F noon-7:30pm. M-F £1.50, concessions £1; Sa-Su £2.50, £1.50.

The Iveagh Bequest, Kenwood House, Hampstead Lane, NW3 (☎8348 1286). Tube: Archway or Golders Green, then #210 to Kenwood. An impeccably maintained 18th-century Neoclassical Adams villa, beautifully located on the Kenwood Estate overlooking Hampstead Heath (see p. 94). Open daily mid-Apr. to Sept. 10am-6pm; Oct. to mid-Apr. 10am-4pm. Free.

Jerwood Space, 171 Union St, SE1. (☎7654 0171). Tube: Southwark. Taking its cues from the Saatchi Gallery (see below), this new venue focuses on the antics of the Young British Artists claque. Most famously, it displays contenders for the Jerwood Painting Prize (on show Sept.-Oct.). Open M-Sa 10am-6pm, Su noon-6pm.

Marlborough Fine Arts, 6 Albermarle St, (☎7629 5161). The biggest contemporary names are sold here. Open M-F 10am-5:30pm, Sa 10am-12:30pm.

October Gallery, 24 Old Gloucester St (☎7242 7367). Tube: Russell Sq. A small venue that mounts the works of international artists. Open Tu-Sa 12:30-5:30pm.

The Percival David Foundation of Chinese Art, 53 Gordon Sq. (☎7387 3909). Tube: Euston Sq., Euston, or Russell Sq. A trove of fabulously rare ceramics touts itself as the finest collection of Chinese ceramics outside China. Its impressive collection includes a blue and white wonderland of Ming ceramics on the second floor. Open M-F 10:30am-5pm. Free.

Royal Academy, Piccadilly, (☎7439 7438) Tube: Green Park. The academy hosts traveling exhibits of the highest order. The whopping annual summer exhibition (June-Aug.) is a London institution—the works of established and unknown contemporary artists festoon every square inch of wall space and all pieces are for sale (at non-budget prices). Open daily M-Sa 10am-6pm, Su 10am-8:30pm. Admission varies by exhibition; average £6, concessions £4. Advance tickets often necessary for popular exhibitions.

Royal Festival Hall Galleries, South Bank Centre, SE1 (☎7960 4242). Tube: Waterloo and follow the signs, or Embankment and cross the Hungerford footbridge. In what is essentially the lobby of the Royal Festival Hall (see p. 100), a display space for contemporary art exhibits. Photography and architecture are the focus. Open daily 10am-10:30pm. Free.

Saatchi Gallery, 98a Boundary Rd, NW8 (☎ 7624 8299). Tube: St. John's Wood or Kilburn Park, or bus #139 from Trafalgar Square or #189 from Oxford Circus. This is art. *This* is beauty! The holdings of enormously influential art-collector Charles Saatchi (he of the eponymous advertising firm). Hot modern art! Hot Young British Artists! Open Sept.-July Th-Su noon-6pm. £4, concessions £2, under 12s free; free for everyone Th.

◙ **Serpentine Gallery,** Off West Carriage Drive, in Kensington Gardens (☎ 7298 1501). Tube: Lancaster Gate. Londoners often rank the Serpentine among their favorite small galleries. The crisp white walls make the perfect space for the gallery's temporary displays of contemporary works. Open daily 10am-6pm. Free.

Special Photographer Company, 21 Kensington Park Rd, W11 (☎ 7221 3489; www.specialphotographers.com). Tube: Ladbroke Grove. Just as its name suggests, focuses on the special photographer deep within us all, ranging from contemporary art to historical exhibits, all of interest to the average person, not just art-a-holics. Open M-Th 10am-6pm, F 10am-5:30pm, Sa 11am-5pm.

Two10 Gallery, 210 Euston Rd, NW1 (☎ 7611 7211; www.wellcome.ac.uk). Tube: Euston or Euston Sq. Rotating exhibitions pertaining to medicine and science. Open M-F 9am-6pm. Free.

◙ **The Wallace Collection,** Hertford House, Manchester Sq., W1 (☎ 7935 0687; www.the-wallace-collection.org.uk). Tube: Bond St. This sumptuous collection was the product of years of acquisition by the 3rd and 4th Marquesses of Hertford and Sir Richard Wallace, the 4th Marquess's son. It holds Old Masters as well as 18th-century French painting and furniture. Outstanding works include Hals's *The Laughing Cavalier,* Velázquez's *Lady With a Fan,* Fragonard's *The Swing,* and Rubens' *Christ on the Cross.* Medieval buffs should note that the house is also home to London's largest armor and weaponry collection. Wheelchair accessible. Tours M-Sa 1pm, W 11:30am and 1pm, Th-F 1pm, Sa 11:30am, Su 3pm. Open M-Sa 10am-5pm, Su 2-5pm. Free.

◙ **Whitechapel Art Gallery,** Whitechapel High St., E1 (☎ 7377 7888). Tube: Aldgate East. The high-ceilinged and sunny galleries of the Whitechapel contain no permanent collection, but host some of Britain's (and the Continent's) most daring exhibitions of contemporary art. Wheelchair accessible. The gallery's hip cafe is open Tu and Th-Su 11am-4:30pm, W 11am-6:30pm. Gallery open Tu and Th-Su 11am-5pm, W 11am-8pm. Free.

Shopping

British imperialism in centuries past made London the ultimate crossroads of world trade. Today, products from all over the world are part of London's consumer economy, while the domestic product continues to be particularly strong on design. Serious shoppers might want to pick up either *Nicholson's Shopping Guide and Streetfinder* (£3) or *Time Out's Directory to London's Shops and Services* (£8). The London **sales** are anxiously awaited affairs involving substantial discounts on large portions of the merchandise as well as extended shopping hours. This is the time to pick up designer fashions at almost-reasonable prices. Most stores have both a winter and a summer sale, usually around **January** and **July;** check newspapers and listings magazines for details, and get to stores early. Tourists who have purchased over £50 worth of goods in one store should ask about getting a refund on the 17.5% VAT (see p. 261). Many stores may be closed on Sunday.

SHOPPING DISTRICTS

Oxford Street. Tube: Bond St., Oxford Circus, or Tottenham Court Rd. Double-decker buses packed end to end, as far as the eye can see, going nowhere fast. And if you thought that was clichéd, wait till you see the stores. Aside from venerable department stores like **Selfridges** and the occasional diversion, like the minimalist **Muji,** uninspiring chains and tourist tat predominate.

Regent Street. Tube: Oxford Circus or Piccadilly Circus. Behind the elegant storefronts and tall windows lie some of the city's oldest and best-known stores, including **Liberty's** and **Hamley's.**

Bond Street. Tube: Bond St. The heart of couture and unjustifiable excess. Old and New Bond St., extending south of Oxford St., are the most prestigious shop addresses in all of London. Here, the glitz of new money means the haughty restraint of old.

Jermyn Street. Tube: Piccadilly Circus or Green Park. The last refuge of the English gentleman, with conservative ties, well-turned shoes, expensive cigars, and fine spirits. Running parallel to Jermyn St., just north, is Piccadilly, home to **Fortnum & Mason** and several other luxury shops.

Knightsbridge. Tube: Knightsbridge. This famously upmarket shopping area is anchored by the city's most celebrated department stores, **Harvey Nichols** and **Harrods**. Sloane St., Knightsbridge, and Brompton Rd. radiate outward from the Tube station.

Kensington High Street. Tube: High St. Kensington. A fairly heterogeneous street at the southwest corner of Kensington Gardens offering a few boutiques, and a wealth of trendy chains.

Covent Garden. Tube: Covent Garden. The hottest proving ground for new designers, Covent Garden is filled with small boutiques vending off-the-wall fashion, as well as massive chains posing as small boutiques. The tamer clothing is what everyone will be wearing in a few years.

Bond Street. Tube: Bond St. The heart of couture and unjustifiable excess. Old and New Bond St., extending south of Oxford St., are the most prestigious shop addresses in all of London. Old Bond street is particularly glitzy—a cloudy Rodeo Drive.

King's Road. Tube: Sloane Sq. Extending west of chic Sloane Sq. (home to **Peter Jones** department store) until World's End, the busy King's Rd. is lined with small stores offering everything from high fashion to cheap knockoffs of American "fashion." The stores are generously interspersed with pubs and cafes. Buses #11, 19, and 22 go up and down the road.

Camden High Street. Tube: Camden Town. Giant, outrageously painted objects (Elvis!) outside can't hide the fact that there's often a sameness to the stores. Still, if you're looking for rebel wear, it's the place to go. Shops cater to the weekend market crowds (p. 141), with shoes, used jeans, leather jackets, and reasonably priced clubwear. That said, it's a good policy to compare the prices here with those at the chain stores in Oxford St. and Covent Garden before buying.

DEPARTMENT STORES

Harrods, 87-135 Brompton Rd., SW3 (☎7730 1234; www.harrods.com). Tube: Knightsbridge. Simply put, this is *the* store in London, perhaps in the world. Their humble motto is *Omnia omnibus ubique*: "All things to all people, everywhere" (presumably all rich people, that is). They can do everything from fit a saddle for your thoroughbred to sell you a Bosendorfer grand piano. English gentlemen keeping a stiff upper lip elsewhere dream of the Harrods food court. The sales (July and January) get so crazy that the police bring out a whole detail to deal with the shoppers. Open M-Tu and Sa 10am-6pm, W-F 10am-7pm. AmEx, DC, MC, V.

Harvey Nichols, 109-125 Knightsbridge, SW3 (☎7235 5000). Tube: Knightsbridge. The trendiest and most expensive of London's department stores. Cell phones ring at "Harvey Nick's" just as often as the registers. Known for interesting and avant-garde window displays that change frequently. Stupendous sale in early July. On the crowded top floor, a branch of Yo! Sushi and an upscale supermarket compete for space with a chic cafe (main courses from £10). Beautify yourself at the Aveda Salon (☎7201 8610) or eat steaming noodles at the downstairs Wagamama (☎7201 8000). Open M, T, Sa 10am-7pm, W-F 10am-8pm, Su noon-6pm. AmEx, DC, MC, V.

Liberty's of London, 210-220 Regent St., W1 (☎7734 1234; www.liberty-of-london.com). Tube: Oxford Circus. Home of the famous Liberty prints, from bolts of fabric to silk ties. Its Tudor Building is worth a wander, and playing dress-up in the hat department is much more acceptable here than at fayre Harrods. Great cosmetics department. Open M-W 10am-6:30pm, Th 10am-8pm, F-Sa 10am-7pm, Su noon-6pm. AmEx, DC, MC, V and most foreign currency.

Marks & Spencer, 458 Oxford St., W1 (☎7935 7954; www.marks-and-spencer.co.uk). Tube: Bond St. or Marble Arch. Also at hundreds of other locations. Brits know it as Marks & Sparks or M&S. Sells well-made in-house goods in a classy but value-conscious manner. The clothes err on the conservative side. Everyone British, including Tony Blair, buys underwear here. Also features a marvelous food department (sandwiches around £2; microwaveable meals £3-4) Open M-F 9am-8pm, Sa 9am-7pm, Su noon-6pm (weekend hours vary slightly). AmEx, MC, V.

Selfridges, 400 Oxford St. (☎7629 1234; www.selfridges.co.uk). Tube: Bond St. There's a reason their yellow shopping bags are ubiquitous around Oxford St.: Selfridges has *everything*. The neo-classical building's vast cosmetics department features every conceivable makeup brand from Bobbi Brown to Miss Mascara; the fashion departments, while not cheap, are extensive and trendy. A bureau de change and tourist office cater to foreign visitors, and 14 cafes and restaurants provide shopping-break sustenance. The food hall holds cheeses, meats, beautifully displayed fruit, a deli, a bakery, a branch of Yo! Sushi, and even an oyster bar. Watch for free samples. Will refund the difference on any item found for less elsewhere. Huge mid-July sale. Open M-W 10am-7pm, Th-F 10am-8pm, Sa 9:30am-7pm, Su noon-6pm. AmEx, DC, MC, V.

Fortnum & Mason, 181 Piccadilly, W1 (☎7734 8040; www.fortnumandmason.co.uk). Tube: Green Park or Piccadilly Circus. Famed for its sumptuous food hall, with liveried clerks, chandeliers, and fountains, occupying the entire ground floor. The upper floors carry clothing, jewelry, and shoes in a posh and sophisticated setting. Open M-Sa 9:30am-6pm. AmEx, DC, MC, V.

CLOTHING

In London you'll find everything from cheap street market clothing to designer boutiques. London's high street clothing chains are fairly adept at adaptations of catwalk styles, making it possible to get quality clothes at reasonable prices especially during **sale season** in January and July. In the past few years, London has made a concerted effort to have its fashion week before that of New York or Paris, trumping the traditional centers of fashion-forward thinking. London's fashion week takes place twice a year: September (for Spring/Summer collections) and March (Autumn/Winter collections). Check the website (www.londonfashionweek.com) for details on getting tickets to the shows, open to the public, which take place on the lawn of the Natural History Museum. *Let's Go* lists only the flagship stores of clothing chains, but if we say "numerous other branches," it's usually safe to assume that there are branches near **Oxford Street** or **Bond Street, Covent Garden, Kensington** or **Knightsbridge,** and **Chelsea.**

Window Shopping

BUDGET CLOTHING

🔲 **Zara,** 118 Regent St., W1 (☎7534 9500). Continental style and adaptations of the latest designer fashions from this Spanish store but at much better prices. Jeans from £25. Open M-W 10am-7pm, Th 10am-8pm, Su noon-6pm.

Amazon, 1-22 Kensington Church St., W8 (no phone). Tube: High St. Kensington. A group of stores, each with a separate facade. The gargantuan collection of men's and women's wear includes designers such as Versace and popular seconds from places like French Connection. Discounts sometimes exceed 50%. Extremely strict exchange policy. Open M-W and F 10:30am-6:30pm, Th 10:30am-7pm, Sa 10am-6pm, Su noon-5pm. MC, V.

Harrods

H&M (Hennes & Mauritz), 261-271 Regent St., W1 (☎7495 4003). Tube: Oxford Circus. Numerous other branches. The Ikea of clothing: Swedish, fairly fashionable, decently priced. Fortunately, their clothes don't require assembly according to strange diagrams. Open M-W and Sa 10am-7pm, Th-F 10am-8pm, Su noon-6pm.

Miss Selfridge, 40 Duke St., W1 (☎7318 3833). Tube: Bond St. Discount clothing for young things, to the side of Selfridges. These clothes won't last forever, but they'll be out of style by the time they fall apart. Open M-W 9:30am-7pm, Th-F 9:30am-8pm, Su noon-6pm. AmEx, MC, V.

Mango, 8-12 Neal St., WC2 (☎7240 6099). Tube: Covent Garden. Comfortable women's clothes from this Spanish chain. Open M-W and F-Sa 10am-7pm, Th 10am-8pm, Su noon-6pm.

Chinatown

MID-PRICED CLOTHING

French Connection (fcuk), 99-103 Long Acre, WC2 (☎ 7379 6560). Tube: Covent Garden. Numerous other branches. Friendly staff and catchy slogans have let fcuk fill the gap in afford-able, trendy urbanwear. Simple designs in dark colors make for a good fcuking buy. Huge sales during January and July when fcukloads of clothes are up to 70% off regular prices. Open M-W 10:30am-7pm, Th 11am-8pm, F-Sa 10:30am-7pm, Su 11am-6pm. AmEx, DC, MC, V.

Jigsaw, 31 Brompton Rd., SW3 (☎ 7584 6226). Tube: Knightsbridge. Numerous other branches. Somewhat pricey, but very stylish men's and women's threads in luscious fabrics (e.g. deliciously soft leather) and muted, subtle colors. Large men's-only store at Floral St. (Tube: Covent Garden). Open M-Tu and Th-F 10:30am-7pm, W 10:30am-7:30pm, Sa 10am-7pm, Su noon-5pm.

Next, 54-58 Kensington High St., W8 (☎ 7938 4211). Tube: High St. Kensington. Numerous other branches. Basic, sophisticated pieces for a wide range of ages. Fair prices for everything from office to beach garb. Open M-W and F-Sa 10am-7pm, Th 10am-8pm, Su 11:30am-6pm.

Hope and Glory, 131a Kensington Church St., W8 (☎ 7727 8424). Tube High St. Kensington. Contemporary fashions with a retro spin. Open M-Sa 10am-6pm, Su noon-5pm.

Ted Baker, 1-2 Langley Court, WC2 (☎ 7497 8862; www.tedbaker.co.uk). Tube: Covent Garden. Also at 5-7 Fouberts Pl., W1 (☎ 7437 5619). Stylish men's and women's clothes, including the famous crisp men's shirts. Open M-W and F 10am-7pm, Th 10am-7:30pm, Sa 10am-6:30pm, Su noon-5pm. AmEx, DC, MC, V.

Levi's, 174 Regent St., W1 (☎ 7292 2500). Yes, it's the same brand of jeans you can get any-where else in the world. But the store itself's worth a browse—there's free use of the Dreamcast and table football, while Vinyl Addiction downstairs sells dance records and CDs. Open M-W 10am-7pm, Th-Sa 10am-8pm, Su noon-6pm.

WOMEN'S CLOTHING

Kookaï, 5-7 Brompton Rd., SW3 (☎ 7581 9633). Tube: Knightsbridge. Numerous other branches. Sexy, billowy clothes at almost-reasonable prices. Kooky details: embroidery, beads, etc. Open M-Tu and Th-Sa 10am-7pm, W 10am-8pm, Su noon-5pm. Major credit cards.

Oasis, 43 James St., WC2 (☎ 7240 7445). Tube: Covent Garden. Numerous other branches. Moderately-priced runway knock-offs. Some work better than others, but all are a look. Open M-W and F 10am-7pm, Th 10am-8pm, Sa 10am-7pm, Su noon-6pm. AmEx, DC, MC, V.

Laura Ashley, 256-258 Regent St., W1 (☎ 7437 9760). Tube: Oxford Circus. Numerous other branches. Inspiration for the decor of B&Bs throughout the UK. Clothes continue to feature flow-ery designs and loose cuts; recent years have seen a move toward simplicity. Open M-Tu 10am-6:30pm, W and F 10am-7pm, Th 10am-8pm, Sa 9:30am-7pm, Su noon-6pm. AmEx, MC, V.

Karen Millen, 22-23 James St., WC2 (☎ 7836 5355). Tube: Covent Garden. Numerous other branches. Elegant cuts and light, luscious colors make for an interesting spin on classic women's wear. Open M-Sa 10am-7pm, Su noon-6pm. AmEx, DC, MC, V.

Monsoon, 264 Oxford St., W1 (☎ 7499 2578). Tube: Oxford Circus. Numerous other branches. Brightly colored (too brightly) feminine wares, often at cut-rate prices. Floaty Indian-print dresses to combat London's frequent tropical days. Open M-Sa 11am-7pm, Su noon-5pm. AmEx, MC, V.

MEN'S CLOTHING

Reiss, 78-79 New Bond St., W1 (☎ 7493 4866; www.reiss.co.uk) Tube: Bond St. Some other branches. One of the most influential trendsetters in men's fashions, using classic fabrics and smooth lines to introduce new styles. They'll be wearing what you buy here next season. Open M-W and F-Sa 10am-7pm, Th 10am-8pm, Su noon-6pm. AmEx, MC, V.

Outrage, 9 Shorts Gardens, WC2 (☎ 7836 5675). Tube: Covent Garden. Practical clothing with flair. Open M-Sa 11am-7pm, Su noon-5pm. AmEx, MC, V.

Sam Walker, 33 Neal St., WC2 (☎ 7240 7800). Tube: Covent Garden. Men's clothing that always satisfies. Colorful shirts and leather goods. Open M-Sa 10am-7pm. Su noon-6pm. AmEx, MC,V.

DESIGNER

❧ **Paul Smith,** 40-44 Floral St., WC2 (☎ 7379 7133; www.paulsmith.co.uk). Tube: Covent Garden. Branches at 122 Kensington Park Rd., W11 (☎ 7727 3553) and 84-86 Sloane Ave., SW3 (☎ 7589 9139). **Sale shop,** 23 Avery Row, W1 (☎ 7493 1287), off Brook St. Tube: Bond St. Paul Smith has defined modern British tailoring as a blend of classic British with influences from the far east and the continent. The cheaper Paul Smith Jeans and R. Newbold can be found around the corner at 9-11 Langley Court, WC2. Open M-W and F 10:30am-6:30pm, Th 10:30am-7pm, Sa 10am-6:30pm. AmEx, MC, V, your right arm.

Nicole Farhi, 158 New Bond St., W1 (☎ 7499 8368). Tube: Bond St. The flagship store for one of the most famous British designers of the 90s. Rich fabrics and textures make for stylishly classic clothes. Open M-W 10am-6pm, Th-Sa 10am-7pm, Su noon-6pm. AmEx, MC, V, your left arm.

Vivienne Westwood, 6 Davies St., W1 (☎ 7629 3757). Tube: Bond St. The quintessential British designer's madcap store, full of her irreverently influential designs. Mostly for women. Open M-W and F-Sa 10am-6pm, Th 10am-7pm. AmEx, MC, V.

Hype Designer Forum, 26-40 Kensington High St., W8 (☎ 7938 4343). Tube: High St. Kensington. A mall of boutiques exhibiting the work of young British designers and larger brands. These garments often appear in the pages of *Vogue* and *Elle*. Open M-W and F 10am-6pm, Th 10am-8pm, Sa 10am-6pm, Su noon-6pm.

VINTAGE AND SECONDHAND

Cornucopia, 12 Upper Tachbrook St., SW1 (☎ 7828 5752). Tube: Victoria. Grande dame of period clothing shops, selling women's attire from 1910-1960. Ball gowns start at £35. Open M-Sa 11am-6pm. MC, V.

Blackout II, 51 Endell St., WC2 (☎ 7240 5006). Tube: Covent Garden. Rummage through this vintage emporium to find duds from the 1940s to the 1970s. Feeling glam rock? Go for it. Some vintage gowns for hire. Open M-F 11am-7pm, Sa 11:30am-6:30pm. AmEx, DC, MC, V.

Origin, 26 Ganton St., W1 (☎ 7437 7338). Tube: Oxford Circus. Proceeds from this dual-sex store benefit Oxfam. Think retro—most threads are from the 60s and 70s. Open M-Sa 11:30am-7pm. MC, V.

CLUBWEAR

❧ **Top Shop/Top Man,** 214 Oxford St., W1 (☎ 7636 7700). Tube: Oxford Circus. Some other branches. An absolute must for the club kid on a budget. This multi-story megastore offers the trendiest inexpensive fashions with something to suit everyone's flamboyant side. Free Playstations, foosball, and Internet access complete the experience. Open M-W and F 9am-8pm, Th and Sa 9am-9pm, Su noon-6pm. AmEx, MC, V.

Cyberdog, 9 Earlham St., WC2 (☎ 7836 7855; www.cyberdog.co.uk). Tube: Leicester Sq. Also at Stables Market, Chalk Farm Rd., Camden Town, NW1. Clubwear displayed as it's meant to be seen—under UV light. Fluorescent-colored T-shirts (£20). Techno always playing and available for sale downstairs. Open M-Sa 11am-7pm, Su 1-6:30pm. AmEx, MC, V.

Diesel, 43 Earlham St., WC2 (☎ 7497 5543; www.diesel.com). Tube: Covent Garden. Pricey, scene-stealing duds, including their famous jeans. Open M-W and Sa 10am-8pm, Th-F 10am-9pm, Su noon-6pm. AmEx, MC, V.

Duffer of St. George, 29 Shorts Gardens, WC2 (☎ 7379 4660). Tube: Covent Garden. The latest streetwear from both the in-store label and others. Somewhat pricey. Attractive shoppers and equally attractive staff attest to Duffer's ability to transform. Open M-F 10:30am-7pm, Sa 10:30am-6:30pm, Su 1-5pm. AmEx, MC, V.

Big Apple, 96 Kensington High St., W8 (☎ 7376 1404). Tube: High St. Kensington. Also at 70 Neal St., WC2 (☎ 7497 0165). Sale racks of tiny tees and daring spandex items. Open M-Sa 10am-7:30pm, Su 11am-7:30pm. AmEx, MC, V.

Urban Outfitters, 36-38 Kensington High St., W8 (☎ 7761 1001). Tube: High St. Kensington. All the kit for scenesters of both sexes. **Carbon Music,** between the ground floor and the basement, has an eclectic selection of vinyl and CDs. Open M-W and F-Sa 10am-7pm, Th 10am-8pm, Su 11am-6pm. AmEx, MC, V.

the BIG $plurge

FLY SHOES

On a long Tube ride, especially at rush hour, it's hard not to notice that Londoners, to a degree unmatched by their continental or American counterparts, wear really, really cool shoes. Even in a city where clothes push the boundaries of outrageous, shoes stand out; to a superlative pair of shoes, clothes are merely an accessory. If feet are your fancy, you'll soon long for your own pair of London-style kicks. However, well-shod feet come at a price. Funky shoes (even if cheaply made) begin around £90. **Shelly's** (p. 132) has branches around London and generally carries the latest styles. You won't go wrong at **Dr. Marten's Department Store Ltd** (p. 132), by now a venerable London institution. Even if it isn't dress shoes you're after, there's plenty of money to be spent on **trainers,** running shoes worn more for fashion than fitness.

Mambo, Thomas Neal's Centre, 37 Earlham St., WC2 (☎7379 6066). Tube: Covent Garden. Branch at 26-27 Carnaby St., W1 (☎7434 2404). London flagship store of the Aussie giant. Bright or garish surfwear, depending on how you look at it. Open M-Sa 10am-7pm, Su noon-6pm.

ACCESSORIES

Accessorize, Unit 22, The Market, Covent Garden, WC2 (☎7240 2107; www.accessorize.co.uk). Tube: Covent Garden. Numerous other branches. The latest trends in accessories interpreted for smaller budgets, organized by color and style. An accessory fetishist's heaven. Open M-Sa 10am-8pm, Su 11am-7pm. AmEx, DC, MC, V.

American Retro, 35 Old Compton St., W1 (☎7734 3477; www.americanretro.com). Tube: Piccadilly Circus or Leicester Sq. From watches to handbags, street-stylish accessories at reasonable prices. Also stocks its own label of clothing and kitschy greeting cards. Open M-F 10:30am-7:30pm, Sa 10:15am-7pm. AmEx, MC, V.

Robot, 37 Floral St., WC2 (☎7836 6156; www.robotshoeslondon.co.uk). Tube: Covent Garden. Who says men can't accessorize? Street-wise fashion, from watches to shoes—they're all here. Open M-Sa 10am-6:30pm, Su noon-5:30pm. AmEx, DC, MC, V.

SHOES

Buffalo, 47-49 Neal St. (☎7379 1051; www.buffaloboots.com). Also at 190 Camden High St., NW1 (☎7424 9014). Want your sneakers to be bright? Two feet tall? Open daily 10:30am-7pm.

Dr. Marten's Dept. Store Ltd, 1-4 King St., WC2 (☎7497 1460). Tube: Covent Garden. Tourist-packed 5-tiered megastore; watches, sunglasses, candles, and of course the hard-as-nails shoes. Buy Docs for everyone you know, from baby to granny. Open M-W and F-Sa 10am-7pm, Th 10:30am-8pm, Su noon-6pm. AmEx, MC, V.

Patrick Cox, 8 Symons St., SW3 (☎7730 6504). Tube: Sloane Sq. One of his shoe lines is appropriately named "Wannabes;" there's often a queue to get into this popular shoe emporium. Moderately priced loafers in wild colors and trendy materials; some can get quite pricey. Open M-Tu and Th-Sa 10am-6pm, W 10am-7pm. AmEx, MC, V.

Office, 43 Kensington High St., W8 (☎7937 7022). Tube: High St. Kensington. Branch on Neal St. (Tube: Covent Garden). **Sale shop** at 61 St. Martin's Ln., WC2 (☎7497 0390; tube: Leicester Sq.). Ultra-trendy mid-range chain. Well-known designers and a hip collection of its own-label stompers. Open daily 10am-6pm. AmEx, MC, V.

Eternity, 46 Oxford St. (☎7580 0890). Tube: Oxford Circus. Although difficult to find (only the "ET" remains on the sign), this shop is worth the search, as the deals here are unbeatable. Italian leather imports go for as little as £20. Open daily 9:30am-7pm.

Shelly's, 266-270 Regent St. (☎7287 0939). Tube: Oxford Circus. Numerous other branches. *The* London shoe store, with the most current styles. Funky shoes at sensible prices. Open M-W and F-Sa 10am-7pm, Th 10am-8pm, Su noon-6pm. AmEx, MC, V.

Swear, 61 Neal St., WC2 (☎ 7240 5313; www.swear-shoes.com). Tube: Covent Garden. This hipper-than-thou footwear boutique takes the high-soled sneaker to new levels, literally and aesthetically. Open M-Sa 11am-7pm, Su 2-6pm.

Offspring, 60 Neal St., WC2 (☎ 7497 2463). Branches at 221 Camden High St. (☎ 7267 9873) and 217 Portobello Rd., W11 (☎ 7221 8424). Sneakers, trainers, sports shoes; call them what you will, Offspring's got them. Open M-W and F-Sa 10am-7pm, Th 10am-7:30pm, Su noon-6pm.

GIFTS

UNDER £5

R. Twining & Co, 216 The Strand, WC2 (☎ 7353 3511). Tube: Charing Cross. This institution of tea honors the leaf that remains the Queen's official brew. A tiny museum in the back traces the tea's lineage. Leaf teas include Earl Grey (£1.45 per 125g), Prince of Wales (£1.50 per 100g), and other regal blends. This may be as close as you get to royalty. Open M-F 9:30am-4:30pm. MC, V.

Paperchase, 213 Tottenham Court Rd., W1 (☎ 7467 6200). Tube: Tottenham Court Rd. Three floors of greeting cards, stationery, and an astounding variety of paper products. Open M, W, and F-Sa 9:30am-6pm, Tu 10am-6pm, Th 9:30am-7:30pm, Su noon-6pm.

Peter Jones, Sloane Sq., SW1 (☎ 7730 3434). Tube: Sloane Sq. Most of the store is too posh for budget travelers, but a la-di-da bone china tea cup (£4.95) might be the perfect gift for mom or granny. Open M-Tu 9:30am-6pm, Th-Sa W 9:30am-7pm.

The Hive Honey Shop, 53 Web's Rd., SW11 (☎ 7924 6233). Rail: Clapham Junction. You don't get much closer to the source than this: the store has a working hive in it. All sorts of bee-based delicacies, medicines, and candles. Jars of seasonal aromatic honeys £2.95-4.95. Open M-Sa 10am-6pm. MC, V.

UNDER £10

The Beer Shop, 14 Pitfield St., N1 (☎ 7739 3701). Tube: Old St. Though the 72-pint cask may prove impractical (really, would it fit in your backpack?), somewhere among the staggering selection of bottles and books on the noble art of brewing you're bound to find a gift for your favorite punter. Variety pack of 4 beers brewed on the premises £7.99. Open M-F 11am-7pm, Sa 10am-4pm. MC, V.

BBC World Service Shop, Bush House, Strand, WC2 (☎ 7557 2576). Tube: Temple. Fill your basket with radio and TV merchandise in this Anglophile paradise. Tapes of classic radio comedy: for dad the antidote to quiz shows, *I'm Sorry, I Haven't a Clue;* for mom, the very English, very witty songs of Victoria Wood; for strange cousin Bob, the manic modern satire *On the Hour.* Tapes £8.99. Open M-Tu and Th-F 9:30am-6pm, W 10am-5:30pm. AmEx, MC, V.

The Conran Shop, 81 Fulham Rd. (☎ 7589 7401). Tube: South Kensington. The flagship store of Britain's design guru. Pop downstairs for stylish gadgets, great-looking stationery, and other design classics, some of which may actually fall within your price range (bottle openers £8-15). Open M, Tu, and F 10am-6pm, W and Th 10am-7pm, Sa 10am-6:30pm, Su 12pm-6pm.

Docklands Shoes

Fortnum and Mason

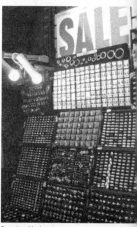

Camden Market

Lillywhite's, 24-36 Lower Regent St., SW1 (☎ 7915 4000). Tube: Piccadilly Circus. London's sporting goods mecca, this is the place to pick up cricket balls (£4-14) and Arsenal football jerseys. End-of-season sales feature bargains like Wimbledon tote bags for £4. Open M-Sa 10am-8pm, Su noon-6pm. AmEx, DC, MC, V.

HEALTH AND BEAUTY

Neal's Yard Stores, Neal's Yard, WC2. Tube: Covent Garden. Feed your body inside and out at this cornucopia of health and beauty shops, including **Neal's Yard Remedies,** 15 Neal's Yard, (☎ 7627 1949), selling a wide range of herbal remedies and essential oils in distinctive cobalt-blue bottles; and **Neal's Yard Therapy Rooms,** 2 Neal's Yard (☎ 7379 7662), carrying the gamut of alternative healing from acupuncture to voice dialogue counseling (1st visit £25-55, later visits £25-40. Open M-F 9am-9:30pm, Sa 1:30-5:30pm).

Vidal Sassoon School of Hairdressing, 56 Davies Mews, W1 (☎ 7318 5205). Tube: Bond St. Become your own offbeat entertainment. Cuts, perms, and colorings at the hand of *un petit Sassoony.* Budget 2-3hr. and £16.50 (concessions £8.25) for a cut and blow dry including consultations with an experienced stylist before the students (most of whom have spent time styling at lesser studios) do their worst. Book well ahead. Open M-F 8:30am-6pm.

Boots. This bright, white pharmacy chain often offers good discounts and its own excellent brand of Boots beauty supplies, including its young and funky "17" line. Branches on almost every high street, generally open M-Sa 9:00am-5:30pm.

Lush, Units 7 and 11, The Piazza, Covent Garden, WC2 (☎ 7240 4570; www.lush.co.uk). Tube: Covent Garden. Branches at 40 Carnaby St., W1 (☎ 7287 5874) and 123 King's Rd., SW3 (☎ 7376 8348). A delicious array of freshly made cosmetics. Slabs of fragrant soaps are almost good enough to eat (£1.20-1.90 for 100g). Open M-Sa 10am-7pm, Su noon-6pm. MC, V.

South Molton Drug Store, 64 South Molton St., W1 (☎ 7493 4156). Tube: Bond St. Crammed with bargain beauty gear. Lipstick and nail polish from 85p, and names like Elizabeth Arden are as much as half-price. Open M-Sa 9am-6pm. AmEx, MC, V.

Space.NK Apothecary, 37 Earlham St., WC2 (☎ 7379 7030). Tube: Covent Garden. One of the trendiest and most expensive places to buy cosmetics; Stila, Kiehl's—all the biggies for scenemakers are here. Some men's stuff too. Open M-W and F-Sa 10am-7pm, Th 10am-7:30pm, Su noon-5pm. AmEx, DC, MC, V.

Penhaligon's, 41 Wellington St., WC2 (☎ 7836 2150). Tube: Covent Garden. Branches on Bond St. and Piccadilly Circus. They supplied Winston Churchill's scented Bath potions, perfumes, and toiletries, all with a Royal Warrant. Open M-Sa 10am-6pm, Su 12:30-5:30pm. AmEx, MC, V.

SPECIALTY SHOPS

INNOCENCE

Hamley's, 188-189 Regent St., W1 (☎ 7734 3161). Tube: Oxford Circus. Even Santa and his elves do their shopping here, in a place most kids would call heaven. London's largest toy shop spans 6 floors filled with every conceivable toy and game. Open M-W 10am-7:30pm, Th-Sa 10am-8pm, Su noon-6pm. Major credit cards.

The Tintin Shop, 34 Floral St., WC2 (☎ 7836 1131; www.thetintinshop.uk.com). Tube: Covent Garden. A store dedicated to everyone's favorite Belgian reporter. All the books in a variety of languages, plus keychains and other Tintin-flavored accessories. Open M-Sa 10am-6pm.

EXPERIENCE

Clone Zone, 64 Old Compton St., W1 (☎ 7287 3530). Tube: Piccadilly Circus or Leicester Sq. Branch at 266 Old Brompton Rd. (☎ 7373 0598). Well-stocked shop for gifts, cards, books, and tons of biker gear. Sex toys and bondage gear in the basement. Pick up club flyers on your way out. Open M-Sa 11am-9pm, Su noon-8pm. AmEx, MC, V.

Honour, 86 Lower Marsh, SE1 (☎ 7401 8220). Tube: Waterloo. One of the few places in London where rubber isn't just the word for eraser. Ground floor stocks wigs and all sorts of PVC gear for fetish trendies; upstairs features bondage gear. Info on upcoming gothic, pagan, and fetish happenings. Open M-F 10:30am-7pm, Sa 11:30am-5pm. AmEx, MC, V.

Into You, 144 St. John St., EC1 (☎ 7253 5085). Tattooing, body-piercing, and related literature and items. If pain is pleasure for you, and permanency doesn't bother you, then take the plunge. Open Tu-F noon-7pm, Sa noon-6pm.

G. Smith and Sons Snuff Shop, 74 Charing Cross Rd., WC2 (☎ 7836 7422). Tube: Leicester Sq. Established in 1869 by George Smith. Buy a can of snuff for £4.95. A pocket tin (75p) will keep you sneezin' through London. Shop doubles as a tobacconist and offers a host of pipes, lighters, and cigars from around the world. Open M-F 9am-6pm, Sa 9:30am-5:30pm.

The Tea and Coffee Plant, 170 Portobello Rd., W8 (☎ 7221 8137). Tube: Ladbroke Grove. This wonderful little shop sells a whole range of fairly traded coffee and tea, much of it organically grown. Mild Guatemalan is a good place to start (£5 per lb.), but cheaper varieties such as Mocha Blend (£2.80 per lb.) are also worth a look. Every Sa they serve what is described as the best coffee in London, made from freshly roasted and drained coffee beans. Mail order available. Open Tu-Th 10:30am-6:30pm, F-Sa 9:15am-6pm.

BOOKSTORES

An exhaustive selection of bookshops lines **Charing Cross Road** between Tottenham Court Rd. and Leicester Sq. and many vend secondhand paperbacks. Cecil Ct., near Leicester Sq., is a treasure trove of tiny shops with specialty bookstores for dance, rare books, travel, etc. Establishments along **Great Russell Street** stock esoteric and specialized books on any subject from Adorno to the Zohar. **Chains** can be found along most main commercial thoroughfares, like Oxford St. and High St. Kensington. Also worth browsing is the **Riverside Walk Market** full of paperbacks and cut-price travel books. (Under Waterloo Bridge. Tube: Waterloo. Sa-Su 10am-5pm.)

GIANT AND CHAIN BOOKSTORES

▨ **Blackwells,** 100 Charing Cross Rd., WC2 (☎ 7292 5100; www.bookshop.blackwell.co.uk). It's academic (mostly). Go for the postmodern theory, stay for the huge selection of fiction. Open M-Sa 9:30am-8:30pm, Su noon-6pm. Amex, MC, V.

▨ **Foyles,** 113-119 Charing Cross Rd., WC1 (☎ 7437 5660). Tube: Tottenham Court Rd. A giant warehouse sprawling over 4 floors. Open M-W and F-Sa 9am-6pm, Th 9am-7pm. AmEx, MC, V.

Dillons, 82 Gower St., WC2 (☎ 7636 1577). Tube: Goodge St. Numerous other branches. One of London's best. Strong on academic subjects, particularly history and politics. Open M-Sa 9:30am-9pm, Su noon-6pm. AmEx, MC, V.

Hatchards, 187 Piccadilly, W1 (☎ 7439 9921; books@hatchards.co.uk; www.hatchards.co.uk). Tube: Green Park. Since 1797, the oldest London bookstore. Four floors of intellectual goodies; particularly strong British history and politics department. Open M and W-Sa 9am-6pm, Tu 9:30am-6pm, Su noon-6pm. AmEx, MC, V.

Waterstone's, 203-206 Piccadilly, WC1 (☎ 7851 2400; www.waterstones.co.uk). Tube: Piccadilly Circus. Numerous other branches. This new store in the heart of all things tourist is one-stop, albeit characterless, book shopping. Open M-Sa 9am-8pm, Su noon-6pm. AmEx, DC, MC, V.

ANTIQUE AND USED BOOKSTORES

▨ **Maggs Brothers,** 50 Berkeley Sq., W1 (☎ 7493 7160). Tube: Green Park. A bibliophile's paradise in an allegedly haunted 18th-century mansion. Tremendous selection of 19th-century travel narratives, illuminated manuscripts, militaria, and autographs. Open M-F 9am-5pm. MC, V.

▨ **Skoob Books,** 15 Sicilian Ave., between Southampton Row and Vernon Pl., WC1 (☎ 7404 3063; books@skoob.com; www.skoob.com). Tube: Holborn. The best used bookstore in Bloomsbury; academic and general interest. Used video section. 10% student discount. Gives coupons for 20% off on your second visit. Open M-Sa 10:30am-6:30pm, Su noon-5pm. AmEx, MC, V.

Bell, Book, and Radmall, 4 Cecil Court, WC2 (☎ 7240 2161). Tube: Leicester Sq. A small antiquarian bookstore with an exceptional selection of first editions and an impressive supply of sci-fi and detective novels. Open M-F 10am-5:30pm, Sa 11am-4pm. AmEx, MC, V.

Bookmongers, 439 Coldharbour Ln., SW9 (☎ 7738 4225). Tube: Brixton. Fabulous secondhand bookstore with a healthy selection of works by African and Caribbean authors. Big selection of books for just 50p in the back. Open M-Sa 10:30am-6:30pm. MC, V.

Southeran's of Sackville Street, 2-5 Sackville St., W1 (☎ 7439 6151). Tube: Piccadilly Circus. Founded in 1761 in York, Southeran's moved to London in 1815 and established itself as a London literary institution. Dickens frequented these silent stacks, and the firm handled the sale of his library after his death in 1870. Strong departments include architecture and literary first editions. Open M-F 9:30am-6pm, Sa 10am-4pm. AmEx, MC, V.

Unsworth Booksellers, 12 Bloomsbury St., WC1. (☎ 7436 9836; www.unsworths.com). Tube: Tottenham Court Rd. 50-90% off publisher's prices on a wide selection of seconds and remainders. Good used books section. Open M-Sa 10am-8pm, Su noon-8pm. AmEx, DC, MC, V.

SPECIAL INTEREST BOOKSTORES

▓ **Books for Cooks,** 4 Blenheim Crescent, W11 (☎ 7221 1992). Tube: Ladbroke Grove. The definitive cookbook shop, including wholefood, vegan, and second-hand cookbooks. Guest chefs serve lunch from the kitchen; book 1 week to 10 days ahead. Open M-Sa 9:30am-6pm. MC, V.

▓ **David Drummond, Theatrical Bookseller and Ephemerist,** 11 Cecil Court, WC2 (☎ 7836 1142). Tube: Leicester Sq. A friendly, fascinating shop crammed with various theatrical paraphernalia, plus early children's books with exquisite color plates, adventure stories, fairy tales, antique postcards, Victorian valentines, and other vintage juvenilia. Open M-F 11am-2:30pm and 3:30-5:45pm, Sa by appointment. AmEx, MC, V.

▓ **Grant and Cutler,** 55-57 Great Marlborough St., W1 (☎ 7734 2012; www.grant-c.demon.co.uk). Tube: Oxford Circus. An impressive store, crammed full of language books and European literature in the original. Open M-W and F-Sa 9am-5:30pm. MC, V.

▓ **Sportspages,** Caxton Walk at 94-96 Charing Cross Rd., WC2 (☎ 7240 9604; info@sportspages.co.uk; www.sportspages.co.uk). Tube: Leicester Sq. Scores of books for both sports fans and professionals on every sport imaginable. Impressive selection of soccer and rugby merchandise, from jerseys to videotapes of classic matches, and a decent sports science section. Kicks off M-Sa 9:30am with the final whistle at 7pm, Su noon-6pm. AmEx, MC, V.

▓ **The Travel Bookshop,** 13-15 Blenheim Crescent, W11 (☎ 7229 5260; www.thetravelbookshop.co.uk). Yes, it's the tiny specialist bookstore featured in *Notting Hill*. No, the people behind the counter rarely look like Hugh Grant. Yes, they stock *Let's Go*. Open M-Sa 10am-6pm.

The BBC World Service Shop. See **Gifts,** p. 133.

Compendium, 234 Camden High St., NW1 (☎ 7485 8944). Tube: Camden Town. This avantgarde bookstore has sections devoted to shamanism, technotheory, anarchism, black and Asian fiction, anarchic technotheory, and Asian shaman fiction. New Age and Egyptology are also well covered. Open M-W 10am-6pm, Th-Sa 10am-7pm, Su noon-6pm. MC, V.

Gay's the Word, 66 Marchmont St., WC1 (☎ 7278 7654; www.gaystheword.co.uk). Tube: Russell Sq. Widest stock of gay and lesbian literature in England; mail order service available. Notice board (including accommodations listings), discussion groups, and readings. Open M-Sa 10am-6:30pm, Su 2-6pm. AmEx, MC, V.

Silver Moon Women's Bookshop, 64-68 Charing Cross Rd., WC2 (☎ 7836 7906; www.silver-moonbookshop.co.uk). Tube: Leicester Sq. A feminist bookstore and the largest women's bookshop in Europe. An exhaustive selection of books by and about women (fiction by women, nonfiction about women written by either sex), the largest lesbian department in Britain, and a nice travel section. Open M-W and F-Sa 10am-6:30pm, Th 10am-8pm, Su noon-6pm. AmEx, MC, V.

Souls of Black Folk, 407 Coldharbour Lane, SW9 (☎ 7738 4141). Tube: Brixton. A friendly neighborhood store stocked high with books on Africa and the Caribbean, as well as fiction by black writers. Cafe serves huge smoothies (£3) named after works by black authors. Open M-Th 11am-10pm, F 11am-3am, Sa 11am-1am, Su 10am-8pm. MC, V.

Zwemmers, 24 Litchfield St., WC2 (☎ 7379 7886; www.zwemmer.com). Tube: Leicester Sq. A multi-store art book empire, headquartered at Litchfield St. The store here, just east of Charing Cross Rd., specializes in books on art. A stone's throw to the south at 80 Charing Cross Rd., the focus is on media (mainly film and photography). 72 Charing Cross Rd. focuses on design. All three open M-F 10am-6:30pm, Sa 10am-6pm. AmEx, MC, V.

RECORD STORES

As anyone who read *High Fidelity* knows, London crawls with music junkies. Fortunately, the city has a record collection to match. Corporate megaliths **HMV, Virgin,** and **Tower Records** fall over each other claiming to be the world's largest record store (they also do brisk business in videos and computer games). Don't expect any bargains, and remember that when it comes to records, "import" means "rip-off."

Vinyl still remains an important part of the London music retail scene. The megastores carry vinyl versions of most major-label releases, but to get those rare promos, white labels, or collectibles, you'll probably have to go to an independent record store. In **Camden Town, Brixton,** and **Ladbroke Grove,** record stores tempt collectors and intimidate browsers with rare vinyl and memorabilia at rock star prices. The best collection of record stores, though, probably at **Berwick Street** in Soho, and **Hanway Street,** off Tottenham Court Rd. If you're looking for a specific type of music, don't be afraid to pop into any of the independents and ask for advice: even if they don't stock it, they'll probably be able to direct you to stores that do. Most of the independent stores also do international mail order. **Street markets** (see p. 141) are another source of music.

MEGASTORES

HMV, 150 Oxford St., W1 (☎ 7631 3423; www.hmv.co.uk). Tube: Oxford Circus. The basement has jazz, classical, world music, and soundtracks. Everything else on the ground floor. Open M-F 9:30am-8pm, Sa 9am-7:30pm, Su noon-6pm. AmEx, DC, MC, V.

Tower Records, 1 Piccadilly Circus, W1 (☎ 7439 2500; www.tower.co.uk). Tube: Piccadilly Circus. This has everything you could ever need or want, including an extensive selection of sheet music and musical bios in the basement. Incredibly helpful staff and huge selection. Good for magazines. Open M-Sa 9am-midnight, Su noon-6pm. AmEx, MC, V.

Stern's Music, 293 Euston Rd. and 74 Warren St., NW1 (☎ 7387 5550; www.sternsmusic.com). Tube: Warren St. The place to go for Afrobeat and other African music, on CD and vinyl. Also stocks music from other countries. Open M-Sa 10:30am-6:30pm.

Uptown Records, 3 D'Arblay St., W1 (☎ 7434 3639; www.uptownrecords.uk.com). Tube: Oxford Circus. UK and US garage feature downstairs. Upstairs, the hip-hop, it don't stop. Open M-W and F-Sa 10:30am-7pm, Th 10:30am-8pm.

Virgin Megastore, 14-16 Oxford St., W1 (☎ 7631 1234). Tube: Tottenham Court Rd. Richard Branson needs more money. Extensive classical music section and a large display of computer games, videos, and books. Open M-Sa 9:30am-9pm, Su noon-6pm. AmEx, MC, V.

SECONDHAND AND SPECIALTY

Black Market, 25 D'Arblay St., W1 (☎ 7437 0478; www.blackmarket.co.uk). Tube: Oxford Circus. A Soho institution: if you're looking for the latest house or garage 12 in., they've got the goods. A phenomenal drum & bass section resides downstairs. Open M-Sa 11am-7pm.

Daddy Kool, basement of 12 Berwick St., W1 (☎ 7437 3535). Tube: Oxford Circus or Piccadilly Circus. Probably Soho's best reggae store, stocking loads of obscure 7 in. and some contemporary dancehall and reggae items. Open M-F 10:30am-7pm, Sa 10am-6pm.

Honest Jon's, 276-278 Portobello Rd., W10 (☎ 8969 9822). Tube: Ladbroke Grove. Still funky after all these years. 276 holds an impressive jazz collection, 278 a wide selection of hip-hop LPs and some decent 12-inch singles, as well as soul and funk holdings. Open M-Sa 10am-6pm, Su 11am-5pm. AmEx, MC, V.

Intoxica!, 231 Portobello Rd., W11 (☎ 7229 8010; www.intoxica.co.uk). Tube: Ladbroke Grove. Enviable stock of surf-rock, rockabilly, film soundtracks, and other exotica. Downstairs jazz, blues, and 60s soul reign. All vinyl. Open M-Sa 10:30am-6:30pm, Su noon-4pm.

Music and Video Exchange, 34-42, 56, 64, and 65 Notting Hill Gate, and 14, 20, and 28-34 Pembridge Rd., W11 (☎ 7221 1444; www.mveshops.co.uk). Tube: Notting Hill Gate. A west London mini-empire, spreading like kudzu near the Tube. Interesting secondhand music and video, plus electronics, musical instruments, clothes, books, and furniture. Open daily 10am-8pm.

on the cheap

STREET CHIC

London's most outrageous fashions aren't always found in the name shops. Frugal fashionistas can find plenty of gear at London's numerous street markets (see p. 138). **Camden Market** and **Portobello Market** are the two main ports of call for quality market shopping. You can purchase an amazing array of items and bargaining is part of the fun: shoes, jackets, homewares, tobacco paraphernalia, vests, records, and most anything else.

If you seek the nightlife but dread the price of club gear, street markets are a great place to begin your search, especially for retro nights. Cool shoes can be found at a bargain as well.

Street markets also provide free people watching and entertainment. Even if you don't buy anything, whiling away a Sunday at Camden is a great time.

Out on the Floor, 10 Inverness St., NW1 (☎7267 5989). Tube: Camden Town. A well-stocked used-CD and vinyl shop. CDs £7.50-12; vinyl from £6. Upstairs mostly jazz and funk, downstairs indie and new wave punk. Open M-F 11am-6pm, Sa-Su 11am-7pm.

Reckless Records, 26 and 30 Berwick St., W1 (☎7437 3362 and 7437 4271; www.reckless.co.uk). Tube: Tottenham Court Rd. Branch at 79 Upper St., N1 (☎7359 0501). Tube: Angel. The DJs' favorite exchange shop, and it shows. Pick up promos (on both vinyl and CD) before their official release. Open daily 10am-7pm. AmEx, MC, V.

Red Records, 500 Brixton Rd., SW2 (☎7274 4476). Tube: Brixton. The sign reads "Black Music Specialists;" inside is an impressive collection of reggae, hip-hop, soul, garage, and jazz. Vinyl, CDs, tapes, and DJ equipment. Open M-Sa 9:30am-8pm. AmEx, MC, V.

Rough Trade, 130 Talbot Rd., W11 (☎7229 8541; www.roughtrade.com). Tube: Ladbroke Grove. Branch at 16 Neal's Yard (☎7240 0105; Tube: Covent Garden), under Slam City Skates. The birthplace of the legendary independent record label. Original snapshots of Johnny Rotten are casually tacked up on the wall next to old posters advertising concerts for Rough Trade bands like The Smiths. Surprising amount of reggae and electronica, plus zines. Open M-Sa 10am-6:30pm, Su 1-5pm. AmEx, MC, V.

Sister Ray, 94 Berwick St., W1 (☎7287 8385). Tube: Piccadilly Circus. Loud music competes with shouts from nearby Berwick St. Market. Let the staff guide you through the collection of indie, 70s/80s rock and punk, and beats. Open M-Sa 10:30am-7pm. AmEx, MC, V.

MARKETS

STREET MARKETS

Time spent bopping around London's street markets is 99% perspiration and 1% inspiration. There are wonderful bargains and must-have gems thrown in with a number of useless knick-knacks. For a complete list of the numerous street markets in the City and East End, see www.britannia.com/travel/london/cockney/markets.html

Bermondsey Market (a.k.a. New Caledonian), Bermondsey Sq. Tube: Bermondsey. Hundreds of stalls selling antiques have been located here since 1949. Real connoisseurs scoff at the Portobello sissies and arrive early (5am) to scout the goods. Open F 5am-2pm.

Berwick Street. Since the 1840s, this street market has rumbled with trade and Cockney accents. Famous for the widest and cheapest selection of fruits and vegetables in central London, the market has expanded to include cheap electricals and a small selection of clothes. The street also boasts an impressive array of record stores and cafes. Open M-Sa 9am-6pm.

Brick Lane, E1. In 1978, the latest immigration wave brought numbers of Bangladeshis. At the heart of the community is this street, which hosts a large weekly market with a South Asian flair (food, rugs, spices, bolts of fabric, strains of sitar), is lined with Indian and Bangladeshi restaurants, colorful textile shops, and grocers. Open Su 8am-2pm.

Brixton Market, Electric Ave., Pope's Rd., and Brixton Station Rd., as well as Granville Arcade and Market Row. Tube: Brixton. Shoppers from all over London mix with local crowds among vendors of food, clothing, and junk, while the record shops provide the soundtrack. Choose from fresh fish, vegetables, and West Indian cuisine, or browse through the stalls of African crafts and discount clothing. Open M-Tu and Th-Sa 8:30am-5pm, W 8:30am-1pm.

Camden Markets, off Camden High St. and Chalk Farm Rd., NW1 (☎7284 2084, stables market ☎7485 5511). Tube: Camden Town or Chalk Farm. Popular crowded place to find anything old or funky. Weekends are best. Open W-Su 9:30am-5:30pm (see p. 83).

Camden Passage, Islington High St., N1. Tube: Angel. Right from the Tube, then right on narrow, pedestrian-only Islington High St. Antiques, prints, and drawings. Open W and Sa 8:30am-3pm, but many start to pack up around 2pm (see p. 82).

Chapel Market (it's the name of the road too). Tube: Angel. Islington's largest street market. Open Tu and Th-Sa 9am-4pm, W and Su 9am-1pm.

Greenwich Market, Greenwich Church St. and College Approach (☎8293 3110). DLR: Cutty Sark. On summer Sundays, the streets are taken over by the young, old, bold, and beautiful seeking the ultimate bargain. Antiques and collectibles dominate Th; F-Su arts and crafts. Open Th-Su 10am-6pm. Greenwich also boasts an **Antique Market,** Burney St. Come in the summer—the number of stalls and bargains dwindles during the winter. Open Sa-Su 9am-5pm.

Petticoat Lane, E1. Tube: Liverpool St., Aldgate, or Aldgate East. Street after street of stalls, mostly cheap clothing and household appliances. The real action begins at about 9:30am. Open Su 9am-2pm; starts shutting down around noon.

Portobello Market, Portobello Rd. Tube: Notting Hill. The market makes this already lively 'hood downright vivacious every Sa. From museum-quality antiques to costume baubles, there's something for every taste and budget (or lack of either). Portobello has hosted freakshows, fortune-tellers, conjurers, and charlatans selling miracle elixirs since the early Victorian age. A look at the tattoo parlors or juice bars hawking Gusto herbal drink today should convince cynics that some things never change. Antique market Sa 7am-5pm. Clothes market F-Sa 8am-3pm. General market open M-W 8am-6pm, Th 9am-1pm, F-Sa 7am-7pm; Sa is the best day.

Spitalfields Market, E1. Tube: Shoreditch or Liverpool St. Formerly the site of London's main wholesale vegetable market, which has since relocated to larger and newer premises in Leyton, E10 (Rail: Leyton). There's still a market at the old site, though, as there has been since 1682; you can find a special item at a good price beneath the soaring glass ceiling of the victorian market building. Lots of veggies and produce. Open M-F 11am-3:30pm, Su10am-3pm.

TRADE MARKETS

London's fresh produce comes in through massive wholesale markets. These markets don't exactly roll out the red carpet for visitors, but they have wall-to-wall atmosphere.

Billingsgate (☎7987 1118). DLR: Canary Wharf or Poplar. This fish market has removed its fishy smells from the old site by St. Magnus Martyr in the City. Open Tu-Sa 5-9am.

Smithfield, Charterhouse St., EC1 (☎7248 0367) Tube: Farringdon or Barbican. Allegedly the largest meat market in the world, sells wholesale only. The market's name is derived from the "smooth field" upon which cattle were sold here in the mid-1800s. Pubs in the area wake up as early as the meat mongers and serve correspondingly flesh-filled breakfasts. Open M-F 4-10am.

RSC in
LONDON'S
LONGEST RUNNING
COMEDY HIT

CRITERION

CRITERION

'A delight'

Tonight
at
8pm

AMERICA

LONDON'S BEST COMEDY

Entertainment

When a man is tired of London, he is tired of life; for there is in London all that life can afford.
—Samuel Johnson, 1777

On any given day or night in London, you can choose from the widest range of entertainment a city can offer. The West End is perhaps the world's theater capital, supplemented by an adventurous "fringe" and an experimental National Theatre. Dance, film, comedy, sports, and countless more happenings will leave you amazed at the variety of listings.

THEATER

The stage for a national dramatic tradition dating from before Shakespeare, London maintains unrivaled standards in theater. The renowned Royal Academy for the Dramatic Arts (RADA) draws students from around the globe, while Hollywood stars prove their "acting cred" in West End plays. Playwrights such as Tom Stoppard, Harold Pinter, and David Hare premier their works in the West End at world class theaters like the National and the Almeida, while young writers and talented independent companies sustain the vibrant fringe theater scene.

Knowing what's on is easy enough: pick up the week's *Time Out*, look through the newspapers' weekend sections, or check out www.officiallondontheatre.co.uk. Knowing what to pick, however, is tougher, given the variety of offerings. *Evening Standard* awards and favorable reviews from the broadsheets are fair indications of quality.

THEATER SPEAK

The **West End** refers not only the part of central London where all the big theatres are but also to all top-class theatres. The **Fringe** is the collective name for the dozens of smaller, less commercial theaters in London: here, you'll find everything from community

on the cheap

cheap theater

Even if you don't have the cash to drive to the theater in a BMW, it's still possible to enjoy London's finest. Buying directly from the box office is almost always cheapest; there may be a small fee if you pay by credit card. For big-name shows, try to get tickets in advance; otherwise, you can go to the theaters early in the morning and try to get a day seat (see Buying Tickets, right). The cheapest seats in most theaters cost about £10, progressing upward to £40 for good stall seats, although previews and matinees (which usually start around 2-3pm) cost a few pounds less. If a show is sold out, returned tickets may be sold (at full price) just before curtain. Many theaters offer cheap student/senior standbys (indicated by "concs," "concessions," or "S" in listings) for around £7-10 shortly before curtain; come two hours beforehand and bring ID. If you are travelling with friends, try asking about group discounts. Day seats (which may provide only a restricted view) are sold at a reduced price to the public from 9 or 10am only on the day of the performance, but to snag one you'll need to queue up a lot earlier than that.

productions to avant-garde experiments. Fixed between those two extremes are **Off-West End** productions, which may lack West End resources but generally feature high quality acting and intelligent writing.

Stalls are seats nearest the stage. **Upper Circle** and **Dress Circle** refer to the balcony seats above the stalls. **Slips** are seats along the top edges of the theater. Slips are usually cheapest but offer the worst views. The **interval** is the time for gin or the loo. You can order interval drinks before the show and find them waiting for you at the end of the bar.

BUYING TICKETS

The **Leicester Square Half Price Ticket Booth,** in the booth topped by a clock tower on the south side of Leicester Square, sells tickets at half-price (plus a £2 booking fee) on the day of the performance, but carries only tickets for certain West End shows, as indicated on the sign outside. The most expensive seats are sold first. Lines are the worst on Saturday. (Open M-Sa noon-6:30pm, Su noon-3pm; cash only.) Legitimate ticket agencies add "booking fees" to the cost of the ticket. They include the **First Call Booking Office** (☎7420 0000), and **Ticketmaster** (☎7344 4444 or 7413 1442; www.ticketmaster.co.uk). To pick up tickets charged to a credit card, you must show the card. For big-name shows, try to get tickets early; as a last chance, go about 2 hours before the show begins and queue for returns. If you have problems with vendors, contact the **Society of London Theatre,** 32 Rose St., WC2E (☎7836 0971; open M-F 10am-6pm).

MAJOR THEATER COMPANIES

Royal Shakespeare Company Barbican Centre, Silk St., EC2 (☎7638 8891 for box office, www.barbican.org.uk). Tube: Barbican or Moorgate. The RSC makes its London home in the two theatres of the Barbican Centre: the **Barbican Theatre** and the **Pit.** The former's futuristic auditorium showcases the Bard's work in style; each row of seats has its own side door (there are no aisles). Forward-leaning balconies guarantee that none of the 1166 seats sit farther than 65 ft. from center stage, and every seat gives a clear view. The Pit provides a more intimate (200-seat) setting. Tickets for the main stage £7.50-24; weekday matinees £6-13; Saturday matinees and previews £8-18. Student and senior citizen standbys available in person or by phone from 9am on the day of the performance, £8 (1 per person). There are always several sign language and audio-described performances during the run of each show. Box office open daily 9am-8pm.

Royal National Theatre, South Bank Centre, SE1 (☎7452 3400; www.nt-online.org). Tube: Waterloo. As you might expect from the "National" part of the name, the RNT's brilliant repertory company puts on a bit of everything on its three stages. All stages offer an unobstructed view. Backstage tours M-Sa £4.75, concessions £3.75. Book in advance; call for times. Box office open M-Sa 10am-8pm.

Olivier and **Lyttelton:** tickets £10-32, day seats (available from 10am on day of performance) £10-14, general standby seats (available 2hr. before show) £12-16, student standby (available 45min. before show) £8-10, standing £4.50-6. Discounted admission for those in wheelchairs (all seats £15-16) and for other disabled people (£8-16). Discounted seats to matinees for under-18s (all seats £9-10) and seniors (£13-14).
Cottesloe: Tickets £10-22. Discounted admission for those in wheelchairs and the visually impaired (all seats £15) and for other disabled people (£8-15). Discounted entry to matinees for under-18s (£9) and seniors (£13).
Shakespeare's Globe Theatre, New Globe Walk, Bankside, SE1 (☎7401 9919 or Ticketmaster☎7316 4703). Tube: London Bridge. Using this reconstruction of the original Globe (where the Bard himself put on some plays) might have been nothing more than a gimmick, but the company employs the 3-tiered open-air space well. Patrons may either purchase spots on the wooden benches or stand through a performance as "groundlings." The latter may actually be preferable: it costs less, allows a historical communion with the Elizabethan peasantry, and puts you much closer to the stage. However, groundlings should prepare for the possibility of rain: umbrellas are prohibited because they impede sight lines. Shows take place May-Sept. Wheelchair access. Box office open M-Sa 10am-8pm, until 6pm by phone.

WEST END THEATERS

Adelphi Theatre, Maiden Lane, WC2R (☎7344 0055). Tube: Charing Cross. Musicals, both new and revivals. Now showing *Chicago.* £16-36.
Albery Theatre, St. Martin's Lane, WC2N (☎7369 1730). Tube: Leicester Sq. Comedies and dramas, old and new, seats £7.50-29.50. Standby for concessions £12.50 30min. before curtain.
Aldwych Theatre, The Strand, WC2B (☎7416 6000) Tube: Covent Garden. Lord Lloyd Webber's *Whistle Down the Wind,* £15-35.
Apollo Theatre, Shaftesbury Ave., W1 (☎7494 5070). Tube: Piccadilly Circus. Super-glitzy venue for popular shows.
Apollo Victoria Theatre, Wilton Rd., SW1 (☎7416 6070). Tube: Victoria. Venue for *Starlight Express,* now in its 16th year. £12.50-30. Concessions 1hr. before performance.
Arts Theatre, 6-7 Great Newport St., WC2 (☎7836 2132). Tube: Leicester Sq. New Dramas and musicals. £15. Children's shows Sept.-May £5-£9.
Cambridge Theatre, Earlham St., WC2 (☎7494 5080). Tube: Covent Garden. *Grease* is the word. £10-30, Sa £12.50-£30. Student standbys M-Th 1hr. before performance.
Criterion Theatre, Piccadilly Circus, W1 (☎7369 1747; www.reduced-shakespeare.co.uk). Tube: Piccadilly Circus. *The Complete Works of William Shakespeare (Abridged).* Tu *The Complete History of America (Abridged).* £6-27.50. Standby for concessions £12.50.
Dominion Theatre, Tottenham Court Rd., W1 (☎7656 1888). Tube: Tottenham Ct. Rd. Notre Dame de Paris. £7.50-37.50.
Theatre Royal, Drury Lane, Catherine St., WC2B (☎7494 5060). Tube: Covent Garden. *Witches of Eastwick.* £7.50-37.50. Student standbys M-Th 1hr. before performance.
Duke of York's Theatre, St. Martin's Lane, WC2 (☎7836 5122). Tube: Leicester Sq. New experimental dramas. £8-32.50.
Duchess Theatre, Catherine St., WC2 (☎7494 5075). Tube: Covent Garden. New dramas and musicals. £15-30. Standby for concessions, £10.
Fortune Theatre, Russell St., WC2 (☎7836 2238). Tube: Covent Garden. *The Woman in Black.* Never screamed in a theater? You will. £9.50-25. Standby for concessions. £10.
Garrick Theatre, Charing Cross Rd., WC2 (☎7494 5085). Tube: Leicester Sq. Revivals of dramas and musicals. £12-25. Standby for concessions. £10.
Gielgud Theatre, 33 Shaftesbury Ave., W1 (☎7494 5065). Tube: Piccadilly Circus. Straight plays, mainly comedies. £17.50-32.50.
Her Majesty's Theatre, Haymarket, SW1 (☎7494 5400). Tube: Piccadilly Circus. *Phantom of the Opera.* £10-35. Book at least a month ahead for Sa night tickets.
London Palladium Theatre, Argyll St., W1 (☎7494 5020). Tube: Oxford Circus. *Saturday Night Fever.* £10-37.50. Student standbys for W matinee £10-£15.
Lyceum Theatre, Wellington St., WC2 (☎7243 9000). Tube: Charing Cross. Musicals. *The Lion King* will most likely hold court through 2001. Call for information. £15-35. Concessions £15 1hr. before performance.

Lyric Theatre Hammersmith, King St., W6 (☎8741 2311; www.lyric.co.uk). Tube: Hammersmith. High-quality repertory comedy and drama. Wheelchair accessible. £8-15, M all tickets £5. Box office open M-W 10am-6pm.

Lyric Shaftesbury Theatre, Shaftesbury Ave., W1 (☎7494 5045). Tube: Piccadilly Circus. *A Busy Day.* £7.50-26.

New London Theatre, Pirker St., WC2 (☎7405 0072). Tube: Covent Garden. *Cats.* £10-37.50

Old Vic, Waterloo Rd., SE1 (☎7928 7616). Tube: Waterloo. One of the most beautiful performance spaces in London. High-brow theater. £7.50-30.

Open Air Theatre, Inner Circle, Regent's Park, NW1 (☎7486 2431; www.open-air-theatre.org.uk). Tube: Baker St. A London institution. 2 Shakespeare plays, a musical, and a kids' show every June to mid-Sept. Wheelchair access; some sign-interpreted performances. £8.50-22.50. Concessions £8 1hr. before curtain; kids' shows (all matinees) £7.50; late night shows £5.

Palace Theatre, Shaftesbury Ave., W1 (☎7434 0909). Tube: Leicester Sq. *Les Miserables.* Actors call them "the Glums." £7-35.

Phoenix Theatre, Charing Cross Rd., WC2 (☎7369 1733). Tube: Leicester Sq. *Blood Brothers.* £11.50-32.50, concessions £12.50.

Prince Edward Theatre, Old Compton St., W1 (☎7447 5400; www.mamma-mia.com). Tube: Leicester Sq. *Mamma Mia!* £15-35.

Prince of Wales Theatre, Coventry St., W1 (☎7839 5972). Tube: Piccadilly Circus. £17.50-37.50. Student standbys £13.

Royal Court Theatre, Sloane Sq. (☎7565 5000; www.royalcourttheatre.com). Tube: Sloane Sq. Affordable, top quality performances in two theatres. Tickets £5-22.50. M all seats £5. Concessions £5, on day of performance. Standing tickets 10p (yup, 10p) 1hr. before performance. Box office open M-Sa 10am-curtain; during non-performance weeks M-F 10am-6pm.

St. Martin's Theatre, West St., WC2 (☎7836 1443). Tube: Leicester Sq. Agatha Christie's *The Mousetrap* in its 5th decade. £11-26.

Savoy Theatre, The Strand, WC2 (☎7836 8888). Tube: Charing Cross. Varied repertory—plays, musicals, and some ballets, mostly contemporary. £12.50-30.

Victoria Palace Theatre, Victoria St., SW1 (☎7834 1317). Tube: Victoria. *Annie.* £10-35. Student standby £15.

Wyndham's Theatre, Charing Cross Rd., WC2 (☎7369 1736). Tube: Leicester Sq. *Art.* £9.50-29.50.

OFF-WEST END THEATERS

The Almeida, Almeida St., N1 (☎7359 4404). Tube: Angel or Highbury & Islington. The theater will close for renovations in February 2001, but the company will put on productions elsewhere; call for details. Tickets £7-25; students and seniors £7-11. Box office open 9:30am-curtain.

Battersea Arts Centre (BAC), Old Town Hall, 176 Lavender Hill, SW11 (☎7223 2223). Rail: Clapham Junction (from Waterloo or Victoria). One of the top fringe venues. Main and 2 studio stages with "mainstream" (radical corruptions of Shakespeare and other canonical texts) and experimental works. In Oct. holds British Festival of Visual Theatre. Tickets £6-13, concessions £4.50-6.50; Tu "pay what you can."

The Bush, Bush Hotel, Shepherd's Bush Green, W12 (☎8743 3388). Tube: Goldhawk Rd. or Shepherd's Bush. Above a branch of O'Neill's. Well-known for innovative plays by new writers. 50p membership fee. Telephone booking M-Sa 10am-6pm. Box office open M-Sa from 6:30pm. £10, concessions £7.

Donmar Warehouse, Earlham St., WC2 (☎7369 1732). Tube: Covent Garden. Mainstream contemporary works. £12-18, concessions £8 1hr. before show.

Drill Hall, 16 Chenies St., WC1 (☎7637 8270). Tube: Goodge St. Politically active productions, often with a gay slant. Vegetarian restaurant downstairs.

The Gate, The Prince Albert, 11 Pembridge Rd., W11 (☎7229 0706). Tube: Notting Hill Gate. Pub-theater hosts mostly new plays. £10, concessions £5. Box office open M-F 10am until 30min. before performance.

Greenwich Theatre, Crooms Hill, SE10 (☎8858 7755). BR: Greenwich. This friendly 423-seat venue mixes West End quality with fringe adventurousness. £9.25-15.50, concessions £5.50-6.50. Call ahead for wheelchair access.

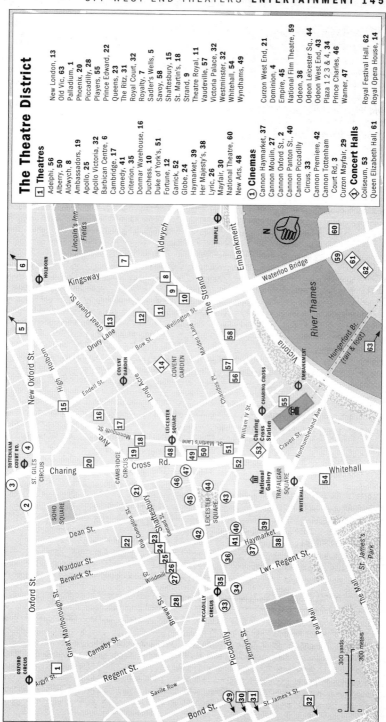

The Theatre District

1 Theatres

Adelphi, **56**
Alberry, **50**
Aldwych, **8**
Ambassadors, **19**
Apollo, **25**
Apollo Victoria, **32**
Barbican Centre, **6**
Cambridge, **17**
Comedy, **41**
Criterion, **35**
Donmar Warehouse, **16**
Duchess, **10**
Duke of York's, **51**
Fortune, **12**
Garrick, **52**
Globe, **24**
Haymarket, **39**
Her Majesty's, **38**
Lyric, **26**
Mayfair, **30**
National Theatre, **60**
New Arts, **48**

New London, **13**
Old Vic, **63**
Palladium, **1**
Phoenix, **20**
Piccadilly, **28**
Players, **55**
Prince Edward, **22**
Queens, **23**
The Ritz, **31**
Royal Court, **32**
Royalty, **7**
Sadler's Wells, **5**
Savoy, **58**
Shaftesbury, **15**
St. Martin's, **18**
Strand, **9**
Theatre Royal, **11**
Vaudeville, **57**
Victoria Palace, **32**
Westminster, **32**
Whitehall, **54**
Wyndhams, **49**

Curzon West End, **21**
Dominion, **4**
Empire, **45**
National Film Theatre, **59**
Odeon, **36**
Odeon Leicester Sq., **44**
Odeon West End, **43**
Plaza 1 2 3 & 4, **34**
Prince Charles, **46**
Warner, **47**

1 Cinemas

Cannon Haymarket, **37**
Cannon Moulin, **27**
Cannon Oxford St., **2**
Cannon Panton St., **40**
Cannon Piccadilly
Circus, **33**
Cannon Premiere, **42**
Cannon Tottenham
Court Rd, **3**
Curzon Mayfair, **29**

⬦ Concert Halls

Coliseum, **53**
Queen Elizabeth Hall, **61**

Royal Festival Hall, **62**
Royal Opera House, **14**

ELECTRIC CO.

The Electric Cinema, on the corner of Blenheim Crescent and Portobello Road, is England's oldest purpose-built cinema. Its history would spell nothing but turmoil to most: During WWI crazed mobs stoned the place, accusing its German manager of communicating to zeppelins overhead; in the 20s the ushers had to spray the audience with pest spray to cut down on flea bites; and during the 40s, the projectionist was serial killer John Christie. After closing in the late 80s, this "temple of cinema" looked like it would succumb to the long goodbye, but in the summer of 2000 it was bought by businessman Peter Simon (founder of Monsoon and Accessorize, see p. 130 and p. 132), and is to be refurbished and reopened in time for Christmas 2000.

Hampstead Theatre, 98 Avenue Rd., NW3 (☎7722 9301). Tube: Swiss Cottage. Alumni include John Malkovich. Tickets £9-17; concessions £6. Box office open M-Sa 10am-7pm.

The King's Head, 115 Upper St., N1 (☎7226 1916). Tube: Angel or Highbury and Islington. When it opened about 30 years ago, the King's Head was London's first pub theatre. Tickets around £15, concessions £10. Box office open M-Sa 10am-8pm, Su 10am-4pm.

Riverside Studios, Crisp Rd., W6 (☎8237 1111; www.riversidestudios.co.uk). Tube: Hammersmith. A mix of theatre, comedy, dance, and even the odd TV show. Box office open noon-9pm.

Tricycle Theatre, 269 Kilburn High Rd., NW6 (☎7328 1000). Tube: Kilburn or buses #98 or 16. A local favorite—some good avant-garde performances. Best known for new black, Jewish, and Irish playwrights. Also an arthouse cinema. Wheelchair accessible £8.50-15, but discounts and concessions bring the prices to as low as £2.50 (check listings). Box office open M-S 10am-8pm.

Young Vic, 66 The Cut, SE1 (☎7928 6363). Tube: Waterloo. Inland from the actual river bank, across from the Old Vic. One of London's most acclaimed Off-West End venues. Seats £6-18. Telephone bookings M-Sa 10am-6pm or 10am to curtain (in person).

FRINGE THEATERS

Trinity Arts Center London, 17 Gloucester Terr., W2. Tube: Paddington, then bus #27. Also served by Buses #7, 23, 36. Community theater based in Paddington—local kid's productions to guest companies. Student discounts. £2.50-7.

Etcetera Theatre, Oxford Arms, 265 Camden High St., NW1 (☎7482 4857). Tube: Camden Town. Frequent presentations of experimental plays. £5-7. Box office open M-Sa 10am-8pm.

Holland Park Open Air Theatre, Holland Park, W8 (☎7602 7856). Tube: Holland Park Open-air stage with opera and ballet in the summer (June to mid-Aug.). Tickets £26, concessions £20. Box office open 10am-curtain (10am-6pm on non-performance days).

Man in the Moon, 392 King's Rd., SW3 (☎7351 2876). Tube: Sloane Sq., then bus #11, 19, or 22. A small pub-theater on its way to greatness.

New End Theatre, 27 New End, NW3 (☎7794 0022). Tube: Hampstead. New and classic works by local and touring companies. £8-14, concessions £6-10. Box office open M-Sa 10am-8pm.

The Old Red Lion, 418 St. John St., EC1 (☎7837 7816). Tube: Angel. One of London's top fringe theaters, usually presenting intriguing plays by new writers. Around £8, concessions £6 Su-Th. Box office open daily 10am-11pm.

Oval House, 52-54 Kennington Oval, SE11 (☎7582 7680). Tube: Oval. Opposite the Oval cricket ground round the corner from the Tube station, with a focus on black, Asian, and gay and lesbian playwrights. £8, concessions £5. Box office open M-F 5-8:30pm.

FILM

London's film scene offers everything. The heart of the celluloid monster is **Leicester Square,** where the latest releases premiere a day before hitting the chains around the city. Among the largest first-run screens are the **Empire** (☎ (0870) 603 4567) and **Odeon Leicester Sq.** The city's main chains are **ABC** (www.abccinemas.co.uk), **Odeon** (☎ (0870) 505 0007; www.odeon.co.uk), **Screen** (www.screencinemas.co.uk), **UCI** (☎ (08700) 102 030), and **UGC** (☎ 0870 907 0716). Tickets to movies in West End cinemas cost £8-10, although tickets screenings before 5pm on weekdays are usually cheaper. UGC sells a ticket allowing you to watch an unlimited number of movies in UGC cinemas for a month (\$30 including West End cinemas, £15 otherwise). The annual **London Film Festival** (www.lff.org.uk), held in November, takes place at the National Film Theatre (see below). While Hollywood shows are released much later in London than in the US, film buffs will be pleased at the large number of repertory cinemas screening classics and obscure arthouse works. Newspapers and *Time Out* carry listings and reviews of other commercial and independent films; try the *Guardian's* Guide section in their Friday edition, or their website at www.filmunlimited.co.uk. Also worth perusing are the ICA and NFT monthly schedules, available on-site (see listings below). Many cinemas have bars and cafés.

ABC Swiss Centre, 10 Wardour St., Leicester Sq., WC2 (☎ 7439 4470). Tube: Leicester Sq. or Piccadilly Circus. New European films and artsy films as well. M £4.30; Tu-Th £4.30 before 5pm, £6.50 after 5pm; F £4.30 before 5pm, £6.70 after 5pm; Sa-Su £6.70.

BFI London IMAX Cinema, South Bank, Waterloo SE1 (☎ 7902 1234). Tube: Waterloo. £6.75, children 5-16 £4.75, second ticket £4; concessions £5.75; children under 5 free.

Ciné Lumière, 17 Queenberry Pl., SW7 (☎ 7838 2144). Tube: South Kensington. Artsy French films, as you might have guessed from the name. Tickets £6, concessions £4.

Curzon Soho, 93-107 Shaftesbury Ave., W1 (☎ 7439 4805; bookings ☎ 7734 2255). Tube: Leicester Sq. Artsy films and a sleek bar. Wheelchair access. £8, £5 M and before 5pm Tu-F; students and seniors £5, children £4. Su double bills £5.

Gate Cinema, 87 Notting Hill Gate, W11 (☎ 7727 4043). Tube: Notting Hill Gate. A Victorian-interior 240-seater cinema with an arthouse selection. £6.50, M-F first film before 3pm £3.50, M-F before 6pm and late shows F and Sa, students, and seniors £3.

Institute of Contemporary Arts (ICA) Cinema, Nash House, The Mall, W1 (☎ 7930 3647). Tube: Charing Cross. Cutting-edge contemporary cinema, plus an extensive list of older arthouse favorites. Before 5pm £4.50, concessions £3.50; after 5pm £6.50, concessions £5.50. Experimental films and classics in the *cinémathèque* £5.

The Lux, 2-4 Hoxton Sq., N1 (☎ 7684 0201). Tube: Old St. While rumors of Hoxton's coolness have been exaggerated, the Lux lives up to its hip reputation. The place to go if you are after something obscure and peculiar. £6, concessions £4. Sometimes closed M-Tu.

Phoenix, 52 High Rd. East Finchley, N2 (info ☎ 8883 2233; box office ☎ 8444 6789). Tube: East Finchley. Sunday double bills mix mainstream hits and classics from around the world. Children's cinema club Sa 11am (no adults without children allowed; £3). Tickets £4.75-5.50, M £3 all day, concessions £3-3.50 (except Sa night).

The Prince Charles, Leicester Pl., WC2 (☎ 7734 9127 or (0901) 272 7007; www.princecharlescinema.com). Tube: Leicester Sq. A Soho institution: 4 shows daily; generally second runs and a few classics for only £2.50-3.50 (M £1.50-2). Originator of hot trend *Sing-a-Long-a-Sound-of-Music*, where von Trappists dress as everything from nuns to "Ray, a drop of golden sun" (F 7:30pm, £12.50; Su 2pm, £10, children always £8). Catch the *Rocky Horror Picture Show,* complete with a live troupe, for £6, concessions £3 every F at 11:45pm.

National Film Theatre (NFT), South Bank Centre, SE1 (☎ 7928 3232; www.bfi.org.uk). Tube: Waterloo, or Embankment and cross the Hungerford footbridge. One of the world's leading cinemas, with a mind-boggling array of films (mostly arthouse favorites and recent raves) in three auditoriums. Program changes daily. Most screenings £6.50, concessions £5.

The Ritzy Cinema, Brixton Oval, Coldharbour Ln., SW2 (☎ 7737 2121, bookings ☎ 7733 2229). Tube: Brixton. This classy picture house shows a combination of artsy and mainstream films in its 5 screens, including a daily "world cinema" matinee (£2) and a kid's show every Sa morning (£1 adult £2). The bar is one of the best among London cinemas. Wheelchair accessible. £6.50 all M shows and Tu-F shows before 6pm £4, students and seniors £3.50 except F-Su after 6pm, under 16 £2.50. Bar open M-Sa 5-11pm, Su 2-10:30pm.

the BIG $plurge

the fat lady sings

Germanophiles and Italophiles might protest that the phrase English opera is an oxymoron: what opera written in a language as cacophonous as English could possibly match the grandeur of a Puccini libretto? Well, they might dirty their tight black jeans when they learn English opera has a rich history beginning in the 18th century. In 1728 **John Gay** satirized English society in the *Beggar's Opera*, written a good half-century before opera galvanized the Continent. Today, anyone expecting stuffy productions of 19th-century works is in for a shock. While Puccini and Verdi continue to be staples of the scene, Operas provide some of the most avant-garde stagings in London. Nudity, profanity, and screeching chords? Welcome to British opera.

Opera is an art form best experienced in style. If you're willing to part with the dosh, a night at the **Royal Opera** (see p. 151) will thrill your eyes and ears. Recently reopened after major renovations, this venerable venue is home to some of Europe's finest opera and ballet. Standbys cost around £12 for ballet and £15 for opera.

A night at the **English National Opera** in the London Coliseum (also on p. 150) is equally enchanting—and it's in English. Standby tickets cost £18.

The Riverside Studio Cinema, Crisp Rd., W6 (☎8237 1111; www.riversidestudios.co.uk). Tube: Hammersmith. Houses both a theater and a repertory cinema which shows great art house films and classics. Box office open noon-9pm. £5, concessions £4, including double bills.

COMEDY

London is laughing its head off—comedy has become as hot as rock'n'roll. For one-man shows, featuring big name stars, check out the **Apollo.** One of the best places to catch new shows (and not just because it's free) is at the **BBC recording studios.** July is a very good month for comedy in London, as many acts preview their work here before taking it up to the Edinburgh Fringe in August. September, some say, is even better than July. Many acts follow up their Edinburgh run with a London show, and by then they've been reviewed to death, so you can be sure you're getting quality.

Canal Cafe Theatre, The Bridge House, Delamere Terrace, W2 (☎7289 6054). Tube: Royal Oak or Warwick Ave. Established venue for up-and-coming comedy, as well as theater and cabaret above a waterside pub in idyllic Little Venice.

Comedy Store, Haymarket House, 1a Oxendon St., SW1 (☎7344 0234). Tube: Piccadilly Circus. The Big One. Stand-up most of the week, W and Su improv. F and Sa shows at 8pm and midnight.

Downstairs at the King's Head, 2 Crouch End Hill, N8 (☎8340 1028). Tube: Finsbury Park. One of the oldest comedy clubs in the city, sometimes known to offer comedic ventriloquism. Shows W-Su 8:30pm, try-out night every other Th. Free-£7, with some concessions.

Hackney Empire, 291 Mare St., E8 (☎8985 2424; www.hackneyempire.co.uk). Tube: Bethnal Green then bus #253 north; Rail: Hackney Central. Buses #30, 38, 242. Beautiful theater hosts popular routines but mostly focuses on comedy theater. £4-25. Prices and hours vary by show. Box office open M-Sa 10am-6pm. MC, V.

Jongleurs at Battersea, 49 Lavender Gdns. SW11, BR: Clapham Jct.; **Jongleurs at Bow Wharf,** 221 Grove Rd., E3, Tube: Mile End; **Jongleurs at Camden Lock,** Middle Yard, Chalk Farm Rd., NW1, Tube: Camden Town (☎7564 2500). Highly successful and popular group of sleek, purpose-built comedy clubs with top line-ups. Shows F-Sa.

Lee Hurst's Backyard Comedy Club, (☎7739 3122), 231 Cambridge Heath Rd., E2. Tube: Bethnal Green. Owned by a successful comedian who fills the place with his top comedy pals.

MUSIC

London's dynamic music scene attracts astonishing diversity. Bengali drummers and South African choirs, Brazilian jazz groups, and Quebecois folk singers share the same stages—and sometimes similar audiences. Unparalleled classical resources include five world-class orchestras, two opera houses, and countless concert halls. See **Nightlife** for details of live **Rock and Pop** (p. 185), **Jazz** (p. 186), and **Folk and Roots** (p. 187).

CLASSICAL

London's world-class orchestras provide only a fraction of the notes that fill its major music centers. London has been the home of some of the great conductors of the century including Sir Thomas Beecham, Otto Klemperer, and Andre Previn. The Barbican Hall and the South Bank Centre host a superb lineup of groups, including the **Academy of St. Martin-in-the-Fields,** the **London Festival Orchestra,** the **London Chamber Orchestra,** the **London Soloists Chamber Orchestra,** the **London Classical Players,** and the **London Mozart Players.** Vladimir Ashkenazy's **Royal Philharmonic Orchestra** and the **BBC Symphony Orchestra** pop up around town as well.

Medieval and Renaissance music still commands a following in England; many London churches offer performances, often at lunchtime. Premier among them are **St. Martin-in-the-Fields,** Trafalgar Sq. (☎ 7839 8362; Tube: Charing Cross); **St. James's Piccadilly,** 197 Piccadilly (☎ 7381 0441; Tube: Piccadilly); and **St. Bride's,** Fleet St. (☎ 7353 1301; Tube: Blackfriars). **St. Paul's boys' choir** sings at the Sunday 5pm service. Watch for the **Academy of Ancient Music,** the **Early Music Consort of London,** and the **Praetorius Ensemble.** Artists from the **Royal College of Music,** Prince Consort Rd., SW7 (☎ 7589 3643; tube: South Kensington) and the **Royal Academy of Music,** Marylebone Rd., NW1 (☎ 7935 5461; Tube: Baker St. or Regent's park) play at their home institutions and at the main city halls. Concerts at these schools are often free—call for details. Check with the **University of London Union,** 1 Malet St., WC1 (☎ 7580 9551; Tube: Goodge St.), for on-campus music there. Although the regular season ends in mid-July, the **Proms** at Royal Albert Hall and a series of festivals on the **South Bank** in July and August take up the slack admirably, offering traditional orchestral music along with more exotic tidbits (see below).

Barbican Hall, Barbican Centre, Silk St., EC2 (☎ 7638 8891; 24-hr. recorded information ☎ 7382 7272; www.barbican.org.uk). Tube: Barbican or Moorgate. The venerable **London Symphony Orchestra** (www.lso.co.uk) is resident here, putting on 85 performances a year; the hall also welcomes a number of guest artists. LSO concerts £6.50-35, under 16 £3, student and senior standby tickets sold shortly before the performance £6-8. Prices may vary for other concerts. Box office open 9am-8pm.

Blackheath Concert Halls, 23 Lee Rd., Blackheath, SE3 (☎ 8463 0100; www.blackheath-halls.com). Rail: Blackheath, then left from the station, or bus #53 from Oxford Circus. Attracts top performers year-round, and serves as a venue for the Greenwich and Docklands Festival (see below). Tickets £2.50-50. Amex, MC, V.

Royal Albert Hall, Kensington Gore, SW7 (☎ 7589 8212; www.royalalberthall.com). Tube: South Kensington or Knightsbridge (buses #9, 10, and 52 go by the Hall from either station). London's premier concert hall, seating 5300. The **Proms** (BBC Henry Wood Promenade Concerts) never fail to enliven London summers; every day for 8 weeks from mid-July to mid-Sept., an impressive roster of musicians performs outstanding programs, including annually commissioned new works. Camaraderie and craziness develop in the long lines for standing room outside. The last night of the Proms traditionally steals the show, with the mass singing of "Land of Hope and Glory" and "Jerusalem." A lottery determines who will be allowed to paint their faces as Union Jacks and "air-conduct" in person. Those who lose can catch the live broadcast in Hyde Park. All the Proms are also broadcast live on BBC Radio 3, 90-93 FM. £5-60. Over 1000 standing tickets in the Arena (the floor of the hall) and the Gallery (the very top of the hall) are available one hour before each concert for just £3, but be ready to queue for longer than that. Tickets for other shows. Box office open daily 9am-9pm.

South Bank Centre (Box office ☎ 7960 4242; £1 booking fee; boxoffice@rfh.org.uk; www.sbc.org.uk). Tube: Waterloo. Three venues host classical shows along with many other diverse groups. The 2500-seat Royal Festival Hall often houses the London Philharmonic and the Philharmonia Orchestra. The 2 other venues in the South Bank Centre, the Queen Elizabeth Hall and the Purcell Room, also host some classical shows. Tickets £10-50. Students, seniors, and children receive a discount for advance tickets, and can queue for standbys (usually a little over half-price) from 5pm on the night of performances. Box office open daily 10am-9pm.

St. John's, Smith Square, SW1. (☎ 7222 1061). Tube: Westminster. A schedule weighted toward chamber groups and soloists. £6-20, concessions for students and seniors.

Wigmore Hall, 36 Wigmore St., W1 (☎ 7935 2141). Tube: Bond St. or Oxford Circus. Elegant venue hosts concerts and chamber music. Tickets £6-35. 1hr. standbys at lowest price. In summer, Su morning coffee concerts begin at 11:30am; £8, coffee free. Closed end of July through Aug. Box office open 10am-5pm.

FOOTBALL FANS ARE COMING HOME

One of the greatest words in english is "hooligan," which commonly refers to a drunk causing mayhem and riots at a football match. In the summer of 2000, the term was on everyone's lips, as England was in the doghouse due to the European Football Championships, where hundreds of hooligans wreaked havoc in the tiny and very afraid Dutch and Belgian towns that hosted the chamionships. What's worse, the latest hooliganism events have been ethnically motivated, and a nasty incident in Istanbul left two Leeds United supporters dead in February 2000. Hundreds of Brits were deported, and a very serious discussion of Britain's "drinking culture" was on every media outlet. What's more, this all came just before the vote for who would host World Cup 2006. England's bid, inevitably, failed. It looks now like a ban from international travel, especially during important matches, is a distinct possibility for those convicted of football hooliganism.

REGULAR OFF-SEASON FESTIVALS

City of London Festival (☎ 7638 8891; www.colf.org). An explosion of activity around the city's grandest monuments: music in the livery halls and churches, plays at various venues, opera, art exhibitions, and walks that often allow access to buildings otherwise closed to the public. Box office (Barbican Centre, Silk St. entrance) open daily 9am-8pm. Many events free, most others £10-40. Booking begins early May.

Greenwich and Docklands International Festival (☎8305 1818; book tickets at ☎8900 0355; www.festival.org.uk). Outdoor concerts, dance and theater from performers across the globe. Closing ceremonies culminate in a spectacular fireworks display. Festival July 6-15, 2001. Free-£20, depending on the event.

Kenwood Lakeside Concerts, at Kenwood, on Hampstead Heath (☎8233 5892, box office ☎7344 4444 for Ticketmaster booking with a £1 service charge). Tube: Golders Green or Archway, then bus #210; or East Finchley, then take a free shuttle bus to Kenwood (5-7:50pm, and after concerts until 10:45pm). Music floats to the audience from a performance shell across the lake while laser shows burn their retinas. Reserved deck chairs £16.50-18, concessions £15. Grass admission £13, concessions £11.50; you can listen from afar for free. Amex, MC, V.

OPERA AND BALLET

Holland Park Theatre, box office in the Visitor Centre (☎7602 7856). Tube: Holland Park. Open-air opera and ballet from a number of companies early June to late Aug., in both English and the original languages. Some dance and classical music, too. Tickets £26, children, seniors, and students £20.50. AmEx, MC, V.

London Coliseum, St. Martin's La., WC2 (☎7632 8300). Tube: Charing Cross or Leicester Sq. The English National Opera's (ENO) repertoire leans toward the contemporary, and all works are sung in English. Seats reserved in advance range approx. £6.50-55. The Half-Price Ticket Booth sells tickets the day of the show if available (see p. 142), or you can show up at the box office weekdays (and Sa matinees) from 10am to claim the 100 day seats in the balcony and 46 in the dress circle. Standbys available 3hr. before curtain (1 per person, £18; Sa available to all, Su-F students and seniors only).

Peacock Theatre, Portugal St. WC2 (☎7314 8800, 7305 1818). Tube: Holborn. Hosts modern and contemporary dance troupes. Box office open daily 8am-8pm.

The Place, 17 Duke's Rd., WC1 (☎7387 0031). Tube: Euston. Britain's national contemporary dance center. Showcases new/experimental dance, independent British dance, Continental and Oriental dance. Put on your boogie shoes for the evening dance classes (around £5, concessions £3; call 387 0161 for details). Performances £4-10.

Royal Opera House, at Covent Garden, Box St.; box office at 48 Floral St., WC2 (☎ 7304 4000). Tube: Covent Garden. Newly refurbished, this grand opera house is home to the **Royal Opera** and the **Royal Ballet**. Ticket prices at this grand old venue do much to keep ballet and opera an amusement of the idle rich. Tickets come in a bewildering variety of prices and flavors; call the box office for ticket prices. Box office open M-Sa 10am-8pm.

Sadler's Wells, Rosebery Ave., EC1 (☎ 7863 8000; www.sadlers-wells.com). Tube: Angel. London's premier space for dance, featuring anything from ballet and contemporary dance. Free bus travel to the theatre; just show your ticket at the ticket office. Tickets £7.50-30; some student and senior tickets £5. Student and senior standbys £7.50-10, available 1hr. before performance. Box office open M-Sa 10am-8:30pm.

OFF THE BEATEN PATH

> London, that great cesspool into which all the loungers and idlers of the Empire are irresistibly drained.
> —Sir Arthur Conan Doyle, A Study in Scarlet

City Farms: Goats, ducks, sheep, poultry, and sometimes cattle, horses, and donkeys bleat, quack, baa, moo, and cluck at **Kentish Town,** 1 Cressfield Close, off Grafton Rd., NW5 (☎ 7916 5420; Tube: Kentish Town; open Tu-Su 9:30am-5:30pm; **pony rides** Su from 1pm); **Freightliners,** Sheringham Rd., N7 (☎ 7609 0467; Tube: Highbury & Islington; open Tu-Su 9am-1pm and 2-5pm); **Hackney,** 1a Goldsmith's Row, E2 (☎ 7729 6381; Tube: Bethnal Green; open Tu-Su 10am-4:30pm); **Mudchute City Farm,** Pier St., E14 (☎ 7515 5901; open daily 8am-5pm, sometimes later on Tu and Th); **Stepping Stones,** Stepney Way, E1 (☎ 7790 8204; tube: Stepney Green; open Tu-Su 10am-6pm); and **Surrey Docks,** Rotherhithe St., SE16 (☎ 7231 1010; tube: Surrey Quays; open Tu-Th and Sa-Su 10am-1pm and 2-5pm). Call to confirm all times. All are free.

The College of Psychic Studies, 16 Queensberry Pl., SW7 (☎ 7589 3292; www.psychic-studies.org.uk). Tube: South Kensington. Increase your psychic sensitivity through lectures (Tu 7pm; £5, concessions £3), musical events (up to £7), and spiritual awareness courses (weekend £28 or £45; 10-week evening courses £80-135). Open M-Th 10am-7:30pm, F 10am-5pm. MC, V.

Islington Arts Factory, 2 Parkhurst Rd., N7 (☎ 7607 0561). Tube: Caledonian Rd. Exit left onto Caledonian Rd. and turn left onto Hillmarton Rd., Islington Arts Factory is in the converted church at the intersection of Camden Rd. and Parkhurst Rd. The Factory offers dance and art classes (£3 term membership fee required to enroll) and sponsors small free exhibitions. For £4.15-7.75 per hr. you can rent a music studio fully equipped with a drumset, P.A., and mikes. Art studios (£6.70 per hr.), dance studios (£9.30-10.30), and darkrooms (£3.60) also available. Open M-Th 10am-9:45pm, F 10am-7:15pm, Sa 2-5:45pm, Su 11am-5:30pm.

London College of Fashion, 20 John Princes St., W1 (☎ 7514 7400). Tube: Oxford Circus. If you want some pampering and have time and a few quid to spare, offer yourself to the students at the LCF's beauty-therapy department. Prices (to cover the cost of products used) start from £3 for a haircut. Open Oct.-June M-F 9am-5pm, but call to make an appointment—no walk-ins.

The Old Bailey (☎ 7248 3277), at the corner of Old Bailey and Newgate St. Tube: St. Paul's. Trial-watching persists as a favorite diversion; the courts fill up whenever a gruesome or scandalous case is in progress. See **Sights,** p. 58.

Speakers' Corner. In the northeast corner of Hyde Park. See **Sights,** p. 79.

Radio and TV Shows. Become part of a live studio audience. Get free tickets for the endless variations on "Master Mind." Write to the **BBC Ticket Unit,** Broadcasting House, Portland Pl., W1; **Thames TV Ticket Unit,** 306 Euston Rd., NW1; or **London Weekend Television,** Kent House, Upper Ground, SE1.

Vidal Sassoon School of Hairdressing, 56 Davies Mews, W1 (☎ 7318 5205). Tube: Bond St. Entertain yourself in front of a mirror for a few hours, entertain everyone else with your funky new haircut when you walk out. See **Health and Beauty,** p. 134.

football match

Football games are tons of fun for the whole family. However, enjoying a day cheering, jeering, and enjoying beer and cigarettes with the kids isn't cheap. Seats cost £10-35 and tickets are available in advance from each club's box office; many have a credit-card telephone booking system. If you're traveling with friends, a match makes a great afternoon out, and really, if you're looking for a good time, £18 is not much more than the cover charge at a fancy club. If you're a parent toting tots with a taste for the sport, a match could provide a cultural experience of sorts, offering just the right mix of familiarity and strangeness. Only a football match gives your child the opportunity to urinate in the same stadium trough as genuine English football hooligans, an experience you'd be hard pressed to give him at the British Museum.

If you find tickets prohibitively expensive, that might not be a bad thing. It isn't always a good idea to smoke and drink with the kids anyway, though cheering and jeering with them is usually better. *Let's Go: Guide to Parenting 2001* recommends more cheering for the kids and jeering at them. Football teams also discourage jeering at the players, even though most are years past childhood.

SPECTATOR SPORTS

ASSOCIATION FOOTBALL

Many evils may arise which God forbid.
—King Edward II, banning football in London, 1314

The all-dominant British sport, football, draws huge crowds—over half a million people attend professional matches in Britain every Saturday during the season. Each club's fans dress with fierce loyalty in team colors. Though mass violence and vandalism at stadiums have dogged the game for years, causing tension between police and fans, the atmosphere in the stands has become a bit tamer now that most stadiums sell seats rather than spaces in the once infamous "terraces," and now that the game is being claimed not only by the middle classes, but also women. For better and often for worse, the English football spirit is alive and well, despite official efforts to dampen enthusiasm. Outbreaks of violence, much of it perpetrated by English fans, cast a sad pall over Euro 2000.

London has been blessed with 13 of the 92 professional teams in England. The big three are **Arsenal,** Highbury Stadium, Avenell Rd., N5 (☎7704 4000; Tube: Arsenal), **Chelsea,** Stamford Bridge, Fulham Rd., SW6 (☎7386 7799; Tube: Fulham Broadway) and **Tottenham Hotspur,** White Hart Lane, 748 High Rd., W17 (☎8365 5000; BR: White Hart Lane). The football scene is very partisan and favorites vary from neighborhood to neighborhood. England plays occasional international matches at the historic but soon to be redesigned **Wembley Stadium,** usually on Wednesday evenings (☎8902 8833; tube: Wembley Park). On a non-professional level, footy is also played in parks all over London: on Sunday morning, the massive grid of pitches on Hackney Marshes are a sight well worth beholding.

RUGBY

The game was spontaneously created when an inspired (or confused) Rugby School student picked up a soccer ball and ran it into the goal. Rugby has since evolved into a complex and subtle game. Rugby League, a professional sport played by teams of thirteen, has traditionally been a northern game. **Wembley Stadium** (above) stages some of the championship matches in May. A random melee of blood, mud, and drinking songs, "rugger" can be incomprehensible to the outsider, yet aesthetically exciting nonetheless. The season runs from September to May. The most significant contests, including the Oxford vs. Cambridge **Varsity match** in December and the springtime **Six Nations Championship** (featuring England, Scotland, Wales, Ireland, France, and Italy) are played at **Twickenham** (☎8831 6666; BR: Twickenham). First-rate games can be seen at one of London's premiere clubs such as **Saracens,** Vicarage Road Stadium, Watford WD1 (☎ (01923) 496 200; Rail: Watford High Street), and **Rosslyn Park,** Priory Ln., Upper Richmond Rd., SW15 (☎ 8876 1879; Rail: Barnes).

CRICKET

Once a synonym for civility, cricket's image has been dulled as modern life overtakes its slow pace. Even so, cricket remains the quintessential English sport, despite (or perhaps because of) the fact that for as long as anyone an remember, the national team has consistently failed to show any sign of improvement against Commonwealth sides intent on taking their post-colonial revenge. It's also probably the only international sport played in starched, pressed trousers and cabled wool sweaters—it may be summer, but this is England. Purists disdain the new one-day matches, with risk-taking players in gaudy colors and quick results. "First Class" matches between county teams amble on for days and often end in draws, while international "Test" matches are played in series that drag on for months (and often still end without a victor). But who cares? The sun is (hopefully) shining, the beer is warm, and there's little enough action that you can read the newspaper and still not miss anything.

Globe Theatre

While attendance at County matches has been falling for years, international games always attract attention, and every summer a touring nation plays England in a series of matches around the country (England reciprocates in the winter). From June to September in 2001, England will take on arch-rivals Australia for cricket's most coveted trophy, the **Ashes,** a sealed urn purported to contain the burnt remains of a cricket bail (a small wooden cylinder placed atop the stumps) used in an international match in 1883. Watch ace Australian bowler Shane Warne demolish the English batting at one of London's two major cricket grounds. **Lord's,** St. John's Wood Rd., NW8 (☎ 7289 1611; Tube: St. John's Wood), is the home turf of the **Marylebone Cricket Club (MCC),** the established governing body of cricket. Archaic stuffiness pervades the MCC; women have yet to see the pavilion's interior. **Foster's Oval,** Kennington Oval, SE11 (☎ 7582 7764; Tube: Oval), home to **Surrey Cricket Club** (tickets ₤7-8), also fields Test Matches (tickets for internationals ₤21-36, book ahead).

Barbican Theatre

TENNIS

Every year, for two weeks in late June and early July tennis buffs all over the world focus their attention on **Wimbledon.** If you want to get in, arrive early (6am); the gate opens at 10:30am (get off the Tube at Southfields or take buses #39, 93 or 200 from central London, which run frequently during the season). Get a copy of the order of play on each court, printed in most newspapers. Outer courts have first-come, first-served seats or standing room only. If you fail to get center or No. 1 court tickets in the morning, try to find the resale booth (usually in Aorangi Park), which sells tickets handed in by those who leave early (open from 2:30pm; tickets ₤5 before 5pm, ₤3 after). Also, on the first Saturday of the championships, 2000 extra center court tickets are put up for sale at the "bargain" price of around ₤25. Call 8971 2473 for ticket information.

Brixton Academy

Food & Drink

Food is incredibly sexy in Britain at the moment, especially in London. Chefs Ainsley Harriot and Jamie Oliver (a.k.a. the "Naked Chef") are TV stars and supermarkets are cool places to be on a Friday night. Even some pubs have gotten in on the act, transforming themselves into so-called gastropubs, although sadly prices have often been transformed in the process. That said, London is still not the Promised Land: the glitz sometimes hides mediocre food, and many restaurants continue to exist solely on the pounds of gullible tourists. What to choose then? If you want the classics of British food, Let's Go's team of cholesterol-oblivious writers have sourced out some of the city's best spots for a **fry-up** (bacon, sausage, eggs, fried bread, beans, and sometimes more: a guaranteed-to-cure-any-hangover killer of a breakfast), **cream tea,** and **fish and chips.** Of course, the true British cuisine might actually be **Indian food**: Prince Charles, when asked for his version of the archetypal British meal, showed he shared popular taste and chose the classic Chicken Tikka Masala. But the city's cosmopolitanism means you can find every international cuisine—from Mediterranean to Malaysian—in London.

The only problem is finding it cheap. Timing is everything for those intending to eat well on a budget. Many good restaurants offer decently-priced set menus and other promotions during lunchtime and in the quieter dinner hours before 7pm (Londoners eat out around 8pm). Call in advance to reserve a table, particularly for evenings and weekends, and specify smoking or non-smoking. Establishments frequently add service charges to bills, but if not, remember that wait staff rely on tips—10% is the current norm.

GROCERIES AND SUPERMARKETS

The cheapest places to get the ingredients for your own meal in London are often the local markets; for a run down of street markets, see **Shopping,** p. 138. If you like all your food under one roof, London's two largest supermarket chains are **Tesco** and **Sainsbury's.**

Larger branches come complete with bakery, cafe, and housewares. Other chains include **Safeway** and **Asda. Waitrose** is a more upmarket supermarket, and is a good source of fancier ingredients. The **Marks and Spencer** food halls are also somewhat pricier, but you get quality for the money. Their branches all over the city include those at 107 Long Acre (across from Covent Garden tube station) and 458 Oxford St. (Tube: Marble Arch). For night owls, the branches of **Hart's** stay open 24 hours. And if you're willing to splurge, the food halls of **Harrods, Harvey Nichols, Selfridges,** and **Fortnum and Mason's** are attractions in their own right.

RESTAURANTS BY TYPE

The restaurants are arranged both by type and by location. **Restaurants: By Type** provides a list of restaurants cross-referenced by food and location. Every restaurant listed in this section is followed by an abbreviated neighborhood label; turn to **Restaurants: By Location** for the full write-up. The restaurants with the thumbs-up symbol next to them are **Let's Go Picks**—the restaurants that we wouldn't miss on a trip to London. The following is a code to the abbreviated neighborhood labels. Also search **www.hardens.com** for a comprehensive restaurant guide to London.

AFRICAN
Mandola — NHB

AMERICAN
Arkansas Cafe — WH
Beverly Hills Bakery — KKHP
Hard Rock Cafe — KKHP
The Nosherie — CL
Star Cafe and Bar — SO
Sticky Fingers — KKHP
Tinseltown — CLAmEx

BELGIAN
Belgo Centraal — CG
Belgo Noord — CD

BREAKFAST
Beverly Hills Bakery — KKHP
Tinseltown — CL
Vingt Quatre — KKHP

CAFES AND SANDWICH SHOPS
Al's Café Bar — CL
Al's Deli — HH
Al-Fresco — WM
Arco Bars — KKHP
Barbican Grill — CL
Buon Appetito — BB
Beverly Hills Bakery — KKHP
Cafe, Bar, & Juice Bar — BR
Café Emm — SO
Café Floris — KKHP
Cafe Roma — SO
Chelsea Bun Diner — CB
Chelsea Kitchen — CB
Field's Sandwiches — CL
Frank's Café — CG
Futures! — CL
Leigh St. Café — BB
Lisboa Patisserie — NHB
Neal's Yard Bakery & Tea Room — CG

Neal's Yard Salad Bar — CG
New Covent Garden Soup Co. — NC
O'Porto Patisserie — NHB
Patisserie Valerie — SO
The Place Below — CL
Polly's Cafe/Tea Room — HH
Pret a Manger — NC
Saints Cafe and Photo Lab — CL
St. John — CL
Square — SO
SWTen — CB
Troubador — EC
Woolley's — BB
World Food Cafe — CG

CARRIBEAN
Coconut Grove — NHB

CHEESE
Neal's Yard Dairy — CG

CHINESE
The Dragon Inn — SO
Kowloon Restaurant — SO
Lok Ho Fook — SO
New Culture Revolution — CB, CD, IS, NHB
Royal China — NHB
1997 Special Zone Restaurant — SO
Wong Kei — SO

CLASSIC ENGLISH
See also **Pubs,** (p. 170)
Chelsea Kitchen — CB
Cockney's Pie and Mash — NHB
Little Bay — HH
Neal's Yard Dairy — CG

CREPES/PANCAKES
Bah Humbug — BR
Le Crêperie de Hampstead — HH
My Old Dutch Pancake House — CB

CL City of London **HO** Holborn **WM** Westminster **CB** Chelsea and Belgravia **KKHP** Kensington, Knightsbridge, Hyde Park **NHB** Notting Hill and Bayswater **MRP** Marylebone and Regent's Park **BB** Bloomsbury **CG** Covent Garden **SO** Soho **MSP** Mayfair, St. James, and Picadilly **NC** Notable Chain **IS** Islington **CD** Camden **HH** Hamstead and Highgate **DL** Docklands **WC** Whitechapel **SSB** South Bank, Southwark **BR** Brixton **GRg** Greenwich **EC** Earl's Court **SHH** Shepherd's Bush, Hammersmith, and Holland Park **RI** Richmond

FISH AND CHIPS

The Fryer's Delight	HO
Geale's	NHB
The Rock & Sole Plaice	CG
Seashell	MRP

FRENCH

Chez Lindsay	RI
est	SO
Le Crêperie de Hampstead	HH
Little Bay	HH
Le Mercury	IS
Patisserie Valerie	SO
Pierre Victoire	NC
Rotisserie Jules	KKHC
Schnecke	SO
Tartuf	IS

GAY AND LESBIAN

Old Compton Cafe	SO

INDIAN/SOUTH ASIAN

Aladin Balti House	WH
Chutney's	BB
Diwana Bhel Poori House	BB
Great Nepalese Restaurant	B&E
Gupta Sweet Centre	B&E
Khan's	NHB
Mandeer	SO
Nazrul	WC
Saffron	EC
Shampan	WC
West End Tandoori	SO

INTERNATIONAL

Bar Room Bar	HH
Giraffe	HH
Mezzo	SO
Ruby in the Dust	CD

ITALIAN/PIZZA

Arco Bar	KKHP
Ask!	MSP, KKHP, WM
Cafe Roma	SO
Cosmoba	BB
Frank's Cafe	CG
Marine Ices	CD
Mille Pini Restaurant	HO
Pizza Express	NC
Square	SO

JAPANESE

Don Zoko	SO
Fujiyama	BR
Noto	CL
Sushi & Sozai	CL
Wagamama	BB, SO, MRP, CT, KKHP
Yo!Sushi	SO

JEWISH

Brick Lane Beigel Bake	WC
Perry's Bakery	EC

JEWISH, CONT.

Spitz	WC

MIDDLE EASTERN

Afghan Kitchen	IS
Angel Mangal	IS
Apadana	KKHP
Istanbul Iskembecisi	IS
Manzara	NHB
Pasha	I
Perry's Bakery	EC
Ranoush Juice	MRP
Sofra	MSP

OPEN LATE

Al's Café Bar	CL
Tinseltown	CL
Vingt Quatre	KKHP
1997 Special Zone Restaurant	SO

POLISH/RUSSIAN

Borshtch 'n' Tears	KKHP
Patio	SHH
Wódka	KKHP

SOUTH AMERICA

La Piragua	CD

SOUTH EAST ASIAN

busuba eathai	SO
Jewel of Siam	NHB
Makan	NHB
Mandalay	MRP
Nusa Dua	SO
Saigon	SO

SPANISH/PORTUGUESE

Bar Gansa	IS
Goya	WM
Lisboa Patisserie	NHB
Lomo	KKHP
O'Porto Patisserie	NHB

SWEETS AND ICE-CREAM

Gupta Sweet Centre	B&E
Lisboa Patisserie	NH&LG
Marine Ices	CD
O'Porto Patisserie	H&LG
Patisserie Valerie	SO

VEGETARIAN

Alara Wholefoods	B&E
Bah Humbug	BR
Chutney's	BB
Diwana Bhel Poori House	BB
Food for Thought	CG
Futures!	CL
The Grain Shop	NHB
Mandeer	SO
Neal's Yard Bakery & Tea Room	CG
Neal's Yard Salad Bar	CG
The Place Below	CL
World Food Cafe	CG

CL City of London **HO** Holborn **WM** Westminster **CB** Chelsea and Belgravia **KKHP** Kensington, Knightsbridge, Hyde Park **NHB** Notting Hill and Bayswater **MRP** Marylebone and Regent's Park **BB** Bloomsbury **CG** Covent Garden **SO** Soho **MSP** Mayfair, St. James, and Picadilly **NC** Notable Chain **IS** Islington **CD** Camden **HH** Hamstead and Highgate **DL** Docklands **WC** Whitechapel **SSB** South Bank, Southwark **BR** Brixton **GRg** Greenwich **EC** Earl's Court **SHH** Shepherd's Bush, Hammersmith, and Holland Park **RI** Richmond

RESTAURANTS BY NEIGHBORHOOD

CENTRAL LONDON

see map pp. 288-289

THE CITY AND CLERKENWELL

The Place Below, in St. Mary-le-Bow crypt, Cheapside. (☎ 7329 0789) Tube: St. Paul's. Generous vegetarian dishes served to City executives in an impressive church crypt. The second dining room moonlights as an ecclesiastical court, where the Archbishop of Canterbury still settles cases pertaining to Anglican law and swears in new bishops a few times a year. Quiche and salad £6, takeaway £4.20. Eat between 11:30am-noon for a £2 discount. Significant takeaway discount. Open M-F 7:30am-2:30pm.

▨ Futures!, 8 Botolph Alley (☎ 7623 4529). Tube: Monument. Off Botolph Ln. Fresh take-away vegetarian breakfast and lunch prepared in a petite kitchen open to view. Daily main dishes, like quiche, £3.40. Spinach pizza £1.85. Branch in Exchange Sq. (behind Liverpool St). Open M-F 7:30-10am and 11:30am-3pm!

Sushi & Sozai, 51a Queen Victoria St. (☎ 7332 0108). Tube: Mansion House. A cheap sushi stand in the City. Medium sushi £4. Large sushi £5. Heated Japanese dishes, including deep-fried pork cutlet and egg on rice, £3. Open M-F 11am-3pm.

Saints Café & Photo Lab, 1 Clerkenwell Rd. (☎ 7490 4199). Tube: Farringdon. Think pub food with an international twist: Sri Lankan fish cakes served with chutney and Thai dressed salad (£4.25), ratatouille and mozzarella pie, with chips (£4.25). After your meal, you can develop your pictures at the Saints photo lab. Cafe open M-F 8am-6pm; hot meals served until 4pm.

Al's Café Bar, 11-13 Exmouth Market (☎ 7837 4821). Tube: Angel or Farringdon. This stylish cafe/bar (with an attached club) is a favorite hangout for magazine journalists. Excellent diner cuisine. £6 lunch specials (M-F noon-6pm) include 6oz. rump steak. Salads £5-6, main courses £6.50-9. English breakfast all day £5.50. Open M 8am-midnight, Tu-F 8am-2am, Sa-Su 10am-midnight. Last orders 1hr. before close. MC, V (for meals above £10).

Tinseltown 24-Hour Diner, 44-46 St. John St. (☎ 7689 2424) Tube: Farringdon. An all-day, all-night American-style diner. Some dishes have film titles for names (Full Monty breakfast £3.50-5). Burgers £5.50, thick, fruity milkshakes £3-3.95.

St. John, 26 St. John St. (☎ 7251 0848). Tube: Farringdon. This airy, classically designed establishment is a strange hybrid of restaurant, bar and bakery. An idiosyncratic and excellent selection of food is available, including smoked eel (£6.70) and winkles (a shellfish). Bar menu. Fresh bread from the bakery £1.20. Restaurant open M-F noon-3pm and 6-11:30pm, Sa 6-11:30pm. Bar open M-F 11am-11pm, Sa 6-11pm.

The Nosherie, 12-13 Greville St. (☎ 7242 1591). Tube: Farringdon or Chancery Ln. Near the jewellers of Hatton Garden, this friendly, unassuming eatery serves classic New York-style deli food and English dishes. Specializes in hot salt beef (corned beef to Americans) from £4.60 (£3.70 takeaway). Fish and chips £3.90 (£2.50 takeaway). Open daily 24hrs. MC, V.

Barbican Grill, 117 Whitecross St. (☎ 7256 6842). Tube: Moorgate. This pleasantly managed, unassuming cafe serves up amazing bargains to its budget-minded student and working crowd. Chicken and chips £3.10. Sandwiches with everything from chicken to salmon, around £1.30. Open M-F 6am-4pm, Sa 6am-11pm.

Field's Sandwiches, 5 St. John St. (☎ 7608 2235). Tube: Barbican. The wooden shelves packed with bric-a-brac lend this sandwich shop a charm its takeaway brethren lack. Quiche £1.20, sandwiches £1-3, samosas 70p. Open M-F 6am-3pm.

Noto, 7 Bread St. (☎ 7329 8056). Tube: St. Paul's or Mansion House. Also at 2-3 Bassishaw Highwalk (☎ 7256 9433). Tube: Moorgate. Step up to the horseshoe-shaped noodle bar, order *ramen* (£5.80-7.60) served in generous portions, slurp it down, pay at the cashier. Life's great when you're a salaryman. Open M-F 11:30am-9pm. Cash only.

HOLBORN

The Fryer's Delight, 19 Theobald's Rd. (☎ 7405 4114). Tube: Holborn. One of the best chippies around. Popular with locals and retro buffs who delight in authentic orange, red, and blue formica. Large portions of fish and chips £2.70 take-away. Quick counter service. Open M-Sa noon-10pm, until 11pm for take-away. No credit cards.

Mille Pini Restaurant, 33 Boswell St. (☎7242 2434). Tube: Holborn. Warm, rustic feel. Offers terrific brick-oven pizza, pasta (£4.50-5.50), and homemade pastries. Divine *tiramisu* £2.50. Open M-F noon-3pm and 6pm-11:30pm, Sa 6pm-11:30pm. Cash only.

WESTMINSTER

Al-Fresco (☎7233 8298). Tube: Victoria. Trendy variations on old standbys. Jacket potato with brie £2.75. Fresh melon juice £1.70. Panini sandwiches £2.80. Open M-F 8 am-5:30 pm, Sa-Su 9am-4:30pm.

Goya, 34 Lupus St. (☎7976 5309). Tube: Pimlico. Corner tapas bar popular with locals for sipping drinks and munching Spanish snacks. Outdoor tables filled on summer nights. Tapas £2.50-4.50. Spanish omelette £2.90. Hearty garlic chicken £4.20. Open daily noon-midnight.

CHELSEA AND BELGRAVIA

◪*Tube: Sloane Sq.*

▨ **New Culture Revolution,** 305 King's Rd. (☎7352 9281). Take a great leap forward and enjoy simple and delicious north Chinese food, mostly noodles and dumplings. Open daily noon-11pm. MC, V. Branches: 43 Parkway, NW1 (☎7267 2700; Tube: Camden Town); 157-159 Notting Hill Gate, W11 (☎7313 9688; Tube: Notting Hill Gate); and 42 Duncan St., N1 (☎7833 9083; Tube: Angel).

My Old Dutch Pancake House, 221 King's Rd. (☎7376 5650). Gorge on hubcap-sized pancakes. Set lunch menu (served weekdays noon-4pm) offers a pancake with your choice of toppings and tea or coffee (£6). Any crepe £5 from 4-7pm. Open M-Th noon-11:30pm, F-Sa noon-midnight, Su 10am-11pm. AmEx, DC, MC, V.

Chelsea Kitchen, 98 King's Rd. (☎7589 1330). Super-cheap food: turkey and mushroom pie, spaghetti bolognese and Spanish omelettes £2.80 or less. Menu changes daily. Set menu £4-5. Breakfast served 8-11:25am. Open M-Sa 8am-11:30pm, Su 9am-11:30pm.

SWTen, 488 King's Rd. (☎7352 4227). Near the World's End. Urbanity at budget prices. Huge sandwiches on crusty bread £1.20-3. Salads £2.80-3.50. Specials (around £3) are a phenomenal value. Take-away discount. Open M-F 8am-4pm.

Chelsea Bun Diner, 9a Limerston St. (☎7352 3635). Variety of sandwiches overflowing with fillings; smoked salmon and avocado, £2.85. Special includes soup, main course, and tea or coffee, £4. English breakfast special £3.35; £2.30 7-10:30am. Open daily 7am-midnight. MC, V.

KENSINGTON, KNIGHTSBRIDGE, AND HYDE PARK

KENSINGTON

◪*Tube: High St. Kensington unless otherwise noted.*

Café Floris, 5 Harrington Rd. (☎7589 3276). A bustling cafe offering large, fresh sandwiches (£1.60-£2.90) and filling breakfasts. Colossal all-day breakfast special (£3.50. Minimum purchase £3 noon-3pm. Open daily 6am-7pm.

Rotisserie Jules, 6-8 Bute St. (☎7584 0600). **Branches** at 338 King's Rd., and at 133 Notting Hill Gate. This lively restaurant serves free-range poultry. Dishes from £4.95. Open daily noon-11:30pm.

Vingt-Quatre, 325 Fulham Rd. (☎7376 7224). Hyper-modern steel tables and chairs give this somewhat pricey diner a space age feel. All-day English breakfast served; small £4.75, large £6.75. Main courses £6.75-9.95. Alcohol served noon-midnight. Open 24hr. MC, V.

Lomo, 222 Fulham Rd. (☎7349 8848). This chic tapas bar, decorated with burnt orange tall tables, opens onto the sidewalk. Hot *chorizo* £3.75, sausages £3.50-5.75. Lunch special £5 for 3 tapas. Happy hour (half price beer and cocktails) 5-7pm. Open M-Sa noon-midnight; Su noon-11:30pm.

Sticky Fingers Cafe, 1a Phillimore Gdns. (☎7938 5338). Former Rolling Stone Bill Wyman operates this memorabilia-crammed diner. Those fearing a Hard Rock Cafe experience shouldn't worry; the only cheese here goes on the burgers (£7.95-8.95 with fries), consistently rated among the best in London. Kids menu: 2 courses and fries £4.95. Open M-Sa noon-11:30pm; Su noon-11pm. AmEx, MC, V.

FLAKES AND SMARTIES

British food has character (of one sort or another), and the traditional snack menu is a unique hodgepodge of sweets, crisps, and squashes. **Cadbury's chocolate** bars include Flake (a stick of flaky chocolate often stuck into an ice cream cone), Crunchie (honeycombed magic), and the classic Dairy Milk. Other favorites include Fruit & Nut, Lunch Break, Aero Bars. **Sweets** come in many forms—the fizzy Refreshers, the chewy Wine Gums, or frosted Fruit Pastilles. Potato chips, or **crisps** as they are known in England, are not just salted, but come in a range of flavors, including Prawn Cocktail, Cheese n' Onion, Chicken, Fruit n' Spice, and Salt n' Vinegar. All this sugar and salt can be washed down with Lilt, a pineapple and grapefruit flavored soda, or a drinkbox-ful of Ribena, a blackcurrant manna from heaven which has to be diluted with water. This latter beverage belongs to a family of drinks known as **squashes,** fruit-based syrups watered down to drink. But the food that expatriate Britons miss most is **Marmite,** a yeast extract which is spread on bread or toast. If you weren't fed Marmite as a baby, you'll never appreciate it; most babies don't either.

Apadana, 351 Kensington High St., W8 (☎7603 3696). Generous quantities of Persian food: *kabab-e kobideh ba nan* (minced lamb kebab with fresh naan bread) £3.90. Other main courses £3.90-4.90. Open daily noon-11pm.

Wódka, 12 St. Alban's Grove (☎7937 6513). Tube: Gloucester Rd. A stylish Polish restaurant that serves delicious cuisine at affordable prices. *Blinis* (crepes filled with various goodies) come with several different toppings, including smoked salmon (£6.90) and aubergine mousse (£5.90). Set lunch £10.90 (two courses). Worth a splurge, especially for meat lovers. Numerous *Wódkas* "on tap" to wash it all down. Open M-F 12:30-2:30pm and 7-11:15pm, Sa-Su 7-11:15pm. AmEx, DC, MC, V.

KNIGHTSBRIDGE

🚇*Tube: Knightsbridge unless otherwise indicated*

Borshtch 'n' Tears, 46 Beauchamp Pl. (☎7589 5003). Tube: Knightsbridge. Here, the atmosphere is more extraordinary than the food—the shashlik (skewer of lamb, £8.95) is decidedly ordinary. Starters £3-6. Most main dishes £7-9. Around 16 varieties of vodka shots (around £2.50). Live music nightly. Cover £1. Last orders 1am. Open daily 6pm-2am Branch, **Borshtch 'n' Cheers,** at 273 King's Rd., Chelsea.

Hard Rock Cafe, 150 Old Park Ln. (☎7629 0382). Tube: Hyde Park Corner. This little-known neighborhood restaurant serves burgers and fries (£7.95) to a small local crowd in an intimate and quiet atmosphere. The perfect eatery for those wishing to avoid lines, loud music, and rock 'n' roll memorabilia. Not. Open Su-Th 11:30am-12:30am, F-Sa 11:30am-1am.

Arco Bars, 46 Hans Crescent (☎7584 6454). The hearty, cheap food, while not particularly outstanding, suits the office crowds and shoppers from nearby Harrods who want a quick meal. The food, Dr. Evil might say, is pretty standard, really: pasta £3.70 or £5.20; sandwiches £4-5.80. Takeaway discount around 20%. Open M-F 7am-6pm, Sa 8am-6pm.

Beverly Hills Bakery, 3 Egerton Terrace (☎7584 4401). All things Californian, from the sunny, colored walls to the natural ingredients in the goodies to the fact that everything is baked on-site. Pecan pie, carrot cake, and cheesecake slices £2.20, take-away £1.80. Muffins £1.10; buy 6 and get the 7th free. Take-away espresso 80p. Open M-Sa 7:30am-6:30pm, Su 8am-6pm.

NOTTING HILL AND BAYSWATER

🍴 **The Grain Shop,** 269a Portobello Rd. (☎7229 5571). Tube: Ladbroke Grove. This take-away sells a surprisingly large array of foods. Organic whole grain breads baked daily on the premises (90p-£1.90 per loaf). Main dishes start at £2.40. Vegan brownies £1. Groceries also available, many organic. Open M-Sa 9:30am-6pm.

🍴 **Cockney's Pie & Mash,** 314 Portobello Rd. (☎8960 9409). Tube: Ladbroke Grove. Cheap, no-nonsense pie and mash (£1.85), with portions of eel (F-Sa only) for a mere £2.70. Open Tu-Sa 11:30am-5:30pm.

Royal China, 13 Queensway (☎ 7221 2535). Tube: Bayswater. For the full Cantonese experience, try the steamed duck's tongue (£1.80) or the marinated chicken feet (£1.80). Generous dishes £10-15. Dim sum served M-Sa noon-5pm, Su 11am-5pm Open M-Th noon-11pm, F-Sa noon-11:30pm, Su 11am-10pm. AmEx, DC, MC, V.

Mandola, 139 Westbourne Grove (☎ 7229 6391). Tube: Bayswater. Simply put, it rocks. A tiny diner that has rapidly shot into trendy eating notoriety, but hasn't raised its prices to match. Salads £3, main dishes £4-8. To finish, try the date mousse (£2.40) and Sudanese coffee, sold in a traditional pot (£3.50; serves 2). Take-away. Open M-Sa noon-11:30pm, Su noon-10:30pm.

Khan's, 13-15 Westbourne Grove (☎ 7727 5240). Tube: Bayswater. Cavernous, noisy, and crowded, Khan's remains a great bargain for Indian food. Though most dishes are still under £4, Khan's charges a £6 per person minimum and a 10% service charge. Uses only *halal* meats. Open daily noon-3pm and 6pm-midnight. AmEx, DC, MC, V.

Manzara, 24 Pembridge Rd. (☎ 7727 3062). Tube: Notting Hill Gate. A wonderful place to refuel after a stroll through Portobello Market. Their speciality is Turkish *pide*, a pizza-like pie. In the afternoon, pizzas are £3.50, sandwiches £2. Vegetarians should try the mixed *meze* (£4.25). Take-away discount. Open daily 7:30am-midnight.

Oporto Patisserie, 62a Golborne Rd. (☎ 8968 8839). Tube: Ladbroke Grove. This *pastelaria*, Portugese to the core, serves pastries crafted from Iberian ingredients. Hearty chicken, fish, or Parma ham sandwiches sold on traditional breads for only £1.40-1.75. Portuguese specialities such as *pasteis de bacalhau* (cod fish cakes) only 75p. Open daily 8am-8pm.

Coconut Grove, 23 All Saints Rd. (☎ 8229 7961). Tube: Westbourne Park or Ladbroke Grove. Behind a rust-red exterior, this candlelit restaurant serves well-prepared jerk chicken (£6.50). Fried plantains £1.80. Take-away slightly cheaper. Open M-Sa 11:30am-11:30pm.

Lisboa Patisserie, 57 Golborne Rd. (☎ 8968 5242). Tube: Ladbroke Grove. Always crowded with nicotine-infused locals, this tiny Portuguese *patisserie* gets started early and is always jumping. Loads of traditional Portuguese pastries; perfect *pastel de nata* (custard tart) melts in your mouth (55p). Glass of coffee 75p. Open daily 8am-8pm.

Makan, 270 Portobello Rd. (☎ 8960 5169). Tube: Ladbroke Grove. Value for money + quality Malaysian food = packed on market days. A wide variety of dishes, from chicken curry to *sambal* prepared with squid or spicy eggplant, around £4-5. Take-away discount 80p. Open M-Sa 11:30am-7:30pm.

Geale's, 2 Farmer St. (☎ 7727 7969). Tube: Notting Hill Gate. An upmarket version of the chippie (it has a wine list), Geale's has won awards for its consistently crispy fish. Fresh haddock and plaice from Grimsby are house specialties. Meals start around £7. Cover charge 15p per person, but takeaway available. Open M-Sa noon-3pm and 6-11pm, Su noon-3pm. AmEx, MC, V.

Jewel of Siam, 39 Hereford Rd. (☎ 7229 4363). Tube: Bayswater. More rhinestone than jewel—well-prepared Thai food in a contrived yet endearing setting. Main courses (£5-6), sumptuous appetizers (£3.50-4.50) and noodle specials (under £5 for both lunch and dinner) are quite satisfying. 10% takeaway discount. Evening cover charge £1. Open M-F noon-2:30pm and 6-11pm, Sa 6-11pm, Su 6-10:30pm. AmEx, MC, V.

MARYLEBONE AND REGENT'S PARK

Mandalay, 444 Edgware Rd. (☎ 7258 3696). Tube: Edgware Rd. It's easy to pass by the ordinary facade of Mandalay, but then this Burmese restaurant is so consistently good it only needs word of mouth to attract customers. Friendly owners explain the intricacies of the dishes. Set lunches are great value: curry and rice £3.50; curry, rice, dessert, and coffee £5.90. Open M-Sa noon-3pm and 6-11pm; last orders 2:30pm and 10:30pm. AmEx, MC, V, DC.

Ranoush Juice, 43 Edgware Rd. (☎ 7723 5929). Tube: Marble Arch. The best Lebanese takeaway on the Edgware Rd (and that's up against some stiff competition). Fortunately, you don't need to spend a fortune to enjoy the very fresh meat of their kebabs and shwarmas (£2.50-4). Wash it all down with the excellent juices (£1.50). Open daily 9:30am-3am. Cash only.

Seashell, 49-51 Lisson Grove (☎ 7224 9000). Tube: Marylebone. Always a contender in the eternal debate over the best fish and chips in London. Get the same high-quality fish from the takeaway for much less than at the restaurant (cod and chips £3.25). Open M-F noon-2:30pm and 5-10:30pm, Sa noon-10:30pm.

▐ ✚ ▐ ⚑ ▐ ⚑ ▐ 📷 ▐ 🏛 ▐ 🛍 ▐ 🎆 ▐ ◯ ▐ 🚩 ▐ 🖼 ▐ ▮ ▐ ⌐ ▐ 🚩 ▮

Sofra, 1 St. Christopher's Pl. See **Mayfair, St. James's, and Picadilly,** p. 165.

Wagamama, 101 Wigmore St. See **Bloomsbury,** below.

BLOOMSBURY

▨ **Wagamama,** 4A Streatham St. (☎ 7323 9223). Tube: Tottenham Ct. Rd. If a restaurant could be a London must-see on the level of Buckingham Palace, this would be it. The waitstaff radio orders to the kitchen and diners slurp happily from massive bowls of ramen at long tables, like extras from *Tampopo*. Noodles in various combinations and permutations, all obscenely tasty (£5-7.25). Open M-Sa noon-11pm, Su 12:30-10pm. AmEx, MC, V. Other branches: 10a Lexington St., W1 (☎ 7292 0990; fax 7734 1815; Tube: Piccadilly Circus); 101 Wigmore St. (☎ 7409 0111; Tube: Marble Arch); 11 Jamestown Rd. (☎ 7428 0800; Tube: Camden Town); and 26 Kensington High St. (☎ 7376 1717; Tube: High St. Kensington).

▨ **Diwana Bhel Poori House,** 121 Drummond St. (☎ 7387 5556). Tube: Warren St. The specialty is *thali* (an assortment of vegetables, rices, sauces, breads, and desserts; £4.50-6.20). The "Chef's Special" is served on weekdays with rice for £4.80. Lunch buffet (served noon-2:30pm, £4.50) includes 4 vegetable dishes, rice, savories, and dessert. Open daily noon-11:30pm. AmEx, MC, V.

Woolley's Salad Shop and Sandwich Bar, 33 Theobald's Rd. (☎ 7405 3028). Tube: Holborn. Fight the tsunami of suits for healthy picnic fare, mostly vegetarian. Mix and match their 10 fresh salads in a variety of sizes (70p-£6.30). The adjoining sandwich shop in back offers everything from chicken *saag* to smoked salmon lovingly swaddled in fresh rolls (£1.70-2.90). Dried fruit, nuts, herbal tea, and *muesli* also for sale. Open M-F 7am-3:30pm.

Buon Appetito, 27 Sicilian Ave. (☎ 7242 7993). Tube: Holborn. Fantastic lunch option near the British Museum. Full breakfast served all day £3.50, sandwiches £1.80-2.90. Open M-Sa 6:15am-4:30pm.

Cosmoba, 9 Cosmo Pl. (☎ 7837 0904). Tube: Russell Sq. Cosmoba's low prices and Italian hospitality have satisfied Londoners for nearly 40 years. Choose from spaghetti, tagliatelle, or penne with a variety of sauces (£3.45-5.30). Open M-Sa 11:30am-3pm and 5:30-11pm. MC, V.

Leigh St Café, 16 Leigh St. (☎ 7387 3393). Tube: Russell Sq. Creative sandwiches and pastries, elegant decor, an enclosed garden in back, and friendly service all make Leigh St Café a good place to experience the British "caff." Sandwiches from 70p, daily pasta selections £3.25. Take-away available. Open M-Su 8am-7pm.

Alara Wholefoods, 58/60 Marchmont (☎ 7837 1172). Tube: Russell Sq. A staples store offering dried fruit, nuts, grains, and a little wholefood propaganda. Most importantly, the take-away kitchen in the back practically gives away jacket potatoes (from 90p), slices of quiche (£1.60), and the hot meal of the day (£3.10 per lb). Open M-F 9:30am-6pm, Sa 10am-6pm. AmEx, MC, V.

Chutney's, 124 Drummond St. (☎ 7338 0604). Tube: Warren St. An upmarket Indian restaurant with down-market prices. £5 all-you-can-eat buffet served M-Sa, noon-2:45pm, 6-11:30pm, and Su noon-10:30pm. Delicious *Dosas* (£3.50-4.30). Lip-smacking mango milkshakes £2. Take-away available 6-11:30pm. Open M-Sa noon-2:45pm and 6-11:30pm, Su noon-10:30pm. AmEx, MC, V.

Great Nepalese Restaurant, 48 Eversholt St. (☎ 7388 6737). Tube: Euston Sq. The food is spicy and the staff is sweet in this family-owned restaurant. Nepalese specialties like *bhutuwa* chicken £4.85. Delicious vegetarian dishes include *aloo bodi tama* (potato, bamboo shoots, and beans) £3. £5.95 set lunch served noon-2:45pm. 10% take-away discount. Open M-Sa noon-2:45pm and 6-11:45pm, Su noon-2:30pm and 6-11:30pm. AmEx, DC, MC, V.

Gupta Sweet Centre, 100 Drummond St. (☎ 7380 1590). Tube: Warren St. Indian sweets to take away. Delicious *chum-chum* (sweet cottage cheese) 30p. *Samosa* 35p. Open M-F 11am-7pm, Sa 10am-7pm, Su noon-7pm.

COVENT GARDEN

🚩*Tube: Covent Garden unless otherwise indicated.*

▨ **Belgo Centraal,** 50 Earlham St. (☎ 7813 2233). Waiters in monk's cowls and great specials make this one of Covent Garden's most popular restaurants. Mondays noon-3pm, all dishes from lobster halves to 6oz. steaks are £5.55. At "lunchtime" (daily noon-5pm), £5 buys you wild boar sausage, Belgian mash, and a beer. During "Beat the Clock," (M-F 6-7:30pm) the time you order is the cost of your meal; order at 6:30, your meal costs £6.30 (choices of *moules-frites*, wild boar sausage, or half a roast chicken, and beer). Open M-Sa noon-11:30pm, Su noon-10:30pm. Wheelchair access. AmEx, MC, V.

Neal's Yard Salad Bar, 2 Neal's Yard (☎ 7836 3233). Take-away or sit outside at this vegetarian's nirvana that's sneeze guards above the average salad bar. The hearty and wholesome hot vegetable dishes cost £4.50-5 (take-away discount 50p). Tempting mix'n' match salads from £2. Eat-in £5 minimum, but the benches nearby count as takeaway. Open M-Sa 10:30am-6pm.

🌠 **World Food Café**, 14-15 Neal's Yard (☎ 7379 0298). A bit pricier than similar peacenik, veggie-loving enclaves, but the food quality explains it all. Features a world-wide array of *meze*, light meals, and appetizing platters (£6-£8). Open M-Sa noon-5pm.

Neal's Yard Bakery & Tearoom, 6 Neal's Yard (☎ 7836 5199). Only organic flour and filtered water are used in the delicious breads here. A small, open-air counter offers a plethora vegetarian dishes with many vegan options. Large loaf £1.90. Beanburger £2.20, take-away £1.80. 50% discount on day-old breads. No smoking. Open M-Sa 10:30am-4:30pm

Belgo Noord

Neal's Yard Dairy, 17 Shorts Gdns. (☎ 7379 7646). This classy cheese shop makes regular purchases from UK farms. Don't miss the homemade yogurt. Open M-Sa 9am-7pm, Su 10am-5pm. **Wholesale location** at 6 Park St. (☎ 7378 8195; Tube: London Bridge) now also does retail (open M-F 10am-6pm).

Food for Thought, 31 Neal St. (☎ 7836 0239). Verdant foliage decorates this aromatic restaurant, which offers large servings of excellent vegetarian and vegan food at moderate prices. Soups, salads, and stir-fries. Daily specials, like chick pea ratatouille, from £3.60. You can sit at slightly cramped wooden tables or take-away a 40-50p discount. Open M-Sa 12pm-8:30pm, Su 12pm.

The Rock and Sole Plaice, 47 Endell St. (☎ 7836 3785). True to its neighborhood, this chippie is older and somewhat pricey. Fortunately, the fish (£5-8) and chunky chips (£1.80) are better than the puns. Downstairs, the underwater scene shows you just what you're eating. Open M-Sa 11am-10:30pm, Su noon-9pm.

Aquarium

Frank's Café, 52 Neal St. (☎ 7836 6345). An old Italian cafe serving homemade pastas at bargain prices (£3-4). Pizza, sandwiches, and breakfast foods available all day. Apple pie with custard (£1.80) is an artery-hardening treat. Take-away discount. Open M-Sa 7:30am-7:30pm.

SOHO AND CHINATOWN

SOHO

🌠 **Yo!Sushi**, 52 Poland St. (☎ 7287 0443). Tube: Oxford Circus. As much an eating experience as a restaurant. Diners sit at an island bar, and pick and choose from dishes placed on a central conveyer belt. Plates are color-coded by price (£1.50-3.50). An electronic drink cart makes its way behind diners delivering liquid delights. Great fun. Open daily noon-midnight. AmEx, MC, V.

🌠 **Don Zoko**, 15 Kingley St. (☎ 7734 1974). Tube: Oxford Circus. This unassuming sushi bar handwrites the menu on strips of paper attached to the wall. Thankfully, an English translation is available, because the made-as-you-order sushi is some of London's best. *Don*

Friend at Hand Pub

the BIG $plurge

Now That's Art

Demian Hirst is one of the most controversial artists working today. A cow has just as much reason to fear ending up in one of his pieces as it would of ending up between hamburger buns. Cows, however, aren't Hirst's only connection to the food industry. His renowned Notting Hill restaurant, **Pharmacy** (p. 173), is outfitted like a chemist's: pill bottles and medicines line the walls, encased in glass. It's an incredible dining experience. However, a trip to Pharmacy is an expensive venture. Fancy vodka drinks, themselves worthy of exhibition, cost around £6. The food in the upstairs restaurant is hardly budget fare—especially if it's been on display before being served. The astounding decor makes having even a drink here well worth it.

Zoko means "rock bottom," and its prices are just that. Sushi £2-4, dishes £3-6.50, beer £1.60-3.90, saki £3.50-5.50 per glass. Open M-F noon-2:30pm and 6-10:30pm; Sa-Su 6-10:30pm. AmEx, MC, V.

Mandeer, 8 Bloomsbury Way (☎ 7242 6202). Tube: Tottenham Court Rd. Mandeer offers some of the best Indian food around and an education about owner Ramesh Patel's Ayurvedic Science of Life. The Northern Indian cuisine is tasty, fresh, organic, and vegetarian. The best deals in the house are the lunch buffet options, which begin at a mere £3.50. The restaurant is also affordable and well worth it. Open M-Sa noon-3pm, 5-10pm.

Saigon, 45 Frith St. (☎ 7437 1672). Tube: Piccadilly Circus or Tottenham Court Rd. Classy decor and mouth-watering aromas are the norm at this renowned Vietnamese restaurant. Large chicken with lemon grass or coconut curry (£5.35) fresh and savory. Seasonal vegetable stir-fry £4.35. Open M-Sa noon-11:30pm. MC, V.

Mezzo, 100 Wardour St. (☎ 7314 4000). Tube: Leicester Sq. Ultra-swank, 2-story mega-restaurant on the former site of the renowned Marquee Club. Doormen, cigarette girls—the whole nine yards and priced accordingly. Come from 5:30-7pm and get a £8.50, 2-course meal in the upstairs "*Mezzonine*." 2-course meal with an Odeon movie ticket £12.50. *Mezzonine* open for lunch M-F noon-3pm, Sa noon-4pm; dinner M-Th 5:30pm-1am, F-Sa 5:30pm-3am. Restaurant open for lunch M-F noon-3pm, Su 12:30-3pm; dinner M-Th 6pm-midnight, F-Sa 6pm-1am, Su 6-10pm. Bar open until 3am F-Sa. MC, V.

Patisserie Valerie, 44 Old Compton St. (☎ 7437 3466). Tube: Leicester Sq. Opened in 1926, this continental patisserie has become a Soho institution. Today, the crowd enjoys the fresh and very tasty, tarts, cakes, breads, and truffles (all £1.20-3). Delectable sandwiches also available (£3.50-5.95). Open M-F 7:30am-10pm, Sa 8am-10pm, Su 9:30am-7pm. **Branches** at 8 Russell St., 105 Marylebone High St., and 66 Portland Pl.

West End Tandoori, 5 Old Compton St. (☎ 7734 1057). Tube: Leicester Sq. The languid Indian music makes dining relaxed. Chicken curry £5.10, vegetarian dishes £3.50-4.75. Open daily noon-2:30pm and 6-11:30pm. AmEx, DC, MC, V.

Old Compton Café, 35 Old Compton St. (☎ 7439 3309). Tube: Leicester Sq. In the geographic epicenter of Soho, *the* gay cafe. Customers (predominantly 20- and 30-somethings) overflow onto the street. Open daily 24hr. No credit cards.

Nusa Dua, 11-12 Dean St. (☎ 7437 3559). Tube: Tottenham Court Rd. Indonesian food in a somewhat cramped space. But the quality of the dishes (£5.10-7.40) more than makes up for it. Set lunches begin at £6; noodle and take-away specials go for £3.95 (noon-7:30pm). Open M-Th noon-2:30pm and 6-11:30pm, F noon-2:30pm and 6pm-midnight, Sa 6pm-midnight, Su 6-11pm. AmEx, MC, V; £15 credit-card minimum.

Council *Travel*

merica's Student Travel Leader for over 50 years

'Happiness is not a destination. It is a method of life"
-Burton Hills

isit us at your nearest office or
online @
www.counciltravel.com

Or call: 1-800-2COUNCIL

It's your world at a discount!

Accepted at over 17,000 locations worldwide.
Great benefits at home and abroad!

Travel in Euro-style by Eurostar™

The whole point of going on holiday is to experience new and exciting things – lik
Eurostar™ – the easiest way to travel between London and Paris or London and Brussel

It's fast (from the heart of Paris to the heart of London in only 3 hours). It's relaxin
comfortable and spacious with courteous staff and excellent service. And it
frequent, with trains leaving Eurostar™ stations up
28 times a day.

Most people, once they've experienced Eurosta
prefer not to travel on anything else. Eurostar™, the
only way to arrive in London, Paris or Brussels.

Café Emm, 17 Frith St. (☎ 7437 0723). Tube: Leicester Sq. Large portions served in an unpretentious atmosphere. All dishes on the rotating specials menu, from vegetarian casseroles to bangers and mash, are £5.50. Last orders 30min. before close. Open M-Th noon-3pm and 5:30-11pm, F noon-3pm and 5:30pm-2am, Sa 5pm-2am, Su 5:30-11pm. MC, V.

The Star Café and Bar, 22 Great Chapel St. (☎ 7437 8788). Tube: Tottenham Court Rd. An American-style diner, complete with tin ads for long-gone brands, with huge American-style portions to match. Baguettes £5.95, omelettes £5.50. Open M-F 7am-4pm.

busaba eathai, 106-110 Wardour St. (☎ 7255 8686). Tube: Tottenham Court Rd. Thai courses (£4.90-7.50) on shared tables. Open M-Th noon-11pm, F-Sa noon-11.30pm, Su noon-10pm.

Café Roma, 37 Berwick St. (☎ 7437 1076). Tube: Oxford Circus. This tiny neighborhood shop offers delicious Italian *ciabatta* sandwiches for around £2 and regular sandwiches for £1.30-£2.50. Savor the *panino vegetariano* (£2.85), enticingly smothered with thick slabs of avocado, tomato, and mozzarella. Full breakfast £3. Open daily 7am-7pm.

est, 54 Frith St. (☎ 7437 0666). Tube: Tottenham Court Rd. The modern wooden furniture gives this brassiere a spacious feeling, making a pleasant contrast from Soho's crowded streets. Main courses £8.20-10.40, pasta dishes £6.20-7.20. The *prix fixe* menu gives you a surprising amount of choice. (£6 for 2 courses; daily noon-7pm). Open noon-midnight.

Schnecke, 58-59 Poland St. (☎ 7287 6666). Tube: Oxford Circus or Tottenham Court Rd. Branch at 80-82 Upper St. Schnecke serves Alsatian food, specializing in *tartes flambees* (thin pastries with either sweet or savory toppings) and sausages. Great beers complement the jovial setting. Open M-Sa 12am-12pm, Su 12pm-10:30pm.

Square, 4 Princes St. (☎ 7409 3455; www.squarespace.com). Tube: Oxford Circus. Square slices of pizza on fluffy dough (£2.25-2.95) plus coffee make a comfortable break from nearby Oxford St. Open M-F 7:30am-5pm.

CHINATOWN

◨Tube: Leicester Sq.

Lok Ho Fook, 4-5 Gerrard St. (☎ 7437 2001). Tube: Leicester Sq. Busy place with good prices and a welcoming atmosphere. Extensive selection of seafood, noodles, and vegetarian dishes (£4-8). Dim sum (£1.40-1.60) is made to order and not strolled around on carts. Helpful staff will aid the novice in selection. Not to be confused with a nearby (and more expensive) place called Lee Ho Fook. Dim served sum until 6pm. Open daily noon-11:45pm. AmEx, DC, MC, V.

Kowloon Restaurant, 21-22 Gerrard St. (☎ 7437 0148). Tube: Leicester Sq. Meal-sized portions of rice noodles (£3.50-6) are served steaming and cheap. Rice dishes also under £4. Tea service available 11:30am-6pm. Satisfy your sweet tooth in the bakery. Open daily noon-11:45pm. AmEx, DC, MC, V.

The Dragon Inn, 12 Gerrard St. (☎ 7494 0869). Tube: Leicester Sq. Traditional Cantonese food. Delicious dim sum dishes served daily 11am-6pm, including a set dim sum for £6 per person (minimum 2 people). Main courses £5.80-9; rice and noodle dishes £4-5.50. Their duck dishes (£6.50) are excellent. Open daily 11am-11:45pm. AmEx, MC, V.

Wong Kei, 41-43 Wardour St (☎ 7437 3071). Tube: Leicester Sq. Three floors of busy (and famously curt) waiters work to make this dimly-lit restaurant one of the best values in Chinatown. Groups with fewer than 8 should expect to share tables. Rice dishes £3.30-4, noodle dishes £2.50-3. Set dinner £6.50 per person (min. 2 people). Open M-Sa noon-11:30pm, Su noon-10:30pm. Cash only.

1997 Special Zone Restaurant, 19 Wardour St. (☎ 7734 2868). Tube: Leicester Sq. The food is par for the course in Chinatown (and you have to bear with the sped-up Cantopop), but it makes a perfect 4am post-club meal. Rice dishes £4.20-5.50, main dishes £6-8. Open 24hr. V, MC.

MAYFAIR, ST. JAMES AND PICADILLY

Sofra, 18 Shepherd St. (☎ 7493 3320). Tube: Green Park/Hyde Park Corner. The house specialty, mixed *meze*, goes for £5.45, while other main courses will run you around £7.45-8.95. Open 12pm-12am. Other **branches** at 36 Tavistock St. (☎ 7240 3773) and 1 St. Christopher's Pl. (☎ 7224 4080; Tube: Bond St.).

Ask! 121-125 Park St. (☎ 7495 7760). Tube: Marble Arch. The hip, metallic look of the Ask! pizza chain is becoming increasingly omnipresent. But with their generous servings of pasta (£5-7) and tasty thin-crusted pizzas (£5-8), who's complaining? Open 12pm-11pm. Numerous **Branches** include: 160-162 Victoria St., 222 Kensington High St., 103 St. John St., and 48 Grafton Way.

NORTH LONDON

ISLINGTON

see map p. 306

🔟*Tube: Angel unless otherwise stated.*

🟦 **Tartuf,** 88 Upper St. (☎ 7288 0954). A convivial Alsatian place that serves excellent *tartes flambées* (£4.90-6.10), rather like pizzas on very thin crusts, except much tastier. All-you-can-eat tartes £8.90. Before 3pm, the £4.90 "lunch express" gets you a savoury *tarte* and a sweet one. Open M-F noon-2:30pm and 5:45-11:30pm, Sa noon-11:30pm, Su noon-11pm.

🟦 **Le Mercury,** 140a Upper St. (☎ 7354 4088). This French restaurant feels like the quintessential Islington gourmet bistro, but with outstandingly low prices. All main courses, including honey-roasted breast of duck, £5.85. Lunch and dinner 3-course *prix fixe* menu changes daily. Kids eat Sunday roast free. Open daily 11am-1am. Reservations recommended for evening. MC, V.

🟦 **Afghan Kitchen,** 35 Islington Green (☎ 7359 8019). This small cafe overlooking Islington Green offers cheap, scrumptious food. Everything on the short menu (8 main dishes, 4 vegetarian and 4 for carnivores; £4.50-5) tastes fresh and comes in very generous portions. The rice (£2) is some of the best in London. Open Tu-Sa noon-3:30pm and 5:30-11pm.

Istanbul Iskembecisi, 9 Stoke Newington Rd. (☎ 7254 7291; www.londraturk.com/istanbuliskembecisi). Rail: Dalston Kingsland, two stops east of Highbury & Islington. Buses #67, 149, and 243. This elegant Stoke Newington restaurant is considered a star by both the local Turkish community and numerous regulars. *Meze* (£2.75-4.75) and deeply flavored main courses (mostly £6-7.50) like *kuzu firin* (stewed leg of lamb) or the more common shish kebab will leave little room for dessert. in any case, there's a complimentary plate of fruit at the end of the meal. Excellent vegetarian selection (£5-6). Open daily noon-5am.

Pasha, 301 Upper St. (☎ 7226 1454). In one of the capital's best Turkish restaurants, the beauty of the simple interior is a perfect setting for excellent classics, like *kleftico* (lamb knuckle; £7.95) or stuffed aubergines (£6.95). Lunch or dinner *meze* (a sampling of appetizers), £9.95. Cover £1. Lunch M-Sa noon-3pm, dinner M-Th 6-11:30pm, F-Sa 6pm-midnight, Su noon-11pm.

La Piragua, 176 Upper St. (☎ 7354 2843). Welcome to South America—all of it! Colombian, Chilean, Venezuelan, and Argentine dishes complement an extensive Latin American wine list. The best deal is the steak: £10 for half a cow. Pork, beans, and plantain all feature heavily on the menu. Main courses £6.50-8. Vegetarian dishes £5.50. Open daily 1pm-midnight.

Angel Mangal, 139 Upper St. (☎ 7359 7777). Thoroughly filling kebabs and great helpings of other Turkish dishes, with tender meat. Most dishes £6-7, including rice, salad, and great, fresh bread. Open daily noon-midnight. MC, V.

CAMDEN TOWN

🔟*Tube: Camden Town unless otherwise indicated*

Bar Gansa, 2 Inverness St. (☎ 7267 8909). Tube: Camden Town. A small tapas bar with bright walls, festive Spanish candles, and Mediterranean ornaments. By night, a raucous international crowd enjoys tapas (£2-3.95) bottled beers (£2.25), sangria (£2.25), and throbbing Latin music. Limited outdoor seating. Open daily 10am-late.

Ruby in the Dust, 102 Camden High St. (☎ 7485 2744). Tube: Camden Town. Bright decor (butterflies and flowers hang from every free inch of plaster) and fun cocktails draw in a twentysomething crowd. Bangers and mash £6.85, burgers £6.55. Brunch 10am-6pm. Wide vegetarian selection. Open M-Th and Su 10am-11pm, F-Sa 10am-11:30pm. AmEx, MC, V.

Marine Ices, 8 Haverstock Hill (☎ 7482 9003). Tube: Chalk Farm. Head left from the station. Superb Italian-style ice cream (£1.25 for a single, £1 each additional scoop) and sundaes. Ice-cream counter open daily 10:30am-11pm. There's an attached restaurant (pizza £5.20-6.60) that's often packed with families, but the food's decidedly ordinary. Open M-F noon-3pm and 5:30-11pm, Sa noon-11pm, Su noon-10pm. MC, V.

Belgo Noord, 72 Chalk Farm Rd. See **Covent Garden,** p. 162.

Wagamama, 11 Jamestown Rd. See **Bloomsbury,** p. 162.

HAMPSTEAD AND HIGHGATE

🚇*Tube: Hampstead unless otherwise noted.*

Pharmacy

🍴 **Le Crêperie de Hampstead,** 77 Hampstead High St. This Hampstead institution is guaranteed nirvana, serving paper-thin Brittany crepes stuffed with fillings both sweet and savory from a tiny van outside the King William IV pub. Crepes £1.55-3.95. Open M-Th 11:45am-11pm, F-Su 11:45am-11:30pm.

🍴 **Giraffe,** 46 Rosslyn Hill (☎7435 0343). World food and world music at prices that are none too worldly. The menu runs the gamut from Cajun fish cakes to *meze.* Innovative breakfasts served M-F 8am-noon. During "Giraffe time" (M-F 6-7pm) a starter and main course cost the same as the time you order: order at 6:30, you pay £6.30. Open M-F 8am-midnight, Sa 9am-midnight, Su 9am-11:30pm. MC, V.

Bar Room Bar, 48 Rossyln Hill (☎8435 0808). Hampstead High St. turns into Rossyln Hill. Forgive the somewhat slow service and soak in the paintings and sculptures for sale in this "art gallery bar." The menu features light salads (£2-6.95) and baby pizzas (£2-3.45) with toppings like crispy duck or portabello with garlic, mozzarella and rosemary. The rear garden, lined with murals, makes for a faboo evening drink. By night, the music blares and the interior is candle-lit. Open M-W noon-11pm, Th noon-midnight, F-Sa noon-1am, Su noon-10:30pm. MC, V.

Wagamama

Little Bay, 228 Belsize Rd. (☎7372 4699). Tube: Kilburn Park. A budget gem, where three courses will set you back a mere £5.50 (before 7pm). And we're not talking about baby courses: very hearty plates of creamy French food and traditional English food. Bring an appetite. Open daily noon-10pm.

Polly's Café/Tea Room, 55 South End Rd. (☎7431 7947). Polly wants a tea room. This cozy enclave selling cheap sandwiches (£2.20-2.85) also provides a perfect retreat when the rains come. Many a budding novelist has sat out writer's block over a pot of Polly's tea (£1.10 per pot); fewer over the smoothies (£2.50). Open daily 8am-7:30pm. MC, V.

Al's Deli, down the alley near the Hampstead Market fruit stall next to 78 Hampstead High St. Cheap and cheerful, a Hampstead institution. One of the freshest and most inexpensive lunches found in this ritzy suburb. The three working-class residents of Hampstead lunch on the benches across from the counter. Sandwiches and pastries under £1.50. Open M-Sa 7am-2pm.

see map p. 305

THE EAST END

WHITECHAPEL

🚇*Tube: Aldgate East.*

Arkansas Café, Old Spitalfields Market. (☎7377 6999). This may not give you a taste of jolly old England, but the Brits are flocking

At Docklands

on the cheap

KOOL KEBAB

The Kebab—known to Londoners as anything ranging from a chewy lump of gristle in pita bread to an ornate concoction involving hummus, meat, and vegetables—is a dietary staple. Kebab shops are ubiquitous and, because of their deliciously high caloric content, offer a satisfying and cheap meal on the go. While Londoners generally choose other forms of takeaway for breakfast and lunch, nothing tops the kebab as an after-pub meal. When the pubs let out, the kebab shops fill up as tipsy pubbers gobble their way to sobriety.

After multiple pints of lager, the kebab begins to tempt like that not-so-attractive person you came to the pub with who has now become that attractive enough person you came to the pub with. Chomping a kebab may be lowering your standards, but hey, at least you won't wake up with it.

here in droves to Bubba and his BBQ pits. Schooled in the art of flesh in Louisiana, Bubba uses nothing but free-range, happy-while-it-lasted meat, and the results are to die for. If your arteries block on-site, the Royal London Hospital is nearby. Open M-F noon-2:30pm, Su 12-4pm. MC, V.

Spitz, 109 Commercial St. (☎ 7247 9747). Inside Spitalfields Market, this elegant bar serves delicious lunches starting at £5. During the weekend, there is live music upstairs, with an emphasis on folk, jazz, and klezmer. Open daily 11am-midnight.

Brick Lane Beigel Bake, 159 Brick Ln. (☎ 7729 0616). This East End gem offers perfect beigels (72p for 6) and stays open all the time. Open daily 24hr.

Shampan, 79 Brick Ln. (☎ 7375 0475). Tube: Aldgate East. A favorite of food critics and City office workers in the know. Balti lamb from £3.95, seafood dishes from £5. Open daily noon-3pm and 6pm-midnight. AmEx, MC, V.

Nazrul, 130 Brick Ln. (☎ 7247 2505). The rapid service means that you don't have to linger if you're pressed for time. Considering the size of the portions, prices are terrifically cheap; Balti menu starts around £3.10. Open M-Th noon-3pm and 5:30pm-midnight, F-Sa noon-3pm and 5:30pm-1am, Su noon-midnight. Cash only.

Aladin Balti House, 132 Brick Ln. (☎ 7247 8210). Must be good if it's the hangout for the Prince of Wales. Get a Camilla Parker Bowl full of food for £3.90. Open M-Th noon-11:30pm, F-Sa noon-midnight. Cash only.

SOUTH AND WEST LONDON

BRIXTON

see maps pp. 310 & 319   🚇 Tube: Brixton

▰ **Café, Bar, and Juice Bar,** 407 Coldharbour Ln. (☎ 7738 4141). This stylish cafe has a wonderful second-hand bookshop, specializing in black and gay issues. Simple vegetarian fare. F live poetry, Su jazz performances. Open M-F 11am-11pm, Sa 11am-2am. AmEx, MC, V.

Bah Humbug, The Crypt, St. Matthew's Church, Brixton Hill (☎ 7738 3184; www.bahhumbug.co.uk). In an atmospheric former church crypt, this is a stylish restaurant serving an eclectic mixture of vegetarian and fish dishes (£7.50-12.90). The savory crepes are particularly tasty: one filled with sauteed zucchini, goat cheese and salsa will set you back £5.80. Open M-F 5pm-midnight, Sa-Su 11am-midnight MC, V.

Fujiyama, 7 Vining St. (☎ 7737 2369; www.new-fujiyama.com). A popular noodle bar. Dishes £4.50-5.50; try the tasty Fujiyama ramen (£5.25). The rice bowls (£4.50-4.90) are equally delicious. Open Su-Th noon-11pm, F and Sa noon-midnight. AmEx, MC, V.

EARL'S COURT

⁊*Tube: Earl's Court*

▨ **Troubador,** 265 Old Brompton Rd. (☎ 7370 1434). Tube: Earl's Court. Assorted snacks, soups, and sandwiches (£3-6), and special breakfasts (£4.50-5) draw scores. Vast selection of coffee drinks. Open daily 9am-midnight. MC, V.

Saffron, 306b Fulham Rd. (☎ 7565 8183). Tube: Earl's Court. Indian restaurant with beautiful design and prices to match. Punjabi tikka (£4). Main courses are up there at £9-12. Open M-Sa 6pm-midnight, Su noon-3pm. AmEx, MC, V.

Perry's Bakery, 151 Earl's Court Rd. (☎ 7370 4825). Tube: Earl's Court. Amiable Bulgarian-Israeli management prides itself on an eclectic menu and fresh baked goods. Straight from Israel comes falafel with know-how (£2.50). £2 eat-in charge. Open daily 6am-midnight.

SHEPHERD'S BUSH, HAMMERSMITH, & HOLLAND PARK

Patio, 5 Goldhawk Rd. (☎ 8743 5194). Tube: Goldhawk Rd. Most of the menu is traditional English fare (main courses £5.50-8), but the main attractions of this Polish restaurant are the specialty dishes—£10.90 gets you 3 excellent courses (ask for the smoked salmon and blini starter) and a shot of vodka. Open noon-3pm and 6pm-midnight. AmEx, DC, MC, V.

RICHMOND

Chez Lindsay, Hill Rise (☎ 8948 7473). Tube: Richmond. A delightful Breton restaurant. While it caters largely to Richmond's moneyed classes (main courses £8.95-15.75), their £5.99 2-course lunch is a bargain. Call ahead. Chef leaves during the afternoon, so some dishes aren't avaiable all day. Lunch M-F 11am-3pm. Open M-Sa 12pm-11pm, S 12pm-10pm.

NOTABLE CHAINS

Prêt-à-Manger. This bustling chrome-adorned sandwich chain has become a London institution. And no wonder: everything Prêt serves is made of the fresh, organic ingredients. Sandwiches £1.35-2.90; eat-in prices are slightly more expensive. Many branches are closed for dinner.

Pierre Victoire. Brasserie chain offers inexpensive Parisian fare in expensive London neighborhoods. Staples like seafood *pot au feu* and mackerel pate. Menu changes daily. 2 course lunch £4.90. MC, V.

Pizza Express (www.pizzaexpress.co.uk). Gourmet establishment serves pizzas and pastas throughout London. Is this the best pizza in London? Quite possibly—this was the one that started the whole hip-pizzeria trend. All pizzas (£5-10) are thin crust and covered in fresh ingredients, like prosciutto, artichoke, and cherry tomato. The branch at 10 Dean St. (☎ 7437 9595) showcases excellent jazz at the **Pizza Express Jazz Club** in the basement. See **Nightlife**, p. 187. MC, V.

New Covent Garden Soup Company, Branch at 23 Fleet St. (☎ 7353 3711) Tube: Temple. Classic and innovative soup flavors, fresh salads and hearty muffins. Soup, chunk of bread, and ice cream or cake £3.50. Open M-F 8am-8pm.

TEA

Under certain circumstances there are few hours in life more agreeable than the hour dedicated to the ceremony known as afternoon tea.
  —Henry James, *Portrait of a Lady*

Quintessentially English, the tradition of afternoon tea is a social ritual combining food, conversation, and of course, a pot of tea--served strong and taken with milk. Don't commit a gaffe by pouring the tea first—aficionados always pour the milk before the tea so as not to scald it. Afternoon **high tea** includes cooked meats, salad, sandwiches, and pastries. **Cream tea,** a specialty of Cornwall and Devon, includes toast, shortbread, crumpets, scones, and jam, accompanied by delicious clotted cream (a cross between whipped cream and butter).

Claridges, Brook St (☎7629 8860). Tube: Bond St. Old-fashioned elegance combined with comfortable sofas and armchairs encourage a long afternoon linger. Smartly dressed waiters pour your tea and present plates of scrumptious sandwiches and pastries. Tea served daily 3pm-5:30pm; book in advance for weekends. £19; with champagne £25. AmEx, DC, MC, V.

The Orangery Tea Room, Kensington Palace, Kensington Gardens (☎7376 0239). Tube: High St. Kensington. Light meals and tea served in the marvelously airy Orangery built for Queen Anne in 1705. Two fruit scones with clotted cream and jam £4. Pot of tea £2.10, set teas from £5.25. Trundle through the gardens afterward, smacking your lips. Open daily 10am-6pm. MC, V.

The Ritz, Piccadilly (☎7493 8181). Tube: Green Park. Universally known as *the* tea experience, and as popular as you might expect it to be. But how often can you say you had tea at The Ritz? Set tea £23.50. Daily 3:30-5pm seatings. Dress code: Jacket and tie. AmEx, DC, MC, V.

The Savoy, Strand (☎7836 4343). Tube: Charing Cross. The elegance of this music-accompanied tea is well worth the splurge. Strict dress code—no jeans or shorts. If gentlemen "forget" their jacket, they'll be forced to borrow a garish red number from the cloakroom (necktie also preferred for gentlemen). £18.50. Tea served daily 3-5:30pm. Sa and Su book ahead. AmEx, DC, MC, V.

PUBS AND BARS

"Did you ever taste beer?"
"I had a sip of it once," said the small servant.
"Here's a state of things!" cried Mr. Swiveller, "She never tasted it—it can't be tasted in a sip!"
    —Charles Dickens, *The Old Curiosity Shop*

London, like much else in life, is far more fun after a few beers. In recognition of this phenomenon, the social institution that is the English pub was created centuries ago, coddling tipplers of all affiliations with mahogany paneling, velvet stools, and brass accents. Sir William Harcourt observed that, "As much of the history of England has been brought about in public houses as in the House of Commons," and this historic import has waned little through the centuries. While taverns and inns no longer serve as staging posts for coaches and horses, pubs remain social and cultural bastions of Britannia. If you're planning serious liver damage check out *Time Out's Guide: Pubs and Bars* (£9), which lists 1000 London watering holes.

WHAT TO DRINK

Beer is the standard pub drink. **Bitter** is the staple of English beer, named for the sharp hoppy aftertaste. "**Real ale,**" naturally carbonated and drawn from a barrel, retains its full flavor. Brown, mild, pale, and India pale ales all have a relatively heavy flavor with noticeable hop. The conspicuous presence of many local ales is thanks to CAMRA, the Campaign for Real Ale, a movement in the 1970s to circumvent big breweries from strong-arming beer-drinkers. **Stout** is rich, dark, creamy, and virtually synonymous with the Irish superstout, Guinness. If you can't stand the heat, try a **lager,** the European equivalent of American beer. **Bottled beer** is always more expensive than draft, and American beers are unusually expensive (in the bizarre utopia of English drinking, Budweiser costs more than Foster's, which in turn costs more than Heineken, which in turn costs more than Guinness). **Cider** is also common in pubs.

WHERE TO DRINK

Let crowd and atmosphere, rather than price, be your guide in selecting a pub. The difference per pint between drinking like a lord and drinking like a pauper is seldom more than 40p—by the time you save up enough to afford that sandwich, you'll have forgotten you wanted it. Pubs closely reflect their neighborhoods: touristy and overpriced near the inner-city train stations, stylish and trendy in the West End, gritty in the East, and suit-packed in the City. Once you've found a good pub, don't be afraid to leave—making a circuit, or pub crawl, is fun, and lets you experience the diversity of a neighborhood's nightlife. More importantly, you can drink an ocean of beer and no one will see just how many pints you've ordered.

WHEN TO DRINK

The "last order" bells that ring through the streets of London at 10:50pm testify to the lamentable truth that British pubs close miserably early. Don't let these bells ring your evening's death knell, however. Begin drinking when the pubs open at 11am. Or hustle to a bar or a club before 11pm, after which raise their cover charges. Though liquor laws continue to relax, most pubs are open only 11 to 12 hours per day. The pubs around Smithfield Market are a notable exception, opening at 7:30am for English breakfast. The average pub serves from 11am to 11pm Monday through Saturday in order to get lunchtime and afternoon business. Sundays, most pubs are open from noon to 10:30pm. More recently, London's pubs are finding ways around closing times—serving food or having an entertainment licence allows an establishment to serve alcohol later, so wine bars are popular and around pub closing time clubs really start to get going.

Pharmacy

PUB GRUB

Pubs can be great places for bargain meals. Pub grub now includes anything from Thai food to burgers, but traditional English food is still a staple at most places. Quality and prices vary greatly, with virtually no relation between the two. Steak and kidney pie or pudding is a mixture of steak and kidney, mushrooms, and pastry or pudding crust. A cornish pasty is filled with potato, onion, and often meat. Shepherd's pie consists of minced beef or lamb with onion, saddled with mashed potatoes, and baked. A ploughman's lunch means portions of bread, cheese, and pickled onions. Mash is British for "mashed potatoes." It comes coated with "liquor," (a parsley-flavored green sauce), with sausages (bangers and mash), or with cabbage (bubble and squeak). Don't expect table service: order from the bar.

Grapes

BARS

If you thirst for cocktails, martinis, or mixed drinks, you're better off visiting a **bar.** London bars offer later hours, higher prices, and less traditional decor—visit them during happy hour (around 5:30-7:30pm) for the best drink deals. The listings below include both bars and pubs; names alone should indicate which is which.

see map pp. 288-289

CENTRAL LONDON

THE CITY OF LONDON

Ye Olde Cheshire Cheese, Wine Office Ct. by 145 Fleet St. (☎ 7353 6170). Tube: Blackfriars or St. Paul's. Classic pub, dating to the 17th century, where Dr. Johnson and Dickens, as well as Americans Mark Twain and Theodore Roosevelt, hung out. Today it's hot among businesspeople and lawyers. Ayingerbrau £1.90. Open M-Sa 11:30am-11pm, Su noon-3pm.

Fuego Bar y Tapas, 1 Pudding Ln. (☎ 7929 3366). Tube: Monument. This snazzy executive watering hole compensates for lack of window space and cavernous basement location with lively evening

Virginia Woolf's

events. Elevated walkway makes for great, smoky disco experience. Spanish music M nights, Th-F disco nights. Tapas £2-4. Dinner main course £6.90-10. Open M-F 11:30am-2am.

The King's Head, 49 Chiswell St. (☎ 7606 9158). Tube: Barbican. This pub's outstanding baguette shop distinguishes it from all the other slot machine-filled City pubs. French bread baked daily on premises. Popular sandwiches include brie and turkey (£2.95). Open M-Sa 11am-11pm, Su noon-10:30pm.

Simpson's, Ball Court, off 38½ Cornhill (☎ 7626 9985). Tube: Bank. "Established 1757" says the sign on the alley leading to this pub; indeed, it remains so traditional a man stands in the door to greet you. The menu is similarly staunchly classic, with hearty dishes such as steak and kidney pie setting you back £5.50-6.90. Open M-F 11:30am-4pm.

The Punch Tavern, 99 Fleet St. (☎7353 6658). Tube: Blackfriars. Old site of the Punch and Judy show. Funky collection of wooden puppet figures—eyes follow you around the room. Better than average pub food; caesar salads and scampi. Pints from £2.10. Food served 11:15am-3pm. Open M-Tu 11am-10pm, W-F 11am-11pm.

HOLBORN

🍺 **Black Friar,** 174 Queen Victoria St. (☎7236 5650). Tube: Blackfriars. One of the most exquisite and fascinating pubs in all of London. The edifice's past purpose as a 12th-century Dominican friary is celebrated not only in the pub's name but in the intriguing arches, mosaics, and reliefs that line the pub's walls. While the carvings look grand, closer examination shows the sense of humor: ironic sayings such as "industry is all" and "finery is foolery" are carved into the side chapel, at the back of the pub. Carlsberg £2.35, Tetley's £2.15. Lunch served 11:30am-2:30pm. Open M-F 11:30am-11pm, Sa noon-5pm, Su noon-4:30pm.

Princess Louise, 208 High Holborn, WC1 (☎7405 8816). Tube: Holborn. This big pub isn't big enough to contain the jovial crowd that assembles after office hours. The pub retains its ornate Victorian grandeur—beautiful tiles and etched mirrors line the walls. Pint of bitter £1.65. Pub grub served noon-9pm. Open M-F 11am-11pm, Sa noon-11pm. AmEx, DC, MC, V.

KENSINGTON, KNIGHTSBRIDGE, AND HYDE PARK

🍺 **The Social,** 5 Little Portland St. (☎7636 4992). Tube: Oxford Circus. Raucous crowd, tiny space, great music, ear-debilitating bass. Manages to be both flashy and welcoming. Perhaps it's the comfort food they serve (eggy bread £2). Pints £2.60-2.70. Open M-Sa noon-midnight, Su 5-10:30pm.

The Scarsdale, 23a Edwardes Sq. (☎7937 1811). Tube: High St. Kensington. When you see people sitting outside in a sea of flowers and ivy, contentedly sipping their pints, well, you've found it. Open M-Sa noon-11pm, Su noon-10:30pm.

The Churchill Arms, 119 Kensington Church (☎7727 4242). Tube: Notting Hill Gate. Comfortable bar decorated with obscure sporting paraphernalia, including commemorations of the Churchill Arms cricket club and a hurling victory. The conservatory is well regarded for cheap, filling meals (main courses under £6). Food served M-Sa noon-2:30pm and 6-9:30pm, Su noon-2:30pm. Open M-Sa 11am-11pm, Su noon-10:30pm

World's End Distillery, 459 King's Rd. (☎7376 8946), near World's End Pass before Edith Grove. Tube: Fulham Broadway (Zone 2). This classy pub dates back to 1689 when it was renowned for its tea garden; now it provides quality pints (£2.20-2.55) in the comfy bookshelf-lined booths. Open M-Sa 11am-11pm, Su noon-10:30pm.

The Goat in Boots, 333 Fulham Rd. (☎7352 1384). Tube: South Kensington. Multi-level bar attracts a young crowd. Drink specials each night (W all shots £1; all drinks 2-for-1). Open M-Sa 11am-11pm, Su noon-10:30pm.

The King's Head and Eight Bells, 50 Cheyne Walk (☎7352 1820). Tube: Sloane Sq. or South Kensington. Richly textured 16th-century pub close to the Thames where Thomas More would have a jar with his dangerous friend Henry VIII. These days, the pub has a more relaxed feel about it. Wide selection of beers on tap, including a decent Belgian selection (Hoegaarden £3.55). Standard pub grub £5.75-6.50. Open M-Sa 11am-11pm, Su noon-10:30pm.

NOTTING HILL AND BAYSWATER

▨ **Pharmacy,** 150 Notting Hill Gate (☎ 7221 2442). Tube: Notting Hill Gate. The lighting makes it a bit too sterile for a long evening of boozing, but walls full of potions make it an intriguing place for a cocktail. Open M-Th noon-3pm and 6pm-1am, F-Sa noon-3pm and 6pm-2am, Su 6-10:30pm. AmEx, MC, V.

▨ **192,** 192 Kensington Park Rd. (☎ 7229 0482). Tube: Ladbroke Grove. Despite 192's popularity amongst area media whores leading to its repeated mention in the *Bridget Jones* books, this wine bar is worth a visit for those looking to model DKNY jeans and D&G crop tops, or eager to check out the expansive wine list (£2.60-6 a glass). Open M-Sa 12:30-11:30pm, Su 12:30-11pm. AmEx, MC, V.

▨ **The Westbourne,** 101 Westbourne Park Villas (☎ 7221 1332). Tube: Westbourne Park. Another fixture of the Notting Hill scene, the Westbourne is a gastro-pub that is notoriously crowded with notoriously attractive area socialites. Bohemian decor inside, and a heated terrace packed to the gills outside—you can't go wrong. Open M 5-11pm, Tu-F noon-11pm, Sa 11am-11pm, Su noon-10:30pm. MC, V.

Ion, 161-165 Ladbroke Grove (☎ 8960 1702). Tube: Ladbroke Grove. After recent renovation, Ion restarted its place in the scenester pantheon, with its retro interior and rumbling overhead train tracks. Pretty standard stuff, with the Notting Hill crowdpacking it in and drinking it down. Reduced drink prices before 9pm. Open M-F 5pm-midnight, Sa-Su noon-midnight. AmEx, MC, V.

Fountain's Abbey, 109 Praed St. (☎ 7402 4916). Tube: Paddington. Across the street from the hospital (St. Mary's) where Alexander Fleming discovered penicillin, Fountain's Abbey is a grade A local—standard decor, decent food, and strangely kitsch 80s pop piped in at high volumes. Open M-Sa 11am-11:30pm, Su noon-10:30pm. AmEx, MC, V.

BLOOMSBURY

Old Crown, 33 New Oxford St. (☎ 7836 9121). Tube: Tottenham Ct. Rd. An interesting mix of a downstairs pub with over-the-top decor, and a dim upstairs lounge, both attended by a fun-loving, boisterous crowd. Cocktails, like the aptly named 'Pirate's of Mens' Pants,' run £4-6. Open M-Sa 11am-11pm. AmEx, MC, V.

Museum Tavern, 49 Great Russell St. (☎ 7242 8987). Tube: Tottenham Ct. Rd. A right proper Victorian pub—by day full of tourists who just can't take any more culture in the British Museum, by night, surprisingly local in crowd. Karl Marx sipped *Bier* here after spending his days in the British Museum reading room. The Star Tavern, which formerly occupied this site, was one of Casanova's rendezvous spots. Open M-Sa 11am-11pm, Su noon-10:30pm. AmEx, MC, V.

The Lamb, 94 Lamb's Conduit St. (☎ 7405 0713). Tube: Russell Sq. In addition to E.M. Forster and other Bloomsbury luminaries, John Wayne tippled here. Food served noon-2:30pm. Open M-Sa 11am-11pm, Su noon-4pm, 7pm-10:30pm. MC, V.

Point 101, 101 New Oxford St. (☎ 7636 7964). Tube: Tottenham Court Rd. Crammed on weekends with affable twenty-somethings (expect a queue), imbibing cocktails (£4-5). Also a good bet for a late-night drink, and they even bring in DJs. Open M-Th 10am-2am, F 10am-2:30am, Su 12pm-12am. AmEx, MC, V.

The Water Rats, 328 Grays Inn Rd. (☎ 7837 7269). Tube: King's Cross/St. Pancras. M-Sa nights a venue for indie, punk, and occasional acoustic gigs. Three bands per night. Marx and Engels debuted many of their proletariat hit songs here. Cover £5, £4 concessions or with flyer. Bands start at 9pm. Open M-Sa 8pm-midnight.

Grafton Arms, 72 Grafton Way (☎ 7387 7923). Tube: Warren St. Off the tourist trail, near Regent's Park. One of the best central London pubs for a relaxed pint. Caters to a lively student crowd (read: cheap beers). Standard pub fare sold all day. Wine bar upstairs and rooftop patio. Open M-Sa 10am-11pm, Su 11am-3pm and 7-10:30pm. MC, V.

COVENT GARDEN

◪*Tube: Covent Garden.*

PUB DISCO!

If you stick around London long enough, you might see your "local" turning into a disco on weekend nights. "Pub discos," basically your local pub plus a DJ spinning thumping hits of the 70s, 80s, and 90s, have become an increasingly common phenomenon, especially in the outer zones where an expensive cab ride or long night bus trek make a night out inconvenient. A north London resident had this to say about disco at her local pub: "The pubs in my neighborhood have tons of older Irish folks in them. Same crowd always. There is one where they always nod and wave to me when I come in and use the restroom while waiting for the bus. On Saturdays, it is disco night, which means they play really naff disco at volumes that must surely cause some of them to have bloody ears, but no one dances. It's just the same crowd of regulars, sitting there, unable to converse due to the stinking disco music." Disco night at the pub are loads of fun, but there's also something fairly comical about the whole thing—the pub, an institution dating from the time of the Magna Carta, seems hardly tailored to a throbbing four-on-the-floor bass beat. Old men sit by as blokes in Addidas track suits eye Essex girls with faux fur and too much eye makeup.

Freud, 198 Shaftesbury Ave. (☎7240 9933). Invigorate your psyche in this downstairs cafe/bar/gallery/hipster hang-out. The bar hosts month-long art shows. A beer here (£2-3) is cheaper than an hour on the couch. Open M-Sa 11am-11pm, Su noon-10:30pm. No credit cards.

Crown and Anchor, 22 Neal St. (☎7836 5649). One of Covent Garden's most popular pubs. A young mix of the down-and-out and the up-and-coming perches on kegs or sits on the cobblestones outside, forming a mellow oasis in the midst of Neal Street's bustling pedestrian zone. Open M-Sa 11am-11pm, Su noon-10:30pm. MC, V.

The Coal Hole, 91 The Strand (☎7836 7503). Red leather couches and a crush of knick-knacks enhance this otherwise standard pub. Ales £2.10-£3.80. Open M-Sa 11am-11pm, Su noon-10:30pm. MC, V.

The Africa Centre. See **Nightlife,** p. 187.

Belushi's, 9 Russell St (☎7240 3411). More of a bar than a pub, and now a restaurant as well. Upbeat Aussie and Kiwi barmen and barmaids serve Budweiser and dance to 80s pop music, making for an unrepentently cheesy good time. Happy hour M-Sa 5-8pm. Open daily 11am-midnight. MC, V.

Lamb and Flag, 33 Rose St. (☎7497 9504). Formerly called the "Bucket of Blood." Site of Dryden's 1679 asswhomping (see **Sights,** p. 84). Traditional old English pub, with no music and two separate sections—the public bar for the working class, and the saloon bar for the businessmen (today the classes mix). Live jazz upstairs Su from 7:30pm. Open M-Th 11am-11pm, F-Sa 11am-10:45pm, Su noon-10:30pm.

Spot, 29 Maiden Ln. (☎7379 5900). Unlike its raucous neighbors, Spot verges on trendy, with loud clubby music, stylish decor, and a crowd of twenty-something regulars. Cocktails around £5. Cover £5 F, Sa. Open M-Sa noon-1am, Su 5pm-1am. AmEx, MC, V,

The White Hart, 191 Drury Ln. (☎7242 3135). Established in 1201, this is the oldest licensed pub in England. Traditional pub fare served alongside hand-pulled ales, as you recline in plush red seats framed by wine-dark wood. Open M-Sa 11am-11pm.

Maple Leaf, 41 Maiden Ln. (☎7240 2843). "The only place outside of North America with Molson on tap" (£2.65 per pint) says it all. Start a rousing chorus of "O Canada," "Tom Sawyer" or "It's All Coming Back to Me" and make some new friends and/or foes. Hockey on TV. Basic pub fare available noon-9:30pm. Open M-F 11am-11pm, Sa noon-11pm, Su noon-10:30pm. AmEx, MC, V.

SOHO

Yo!Below, 52 Poland St. (☎7439 3660). Tube: Oxford Circus. Located below Yo!Sushi. Customers sit on cushions on the floor and dispense their own beer from taps at the table. Free massages and tea ceremonies, along with karaoke singing staff make for a great night out. Open M-Su noon-midnight. AmEx, MC, V.

The Three Greyhounds, 25 Greek St. (☎7287 0754). Tube: Leicester Sq. This tiny, Tudor-front pub provides personality and a welcome respite from the endless posturing of Soho. Open M-Sa 11am-11pm, Su noon-10:30pm.

The Coach and Horses, Bruton St. (☎7629 4123). Tube: Bond St. A tiny Tudor house that looks somewhat out of place near the boutiques of New Bond St. The Queen was born nearby, on 17 Bruton St. Foster's £2.27. Open M-F 11am-11pm, Sa 11am-8pm.

The Dog and Duck, 18 Bateman St. (☎7437 4447). Tube: Tottenham Ct. Rd. A frequent winner of the Best Pub in Soho award, its size keeps the crowd down (or at least out on the street). Local professionals squeeze in at lunch for the cheap pints (Carlsberg £2.50). Evenings bring locals, actors on the way home, and, yes, some tourists. Why dog and duck? Look closely at the tiles that line the walls. Open M-F noon-11pm, Sa 5-11pm, Su 6-10:30pm.

The Salisbury, 90 St. Martin's Ln. (☎7836 5863). Tube: Leicester Sq. A dramatically decorated pub in the heart of the theater district. Business people and tourists by day, a younger crowd by night. Bitter £2.18, Ale £2.51. Open M-Sa noon-11pm, Su noon-10:30pm.

Sherlock Holmes, 10 Northumberland St., WC2 (☎7930 2644). Tube: Charing Cross. Near Great Scotland Yard, in what used to be the Northumberland Hotel, mentioned in the *Hound of the Baskervilles*. Upstairs replicates Holmes' 221b Baker St. den. Plenty of relics to thrill Holmes fiends—tobacco in the slipper, correspondence affixed to the mantelpiece with a dagger, and the Hound of the Baskervilles's head. Sherlock Holmes Ale £2.20. Open M-Sa 11am-11pm, Su noon-10:30pm.

Comptons of Soho, 53 Old Compton St. See **Nightlife,** p. 179.

Admiral Duncan, 54 Old Compton St. See **Nightlife,** p. 178.

MAYFAIR, ST. JAMES'S, AND PICADILLY

Ye Grapes, Shepherd Market (☎7499 1563) Tube: Green Park. In a corner of the pedestrianised Shepherd Market area, Ye Grapes has a village pub feel to it. Fortunately, pints are decently priced (£2.75). Open M-Sa 11am-11pm, Su noon-11pm.

NORTH LONDON

ISLINGTON

🚇*Tube: Angel unless otherwise indicated*

see map p. 306

🚽 **Filthy MacNasty's Whiskey Café,** 68 Amwell St. (☎7837 6067). St. Augustine's "O lord make me pure but not just yet," sits above the patrons of this famously small and friendly Irish pub. Renowned for traditional Irish music Su, and one of Shane Macgowan's favorite pubs. Live readings and music every M, and W-Th. Guinness £2.20. Wheelchair accessible. Open daily noon-11pm.

Bierodrome, 173 Upper St. (☎7226 5835). Started by the Belgo people (see p. 156), so the bar menu is the traditional Belgian fries and mussels; here, though, the focus is the beer.

Duke of Cambridge, 30 St. Peter's St. (☎7359 3066). No music, but a constant hum of chat and laughter of small groups of friends. Young and friendly staff justifiably proud of delicious food and drink, all organic and additive-free. Freedom organic lager £2.80. Good wine selection £10-40, organic fruit juice £2-2.50. Hurrah and huzzah, there's even a non-smoking section. Food served 12:30-3pm and 6:30-10:30pm.

The Marquess, 32 Canonbury St. (☎7354 2975). Tube: Highbury and Islington or Rail: Essex Rd. This Canonbury neighborhood pub was once voted Best Real Ale pub in North London by CAMRA (Campaign for Real Ale), the pressure group that saved British brewing from a weak and watery grave. Bitter £2, lager £2.20. Open M-Sa 11am-11pm, Su noon-10:30pm.

The King's Head, 115 Upper St. (☎7226 1916). Famous for its pub theatre (see **Entertainment,** p. 146), which takes place both in the evening and at lunchtime, the King's Head is also a charming place for a late-night pint (£2.40). Open Su-Th 11am-1am, F-Sa 11am-2am.

The Camden Head, Camden Passage (☎7359 0851). Very much a traditional pub feel, with snug booths and large outdoor area. Fosters £2.23. Tu comedy nights. Food served M-W 11am-

OF DOGS AND DUCKS

Pubs are an aspect of London that is impossible to miss—there's a place to tipple on virtually every street corner. With titles like "The Doghouse," pub names, however, appear to be mysteriously unrelated to the offerings inside. That's not usually the case. Pub names with the word "bell" in them often referred to nearby church or monastery ringers; Christian religious icons such as lambs and doves soon found their way onto pub signs, then into the names themselves. Even the unlikely name "The Bull" has a religious derivative, "bull" being a corruption of the Latin word for monastery.

Pubs also tried to align themselves with nobility; some, like the "King William IV" pub, are named after individual royal figures. It was often too impractical, however, to constantly shift names with the political tides, so many pubs adopted general terms associated with the monarchy, such as "The Crown" and "The King's Head." To align themselves with noble families, pubs often took the names of the creatures that appeared on a family coat-of-arms; the lion was a popular example of this phenomenon.

9pm, Th-Sa 11am-6pm, Su noon-6pm. Open M-Sa 11am-11:30pm, Su noon-11pm.

The Mitre, 130 Upper St. (☎7704 7641). The Mitre is loud, packed with students and game machines, and has a wide range of drink specials—just how its young patrons like it. The huge beer garden with outdoor billiard table is popular on F and Sa DJ nights. Carling £2. Open M-Th noon-midnight, F-Sa noon-1am, Su noon-10:30pm.

Nu Bar, 196 Essex Rd. See **p. 183**.

CAMDEN TOWN

The Engineer, 65 Gloucester Ave. (☎7722 0950). Tube: Chalk Farm. A thousand miles away from boisterous Camden, join the beautiful Luvvies at this classic pub. A bright atmosphere and a sumptuous back garden makes everybody feel relaxed. Pints £2.50. Wheelchair accessible. Open M-Sa 9am-11pm, Su 9am-10:30. MC, V.

Dublin Castle, 94 Parkway. See **Nightlife,** p. 186.

Liberty's, 100 Camden High St. (☎7485 4019). Tube: Camden Town. This cool, airy pub manages to maintain a chilled atmosphere even on a Friday night. The speedy bar staff even make time to empty your crisps into a little bowl. Said to serve the best pint of Guinness in North London. Pints start at £2.25, Open M-Sa noon-11pm, Su noon-10:30pm.

HAMPSTEAD AND HIGHGATE

The Holly Bush, 22 Holly Mount (☎7435 2892). Tube: Hampstead. The quintessential snug Hampstead pub in a quaint cul-de-sac. Currently undergoing renovations. A maze of glass, the Bush serves pints from £1.95. Open M-F noon-3pm and 5:00-11pm, Sa noon-4pm and 6-11pm, Su noon-10:30pm. MC, V.

EAST LONDON

WHITECHAPEL

◪ Shoreditch Electricity Showrooms, 39a Hoxton Sq. (☎7739 6934). Tube: Old St. If you wanted to know where the super-cool go, this is the answer. Cocktails £6, beers £2.30 and up. Open Tu, W noon-11pm, Th 12am-12pm, F-Sa 12am-1am, Su noon-10:30pm. MC, V.

see map p. 305

Cantaloupe, 35-42 Charlotte Rd. (☎7613 4411). Tube: Old St. right. Cantaloupe is almost strictly Londoners, drinking at the long wooden tables, and eating so-so tapas at the bar or at the restaurant in back. Open M-F 11am-midnight, Sa 2pm-midnight, Su noon-11:30pm. MC, V.

The Vibe Bar, The Brewery, 91-95 Brick Ln. (☎7377 2899). Young, fun, and loud, with DJ's day and night. Plop on a comfy sofa, tackle a game at a Playstation or check your email for free when you buy a drink. Disabled access. Open M-Sa 11am-11pm, Su noon-10:30pm. AmEx, MC, V.

The Blind Beggar, 337 Whitechapel Rd. (☎ 7247 6195). Tube: Whitechapel. You may be sitting where George Conell sat when he was gunned down by rival Bethnal Green gangster Ronnie Kray in 1966. Keep your head low. Spacious pub with conservatory and garden. Open M-Sa 11am-11pm, Su noon-10:30pm.

DOCKLANDS

▣ **Prospect of Whitby,** 57 Wapping Wall (☎ 7481 1095). Tube: Wapping. Open ceilings and rustic flagstone bar in a building dating from 1520 pale next to the glorious Thamescape. Lunch served noon-2:30pm, dinner 6-9pm daily. Open M-F 11:30am-3pm and 5:30pm-11pm, Sa 11:30am-11pm, Su noon-10:30pm. AmEx, DC, MC, V.

▣ **Gun,** 27 Coldharbour, E14 (☎ 7987 1692). DLR: Blackwall. A contender for best view amongst the docks, with a view of the Dome and the West India Docks. Open M-Sa 11am-11pm, Su noon-10:30pm. MC, V.

see map p. 319

SOUTH LONDON

SOUTH BANK AND SOUTHWARK

▣ **The Fire Station,** 150 Waterloo Rd. (☎ 7620 2226). Tube: Waterloo, behind the station. In converted Edwardian fire station, the food menu that changes twice daily. Main dishes, from pork and leek sausages to salmon steaks, are excellent but pricey (£7-12). Open M-Sa noon-2:45pm and 5:30-11pm, Su noon-9:30pm. AmEx, MC, V.

▣ **Tas,** 33 The Cut (☎ 7928 2111). Tube: Waterloo. Tas manages to serve gourmet quality Turkish and Mediterranean food at low prices. Starter and main for a scandalously low £6.45. Rejoice! Open M-Sa noon-11:30pm, Su noon-10:30pm. AmEx, MC, V.

▣ **Cubana,** 48 Lower Marsh. (☎ 7928 8778). Tube: Waterloo. Staff keep The People happy with fresh, spiky cocktails, live salsa music W nights, a cheap and intriguing menu (crab and papaya salad £6.95), and a wide selection of edible cigars. Open M-Sa noon-midnight. AmEx, MC, V.

▣ **Bread and Roses,** 68 Clapham Manor St. (☎ 7498 1779). Tube: Clapham Common. With socialist roots and pinko leanings, Bread and Roses has a history of liquoring up the people. Primarily trad pub that has great beers (Smile's Workers' Ale £2) and often hosts theater and music; call for a schedule. Open M-Sa 11am-11pm, Su noon-10:30pm. MC, V.

The Dickens Inn, St. Katherine's Way (☎ 7488 2208). Tube: Tower Hill or DLR: Tower Gateway. Before entering the Dickens to have a drink, imagine 18th-century traders milling about on one of the 3-story balconies. Open M-Sa 11am-11pm, Su noon-10:30pm. AmEx, DC, MC, V.

George Inn, 77 Borough High St. (☎ 7407 2056). Tube: Borough. London's only surviving 17th-century galleried coaching inn, with multiple bars. Ever-changing guest beers make cameos (£2.30-2.60). Non-smoking room. Open M-Sa 11am-11pm, Su noon–10:30pm. MC, V

BRIXTON

Bug Bar, The Crypt, St. Matthew's Church, Brixton Hill. See **Nightlife,** p. 182.

The Dogstar, 389 Coldharbour Ln. See **Nightlife,** p. 182.

Fridge Bar, 1 Town Hall Parade, Brixton Hill. See **Nightlife,** p. 183.

Satay Bar, 447-450 Coldharbour Ln. (☎ 7326 5001). Tube: Brixton. One of Brixton's more relaxed bars. A nice selection of Southeast Asian beers on tap (Tiger £2.50). Open M-Th 6-pm-11pm, F-Sa 6pm-1am, Su 6pm-10pm.

GREENWICH

North Pole, 131 Greenwich High Rd. (☎ 8853 3020). DLR: Greenwich. North Pole is a freehouse serving a gamut of beers, including Leffe and Stella (£2.50-3). Open M 5:30-11pm, Tu-Sa noon-11pm, Su noon-10:30pm. AmEx, MC, V.

LATE NIGHT ROW

Everyone bemoans the early closing time of 11pm imposed on pubs K-wide as a ma or style-cramper. In the last few years, there has been discussion of changing these laws, instituted during WWI to keep munitions workers from staying out too late (Whoops . . . Boom), though now clearly unnnecessary. However, Westminster City Council recently instituted a ban in Covent Garden on the ever-proliferating way around these rules, the late license. Only those bars and pubs that currently possess them will be allowed to stay open past the standard closing times, and therefore will become even more crowded. In addition, at least on the record, no venue in Covent Garden is allowed to remain open past 1am, although the enforcement of this will likely be spotty. The measure was a result of complaints by area residents, and a step towards trying to prevent a 24-hour society. Very British indeed.

WINE BARS

Vinopolis, City of Wine, 1 Bank End (☎0870 444 4777; www.vinopolis.co.uk). Tube: London Bridge. With a ticket to this Dionysian Disneyland guests are treated to an interactive (yes, that means samples) tour of the world's wine history and offerings. £11.50, under 18 £4.50, £1 discount for advance booking. Open daily 10am-5pm; last entry 4:30pm.

Vats, 51 Lamb's Conduit St. (☎7242 8963). Tube: Russell Square. Knowedgable staff willing to give suggestions for the best wines on a budget. Open M-F noon-11pm. AmEx, MC, V.

Bleeding Heart Bistro, Bleeding Heart Yard, off Greville St. (☎7242 2056). Tube: Farringdon. A tremendous cellar coupled with tremendous food may give you a coronary, but the price tag on the wines at the upper end of the bistro's selection most definitely will. Glass £4-5, bottles £11 on up. Open M-F noon-11pm. AmEx, MC, V.

Odette's Wine Bar, 130 Regent's Park Rd. (☎7722 5388). Tube: Chalk Farm. Full of little corners and crannies, Odette's makes for serious date action. Two dozen wines to be had by the glass £3-5. Open M-Sa 12:30-3pm and 5:30-11pm. AmEx, MC, V.

Albertine, 1 Wood Lane (☎8743 9593). Tube: Shepherd's Bush. 50 wines beckon, many by the glass (£2.20-4.20). Good for a romantic piss-up. Open M-F 11am-11pm, Sa 6:30-11pm. MC, V.

GAY AND LESBIAN BARS

see map pp. 292-293

GAY

Ku Bar, 75 Charing Cross Rd., WC2 (☎7437 4303; www.ku-bar.co.uk). Tube: Leicester Sq. Attracts well-dressed, younger gay men and those that love them. The crowd frequently spills onto the street, attesting to the popularity of this pre-club venue. Beer £2.25. Open M-Sa 12:30-11pm, Su 12:30-10:30pm.

Admiral Duncan, 54 Old Compton St., W1 (☎7437 5300). Tube: Leicester Sq. or Piccadilly Circus. Always a popular hangout, now forever noted as a defiant symbol against intolerance. Since the 1999 bombing here, the pub's been renovated and still pulls in the crowds. Foster's £2.37. Open M-Sa 11am-11pm, Su noon-10:30pm.

The Box, Seven Dials, 32-34 Monmouth St. See **Nightlife,** p. 185.

Brief Encounter, 42 St. Martin's Ln. In the same building as Ian Schrager's ultra-chic St. Martin's Lane hotel. Encounters as brief as you choose. Open M-Sa 3-11pm, Su 5-10:30pm.

Comptons of Soho, 53 Old Compton St. (☎7479 7461). Tube: Leicester Sq. or Piccadilly Circus. Soho's "official" gay pub is always busy, with a mostly male crowd of all ages. Horseshoe-shaped bar encourages the exchange of meaningful glances, while upstairs offers a more mellow scene. Open M-Sa 11am-11pm, Su noon-10:30pm.

Kudos, 10 Adelaide St. (☎7379 4573). Tube: Charing Cross. Split-level bar filled with a well-dressed crowd. Open M-Sa 10am-11pm, Su 10am-10:30pm.

79 CXR, 79 Charing Cross Rd. (☎7734 0769). Tube: Leicester Sq. A gay pub that attracts an older crowd. Less posing, less attitude. Open 1pm-2am M-Th, 1pm-3am F-Sa, Su 1pm-10:30pm.

see map pp. 292-293

LESBIAN

🔲 **The Candy Bar,** 4 Carlisle St., W1 (☎7494 4041). Tube: Tottenham Ct. Rd. Three floors of women (men welcome as guests) at London's first and the UK's original 7 days a week lesbian bar. Bar downstairs becomes dance floor W-Sa. Cover £5 F and Sa after 10pm. Bar open M-Th 5-midnight, F 5pm-2am, Sa 11am-11pm, Su 5-10:30pm. Club open M-Th 8pm-12am, F-Sa 8pm-2am, Su 7-11pm.

🔲 **Vespa Lounge,** St. Giles High St. (☎7240 1860). Tube: Tottenham Court Rd., under the giant skyscraper, on the backside. A newcomer to the lipstick lesbian scene, but definitely a keeper, and always packed at weekends. Men welcome as guests. Open daily 6-11pm.

4UGirl, at The Seen, 93 Dean St., W1 (☎0956 514 574; wowbar@dircon.co.uk). Tube: Tottenham Court Rd. A dimly lit basement lounge and dance floor sweats and shakes it in this self-titled "glamour dyke dive," every Saturday. Men welcome as guests. Drinks £2 from 10-11pm. Cover £4 before 11pm, then £5. Open Sa 10pm-3am.

Nightlife

NIGHTCLUBS

I like the nightlife. I like to boogie.
— Rumor attributes this to Winston Churchill

Every major DJ in the world either lives in London or makes frequent visits to the city. While the US may have introduced house music to the world, the UK has taken the lead in developing and experimenting with new types of dance music. Take advantage of your tourist status and party during the week—though there are fewer options, London has enough tourists, slackers, and devoted party people to pack a few clubs even Sunday through Wednesday. If you want go out with the rest of the city on Friday and Saturday, show up before the pubs close—perverse things happen to cover charges after 11pm.

Fashion evolves and revolves, but black (and simple) is always in, and dress codes are rarely more elaborate than standard London wear (an elusive concept). In a scene striving to exude effortless extravagance, budget clubbing is a bit difficult. If bouncers tell you "members and regulars only," they don't think you belong; but if you persist you may be able to talk your way in. If there's no queue and it's less than two hours before closing, you may not have to pay full cover, so try to strike a deal. If you see a cover price prefixed by "NUS (National Union of Students)," an ISIC card may fetch a discount.

Planning is important for the discriminating budget clubber. Look before you leap, and especially before you drink. It's best to avoid the bright glitzy clubs in Leicester Square (e.g. Equinox and Hippodrome), which are crowded with out-of-town English youth looking to get lucky. *Time Out* is the undisputed scene cop, and their starred picks of the day are usually a safe bet. Many clubs have after-hours parties called "chill outs," usually 6am-noon. For those who choose not to stay out until the morning hours, remember that the tube shuts down shortly after midnight and black cabs are especially hard to find when clubs are closing. Some late-night frolickers catch "minicabs," unmarked cars that sometimes wait outside clubs; negotiate a price before you get in, and be wary of riding alone. It's advisable to arrange transportation in advance or acquaint yourself with the extensive network of night buses (information 7222 1234). Listings include some of the night bus routes that connect to venues outside of central London, but routes change and a quick double-check is recommended.

The Africa Centre, 38 King St., WC2 (☎ 7836 1973). Tube: Covent Garden. Art center by day, psychedelic, blacklit den of funk by night. Live African and samba music at the "Lompopo Club" most F, some Sa. F and Sa 9pm-3am. £7-8 in advance, £10 at the door.

The Aquarium, 256 Old St., EC1 (☎ 7251 6136). Tube: Old Street. Ultra-trendy club comes complete with swimming pool for club kids to take a dip in. Caters to a twenty-something crowd. Open Th 9am-3pm, F (garage) 10pm-4am, Sa (house) 10am-5pm. £5-15.

The Astoria (LA1), 157 Charing Cross Rd., WC2 (☎ 7434 0403). Tube: Tottenham Court Rd. From the station, take Charing Cross towards Soho. Megavenue (capacity 2000), hosts frequent live acts as well as Jeremy Joseph's popular *G.A.Y.* In the basement is the **LA2,** whose Sa *Carwash* requires a costume and a love of the 1970s. £7-14.

Bagleys, York Way, N1 (☎ 7278 2777). Tube: Kings Cross. This former movie studio is London's biggest club venue (capacity 3000). Four cavernous rooms with garage, house and old school raves. Open F 10pm-6am, Sa 10pm-8am. £10-14. **Be careful around King's Cross at night.**

Bar Rumba, 35 Shaftesbury Ave., W1 (☎ 7287 2715). Tube: Piccadilly Circus. Brilliant nights out in a cozy underground space: *Garage City* (Sa) features house, garage, and a well-dressed crowd. It's also home to *This!,* one of London's best Mondays, where Gilles Peterson, head of Talkin' Loud Records, plays his mix of drum and bass, jazz, and funk. Open M-Tu and Th-F 10pm-3am, W 10pm-3:30am, Sa 10pm-4am, Su 8pm-1:30am. £4-12.

Bug Bar, The Crypt, St. Matthew's Church, Brixton Hill, SW2 (☎ 7738 3184; www.bugbar.co.uk). Tube: Brixton. Maybe it's become cliché to talk about the "vibe" of a bar, but if any place has vibe, this converted church crypt does. Bar food comes from adjacent restaurant Bah Humbug, and is all the better for it. DJs spin on Th-Su. Open M-W 7pm-1am, Th and Su 7pm-2am, F-Sa 7pm-3am. F-Sa £5, £3 before 11pm.

Camden Palace, 1A Camden High St., NW1 (☎ 7387 0428) Tube: Morning Crescent. Huge and hugely popular with tourists and locals alike. *Peach* (F) packs 'em in with house and garage, while *Feet First* (Tu) does the same with indie, Britpop, and the occasional live act. Open Tu 10pm-2am, F-Sa 10pm-6am. £2-10.

Cube Bar, 135 Finchley Rd., NW3 (☎ 7483 2393). Tube: Swiss Cottage. A hit among youngish North Londoners, Cube Bar is a converted bank with a garishly painted ground-floor bar with DJ, a gallery space and lounge upstairs, and a small basement bar. Happy hour (5-10pm) knocks down cocktails prices from £5-£6 to £3.50. Open Th 5pm-midnight, F-Sa 5pm-1am. MC, V.

The Dogstar, 389 Coldharbour Ln., SW9 (☎ 7733 7515; www.dogstarbar.co.uk). Tube: Brixton. A strong emphasis on the "club" part of club-bar, with DJs every night and a large central space to shake it. Open Su-Th noon-2:30am, F-Sa noon-4:30am.

Dust, 27 Clerkenwell Rd., EC1 (☎ 7490 5120). Tube: Farringdon. Glittery walls vibrate to house and salsa music at nights when this pub morphs into a club. Program changes regularly, so call ahead. Open M-W 11am-11pm, Th 11am-midnight, F 6pm-midnight, Sa noon-2am. Free-£3.

The End, 18A West Central St., WC1 (☎ 7419 9199). Tube: Tottenham Court Rd. The End possesses not only the most beautiful sound system of all the London clubs (nasal hairs will vibrate) but also a decidedly stylish interior, and friendly group of staff and patrons. Shocking. *Atelier* (Th) is a gay-friendly and style-conscious festival of funky house, while *Twice as Nice* (Su) is straighter, but not narrower. Th, all drinks £1.50 before 11pm. Open Th 9pm-3:30am, F-Su 9pm-6am. £5-20, Th and some other nights free with flyer before 11pm.

Electric Ballroom, 184 Camden High St., NW1 (☎ 7485 9006). Tube: Camden Town. Cheap and fun. *Saturday Night Fever* free to those decked out in suitable 70s attire. For clubbers who despise natural fibers. Open F-Sa 10:30pm-2:30am. £8.

Fabric, 77a Charterhouse St., EC1 (☎ 7490 0444). Tube: Farringdon. Three enormous caves of pumping London youth. No place like their co-ed toilets to find a new friend. Pass the lipstick. Su nights "polysexual extravaganzas." Open F-Su 10pm-5am. £10-15.

The Fridge, Town Hall Parade, Brixton Hill, SW2 (☎ 7326 5100; www.fridge.co.uk). Tube: Brixton. Out of the station, cross the street and walk to the left. Walk up Brixton Hill. The long line is the one you're looking for. Converted cinema hosts some of the most popular nights in London, announcing them on the marquee. Open F-Sa 10pm-6am. £8-12. If you're stumbling out of the club and can't take the glare of sunlight, head next-door for the after party at the **Fridge Bar,** with a long bar and a music policy that leans heavily towards soul and R&B. DJs spin Th-M. Open M-Th 6pm-2:30am, F 6pm-4am, Sa 5:30am-noon and 6pm-4am, Su 5:30am-noon and 6pm-3am. £5 F-Sa after 10pm, Su after 9pm; £3 F-Sa 9-10pm, Sa 5:30am-noon and 9-10pm.

The Hanover Grand, 6 Hanover St., W1 (☎ 7499 7977). Tube: Oxford Circus. Multiple floors crammed full of well-dressed people. Getting in, however, may take ages—plan to go early, even on weekdays. Open W (hiphop and UK garage) 10:30pm-3:30am, F (garage) 10pm-4am, and Sa (house) 10:30pm-5:30am. £3-15.

100 Club

Legends, 29-30 Old Burlington St., W1 (☎ 7437 9933; www.legends.co.uk). Tube: Green Park or Piccadilly Circus. A triumph of style over substance. Depending on when you go, the house and garage can be too mainstream for tastes, but it's a beautiful space, with plush seats, aluminum stairs, and a great windowed bar. Open Th 6pm-3am, F 6pm-4am, Sa 9pm-4am.

Leopard Lounge, The Broadway, Fulham Rd., SW6 (☎ 7385 0834). Tube: Fulham Broadway. Jungle-themed glamour club that does a 70s party Th. Otherwise, house is in-house. Open most nights 10pm-3am, but varies. £6-12.

Limelight, 136 Shaftesbury Ave., WC2 (☎ 7434 0572). Tube: Leicester Sq. Converted church provides a religious club experience. Open M-Th and Su 10pm-3am, F 10pm-3:30am, Sa 9pm-3:30am.

Mass, St. Matthew's Church, Brixton Hill (☎ 7737 1016; www.massclub.co.uk). Tube: Brixton. In a converted church, up what feels like more spiral stairs than a Tube station emergency exit. Open F 10pm-5am, Sa 9pm-6am.

The Fridge

Ministry of Sound, 103 Gaunt St., SE1 (☎ 7378 6528; www.ministryofsound.co.uk). Tube: Elephant and Castle. Take the exit for South Bank University. The granddaddy of all serious clubbing. Open F 10:30pm-6:30am, Sa midnight-9am. Cover £10-15.

Notting Hill Arts Club, 21 Notting Hill Gate, W11 (☎ 7460 4459). Tube: Notting Hill Gate. Hard beats fill the basement dance floor. Soul, Latin, jazz, house. £3-5. Open M-Sa 5pm-1am, Su 4pm-11pm. £3-5 M-Sa after 8pm, Su after 7pm.

Nu Bar, 196 Essex Rd., N1 (☎ 7354 8886). Tube: Angel or Highbury & Islington. Loads of couches make for a great lounging space. DJs spin music every night from the booth above the bar. Open M-Th 4-11pm, F noon-11pm, Sa 11am-11pm, Su noon-10:30pm.

The Office, 3-5 Rathbone Pl. (☎ 7636 1598). Tube: Tottenham Court Rd.By day it's a restaurant/bar, by night a 300-capacity club that pulls in a twentysomething crowd. DJs spin on Th (R&B, house, and garage), F (70s and 80s) and Sa (80s) nights, and on Su "recovery

Hippodrome

on the cheap

Big Night

So you've decided that weekend club prices are ridiculously high? That shouldn't put you off going out altogether; London's weekday scene has some great deals. Below are our picks of the best London club nights, all of which should cost under a fiver to get into.

Sundays: *Lazy Dog* at Notting Hill Arts Club (p. 183).

Mondays: *THIS!* (That's How It Is) at Bar Rumba (p. 182).

Tuesdays: *Feet First* at the Camden Palace (p. 182)

Wednesdays: *Fresh and Funky* at the Hanover Grand (p. 183)

Thursdays: *Atelier* at the End (p. 182)

parties," beginning at 6.30am. Cover £4-9 on Th-Sa nights. Open daily noon-3am, some Su from 6:30am.

Roof Gardens, 99 Kensington High St., entrance on Derry St., W8 (☎7937 7994). Tube: High St. Kensington. This bar-restaurant offers a beautiful view in an upscale neighborhood. All are dressed to match. Open for club nights Th and Sa, but non-members must eat in the chi-chi restaurant to get in. Reservations a must: dinner is at 8:30pm. Club open 11pm-3am.

Salsa!, 96 Charing Cross Rd., WC2 (☎7379 3277). Tube: Leicester Square. Attracts lovers and looking-for-love-ers alike. Partners not needed, they'll find you. Beware lest the roaming tequila shot ladies lead you to perdition. Open M-Sa 5:30pm-2am, last admission midnight. M-Th £4, students £2; F-Sa £8, before 9pm £4.

Subterania, 12 Acklam Rd., W10 (☎8960 4590). Tube: Ladbroke Grove. One of West London's finest clubs, tucked in under the Westway flyover (hence the name). Peek at the well-dressed crowds below from the balcony. *Rotation* (F) is a major crowd-puller. Reggae W, hiphop and garage F, garage and house Sa. Open W 10pm-2am, F-Sa 10pm-3am. £5-10; go early for cheaper cover.

Turnmills, 63B Clerkenwell Rd., EC1 (☎7250 3409). Tube: Farringdon. Walk up Turnmill St. and turn right onto Clerkenwell Rd. *Trade* gets kickin' at 3am and keeps on kickin' until noon. Get there early or late to avoid long queues, or reserve in advance. Open F-Sa 3am-noon. £10.

Velvet Room, 143 Charing Cross Rd., WC2 (☎7439 4655). Tube: Tottenham Court Rd. A hoity-toity club-bar with a big-time drum'n'bass night *Swerve* (W) and deep house at *Ultimate BASE* (Th). Dress like you mean it. Generally open 8pm-3am. £4-6; student discounts.

The Wag Club, 35 Wardour St., W1 (☎7437 5534). Tube: Piccadilly Circus. The Whiskey-a-go-go, name duly abbreviated, continues to go strong, although its location means it can get quite touristy. Tu house, W rock, Th indie, F 70s and 80s, Sa 60s R&B. Open F-Sa 10pm-4am. Tu and Th 10pm-3am, W 10pm-3:30am. £4-10.

WKD, 18 Kentish Town Rd., NW1 (☎7267 1869). Tube: Camden Town. Two floors of "cafe-music-club." DJs most nights. Open Su-Th 9am-2:30pm, F-Sa 9am-3pm.

BI, GAY, AND LESBIAN NIGHTLIFE

For details about London's gay and lesbian nightlife scene, check out Boyz (www.boyz.co.uk) or QX (www.qxmag.co.uk), available free at many gay bars.

"Atelier," Thursday at The End, 18 West Central St., WC1 (☎7419 9199). Tube: Tottenham Court Rd. Dressing up is essential. £5, free with flyer from pre-party at **Manto**, 30 Old Compton St.

The Black Cap, 171 Camden High St., NW1 (☎ 7428 2721). Tube: Camden Town. North London's best-known drag bar. Live shows every night attract a mixed male and female crowd. When the shows aren't on, a DJ plays Top 40. M "oldies and trash" night is a favorite. Open M-Th 9pm-2am, F-Sa 9pm-3am, Su noon-3pm and 7pm-midnight. Tu-Sa £2-4, free before 11pm.

The Box, Seven Dials, 32-34 Monmouth St., WC2 (☎ 7240 5828). Tube: Covent Garden or Leicester Sq. Intimate and stylish gay/mixed bar and brasserie. Menus change to match the season (main courses £6-9). Fun, hip clientele of both genders and all races. The dance floor downstairs makes this an excellent venue for a night of dancing and drinking (lager £2.50). Open M-Sa 11am-11pm, Su 7-10:30pm. MC, V.

Freedom, 60-66 Wardour St., W1 (☎ 7734 0071). Tube: Piccadilly Circus. A very trendy (look the part!) cafe-bar that draws in a mixed crowd for cocktails. DJs and dancing space below.

Heaven, Under The Arches, Craven St., WC2 (☎ 7930 2020; www.heaven-london.com). Tube: Charing Cross or Embankment. The most famous gay disco in Britain, if not the world. On the busiest nights, 5 dance floors are open. Open M, W, F-Sa, some Tu and Th 10pm-5am. AmEx, MC, V. £1-12; frequent concessions, some nights half-price or free!

"G.A.Y.," at the London Astoria 2, 157 Charing Cross Rd., WC2 (☎ 7734 6963). Tube: Tottenham Court Rd. A 3-nights-a-week pop extravaganza amidst chrome and mirrored disco balls. Unpretentious clientele (mixed in both gender and orientation). Open Th 10:30pm-4am, F 11pm-4am, Sa 10:30pm-5am. M £3; students or with flyer £1; Th £3, free with flyer; Sa £6, with flyer £5.

Popstarz Liquid Lounge, 275 Pentonville Rd., N1 (☎ 7837 6900). Tube: King's Cross. Indie music and 80s relics. *Miss-shapen* (Sa) provides a haven for emphatically non-beautiful people and those who dislike the attitude side of the gay scene; mostly female. Early scene is more chilled. Open M-Th 5.30pm-2am, F 5.30pm-1am, Sa 5.30pm-3am, Su 5.30pm-1am. £3-5.

Rupert Street, 50 Rupert St., W1 (☎ 7292 7141). Tube: Piccadilly Circus. Trends meet suits in this upscale bar, bursting at the seams on weekend nights. Open M-Sa noon-11pm, Su noon-10:30pm.

The Village Soho, 81 Wardour St., W1 (☎ 7434 2124). Tube: Piccadilly Circus. In the heart of Soho, this expansive bar caters to a wide range of mixed clientele. Gothic candelabras shed warm light upon the masses. Open M-Sa 2pm-1am, Su 2-10:30pm.

ROCK AND POP

Major venues for rock concerts include the indoor **Wembley Arena** and the huge outdoor **Wembley Stadium,** the **Royal Albert Hall,** and the **Forum.** In the summer, outdoor arenas such as **Finsbury Park** become venues for major concerts and festivals.

Apollo Hammersmith, Queen Caroline St., W6 (☎ 7416 6080; www.tickets-direct.com). Tube: Hammersmith. Mainstream rock. Tickets £14.50-£35. Phone bookings 24hr. MC, V.

Astoria (LA1), 157 Charing Cross Rd., WC2 (☎ 7434 0403). Tube: Tottenham Court Rd. Hot and sweaty rock. Two halls have capacity

Jazz Cafe

Electric Ballroom

Riverboat Party

for 2000 and 1000 apiece. Club nights on weekends; gay night Sa (See **G.A.Y.**, p. 185). Box office open M-Sa 10:30am-5:30pm; phone bookings M-Sa 9am-7:30pm. £8-15. AmEx, MC, V.

Borderline, Orange Yard, Manette St., off Charing Cross Rd., WC2 (☎7734 2095; www.border-line.co.uk). Tube: Tottenham Court Rd. British record companies test new rock and pop talent in this basement club. Sometimes the site of secret concerts by famous rockers. £5-10 in advance, student discount £5. Box office open M-F 4-7:30pm. MC, V.

Brixton Academy, 211 Stockwell Rd., SW9 (☎7771 2000). Tube: Brixton. Time-honored venue hosts a variety of music, including rock, reggae, rap, and alternative. 4300 capacity. Box office open M-F 10am-8pm, Sa noon-6pm; phone bookings M-F 10am-6pm, Sa noon-6pm. £8-25. MC, V; cash only at the door.

Dublin Castle, 94 Parkway, NW1 (☎7485 1773). Tube: Camden Town. Irish pub facade hides one of London's most legendary indie clubs. A no-holds-barred joint. 3-4 bands per night. £3.50-5. Open daily 11am-midnight; music M-Sa 9pm-midnight, Su 8:30-11pm.

Forum, 9-17 Highgate Rd., NW5 (☎7284 1001, box office ☎7344 0044). Tube: Kentish Town. Turn right out of tube station. Top-notch audio system in a popular venue. Open Su-Th 7-11pm, F-Sa 7pm-2am. £5-15. Amex, MC, V.

The Garage, 20-22 Highbury Corner, N5 (☎8963 0940, box office ☎7344 0044). Tube: Highbury and Islington. Club/performance space with decent views that attracts big names, but patrons complain about its sound system. Rock, pop, and indie bands most nights. Music starts 8pm. £4-10. Amex, MC, V.

London Palladium, 8 Argyll St., W1 (☎7494 5020). Tube: Oxford Circus. Primarily a theater venue. Music usually starts at 7:30pm. Capacity 2300. £10-35. AmEx, MC, V.

Mean Fiddler, 22-28a Harlesden High St., NW10 (☎8963 0940). Tube: Willesden Junction. Cavernous club with good bars, mixing country & western, folk, and indie. £3-15. M-Th and Su 8pm-2am, F-Sa 8:30pm-3am. AmEx, MC, V.

Rock Garden, The Piazza, Covent Garden, WC2 (☎8836 4052; www.rockgarden.co.uk). Tube: Covent Garden. A variety of one-off new bands play nightly—rock, indie, acid jazz, soul. Happy hour daily 5-8pm, free admission and cheap drinks. Open M-Th 5pm-3am, F-Sa 5pm-4am, Su 7pm-midnight. £5, concessions £4; F-Sa after 10pm £8-10. AmEx, MC, V.

Royal Albert Hall, Kensington Gore. (See **Classical Music,** p. 149.)

Shepherd's Bush Empire, Shepherds Bush Green, W12 (☎7771 2000). Tube: Shepherds Bush. Hosts dorky-cool musicians like David Byrne, the Proclaimers, and Boy George. 2000 capacity, with 6 bars. Box office open M-F 10am-6pm, Sa noon-6pm; phones bookings M-F 10am-8pm, Sa noon-6pm. MC, V. £5-20.

The Water Rats, 328 Grays Inn Rd. (See **Food and Drink,** p. 173.)

JAZZ

Ronnie Scott's, 47 Frith St., W1 (☎7439 0747; fax 7437 5081). Tube: Leicester Sq. or Piccadilly Circus. The most famous jazz club in London and one of the oldest in the world has seen the likes of Ella Fitzgerald and Dizzy Gillespie. Expensive food (but don't overlook the cheaper starters) and great music. Waiters masterfully keep noisy clients from ruining the music by politely telling them to shut up. Reservations essential. Box office open M-Sa 11am-6pm. Music M-Sa 9:45pm-2:30am. Open M-Sa 8:30pm-3am, Su 7:30-11:30pm. £15 M-Th, £20 F-Sa; students £9 M-W. AmEx, MC, V.

100 Club, 100 Oxford St., W1 (☎7636 0933). Tube: Tottenham Court Rd. Offerings vary from traditional modern jazz, swing, and blues to indie rock and comedy, all hidden behind a battered doorway. Staged one of the Sex Pistols' 1st gigs. Regular nights include jazz dance parties F, swing jazz Sa, rhythm and blues Su, "Stompin" swing dance M. Cover usually £6-10. Free sessions F at lunch. Open Su-Th 7:30pm-midnight, F-Sa 7:30pm-2am.

606 Club, 90 Lots Rd., SW10 (☎7352 5953; www.606club.co.uk). Tube: Fulham Broadway or Earl's Court. Over 40 bands per month, from blossoming talent to household names in diverse styles; check website for listings. Singers Su nights, blues last M of month, jam session 2nd Th, Latin last F of the month. Bookings essential F-Sa. Music M-W 7:30pm-1am, Th 8:15pm-1am, F-

Sa 8:15pm-2am, Su 8:15pm-midnight. "Optional music charge" added to bill. F-Sa £6, Su-Th £5, no cover at the door. MC, V.

Jazz Café, 5 Parkway, Camden Town, NW1 (☎ 7916 6060; bookings via Ticketmaster ☎ 7344 0044 24hr.; www.jazzcafe.co.uk). Tube: Camden Town. Night Bus #N93. Converted bank hosts top jazz, soul, funk, Latin, and Brazilian. Recent acts include Astrud Gilberto and Terence Blanchard. Balcony restaurant (main courses £14.50). Music nightly. Regular club nights: *Wah Wah* F, *Messin around* jazz dance with live floor show Sa. Open Su-Th 7pm-1am, F-Sa 7pm-2am. Gigs £6-18; club £7 (£5 with flyer) after 10:30pm. MC, V.

Pizza Express Jazz Club, 10 Dean St., W1 (☎ 7439 8722). Tube: Tottenham Court Rd. or Leicester Sq. Packed club beneath a pizzeria. Fantastic groups and occasional greats; get there early or reserve ahead. Music nightly 9pm-midnight; doors open 7:45pm. Restaurant open daily 11:30am-12:30am. £10-20. AmEx, MC, V.

FOLK, WORLD, AND ROOTS

The Africa Centre, 38 King St., WC2 (See **Nightclubs,** p. 181.)

Cecil Sharpe House, 2 Regent's Park Rd., NW1 (☎ 7485 2206). Tube: Camden Town. Happening folk scene includes singing and dancing lessons. Open M 7-11pm.

Halfway House, 142 The Broadway, West Ealing, W13 (☎ 8567 0236). Tube: Ealing Broadway. Irish, Cajun, and blues. Music F-Su. Open M-Sa 11am-midnight, Su noon-10:30pm. Free-£3.

Hammersmith and Fulham Irish Centre, Black's Road, Hammersmith, W6 (☎ 8563 8232). Tube: Hammersmith. Large hall hosting traditional Irish bands on weekends. Become a "friend" of the center and receive a monthly program. Music starts 8:30pm. £3-6.

Swan, 215 Clapham Rd., SW9 (☎ 7978 9778) Tube: Stockwell. Enormous pub (holds more than 1000) offering traditional Irish and variations seven nights a week. Music starts around 9:30pm. Open M-W 5pm-midnight, Th 5pm-2am, F 5pm-3am, Sa 7pm-3am, Su 7pm-2am. £2-6 after 9pm Th-Su, otherwise free.

Troubadour Coffee House, 265 Old Brompton Rd., SW5 (☎ 7370 1434). Tube: Earl's Court. Acoustic entertainment served up in a warm cafe. Bob Dylan and Paul Simon played here early in their careers. Lots of variety; from comedy to theatre to jazz. M attracts poets, F offers jazz, Sa folk bands. Entertainment starts 8:30pm. Open 8pm-11pm. £4-8.

Bar Rhumba

Heaven

Garage

Daytripping

London is a splendid place to live for those who can get out of it.
—Lord Balfour, Observer Sayings of the Week, Oct. 1, 1944

WINDSOR AND ETON

The town of Windsor, and the attached village of Eton, are completely overshadowed by its two bastions of the British class system, Windsor Castle and Eton College. Windsor itself was built up around the castle during the Middle Ages, and is now filled with specialty shops, tea houses, and pubs, all of which are charming enough but worth overlooking for the stupendous sights nearby.

GETTING THERE

Trains (☎ (08457) 484950) go from **Victoria** and **Paddington** to **Windsor and Eton Central** with a change in **Slough,** and direct from **Waterloo** to **Windsor and Eton Riverside** (50min., every 30min., day return £5.70); both stations are within walking distance of the castle. **Green Line coaches** (☎ 8668 7261) #700 and 702 leave for Windsor from their station on **Eccleston Bridge,** behind Victoria Station (50min.-1½hr., day return £4.35-5.50). **Phone Code:** 01753.

FOOD

The Waterman's Arms is just over the bridge into Eton and to the left at Brocas St. next to the Eton College Boat House. A traditional public house (circa 1542), it's still a local favorite. (☎ 861001. Guinness £2.05. Open M-Sa noon-2:30pm and 6-11pm, Su noon-3pm and 7-10pm.) **Michael's The Eton Bakery,** 43 Eton High St., is an old-time, neighborhood bakery. You can buy stale bread to feed the ducks for 10p. (☎ 864725. Take-away only. Open M-F 7:30am-5pm, Sa 7:30am-4:30pm, Su 11am-4:30pm.)

SIGHTS

WINDSOR CASTLE

▮☎(01753) 868 286 or (01753) 831 118 for 24hr. information. Always call to check that the castle is not closed for state visits. Most of the castle is wheelchair accessible—call ☎ (01753) 868 286, ext. 2235 for details. Open daily Apr.-Oct. 10am-5:30pm, last entry 4pm; Nov.-Mar. 10am-4pm; last entry 3pm. £10, over 60 £7.50, under 17 £5, families £22.50.

Within these ancient stone walls lie some of the most sumptuous rooms in Europe and some of the rarest artworks in the Western world. But beyond the velvet and fine art, this castle's charm lies in its location high above the Thames, and the thousands of arms that bedeck its walls. Built by William the Conqueror as a fortress rather than as a residence, it has grown over nine centuries into the world's largest inhabited castle.

Be aware that Windsor is a working castle, which may sound a little strange in this day and age, but only means that various members of the Royal Family reside here on weekends and for various special ceremonies. The practical consequence of the Royals' residence is that, often without warning, large areas of the castle will be unavailable to visitors. The steep admission prices will be lowered, but it is wise to call before visiting to check that the areas you want to see are open.

UPPER AND LOWER WARD. On passing through Norman Tower and Gate (built by Edward III from 1359-60) you enter the **upper ward,** where many of the rooms are open to the public, including the elegantly furnished **state apartments,** which are mostly used for ceremonial occasions and official entertainment. The rooms are richly decorated with artwork from the massive Royal Collection, including works by Holbein, Rubens, Rembrandt, and an entire room of Van Dycks. A stroll down to the **lower ward** will bring you to **St. George's Chapel,** a sumptuous 15th-century building with delicate fan vaulting and an amazing wall of stained glass dedicated to the Order of the Garter. Most recently used for the marriage of Sophie and Prince Edward, the chapel's intimate atmosphere is born from its role as the repository of the bones of Edward's ancestors. Ten sovereigns rest here in all, including George V, Queen Mary, Edward IV, Charles I, and Henry VI. Henry VIII rests below a remarkably humble stone.

ETON COLLEGE. Eton College is still England's preeminent public (which is to say, private) school, founded by Henry VI in 1440, and at present is attended by Princes William and Harry. The Queen is the sole (honorary) female Old Etonian. Eton boys still wear tailcoats to every class and solemnly raise one finger in greeting to any teacher on the street. Despite its position at the apex of the British class system, Eton has molded some notable dissidents and revolutionaries—Percy Bysshe Shelley, Aldous Huxley, George Orwell, and even former Liberal Party leader Jeremy Thorpe. *(10min. down Thames St. from the castle, across the river. ☎(01753) 671 177. Open daily July-Aug. and late Mar. to mid-Apr. 10:30am-4:30pm; other times 2-4:30pm. Tours daily 2:15 and 3:15pm; £3.60, under 16 £3. Admission £2.60, under 16 £2.)*

LEGOLAND WINDSOR. This high-class amusement park, is a recent (1996), whimsical, and expensive addition to the area. Beautifully landscaped and wonderfully staffed, it is guaranteed to thrill the 11-and-under set with rides, playgrounds and circuses. Adults will be amazed by **Miniland,** which took 100 workers, three years, and 25 million blocks to build. *(Take the shuttle from Riverside station; £1. ☎(0990) 040 404. Open daily Mar. 14-Nov. 1 and Oct. weekends 10am-6pm; July 18-Aug. 31 10am-8pm. £16.50, children £13.50, seniors £10.50.)*

BRIGHTON

The undisputed home of the dirty weekend, Brighton (pop. 180,000) sparkles with a risqué, tawdry luster. According to legend, the future King George IV sidled into Brighton around 1784 for some hanky-panky. Having staged a fake wedding with a certain "Mrs. Jones" (Maria Fitzherbert), he headed off to the farmhouse known today as the Royal Pavilion, and the royal rumpus began. Since then, Brighton has turned a blind eye to some of the more outrageous activities that occur along its shores; holiday-goers and locals alike peel it off—all of it—at England's first bathing beach. Kemp Town (jokingly

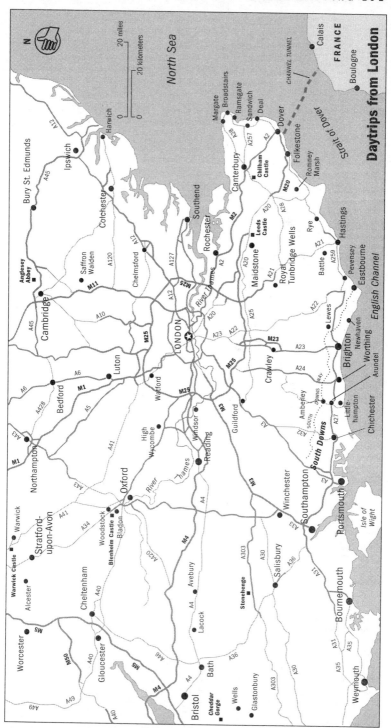

Daytrips from London

called Camp Town), among other areas of Brighton, has a thriving gay and lesbian population, while the immense student crowd, augmented by flocks of foreign youth purportedly learning English, feeds Brighton's decadent clubbing scene. The ancient, narrow streets that make up the Lanes district provide an anarchic setting for Brighton's wild behavior. Lovingly known as "London-by-the-Sea," Brighton's open demeanor and youthful spirit make for a memorable sojourn for adventurous travelers.

ORIENTATION AND PRACTICAL INFORMATION

Trains from London (☎ (08457) 484950; 1¼hr., at least 6 per hr., £9.90) arrive at the station at the north end of **Queen's Rd.,** about 10min. from the town center and waterfront. (Ticket office open 24hr.; Travel Centre open M-Sa 8:15am-6pm.) **National Express buses** (☎ (08705) 808080) arrive at **Pool Valley,** at the southern angle of Old Steine, from **Victoria** (2hr., 15 per day, £8 return). **Old Steine,** a road/square, runs in front of the Royal Pavilion, while **King's Rd.** runs along the waterfront. The **tourist information centre,** 10 Bartholomew Sq., is south along **Queen's Rd.** toward the water. Turn left onto **North St.** (not to be confused with North Rd. or North Laine) and continue until you reach **Ship St.;** turn right and proceed along to **Prince Albert St.** The staff books National Express tickets and gives out free street maps. **Walking tours** start here June through August Thursday at 11am and cost £3. (☎ (0906) 711 2255. Open M-Tu and Th-F 9am-5pm, W and Sa 10am-5pm, Su 10am-4pm.) The **police** (☎ 606744) are at John St. The **Royal Sussex County Hospital** (☎ 696955) is on Eastern Rd., parallel to Marine Parade. **Phone Code:** 01273.

ACCOMMODATIONS AND FOOD

Brighton Backpackers Hostel, 75-76 Middle St., is *the* place to meet others in Brighton, although outgoing atmosphere may not suit reclusive travelers. It offers a TV lounge, pool table, and Internet access. The quieter **annex** faces the ocean. (☎ 777 717. Coed and single-sex dorms. Kitchen and laundry. No curfew. Dorms £10-11, weekly £55-60; doubles £25.) The **YHA Youth Hostel,** Patcham Pl., is 4 mi. north on London Rd. Take Patcham bus #5 or 5A from Old Steine in front of the Royal Pavilion (stop E) to the Black Lion Hotel (£1.25). Don't stay here if you want to party late. (☎ 556196. Laundry facilities. Reception closed 10am-1pm. Curfew 11pm. Often full; call ahead in July-Aug. Closed Jan. Dorms £10.15, under 18 £6.85.)

   Food for Friends, 17a-18 Prince Albert St., offers cheap, well-cooked, well-seasoned vegetarian food in a breezy, easy atmosphere. Daily salad specials (£2.25-3.55) send taste buds straight to heaven. The "Taster" (£5.20) offers a bit of all the day's main courses. (☎ 202310. Open M-Sa 8am-10pm, Su 9:15am-10pm. 20% student discount.) On the fringe of the Lanes, open-air **Donatello,** 1-3 Brighton Pl., makes a hot people-watching spot. Try the £6.40 three-course lunch special or a delicious pizza for £4-6. (☎ 775477. Reservations advised. Open daily 11:30am-11:30pm.)

SIGHTS AND ENTERTAINMENT

In 1750, Dr. Richard Russell wrote a treatise on the merits of drinking and bathing in sea water, beginning Brighton's transformation from the sleepy village of Brighthelmstone to England's "center of fame and fashion". The main attraction in Brighton today remains the **beach.** Even though the weather can be nippy even in June and July, and the closest thing to sand are the fist-sized brown rocks, beach-goers gamely put on bikinis and fight for their spot on the crowded shore. The extravagant **Royal Pavilion** seems to have created much of Brighton's present brand of gaudiness. George IV, then Prince of Wales, and architect John Nash turned an ordinary farm villa into the Oriental/Indian/Gothic/Georgian palace visible today. (☎ 290900. Audio tour £1. Partial wheelchair access. Open daily June-Sept. 10am-6pm; Oct.-May 10am-5pm. £4.90, concessions £3.55.) The gaudiness permeates to the beachfront, where **Palace Pier,** the fourth largest tour attraction in England, is a mecca of slot machines and video games. **Volk's Railway,** an early electric train, shuttles along the waterfront. (☎ 681061. Runs Apr.-Sept. daily 11am-6pm. Rides £1.10, children 60p.)

   Brighton has a dizzying array of nighttime choices. *The Punter*, a local monthly found at newsagents and record stores, details evening events, and *What's On*, a poster-sized flysheet found at music stores and pubs, points the hedonist the right way. Gay and lesbian venues can be found in the latest issues of *Gay Times* ($2.50) or *Capital Gay* (free), available at newsstands. Many **pubs** offer fantastic drink specials on weekdays to attract students. Pub-crawling in the Lanes is a good bet on any night, and **Fortune of War,** 157 King's Road Arches, is always a lucky choice. (☎205065. Open M-Sa 10:30am-11pm, Su 11am-10:30pm.) Brighton's the hometown of the dance record label **Skint Records,** so these Brightonians know a thing or two about **clubs.** Most clubs are open M-Sa 10pm-2am, and many offer student discounts on weeknights. **The Beach,** 171-181 King's Road Arches (☎722 272), adds big beat to the music on the shore.

CANTERBURY

Flung somewhere between the cathedral and the open road, the soul of Canterbury is as flighty as the city's itinerant visitors. Archbishop Thomas à Becket met his demise in Canterbury Cathedral in 1170 after an irate Henry II asked, "Will no one rid me of this troublesome priest?" and a few of his henchmen took the hint. In the near millennium since, the site of one of British history's most gruesome executions has become the focus of many pilgrimages dedicated to the "the hooly blisful martir." Geoffrey Chaucer saw enough irony in pilgrim flocks to capture them in his *Canterbury Tales.*

Ashmolean Museum

ORIENTATION AND PRACTICAL INFORMATION

Connex South Trains (☎(08457) 484950) run every hour from **Charing Cross** and **Waterloo** to **Canterbury West,** Station Rd. West, off St. Dunstan's St. (1½hr.; £15.30, day return £15.80). **National Express buses** (☎(08705) 808080) come from **London Victoria** every hour (2hr., £6-8) to the St. George's Ln. bus station. Canterbury is roughly circular, as defined by the eroding city wall. An unbroken street crosses the city from northwest to southeast, changing names from **St. Peter's St.** to **High St.** to **The Parade** to **St. George's St.** The cathedral looms in the northeast quadrant. The **tourist information centre** is at 34 St. Margaret's St. and gives out a free mini-guide. (☎766 567. Open daily Apr.-Aug. 9:30am-5:30pm; Sept.-Mar. 9:30am-5pm.) You can rent bikes at **Byways Bicycle Hire,** 2 Admiralty Walk. The owner delivers from his home office; just call at any reasonable hour. (☎ 277397. £10 per day, £50 per week. £50 deposit per bicycle.) **Phone Code:** 01227.

All Souls College

ACCOMMODATIONS AND FOOD

🛏 **Hampton House,** 40 New Dover Rd., is a luxurious house with comfortable, quiet, Laura Ashley-esque rooms; the orthopedic mattresses are heaven. (☎ 464912. £20-25 per person. Singles more expensive in summer. Off-season prices vary.) The **YHA Youth Hostel,** 54 New Dover Rd., is ¾ mi. from East Station and ½ mi. southeast of the bus station. The relaxing lounge offers Internet access at 50p per six minutes. (☎ 462911; fax 470752; email canterbury@yha.org.uk. 86 beds. Laundry facilities. Lockers £1 plus deposit. Self-catering

Pembroke College

OXFORD MADE EASY

Oxford undergraduates study for three years, each year consisting of three eight-week terms; more time is spent on holiday than at school. The university itself has no official, central campus. Though central facilities—libraries, laboratories, and faculties—are established and maintained by the university, Oxford's independent colleges, where students live and learn simultaneously (at least in theory), are scattered throughout the city. Students must dress in formal wear called sub fusc for all official University events, including exams; carnations are obligatory. At the end of their last academic year, students from all the colleges assemble for degree examinations, a gruelling three-week ordeal that takes place in the Examination Schools on High Street in late June and early July. Each year, university authorities do their best to quell the vigorous post-examination celebrations in the street. Each year they fail. The authorities, that is.

kitchen; meals also available. Bureau de change. Reception open 7:30-10am and 1-11pm. In summer book a week ahead. Call for off-season openings. Dorms £10.85, under 18 £7.40.)

Bakeries and sweet shops please the palates of weary pilgrims around the cathedral. Pubs, restaurants, and fast-food dens crowd High St. **Marlowe's**, 55 St. Peter's St., offers an eclectic mix of vegetarian and beefy English, American, and Mexican food in a friendly setting. Choose from 8 toppings for 8 oz. burgers (£6.60), or select one of 18 vegetarian dishes. (☎ 462194. Open daily 11:30am-10:30pm.)

SIGHTS

CANTERBURY CATHEDRAL

☎ 762862. www.canterbury-cathedral.org. Cathedral open Easter-Sept. M-Sa 9am-6:30pm, Su 12:30-2:30 and 4:30-5:30pm; Oct.-Easter M-Sa 9am-5pm, Su 12:30-2:30 and 4:30-5:30pm. Evensong services M-F 5:30pm, Sa 3:15pm, Su 6:30pm. Precincts open daily 7am-9pm. Tours (75min.) 4 per day, fewer off-season; check the nave or welcome center for times; £3, students and seniors £2, children £1.20. Self-guided tour booklet £1.25. Audio tour (25min.) £2.50. £3, concessions £2. Visitors are charged at the gate; after hours you may be able to wander into the precincts for free, but probably not into the building, unless you happen to be an Anglican bishop. Wheelchair accessible.

Money collected from pilgrims built much of Canterbury Cathedral's splendors, including the early Gothic nave, constructed mostly between the 13th and 15th centuries on a site allegedly first consecrated by St. Augustine 700 years earlier. Among the nave's entombed inhabitants are Henry IV, his wife Joan of Navarre, and the Black Prince. A taste for the macabre has drawn the morbidly curious to the cathedral since 1170, when Archbishop Thomas à Becket was beheaded here with a strike so forceful it broke the blade of the axe. The murder site today is closed off by a rail—a kind of permanent police line—around the Altar of the Sword's Point. Travelers with a taste for the gruesome can view a 14-minute audio-visual recreation of the homicide just off the cloisters. *(Shown continuously 10am-4pm. £1, students and seniors 70p, children 50p.)* In the adjacent **Trinity Chapel,** a candle marks where Becket's body lay until 1538, when Henry VIII burned his remains to show how he dealt with bishops who crossed the king.

In a building beset with fire and rebuilt again and again, the **Norman crypt,** a huge 12th-century chapel, remains intact. The **Corona Tower,** 105 steps above the easternmost apse, recently reopened after renovations. *(60p, children 30p.)* Under the **Bell Harry Tower**—at the crossing of the nave and western transepts—perpendicular arches support intricate 15th-century fan vaulting. The cathedral's **welcome center,** also a gift shop, dispenses information and pamphlets for 20p-£2.50. *(Open M-Sa 9am-4pm.)* **Guided tours** supplant the sparsely posted information about the building.

OTHER SIGHTS

At **The Canterbury Tales**, be entertained by the gap-toothed Wife of Bath and her companions in an abbreviated Modern English version of Chaucer's bawdy *Tales*—complete with the scent of sweat, hay, and general grime. *(St. Margaret's St. ☎479 227. Open daily July-Aug. 9am-5.30pm; Mar.-June and Sept.-Oct. 9:30am-5:30pm; Nov.-Feb. Su-F 10am-4:30pm, Sa 9:30am-5:30pm. £5.55, concessions £4.60.)* Little remains of **St. Augustine's abbey,** built in AD 598, but you can view older Roman ruins and the site of St. Augustine's first tomb. Exhibits from the site's excavation and the free audio tour reveal the abbey's past as a burial place, a royal palace, and a pleasure garden. *(Outside the city wall near the cathedral. ☎ 767345. Open daily Apr.-Oct. 10am-6pm; Nov.-Mar. 10am-4pm. £2.50, students and seniors £1.90, children £1.30. Wheelchair accessible.)*

OXFORD

Almost 900 years of scholarship lie behind Oxford. It was in 1167 that Henry II founded the actual university, Britain's first and one of the earliest in Europe. Today, despite the mass of tourists, Oxford has an irrepressible grandeur, and there are pockets of respite to charm and edify the academic pilgrim: the basement room of Blackwell's Bookshop, the impeccable galleries of the Ashmolean, and the perfectly maintained quadrangles of Oxford's 39 colleges.

St. Mary's Church

GETTING THERE AND AROUND

Thames Trains run every 30 minutes from **Paddington** (1hr., day return £14.80) to Oxford's **train station**, at Park End, west of Carfax (ticket office open M-F 6am-8pm, Sa 6:45am-8pm, Su 7:45am-8pm). The **Oxford Tube** (☎772250) sends **buses** to the bus station at **Gloucester Green** from **Victoria** (1½hr.; 1-6 per hr.; next-day return £7.50, concessions £6.50, period return £9.50). The local bus companies **Oxford Bus Company** (☎785400) and **Stagecoach Oxford** (☎772250) have swift and frequent service. Most local services board on the streets around Carfax, and fares are low (most are 70p singles). Day and week passes are available and worth the purchase; buy them from the bus driver or at the bus station.

St. John's College

PRACTICAL INFORMATION

Queen St., High St., St. Aldates St., and **Cornmarket St.** meet at right angles at **Carfax,** the town center and site of the colossal Carfax Tower. Most of the colleges are all within a mile of each other, lying mainly to the east along High St. and Broad St. The **Tourist Information Centre** (TIC), Old School, Gloucester Green, beside the bus station, is a pamphleteer's paradise. The £1 street map and guide includes a valuable index. (☎ 726871. Open M-Sa 9:30am-5pm; Easter-Oct. also Su 10am-3:30pm.) A two-hour **walking tour** leaves the tourist information center two to five times daily, and is the only means of access to some colleges. Tours run between 10:30am and 2pm. (£4.50, children £3.) **The Oxford Classic Tour** runs a bus tour of the city. (☎(01235) 240105. £7, students and seniors £5, children £2.) The **police** are at the corner of St. Aldates and Speedwell St. (☎266000). Take bus #13B or 14A to reach **John Radcliffe Hospital,** Headley Way (☎741166). **Phone Code:** 01865.

Catte Street

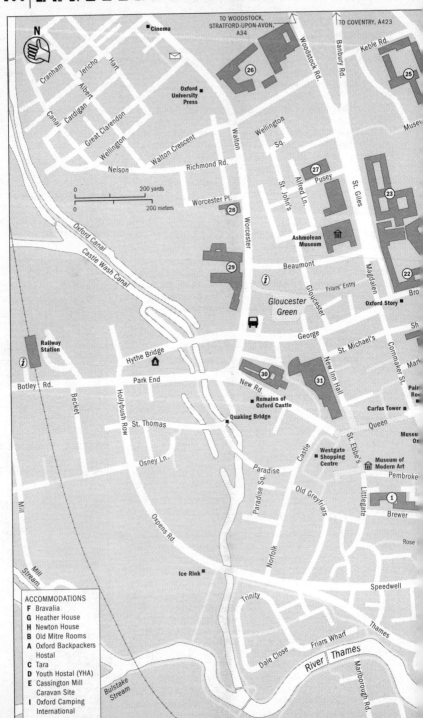

TO WOODSTOCK,
STRATFORD-UPON-AVON,
A34

TO COVENTRY, A423

Cinema

N

Cranham
Jericho
Hart
Albert
Cardigan
Canal
Great Clarendon
Wellington
Nelson

Walton Crescent
Richmond Rd.

Oxford
University
Press

Keble Rd.

26

25

Woodstock Rd.
Banbury Rd.

Muse

Walton

Wellington
Sq.

Worcester Pl.

28

200 yards
200 meters

Worcester

27

Pusey

Alfred Ln.
St. John's

St. Giles

23

Castle Wash Canal
Oxford Canal

29

Beaumont

Ashmolean
Museum

Magdalen

22

Bro

Gloucester
Green

Friars' Entry

Oxford Story

Gloucester

Sh

Railway
Station

Hythe Bridge

George

St. Michael's

Botley Rd.

Park End

New Rd.

New Inn Hall

Connmaker St.

Mar

Becket
Hollybush Row

30

31

Palr
Ro

St. Thomas

Remains of
Oxford Castle

Quaking Bridge

Carfax Tower

Queen

Museu
Ox

Osney Ln.

Oxpens Rd.

Paradise

Castle

St. Ebbe's

Westgate
Shopping
Centre

Museum of
Modern Art

Paradise Sq.

Old Greyfriars

Pembroke

Littlegate

1

Brewer

Mill Stream

Ice Rink

Norfolk

Rose

Trinity

Speedwell

ACCOMMODATIONS
F Bravalia
G Heather House
H Newton House
B Old Mitre Rooms
A Oxford Backpackers
  Hostal
C Tara
D Youth Hostal (YHA)
E Cassington Mill
  Caravan Site
I Oxford Camping
  International

Dale Close

Friars Wharf

River Thames

Marlborough Rd.

Bulstake Stream

ALPS   ASPEN

AT&T Direct Service

AT&T Direct Service access numbers are the easy way to call home from anywhere.

Global connection with the AT&T Network | **AT&T** direct service

www.att.com/traveler

AT&T Direct® Service

The easy way to call home from anywhere.

AT&T Access Numbers

Austria ● 0800-200-288	France 0800-99-00-11
Belarus × ....8 ♦ 800-101	Gambia ● 00111
Belgium ● 0-800-100-10	Germany 0800-2255-288
Bosnia ▲ 00-800-0010	Ghana 0191
Bulgaria ▲ 00-800-0010	Gibraltar 8800
Cyprus ● 080-900-10	Greece ● 00-800-1311
Czech Rep. ▲00-42-000-101	Hungary ● 06-800-01111
Denmark 8001-0010	Iceland ● 800-9001
Egypt ●(Cairo) ∓....510-0200	Ireland ✓.....1-800-550-000
Finland ● 0800-110-015	Israel 1-800-94-94-949

AT&T Direct® Service

The easy way to call home from anywhere.

AT&T Access Numbers

Austria ● 0800-200-288	France 0800-99-00-11
Belarus × ....8 ♦ 800-101	Gambia ● 00111
Belgium ● 0-800-100-10	Germany 0800-2255-288
Bosnia ▲ 00-800-0010	Ghana 0191
Bulgaria ▲ 00-800-0010	Gibraltar 8800
Cyprus ● 080-900-10	Greece ● 00-800-1311
Czech Rep. ▲00-42-000-101	Hungary ● 06-800-01111
Denmark 8001-0010	Iceland ● 800-9001
Egypt ●(Cairo) ∓....510-0200	Ireland ✓.....1-800-550-000
Finland ● 0800-110-015	Israel 1-800-94-94-949

The best way to keep in touch when you're traveling overseas is with **AT&T Direct**® Service. It's the easy way to call your loved ones back home from just about anywhere in the world. Just cut out the wallet guide below and use it wherever your travels take you.

For a list of AT&T Access Numbers, tear out the attached wallet guide.

AT&T

Italy ● 172-1011	Russia (Moscow) ▶▲●755-5042
Luxembourg ╈ ..800-2-0111	(St. Petersbg.)▶▲● ..325-5042
Macedonia ● ..99-800-4288	Slovakia ▲ ..00-42-100-101
Malta 0800-890-110	South Africa ..0800-99-0123
Monaco ● 800-90-288	Spain 900-99-00-11
Morocco 002-11-0011	Sweden 020-799-111
Netherlands ● ...0800-022-9111	Switzerland ● 0800-89-0011
Norway 800-190-11	Turkey ● 00-800-12277
Poland ▲● ..00-800-111-1111	Ukraine ▲ ....8╈100-11
Portugal ▲ 800-800-128	U.A. Emirates ● 800-121
Romania ●......01-800-4288	U.K..............0800-89-0011

FOR EASY CALLING WORLDWIDE

1. Just dial the AT&T Access Number for the country you are calling from.
2. Dial the phone number you're calling.   *3.* Dial your card number.

For access numbers not listed ask any operator for **AT&T Direct**® Service.
In the U.S. call 1-800-331-1140 for a wallet guide listing all worldwide AT&T Access Numbers.
Visit our Web site at: **www.att.com/traveler**
Bold-faced countries permit country-to-country calling outside the U.S.
- ● Public phones require coin or card deposit to place call.
- ▲ May not be available from every phone/payphone.
- ╈ Public phones and select hotels.
- ◆ Await second dial tone.
- ▶ Additional charges apply when calling from outside the city.
- ╈ Outside of Cairo, dial "02" first.
- ✘ Not available from public phones or all areas.
- ✔ Use U.K. access number in N. Ireland.

When placing an international call *from* the U.S., dial 1 800 CALL ATT.

EMEA   © 8/00 AT&T

Italy ● 172-1011	Russia (Moscow) ▶▲●755-5042
Luxembourg ╈ ..800-2-0111	(St. Petersbg.)▶▲● ..325-5042
Macedonia ● ..99-800-4288	Slovakia ▲ ..00-42-100-101
Malta 0800-890-110	South Africa ..0800-99-0123
Monaco ● 800-90-288	Spain 900-99-00-11
Morocco 002-11-0011	Sweden 020-799-111
Netherlands ● ...0800-022-9111	Switzerland ● 0800-89-0011
Norway 800-190-11	Turkey ● 00-800-12277
Poland ▲● ..00-800-111-1111	Ukraine ▲ ....8╈100-11
Portugal ▲ 800-800-128	U.A. Emirates ● 800-121
Romania ●......01-800-4288	U.K..............0800-89-0011

FOR EASY CALLING WORLDWIDE

1. Just dial the AT&T Access Number for the country you are calling from.
2. Dial the phone number you're calling.   *3.* Dial your card number.

For access numbers not listed ask any operator for **AT&T Direct**® Service.
In the U.S. call 1-800-331-1140 for a wallet guide listing all worldwide AT&T Access Numbers.
Visit our Web site at: **www.att.com/traveler**
Bold-faced countries permit country-to-country calling outside the U.S.
- ● Public phones require coin or card deposit to place call.
- ▲ May not be available from every phone/payphone.
- ╈ Public phones and select hotels.
- ◆ Await second dial tone.
- ▶ Additional charges apply when calling from outside the city.
- ╈ Outside of Cairo, dial "02" first.
- ✘ Not available from public phones or all areas.
- ✔ Use U.K. access number in N. Ireland.

When placing an international call *from* the U.S., dial 1 800 CALL ATT.

EMEA   © 8/00 AT&T

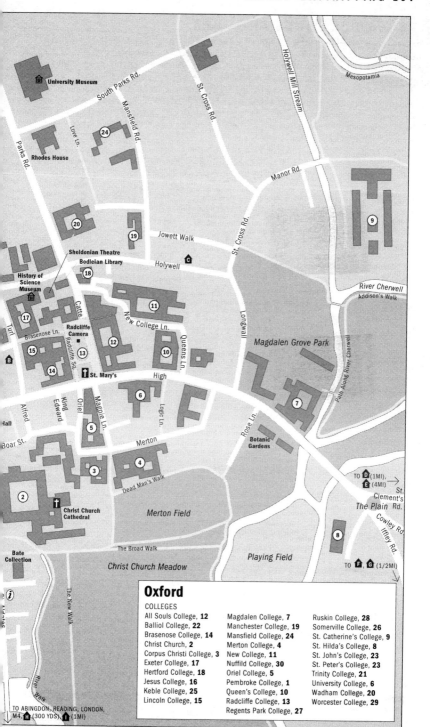

University Museum

South Parks Rd.

St. Cross Rd.

Holywell Mill Stream

Mesopotamia

Parks Rd.

Love Ln.

Mansfield Rd.

Rhodes House

24

Manor Rd.

20

19

Jowett Walk

St. Cross Rd.

9

Sheldonian Theatre
Bodleian Library

Holywell

C

18

River Cherwell

Addison's Walk

History of
Science
Museum

17

Catte

New College Ln.

11

B

Brasenose Ln.

Radcliffe
Camera

Radcliffe Sq.

12

Longwall

Magdalen Grove Park

Turl

15

13

10

Queens Ln.

14

St. Mary's

High

Path Along River Cherwell

6

King Edward

Oriel

Magpie Ln.

Logic Ln.

7

Alfred

5

Rose Ln.

Hall

Boar St.

Merton

Botanic
Gardens

3

4

TO **D** (1MI),
E (4MI)

Dead Man's Walk

St.
Clement's
The Plain Rd.

2

Christ Church
Cathedral

Cowley Rd.

Merton Field

8

Iffley Rd.

Bate
Collection

The Broad Walk

Playing Field

TO **F**, **G** (1/2MI)

i

Christ Church Meadow

The New Walk

Oxford

COLLEGES

All Souls College, **12**	Magdalen College, **7**	Ruskin College, **28**
Balliol College, **22**	Manchester College, **19**	Somerville College, **26**
Brasenose College, **14**	Mansfield College, **24**	St. Catherine's College, **9**
Christ Church, **2**	Merton College, **4**	St. Hilda's College, **8**
Corpus Christi College, **3**	New College, **11**	St. John's College, **23**
Exeter College, **17**	Nuffild College, **30**	St. Peter's College, **23**
Hertford College, **18**	Oriel College, **5**	Trinity College, **21**
Jesus College, **16**	Pembroke College, **1**	University College, **6**
Keble College, **25**	Queen's College, **10**	Wadham College, **20**
Lincoln College, **15**	Radcliffe College, **13**	Worcester College, **29**
	Regents Park College, **27**	

River Walk

TO ABINGDON, READING, LONDON,
M4, **H** (300 YDS), **↑** (1MI)

ACCOMMODATIONS AND PUBS

Book accommodations **at least a week ahead** from June to September, especially for singles, and be prepared to mail in a deposit or give a credit card number. To get to the **YHA Youth Hostel**, 32 Jack Straw's Ln., Headington, catch bus #13 heading away from Carfax on High St. (4 per hr., last bus 11:10pm; 70p, return £1.10) and ask the driver to stop at Jack Straw's Ln.; it's a further eight minutes up the hill. (☎ 762997. Generous facilities. Dorms £10.85, under 18 £7.45, student ID £1 off.) **Oxford Backpackers Hotel**, 9a Hythe Bridge St., is right between the bus and train stations. This independent hostel combines good prices and a great locale. Lively, social vibes. (☎ 721761. Foreign passport required. Dorms £11-12.)

Turf Tavern, 4 Bath Pl., off Holywell St., is arguably the most popular student bar in Oxford (they call it "the Turf"). This sprawling, cavernous 13th-century pub is tucked into an alleyway against the ruins of the city wall. (☎ 243235. Open M-Sa 11am-11pm, Su noon-10:30pm. Hot food served in back room noon-8pm.) **The Eagle and Child**, 49 St. Giles, is one of Oxford's most historic pubs. This archipelago of paneled alcoves moistened the tongues of C.S. Lewis and J.R.R. Tolkien for a quarter-century. (☎ 310154. Open M-Sa 11am-11pm, Su 11am-10:30pm. Food served noon-2:30pm and 5-7:30pm.)

SIGHTS

Apparently this is a college town. To get around, the tourist information centre sells the *Welcome to Oxford* guide (£1), which lists the colleges' public visiting hours, although these are often curtailed without prior notice.

CARFAX TOWER AND OXFORD STORY. A hike up **Carfax Tower**'s 99 spiral steps gives a grand view of the city from the only present reminder of the medieval St. Martin's Church. Admire the bell-ringing chamber as you climb. (☎ 792653. Open daily Apr.-Oct. 10am-5:30pm; Nov.-Mar. 10am-3:30pm. £1.20, under 16 60p.) The excessive **Oxford Story**, 6 Broad St., hauls visitors around on medieval-style "desks" through dioramas recreating Oxford's past. (☎ 790055. Open July-Aug. daily 9am-6pm; Apr.-June and Sept.-Oct. daily 9:30am-5pm; Nov.-Mar. M-F 10am-4:30pm, Sa-Su 10am-5pm. £5.70, concessions £4.70.)

ASHMOLEAN MUSEUM. The imposing Ashmolean, the finest classical collection outside London, was Britain's first public museum when it opened in 1683. Leonardo, Monet, Manet, Van Gogh, Michelangelo, Rodin, and Matisse convene for the permanent collection. While the museum is being renovated, the entire collection is on display. The **Cast Gallery**, behind the museum, has over 250 casts of Greek sculptures. (Beaumont St. ☎ 278000. Open Tu-Sa 10am-5pm, Su 2-5pm. Extended summer hours; call for details. Free.)

BODLEIAN LIBRARY. Oxford's principal library with over five million books. As a copyright library, the Bodleian receives copies of every book printed in Britain. Admission to the reading rooms by ticket only. (Catte St. ☎ 277165. Library open M-F 9am-6pm, Sa 9am-1pm. Tours leave from the Divinity School, across the street; in summer M-F 4 per day, Sa-Su 2 per day; in winter 2 per day. Tours £3.50.)

CHRIST CHURCH COLLEGE. An intimidating pile of stone dwarfing the other colleges, "The House" has Oxford's grandest quad and its most socially distinguished students. In June, hush while navigating the narrow strip open to tourists or face rebukes by undergrads prepping for exams. Charles I made Christ Church his capital during the Civil War. **Tom Quad** adjoins the Chapel grounds. The quad takes its name from **Great Tom**, the seven-ton bell in Tom Tower, rung faithfully at 9:05pm (the original undergraduate curfew) every evening since 1682. (☎ 276492. Open M-Sa 9:30am-5:30pm, Su 11:30am-5:30pm; closed Christmas. Services Su 8, 10am, 11:15am, and 6pm; weekdays 7:30am and 6pm. £2.50, concessions £1.50, families £6.)

OTHER COLLEGES. Merton College features a fine garden and a 14th-century library holding the first printed Welsh Bible. It's also home to the 14th-century **Mob Quad**, Oxford's oldest, and **St. Alban's**, which has some of the University's best gargoyles. (Off Merton St. ☎ 276310. Open M-F 2-4pm, Sa-Su 10am-4pm. Closed around Easter and Christmas, and sometimes on Sa. Free.) Soot-blackened **University College** dates from 1249 and vies with Merton for the title of oldest college. (High St. ☎ 276619. Closed to public.) Candidates who survive the difficult admission exams into **All Souls** graduate college get invited to dinner only to be reminded that they are "well-born, well-bred, and only moderately learned." The **Great Quad,** with its fastidious lawn and two spare spires, may be Oxford's most serene, ordered space. *(Corner of High St. and Catte St. ☎ 279379. Open M-F 2-4:30pm; closed Aug. Free.)* A statue of Queen Caroline (wife of George II) crowns the front gate of **Queen's College.** Around since 1341, Queen's was rebuilt by Wren and Hawksmoor in glorious orange, white, and gold. *(High St. ☎ 279121. Closed to the public, except for those on authorized tours from the tourist information center.)* Extensive grounds surround the flower-laced quads of **Magdalen College** (MAUD-lin), traditionally considered Oxford's handsomest. *(High St. ☎ 276000. Open July-Sept. M-F noon-6pm, Sa-Su 2-6pm; Oct.-June daily 2-5pm. Apr.-Sept. £2, concessions £1; Oct.-Mar. free.)* Founded in 1555, **Trinity College** has a splendid Baroque chapel, including a limewood altarpiece and cedar lattices, with cherubim everywhere. *(Broad St. ☎ 279900. Open daily 10:30am-noon and 2-4pm. £2, concessions £1.)* Students at **Balliol** preserve a semblance of tradition by hurling bricks over the wall at their Trinity rivals. The interior gates of the college still bear scorch marks where 16th-century Protestants were burned, while a mulberry tree planted by Elizabeth I still shades students. Matthew Arnold, Aldous Huxley, and Adam Smith were Balliol men. *(Broad St. ☎ 277777. Open term-time daily 2-5pm. £1, students and children free.)* Named for its late founding in 1379, **New College** is now one of Oxford's most prestigious. A croquet garden is encircled by part of the **old city wall,** and every three years the mayor of Oxford visits to ascertain the wall's state of repair. *(New College Ln. ☎ 279555. Open daily Easter-Oct. 11am-5pm; Nov.-Easter 2-4pm, use the Holywell St. Gate. £1.50.)*

ENTERTAINMENT

Pick up *This Month in Oxford* from the tourist information centre. Classical music and theatrical performances often offer concession prices. Public transit in Oxford shuts down sometime after 11pm, but the action keeps going. The **Zodiac,** 193 Cowley Rd. (☎ 726336), has themes every night and the best bands around, for a cover of £5 and up. A more traditional pastime is **punting** on the River Thames (known in Oxford as the Isis) or on the River Cherwell (CHAR-wul). Magdalen Bridge Boat Co., Magdalen Bridge, east of Carfax along High St., rents from March to November. (☎ 202643. M-F £9 per hr., Sa-Su £10 per hr., deposit £20 plus ID. Open daily 10am-9pm.)

STRATFORD-UPON-AVON

ORIENTATION AND PRACTICAL INFORMATION

The **train station** is at Station Rd., off Alcester Rd. **Thames Trains** (☎ (08457) 484950) run from **Paddington** (2¼hr., 7-10 per day, £22.50 return). **National Express** (☎ (08705) 808080) runs **buses** from **Victoria** to the Riverside Car Park, off Bridgeway Rd. by the Leisure Centre (3hr., 3-4 per day, £11). Local **Stratford Blue** buses stop on Wood St. **Main Taxis** (☎ 415111) and **Taxiline** (☎ 266100) both run 24hr. To get to the **tourist information centre,** Bridgefoot, cross Warwick Rd. at Bridge St. toward the waterside park. It books accommodations for £3 plus a 10% deposit on the entire stay. (☎ 293127; bed booking hotline ☎ 415061. Open Apr.-Oct. M-Sa 9am-6pm, Su 11am-5pm; Nov.-Mar. M-Sa 9am-5pm.) **Guide Friday,** Civic Hall, 14 Rother St., runs tours to all of Shakespeare's houses, departing daily 4-5 times per hour from shrines around town. (☎ 294466. £8.50, students and seniors £7, children under 12 £2.50.) The **police** are at Rother St. (☎ 414111), up Greenhill St. The **Stratford-upon-Avon Hospital** is on Arden St. (☎ 205831), off Alcester Rd. **Phone Code:** 01789.

ACCOMMODATIONS AND FOOD

To B&B or not to B&B? This hamlet has tons of them, but singles are hard to find. In summer, 'tis nobler to make advance reservations by phone. The **YHA Youth Hostel,** Hemmingford House, Wellesbourne Rd., Alveston, is 2 mi. from Stratford. Follow the B4086 or take bus #X18 from the Bridge St. bus stop (1 per hr., £1.70). The friendly staff dishes out full English breakfasts. (☎ 297093; stratford@yha.org.uk. Reception open 24hr. Dorms £14.90, students £13.90, children £11.20.) **Stratford Backpackers Hotel,** 33 Greenhill St., has clean and comfortable rooms, a kitchen, and a small common room. (☎/fax 263838. Photo ID required. Dorms £12.)

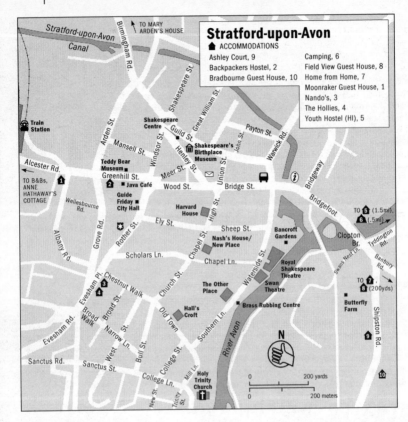

Stratford-upon-Avon

ACCOMMODATIONS

Ashley Court, 9
Backpackers Hostel, 2
Bradbourne Guest House, 10

Camping, 6
Field View Guest House, 8
Home from Home, 7
Moonraker Guest House, 1
Nando's, 3
The Hollies, 4
Youth Hostel (HI), 5

Faux Tudor fast food and pub grub clogs the Bard's hometown. **Hussain's Indian Cuisine,** 6a Chapel St., is probably Stratford's best Indian cuisine, with a slew of tandoori prepared as you like it. Get a three-course lunch for £6, or a fabulous chicken tikka masala. (☎267506. *Main courses £6 and up. 15% discount for takeaway. Open Th-Su 12:30-2:30pm and daily 5pm-midnight.*)

SIGHTS AND ENTERTAINMENT

Several official **Shakespeare properties** (☎204016) grace the town and environs, including Shakespeare's Birthplace, Hall's Croft, and Anne Hathaway's Cottage. Diehard fans should buy the **combination ticket,** a savings of £8 if you make it to every shrine. (*£12, students and seniors £11, children £6.*)

SHAKESPEARE SIGHTS. Half period recreation and half Shakespeare life-and-work exhibition, **Shakespeare's birthplace** includes an exhibit on the glove-making career of Will's father. Sign the guestbook and enter the company of such distinguished pilgrims as Charles Dickens. (*Henley St. ☎204016. Open Mar. 20-Oct. 19 M-Sa 9am-5pm, Su 9:30am-5pm; Oct. 20-Mar. 19 M-Sa 9:30am-4pm, Su 10am-4pm. Partial wheelchair access. £5.50, children £2.50, families £14.*) The least crowded way to pay homage to the institution himself is to visit **Shakespeare's grave** in **Holy Trinity Church,** though massive tour groups still pack the arched door at peak hours. (*Trinity St. £1, students and children 50p.*) Ill-marked footpaths lead to **Anne Hathaway's Cottage,** the birthplace of Shakespeare's wife, about 1 mi. from Stratford in Shottery. (☎292100. *Open Mar.-Oct. daily 9am-5pm; Nov.-Feb. daily 9:30am-4:30pm. £4.20, students and seniors £3.70, children £1.70.*) Dr. John Hall married Susanna, Shakespeare's oldest daughter. Aside from that connection to the Bard, Dr. Hall garnered fame in his own right by being one of the first doctors to keep detailed records of his patients, and **Hall's Croft** features an exhibit on medicine in Shakespeare's time. *(Old Town. Open Mar. 20-Oct. 19 M-Sa 9:30am-5pm, Su 10am-5pm; Oct. 20-Mar. 19 M-Sa 10am-4pm, Su 10:30am-4pm. £3.50, children £1.70, families £8.50.)*

THE ROYAL SHAKESPEARE COMPANY. One of the world's most acclaimed repertories, the RSC sells well over one million tickets each year and claims Kenneth Branagh and Ralph Fiennes as recent sons. It performs in three Stratford theaters. The boards of the **Royal Shakespeare Theatre,** on Waterside, are graced only by the great man's plays. Behind the RST is the smaller and more intimate **Swan,** which showcases RSC productions of Renaissance and Restoration plays. **The Other Place,** on Southern Ln., is the RSC's newest branch, performing modern dramas in an experimental black-box theater.

A group gathers outside about 20 minutes before opening for same-day sales (matinee tickets are easier to get). **Disabled travelers** should call to advise the box office of their needs—certain seats are wheelchair accessible, while some performances feature sign language interpretation or audio description. The RSC also offers **backstage tours** that cram camera-happy groups into the wooden "O"s of the RST and the Swan. *(Box office in the foyer of the Royal Shakespeare Theatre on Waterside handles ticketing for all three theaters. ☎403403, 24hr. recording ☎403404; www.rsc.org.uk. Open M-Sa 9am-8pm. RST tickets £5-40; Swan £5-36; Other Place £10-20. RST and Swan have £5 standing tickets; under 25s get half-price same-day tickets; £8-12 student and senior standbys exist in principle—be ready to pounce. Backstage tours daily 1:30pm, 5:30pm, and after performances; call ☎412602 for details. £4, students and seniors £3.)*

Royal Blenheim

NEAR STRATFORD: WARWICK CASTLE

Many historians, architects, and P.R. hacks regard **Warwick Castle** as England's finest medieval castle. Climb the 530 steps to the top of the towers and see the countryside unfold like a fairytale kingdom of hobbits and elves. The dungeons are filled with life-sized wax figures of people preparing for battle, while "knights" and "craftsmen" talk about their trades. *(Trains run to Warwick from London Marylebone (2½hr., 2 per hr., £24.50, day return £19.50) and Stratford (20 min., 1 per hr., £2.50). ☎406600; www.warwick-castle.co.uk. Open daily Apr.-Oct. 10am-6pm; Nov.-Mar. 10am-5pm. Limited wheelchair access. £10.95, students and seniors £7.85, children £6.50.)*

Sheldonian Theatre

CAMBRIDGE

Cambridge (pop. 105,000) has weathered many winds of change over the years. Once invaded by Romans, this trading town endured a series of nasty Viking raids before the Normans arrived in the 11th century. The 13th century brought Oxford's refugees to the banks of the Cam, an influx that would permanently alter the city more than any military conquest. Cambridge is feistily determined to remain under its pastoral academic robes, in contrast to museum-oriented metropolitan Oxford. At exams' end, the city explodes with gin-soaked glee, and **May Week** (in mid-June, naturally) launches a dizzying schedule of cocktail parties in celebration of pending graduation ceremonies.

Shopping in Oxford

ORIENTATION AND PRACTICAL INFORMATION

Trains (☎(0345) 484950) run from both **King's Cross** (45min., 2 per hr., £14.50) and **Liverpool St.** (1¼hr., 2 per hr., £18.80). To get to the heart of things from the **train station** on **Station Rd.**, turn right onto **Hills Rd.**, and continue straight ahead, or take the **Cambus** shuttle (every 6min.). **National Express buses** (☎(08705) 808080) run to the **Drummond St. station** from **Victoria** (2hr., 17 per day, from £8). From Drummer St., a hop-skip-and-jump down **Emmanuel St.** will land you right in the shopping district near the **tourist information centre**, on Wheeler St., south of Market Square. The staff books rooms for £3 and a 10% deposit on the first night's stay, and runs an advance booking hotline 5 days or more in advance. They also sell 40p mini-guides and 20p town maps. (☎322640; booking hotline ☎457581, M-F 9:30am-4pm. Open Apr.-Oct. M-F 10am-5:30pm, Sa 10am-5pm, Su 11am-4pm; Nov.-Mar. M-F 10am-5:30pm, Sa 10am-5pm.) Informative two-hour **walking tours** of the city and some colleges leave from the tourist information centre. Tours are well narrated but usually enter only one college—usually King's. (£7, children £4). **Guide Friday** (☎362444) runs one-hour **bus tours** every 15-30min.; jump on at any stop. (Tours run Apr.-Oct. £8.50, students and seniors £7, children £2.50, families £19.50) The **police station** is on Parkside (☎358966). **Addenbrookes Hospital** is at Hills Rd. (☎245151); catch Cambus #4, 5, or 5a from Emmanuel St. (£1) and get off where Hills Rd. intersects Long Rd. **Phone Code:** 01223.

ACCOMMODATIONS AND FOOD

The lesson this university town teaches budget travelers is to book ahead, especially in summer. At **Tenison Towers Guest House**, 148 Tenison Rd., fresh flowers grace airy rooms two blocks from the train station. (☎566511. Singles £22; doubles £36, with shower £42.) At the **YHA Youth Hostel**, 97 Tenison Rd., the friendly staff foster a welcoming atmosphere, although more showers wouldn't hurt. (☎354601; fax 312780; cambridge@yha.org.uk. 100 beds. No curfew or lockout. Crowded Mar.-Oct.; call a week ahead. Dorms £15.10, under 18 £11.40.)

Cooking for yourself or buying pub grub are good budget options in Cambridge. The market in **Market Sq.** has bright pyramids of fruit and vegetables. (Market open M-Sa 9:30am-4:30pm.) Indian and Greek restaurants abound, and south of town, **Hills Rd.** and **Mills Rd.** brim with good, cheap restaurants. **Nadia's**, 11 St. John's St., is an uncommonly good bakery. **King St.** is home to a number of pubs. Have a quick pint in Cambridge's oldest pub, **The Eagle** (☎505020), on Benet St. This was where Watson and Crick first rushed in to announce their discovery of the DNA double helix.

SIGHTS AND ENTERTAINMENT

Most university buildings line the east side of the Cam between Magdalene Bridge and Silver St. Visitors can enter most college grounds from 9am to 5:30pm, though many close during the Easter term and virtually all close during exam period (mid-May to mid-June). Call ☎331100 for hours. If you have time for only a few colleges, **King's, Trinity, St. John's, Queens', Christ's**, and **Jesus** should top your list.

KING'S COLLEGE. Founded by Henry VI in 1441, King's College is one of the best-known Cambridge colleges, with spectacular river-side gardens such as the **Back Lawn**. The real draw, however is **King's College Chapel**. The interior of the chapel consists of one huge chamber cleft by a carved wooden choir screen. Behind the altar hangs Rubens' magnificent *Adoration of the Magi* (1639), a gift to the College and the most expensive painting ever auctioned at the time of its purchase. Enjoy the classic view of the chapel and of the adjacent **Gibbs Building** from the river. As you picnic by the water, think of those who have gone before you: E.M. Forster based *The Longest Journey* on his King's days, and Salman Rushdie also felt the college's grounds beneath his feet. In early June the university posts the final grades of every student in the Georgian **Senate House** opposite the chapel; about a week later, degree ceremonies are held there. *(King's Parade. ☎331100. Chapel and grounds open M-Sa 9:30am-4:30pm, Su 9:30am-2:30pm. Listing of chapel services and musical events available at porter's lodge for £1. Evensong 5:30pm most nights. Tours arranged through the TIC. £3.50, students and children £2.50, under 12 free with adults.)*

TRINITY COLLEGE. Founded in 1546 by Henry VIII, Trinity is the largest and wealthiest of Cambridge's colleges. The alma mater of Sir Isaac Newton, who lived in E stair-

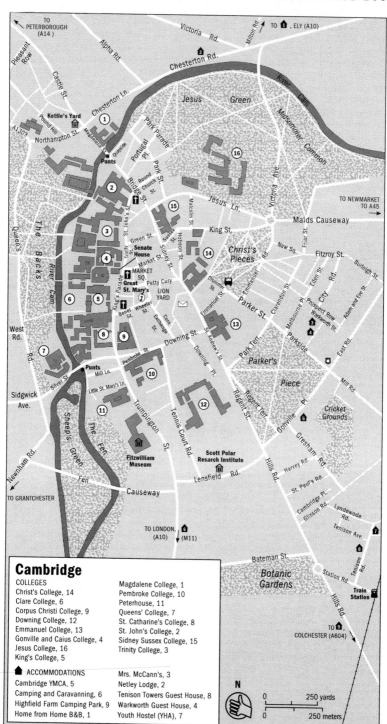

Victoria Rd.

TO ⌂, ELY (A10)

Milton Rd.

Pleasant Row

Alpha Rd

Chesterton Rd.

Castle St.

Chesterton Ln.

A1303

Pound Hill

Kettle's Yard

Northampton St.

Punts

Portugal Pl.

Park Parade

Jesus   Green

River Cam

Midsummer Common

1 Magdalene

Bridge St.

Round Church St.

Church St.

16

Jesus Ln.

TO NEWMARKET
TO A45

Malds Causeway

2

St. John's St.

Green St.

Trinity St.

15

Malcolm St.

Sidney St.

Hobson St.

King St.

Christ's Pieces

New Sq.

Fitzroy St.

Burleigh St.

Eden St.

Friar St.

City Rd.

3

Senate House

4

Market St.

Petty Cury

14

Drummer St.

Emmanuel St.

Parker St.

Clarendon St.

Melbourne Pl.

Prospect Row

Warkworth St.

Adam and Eve St.

East Rd.

MARKET SQ

Great St. Mary's

LION YARD

6   5

King's Parade

Benet St.

Wheeler St.

Corn Exchange St.

Downing St.

St. Andrew's St.

13

Park Terr.

Parker's Piece

Parkside

Mill Rd.

8   9

Pembroke St.

Downing Pl.

Downing St.

Regent Terr.

Gonville Pl.

7

West Rd.

Punts

Mill Ln.

Silver St.

Little St. Mary's Ln.

10

Trumpington St.

Tennis Court Rd.

12

Regent St.

Cricket Grounds

Gresham Rd.

Sidgwick Ave.

11

Fitzwilliam Museum

Scott Polar Research Institute

Lensfield Rd.

Harvey Rd.

Hills Rd.

The Backs

Queens'

River Cam

Sheep's Green

The Fen

Newnham Rd.

Fen Causeway

TO GRANTCHESTER

TO LONDON, (A10) ⌂
(M11)

Bateman St.

St. Paul's Rd.

Cambridge Pl.

Glisson Rd.

Lyndewode Rd.

Tenison Ave.

Tenison Rd.

Station Rd.

Botanic Gardens

Train Station

Hills Rd.

TO ⌂, COLCHESTER (A604)

Cambridge

COLLEGES

Christ's College, 14
Clare College, 6
Corpus Christi College, 9
Downing College, 12
Emmanuel College, 13
Gonville and Caius College, 4
Jesus College, 16
King's College, 5

Magdalene College, 1
Pembroke College, 10
Peterhouse, 11
Queens' College, 7
St. Catharine's College, 8
St. John's College, 2
Sidney Sussex College, 15
Trinity College, 3

ACCOMMODATIONS

Cambridge YMCA, 5
Camping and Caravanning, 6
Highfield Farm Camping Park, 9
Home from Home B&B, 1

Mrs. McCann's, 3
Netley Lodge, 2
Tenison Towers Guest House, 8
Warkworth Guest House, 4
Youth Hostel (YHA), 7

N

0 ___ 250 yards
0 ___ 250 meters

case for 30 years, the College of the Holy and Undivided Trinity boasts an illustrious list of alumni: Byron, Tennyson, Nabokov, Russell, Wittgenstein, and Nehru all studied here. Byron lived in Nevile's Court, where he shared his rooms with a pet bear—college regulations only forebade cats and dogs—whom he claimed would take his fellowship exams for him. The pride of the college is the magnificent **Wren Library,** named (you guessed it) after its architect. Treasures inside include A.A. Milne's handwritten manuscript of *Winnie the Pooh* and Newton's own copy of his *Principia.(Trinity St. ☎338400. Chapel and courtyard open daily 10am-5pm. Wren Library open M-F noon-2pm, Sa 10:30am-12:30pm. Easter-Oct. £1.75, otherwise free.)*

ST. JOHN'S COLLEGE. Established in 1511 by Lady Margaret Beaufort, mother of Henry VIII, St. John's is one of seven Cambridge colleges founded by women (but *for* men). The Bridge of Sighs connects the older part of the college to the towering neo-Gothic extravagance of **New Court,** which is likened by some to a wedding cake in silhouette. The **School of Pythagoras,** a 12th-century pile of wood and stone rumored to be the oldest complete building in Cambridge, hides in St. John's Gardens. *(St. John's St. ☎338600. Chapel and grounds open daily 10am-4:45pm. Evensong 6:30pm most nights. £1.75, seniors and children £1, families £3.50.)*

FITZWILLIAM MUSEUM. The mosaic tile floors could be a display of their own, and the grand entrance hall, lined with marble busts and austere columns, is equally impressive. Egyptian, Chinese, Japanese and Greek antiquities bide their time downstairs. The **Founder's Library** houses an intimate collection of French Impressionists, while the drawing room displays William Blake's books and woodcuts. *(Trumpington St. ☎332900. Open Tu-Sa 10am-5pm, Su 2:15-5pm. Guided tours Sa 2:30pm. Free, but suggested donation £3. Tours £3.)*

OTHER MAJOR COLLEGES. Founded not once, but twice—by painted Queen Margaret of Anjou in 1448 and again by Elizabeth Woodville in 1465—**Queens' College** has the only unaltered Tudor courtyard in Cambridge, housing the half-timbered President's Gallery. The **Mathematical Bridge** was built in 1749 without a single bolt or nail, relying on mathematical principle. A meddling Victorian took apart the bridge to see how it worked and the inevitable occurred—he couldn't put it back together without using steel rivets. *(Silver St. ☎335511. College open Mar.-Oct. daily 10am-4.30pm. Closed during exams. £1.)* Founded as "God's-house" in 1448 and renamed in 1505, **Christ's College** has since won fame for its association with John Milton and for its gardens. Charles Darwin dilly-dallied through Christ's—his rooms (unmarked and closed to visitors) were on G staircase in First Court. *(St. Andrews St. ☎334900. Gardens open in summer M-F 9:30am-noon; term-time M-F 9:30am-4:30pm. Free.)* **Jesus College** has preserved an enormous amount of unaltered medieval work from as far back as 1496. Beyond the long, high-walled walk called the "Chimny" lies a three-sided court fringed with colorful gardens. Sterne and Coleridge were Jesus alumni. *(Jesus Ln. ☎339339. Courtyard open 9am-6pm; closed during exams to groups of 3 or more.)* Inhabiting buildings from a 15th-century Benedictine hostel, **Magdalene College** (MAUD-lin), sometime teaching home of Christian allegorist C.S. Lewis, has retained its religious emphasis. Take a peek at the **Pepys Library** in the second court. Pepys wrote his diaries in shorthand, which later took three years to decipher. *(Magdalene St. ☎332100. Library open Easter-Aug. 11:30am-12:30pm and 2:30-3:30pm; Sept.-Easter M-Sa 11:30am-12.30pm. Courtyards closed during exams. Free.)* Thomas Gray wrote *Elegy in a Country Churchyard* while staying in **Peterhouse,** Trumpington St., the oldest and smallest college, founded in 1294. *(☎338200. Call for opening hours.)* **Pembroke College** harbors the earliest architectural effort of Sir Christopher Wren and counts Ted Hughes and Eric Idle among its grads. *(☎338100. Courtyard open until 6pm; closed during exams. Call ahead for hours.)* A Wren chapel designed by the front court of **Emmanuel College,** St. Andrews St., is known fondly to its residents as "Emma." *(☎334200. Courtyard open until 6pm.)*

For a college town, Cambridge is rather bereft of nightlife—these kids take their studies seriously. The **Boat Race,** 170 East Rd., a packed and popular joint neat the police station, features a variety of music nightly. *(☎508533. Usually free, but call ahead.)* **Punts** (flat-bottomed boats propelled by a pole) are a favored form of entertainment. **Tyrell's,** Magdalene Bridge (☎(01480) 413517), has punts for $8 an hour plus $40 deposit. At **Scudamore's,** Silver St. Bridge (☎359750), punts cost $10 an hour plus $50 deposit.

LIVERPOOL

On the banks of the Mersey, Liverpool (pop. 520,000) was on its way to becoming an important port as early as 1715, when it opened England's first commercial docks. Much of its early wealth was amassed through the slave trade, but it was the successful Lancashire cotton industry that bolstered the city's growth. The city's docks also served as the departure point for many an emigrant bound for North America or the Antipodes. However, Liverpool's shipping dominance drew unfortunate attention in World War II as it became Britain's second most heavily bombed city. In the 1980s, high unemployment rates and local government scandals inhibited the revival of prosperity and enthusiasm. Despite the enduring poverty of some of the city's outlying suburbs, central Liverpool is becoming increasingly vibrant. A transformed Albert Dock studded with restaurants and museums, two enormous cathedrals, and a wild nightlife scene make Liverpool a great destination for travelers. Scousers—as Liverpudlians are colloquially known—are usually happy to introduce you to their Scouse dialect and humor, and to discuss the relative merits of Liverpool's two football teams. Oh, yeah—and the Beatles.

TICKET TO RIDE

Trains: Lime St. Station. Ticket office open M-Sa 5:15am-12:30am, Su 7:15am-12:30pm. (☎(08457) 484950) from **Euston** (2hr., 1 per hr., £44, £19 Virgin Value fare available if purchased by 6pm previous day). The smaller **Moorfields, James St.,** and **Central** train stations serve mainly as transfer points to local **Merseyrail** trains, including service to Chester and Crewe.

Buses: Norton St. Coach Station services **National Express** (☎(08705) 808080) from **Victoria** (4-5hr., 6 per day, day return £15, return £24)

Local Transportation: Private buses blanket the city and the surrounding Merseyside area. Consult the transport mavens at **Mersey Travel** (☎236 7676), in the tourist information centre. Open daily 8am-8pm.

Taxis: Local taxis are cheap and efficient. Try **Mersey Cabs** (☎298 2222).

HELP!

Although Liverpool is part of a vast metropolitan area sprawling across the River Mersey, its central district is pedestrian-friendly. The city has two clusters of museums: those on **William Brown St.,** near the main train station at Lime St., and those at **Albert Dock,** on the river. These flank the central shopping district, whose central axis comprises **Bold St., Church St.,** and **Lord St.** Most sights are within a 20-minute walk of the Lime St. train station.

Tourist Information Centre: Merseyside Welcome Centre (☎709 3631; fax 708 0204; www.merseyside.org.uk), in Queen Sq. Sells the handy *Visitor Guide to Liverpool and Merseyside* (£1), which contains lists of sights in the county and a map of the city. Books beds for a 10% deposit. Open M-Sa 10am-5:30pm, Su 10am-4:30pm. A smaller **branch** is at Atlantic Pavilion, Albert Dock (☎708 8854). Same hours.

Tours: Roll up for the big yellow-and-blue bus of the **Magical Mystery Tour** (☎236 9091), which leaves for the city's Beatles sites daily at 2:30pm from Albert Dock and the Welcome Centre (2hr., £10.95; definitely book ahead). **Phil Hughes** (☎228 4565 or (0961) 511223) runs an excellent Beatles tour, taking you *everywhere* that's connected with Liverpool's favorite sons in an 8-seat minivan (2hr., call for times, £9). Numerous other bus tours (from £4) and walking tours (£1) rotate throughout the summer; the tourist information centre has the leaflets if you have the feet. Ferry across the Mersey with the river cruises of **Mersey Ferries.** (☎333 1444. 50min. £3.50, concessions £2.50.)

Police: Canning Pl. (☎709 6010).

Hospital: Royal Liverpool Hospital, Prescot St. (☎706 2000), ½ mi. from the train station.

Internet Access: Central Library, William Brown St. The computer room is up the stairs on the left. Friendly staff, several computers. £1 per 30min. Open M-Sa 9am-5:30pm.

Post Office: 42-44 Houghton Way (☎708 4165), in St. John's Shopping Centre. **Postal Code:** L1. **Telephone Code:** 0151.

A HARD DAY'S NIGHT

Your best bet for cheap accommodations lies east of the city center. **Lord Nelson St.**, adjacent to the train station, is lined with modest hotels, and similar establishments are found along **Mount Pleasant**, one block from Brownlow Hill and the bus stop. Stay only at places approved by the tourist information centre (TIC). Both of Liverpool's hostels are full of young music-loving travelers, making for great room- and pub-mates. Demand for rooms is highest in summer, as well as in early April when jockeys and gamblers gallop into town for the Grand National Race.

Embassie Youth Hostel, 1 Falkner Sq. (☎ 707 1089). 15-20min. walk from the bus or train stations or a £2 taxi ride. Feels like a laid-back student's flat, with laundry, TV lounge, pool table, and kitchen, as well as all the toast and jam you can eat, all day, every day. One of England's friendliest hostels—ask the energetic staff for pub-crawling tips, or ask Kevin to tell you about the time his band outplaced John Lennon's in a talent competition. No lockout, curfew, or checkout time. Dorms £12.50 first night, £11.50 each additional night.

YHA Liverpool, 24 Tabley St., The Wapping (☎ 709 8888; fax 709 0417; liverpool@yha.org.uk). Spanking new, with comfortable, large, and clean rooms and friendly staff. Ideal location next to Albert Dock. Laundry and kitchen facilities. No lockout. Dorms £17.40, under 18 £13.10.

YWCA, 1 Rodney St. (☎ 709 7791), just off Mt. Pleasant. For both men and women. Renovated rooms are sparkling clean, attractively decorated, and surprisingly spacious, with firm beds. Kitchen, limited laundry facilities (no soap or change available), and hot showers. Key deposit £15 for stays longer than 5 nights. No lockout or curfew. £12 per person; discounted weekly rates.

SAVOY TRUFFLE

Trendy vegetarian cafes and reasonably priced Indian restaurants line **Bold St.** and **Hardman St.**, while cheap takeouts crowd **Hardnon St.** and **Berry St.** Liverpool parties late, and many restaurants stay open until 3am. Self-caterers should try **St. John's Market**, sprawled across the top of St. John's shopping mall, for fresh produce and local color.

Metz Café-Bar, Rainford Gdns. (☎ 227 2282), off Mathew St. "Don't discriminate, integrate," they proclaim. At this gay-friendly candlelit underground establishment, everyone's welcome to taste their esoteric and tasty lunch sandwich and soup combos (£4.25; served noon-7pm). Dinner's delightful too, but more expensive (*starigrad* lamb £9.50). Open M-Th noon-11pm, F-Sa noon-midnight, Su noon-10:30pm.

not sushi, Exchange St. East (☎ 709 8894), near Dale St. Opposite the town hall. Watch chefs prepare the primarily Japanese dishes (main courses £5.95-6.95) through huge glass windows as you slurp your noodles. Open M-Sa 11am-11:30pm.

Hub Café Bar, Berry St. (☎ 707 9495). Furniture made out of bicycle parts in a cafe that dishes out light veggie and vegan meals (£1.50-3); the quality of the food spokes for itself. Open M-Sa 10am-6pm.

MAGICAL MYSTERY TOUR

Many museums come under the **Eight-Museum Pass** (£3, students and seniors £1.50, children under 16 free); paying for entry into any one museum lets you into all the museums for a year. Visitors intending to visit only the attractions on the dock can purchase a **Waterfront Pass** (£9.99, concessions £6) from the Atlantic Pavilion branch of the tourist information centre, which includes admission to the Beatles Story, the Merseyside Maritime Museum, the Museum of Liverpool Life, and a Mersey Ferries cruise.

TATE GALLERY. The Liverpool branch of the London institution contains a select and impressive range of 20th-century artwork. British artists such as Lucian Freud, Damien Hirst, and Francis Bacon dominate the ground floor, while the floor above shows an annually-rotating exhibition selected from the Gallery's archives. By prior arrangement, the staff will fit the visually impaired with special gloves and allow them to touch some of the art. (*Albert Dock. ☎ 709 3223. Open Tu-Su 10am-6pm. Wheelchair access. Free; some special exhibits £3, concessions £1.*)

MERSEYSIDE MARITIME MUSEUM. The six floors of this museum, which recreate something of the horror of the slave trade and the carnage of the Battle of Britain, are impressive. Wander through the cramped hull of a slave trader's ship, or down a dimly lit dockside street to the voices of desperate emigrants, waiting to leave to the New

World. A floor above, fans of a certain movie starring Leonardo DiCaprio can check items recovered from the "unsinkable" ship. (*Albert Dock.* ☎ *478 4499. Open daily 10am-5pm, last admission 4pm. Admission with Eight-Museum Pass.*)

THE BEATLES STORY. This exhibit includes recreations of Hamburg, the Cavern Club (complete with the disinfectant "basement smells"), and a shiny Yellow Submarine. (*Albert Dock.* ☎ *709 1963. Open daily Apr.-Oct. 10am-6pm; Nov.-Mar. 10am-5pm. £6.95, concessions £4.95, families £17.*) For other Beatles-themed locales, pick up the **Beatles Map** (£2.50) at the tourist information centre: it takes you down to Strawberry Fields and Penny Lane. Souvenir hunters can raid the **Beatles Shop,** stuffed with memorabilia. (*31 Mathew St.* ☎ *236 9091. Open M-Sa 9:30am-5:30pm, Su 11am-4pm.*)

LIVERPOOL CATHEDRAL. Begun in 1904 and completed in 1978, this Anglican cathedral is *vast,* featuring the highest Gothic arches ever built (107 ft.), the largest vault and organ (9704 pipes), and the highest and heaviest bells in the world. Take two lifts and climb the final 108 stairs to the top of the tower for a view stretching to Wales. (*Upper Duke St.* ☎ *709 6271. Cathedral open daily 9am-6pm; tower open daily 11am-4pm, weather permitting. Cathedral free. Tower admission £2, children £1.*)

WALKER ART GALLERY. This stately gallery houses a huge collection of works dating from 1300 and including a variety of impressive post-Impressionist and pre-Raphaelite paintings. (*William Brown St.* ☎ *478 4199. Open M-Sa 10am-5pm, Su noon-5pm. Admission with Eight-Museum Pass.*)

CONSERVATION CENTRE. A small interactive museum on the ground floor of the conservation studios and labs for the National Museum and Galleries of Merseyside, the Centre allows insight into the decisions and processes of art conservation, restoration, and preservation. The hands-on exhibits are particularly engaging for children. (*Whitechapel.* ☎ *478 4999. Open M-Sa 10am-5pm, Su noon-5pm. Admission with Eight-Museum Pass. Tours W and Sa 2pm and 3pm for extra charge.*)

THE MUSEUM OF LIVERPOOL LIFE. This museum traces Liverpool's history of stormy labor struggles and race relations, as well as the city's sporting heritage. A TV runs footage of legendary football matches between Liverpool and Everton, while a plaque marks out Grand National-winning horses. (*Albert Dock.* ☎ *478 4080. Open daily 10am-5pm, last admission 4pm. Admission with Eight-Museum Pass.*)

LIVERPOOL MUSEUM. A natural history exhibit with a carved narwhal horn, a vivarium with live animals including fire-bellied toads, and a planetarium fill this museum located near the Walker Art Gallery. It's still open despite renovations. (☎ *478 4399. Open same hours as the Walker. Admission with Eight-Museum Pass.*)

LIVERPOOL AND EVERTON FOOTBALL CLUBS. If you're not here for the Beatles, you're probably here for the football. The rivalry between the city's two main clubs is one of the country's deepest and most passionate. **Liverpool** and **Everton** both offer tours of their grounds (Goodison Park and Anfield respectively) as well as match tickets when available. (*Both stadiums can be reached by bus #26 from the city center. Liverpool* ☎ *260 6677. Everton* ☎ *330 2266. Tours from £5. Tickets from £14.*)

COME TOGETHER

Pubs teem in almost every street in Liverpool. Two of the city's most notable products—football fans and rock musicians—were born in the pub culture. Liverpool has continued to incorporate these traditions into its present pub renaissance. **Slater St.** in particular brims with £1 pints.

The Jacaranda, Slater St. (☎ 708 0233). The site of the first paid Beatles gig, the Jacaranda has a basement where the Beatles did the original paint work. Live bands still play, and a small dance floor lets you kick loose. Open M-Sa noon-2am.

The Philharmonic, 36 Hope St. (☎ 709 1163). John Lennon once said that the worst thing about being famous was "not being able to get a quiet pint at the Phil." The non-celebrities among us can still get that silent beer, and at reasonable prices (drafts £1.60). Worth going into just to see some of Britain's most ornate bathrooms. Open M-Sa 11:30am-11pm, Su 7-10:30pm.

Baa Bar, 43-45 Fleet St. (☎ 707 0610), off Bold St. Attracts a far-from-sheepish lesbian, gay, and trendy crowd for cappuccino during the day and cheap beer at night. Open M-Sa 10am-2am.

PLEASE PLEASE ME

Liverpool has a thriving arts and nightlife scene. The free monthly *Ink*, available at the tourist information centre and many cafes, offers the most up-to-date arts information, as does the *Liverpool Echo*, an evening newspaper sold by street corner vendors that also includes local news (30p).

Cream (☎ 709 1693), in Wolstonholme Sq. off Parr St. In a word, *brilliant*. The queue goes on forever, because people travel from all over Britain (and the world) to come to this nationally-renowned superclub. Steep prices, but an amazing party. Cover £11. Open Sa, plus last F of the month, 10pm-4am.

The Cavern Club, 10 Mathew St. (☎ 236 9091). On the site where the Fab Four gained prominence, and with the same decor, the Cavern now plays regular club music. Club open M and Th-Sa 9pm-2am, pub open from noon. Free admission before 10pm. Live music Sa 2-6pm.

Heebiejebees, 80-82 Seel St. (☎ 709 2666). Billed as "the house that jazz built," this gritty club also plays everything from French pop to Jungle. No cover. Open M and W-Sa.

BATH

A visit to the elegant spa city of Bath (pop. 83,000) remains *de rigeur*, even if it is now more of a museum—or perhaps a museum's gift shop—than a resort. But expensive trinkets can't conceal Bath's underlying sophistication. Early in their occupation of Britain, the Romans built an elaborate complex of baths to house the curative waters at the town they called *Aquae Sulis*, and the excavated remains of that complex draw in visitors today. Queen Anne's visit to the hot springs here in 1701 reestablished the city's prominence, making it a meeting place for 18th-century artists, politicians, and intellectuals.

ORIENTATION AND PRACTICAL INFORMATION

Trains (☎ (08457) 484950) arrive from **London Paddington** (1½hr., 2 per hr., £34) and **London Waterloo** (2¼hr., 4 per day, £21). **National Express** office open M-Sa 8:30am-5pm.) **National Express** (☎ (08705) 808080) runs from **London Victoria** (3hr., 9 per day, £11.50).

To reach the **tourist information centre,** Abbey Chambers, Abbey Churchyard, from the bus or train stations, walk up Manvers St. to the Terrace Walk roundabout and turn left onto York St. (☎ 477101; fax 477787; www.visitbath.co.uk. Open May-Sept. M-Sa 9:30am-6pm, Su 10am-4pm; Oct.-Apr. M-Sa 9:30am-5pm, Su 10am-4pm.) Free guided **walking tours** given by the Mayor's Honorary Guides depart from the Abbey Churchyard daily at 10:30am and 2pm. The **police** are on Manvers St. (☎ 444343), just up from the train and bus stations. To get to **Royal United Hospital,** Coombe Park, in Weston (☎ 428331), take bus #14, 16, or 17 from the train or bus station. **Phone Code:** 01225.

ACCOMMODATIONS

Bath's well-to-do visitors drive up B&B prices—expect to pay £18 and up. B&Bs cluster on **Pulteney Rd.** and **Pulteney Gdns.** For a more relaxed setting, continue past Pulteney Gdns. (or take the footpath from behind the rail station) to **Widcombe Hill.** The steep climb has prices to match. A walk west toward Royal Victoria Park on **Crescent Gdns.** will reveal another front of B&Bs.

YHA Youth Hostel, Bathwick Hill (☎ 465674). From North Parade Rd., turn left onto Pulteney Rd., then right onto Bathwick Hill. A footpath leads up the steep hill to the hostel (20min.). Badgerline "University" bus #18 (6 per hr. until midnight; £1 return) runs to the hostel from the bus station or the Orange Grove roundabout. Secluded mansion overlooking the city. 124 beds. TV. No lockout, no curfew. Laundry service. In summer reserve a week in advance. Dorms £11, under 18 £7.75.

Mrs. Rowe, 7 Widcombe Crescent (☎ 422726). Proceed up Widcombe Hill and turn right. In the southeast, uphill from the stations and 10min. from town center. The height of elegance with a view to match. Singles £26; twins £44; doubles with bath £46.

The White Guest House, 23 Pulteney Gdns. (☎ 426075). From North Parade Rd., turn right at the traffic light; Pulteney Gdns. is the second left. A homey B&B with a patio filled with flowers. All rooms have TVs and bath. Kind proprietors will knock 10% off if you stay 3 or more nights. Singles £25-30; doubles £45-50. Prices lower Nov.-Apr.

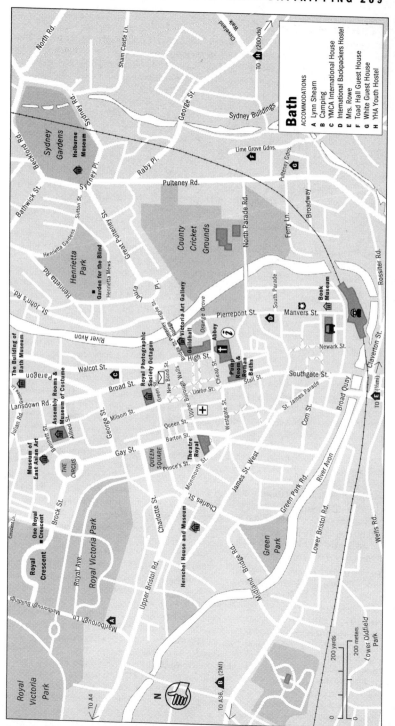

Bath

ACCOMMODATIONS
A Lynn Shearn
B Camping
C YMCA International House
D International Backpackers Hostel
E Mrs. Rowe
F Toad Hall Guest House
G White Guest House
H YHA Youth Hostel

FOOD AND DRINK

Meals in Bath can be elegant (and pricey) affairs, but your wallet doesn't have to float after a meal; several decent cafes and restaurants populate the city. On Sundays, many pubs offer three-course lunches at bargain prices. Salivate over the impressive French creations at **Tilleys Bistro**, 3 North Parade Passage, including mushroom crepes for under £5. (☎484200. Open M-Sa noon-2:30pm and 6:30-11pm, Su 6:30-10:30pm.) The casual atmosphere and satisfying fare at the **Adventure Cafe**, 5 Princes Buildings, will take out the worry out of any lunching expedition; the sandwiches are a steal at £2.50-3.75. **The Pump Room**, Abbey Churchyard, elegantly exercises its monopoly over Bath Spa drinking water (one glass 45p) in a palatial Victorian ballroom. Cream tea (£6.75) is served from 2:30pm until closing; weekend reservations are essential. (☎444477. Open daily Apr.-Sept. 9am-6pm; Oct.-Mar. 9:30am-5pm.)

If you're looking for drinks of another sort, **The Boater**, 9 Argyle St. (☎464211), overlooks the river with outdoor seating and a view of the lit-up Pulteney Bridge. The Garrick's Head, St. John's Pl. (☎448819), is a scoping ground for the stage door of the Theatre Royal. The Pig and Fiddle, on the corner of Saracen St. and Broad St., brings in a young crowd for pints around a large patio.

SIGHTS

THE ROMAN BATHS. In 1880, sewer diggers inadvertently uncovered the first glimpse of what recent excavation has shown to be a splendid model of advanced Roman engineering. The **Roman Baths Museum** displays the complexity of Roman engineering, including central heating and internal plumbing. Bath flourished for nearly 400 years as a Roman spa city. Read the various recovered curses (in Latin or in English) that Romans cast into Minerva's spring. Tradition maintained that if the written curse floated on the water, it would be visited back upon the curser. The Romans neatly avoided this by writing their ill wishes on lead. (Stall St. ☎477759. Open Apr.-July and Sept. daily 9am-6pm; Aug. 9am-6pm and 8-10pm; Oct.-Mar. 9:30am-5pm; last admission 30min. before closing. Partial wheelchair access. Admission includes guided tours, which run hourly from the main pool, and audio tours. £6.70, seniors £6, children £4, families £17; or buy a joint ticket to the Baths and the Museum of Costume, £8.70, seniors £7.80, children £5.20, families £22.60.)

BATH ABBEY AND HERITAGE VAULTS. On a site that once contained a Saxon cathedral three times as large, the 15th-century **abbey** still towers over its neighbors, beckoning to visitors across the skyline. An anomaly among the city's 1st-century Roman and 18th-century Georgian sights, the abbey saw the crowning of Edgar, "first king of all England," in AD 973. The whimsical west facade sports angels climbing ladders up to heaven and two angels climbing down. Tombstones cover every possible surface in the church save the sanctuary and ceiling. (Next to the Baths. ☎477752. Open daily 9am-4:30pm. Requested donation £1.50.) Below the Abbey, the **Heritage Vaults** detail the abbey's history and its importance to Bath. Among the exhibits are statues from the original facade (including an angel in a nosedive) and a fascinating disappearing diorama. (☎422462. Open M-Sa 10am-4pm. Wheelchair access. Admission £2, students, seniors, and children £1.)

MUSEUM OF COSTUME. The museum houses a parade of 400 years of catwalks and a phenomenal collection of wedding gowns, including a "generously cut" number worn by Queen Victoria. (Bennett St. ☎477752. Open daily 10am-5pm. Wheelchair access. £3.90, seniors £3.50, children £2.70; or by joint ticket with the Roman Baths—see above.) The clothes are in the basement of the **Assembly Rooms,** which staged fashionable events in the late 18th century. Although World War II ravaged the rooms, renovations duplicate the originals in fine detail. (☎477789. Open daily 10am-5pm. Free.)

HISTORIC BUILDINGS. Walk up Gay St. to **The Circus,** in the city's northwest corner, which has attracted illustrious residents for two centuries. Blue plaques mark the houses of Thomas Gainsborough and William Pitt (MP for Bath). Proceed from there up Brock St. to Royal Crescent, a half-moon of Georgian townhouses, stopping at the oasis of book and art stores at **Margaret's Building** on the way. The interior of **One Royal Crescent** has been painstakingly restored by the Bath Preservation Trust to a near-perfect replica of a 1770 townhouse. (1 Royal Crescent. ☎428126. Open mid-Feb. to Oct. Tu-Su 10:30am-5pm; Nov. Tu-Su 10:30am-4pm. £4, concessions £3.50, families £10.) Climb the 156 steps of **Beckford's Tower** for stupendous views. (Lansdowne Rd. ☎338727. £2, concessions £1).

ENTERTAINMENT

The **Paragon Wine Bar,** 1a The Paragon (☎466212) holds an eclectic set of laid-back drinkers and talkers. **The Bell,** 103 Walcot St., features live music. (☎460426. Open daily 11am-11pm.) **The Hat and Feather,** 14 London St., further down Walcot St., mixes house, reggae and DJ concoctions. (☎425672. Open daily 11am-11pm.) For clubs, try **Cadillacs** on Walcot St., just behind The Bell, where standard chart music is spun.

STONEHENGE

Perhaps the gentle giants on Salisbury's windswept plain will remain fascinating for millennia to come, both for their mystery and their sheer longevity. A submerged colossus amid swaying grass and indifferent sheep, Stonehenge stands unperturbed by 50mph whipping winds and the legions of people who have been by its side for over 5000 years. The present stones—22 ft. high—comprise the fifth temple constructed on the site. The first probably consisted of an arch and circular earthwork furrowed in 3050 BC, and was in use for about 500 years. Its relics are the **Aubrey Holes** (white patches in the earth) and the **Heel Stone** (the isolated, rough block standing outside the circle). The next monument consisted of about 60 stones imported up the River Avon from Wales around 2100 BC, used to mark astronomical directions. This may once have been composed of two concentric circles and two horseshoes of megaliths, both enclosed by earthworks.

Admission to Stonehenge includes a helpful 40min. English Heritage **audio tour,** although the effect may be more haunting than Stonehenge itself—a bizarre march of tourists who seem to be engaged in business calls. (☎(01980) 625368. Open daily June-Aug. 9am-7pm; mid-Mar. to May and Sept. to mid-Oct. 9:30am-6pm; mid-Oct. to mid-Mar. 9:30am-4pm. Wheelchair access. £4, students and seniors £3, children £2, families £10.)

Getting to Stonehenge doesn't require much effort if you aren't carting 45-ton rocks. Take a **train** (☎(08457) 484950) to **Salisbury** from **Victoria** (1½hr,. 1 per hr., £22-30); or take a **National Express** (☎(08705) 808080) coach from **Victoria,** 2¾hr., 4per day, £11.50, return £12.50. From Salisbury center or from the train station, transfer to any **Wilts & Dorset bus** to Stonehenge, including service #3 (40min., return £4.80). Ask for an **Explorer** pass, which costs the same as a regular return ticket.

ALTHORP

The ancestral home of the Spencer family took on special significance with the death of Princess Diana. Under the guidance of Diana's brother Charles, this classic English country house and 300 acres of sheep-speckled fields have been transformed into a shrine where the people can remember the "People's Princess."

In the darkened rooms of **Diana: a Celebration,** the late princess comes alive in continuous film clip; also on display are her letters, childhood mementos (the most recent addition is her christening robe), and wedding wear, including her wedding gown with its 25 ft. train and two bridesmaid's dresses. An autographed copy of Elton John's *Candle in the Wind,* sung at Diana's funeral, is prominently displayed. The converted stables also house a **cafe,** which still retains some of the stable interior, and serves the usual selection of sandwiches (£2), tea (85p), and snacks. There's no undignified rummaging in the **gift shop;** pick out your Althorp and English Rose memorabilia from the catalogue provided and request them from the cashier. Tickets to Althorp must be booked in advance; Call the 24-hour booking line at ☎(01604) 592 020. You will be asked to specify a morning (9am) or afternoon (1pm) ticket; the last admission is at 4pm. (Grounds open daily July 1-Aug. 30, 9am-5pm. £9.50, senior citizens £7, children 5-17 £5).

Trains arrive from **Euston** (1-1½hr., 1 every hour, £14). A special shuttle service (15 min., £3.20 return) brings visitors from the train station directly to Althorp, leaving from the train station at 8:45am, 9:40am, 12:45pm, and 1:45pm. **Buses** roll in from **Victoria** (2 hr., 6 daily, £11). The nearest **tourist office** is located in Northampton at St. Gile's Square. (☎(01604) 622 677; email tic@northampton.gov.uk. Open M-F 9:30am-5pm, Sa 9:30am-4pm; June-Aug. Su noon-4pm.)

Planning Your Trip

DOCUMENTS AND FORMALITIES

PASSPORTS

REQUIREMENTS. Citizens of all non-EU countries need valid passports to enter Britain and to re-enter their own country. Britain does not allow entrance if the holder's passport expires in under six months; returning home with an expired passport is illegal, and may result in a fine.

PHOTOCOPIES. It is a good idea to photocopy the page of your passport that contains your photograph, passport number, and other identifying information, along with other important documents such as visas, travel insurance policies, airplane tickets, credit card numbers, and traveler's check serial numbers. Carry one set of copies in a safe place apart from the originals and leave another set at home.

LOST PASSPORTS. If you lose your passport, immediately notify the local police and the nearest embassy or consulate of your home government. To ensure that it's replaced quickly, you will need to know all information previously recorded and show identification and proof of citizenship. In some cases, a replacement may take weeks to process, and it may be valid only for a limited time. Any visas stamped in your old passport will be lost. **In an emergency, ask for immediate temporary traveling papers that will permit you to re-enter your home country.**

NEW PASSPORTS. Applications for new passports or renewals should be filed several weeks or months in advance of your planned departure date—remember that you are relying on government agencies to complete these transactions. Most passport offices do offer emergency passport services for an extra charge.

Australia Citizens must apply for a passport in person at a post office, a passport office, or an Australian diplomatic mission overseas. Passport offices are located in Adelaide, Brisbane, Canberra, Darwin, Hobart, Melbourne, Newcastle, Perth, and Sydney. New adult passports cost AUS$128 (for a 32-page passport) or AUS$194 (64-page) and a child's is AUS$64 (32-page) or AUS$96 (64-page). Adult passports are valid for 10 years and child passports for 5 years. For more info, call toll-free (in Australia) ☎ 131 232 or visit www.dfat.gov.au/passports.

Canada Application forms are available at all passport offices, Canadian missions, many travel agencies, and Northern Stores in northern communities. Passports cost CDN$60 for a 24-page passport and CDN$62 for a 48-page passport, plus a CDN$25 consular fee. Passports are valid for 5 years and not renewable. For additional info, contact the Canadian Passport Office, Department of Foreign Affairs and International Trade, Ottawa, ON, K1A 0G3 (☎(613) 994-3500; www.dfait-maeci.gc.ca/passport.htm). Travelers may also call 800-567-6868 (24hr.); in Toronto, (416) 973-3251; in Vancouver, (604) 586-2500; in Montreal, (514) 283-2152.

Ireland Citizens can apply for a passport by mail to either the Department of Foreign Affairs, Passport Office, Setanta Centre, Molesworth St., Dublin 2 (☎(01) 671 1633; fax 671 1092; www.irlgov.ie/iveagh), or the Passport Office, Irish Life Building, 1A South Mall, Cork (☎(021) 27 25 25). Applications at Garda stations and post offices, or request one from a passport office. 32-page passports cost IR£45 and 48-page passports IR£55. Both are valid for 10 years. Citizens under 18 or over 65 can request a 3-year passport that costs IR£10.

New Zealand Application forms for passports are available in New Zealand from most travel agents. Applications may be forwarded to the Passport Office, P.O. Box 10526, Wellington, New Zealand (☎0800 22 50 50; www.passports.govt.nz). Standard processing time in New Zealand is 10 working days for correct applications. The fees are adult NZ$80 and child NZ$40. Expedited and emergency services cost more (urgent service NZ$160 adult, NZ$120 children; callout service NZ$330 adult, NZ$290 child). Adult passports are valid for up to 10 years. Children must apply for their own passports, which are valid for up to 5 years. Standard service processes passport requests in 10 working days.

South Africa South African passports are issued only in Pretoria. However, all applications must still be submitted or forwarded to the applicable office of a South African consulate. Tourist passports, valid for 10 years, cost around SAR80. Children under 16 must be issued their own passports, valid for 5 years, which cost around SAR60. Time for the completion of an application is normally at least 3 months from the time of submission. For further information, contact the nearest Department of Home Affairs Office (www.southafrica-newyork.net/passport.htm).

United States Citizens may apply for a passport at any federal or state courthouse or post office authorized to accept passport applications, or at a US Passport Agency, located in most major cities. Refer to the "US Government, State Department" section of the telephone directory or the local post office for addresses. Passports are valid for 10 years (5 years if under 16) and cost US$60 (under 16 US$40). Passports may be renewed by mail or in person for US$40. Processing takes 3-4 weeks. For more info, contact the US Passport Information's 24hr. recorded message (☎(202) 647-0518) or look on the web at http://travel.state.gov/passport_services.html.

IDENTIFICATION

When you travel, always carry two or more forms of identification on your person, including at least one photo ID; a passport combined with a driver's license or birth certificate is usually adequate. Many establishments, especially banks, may require several IDs in order to cash traveler's checks. Never carry all your forms of ID together; split them up in case of theft or loss. It is useful to bring extra passport-size photos to affix to the various IDs or passes you may acquire along the way.

STUDENT AND TEACHER IDENTIFICATION. The **International Student Identity Card (ISIC)**, the most widely accepted form of student ID, provides discounts on sights, accommodations, food, and transport. The ISIC is preferable to an institution-specific card (such as a university ID) because it is more likely to be recognized (and honored) abroad. All cardholders have access to a 24-hour emergency helpline for medical, legal, and financial emergencies (in North America call ☎ (877) 370-ISIC, elsewhere call US collect ☎+1 (715) 345-0505), and US cardholders are also eligible for insurance benefits (see

Insurance, p. 223). Many student travel agencies issue ISICs, including STA Travel in Australia and New Zealand; Travel CUTS in Canada; usit in the Republic of Ireland and Northern Ireland; SASTS in South Africa; Campus Travel and STA Travel in the UK; Council Travel (www.counciltravel.com/idcards/default.asp) and STA Travel in the US (see p. 227). The card is valid from September of one year to December of the following year and costs AUS$15, CDN$15, or US$22. Applicants must be degree-seeking students of a secondary or post-secondary school and must be of at least 12 years of age. Because of the proliferation of fake ISICs, some services (particularly airlines) require additional proof of student identity, such as a school ID or a letter attesting to your student status, signed by your registrar and stamped with your school seal. The **International Teacher Identity Card (ITIC)** offers the same insurance coverage as well as similar but limited discounts. The fee is AUS$13, UK£5, or US$22. For more info, contact the **International Student Travel Confederation (ISTC),** Herengracht 479, 1017 BS Amsterdam, Netherlands (☎+31 (20) 421 28 00; fax 421 28 10; email istcinfo@istc.org; www.istc.org).

YOUTH IDENTIFICATION. The International Student Travel Confederation issues a discount card to travelers who are 25 years old or under, but are not students. This one-year **International Youth Travel Card** (IYTC; formerly the GO 25 Card) offers many of the same benefits as the ISIC. Most organizations that sell the ISIC also sell the IYTC (US$22).

VISAS

EU citizens do not need a visa to enter Britain or Ireland. For visits of less than six months, citizens of Australia, Canada, New Zealand, South Africa, and the US do not need a visa to enter; neither do citizens of Israel, Japan, Malaysia, Mexico, Singapore, and many Caribbean and Pacific countries. Citizens of most other countries need a visa to enter Britain and Ireland. Visas cost £35 for a one-time pass and allow you to spend varying amounts of time in the UK depending on your country of origin. Visas can be purchased from your nearest British consulate. The **Center for International Business and Travel (CIBT)** (☎800-925-2428) secures visas for traveling U.S. citizens with a variable service charge. If you need a **visa extension,** contact the Home Office (☎(08706) 067766) Immigration and Nationality Directorate Lunar House, Wellesley Rd., Croydon CR9 1AT.

CUSTOMS

Upon entering Britain, you must declare certain items from abroad and pay a duty on the value of those articles that exceed the allowance established by the UK's customs service. It's wise to make a list, including serial numbers, of any valuables you carry from home; registering this list with customs before your departure and having an official stamp will avoid import duty charges and ensure an easy passage on your return. Be especially careful to document items made abroad. If applicable, apply for a **Value-Added Tax (VAT) refund** (see **Taxes,** p. 220).

ENTRANCE REQUIREMENTS

Passports (p. 213). All non-EU citizens entering the UK need a passport; EU citizens require either a passport or an EU-government ID card. **Visas** (p. 215). Citizens of most western countries do not need visas to enter the UK If you are unsure, call the local embassy or see http://visa.fco.gov.uk for British immigration rules.

Inoculations: No inoculations are necessary for visiting Britain.

Work Permit (p. 215). Required for all non-EU citizens planning to work in Britain.

If you are arriving in Britain from the EU, Australia, or New Zealand and wish to bring along your pet, you may be able to avoid having to place the pet in quarantine by participating in the new **PETS** "pet passport" trial scheme. Provided you are able to have your pooch or feline friend microchipped, vaccinated, bloodtested, and certified against tapeworm and ticks six months before entering the UK, you should be able to avoid pet quarantine. Consult www.maff.gov.uk/animalh/quarantine for more details.

Upon returning home, you must declare all articles acquired abroad and pay a **duty** on the value of articles that exceed the allowance established by your country's customs service. Goods and gifts purchased at **duty-free** shops abroad are not exempt from duty or sales tax at your point of return; you must declare these items as well. For more specific information on customs requirements, contact the following information centers:

Australia: Australian Customs National Information Line (in Australia call ☎(01) 30 03 63, from elsewhere ☎ +61 (2) 6275 6666; www.customs.gov.au).

Canada: Canadian Customs, 2265 St. Laurent Blvd., Ottawa, ON K1G 4K3 (☎(800) 461-9999 (24hr.) or (613) 993-0534; www.revcan.ca).

Ireland: Customs Information Office, Irish Life Centre, Lower Abbey St., Dublin 1 (☎(01) 878 8811; fax 878 0836; taxes@revenue.iol.ie; www.revenue.ie/customs.htm).

New Zealand: New Zealand Customhouse, 17-21 Whitmore St., Box 2218, Wellington (☎(04) 473 6099; fax 473 7370; www.customs.govt.nz).

South Africa: Commissioner for Customs and Excise, Privat Bag X47, Pretoria 0001 (☎(012) 314 9911; fax 328 6478; www.gov.za).

United Kingdom: Her Majesty's Customs and Excise, Passenger Enquiry Team, Wayfarer House, Great South West Road, Feltham, Middlesex TW14 8NP (☎(020) 8910 3744; fax 8910 3933; www.hmce.gov.uk).

United States: US Customs Service, 1330 Pennsylvania Ave. NW, Washington, D.C. 20229 (☎(202) 354-1000; fax 354-1010; www.customs.gov).

MONEY

London's reputation as one of the most expensive cities in the world is well-deserved. If you stay in hostels and prepare your own food, expect to spend anywhere from UK£30-40 per person per day. **Accommodations** start at around £14 per night for a hostel or dormitory room and £40 or more for a Bed and Breakfast, while a basic sit-down meal costs around £8-10. The currency chart is based on exchange rates from August 2000.

CURRENCY	THE BRITISH POUND STERLING	
	US$1 = £0.66	£1 = US$1.51
	CDN$1 = £0.45	£1 = CDN$2.22
	IR£1 = £0.80	£1 = IR£1.25
	AUS$1 = £0.39	£1 = AUS$2.56
	NZ$1 = £.31	£1 = NZ$3.21
	SAR1=£0.09	£1 = SAR10.55

As a general rule, using your cash card to withdraw money from an account at home gets you the best exchange rate. Cash machines also save you a trip to the bureaux de change and the trouble of carrying large amounts of cash. However, you should bring enough foreign currency to last for the first 24 to 72 hours of a trip to avoid being penniless should you arrive after bank hours or on a holiday. Travelers from the US can get foreign currency from the comfort of home: **International Currency Express** (☎(888) 278-6628) delivers foreign currency or traveler's checks overnight (US$15) or 2nd-day (US$12) at competitive exchange rates.

When changing money abroad, try to go only to banks or bureaux de change that have at most a 5% margin between their buy and sell prices. Since you lose money with every transaction, **convert large sums** (unless the currency is depreciating rapidly), **but no more than you'll need.** If you use traveler's checks or bills, carry some in small denominations for times when you are forced to exchange money at disadvantageous rates, but bring a range of denominations since charges may be levied per check cashed. Store your money in a variety of forms; ideally, you will at any given time be carrying some cash, some traveler's checks, and a cash and/or credit card.

TRAVELER'S CHECKS

Traveler's checks (**American Express** and **Visa** are the most recognized) are one of the safest and least troublesome means of carrying funds. Several agencies and banks sell them for a small commission. Each agency provides refunds if your checks are lost or stolen, and many provide additional services, such as toll-free refund hotlines abroad, emergency message services, and stolen credit card assistance.

Hackney Carriage

While traveling, keep check receipts and a record of which checks you've cashed separate from the checks themselves. Also leave a list of check numbers with someone at home. Never countersign checks until you're ready to cash them, and always bring your passport with you to cash them. If your checks are lost or stolen, immediately contact a refund center of the issuing company to be reimbursed; they may require a police report verifying the loss or theft. Less-touristed countries may not have refund centers at all, in which case you might have to wait to be reimbursed. Ask about toll-free refund hotlines and the location of refund centers when purchasing checks, and always carry emergency cash.

American Express: Call ☎ 800 251 902 in Australia; in New Zealand ☎ 0800 441 068; in the UK ☎ (0800) 52 13 13; in the US and Canada ☎ 800-221-7282. Elsewhere, call US collect ☎ 1-801-964-6665; www.aexp.com. American Express traveler's checks are available in British pounds. Checks can be purchased for a small fee (1-4%) at American Express Travel Service Offices, banks, and American Automobile Association offices. AAA members can buy them commission-free. American Express offices cash their checks commission-free (except where prohibited by national governments), but often at slightly worse rates than banks.

Look Right

Citicorp: Call ☎ 800-645-6556 in the US and Canada; in Europe, the Middle East, or Africa, call the London office at ☎ 7508 7007 or 0800 622 887; from elsewhere, call US collect ☎ 1-813-623-1709. Traveler's checks in English pounds. Commission 1-2%. Purchase checks at Citibank branches. 332 Oxford St., W1 (☎ 7508 1201) Tube: Tottenham Court; 336 Strand WC2 (☎ 7500 9906) Tube: Charing Cross. Open Mon-Fri 9am-5pm.

Thomas Cook MasterCard: From the US, Canada, or Caribbean call ☎ 800-223-7373; from the UK call ☎ (0800) 622 101; from elsewhere, call ☎ 44 1733 318 950 toll free; www.us.thomascook.com. Commission 2%. Checks cashed commission-free.

Visa: Call 800-227-6811 in the US; in the UK (0800) 895 078; from elsewhere, call 44 1733 318 949 and reverse the charges. Any of the above numbers can tell you the location of their nearest office. Checks available at Barclay's branches.

Heathrow

Money From Home In Minutes.

If you're stuck for cash on your travels, don't panic. Millions of people trust Western Union to transfer money in minutes to 176 countries and over 78,000 locations worldwide. Our record of safety and reliability is second to none. For more information, call Western Union: USA 1-800-325-6000, Canada 1-800-235-0000. Wherever you are, you're never far from home.

www.westernunion.com

WESTERN UNION | MONEY TRANSFER

The fastest way to send money worldwide.

CREDIT CARDS

Credit cards often offer superior exchange rates—up to 5% better than the retail rate used by banks and other currency exchange establishments. Credit cards may also offer services such as insurance or emergency help, and are sometimes required to reserve hotel rooms or rental cars. **MasterCard** and **Visa** (a.k.a. Barclaycard) are the most welcomed; **American Express** cards work at some cash machines and at AmEx offices and major airports. However, budget travelers will probably find that few of the establishments they frequent will accept credit cards.

Credit cards are also useful for **cash advances,** which allow you to withdraw pounds from associated banks and cash machines instantly. However, transaction fees for all credit card advances (up to US$10 per advance, plus 2-3% extra on foreign transactions after conversion) tend to make credit cards a more costly way of withdrawing cash than cash machines or travelers checks. In an emergency, however, the transaction fee may prove worth the cost. To be eligible for an advance, you'll need to get a **Personal Identification Number (PIN)** from your credit card company (see **Cash Cards,** below). Be sure to check with your credit card company before you leave home; in certain circumstances companies have started to charge a foreign transaction fee.

CASH CARDS (ATM CARDS)

Cash (ATM) cards are widespread in Britain; to find one, ask for the nearest **cash machines**. Depending on the system that your home bank uses, you can probably access your own personal bank account whenever you need money. There is often a limit on the amount of money you can withdraw per day (usually about US$500, depending on the type of card and account), banks usually attach rapacious fees (US$5 is not unheard of) to overseas transactions, and computer networks sometimes fail. If you're traveling from the US or Canada, memorize your PIN code in numeral form since machines elsewhere often don't have letters on their keys. If your PIN is longer than four digits, ask your bank whether the first four digits will work, or whether you need a new number.

The two major international money networks are **Cirrus** (US ☎ 800-4-CIRRUS (424-7787)) and **PLUS** (US ☎ 800-843-7587 for the "Voice Response Unit Locator"). These numbers direct you to nearby cash machines; alternatively, check the web (www.visa.com/pd/atm or www.mastercard.com/atm).

Visa TravelMoney (for customer assistance call 0800-963-833) is a system allowing you to access money from any Visa cash machine, common throughout London. You deposit an amount before you travel (plus a small administration fee), and you can withdraw up to that sum. The cards, which give you the same favorable exchange rate for withdrawals as a regular Visa, are especially useful if you plan to travel through many countries. Check with your local bank to see if it issues TravelMoney cards. **Road Cash** (US ☎ (877) 762-3227; www.roadcash.com) issues cards in the US with a minimum US$300 deposit.

2 ESSENTIAL INFORMATION

PACKING

Pack lightly; the rest is commentary. Remember that you can buy anything you'll need in London. One tried-and-true method of packing is to set out everything you think you'll need, then pack half of it— and twice the money. For a long stay in London, you might prefer a **suitcase** to a conspicuous backpack. If you'll be on the move frequently, go with the pack. Don't forget a small **daypack** for carrying things around. Keep some money, passport, and other valuables with you in a purse, neck pouch, or money belt. For added security, bring a combination lock for your bag and for hostel lockers.

Nothing will serve you more loyally in London than comfortable **walking shoes** and a folding **umbrella.** Bring a light sweater (even in summer), an alarm clock, and a raincoat. Despite its rainy reputation, London can get sunny in summer—pack sunscreen and sunglasses.

FILM AND VIDEOTAPE

Film in London generally costs US$7 for a roll of 24 exposures. If you're not a serious photographer, you might consider bringing a **disposable camera** or two rather than an expensive permanent one.

The UK uses the PAL system for **videotapes,** not the NTSC system used in North America. Unless you find tapes specially marked "NTSC," forking over the money for the *Absolutely Fabulous* series may not be such a good idea.

GETTING MONEY FROM HOME

AMERICAN EXPRESS. Cardholders can withdraw up to US$1000 every seven days from their checking accounts at any of AmEx's major offices and many of its representatives' offices; AmEx also offers Express Cash at their (rare) cash machines in Britain. There is a 3% transaction fee for each cash withdrawal, with a US$3 minimum fee. To enroll in Express Cash, card members may call ☎800-CASH NOW (227-4669) in the US; outside the US call collect ☎ +1-336-333-3211.

WESTERN UNION. Travelers from the US, Canada, and the UK can wire money abroad through Western Union's international money transfer services. In the US call ☎(800) 325-6000; in Canada ☎(800) 235-0000; in the UK ☎(0800) 833 833. To wire money within the US using a credit card (Visa, MsterCard, Discover), call ☎(800) CALL-CASH (225-5227). The rates for sending cash are generally US$10-11 cheaper than with a credit card, and the money is usually available at the place you're sending it to within an hour. To locate the nearest Western Union location, consult www.westernunion.com.

US STATE DEPARTMENT (US CITIZENS ONLY). In emergencies, US citizens can have money sent via the State Department. For US$15, they will forward money within hours to the nearest consular office, which will disburse it according to instructions. The office serves only Americans in the direst of straits abroad; non-American travelers should contact their embassies for information on wiring cash. Check with the State Department or the nearest US embassy or consulate for the quickest way to have the money sent. Contact the Overseas Citizens Service, American Citizens Services, Consular Affairs, Room 4811, US Department of State, Washington, D.C. 20520 (☎(202) 647-5225; nights, Sundays, and holidays (202) 647-4000; fax (on demand only) 647-3000; travel.state.gov).

COSTS

The cost of your trip will vary considerably, depending on where you go, how you travel, and where you stay. The single biggest cost of your trip will probably be your round-trip (return) airfare to London. Before you go, spend some time calculating a reasonable per-day budget that will meet your needs. To give you a general idea, a bare-bones day in London (camping or sleeping in hostels/guesthouses, buying food at supermarkets) would cost about US$60; a slightly more comfortable day (sleeping in hostels/guesthouses and the occasional budget hotel, eating one meal a day at a restaurant, going out at night) would run around US$90; and for a luxurious day, the sky's the limit. Also, don't forget to factor in emergency reserve funds (at least US$200) when planning how much money you'll need.

STAYING ON A BUDGET

Given that saving a few dollars a day over the course of your trip can pay for days or weeks of additional travel, the art of penny-pinching is well worth learning. Learn to take advantage of freebies: **museums** are often free once a week, and cities often host free open-air concerts and/or cultural events. You can split **accommodation** costs (in hotels and some hostels with trustworthy fellow travelers; multi-bed rooms always work out cheaper per person than singles. The same principle will also work for cutting down on the cost of **meals**. Instead of eating out, buy food in supermarkets. That said, don't go overboard; though staying within your budget is important, don't do so at the expense of your sanity or health.

TIPPING AND TAXES

Tips in restaurants are usually included in the bill, but check carefully. If not included, you should tip 10-15%. Tipping bartenders is not expected, and rarely practiced. Tour guides and theater ushers are also never tipped. Taxi drivers should receive a 10% tip and bellhops and chambermaids usually expect somewhere between £1 and £3.

Britain charges **value-added tax (VAT)**, a national sales tax of 17.5%, on everything except books, medicine, food, and children's clothes. All prices in the UK include VAT. The prices stated in *Let's Go* include VAT unless otherwise specified. Visitors to the UK can get a VAT refund through the **Retail Export Scheme**. Ask the shopkeeper for the appro priate form, which immigration officials will sign and stamp when you leave the country. Not all shops participate in the scheme and of those that do, many have a purchase minimum of $50-100 before they offer refunds, and often, an administrative fee will be deducted from your refund. At the airport, look for the TaxFree Refund desk. It is easiest to keep purchased items in a carry-on, as an officer will inspect your baggage to make sure the items in question are leaving the country, after which your forms will be validated. At peak hours, this additional process may add as much as an hour to your airport time. Once you have checked in and passed security, you may mail your refund directly from the airport or wait until you get home. To obtain the refund by check or credit card, send the form back in the envelope provided and the shop-keeper will then send your refund; note, however, that a service charge will be deducted from your refund. You must leave the country within three months of your purchase to claim a VAT refund.

SAFETY AND SECURITY
◼ THE NATIONAL EMERGENCY NUMBER IN THE UK IS 999.

As big cities go, London is relatively safe and even the bobbies (police) are typically unarmed. Violent crime is rare, but **pickpocketing** and **bagsnatching,** particularly in heavily touristed areas and the Underground, is fairly common. Tube stops will post visible warnings if thieves have been particularly active (see **Women Travelers,** p. 233). It's hard to wander into questionable neighborhoods—these areas, in parts of Hackney, Tottenham, and South London, lie well away from central London.

PERSONAL SAFETY

BLENDING IN. Never admit that you're traveling alone. When walking at night, stick to busy, well-lit streets and avoid dark alleyways. Do not attempt to cross through parks, parking lots, or other large, deserted areas. Familiarize yourself with your surroundings before setting out; if you must check a map on the street, duck into a cafe or shop (but don't forget that even Londoners rely on their A-Z maps). Look for children playing, women walking in the open, and other signs of an active community. If you feel uncomfortable, leave as quickly and directly as you can.

EXPLORING. Extra vigilance is always wise. Carry a whistle on your keychain or a rape alarm and don't hesitate to use them in an emergency. Guns, mace, and pepper sprays are illegal in Britain. If you are need of help, **dial 999** on any phone to reach police, fire or ambulance. Think twice about entering potentially problematic neighborhoods like Hackney, Tottenham, and South London, particularly at night.

For the love of god, look right! British drivers travel on the left side of the road, meaning that they'll be speeding towards pedestrians from a different direction than many visitors will expect. It's a testament to the competence of London drivers that more tourists aren't killed by stepping unwittingly into traffic. Don't go out like a sucker—signs at your feet tell you which way to look. Obey them.

𝑖 ESSENTIAL
INFORMATION

PERSONAL SAFETY

The following government offices provide travel information and advisories by telephone or on their websites:

Australian Department of Foreign Affairs and Trade. ☎ (2) 6261 1111. www.dfat.gov.au.

Canadian Department of Foreign Affairs and International Trade (DFAIT). ☎ 800-267-8376 or (613) 944-4000 from Ottawa. www.dfait-maeci.gc.ca. Call for their free booklet, *Bon Voyage...But.*

United Kingdom Foreign and Commonwealth Office. ☎ (020) 7238 4503. www.fco.gov.uk.

United States Department of State. ☎ (202) 647-5225. travel.state.gov. For their publication *A Safe Trip Abroad,* call (202) 512-1800.

ELECTRIC CURRENT

In London, electric current is 240 volts AC, enough to fry any 110V North American appliance. 240V appliances don't like 110V current, either. Visit a hardware store for an adapter (which changes the shape of the plug) and a converter (which changes the voltage). Don't make the mistake of using only an adapter (unless appliance instructions explicitly state otherwise).

SELF-DEFENSE COURSES. There is no sure-fire set of precautions that will protect you from the situations you might encounter when you travel. A good self-defense course will give you more concrete ways to react to different types of aggression. **Impact, Prepare,** and **Model Mugging** can refer you to local self-defense courses in the United States (☎ 800-345-5425). Workshop (2-3 hours) start at US$50; full courses run US$350-500.

TERRORISM. Though there has been a history of violent activity tied to the political situation in Northern Ireland, the main paramilitary groups as of spring 1999 were observing a cease-fire, and things are relatively quiet in London. Nevertheless, vigilance is always called for. If you see an abandoned suitcase or package, always notify the nearest law enforcement officer. The Underground is often delayed due to suspicious objects. Issues closer to London have also motivated bombings. During spring 1999, a nail bomb exploded in a Brixton market, wounding 39. The attack was said to have been racially motivated. Soho's Admiral Duncan Pub, a popular gay spot, was also attacked.

FINANCIAL SECURITY

There are a few steps you can take to minimize the financial risk associated with traveling. First, **don't put a wallet with money in your back pocket,** and don't keep your valuables (money, important documents) in one place. Carry as little as possible and avoid counting money in public. If you carry a purse, buy a sturdy one with a secure clasp and carry it crosswise on the side away from the street with the clasp against you. Second, **use a money belt**—it's the best way to carry cash, traveler's checks, and credit/cash cards. Third, **keep a small cash reserve separate from your primary stash.** This should entail about $35 sewn into or stored in the depths of your pack, along with your traveler's check numbers and important photocopies. Fourth, **bring as little with you on your trip as possible.** Leave expensive watches, jewelry, cameras, and electronic equipment at home; chances are you'd break them, lose them, or get sick of lugging them around anyway. And finally, buy a few combination **padlocks** to secure your belongings either in your pack—which you should **never leave unattended**—or in a hostel or train station locker.

DRUGS AND ALCOHOL

A meek "I didn't know it was illegal" will not suffice. Penalties for possession, trafficking or use of illegal drugs are incredibly severe, and you may face being expelled or imprisoned if caught. If you carry **prescription drugs,** it is vital to have a copy of the prescriptions and a note from a doctor. If you buy illegal drugs, you don't always know what you're getting, especially if you buy in a club. Visitors should **avoid public drunkenness;** not only is it unseemly, it's against the law.

HEALTH

For listings of **hospitals, emergency rooms,** and **medical hotlines** in London, see the **Service Directory,** p. 271.

Preparation can help minimize the likelihood of getting sick. For minor health problems, you may want to bring motion sickness remedy, sunscreen, tweezers, aspirin or other pain killers, antibiotic cream, and other necessities. **Contact lens** wearers should bring an extra pair, a copy of the prescription, a pair of glasses, extra solution, and eyedrops. Bear in mind that you can purchase most of these products in London, but if you need a prescription, bring it with you

In your **passport,** write the names of any people you wish to be contacted in case of a medical emergency, and also list any **allergies** or medical conditions you would want doctors to be aware of. Allergy sufferers might want to obtain a full supply of any necessary medication before the trip. Carry up-to-date, legible prescriptions or a statement from your doctor stating the medication's trade name, manufacturer, chemical name, and dosage. While traveling, keep all medication with you in your carry-on bags.

Despite London's foggy reputation, during the summer **sunburn** and **heat exhaustion** are possible even on cloudy days. Drinking plenty of clear fluids will help you stay hydrated. If you're prone to sunburn, apply sunscreen liberally and often to avoid burns.

MEDICAL ASSISTANCE

Medical aid is readily available and of the quality you would expect in a major Western European city. For minor ailments, **chemists** (drugstores) are plentiful although generally not open late. Individual chemists can often be recognized by the green cross hanging outside the store; branches of the **Boots** chain can be found in most neighborhoods. If you need urgent medical attention, most large hospitals have **24hr. Emergency Rooms** (called Casualty or Accident & Emergency); a list is given in the **Service Directory,** p. 273. In an **emergency,** call 999 from any phone to request an ambulance.

MEDICAL CONDITIONS

Americans with medical conditions (e.g. diabetes, allergies to antibiotics, epilepsy, and heart conditions) may want to obtain a stainless steel **Medic Alert** identification tag (US$35 the first year, $15 annually thereafter), which identifies the condition. Medical Alert's hotline provides vital medical information (e.g. allergies to drugs, your primary physician, next of kin) in the event of an emergency. For more information, contact the Medic Alert Foundation, 2323 Colorado Ave., Turlock, CA 95382 (☎800-825-3785; www.medicalert.org).

Diabetics can contact **Diabetes UK** (☎(0800 013 4443) for information or before traveling the **American Diabetes Association,** 1701 North Beauregard St., Alexandria, VA 22311 (☎800-232-3472; www.diabetes.org), to receive copies of the article "Travel and Diabetes" and a diabetic ID card. Those Down Under can contact **Diabetes Australia,** Churchill House, 1st fl., 218 Northbourne Ave., Braddon, ACT 2612 (☎(02) 6230 1155).

AIDS, HIV, AND STDS

Acquired Immune Deficiency Syndrome (AIDS) is a problem in the UK, just as it is around the world; estimates fix the HIV-positive percentage of adults in Britain at 0.09%. Never share needles and never have sex without using a condom. **Condoms** are available at pharmacies like Boots. Currently the UK has restrictions on **HIV positive** travelers; if you appear unwell you may be tested on entrance and a positive result may block your entrance to Britain.

WOMEN'S HEALTH

Women on oral contraceptives should bring enough to allow for possible loss or extended stays. Bring a prescription, since forms vary a good deal.

Abortion is legal in Britain (and free to British citizens on the NHS). Women who need an abortion should contact the **International Planned Parenthood Federation,** European Regional Office, Regent's College Inner Circle, Regent's Park, NW1 (☎7487 7900; www.ippf.org), for more information.

For more general care, the **Audre Lorde Clinic,** at the Ambrose King Centre, Royal London Hospital, E1 (☎7377 7312; Tube: Whitechapel), and the **Bernhard Clinic,** West London Centre for Sexual Health, Charing Cross Hospital, Fulham Palace Rd, W6 (☎8846 1576; Tube: Baron's Court or Hammersmith), are female-staffed facilities offering smear tests, screenings for HIV, STDs, and infections, breast exams, advice, and counseling for lesbians. (Audre Lorde open F 10am-5pm; Bernhard open W 2-4:30pm and 5:30-6.30pm; call for appointments M-F.)

INSURANCE

Travel insurance generally covers four basic areas: medical/health problems, property loss, trip cancellation/interruption, and emergency evacuation. Although your regular insurance policies may well extend to travel-related accidents, you may consider purchasing travel insurance if the cost of potential trip cancellation/interruption is greater than you can absorb.

Medical insurance (especially university policies) often covers costs incurred abroad; check with your provider. **Medicare does not cover foreign travel.** Canadians are protected by their home province's health insurance plan for up to 90 days after leaving the country; check with the provincial Ministry of Health or Health Plan Headquarters for details. Australians traveling in the UK are entitled to many of the services that they would receive at home as part of the Reciprocal Health Care Agreement. **Homeowners' insurance** often covers theft during travel and loss of travel documents (passport, plane ticket, railpass, etc.) up to US\$500.

ISIC and **ITIC** provide basic insurance benefits, including US\$100 per day of in-hospital sickness for a maximum of 60 days, US\$3000 of accident-related medical reimbursement, and US\$25,000 for emergency medical transport (see **Identification**, p. 214). Cardholders have access to a toll-free 24-hour helpline (☎ (020) 8666 9205) whose staff can provide assistance in medical, legal, and financial emergencies overseas **American Express** (☎ 800-528-4800) grants most cardholders automatic car rental insurance (collision and theft, but not liability) and travel accident coverage of US\$100,000 on flight purchases made with the card.

Most student travel agencies (see p. 214) will supplement your basic insurance coverage. For more information, contact **Globalcare Travel Insurance** (☎ 800-821-2488) in the US or Canada or **CIC Insurance** (☎ (02) 9202 8000) in Australia.

INSURANCE PROVIDERS. Council and **STA** (see p. 227) offer a range of plans that can supplement your basic coverage. Other private insurance providers in the **US** and **Canada** include: **Access America** (☎ (800) 284-8300); **Berkely Group/Carefree Travel Insurance** (☎ (800) 323-3149; www.berkely.com); **Globalcare Travel Insurance** (☎ (800) 821-2488; www.globalcare-cocco.com); and **Travel Assistance International** (☎ (800) 821-2828; www.worldwide-assistance.com).

KEEPING IN TOUCH
MAIL

SENDING MAIL TO AND RECEIVING MAIL IN LONDON. Airmail letters under 1oz. between North America and London take 3 to 5 days and cost US\$1 or CDN\$0.95. Allow at least 5 to 7 days from Australia (postage AUS\$1.20 for small letters up to 20 grams, AUS\$1.50 for large letters up to 20 grams). Envelopes should be marked "air mail" or "par avion" to avoid having letters sent by sea. Sending by sea **(surface mail)** is the cheapest and slowest way to send mail. It takes one to three months to cross the Atlantic and two to four to cross the Pacific. When ordering books and materials from abroad, always include one or two **International Reply Coupons (IRCs)**—a way of providing the postage to cover delivery. IRCs should be available from your local post office (60p or US\$1.05). The characters before the space in British **postal codes** refer to the postal district; the characters after identify the exact street or building. London encompasses several postal districts (there are at least five King Streets, for instance). To get exact postal codes call ☎ (0345) 223344 or check www.royalmail.co.uk.

SENDING MAIL HOME FROM BRITAIN. The **Royal Mail** (☎ (0345) 223344; www.royalmail.co.uk) runs Britain's post offices. **Aerogrammes,** printed sheets that fold into envelopes and travel via airmail, are available at post offices. Most post offices refuse to send aerogrammes with enclosures. Airmail from the UK averages 5 to 7 days.

To send a postcard to an international destination from the UK costs 38p, an airmail letter up to 10g is 44p, and from 10-20g costs 64p.

TELEPHONES

The London **area code** is **020**. This new phone code was instituted last year, but you may still see the old 0171 and 0181 phone codes on store fronts.

CALLING HOME FROM BRITAIN

A **calling card** allows you to charge all your calls to an account. **To obtain a calling card** from your national telecommunications service before you leave home, contact the appropriate company: **USA: AT&T** (☎ 888-288-4685); **Sprint** (☎ 800-877-4646); or **MCI** (☎ 800-444-4141); from abroad dial the country's MCI access number); **Canada:** Bell Canada **Canada Direct** (☎ 800-565-4708); **Ireland:** Telecom Éireann **Ireland Direct** (☎ (800) 250 250); **Australia:** Telstra **Australia Direct** (☎ 13 22 00); **New Zealand:** Telecom New Zealand (☎ (800) 000 000); **South Africa: Telkom South Africa** (☎ 09 03).

The international rates for dialing directly are often higher than calling cards. If you dial **direct**, you must first insert the appropriate amount of money, a BT phonecard, dial 00 (the international access code in Britain), then dial the country code and number of your home. BT (British Telecom) publishes a simple pamphlet about how to make international calls from any phone (available at tourist offices and most hotels). **Country codes** include: Australia 61; Ireland 353; New Zealand 64; South Africa 27; US and Canada 1. Many BT phone booths have country codes listed inside. Phone rates tend to be highest in the day, lower after 6pm, and lowest on Sunday and late at night.

Many news agents in London sell **prepaid international phonecards,** such as those offered by Swiftlink. These carry a certain amount of phone time and are usually the cheapest way to make international phone calls. However, they may carry a minimum charge per call, which makes quick calls less cost-effective. To make a phone call using these cards, dial the toll-free access number from any phone, and follow the instructions on the card. Stores such as **Call Shop** offer cheap international calls from their booths, and can be found in parts of London with large numbers of tourists and/or immigrants.

The expensive alternative to dialing direct or using a calling card is using an international operator to place a **collect call.** The **international operator** in Britain can be reached by dialing **155.** Alternatively, dialing the appropriate service provider will connect you to an operator from your home nation who will usually place a (pricey) collect call for you even if you don't have one of their calling cards.

CALLING WITHIN THE UK

Certain British **phone codes** should be noted. **Premium rate calls**—calls that cost about 50p a minute—can be identified by their 0891 phone code, while **toll-free** numbers have either a 0500 or an 0800 code. Calls to the 0345 and 0845 codes charged at the **local call rate,** while the 08705 and 0990 phone codes are charged at the **national call rate.** Your new-found London friends might give you their **mobile phone** (cellphone) number, recognizable by the phone codes, which begin with 077, 078, and 069. Calling a mobile phone is significantly more expensive than placing a regular call. Call **192** for directory inquiries.

PUBLIC PHONES IN BRITAIN. Public pay phones in Britain are mostly run by British Telecom (BT), recognizable by the piper logo. Many public phones in the UK now only accept **phonecards,** available at any convenience store or chemist. The BT phonecard (£2-20), is probably the most useful one to buy. It's still a good idea to carry some change, since non-BT phones will not accept the phonecards.

Public phones charge 10p for local calls, and don't accept 1p, 2p, or 5p coins. The dial tone is a continuous purring sound; a repeated double-purr means the line is ringing. A series of harsh beeps will warn you to insert more money when your time is up. For the rest of the call, the digital display ticks off your credit in suspenseful 1p increments. Once you

---

i **ESSENTIAL**
INFORMATION

GENERAL DELIVERY (POSTE RESTANTE)

If you have no fixed address while in London, you can receive mail through the British post offices' **Poste Restante** (General Delivery) service. If you were sending a letter to John Smith in London, you'd mark the envelope John SMITH, Poste Restante, London SW1, United Kingdom. The mail will go to a special desk in the central post office unless you specify a post office by street address or postal code.

When in London, send mail to Poste Restante, Trafalgar Square Post Office, 24-28 William IV St., WC2N 4DL (☎ 7484 9304; Tube: Charing Cross; M-F 8am-8pm, Sa 9am-8pm)—all general delivery to unspecified post offices ends up here. Post offices will *not* accept FedEx or other non-postal services. When picking up your mail, bring a form of photo ID, preferably a passport. There is generally no surcharge unless the sender has not paid enough postage. Post offices usually hold *Poste Restante* mail for a month.

Call the USA

"feel free to call"

1 800 COLLECT

1-800-COLLECT

When in Ireland
Dial: 1-800-COLLECT (265 5328)

When in N. Ireland, UK & Europe
Dial: 00-800-COLLECT USA (265 5328 872)

Member of
Dublin Tourism

Australia	0011 800 265 5328 872
Finland	990 800 265 5328 872
Hong Kong	001 800 265 5328 872
Israel	014 800 265 5328 872
Japan	0061 800 265 5328 872
New Zealand	0011 800 265 5328 872

hang up, your remaining phonecard credit is rounded down to the nearest 10p, or unused coins are returned. Payphones do *not* return change—if you only make 22p worth of calls using a 50p coin, the remaining 28p is gone once you put the receiver down. Phone rates tend to be highest in the morning, lower in the evening, and lowest on Sunday and late at night.

EMAIL AND INTERNET

The UK is one of the world's most on-line countries, and cybercafes are fairly easy to find in London. The popular **EasyEverything** cybercafes charge a miniscule £1 for 1-2 hours, and many cybercafes are beginning to follow suit. Most cybercafes charge only for time used, not the whole hour. *Let's Go: London* lists cybercafes in the **Service Directory,** p. 271. Many hostels are also starting to offer email services to their residents, charging about the same rates; where applicable *Let's Go* lists such services.

GETTING THERE BY PLANE

When it comes to airfare, a little effort can save you a bundle. Tickets bought from consolidators and standby seating are good deals, but last-minute specials, airfare wars, and charter flights often beat these fares. The key is to hunt around, be flexible, and be persistent about discounts. Seniors and those under 26 should never pay full price for a ticket.

DETAILS AND TIPS

Timing: Airfares to London peak between June and mid-Sept. and at Christmas is also an expensive time to travel. Midweek (M-Th morning) round-trip flights run US$40-50 cheaper than weekend flights.

Boarding: Pick up tickets for international flights well in advance of the departure date, and confirm by phone within 72 hours of departure. Most airlines require that passengers arrive at the airport at least two hours before departure.

Fares: Student tickets from the **US** cost up to US$500 during the offseason and up to US$700 during the summer.

BUDGET AND STUDENT TRAVEL AGENCIES

Students and under-26s holding **ISIC and IYTC cards** (see **Identification,** p. 214), respectively, qualify for big discounts from student travel agencies. Most flights from budget agencies are on major airlines, but in peak season some may sell seats on charter flights.

Campus/Usit Youth and Student Travel (www.usitcampus.co.uk). In UK call (0870) 240 1010; in North America call 7730 21 01; worldwide call 7730 81 11. Offices include: 19-21 Aston Quay, O'Connell Bridge, **Dublin** 2 (☎(01) 677-8117; fax 679-8833); 52 Grosvenor Gardens, **London** SW1W OAG; New York Student Center, 895 Amsterdam Ave., **New York,** NY, 10025 (☎(212) 663-5435; email usitny@aol.com). Additional offices in Cork, Galway, Limerick, Waterford, Coleraine, Derry, Belfast, and Greece.

Council Travel (www.counciltravel.com). US offices include: Emory Village, 1561 N. Decatur Rd., **Atlanta,** GA 30307 (☎(404) 377-

9997); 273 Newbury St., **Boston,** MA 02116 (☎(617) 266-1926); 1160 N. State St., **Chicago,** IL 60610 (☎(312) 951-0585); 10904 Lindbrook Dr., **Los Angeles,** CA 90024 (☎(310) 208-3551); 205 E. 42nd St., **New York,** NY 10017 (☎(212) 822-2700); 530 Bush St., **San Francisco,** CA 94108 (☎(415) 421-3473); 1314 NE 43rd St. #210, **Seattle,** WA 98105 (☎(206) 632-2448); 3300 M St. NW, **Washington, D.C.** 20007 (☎(202) 337-6464). **For US cities not listed,** call 800-2-COUNCIL (226-8624). Also 28A Poland St. (Oxford Circus), **London,** W1V 3DB (☎(0171) 287 3337), **Paris** (☎(144) 41 &% 89), and **Munich** (☎(089) 39 50 22).

CTS Travel, 44 Goodge St., W1 (☎7636 0031; fax 7637 5328; email ctsinfo@ctstravel.com.uk).

STA Travel, 6560 Scottsdale Rd. #F100, Scottsdale, AZ 85253 (☎800-777-0112 fax (602) 922-0793; www.sta-travel.com). US offices include: 297 Newbury Street, **Boston,** MA 02115 (☎(617) 266-6014); 429 S. Dearborn St., **Chicago,** IL 60605 (☎(312) 786-9050); 7202 Melrose Ave., **Los Angeles,** CA 90046 (☎(323) 934-8722); 10 Downing St., **New York,** NY 10014 (☎(212) 627-3111); 4341 University Way NE, **Seattle,** WA 98105 (☎(206) 633-5000); 2401 Pennsylvania Ave., Ste. G, **Washington, D.C.** 20037 (☎(202) 887-0912); 51 Grant Ave., **San Francisco,** CA 94108 (☎(415) 391-8407). In the UK, 6 Wrights Ln., **London** W8 6TA (☎7938 47 11 for North American travel). In New Zealand, 10 High St., **Auckland** (☎(09) 309 04 58). In Australia, 222 Faraday St., **Melbourne** VIC 3053 (☎(03) 9349 2411).

Travel CUTS (Canadian Universities Travel Services Limited), 187 College St., Toronto, Ont. M5T 1P7 (☎(416) 979-2406; fax 979-8167; www.travelcuts.com). 40 offices in Canada. Also in the UK, 295-A Regent St., **London** W1R 7YA (☎(0171) 255 19 44).

Wasteels, Victoria Station, London, UK SW1V 1JT (☎7834 70 66; fax 630 76 28; www.wasteels.dk/uk). Sells BIJ tickets, which are discounted (30-45% off regular fare) 2nd class international tickets with unlimited stopovers for the under 26; sold only in Europe.

COMMERCIAL AIRLINES

The commercial airlines' lowest regular offer is the **APEX** (Advance Purchase Excursion) fare, which provides confirmed reservations and allows "open-jaw" tickets. Generally, reservations must be made 7 to 21 days in advance, with 7- to 14-day minimum and up to 90-day maximum-stay limits, and hefty cancellation and change penalties (fees rise in summer). Book peak-season APEX fares early, since by May you will have a hard time getting the departure date you want. Popular carriers to London include:

Air New Zealand: NZ ☎0800 737 000, AU ☎13 24 76; www.nzair.co.nz.
American Airlines: US ☎800-433-7300; www.americanair.com.
British Airways: US ☎800-247-9297, AU (02) 9258 3300), NZ (09) 356 8690; www.british-airways.com.
Canadian Airlines: CA ☎800-665-117; www.cdnair.ca.
Continental Airlines: US ☎800-525-0280; www.continental.com.
Delta Airlines: US ☎800-221-1212; www.delta-air.com.
Qantas: Australia ☎13 1211; NZ ☎0800 808 767; www.quantas.com.au.
South African Airlines: www.saa.co.za.
United Airlines: ☎800 241 6522; www.ual.com.
Virgin Atlantic: ☎800-862-8621; www.fly.virgin.com.

DISCOUNT AIRLINES

If you're traveling from Europe and can book in advance (sometimes *way* in advance) and/or travel at odd hours, the popular new **discount airlines** may be the least costly way of arriving in London. They also allow for cheap quick jaunts back onto the continent. Remember that saving money often means cutting back on frills—food and drinks don't always come free on these flights. Most offer return flights for US$100-200 depending on destination and date of travel. The following airlines offer cheap fares to a variety of European destinations:

British Midland (☎(0870) 607 0555 for reservations; US ☎800 788 0555; www.britishmidland.com)

easyJet (☎(0870) 600 0000; www.easyjet.com)

go (☎(08456) 054 321; internationally (44) 1279 666388; www.go-fly.com)

Ryanair (☎(0541) 569569; www.ryanair.ie)

Virgin Express (UK ☎7744 0004; www.virgin-express.com)

OTHER CHEAP ALTERNATIVES

AIR COURIER FLIGHTS. Couriers help transport cargo on international flights by guaranteeing delivery of the baggage claim slips from the company to a representative overseas. Generally, couriers must travel light and deal with complex restrictions on their flight. Most are round-trip only with short fixed-length stays (usually one week) and a limit of one ticket per issue. Most flights also operate only out of major cities. Generally, you must be over 21 (in some cases 18), have a valid passport, and procure a visa, if necessary. Groups such as the **Air Courier Association** (US ☎800-282-1202; www.aircourier.org) and the **International Association of Air Travel Couriers,** 220 South Dixie Hwy., P.O. Box 1349, Lake Worth, FL 33460 (US ☎(561) 582-8320; email iaatc@courier.org; www.courier.org) provide members with lists of opportunities and courier brokers worldwide for an annual fee. For more information, consult *Air Courier Bargains*, by Kelly Monaghan (US$15) or the *Courier Air Travel Handbook* by Mark Field (US$13).

CHARTER FLIGHTS. Charters are flights a tour operator contracts with an airline to fly extra loads of passengers during peak season. Charters can sometimes be cheaper than flights on scheduled airlines, some operate nonstop, and restrictions on minimum advance-purchase and minimum stay are more lenient. However, charter flights fly less frequently than major airlines, make refunds difficult, and are almost always full. Schedules and itineraries may also change or be cancelled at the last moment without a full refund, and check-in, boarding, and baggage claim are often much slower. **Discount clubs** and **fare brokers** offer members savings on last-minute charter and tour deals. Study their contracts closely; you don't want to end up with an unwanted layover. **Travelers Advantage,** Stamford, CT (☎800-548-1116; www.travelersadvantage.com; US$60 annual fee includes newsletters, and cheap flight directories) specializes in European travel.

STANDBY FLIGHTS. To travel standby, you will need considerable flexibility in the dates and cities of your arrival and departure. Companies that specialize in standby flights don't sell tickets but rather the promise that you will get to your destination (or near your destination) within a certain window of time (anywhere from 1-5 days). It is difficult to receive refunds, and clients' vouchers will not be honored when an airline fails to receive payment in time. **Airhitch,** 2641 Broadway, 3rd Fl., New York, NY 10025 (☎800-326-2009 or (212) 864-2000; fax 864-5489; www.airhitch.org); also in Los Angeles, CA (☎(310) 726-5000); Paris (☎01 47 00 16 30); and Amsterdam (☎20 626 32 20). Flights to Europe cost US$159 each way when departing from the Northeast.

TICKET CONSOLIDATORS. Ticket consolidators, or **"bucket shops,"** buy unsold tickets in bulk from commercial airlines and sell them at discounted rates. The best place to look is in the Sunday travel section of any major newspaper, where many bucket shops place tiny ads. Call quickly, as availability is typically extremely limited. Not all bucket shops are reliable establishments, so insist on a receipt that gives full details of restrictions, refunds, and tickets, and pay by credit card. For more information, check the website **Consolidators FAQ** (www.travel-library.com/air-travel/consolidators.html).

BY TRAIN

The **Eurostar** (In the UK, ☎(0990) 186186 or (01233) 617 575; in the US, 800 387 6782; www.eurostar.com) speeds passengers to and from Paris, Disneyland Paris, Brussels, Lille, Calais, and Bourg-St.-Maurice to **Waterloo station in London** (Tube: Waterloo). Major railpasses (such as Eurail and Britrail) entitle you to discounts. Trains to and from Paris leave every hour Monday-Saturday from 5am-8pm and Sundays 7am-8pm for their 3 hour trip. Special coaches are equipped for wheelchair-bound customers and reduced fares are available for both the disabled and their escorts. Fares are not cheap (£169 for a roundtrip weekender fare, £249 for standard). Check for student discounts.

BRITRAIL PASSES

If you plan to travel a great deal on trains within Britain, the **BritRail Pass** (www.britrail.com) can be a good buy. Eurail passes are *not* valid in Britain, but there's often a discount on BritRail passes if you purchase the two simultaneously. BritRail passes are only available outside Britain; *you must buy them before traveling to Britain.* They allow unlimited train travel in England, Wales, and Scotland, regardless of which company is operating the trains, but do not allow free travel in Northern Ireland, or on the Eurostar.

BRITRAIL PASS PRICES	8 days	15 days	22 days	1 month
Britrail Classic 1st class	US$400	US$600	US$760	US$900
Britrail Classic Standard (2nd) class	US$265	US$400	US$505	US$600
Youth Britrail Classic (standard class only)	US$215	US$280	US$355	US$420
Senior Britrail Classic (first class only)	US$340	US$510	US$645	US$765

BRITRAIL DISTRIBUTORS

Passes and additional details on discounts are available from most travel agents (see p. 227). The distributors listed below will either sell you passes directly, or tell you the nearest place to buy passes.

Australia: Rail Plus, Level 3, 459 Little Collins Street, Melbourne, Victoria 3000 (☎(09) 9642 8644; fax 9642 8403; www.railplus.com; email info@railplus.com.au). **Concorde International Travel** (Rail Tickets), Level 9, 310 King Street, Melbourne Victoria 3000 (☎(03) 9920 3833; fax 9920 3822; email: railpass@railtickets.com.au).

Canada and the US: Rail Europe, 226 Westchester Ave., White Plains, NY 10604 (☎800-438-7245; www.raileurope.com), is the North American distributor of BritRail products. Or try **Rail Pass Express** (☎800-722-7151; www.railpass.com).

Ireland: BritRail Ireland, 123 Lower Baggot Street, Dublin 2 (☎(01) 661 2866; fax 661 8536).

New Zealand: Holiday Shoppe (☎0800 72 94 35) or **Budget Travel** (☎0800 808 040).

South Africa: World Travel Agency, (☎(021) 252470; fax 21 217868),

BY BUS

Long-distance buses (known as **coaches** in the UK) arrive in London at **Victoria Coach Station,** 164 Buckingham Palace Rd. SW1 (☎7730 3466; Tube: Victoria). **National Express** (☎(08705) 808080; www.nationalexpress.co.uk), is the principal operator of long-distance coach services from Britain. **Eurolines** (☎(01582) 404511) runs coaches into Victoria from Europe.

SPECIFIC CONCERNS

If you need confidential help with emotional problems, the national **Samaritans** phone number in the UK is (0345) 909090. They can also refer you to the appropriate sources.

WOMEN TRAVELERS

London is one of the world's best destinations for women travelers. Of course, women exploring any area on their own face additional safety concerns. Use common sense and don't be afraid to trust your instincts: if you'd feel better somewhere else, move on.

You may want to consider staying in hostels that offer single rooms that lock from the inside or religious organizations that offer rooms for women only. Try and find accommodation within ten minutes walk of a tube station and avoid empty carriages when using the underground at night. **Lady Cabs** (☎254 3501) is a London-based women's taxi service (drivers and passengers are female; open M-Th 8am-midnight, F 8am-1am, Sa 9am-1am, Su 10am-5pm).

When traveling, always carry extra money for a phone call, bus, or taxi. **Hitching** is never safe for lone women, or even for two women traveling together. Look as if you know where you're going (even when you don't) and approach older women or couples for directions if you're lost or feel uncomfortable.

Women may face some specific health concerns when traveling (see **Women's Health,** p. 223). **London Women's Aid** (☎7392 2092) offers 24-hour support for victims of violence, and the **Rape and Sexual Abuse Support Center** (☎8239 1122) hotline is answered from Monday to Friday noon-2:30pm and 7-9:30pm, weekends and bank holidays 2:30-5pm. The **Audre Lorde Clinic,** at the Ambrose King Centre, Royal London Hospital, E1 (☎377 7312; tube: Whitechapel), and the **Bernhard Clinic,** West London Centre for Sexual Health, Charing Cross Hospital, Fulham Palace Rd., W6 (☎(8) 846 1576; tube: Baron's Court or Hammersmith), are female-staffed facilities offering screenings for STDs and vaginal infections, counseling for lesbians, breast exams, HIV tests, and advice. (Audre Lorde open F 10am-5pm, Bernhard open W 2-4:30pm, and 5:30-6.30pm; call for appointments M-F.) A self-defense course will not only prepare you for a potential attack, but may raise your level of awareness of your surroundings as well as your confidence.

FURTHER READING

A Journey of One's Own: Uncommon Advice for the Independent Woman Traveler, Thalia Zepatos. Eighth Mountain Press (US$17).

Adventures in Good Company: The Complete Guide to Women's Tours and Outdoor Trips, Thalia Zepatos. Eighth Mountain Press (US$7).

Active Women Vacation Guide, Evelyn Kaye. Blue Panda Publications (US$18).

BISEXUAL, GAY, AND LESBIAN TRAVELERS

See **Service Directory**, p. 273, for London-specific information. Listed below are organizations which offer materials addressing **general concerns** about gay and lesbian travel.

Gay's the Word, 66 Marchmont St, London WC1N 1AB (☎7278 7654; sales@gaystheword.co.uk; www.gaystheword.co.uk). The largest gay and lesbian bookshop in the UK, with both fiction and non-fiction titles. Mail-order service available.

Giovanni's Room, 345 S. 12th St., Philadelphia, PA 19107, USA (☎(215) 923-2960; fax 923-0813; www.queerbooks.com). An international lesbian/feminist and gay bookstore with mail-order service (carries many of the publications listed below).

International Gay and Lesbian Travel Association, 4331 N. Federal Hwy., #304, Fort Lauderdale, FL 33308, USA (☎(954) 776-2626; fax 776-3303; www.iglta.com). An organization of over 1350 companies serving gay and lesbian travelers worldwide.

International Lesbian and Gay Association (ILGA), 81 rue Marché-au-Charbon, B-1000 Brussels, Belgium (tel./fax +32 (2) 502 24 71; www.ilga.org). Not a travel service; provides political information, such as homosexuality laws of individual countries.

FURTHER READING

Spartacus International Gay Guide. Bruno Gmunder Verlag. (US$33).

Damron Men's Guide, Damron's Accommodations. Damron Travel Guides (US$14-19). For more info, call US ☎(415) 255-0404 or (800) 462-6654 or check their website (www.damron.com).

Ferrari Guides' Gay Travel A to Z, Ferrari Guides' Men's Travel in Your Pocket, Ferrari Guides' Women's Travel in Your Pocket, and *Ferrari Guides' Inn Places.* Ferrari Guides (US$14-16). For more info, call (602) 863-2408 or (800) 962-2912 or try www.q-net.com.

SOLO TRAVELERS

There are many benefits to traveling alone, among them greater independence and challenge. As a lone traveler, you have greater opportunity to interact with the residents of the region you're visiting. On the other hand, solo travelers are more vulnerable targets of harassment and theft. Lone travelers need to be well-organized and look confident at all times. Try not to stand out as a tourist, and be careful in deserted or very crowded areas. Maintain regular contact with someone at home who knows your itinerary.

A number of organizations supply information for solo travelers, and others find travel companions for those who don't want to go alone. Two are *Traveling Solo*, Eleanor Berman (Globe Pequot; US$17); and *The Single Traveler Newsletter*, P.O. Box 682, Ross, CA 94957 (☎(415) 389-0227; 6 issues US$29).

OLDER TRAVELERS

A wide array of discounts (called **concessions**) are available with proof of senior citizen status. These are often denoted **"OAP"** (old-age pensioners). Although descent into the underground is usually by escalator or elevator, most tube stations involve some stairclimbing. However, most of London's major attractions can be seen from the top of a double-decker tour bus, and most of these allow you to get on and off as often as you like. A useful resource while traveling in Britain is **Age Concern** (☎8765 7200; 9:15am-5:15pm M-F). Two British magazines targeted to the growing older population are *Yours*, brimming with nostalgia, and Richard Ingrams' hilariously dour *The Oldie*.

Agencies for senior group travel are growing in enrollment and popularity. These are only a few:

Travel Companion Exchange, P.O. Box 833, Amityville, NY 11701, USA (☎(631) 454-0880 or 800-392-1256; www.whytravelalone.com; membership US$48).

Solo Travel Network, P.O. Box 29088, Delamont RPO, Vancouver, BC V6J 5C2 (☎/fax (604) 737-7791; www.cstn.org; membership US$25-35).

Elderhostel, 75 Federal St., Boston, MA 02110, USA (☎(617) 426-7788 or (877) 426-2166; email registration@elderhostel.org; www.elderhostel.org). Organizes 1- to 4-week "educational adventures" in London on varied subjects for those 55+.

The Mature Traveler, P.O. Box 50400, Reno, NV 89513, USA (☎(775) 786-7419, credit card orders (800) 460-6676). Deals, discounts, and packages for the 50+ traveler. Subscription $30.

TRAVELERS WITH DISABILITIES

A phenomenally useful guide to London for people with any sort of mobility impairment is Couch's *Access in London*, an in-depth guide to accommodations, transport, and accessibility. (Order from Access Project, 39 Bradley Gardens, West Ealing, London W13 8HE. £7.95 donation.) Another excellent resource is *Tripscope* (☎8994 9294; fax 8994 3618; email tripscope@cableinet.co.uk.), a not-for-profit agency that provides excellent, free advice and helpful phone numbers for travel throughout the UK. *London For All* is a booklet on transport, tours, and hotels published by the London Tourist Board and available at Tourist Information Centres.

Those with disabilities should inform airlines and hotels of their disabilities when making arrangements for travel; some time may be needed to prepare special accommodations. Call ahead to restaurants, hotels, parks, and other facilities to find out about the existence of ramps, the widths of doors, the dimensions of elevators, etc. Britain has strict quarantine regulations on animals entering the country to avoid rabies; **guide dogs (seeing-eye dogs)** fall under the new PETS regulations (p. 216); guide dogs coming from EU countries, Australia and New Zealand can avoid quarantine by being microchipped, vaccinated, bloodtested, and certified against tapeworm and ticks before entering the UK. Guide dogs from all other countries will be quarantined for six months. Call the PETS helpline at (087) 0241 1710 or consult www.maff.gov.uk/animalh/quarantine.

A resource that may make your trip to London easier is the RADAR Toilet Key, which is a key that literally opens the door to disabled loos throughout the UK. For more information, contact RADAR, 12 City Forum, 250 City Rd., London EC1V 8AF (☎7250 3222). Send £2.50 along with a letter stating your disability.

For equipment repair and hire, try **Direct Mobility Hire,** 8, Cheapside, Palmers Green N13 (☎7924 4058). Their list of products is geared toward outpatients, so it extends beyond wheelchairs, and they offer a delivery service.

The **"Arts Access"** section at the beginning of the London telephone books details special services available at theaters, cinemas, and concert halls around London. Call **Artsline,** 5 Crowndale Rd, NW1 (☎7388 2227), for entertainment accessibility information (M-F 9:30am-5:30pm). **Shape** (☎7700 8138) offers very cheap tickets to accessible arts events through a membership scheme, as well as providing transport and escorts.

GETTING AROUND LONDON

Many transportation companies in Britain are very conscientious about providing facilities and services to meet the needs of travelers with disabilities. It is strongly recommended that you notify a bus or coach company of your plans ahead of time so that they will have staff ready to assist you; most train operators require advance notice, especially for those using wheelchairs. Not all stations are accessible; write for the pamphlet *British Rail and Disabled Travelers.*

There are networks of **Mobility Buses** in outer London, which are fully wheelchair accessible and available to anyone getting on and off. One route, Bus #139, which covers central London, has **low-floor Buses,** which are accessible to those in wheelchairs and are also available to parents pushing prams. **Stationlink** coaches are fully accessible low-floor buses which run at hourly intervals along a route between the main line terminals. Another good method of transport is the **Docklands Light Railway,** which is fully wheelchair accessible, including all stations. Mobility-impaired travelers may have problems on the **Underground;** with their stairs and miles of foot tunnels, few of the ancient stations are easily navigated. The newer stations being built for the Jubilee and East London extensions will be fully wheelchair accessible. For more information on travel by Underground and bus, pick up the free *Access Around London* booklet from tourist offices and London Transport Information Centres, or by post from the Unit for Disabled Passengers (London Transport, 172 Buckingham Palace Rd, London SW1W 9TN; ☎7918 3312; fax 7918 3876). London Transport's 24-hour travel information hotline is also useful (☎7222 1234). Perhaps your best bet for traveling around central London is by black cab, most of which can accommodate wheelchairs (see **Taxicabs,** p. 28).

kids
in the city

Where to Stay with Kids

Let's Go recommends the following accommodations for families:

King's Cross/St. Pancras, 79-81 Euston Rd, N1 (☎7388 9998; fax 7388 6766; stpancras@yha.org.uk; see p. 251)

Jurys Inn, 60 Pentonville Rd., N1 (☎7282 5500; fax 7282 5511; www.jurys.com).(p. 255)

If you need some time to yourself, **Pippa Pop-Ins,** 430 Fulham Rd., SW6 (☎7385 2458; Tube: Fulham Broadway) runs a daytime nursery from Monday to Friday, taking care of your kids between 9am and 6pm (£55, including lunch and tea).

Several **car rental agencies,** such as **Wheelchair Travel** in Surrey (☎(01483) 233 640; fax (01483) 237 772; www.wheelchair-travel.co.uk; info@wheelchair-travel.co.uk) can provide hand-controlled cars, taxi service, and more.

USEFUL ORGANIZATIONS

Mobility International USA (MIUSA), P.O. Box 10767, Eugene, OR 97440, USA (☎(541) 343-1284 voice and TDD; fax 343-6812; email info@miusa.org; www.miusa.org). Sells *A World of Options: A Guide to International Educational Exchange, Community Service, and Travel for Persons with Disabilities* (US$35).

Moss Rehab Hospital Travel Information Service (☎(215) 456-9600 or (800) CALL-MOSS; email netstaff@mossresourcenet.org; www.mossresourcenet.org). An information resource on travel-related concerns for the disabled.

Society for the Advancement of Travel for the Handicapped (SATH), 347 Fifth Ave., #610, New York, NY 10016 (☎(212) 447-7284; www.sath.org). An advocacy group that publishes the quarterly travel magazine *OPEN WORLD* (free for members, US$13 for nonmembers). Also publishes a wide range of info sheets on disability travel facilitation and destinations. Annual membership US$45, students and seniors US$30.

TOUR AGENCIES

Directions Unlimited, 123 Green Ln., Bedford Hills, NY 10507, USA (☎(914) 241-1700 or (800) 533-5343; www.travel-cruises.com). Specializes in arranging individual and group vacations, tours, and cruises for the physically disabled.

The Guided Tour Inc., 7900 Old York Rd., #114B, Elkins Park, PA 19027, USA (☎(800) 783-5841 or (215) 782-1370; www.guidedtour.com). Organizes travel programs for persons with developmental and physical challenges around London.

FURTHER READING

Access in London, Gordon Couch. Cimino Publishing Group (US$12).

Resource Directory for the Disabled, Richard Neil Shrout. Facts on file (US$45).

Wheelchair Through Europe, Annie Mackin. Graphic Language Press (US ☎(760) 944-9594; niteowl@cts.com; US$13).

MINORITY TRAVELERS

It's very hard to look like a foreigner in London. The most multi-ethnic European city, it's home to dozens of languages and all major religions. As such, it's also one of the most cosmopolitan, and you should not feel threatened. That's not to say that London does not have problems with racism, only that as a traveler you should not feel its effects. There are few resources specifically oriented toward minority travelers; in cases of harassment or assault, contact the police or the **Commission for Racial Equality,** Elliot House, 10-12 Allington St., London SW1E 5EH (☎7828 7022; www.cre.gov.uk). Alternatively, the **National Council for Civil Liberties** (21 Tabard

St, SE1 4LA. Tube: Borough) gives advice on dealing with discrimination, excluding education and housing, by letter only.

TRAVELERS WITH CHILDREN

Family vacations often require that you slow your pace and always require that you plan ahead. When deciding where to stay, remember the special needs of young children; if you pick a B&B or small hotel, call ahead and make sure it's child-friendly. If you rent a car, make sure the rental company provides a car seat for younger children. Be sure that your child carries some sort of ID in case of an emergency or in case he or she gets lost.

Museums, tourist attractions, accommodations, and restaurants often offer discounts for children. Children under two generally fly for 10% of the adult airfare on international flights (this does not necessarily include a seat). International fares are usually discounted 25% for children ages two to 11. Finding a private place for **breast feeding** is often a problem while traveling, so pack accordingly. London has an endless number of activities to entertain children, from parks, farms, and zoos to museums with interactive exhibits. The London Tourist Board publishes the brochure "Where to Take Children," filled with child-friendly sights, restaurants, and services, available at any London Tourist Centre. For up-to-date information on entertainment for kids, call Kidsline (☎ 7222 8070) or the London Tourist Board's Children's Information line (☎ (0839) 123 404). Most sights and museums offer discounted family and child admission prices, and many offer special exhibits and events specifically for children.

FURTHER READING

Take Your Kids to Europe, Cynthia W. Harriman. Globe Pequot (US$17).
Have Kid, Will Travel: 101 Survival Strategies for Vacationing With Babies and Young Children, Claire and Lucille Tristram. Andrews and McMeel (US$9).
Trouble Free Travel with Children, Vicki Lansky. Book Peddlers (US$9).

DIETARY CONCERNS

Vegetarians should have no problem finding exciting cuisine, or having to explain that vegetarian means no ham. Travelers who keep **kosher** should contact synagogues in larger cities for information on kosher restaurants; your own synagogue or college Hillel should have access to lists of Jewish institutions across the nation. North London generally, and Golders Green, with a significant Orthodox community in particular are good for Kosher restaurants and grocers. **The Jewish Travel Guide** lists kosher restaurants. It is available in the UK from Vallentine-Mitchell Publishers, Newbury House 890-900, Eastern Ave, Newbury Park, Ilford, Essex, UK IG2 7HH (☎ 8599 8866; fax 8599 09 84); in the US ($16) from ISBS, 5804 NE Hassallo St, Portland, OR 97213 (☎ 800 944 6190).

For **further reading**, try *The Vegan Travel Guide: UK and Southern Ireland* (Book Publishing Co.; US$15), or *Europe on 10 Salads a Day*, Greg and Mary Jane Edwards (Mustang Publishing; US$10).

ALTERNATIVES TO TOURISM

Information on studying, working, and volunteering in London can be found in **Living in London**, p. 261. For an extensive listing of "off-the-beaten-track" and specialty travel opportunities, try the **Specialty Travel Index,** 305 San Anselmo Ave., #313, San Anselmo, CA 94960, USA (☎ (888) 624-4030 or (415) 455-1643; www.spectrav.com; US$6). **Transitions Abroad** (www.transabroad.com) publishes an on-line newsletter for work, study, and specialized travel abroad.

ADDITIONAL INFORMATION
TIME ZONES

Greenwich Mean Time (GMT), the standard by which much of the world sets its clocks, is used in Britain during the winter months; from late March to late Oct, the UK puts its clocks one hour forward onto British Summer Time. The time in London is generally 1hr. behind Paris and five hours ahead of New York.

TOURIST OFFICES

For a comprehensive list of tourist information centers in London, see **Service Directory,** p. 275. The British Tourist Authority (BTA; www.visitbritain.com) sells the **Great British Heritage Pass,** a useful pass that gets you into all National Trust, English Heritage, Historic Scotland, and CADW (Welsh Historic Monuments) properties throughout Britain (7 days US$48, 15 days $70).

Australia, Level 16, Gateway Bldg, 1 Macquarie Pl., Sydney NSW 2000 (☎(02) 9377 4400).
Canada, 111 Avenue Rd, Suite 450, Toronto M5R 3J8 (☎888-847-4885 or (416) 925-6326).
Ireland, 18/19 College Green, Dublin 2 (☎(01) 670 8000).
New Zealand, Dilworth Bldg, Suite. 305, Corner Customs and Queen St, Auckland 1 (☎(09) 303 1446).
South Africa, Lancaster Gate, Hyde Lane Manor, Hyde Park, Sandton 2196 (☎(011) 325 0343; fax 325 0344).
US, 551 Fifth Ave, Suite 701, New York, NY 10176 (☎800-462-2748 or (212) 986-2200).

BRITISH EMBASSIES AND CONSULATES

Australia, British High Commission, Commonwealth Ave., Yarralumla, Canberra, ACT 2600 (☎(02) 6270 6666).
Canada, British Consulate-General, British Trade & Investment Office, 777 Bay St., Ste. 2800, Toronto, Ont. M5G 2G2 (☎(416) 593-1290).
Ireland, British Embassy, 29 Merrion Rd, Ballsbridge, Dublin 4 (☎(01) 205 3700; fax 205 3885).
New Zealand, British Consulate-General, 17th fl., Fay Richwhite Bldg, 151 Queen St, Auckland 1 (☎(09) 303 2973).
South Africa, British High Commission, Liberty Life Pl., Glyn St., Hatfield 0083, Pretoria.

US, British Consulate, 19 Observatory Circle, NW, Washington, D.C. 20008. British Embassy, 3100 Massachusetts Ave., NW, Washington D.C. 20008 (☎(202) 462-1340); www.britain-info.org/bis/embassy/embassy.htm.

USEFUL PUBLICATIONS

LOCAL RESOURCES
Time Out publishes a weekly entertainment guide to London and the surrounding area.
The Independent Newspaper offers an entertainment and events supplement every Th; **The Guardian** does the same every Sa.

TRAVEL BOOK AND MAP PUBLISHERS
Hunter Publishing, 130 Campus Dr., Edison, NJ 08818, USA (☎(800) 255 0343; www.hunter-publishing.com). Has an extensive catalog of travel books, guides, language tapes, and maps.
Hippocrene Books, Inc., 171 Madison Ave., New York, NY 10016 (☎(212) 685 4371; orders (718) 454-2366; fax 454-1391; contact@hippocrenebooks.com; www.netcom.com/~hippocre). Reference books, travel guides, and dictionaries and learning guides for over 100 languages.
Rand McNally, 150 S. Wacker Dr., Chicago, IL 60606 (☎800 234 0679 or (312) 332 2009; fax 443-9540; email storekeeper@randmcnally.com; www.randmcnally.com), publishes a number of comprehensive road atlases (each US$10).

THE WORLD WIDE WEB

Armchair travelers rejoice. You can plan for much of your trip without getting out of your pajamas by using the vast resources of the world wide web. *Let's Go: London* lists web sites throughout the book whenever available, but here are a few of the best.
TimeOut London (www.timeout.com/london) is the website for the popular TimeOut magazine. Contains links to music, fashion, student, tourist sites, and all the scenes fit to be seen in.
LondonNet (www.londonnet.co.uk) has all the latest weather, news, and sports info, plus hotels, entertainment and shopping. Also offers occasional chat rooms and information on the London job scene.
The Gay London Guide (http://home.clara.net/mike.pl) has links to gay London, as well as a good number of resources and hotlines for gays and lesbians in London. Also lists gay-friendly pubs and clubs in all areas of the city.
The London Transport Authority (www.londontransport.co.uk) has all the information on trains, buses and the Underground that you will need to plan your trip.
London Theatre (www.officiallondontheatre.co.uk) has a complete list of all West End shows, including times, prices, dates, locations and contact numbers.
The CIA World Factbook (www.odci.gov/cia/publications/factbook/index.html) has tons of vital statistics on the UK. Check it out for an overview of England's economy and an explanation of its system of government.

AND OUR PERSONAL FAVORITE...
Let's Go: www.letsgo.com. Our recently revamped website features photos and streaming video, info about our books, a travel forum buzzing with stories and tips, and links that will help you find everything you could ever want to know about Britain and Ireland.

FURTHER READING
How to Plan Your Dream Vacation Using the Web. Elizabeth Dempsey. Coriolis Group (US$25).
Nettravel: How Travelers Use the Internet, Michael Shapiro. O'Reilly & Associates. (US$25).
Travel Planning Online for Dummies, Noah Vadnai. IDG Books. (US$25).

Accommodations

To sleep in London, however, is an art which a foreigner must acquire by time and habit.
—Robert Southey, 1807

Sorry folks, but this isn't going to be pretty. Just as real estate prices make Londoners clutch their heads and scream, hotels and hostels are incredibly expensive. The further bad news is that high prices are not often a sign of quality, with grotty or, at best, achingly kitsch interiors, surly staff, and draconian payment procedures being the norms. No matter where you plan to stay, it is essential to plan ahead, especially in July and August when London's hotels are bursting with visitors. It's worth the price of a phone call or fax to confirm a booking. The proprietor should specify the deposit amount (usually one night's stay) and advise the best way to make the deposit. More and more hotels and most HI hostels accept credit card phone and internet reservations. The **Tourist Information Centre Accommodations Service** at Victoria Station can help you find a room (see **Tourist Information**, p. 275).

Accommodations in this chapter are grouped by neighborhood and by type; for a listing of accommodations by price, see the box on p. 245. Within each grouping, accommodations are listed in order of preference, starting with the best; listings marked with a thumb-pick (🖜) are exceptional values, worthy of special mention. For information on how to find **Long-term accommodations,** see **Living in London, p. 266**.

TYPES OF ACCOMMODATIONS

London offers a wide range of accommodations to suit travelers with different social needs, attachments to privacy, and capacities for roughing it. In addition to hotels, the most expensive category, there are three major accommodation types suited to the budgeteer; hostels, halls of residence, and bed and breakfasts; these are described below.

Most accommodations accept credit cards. However, if you pay with plastic a 2-4% **surcharge** will likely be added to your bill by the hotel or hostel. If you are making reservations in person, be sure to look at a room before agreeing to take it. If you arrive on a hotel's doorstep in the afternoon or evening looking for a night's lodging, **haggling** over the price can often save you a few quid—after all if you don't take the room, it'll likely go empty. Some proprietors grant **rate reductions** for stays over a week or during the off season. Off season is from October through March (although September, April, and May are slow enough that you may be able to wrangle a few pounds' discount). In winter, be sure to check whether the room will be heated. If you are an American who doesn't like stairs, keep in mind that "1st floor" to the rest of the world means 2nd floor to you.

HOSTELS

Hostels are low-priced, dorm-style accommodations generally geared toward young travelers. If you are traveling alone or in a small group, a hostel is your cheapest option. You'll sleep in a room with anywhere from three to 15 other travelers; some hostels offer private rooms for two at a slightly higher cost. You'll also share a bathroom with your new roommates and often with guests from several rooms. Hostels are places where globetrotters can swap information and meet new traveling companions, a social dimension as important to their guests as their low prices.

There are two flavors of hostel: **Hostelling International (HI)/Youth Hostel Association (YHA) hostels** and **private hostels.** HI/YHA hostels generally cost more than private ones, but are usually cleaner and often have spectacular locations. On the other hand, they tend to be more institutional-feeling, and draw a less bohemian crowd. The HI/YHA hostels require membership (see HI Hostels listings below for more information) and some have curfews. The staff in HI/YHA hostels are usually extremely knowledgeable about the area and many can arrange activities for guests. Bathrooms and common spaces are well maintained.

HI/YHA HOSTELS

▐*Reservations at HI/YHA hostels can be made through a central booking agency and online: ☎ 7373 3400; lonres@yha.org.uk; www.yha.org.uk. Telephone bookings taken M-Sa 9am-5pm*

Staying at Hostelling International/YHA hostels is restricted to **Hostelling International** or **Youth Hostel Association members.** You can join at YHA London Headquarters or at the hostels themselves for £12, under 18 £6. An **International Guest Pass** (£1.90) permits non-members not resident in England or Wales to stay at hostels, though often at slightly higher rates. Buy six guest passes and you automatically become a full member.

The cheerful staff members, often international travelers themselves, keep London HI/YHA hostels clean and refreshingly well managed. They can also often provide a range of helpful information on the hostel's environs. Plan ahead; London hostels are exceptionally crowded. During the summer, beds fill up months in advance. In recent years, hostels have not always been able to accommodate every written request for reservations, much less on-the-spot inquiries. But hostels frequently hold some beds free until a few days before—it's always worth checking. To secure a place, show up as early as possible and expect to stand in line, or book in advance with a credit card at the number or website above; you can also write to the warden of the individual hostel.

All hostels are equipped with large **lockers** that require a padlock. Bring your own or purchase one from the hostel for £3. London hostels do not charge for a sheet or sleeping bag. Most have laundry facilities and some kitchen equipment. Theater tickets and discounted attraction tickets are available.

The **YHA London Information Office and Adventure Shop,** 14 Southampton St, WC2, has information on hostels and sells hostelling memberships and supplies. Cardholders receive a 10% discount on anything in the Adventure Shop. (☎ 7836 8541 or 7374 0547 for office. Tube: Covent Garden. Open M-Th 10am-6pm, F 10am-7pm, Sa 9:30am-6pm, Su 11am-4pm.) YHA shops are also found at: 174 Kensington High St. (☎ 7938 2948; Tube: High St. Kensington; open M-W 10am-6pm, Th-F 10am-7pm, Sa 9am-6:30pm, Su 11am-5pm); and 52 Grosvenor Gardens (☎7823 4739; Tube: Victoria; open M-W and F 8:30am-6pm, Th 8:30am-8pm, Sa-Su 10am-5pm).

UNIVERSITY RESIDENCE HALLS

London's colleges and universities rent out rooms in their halls of residence over the summer, Christmas, and Easter vacations. If you have a student ID, you may be able to find a bargain—in some cases, you can get a private single for the same price you'd pay for a bed in a hostel dorm. Rates are a bit higher without student ID, but are still affordable for those traveling alone. Rooms tend to be fairly ascetic—standard student digs—and clean. Some of the halls include breakfast in the price of the room. Generally halls offer rooms to individuals for two or three months over the summer, so calling or writing way ahead is essential. Some halls keep a few rooms for travelers throughout the year.

COLLEGE ACCOMMODATIONS OFFICES

Many of London's colleges run a **central accommodations office.** While you're usually expected to book through the individual halls, these offices can direct you to the numerous halls run by each college, including a few halls that may only be open.

University College London Residential Services, John Dodgson House, 24-36 Bidborough St., WC1 (☎7554 7780; fax 7554 7781). Tube: King's Cross/St. Pancras. Runs 8 halls, mostly around Bloomsbury. Only 4, however, are available to individual travellers. Rooms available Apr and mid-June to mid-Sept. Office open M-F 9am-5pm.

King's Campus Vacation Bureau, 127 Stamford St., SE1 (☎7928 3777; fax 7928 5777; vac.bureau@kcl.ac.uk; www.kcl.ac.uk). Tube: Waterloo. Accommodations at the halls of King's College London, including **Wellington Hall** (see p. 247). Rooms available around Easter and mid-June to mid-Sept. 10% discount for stays of 7 nights or more.

BED AND BREAKFAST HOTELS

Bed and Breakfasts are smallish hotels run by a family or a proprietor who will provide—surprise!—a bed and breakfast. The term "B&B" encompasses budget hotels of wildly varying quality and personality. Some are nothing more than budget hotels that serve breakfast—don't expect snug, quaint lodgings. Rooms in these lesser-quality B&Bs can be small, dreary, and bare, although you can usually count on a sink and tea/coffee-making facilities. However, some B&Bs are much nicer, offering warm comforters and charming decorative details. Due to the highly variable character of B&Bs, investigate all of your options before choosing one. A **basic room** means that you share the use of a shower and toilet in the hall. A room **with bath** contains a private shower or bath and a toilet, and tends to cost £10-20 more. Be aware, however, that in-room showers are often awkward prefab units jammed into a corner. **Family room** in B&B lingo generally means a quad or quint with at least one double bed and some single beds. A group of two or more may find that sharing a room in a moderately-priced B&B costs less than staying in some hostels. Most B&Bs serve the full **English breakfast**—eggs, bacon, toast, fried toast, baked beans, a peculiarly prepared tomato (baked or stewed), and tea or coffee. **Continental breakfast** means some form of bread, cereal, and hot beverage.

ACCOMMODATIONS DISTRICTS

When contemplating where to stay, tourists should take into consideration what sorts of fun they'll be having in London. Some districts are better for those interested in being close to the sights; others are more geared toward those who like nightlife. Bargain seekers, however, should keep in mind that the further out you go, the better the prices, and often, the nicer the neighborhoods. Lest the length of a commute to sights deter you, be forewarned that public transport in London is tremendously slow, no matter where you're going, and central London is even slower, due to nightmarish traffic.

What follows is a thumbnail sketch of the areas in which travelers are most likely to bunk down. London is not very well-served by public transportation after midnight, so if you're staying in the outskirts and plan to stay out late, you'll have to swallow a huge wait for a night bus or an expensive cab ride. For a more detailed overview of London neighborhoods, see **Once in London, p. 19.**

CENTRAL LONDON

CITY OF LONDON. Places to stay are scarce in the City, with most available space gobbled up by offices. However, many sights are nearby and the region is very well-served by the Tube and buses, particularly on weekdays.

HOLBORN. Few accommodations grace this center of London's legal practice. But the area is close to central London's major sights and well-served by public transport.

WESTMINSTER. The area near Victoria station is full of budget hotels. Play them off each other—show reluctance to take a room, and you may see prices plummet, especially in the off-season. Popular hotels will fill up weeks in advance; call ahead. Hotels closer to Pimlico are nicer than those near Victoria Station.

KENSINGTON, KNIGHTSBRIDGE, AND HYDE PARK. Kensington is not the cheapest part of town to stay in, to say the least. Still, it's conveniently close to the stunning array of museums that line the southwest side of Hyde Park, as well as the huge department stores in Knightsbridge. The sprinkling of B&Bs on Vicarage Gate, off Kensington Church St. (Tube: High St. Kensington), deliver a modicum of luxury at surprisingly affordable prices. Other spots for B&Bs are Cromwell Rd. and Gloucester Rd. (Tube: Gloucester Rd.). Be aware that Cromwell Rd., though centrally located, is a very busy, noisy, and dirty street. If these options fail, Earl's Court and Bayswater are close by.

MARYLEBONE AND REGENT'S PARK. A few hotels can be found near Marble Arch, in the sidestreets off the **Edgware Road**. It's convenient to Oxford St. and Hyde Park, and numerous night buses serve the area. The hotels themselves can be fairly uninspiring.

BLOOMSBURY. Quiet (too quiet?) residential streets lined with B&Bs, a few halls of residence, and a few hostels. This moderately expensive area is within walking distance of Drummond St. (home of outstanding Indian restaurants) to the north and Covent Garden to the south; the British Museum is right next door. West End theaters are also within reach, either a longish walk or short bus ride away. The closer the accommodation is to the King's Cross, St. Pancras, and Euston train-station triumvirate, the scuzzier the neighborhood tends to be, especially after dark.

SOHO. Sure, you want to stay in Soho and conveniently stagger home from the bars every night. But good luck finding a hotel anywhere—there are few hotels of any sort in the area. If you gain access to a film star's fortune, there's **Hazlitt's,** 6 Frith St. (☎ 7437 1771). Fortunately for night owls, the area is extremely well-served by public transport, and in any case the numerous B&Bs and hostels of Bloomsbury are close by.

OUTSIDE CENTRAL LONDON

ISLINGTON. A number of budget accommodations are found around Islington. You'll be farther from central London than you'd be in any of the neighborhoods above, but you'll be smack in the middle of one of the city's most exciting neighborhoods.

HAMPSTEAD AND HIGHGATE. This area contains a few pleasant B&Bs, a few hostels, and a number of residence halls. Prices tend to offer outstanding value (by London standards), although the long commute can make it difficult to take advantage of nightlife.

DOCKLANDS. Few budget accommodations have found their way to the Docklands. The few that have, however, are quality. You'll be near Greenwich and the action south of the Thames.

BRIXTON. Staying in Brixton will put you within walking distance of some of London's best nightlife, a short tube ride away from sights on the South Bank, and a slightly longer ride away from major central London sights.

EARL'S COURT. This area feeds on the budget tourist trade, spewing forth travel agencies, souvenir shops, and bureaux de change. Some streets seem to be solely populated by B&Bs and hostels. The area has a vibrant gay and lesbian population and is also a tremendously popular destination for Aussie travelers cooling their heels in London (so much so that in the 1970s, it gained the nickname "Kangaroo Valley"). The police have recently installed closed-circuit video cameras around the neighborhood, but be careful at night. Also, beware of over eager guides willing to lead you from the station to a hostel. Some B&Bs in this area conceal grimy rooms behind fancy lobbies and well-dressed staff. Always ask to see a room.

SHEPHERD'S BUSH, HAMMERSMITH, & HOLLAND PARK. A plethora of B&Bs (some excellent, others less so) line Shepherd's Bush Rd., which stretches between Shepherd's Bush Green and the Hammersmith Tube stations. While it's a bit of a schlepp to the center, transport links are good, rooms are usually cheaper, and you usually get a private bathroom.

ACCOMMODATIONS BY PRICE

For full listings of the establishments mentioned here, look under the appropriate neighborhood in **Accommodations by Neighborhood,** p. 245. Establishments are grouped according to the least expensive one night stay for travelers over 18.

UNDER £20		£30-40	
International Students House	MRP	Arosfa	BB
Ashlee House	BB	Ridgemount Hotel	BB
Astor's Museum Inn	HB	Langland Hotel	BB
Tonbridge Club	BB	Cosmo/Bedford House Hotel	BB
Hampstead Heath	HH	Hotel Apollo	BB
YHA Holland House	SBHH	Alhambra Hotel	BB
Tent City—Hackney	GL	Kandara Guesthouse	IS
Crystal Palace caravan Club Site	GL	Oxford Hotel	EC
		Lord Jim Hotel	EC
£20-30		Beaver Hotel	EC
YHA City of London	CL	Oakley Hotel	EC
Finsbury Residences	CL	Dalmacia Hotel	EC
Wellington Hall	WM	Star Hotel	SBHH
Queen Alexandra's House	MRP	Hotel Orlando	SBHH
King's Cross/St. Pancras	BB		
Passfield Hall	BB	**OVER £40**	
John Adams Hall	BB	Alexander Hotel	WM
Connaught Hall	BB	Dover HotelWMStanley House HotelS	WM
Commonwealth Hall	BB	Surtees Hotel	WM
Carr-Saunders Hall	BB	Melita House Hotel	WM
Central University of Iowa Hostel	BB	Abbey House Hotel	KKH
Jesmond Dene Hotel	BB	Vicarage HotelK	KH
YHA Oxford Street	SO	Swiss House Hotel	KKH
Walter Sickert Hall	IS	Hotel Europe	KKH
Five Kings Guesthouse	IS	Ashburn HotelK	KHP
Rosebery Hall	IS	Glynne Court Hotel	MRP
YHA Rotherhithe	DL	Redland House Hotel	MRP
Half Moon Hotel	EC	Mentone Hotel	BB
Windsor Guest House	SBHH	George Hotel	BB
Hotel 65	SBHH	Crescent Hotel	BB
		Jenkins Hotel	BB
£30-40		Ruskin Hotel	BB
Hotel Strand Continental	HB	Outlet	SO
Luna and Simone Hotel	WM	Jury's Inn	IS
Melbourne House	WM	Number 7	BX
Georgian House Hotel	WM	Mowbray Court Hotel	EC
Oxford House	WM	Philbeach Hotel	EC
Imperial College Accommodation Link	KKH		

CL City of London **HO** Holborn **WM** Westminster **CB** Chelsea and Belgravia **KKHP** Kensington, Knightsbridge, Hyde Park **NHB** Notting Hill and Bayswater **MRP** Marylebone and Regent's Park **BB** Bloomsbury **CG** Covent Garden **SO** Soho **MSP** Mayfair, St. James, and Picadilly **NC** Notable Chain **IS** Islington **CD** Camden **HH** Hamstead and Highgate **DL** Docklands **WC** Whitechapel **SSB** South Bank, Southwark **BR** Brixton **GRg** Greenwich **EC** Earl's Court **SHH** Shepherd's Bush, Hammersmith, and Holland Park **RI** Richmond

ACCOMMODATIONS BY NEIGHBORHOOD
CENTRAL LONDON

THE CITY OF LONDON

see map p. 300

HOSTELS

▨ **YHA City of London,** 36 Carter Ln., EC4 (☎ 7236 4965; fax 7236 7681). Tube: St. Paul's. Sleep in quiet comfort a stone's throw from St. Paul's. Scrupulously clean, with a full range of services, including secure luggage storage, currency exchange, laundry facilities (£1.50 for washers), Internet access (£5 per hr.), and theater box office. A canteen offers inexpensive set lunches and dinners. Rooms (all single-sex) contain 1-15 beds. Many feature the less-than-ideal triple-decker bunk beds common in London YHA hostels. 24hr. security. Reception 7am-11pm. Dorms £20.50, under 18 £18.70; 5- to 8- bed dorms £22.95, under 18 £19.70; 3- to 4- bed dorms £20.80, under 18 £24.10; singles £26.80, £23.30; doubles and twins (some with TV) £52.10, £44.60. Private rooms £50-135, families £40-120. MC, V.

RESIDENCE HALLS

▨ **Finsbury Residences** (City University), 15 Bastwick St., (☎ 7477 8811; fax 7477 8810; www.city.ac.uk/ems). Tube: Barbican. Walk up Aldersgate St. and Goswell Rd.; Bastwick St. is on the right. Cheap, clean, basic accommodation within walking distance of both the City and the nightlife of Islington and Clerkenwell. Admittedly, the tower block setting is unattractive, but recent renovations have made the inside very pleasant. Good service for a university accommodation: the staff are helpful and welcoming, and there are fresh towels. Breakfast. Licensed bar, lounge, TV room and laundry. Rooms include phone, desk, basin, and closet. Available around Easter and summer. Max. stay 3 weeks. Singles £21.

HOLBORN

see map pp. 296-297

RESIDENCE HALLS

High Holborn Residence, 178 High Holborn, WC1 (☎ 7379 5589; fax 7379 5640). Tube: Holborn. A comfortable, modern, and extremely well-located place. Rooms come with phones, and each flat has a kitchen. Laundry, lounge, and bar facilities. Excellent wheelchair facilities. Full English breakfast. Open mid-June to September (peak rates in July). Singles £27-34; twins £46-57, with bath £56-67; triples with bath £66-77. MC, V.

BED AND BREAKFAST HOTELS

Hotel Strand Continental, 143 Strand, WC2 (☎ 7836 4880; fax 7379 6105), Tube: Covent Garden, Charing Cross, or buses #501, 505, 176 or 188 from Waterloo Station. Descriptions like "stylish," "recently renovated," or "upscale," don't apply to this hotel, but for practical types who want a clean place to crash that is very close to the action, this is a good deal. Small but workable rooms, no en suite bathrooms. All rooms have sinks and heating. TV lounge takes advantage of the building's leaded and stained glass windows. Singles £32, doubles £40, twin £45, family room £50.

WESTMINSTER

see map p. 68

RESIDENCE HALLS

Wellington Hall, 71 Vincent Sq. (☎ 7834 4740; fax 7233 7709; reservations ☎ 7928 3777). Tube: Victoria. An Edwardian building on a beautiful square near Victoria station. TV lounge, library, and bar. English breakfast. Laundry. Rooms available around Easter and mid-June to mid-Sept. Singles £26; twins £40. 10% discount for stays longer than a week.

BED AND BREAKFAST HOTELS

▨ **Luna and Simone Hotel,** 47-49 Belgrave Rd. (☎ 7834 5897; fax 7828 2474; lunasimone@talk21.com). Tube: Victoria. Fabulous! Stylish, fun, and immaculately maintained; the area's best option. Yellow and blue rooms all come with TV, phones, hair dryers, and firm mat-

tresses. English breakfast in sleek dining room. Luggage storage. Recommended to book ahead 1 month. Singles £28-34; doubles £48-60, with bath £50-75; triples £65-80, with shower £75-95. 10% discount for long-term stays. Winter discount. MC, V.

 Melbourne House, 79 Belgrave Rd. (☎ 7828 3516; fax 7828 7120; melbourne.househotel@virgin.net). Tube: Pimlico. An extraordinarily clean, well-kept establishment. The rooms are spacious, all non-smoking, and have TV, phone, and hot pot. English breakfast served 7:30-8:45am. Free luggage storage. Book ahead with credit card. 48hr. cancellation fee. Singles £30, with bath £50-55; doubles or twins with bath £70-75; triples with bath £90-95; family quad with bath £100-110. Cash preferred.

Alexander Hotel, 13 Belgrave Rd. (☎ 7834 9738; fax 7630 9630, www.alexanderhotel.co.uk). Tube: Pimlico. Sumptously carpeted rooms are slightly crunched but attractive and sparkling clean throughout. All with satellite TV, radio, and private bath. TV lounge. English breakfast served 7:30-9am. Check-out 11am. Singles £45; Doubles and twins £60-65; triples £75-80; family rooms £80-110. Winter discount. MC, V.

Dover Hotel, 42/44 Belgrave Rd. (☎ 7821 9085; fax 7834 6425; dover@rooms.demon.co.uk). Tube: Pimlico. All rooms and facilities are all clean and in good condition and have bathrooms. Continental breakfast served 7:30-9:30am. Singles £40-55; doubles and twins £50-70; triples £60-75; quads £70-100; quints £80-110. AmEx, DC, MC, V.

Stanley House Hotel, 19-21 Belgrave Rd. (☎ 7834 5042 or 7834 8439). Tube: Pimlico. Ceilings lower and rooms get smaller as you go up. Test mattresses before you rest to get the best. English breakfast. TV lounge. 24hr. reception. Book 2 weeks in advance. Singles £42, with shower £50; doubles £50, with shower or bath £60; family rooms £25 per person. AmEx, MC, V.

Georgian House Hotel, 35 St. George's Dr. (☎ 7834 1438; fax 7976 6085; georgian@wild-net.co.uk; www.georgianhousehotel.co.uk). Tube: Victoria. Terrific discounts on on the 3rd and 4th floor rooms. Spacious rooms rooms come with TV, phone, and hot pot. English breakfast. Reception 8am-11pm. Singles £30, students £24, with bath £48, in annex £42; doubles with bath £65, students £38, in annex £54; triples with bath £78, students £59, in annex £69; quads £88, students £65, in annex en suite £79. MC, V.

Surtees Hotel, 94 Warwick Way. (☎ 7834 7163 or 7834 7394; fax 7460 8747, www.zen-dens.uninet.co.uk/surtees). Tube: Pimlico. Pleasantly decorated rooms with comfy beds, radio, and color TV. Great breakfast included. Singles with shower and toilet in corner £50; doubles £50, with shower and toilet £65; triples with shower and toilet £80; family rooms with shower and toilet £90-120. Long-term prices negotiable. AmEx, MC, V. 5% surcharge for credit cards.

Melita House Hotel, 33-35 Charlwood St. (☎ 7828 0471 or 7834 1387; fax 7932 0988; reserve@melita.co.uk; www.melita.co.uk). Tube: Pimlico. Charming manicuried entrance leads to a sunny yellow lounge and new dining room. Pleasant non-smoking rooms with private bathrooms. TV, hair dryer, telephone, refrigerator and digital safe in each room. English breakfast included. Singles £50-60; doubles £75-85, twins £70-85; triples £85-£90; quads £95-110. Discount for stays over 1 week. AmEx, MC, V. 5% surcharge for credit cards.

Oxford House, 92-94 Cambridge St. (☎ 7834 9681; fax 7834 0225), close to the church. Tube: Victoria. Comfortable, clean, freshly painted rooms. English breakfast served 7:30-8:45am. Reserve 3-4 weeks ahead. Singles £40; doubles £48-50; triples £63-66; quads £84-86. Must pay the day before departure. MC, V.

KENSINGTON, KNIGHTSBRIDGE, AND HYDE PARK

RESIDENCE HALLS

Imperial College Accommodation Link, Prince's Gardens. (☎ 7594 9507 or 7594 9511; fax 7594 9504; reservations@ic.ac.uk; www.ad.ic.ac.uk/conferences). Tube: South Kensington. Well-equipped halls close to the South Kensington museums and Kensington Gardens. Laundry. Phone and Internet access to were being added to some rooms at the time of writing. Full breakfast included. Wheelchair access. Open April and July-Sept. Singles £35, twins £55. MC, V.

see map p. 313

BED AND BREAKFAST HOTELS

 Abbey House Hotel, 11 Vicarage Gate. (☎ 7727 2594) Tube: High St. Kensington. The elegant black and white marble entrance to this historical house makes you feel like royalty. After you check in, the owners (who live in-house) or an assistant will spend 20min. giving you an introduction to London. The hotel achieves a level of comfort unrivaled at these prices. 24hr. tea, coffee, and ice room. Palatial pastel rooms with color TVs, washbasins, towels and soap, and billowing curtains. English breakfast. Reception 8:30am-10pm. Book far ahead. Singles £43; doubles £68; triples £85; quads £95; quints £105. Weekly rates in winter only. No credit cards.

Vicarage Hotel, 10 Vicarage Gate. (☎ 7229 4030; fax 7792 5989; reception@londonvicaragehotel.com; londonvicaragehotel.com). Tube: High St. Kensington. The stately foyer and breakfast room are surpassed only by the comfortable bedrooms and spotless bathrooms. Singles £45; doubles and twins £74, with bath and TV £98; triples £90; family rooms £98. No credit cards.

Swiss House Hotel, 171 Old Brompton Rd. (☎ 7373 2769; fax 7373 4983; recep@swiss-hh.demon.co.uk). Tube: Gloucester Rd. A beautiful, plant-filled B&B with 16 airy, spacious rooms, most with fireplaces. Cable TV, telephone, and tea-and-coffee facilities included. Fax and Internet access. All rooms have showers. Continental breakfast included. English breakfast £6. Reception open M-F 7:30am-11pm, Sa-Su 8am-11pm. Singles £46, with toilet £65; doubles/twins (all with bath) £80-90; triples (all with bath) £104; quads (all with bath) £118. 5% discount for stays over a week in the off-season. 5% discount for cash payments. AmEx, MC, V, DC.

Hotel Europe, 131-137 Cromwell Rd. (☎ 7598 7979; fax 7598 7981; reservations@hoteleurope.co.uk) Tube: Gloucester Rd. Clean, medium-sized (100 rooms) hotel. Can be a bit noisy along this main drag. Sleek bar. Safety deposit box £0.50. Continental breakfast. Singles with bath £70-80; twins or doubles with bath £85-95; triples £95; quads £105. All prices listed for rooms with private bathrooms. Call for prices of rooms with shared bathrooms. AmEx, MC, V.

Ashburn Hotel, 111 Cromwell Rd. (☎ 7370 3321; fax 7370 2360; www.ashburn-hotel.co.uk). Tube: Gloucester Rd. All rooms have attached phones, and TVs. Continental breakfast included; full English breakfast £3.50. Singles £60; doubles £75; triples £89; quads £95.

MARYLEBONE AND REGENT'S PARK

RESIDENCE HALLS

see map p. 303

International Student House, 229 Great Portland St. (☎ 7631 8300, or 7631 8310; fax 7631 8315; email accom@ish.org.uk; www.ish.org.uk). Tube: Great Portland St. A thriving international metropolis with its own films, concerts, discos, study groups, athletic contests, expeditions, and parties. Over 500 beds. The bar in the lobby has a huge TV and serves £1.80 pints from 5-11pm weekdays, F-Sa 5pm-2am. Lockable cupboards in dorms, laundry facilities, currency exchange, and Internet access. Continental breakfast provided except for those in dorms. No curfew. Reserve at least 1 month ahead, earlier during academic year. Dorms £10; singles £30, with bath and phone £32.50; twins £44, with bath and phone £50; triples £52.50. MC, V.

Queen Alexandra's House, Kensington Gore. (☎ 7589 1120; fax 7589 3177). Tube: South Kensington. **Women only.** Magnificent Victorian building directly across from Kensington Gardens. Kitchen, laundry, sitting room, and 20 piano-filled music rooms. Common showers/lavatories. No visitors 11pm-10am. Continental breakfast included. 2-night minimum stay. Write weeks in advance for a booking form; fax is best. Cozy singles £25; weekly rates for stays over 2 weeks £150 per week upon availability, including breakfast and dinner. No credit cards.

BED AND BREAKFAST HOTELS

Edward Lear Hotel, 28-30 Seymour St. (☎ 7402 5401; fax 7706 3766; edwardlear@aol.com; www.edlear.com). Tube: Marble Arch. Comfortable rooms and friendly staff. All rooms with TVs, radios, and phones. Singles £48, with shower £58, with bath and toilet £74.50. Doubles and twins £67.50, £81.50, £92.50. Triples £81.50, £91.50, £102.50. Family rooms with bath £99.50, with bath and toilet £109.50.

Glynne Court Hotel, 41 Great Cumberland Pl. (☎ 7262 4344; fax 7724 2071). Tube: Marble Arch. No great shakes, but still, rooms have attached baths, TVs, and phones. Singles £55, doubles £70, triples £85, family rooms £100. AmEx, DC, MC, V (4% surcharge).

Redland House Hotel, 52 Kendal St. (☎ 7723 7118; fax 7402 9049). Tube: Marble Arch. A functional B&B. Singles £44, with shower £65; doubles and twins £56, with shower £80; triples £80; family rooms £90. MC, V (4% surcharge).

BLOOMSBURY

see map pp. 296-297

HOSTELS

YHA King's Cross/St. Pancras, 79-81 Euston Rd. (☎7388 9998; fax 7388 6766; stpancras@yha.org.uk). Tube: King's Cross/St. Pancras. New, comfortable beds, sparkling bathrooms, and an airport-like lounge. Some rooms even come with air-conditioning. Numerous family rooms. Premium rooms include bathroom, TV, and coffee/tea facilities. Dinner (£4) from 6-9pm. Full English breakfast. Luggage storage. Laundry, email, and kitchen facilities. Max. stay 1 week. Book way in advance. Dorm £23, under 18 £19.70; 2-bed family rooms £40; 4-bed £80; 5-bed £100; premium double £53; premium quad £100. MC, V.

Ashlee House, 261-65 Gray's Inn Rd. (☎7833 9400; fax 7833 6777; info@ashleehouse.co.uk; www.ashleehouse.co.uk). Tube: King's Cross. Clean, bright rooms within easy walking distance of King's Cross (which is good and bad). Some rooms have skylights, all have washbasins and central heating. No hot water noon-6pm. Generous breakfast (served M-F 7:30-9.30am, Sa-Su 8-10am). Secure luggage room, laundry, kitchens, and email. Linen provided. Spacious reception area open 24hr. Check-out 10am. Summer prices Apr 1-Oct 31. Dorms £13 Apr.-Oct., £15; 4- and 6-bed rooms £17,19; twins £22, 24. All prices per person.

Astor's Museum Inn, 27 Montague St. (☎7580 5360; fax 7636 7948; astorhostels@msn.com; www.astorhostels.com). Tube: Russell Sq. Across the street from the British Museum. A proper hostel—a fun, party crowd rocks these well-worn digs. Coed dorms almost inevitable. Kitchen, cable TV. Continental breakfast. Linens provided. 24hr. reception. No curfew. Book 1 month ahead. 4-10 bed dorms £14-£16; doubles £40, triples £51. Discounts available Oct.-Mar., including a weekly dorm rate of £70. MC, V. No surcharge if greater than £30.

Central University of Iowa Hostel, 7 Bedford Pl. (☎/fax 7580 1121). Tube: Tottenham Court Rd. or Russell Sq. On a quiet street near the British Museum. Spartan, narrow dorm rooms with bunk beds and washbasins. Continental breakfast. Laundry facilities, towels and linen, TV lounge. Twins £22; 4-8 bed room £20. £10 key deposit. Reception 9am-10:30pm. No curfew. Open approximately May 20-Aug. 20. MC, V.

Tonbridge Club, 120 Cromer St. (☎7837 4406). Tube: King's Cross/St. Pancras. Follow Euston Rd. towards the British Library and turn left onto Judd St.; the hostel is 3 blocks down on the left. Students and those with non-British passports only. A clean, no frills place to sleep and shower. Men sleep in basement gym, women in karate-club hall. Pool tables, TV, video games. Daytime storage space. Blankets and foam pads provided. Lockout 9am-9pm; lights-out 11:30pm; midnight curfew. Floor space £5.

RESIDENCE HALLS

Passfield Hall, 1-7 Endsleigh Pl., WC1 (☎7387 3584; fax 7387 0419; www.lse.ac.uk/vacations). Tube: Euston. Rooms vary in size; all have desks and phones (incoming calls only). English breakfast included. Laundry and kitchen facilities. Singles £25, twins £44, triples £57. MC, V.

John Adams Hall, 15-23 Endsleigh St., WC1 (☎7387 4086; fax 7383 0164; jah@ioe.ac.uk; www.ioe.ac.uk). Tube: Euston Sq. An elegant if somewhat old-looking Georgian building with small, wrought-iron balconies. Singles are small and simple. TV lounge, pianos. Laundry facilities. English breakfast included. Open July-Sept. and Easter. Singles £24, twins £42, triples £59. Discounts for students, stays of 6 nights or more, and in the off-season. MC, V.

Connaught Hall, 36-45 Tavistock Sq., WC1 (☎7685 2800; fax 7383 4109). Tube: Euston Sq. or Russell Sq. Quiet atmosphere, overlooking a garden. Rooms have sinks and desks. Reading rooms and laundry. English breakfast included. Wheelchair accessible. Open Easter and July-Aug. Singles £22.50, twins £40. No credit cards.

Commonwealth Hall, 1-11 Cartwright Gardens, WC1 (☎7685 3500). Tube: Russell Sq. Try to get a room overlooking the tennis courts of Cartwright Gardens. Sports facilities and TV lounge, music rooms, and a bar. Open Easter, July-Sept., and Christmas. Singles £25, twins £50. Students discount. Reservations required.

Carr-Saunders Hall, 18-24 Fitzroy St. (☎7574 5300; fax 7580 4718; saunders@lse.ac.uk; www.lse.ac.uk/halls). Tube: Warren St. Rooms come with a sink, phones, and desk. English breakfast included. Internet access. Reception open Su-Th 8:30am-midnight, F-Sa 8:30am-2am. Open Easter and July-Sept. Singles £27; twins £45. MC, V.

BED AND BREAKFAST HOTELS

Arosfa Hotel, 83 Gower St. (☎/fax 7636 2115). Tube: Tottenham Court Rd. The name is Welsh for "place to rest," and it lives up to its name admirably by offering spacious rooms, immaculate facilities, and furnishings. All rooms with TV and sink. No smoking. Full English breakfast included. Singles £35; doubles £48, with bath £63; triples £65, £76; quad with bath £88. MC, V with 2% surcharge.

Euro Hotel, 51-53 Cartwright Gdns., WC1 (☎ 7387 4321; fax 7383 5044; reception@eurohotel.co.uk; www.eurohotel.co.uk). Tube: Russell Sq. Large, high-ceilinged rooms with cable TV, radio, kettle, phone, and sink. Sparkling, spacious bathroom facilities. Free email. Full English breakfast included. Singles £46, with bath £68; doubles £65, £85; triples £79, £99; quads £88, £108. Under 13 sharing with adults £10. AmEx, MC, V.

Ridgemount Hotel, 65-67 Gower St. (☎ 7636 1141 or 7580 7060; fax 7636 2558). Tube: Tottenham Court Rd. Charming staff keep the loyal guests happy and the well-kept hotel radiantly clean. Snug singles with TVs. Garden in back, free tea and coffee in the TV lounge. English breakfast included. Laundry service £3. Book ahead. Singles £32, with shower £43; doubles £48, £62; triples £63, £75; quads £72, £86; quints £78, £89. MC, V.

The Langland Hotel, 29-31 Gower St. (☎ 7636 5801; fax 7580 2227; sarah@langlandhotel.freeserve.co.uk; www.langlandhotel.com). Tube: Euston. Renovations have added bathrooms to many of the rooms and TVs to all. Cable TV lounge with comfy blue sofas. English breakfast. Laundry facilities. Winter and long-term student discounts. Singles £40; doubles £50, with bath £70; triples £70; quads £90; quints £110. Rooms with bath range £60-£120. AmEx, MC, V.

Cosmo/Bedford House Hotel, 27 Bloomsbury Sq. (☎ 7636 4661; fax 7636 0577; cosmo.bedford.hotel@dial.pipex.com). Tube: Holborn. Location prevails over decoration in this family run establishment with neat, comfortable rooms that come with color TVs, and sinks. Some rooms overlook a tree-filled garden (one in particular has its own private garden); others look out onto the square. Continental breakfast. Singles £36, with bath £48; doubles £58, £70; triples £75, £85; quad £85, £90. AmEx, DC, MC, V. 5% credit card surcharge.

Mentone Hotel, 54-56 Cartwright Gdns. (☎ 7387 3927; fax 7388 4671; mentonehotel@compuserve.com; ourworld.compuserve.com/homepages/MentoneHotel). Tube: Russell Sq. Flowers cover the exterior, floral prints the interior. All rooms have phone, color TV and tea/coffee makers,

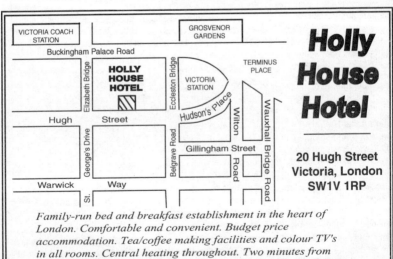

and the majority come with private bath. Airport shuttle available with advance reservation (from Heathrow £24, Stansted £43, Luton £34, Gatwick £40). English breakfast included. Singles £42, with bath £60; doubles with bath £79; triples with bath £90; quads with bath £99. Reduced rates for longer stays in Dec.-Apr. AmEx, DC, MC, V.

George Hotel, 58-60 Cartwright Gdns. (☎7387 8777; fax 7387 8666; ghotel@aol.com; www.georgehotel.com). Tube: Russell Sq. Homey dining hall, high ceilings, and track lighting. All rooms have phone, cable TV, and kettles. Hair dryers, irons, and email available upon request. English breakfast included. Singles from £50; doubles £70, with shower £75, with shower and toilet £85; triples £82, £90, £100; quads £95. Children under 12 £9.50. 10% discount for stays of 1 week or longer. MC, V.

Crescent Hotel, 49-50 Cartwright Gdns. (☎7387 1515; fax 7383 2054; general.enquiries@crescenthotelsoflondon.com; www.crescenthotelsoflondon.com). Tube: Russell Sq. An elegant lobby and swanky breakfast room have made this hotel a favorite of Bloomsbury visitors. Tea/coffee makers, sinks, and TVs in each room, hairdryers and alarm clocks on request. English breakfast included. Singles from £43, with shower £48, with bath £70; doubles with bath £82; triples with bath £93; quads with bath £105. More for one night stays; discounts for over a week. MC, V.

Jenkins Hotel, 45 Cartwright Gdns. (☎7387 2067; fax 7383 3139; www.jenkinshotel.demon.co.uk; reservations@jenkinshotel.demon.co.uk). B&B featured in the Agatha Christie TV series *Poirot*. If that isn't a ringing endorsement, what is? Tidy pastel rooms, phones, safes, teapots, TV, hairdryers, sinks, and fridges. No smoking. English breakfast included. Book ahead. Singles £52, with bath £72; doubles £72, £82; triples with bath £90. MC, V.

Ruskin Hotel, 23-24 Montague St. (☎7636 7388; fax 7323 1662). Tube: Holborn. Prime position across the street from the British Museum. Meticulously upkept rooms include kettles, sinks, phones, and hair dryers. TV lounge with elegant glass lamps. Lovely back garden. English breakfast included. Singles £45; doubles £64, with bath £79; triples £80, £89. AmEx, MC, V.

Celtic Hotel, 62 Guilford St. (☎7837 9258 or 7837 6737). Tube: Russell Sq. Provides basic rooms and clean facilities. They don't give room keys but will open the door for guests 24hr. Streetside rooms can be a bit noisy. TV lounge. Full English breakfast included. Singles £38.50; doubles £50.50; triples £70; quads £80; quints £100. No credit cards.

Jesmond Dene Hotel, 27 Argyle St. (☎7837 4654; fax 7833 1633; JesmondDeneHotel@msn.com; www.scoot.co.uk/jesmond-dene). Tube: King's Cross-St. Pancras. Black-and-white rooms with sinks and large TVs are slightly worn but scrupulously clean. Not the loveliest neighborhood. English breakfast. Reserve 2 weeks in advance. Singles £30; doubles £42, with shower £55; triples £60, £75; quads with bath £90; quints £95. MC, V (4% surcharge).

Hotel Apollo, 43 Argyle St. (☎7837 5489; fax 7916 1862; apollohotel@msn.com). Tube: King's Cross-St. Pancras. A smaller hotel run by the same friendly people as the Jesmond Dene; reception for both is also located there. Clean, basic rooms, all with sinks and TVs. Singles £30, with shower £35; doubles £40, £55. MC, V (4% surcharge).

Alhambra Hotel, 17-19 Argyle St. (☎7837 9575; fax 7916 2476; postmaster@alhambrahotel.demon.co.uk; www.smoothhound.co.uk/hotels/alhambra.html). Tube: King's Cross/St. Pancras. The rooms in the main building are pained by clashing decor but very clean; rooms in the refurbished annex across the street are a step up and come with bathrooms. Sinks and TVs in all rooms. Cozy dining room. Not the loveliest neighborhood. English breakfast. Singles £32, with shower £42, with bath £60; doubles £44, with shower £50, with bath £60; triples £62, with bath £77; quads with bath £92. AmEx, MC, V (4% surcharge).

SOHO

see map pp. 292-293

HOSTELS

YHA Oxford Street, 14-18 Noel St. (☎7734 1618; fax 7734 1657; oxfordst@yha.org.uk). Tube: Oxford Circus. As close as you can possibly get to the Soho action. The reception is on the 3rd floor; an elevator takes you up. Facilities include spacious TV lounge with plenty of comfortable couches, clean and fully equipped kitchen with microwave, laundry facilities, Internet access, and currency exchange. Rooms have large storage lockers, but you must bring your own padlock. Packed continental breakfast £3.20. Book at least 3-4 weeks in advance—very few walk-ins accepted. Full payment required to secure a reservation. No children under 6. Reception open 7am-11pm. 24hr. security; no curfew. 2-bed dorms £21.80; 3-4 bed dorms £20.55, under 18 £16.85. MC, V.

APARTMENT AGENCIES

Outlet, 32 Old Compton St. (☎7287 4244; fax 7734 2249; homes@outlet.co.uk; www.outlet.co.uk). Tube: Tottenham Court Rd. or Leicester Sq. Manages various holiday apartments for gay men and lesbians. All flats are around Soho; see website for pictures. Office open M-F 10am-7pm, Sa noon-5pm. Book well in advance. Self-contained studio flats £75-84, 1-bedroom flats £99-105. Shared accommodation (sharing a kitchen and bathroom) £45-60. Also has listings for longer-term stays.

OUTSIDE CENTRAL LONDON

ISLINGTON

RESIDENCE HALLS

Rosebery Hall, 90 Rosebery Ave., EC1 (☎7278 3251; fax 7278 2068). Tube: Angel. Exit left from the Tube station and go down St. John St.; Rosebery Ave. is on the right. A standard student hall, cinderblock walls and all. Economy twins are cheap but cramped. Kitchen, bar, TV room. Full breakfast included. see map pp. 308-309

Laundry. Reception open 7:30am-11:30pm. Available Mar.-Apr. and mid-June to Sept. Singles £26-31; economy twins £36; twins £46, with bath £57; triples £55. MC, V.

BED AND BREAKFAST HOTELS

▧ **Kandara Guesthouse,** 68 Ockendon Rd. (☎7226 5721; fax 7226 3379; admin@kandara.co.uk; www.kandara.co.uk). Tube: Highbury & Islington. Those with luggage may prefer to take bus #73, which stops close by on Essex Rd., from King's Cross or Angel. A bit far from the Tube, but well-served by buses. An exceedingly pleasant family-run B&B, with well-equipped, spacious rooms and shared bathrooms that are modern and bright. All rooms have TVs, washbasins, and tea- and coffee-making facilities. Prices depend on time of year and length of stay; booking early tends to get you lower prices. Breakfast (including vegetarian options) included. Singles £37-44; doubles and twins £49-57; triples £58-66. MC, V.

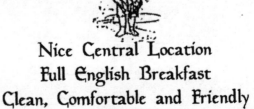

Walter Sickert Hall, 29 Graham St. (☎7477 8822; fax 7477 8825; www.city.ac.uk). Tube: Angel. Exit the station heading left; turn left onto City Rd.; Graham St. will be on the left just before the canal. Buses #43 and #214 go close by from the Tube station. Between Islington and the City. A great value. All rooms come with bath, kettle, phone, desks, and bookshelves. About 220 units. TV rooms. 24hr. security. In-room continental breakfast. Laundry facilities. Singles £30; doubles £50. "Executive" singles (with TVs and other amenities) £38; doubles £55. MC, V.

Five Kings Guesthouse, 59 Anson Rd. (☎7607 3996; fax 7609 5554). Tube: Tufnell Park. Quite far from central London, which may deter those intending to stay out late. All rooms have TVs, washbasins, and desks. Singles £25, with bath £28. Twins/doubles £38, with bath £44. Family rooms £48, with bath £63. 10% student discount. MC, V.

Jurys Inn, 60 Pentonville Rd. (☎7282 5500; fax 7282 5511; www.jurys.com). Tube: Angel. Exit left from the station, and turn right onto Pentonville Rd. While three-star hotels don't usually find their way into *Let's Go*'s listings, Jurys Inn's policy of charging on a per-room basis makes it an excellent deal for families and people in groups of 3. Comfortable beds and duvets. As you might expect, each of the 229 rooms comes with a bathroom, phone (and modem point), and satellite TV. Rooms are arranged either with a double bed and a single bed (for up to 3 adults) or with a double bed and a pull-out couch (for 2 adults and 2 children). Continental breakfast £5, English breakfast £6. Rooms £84.

HAMPSTEAD AND HIGHGATE

HOSTELS

🗺 **Hampstead Heath,** 4 Wellgarth Rd. (☎8458 9054 or ☎8458 7096; fax 8209 0546; hampstead@yha.org.uk). Tube: Hampstead or Golders Green, then bus #210 or 268 toward Hampstead, or on foot (uphill) turning right from Hampstead station onto Heath St, which becomes North End Rd., then right again onto Wellgarth Rd., a 15-20min. walk. A beautiful,

see map p. 318   sprawling hostel with Internet and fax access, a restaurant, parking, and video games. English breakfast included. Laundry. 24hr. security and reception. Lockers available. 200 beds in cabin-like rooms. No curfew. Book in advance. 2- to 6-bed dorms £19.70, under 18 £17.30. Family bunk rooms: doubles £35; triples £51.95; quads £68.95; quints £85.95; 6-bed £100. MC, V.

DOCKLANDS

HOSTELS

YHA Rotherhithe, 20 Salter Rd. (☎7232 2114; fax 7237 2919; rotherhithe@yha.org.uk). Tube: Rotherhithe or Canada Water. Buses 381 from Waterloo stops directly in front. This modern, somewhat impersonal 320-bed hostel is a trip into futuristic living. Kitchen. Breakfast (English or continental) included. Laundry. Other facilities include: internet, currency

see map p. 319   exchange, restaurant, and bar. All rooms with bath. Bigger rooms have triple bunks. Book ahead. 6- to 10-bed dorms £22.95, under 18 £19.70; 4-bed dorms £23; 2-bed dorms £25; family bunk room (1 child under 16, at least) double £40, quad £80, 6 beds £120. Wheelchair accessible. Amex, MC, V.

BRIXTON

BED AND BREAKFAST HOTELS

Number 7, 7 Josephine Ave. (☎8674 1880; hotel@no7.com; www.no7.com). Tube: Brixton. This gay B&B is within walking distance of the clubs but far away enough to avoid the noise. Rooms include TV, dataport, phones, and bath. Breakfast included. Singles from £59; doubles £79; triples, £119; quads £129. Major credit cards.

see map p. 318

EARL'S COURT

BED AND BREAKFAST HOTELS
All accommodations are near Tube: Earl's Court.

🔲 **Oxford Hotel,** 24 Penywern Rd. (☎ 7370 1161; fax 7373 8256; Oxford-hotel@btinternet.com). Clean rooms installed with new beds are repainted every year. The stylish dining room includes a bar. Breakfast 7:30-9:30am. Luggage storage and safe. 24hr. reception. Singles with shower £34, with bath £47; doubles £53, with bath £63; triples £63, with bath £73; quads with shower £75, with bath £85; quints with shower £95, with bath £105. Winter and weekly rates may be 10-15% lower. Reserve ahead. Amex, MC, V.

see map pp. 310-311

🔲 **Mowbray Court Hotel,** 28-32 Penywern Rd. (☎ 7373 8285 or 7370 3690; fax 7370 5693; mowbraycrthot@hotmail.com; www.m-c-hotel.mcmail.com). Staff this helpful is a rarity in London; wake-up calls, tour arrangements, taxicabs, theater bookings, and dry cleaning. Rooms are equipped with firm mattresses, towels, shampoo, hair dryers, TV, radio, trouser press, telephone, the Bible, and *The Teachings of Buddha.* Internet access. Reserve ahead; no deposit required. In-room safes £2 per day. Singles £45, with bath £52; doubles £56, with bath £67; triples £69, with bath £80; family rooms for 4 people £84, with bath £95; for 5 £100, with bath £110; for 6 £115, with bath £125. Negotiable discounts. AmEx, DC, MC, V.

Beaver Hotel, 57-59 Philbeach Gdns. (☎ 7373 4553; fax 7373 4555). Plush lounge with polished wood floors and cable TV. Lift access. All rooms have desks, phones, hair dryers, and coordinated linens. All bathrooms are a study in cleanliness. Wheelchair accessible. Parking £5. Singles £38, with bath £55; doubles £45, with bath £80; triples with bath £90. English breakfast served in lovely room 7:30-9:30am. Reserve several weeks ahead. AmEx, DC, MC, V.

Philbeach Hotel, 30-31 Philbeach Gdns. (☎ 7373 1244; fax 7244 0149; www.philbeachho-tel.freesere.). The largest gay B&B in England, popular with all genders. Jimmy's Bar downstairs is residents-only. Internet access. Continental breakfast included. Book 1 week ahead. Budget single £30, else £35-50, with shower £50-60; doubles £65, with bath £85; triple £75, £90; AmEx, DC, MC, V.

Half Moon Hotel, 10 Earl's Ct. Sq., SW5 (☎ 7373 9956; fax 7373 8456). From Earl's Court tube, take a right, and Earl's Court Sq. is the second right. Looks like a two-star, charges like a budget. Singles £30, with shower £45; doubles £55, with bath £60; triples £65, with bath £80; quads with shower £100. Continental breakfast included. MC, V with 4% surcharge.

Lord Jim Hotel, 23-25 Penywern Rd. (☎ 7370 6071; fax 7373 8919; taher_tayeb@com-puserve.com). If you don't mind small bedrooms, this hotel offers prices about £5-10 lower than competitors. Internet access. Super-clean rooms include phone, TV, and hair dryer. Singles £32, with shower £48; doubles £45, with shower £52, with bath £59; triples £52, with shower £60, with bath £68. Special rate promotions for stays over 5 nights and in the off season. Group rates from £12 per person. Continental breakfast included. 1 night's deposit required to secure reservation. 5% surcharge for credit cards. AmEx, MC, V.

Court Hotel, 194-196 Earl's Ct. Rd. (☎ 7373 0027; fax 7912 9500). This hostel couldn't be closer to the Tube station, and is a good choice for those unbothered by clutter. All single, double, and twin rooms have TV and tea/coffee set. No rooms have bunk beds but all have phones that take incoming calls. Gleaming bathrooms. Full kitchen facilities, internet access, and TV lounge. Safe available for valuables. Reception 24hr. No curfew. No reservations; call for availability. 4-bed dorm (single-sex and co-ed) £13-15; singles £26-30; doubles £35-40. Weekly: dorm £94; singles £180; doubles £240. Off-season and long-term discounts. AmEx, MC, V.

Ayers Rock Hotel, 16 Longridge Rd., SW5 (☎ 7373 2944; www.iliv4now.com). The name indicates what kind of clientele it pulls in. Large reception and fantastic purple lounge/TV area full of rugby fanatics. Free tea and coffee. Most rooms have fridges, but tended to be cramped. Basic accommodations cater to a backpacker crowd. 4- to 6-bed dorm from £12. Weekly: dorms from £60, £160.

SHEPHERD'S BUSH, HAMMERSMITH, AND HOLLAND PARK

see map pp. 310-311

HOSTELS

YHA Holland House, Holland Walk, W8 (☎ 7937 0748; fax 7376 0667; hollandhouse@yha.org.uk). Tube: High St. Kensington or Holland Park. Part of this hostel is a handsome 1607 Jacobean mansion. Rooms are clean and spacious, contain standard YHA beds, and have storage lockers—bring a padlock. Cooked breakfast included. Laundry and kitchen facilities. Free daytime luggage storage. 24hr. access. Dorms £19.95, under 18 £17.95. MC, V.

BED AND BREAKFAST HOTELS

Dalmacia Hotel, 71 Shepherd's Bush Rd. (☎ 7603 2887; fax 7602 9226; dalmacia@virginbiz.net; www.cityscan.co.uk/sites/3247). Tube: Goldhawk Rd. Large doubles, freshly redone rooms, and good service all make this a place to recommend. Nirvana stayed here before they became famous. Email and drink machine in the lobby. All rooms have satellite TV, phone, hairdryer, and bath. Singles £39; twins and doubles £59; triples £79. Cash discount. AmEx, MC, V.

Star Hotel, 97-99 Shepherd's Bush Rd. (☎ 7603 2755; fax 7603 0948). Tube: Hammersmith. A very clean B&B, with new furnishings and spacious rooms. All rooms with TVs and bath. Singles £35; doubles/twins £55; triples £95. Discounts for stays over 3 nights.

Hotel Orlando, 83 Shepherd's Bush Rd. (☎/fax 7603 4890; hotelorlando@supanet.com; www.hotelorlando.co.uk/home.htm). Tube: Goldhawk Rd. or Shepherd's Bush. The name comes from a surname, not from the Florida city. All rooms with TV, phone, radio, and sparkling clean bathrooms. Singles £35; doubles/twins £48; triples £66; family rooms £88. AmEx, MC, V.

Windsor Guest House, 43 Shepherd's Bush Rd. (☎/fax 7603 2116; neven@windsorghs.freeserve.co.uk). Tube: Goldhawk Rd. Rooms aren't terribly large, but the prices are reasonable. All rooms with TV and bath. Singles £25; doubles/twins £45; triples £67.50; "basic" rooms (with showers but no attached toilets) are cheaper. No credit cards.

Hotel 65, 65 Shepherd's Bush Rd. (☎7603 5634; fax 7603 4933; bookings@hotel65.demon.co.uk; www.hotel65.com). Tube: Goldhawk Rd. Singles £30, with bath £40; twins with bath £40; doubles with bath £50; triples £69. AmEx, DC, MC, V.

CAMPING

Camping in London provides the cheapest sleep, and the showers and toilets are similar to the ones in most hostels. In summer months, the few campsites near London fill up. You'll have to make reservations one to two weeks in advance.

Tent City—Hackney, Millfields Rd. (☎8749 9074; tentcity@btinternet.com; www.btinternet.com/~tentcity). Bus #38 from Victoria or Piccadilly Circus to Clapton Pond, and walk down Millfields Rd.; or Bus #242 from Liverpool St. Station to Millfields Rd., and cross bridge to Hackney Marshes. A canal-side campsite in a nature reserve, 4 mi. from London. Pitch your own or rest under their big top tents. Free hot showers, baggage storage, shop, snack bar, **laundry,** and cooking facilities. BBQs every Sa night. Inconvenient for public transport. £5 per person, children £2.50, under 5 free. Open 24hr. Open June-Aug.

Crystal Palace Caravan Club Site, Crystal Palace Parade (☎8778 7155). Tube: Brixton, then Bus #3 to Crystal Palace Tower. 8 mi. from London. Wonderfully close to the healthful activities at the Crystal Palace National Sports Centre. Showers and laundry facilities. You must bring your own tent. 21-day max. stay. Wheelchair accessible. £4 per person, children £1.20. Large tents £4, small tents £2. All visitors (even pedestrians) pay additional parking fees: caravan £5 (£4 for members—ask about membership at the site); tent with car £3.50; tent with motorcycle £2.50; tent with backpacker £2. Lower fees Oct.-Apr. Open year-round.

The MCI WorldCom Card.
The easy way to call when traveling worldwide.

MCI WORLDCOM *WORLDPHONE.*

1·800·888·8000

J. L. SMITH

The MCI WorldCom Card gives you...

- Access to the US and other countries worldwide.
- Customer Service 24 hours a day
- Operators who speak your language
- Great MCI WorldCom rates and no sign-up fees

For more information or to apply for a Card call:
1-800-955-0925

Outside the U.S., call MCI WorldCom collect (reverse charge) at:
1-712-943-6839

COUNTRY	WORLDPHONE TOLL-FREE ACCESS #
Argentina (CC)	
Using Telefonica	0800-222-6249
Using Telecom	0800-555-1002
Australia (CC) ♦	
Using OPTUS	1-800-551-111
Using TELSTRA	1-800-881-100
Austria (CC) ♦	0800-200-235
Bahamas (CC) +	1-800-888-8000
Belgium (CC) ♦	0800-10012
Bermuda (CC) +	1-800-888-8000
Bolivia (CC) ♦	0-800-2222
Brazil (CC)	000-8012
British Virgin Islands +	1-800-888-8000
Canada (CC)	1-800-888-8000
Cayman Islands +	1-800-888-8000
Chile (CC)	
Using CTC	800-207-300
Using ENTEL	800-360-180
China ♦	108-12
Mandarin Speaking Operator	108-17
Colombia (CC) ♦	980-9-16-0001
Collect Access in Spanish	980-9-16-1111
Costa Rica ♦	0800-012-2222
Czech Republic (CC) ♦	00-42-000112
Denmark (CC) ♦	8001-0022
Dominica+	1-800-888-8000
Dominican Republic (CC) +	
Collect Access	1-800-888-8000
Collect Access in Spanish	1121

COUNTRY	ACCESS #
Ecuador (CC) +	999-170
El Salvador (CC)	800-1767
Finland (CC) ♦	08001-102-80
France (CC) ♦	0-800-99-0019
French Guiana (CC)	0-800-99-0019
Germany (CC)	0800-888-8000
Greece (CC) ♦	00-800-1211
Guam (CC) ♦	1-800-888-8000
Guatemala (CC) ♦	99-99-189
Haiti +	
Collect Access	193
Collect access in Creole	190
Honduras +	8000-122
Hong Kong (CC)	800-96-1121
Hungary (CC) ♦	06*-800-01411
India (CC)	000-127
Collect access	000-126
Ireland (CC)	1-800-55-1001
Israel (CC)	1-800-920-2727
Italy (CC) ♦	172-1022
Jamaica +	
Collect Access	1-800-888-8000
From pay phones	#2
Japan (CC) ♦	
Using KDD	00539-121 ▶
Using IDC	0066-55-121 ▶
Using JT	0044-11-121

COUNTRY	ACCESS #
Korea (CC)	
To call using KT	00729-14
Using DACOM	00309-12
Phone Booths +	
Press red button ,03,then*	
Military Bases	550-2255
Luxembourg (CC)	8002-0112
Malaysia (CC) ♦	1-800-80-0012
Mexico (CC)	01-800-021-8000
Monaco (CC) ♦	800-90-019
Netherlands (CC) ♦	0800-022-91-22
New Zealand (CC)	000-912
Nicaragua (CC)	166
Norway (CC) ♦	800-19912
Panama	00800-001-0108
Philippines (CC) ♦	
Using PLDT	105-14
Filipino speaking operator	105-15
Using Bayantel	1237-14
Using Bayantel (Filipino)	1237-77
Using ETPI (English)	1066-14
Poland (CC) +	800-111-21-22
Portugal (CC) +	800-800-123
Romania (CC) +	01-800-1800
Russia (CC) + ♦	
Russian speaking operator	
	747-3320
Using Rostelcom	747-3322
Using Sovintel	960-2222
Saudi Arabia (CC)	1-800-11

COUNTRY	WORLDPHONE TOLL-FREE ACCESS #
Singapore (CC)	8000-112-112
Slovak Republic (CC)	08000-00112
South Africa (CC)	0800-99-0011
Spain (CC)	900-99-0014
St. Lucia +	1-800-888-8000
Sweden (CC) ♦	020-795-922
Switzerland (CC) ♦	0800-89-0222
Taiwan (CC) ♦	0080-13-4567
Thailand (CC)	001-999-1-2001
Turkey (CC) ♦	00-8001-1177
United Kingdom (CC)	
Using BT	0800-89-0222
Using C & W	0500-89-0222
Venezuela (CC) + ♦	800-1114-0
Vietnam + ●	1201-1022

KEY
Note: Automation available from most locations. Countries where automation is not yet available are shown in *Italic*
(CC) Country-to-country calling available.
+ Limited availability.
✻ Not available from public pay phones.
▶ Public phones may require deposit of coin or phone card for dial tone.
♦ Local service fee in U.S. currency required to complete call.
▶ Regulation does not permit Intra-Japan Calls.
* Wait for second dial tone.
■ Local surcharge may apply.
Hint: For Puerto Rico and Caribbean Islands not listed above, you can use 1-800-888-8000 as the WorldPhone access number.

WORLDWIDE CALLING MADE EASY

The MCI WorldCom Card, designed specifically to keep you in touch with the people that matter the most to you.

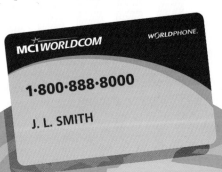

MCI WORLDCOM · WORLDPHONE.
1·800·888·8000
J. L. SMITH

www.wcom.com/worldphone

Please tear off this card and keep it in your wallet as a reference guide for convenient U.S. and worldwide calling with the MCI WorldCom Card.

HOW TO MAKE CALLS USING YOUR MCI WORLDCOM CARD

> **When calling from the U.S., Puerto Rico, the U.S. Virgin Islands or Canada** to virtually anywhere in the world:

1. Dial 1-800-888-8000
2. Enter your card number + PIN, listen for the dial tone
3. Dial the number you are calling :
   Domestic Calls: Area Code + Phone number
   International Calls:
   011+ Country Code + City Code + Phone Number

> **When calling from outside the U.S.**, use WorldPhone from over 125 countries and places worldwide:

1. Dial the WorldPhone toll-free access number of the country you are calling from.
2. Follow the voice instructions or hold for a WorldPhone operator to complete the call

> **For calls from your hotel:**

1. Obtain an outside line.
2. Follow the instructions above on how to place a call.
   Note: If your hotel blocks the use of your MCI WorldCom Card, you may have to use an alternative location to place your call.

RECEIVING INTERNATIONAL COLLECT CALLS*

Have family and friends call you collect at home using WorldPhone Service and pay the same low rate as if you called them.

1. Provide them with the WorldPhone access number for the country they are calling from (In the U.S., 1-800-888-8000; for international access numbers see reverse side).
2. Have them dial that access number, wait for an operator, and ask to call you collect at your home number.

For U.S. based customers only.

START USING YOUR MCI WORLDCOM CARD TODAY. MCI WORLDCOM STEPSAVERS℠

Get the same low rate per country as on calls from home, when you:

1. **Receive international collect calls to your home** using WorldPhone access numbers

2. **Make international calls with your MCI WorldCom Card** from the U.S.*

3. **Call back to anywhere in the U.S. from Abroad** using your MCI WorldCom Card and WorldPhone access numbers.

An additional charge applies to calls from U.S. pay phones.

WorldPhone Overseas Laptop Connection Tips —
Visit our website, www.wcom.com/worldphone, to learn how to access the Internet and email via your laptop when traveling abroad using the MCI WorldCom Card and WorldPhone access numbers.

Travelers Assist® — When you are overseas, get emergency interpretation assistance and local medical, legal, and entertainment referrals. Simply dial the country's toll-free access number.

Planning a Trip?—Call the WorldPhone customer service hotline at 1-800-736-1828 for new and updated country access availability or visit our website:

www.wcom.com/worldphone

MCI WorldCom Worldphone Access Numbers

Easy Worldwide Calling

MCI WORLDCOM
1·800·888·8000
J. L. SMITH

MCI WORLDCOM.™

Living in London

Maybe you're starting a job after college, taking time off, or just passing through for a few months. There's no better way to understand London than to live there. Waiting patiently with after work commuters for a Central Line train is as London as anything a mere tourist would experience, and seeing your name on a BT phone bill brings a strange rush: it shows you've become part of London life in a small but significant way. London, celebrated and mythologized in brochures and travel guides, is really just a city. And as such, it presents the challenges you'd expect—it's crowded and dirty, high rents might mean a long commute to work, and the crowds can make any loneliness acute.

It may be hard to come to London alone, but you'll probably meet plenty of people at work. Paging through *Time Out* to find activities (dance classes, film festivals, athletic events) can help you meet people with similar interests. London offers plenty of inexpensive weekend and weeknight activities and the more you take advantage of these, the fewer evenings you'll spend eating baked beans and sipping lager in front of the BBC. Plus you'll see the sides of London that only living there reveals.

LONG-TERM VISAS AND EMPLOYMENT

EU citizens do not need visas to live or work in Britain; while citizens of numerous countries, including Australia, Canada, New Zealand, South Africa, and the USA, do not need visas for visits of under 6 months, all non-EU citizens planning to stay longer than 6 months must obtain a long-stay visa before their arrival in the UK. For details of how to obtain a British visa, see **Planning you trip**, p. 215. A tourist visa does not permit you to accept any type of paid employment, however. Non-EU citizens intending to work in the UK must also apply for and obtain a **work permit** before their arrival; see below for details.

BRITISH	AMERICAN
aubergine	eggplant
banger	sausage
bap	soft bun
barmy	insane, erratic
bathroom	room containing a bathtub
bed-sit, or bed sitter	one-room apartment
bird	girl
biro	ballpoint pen
bit of alright	attractive (of girls)
biscuit	a cookie or cracker
bloke	guy
bobby	police officer
give a bollocking to	shout at
bonnet	car hood
boot	car trunk
braces	suspenders
bubble and squeak	cabbage and mashed potatoes
bum bag	fanny pack
busker	street musician
caravan	trailer, mobile home
car park	parking lot
cheeky	mischievous
cheers, cheerio	thank you, goodbye
chemist, chemist's	pharmacist, pharmacy
chips	french fries
chuffed	happy
circle	theater balcony
coach	inter-city bus
concession, "concs"	discount on admission
courgette	zucchini
crisps	potato chips
dicey, dodgy	problematic, sketchy
the dog's bollocks	the best
dosh, dough	money
ensuite	with atttached bathroom
fag	cigarette
fanny	vagina
first floor	second floor
fortnight	two weeks
full stop	period (punctuation)
geezer	man
gob	mouth
grotty	grungy
governor (pron. "guvnah" or "guv")	boss

OBTAINING A WORK PERMIT

Unless you're an EU citizen, you need a work permit to legally work in Britain. **EU citizens** can work anywhere in the EU, and if your parents were born in an EU country, you may be able to claim dual citizenship or the right to a work permit. If your parents were born in Britain, you may be eligible for a British passport, which allows unrestricted employment. If your grandparents are British, you can apply for a Right of Abode visa ($50), which allows you to stay and work for up to 4 years in Britain without a permit. Citizens of certain **Commonwealth countries** (including Australia, Canada, New Zealand, and South Africa) between 17-27 can apply for a **working holiday visa** at their local British embassy ($33). This allows you to work in Britain during a visit of up to 2 years if the employment you take is "incidental to your holiday." **American citizens** who are full-time students at American universities and are older than 18 can apply for a **Blue Card Permit** from BUNAC (see **Finding Work**, below), which allows them to work for up to 6 months.

Non-EU and non-Commonwealth job-seekers must have their prospective employers apply for a work permit or apply themselves with supporting papers from the prospective employers. The real catch-22 is that normally one must physically enter the country in order to have immigration officials validate your work permit papers and note your status in your passport. This means if you can't set up a job from afar and have the permit sent to you, you must enter the country to look for a job, find an employer, have them start the permit process, then *leave* the country until the permit is sent to you (up to 6 weeks), and finally return and start work.

FINDING WORK

One foolproof way to immerse yourself in a foreign culture is to become part of its economy. It's easy to find a **temporary job,** especially with London's booming economy, but it may not pay much. If you are a US citizen and a full-time, degree-seeking student at a US university, the simplest way to get a job abroad is through work-permit programs run by **British Universities North America Club (BUNAC)** and its member organizations. For a US$225 application fee, BUNAC can secure participants six-month work permits and offers information and assistance in finding work and housing, along with other perks. BUNAC also administers programs for residents of Australia, New Zealand, and South Africa. For more information contact BUNAC at 16 Bowling Green Ln., London EC1R 0QH (☎ 7251 3472 or US ☎ 800-GO-BUNAC (462-8622); BUNAC@easynet.co.uk; www.bunac.org.uk).

WORK/TRAVEL PROGRAMS

The following organizations arrange work exchanges in the UK for foreigners:

Accord Cultural Exchange, 750 La Playa, San Francisco, CA 94121, USA (☎ (415) 386-6203); www.cognitext.com/accord). US$40 application fee.

interExchange, 161 Sixth Ave, New York, NY 10013 (☎ (212) 924-0446; fax 924-0575; www.interexchange.org).

Childcare International, Trafalgar House, Grenville Pl., London NW7 3SA (☎ 8906 3116; fax 8906 3461; www.childint.co.uk). £100 application fee.

International Exchange Programs (IEP), 196 Albert Rd., South Melbourne, Victoria 3205, Australia (☎ (03) 9690 5890), and P.O. Box 1786, Shortland St., Auckland, New Zealand (☎ (09) 366 6255; www.iepnz.co.nz). Work/travel programs in Britain for Australians and Kiwis.

International Schools Services, Educational Staffing Program, P.O. Box 5910, Princeton, NJ 08543 (☎ (609) 452-0990; fax 452-2690; edustaffing@iss.edu; www.iss.edu). Recruits teachers and school administrators. Applicants must have a bachelor's degree and 2 years' experience. US$100 application fee. Publishes *The ISS Directory of Overseas Schools* (US$35).

South Africa Student Travel Services, 8th Fl., J.H. Isaacs House, 5 Heerengracht, Foreshore, Cape Town 8001 (☎ (021) 418 3794; www.sasts.org.za). *Work and Travel Britain* program helps South Africans on the two-year working holiday visa find jobs and meet up with other participants.

Vacation Work Publications, 9 Park End St., Oxford OX1 1HJ, UK (☎ (01865) 24 19 78; fax 79 08 85). Publishes a wide variety of guides and directories with job listings and info for the working traveler, including *Teaching English Abroad* (£10; postage £2.50, £1.50 within UK) and *The Au Pair and Nanny's Guide to Working Abroad* (£9; postage £2.50, £1.50). Opportunities for summer or full-time work in numerous countries. Write for a catalogue.

OPTIONS FOR WORK

INTERNSHIPS

Finding an internship in London is not difficult—finding a paid one is. Interning has its resume-boosting perks (just ask Monica Lewinsky) but hey, you don't get paid, and photocopiers are no different in Britain from anywhere else in the

BRITISH	ENGLISH
high street	main street
hire	rent
holiday	vacation
hoover	vacuum cleaner, to vacuum
holiday	vacation
ice lolly	popsicle
interval	intermission
jumble sale	yard sale
jumper	sweater
kip	sleep
knackered	tired, worn out
knob	penis, awkward person
knock up	to knock on someone's door
lavatory, loo	restroom
lay-by	roadside turnout
leader (in newspaper)	editorial
legless	drunk
to let	to rent (property)
lift	elevator
lorry	truck
luvvly-jubbly	great
mad	crazy
mate	pal
motorway	highway
mobile phone	cellphone
naff	shabby or cheap
pants	underpants
petrol	gasoline
phone box, call box	telephone booth
take the piss, take the mick	make fun
pissed	drunk
prat	stupid person
plaster	Band-Aid
prawn	shrimp
props	pub regulars
pudding	dessert
pull	to "score"
public schools	the most prestigious private schools
punter	average person, customer
quid	pound (in money)
queue up, queue	line up, a line
quay (pronounced "key")	river bank
return ticket	round-trip ticket

on the cheap

Fringe Benefits

If you're put off by the exorbitant rent charged for Zone 1 digs, think about living farther out. Sure, living in Zone 1 puts you right near the action and probably close to work; but living in an outer Zone has a number of advantages. First of all, rents are cheaper—it's possible to find a comfortable pad for the same price you'd pay for a Zone 1 hole-in-the-wall. Still, you have to look around. The outer Zones are pocked with a number of ugly blocks of flats. Don't let that discourage you—many flats in the areas that were once London suburbs are as charming as they are cheap.

If you're looking in the outer Zones, try to find something near a tube station: buses are erratic and slow, and living near the Underground means that if you're no farther out than Zone 3, you're probably not more than 30 minutes outside central London.

Price isn't the only reason to live outside Zone 1. You might find that if you life in an outer Zone you'll experience a side of London your study abroad friends won't. Leaving Zone 1, London's polish gives way to grit. In east London especially, immigrants add international flavor to many neighborhoods. You'll see how London works as a city, not just a tourist trap.

world. Companies might not even pay your dry-cleaning bills. But if you are interested in interning, use your college career office and the Internet to investiage options. Then send out reams of CVs (*curriculum vitae;* the British term for a resume). MPs (Members of Parliament) take interns, and a number of other governmental internships are available as well.

VOLUNTEERING

Volunteer jobs are fairly easy to secure. However, if you receive room and board in exchange for your labor, you are considered to be employed and must get a work visa. You can sometimes avoid the high application fees charged by organizations by contacting the individual workcamps directly.

Council has a Voluntary Services Dept., 205 E. 42nd St., New York, NY 10017 (☎(888) COUNCIL (268-6245); fax (212) 822-2699; info@ciee.org; www.ciee.org), which offers 2- to 4-week environmental or community services projects.

Service Civil International Voluntary Service, 5474 Walnut Level Rd., Crozet, VA 22932 (☎(804) 823-1826; fax 823-5027; sciivsusa@igc.apc.org; wworks.com/~sciivs). Workcamp placements for ages 18 and over. Local organizations sponsor groups for physical or social work.

Volunteers for Peace, 43 Tiffany Rd., Belmont, VT 05730 (☎(802) 259-2759; fax 259-2922; vfp@vfp.org; www.vfp.org). A nonprofit organization that arranges speedy placement in 2-3 week workcamps comprising 10-15 people. VFP offers over 1000 programs in 70 nations. Complete and up-to-date listings are in the annual International Workcamp Directory (US$15). Registration fee US$200. Some work camps are open to 16- and 17-year-olds for US$225. Free newsletter.

FURTHER READING

Summer Jobs: Britain (US$17), lists roughly 30,000 jobs in the UK.

International Jobs: Where they Are, How to Get Them, by Eric Kocher and Nina Segal. Perseus Books (US$16).

How to Get a Job in Europe, Robert Sanborn. Surrey Books (£16.50 or US$22).

Work Abroad, by Clayton Hubbs. Transitions Abroad (US$16).

Overseas Summer Jobs 1999 and *Directory of Jobs and Careers Abroad.* Peterson's (US$17-18).

International Directory of Voluntary Work, by Victoria Pybus (Vacation Work Publications; £10.99 or US$15.95).

STUDYING IN LONDON

It's not difficult to spend a summer, term, or year studying in London under the auspices of a well-established program. Enrolling as a full-time student, however, is somewhat trickier; admission requirements can be hard to meet unless you attended a British secondary school, and only a limited number of foreign students are accepted each year. Once accepted on a course, you'll need to get an official letter from university and proof of financial support to be admitted to the UK. **Council** sponsors over 40 study abroad programs throughout the world.

American Institute for Foreign Study, College Division, 102 Greenwich Ave, Greenwich, CT 06830 (☎(800) 727-2437 ext. 6084; www.aifs.com). Organizes programs for high school and college study in universities.

Association of Commonwealth Universities, John Foster House, 36 Gordon Sq., London WC1H OPF (☎7387 8572; fax 7387 2655; info@acu.ac.uk; www.acu.ac.uk). Administers scholarship programs like British Marshall scholarships and publishes information about Commonwealth universities. Library open T-Th 10am-1pm and 2-4pm.

Beaver College Center for Education Abroad, 450 S. Easton Rd., Glenside, PA 19038-3295 (☎(800) 755-5607 or 888-BEAVER; fax (215) 572-2174; cea@beaver.edu; www.beaver.edu/cea). Applicants must have completed three full semesters at an accredited university.

Central College Abroad, Office of International Education, 812 University, Pella, IA 50219 (☎(800) 831-3629; fax (515) 628-5375; studyabroad@central.edu; www.studyabroad.com/central/). Applicants must be at least 18 years old, have completed their 1st year of college, and have a minimum 2.5 GPA.

Universities and Colleges Admissions Services (UCAS), Fulton House, Jewssop, Cheltenham GL50 3SH, UK (☎(01242) 22 77 88). Provides information and handles admissions to all full-time undergraduate courses at universities and their affiliated colleges in the UK.

UKCOSA/United Kingdom Council for International Education, 9-17 St. Albans Pl., London N1 0NX (☎7226 3762; advice line 7354 5210; www.britcoun.org/website/ukcosa/index.htm). Advises prospective and current students on immigration, finance, and more.

THE BRITISH COUNCIL

The British Council is the arm of the government charged with promoting education opportunities in Britain, among other responsibilities. Its offices are an invaluable source of information for those intending to study in Britain at a secondary school or university level, or for those enrolling in language classes in Britain. For their numerous branches in countries not listed here, call the London office or check out their website at www.britishcouncil.org.

BRITISH	ENGLISH
ring up	telephone
roundabout	rotary intersection
rubber	eraser
sack , give the sack	to fire someone
self-catering	with kitchen facilities
serviette	napkin
shag, shagging	sex, having sex
single carriageway	non-divided highway
single ticket	one-way ticket
snog	to kiss
sod it	forget it
spotted dick	steamed sponge pudding with raisins
stalls	orchestra seats
sultanas	a type of raisin
suspenders	garters
subway	pedestrian underpass
sweets	candy
swish	swanky
ta, ta-ta	thank you, goodbye
tariff	cost
toilet	restroom
torch	flashlight
tosser	literally, masturbator; ses prat
trainers	sneakers
trousers	pants
tube/Underground	London subway
vest	undershirt
waistcoat	men's vest
wanker	see tosser
way out	exit
WC	restroom
wellies, Wellington boots	waterproof boots
yob	prole, uncultured person
zed	the letter Z
zebra crossing	crosswalk

BRITISH	PRONOUNCED
Berkeley	BARK-lee
Berkshire	BARK-sher
Birmingham	BIRM-ing-um
Derby	DAR-bee
Dulwich	DULL-ich
Edinburgh	ED-in-bur-ra
Gloucester	GLOS-ter
Greenwich	GREN-ich
Grosvernor	GRO-vna
Islington	IHZ-ling-tun
Leicester	LES-ter
Maryleborn	MAR-lee-bun
Magdalen	MAUD-lin
quay	KEY
Norwich	NOR-ich
Salisbury	SAULS-bree
Southwark	SUTH-uk
Thames	TEMS
Worcester	WOO-ster

London Office: 10 Spring Gdns, London SW1A 2BN (☎(0161) 957 7755 for inquiries; ☎7389 4383).

Australia: Suite 401, Level 4, Edgecliff Centre, 203-233 New South Head Rd. (PO Box 88), Edgecliff NSW 2027 (☎(02) 9326 2022; www.bc.org.au).

Canada: 80 Elgin St., Ottawa, Ontario K1P 5K7 (☎613 237 1530).

New Zealand: 44 Hill St., P.O. Box 1812, Wellington (☎(04) 472 6049; www.britishcouncil.org.nz).

South Africa: 76 Juta St., Braamfontein, Johannesburg 2017 (☎(011) 403 3316).

United States: 3100 Massachusetts Ave. N.W., Washington, D.C. 20008 (☎202 588 6500; www.british-council-usa.org).

FURTHER INFORMATION

www.studyabroad.com

Academic Year Abroad 2000/2001. Institute of International Education Books (US$45).

Vacation Study Abroad 2000/2001. Institute of International Education Books (US$43).

Peterson's Study Abroad 2001. Peterson's (US$30).

Peterson's Summer Study Abroad 2001. Peterson's (US$30)

LONG-TERM ACCOMMODATIONS

Finding a flat in London is easy; finding an affordable one is an entirely different game. People on budgets will probably have to rent a **bedsit** (a small room in a private house, with access to a kitchen and bathroom) or join in a **flatshare** (i.e. splitting the rent and utilities for a flat with other people). Expect to pay £60-80 a week at the very least, a figure which rises as you get closer to central London. **Short-term stays** cost more, and most landlords won't lease for less than a month. You'll generally have to pay one month's advance rent and another month's rent as deposit. Check which **transport zone** your flat is in; this will affect your bus or tube fare.

Do-it-yourselfers willing to put in some time and footwork should rush to the newsagent the morning that London's **small-ads papers** are published, and immediately begin calling. **Loot** (☎(08700) 434434; www.loot.com) is published daily, as is the **Evening Standard** (which, despite its name, can be bought in the morning). Both have the best listings for short (1-2 month) rentals. **Capital FM** and the **Guardian** jointly publish a flatshare list in the *Space* supplement of the Thursday edition of the Guardian. The latest lists can be picked up at the **Capital FM Foyer,** 29-30 Leicester Sq. (Tube: Leicester Sq.) on Wednesday at 6pm. Other sources of vacancies are **Time Out** (out on Tuesday) and **NME** (Thursday). Bulletin boards in small grocery shops frequently list available rooms and flats, as do the classified sections of major and local newspapers. Beware of ads placed by **accommodations agencies;** they may try to sell you something more expensive when you call. Though they save a lot of legwork, agencies generally charge one or two weeks' rent as a fee, and it's in their interest to find high-priced accommodations. Note that it is illegal for accommodation agencies to charge you money just for supplying a list of addresses or registering with them; they may only charge you after you rent the room. You may want to register with several agencies. Many London boroughs run **information offices,** which often have listings of reliable local agencies.

ACCOMMODATIONS AGENCIES

Jenny Jones Accommodations Agency, 40 South Molton St., W1 (☎ 7493 4801). Tube: Bond St. Charges the fee to the landlord instead of the tenant. Suburban bedsits from £60-65 per week; check several times for a central location (£80-130 per week). Open M-F 10am-5:30pm.

University of London Accommodations Office, University of London Senate House, Room B, Malet St., WC1 (☎ 7862 8880; fax 7862 8084; ulao@accom.lon.ac.uk; www.lon.ac.uk/accom). Tube: Russell Sq. Students should begin their search at this wonderful place, which has lists of private accommodations available for summer stays beginning in June, and have similar lists of university-affiliated housing for the summer (late June-Oct.), Christmas (mid-Dec. to mid-Jan., and Easter (mid-March to April) holidays. Sometimes "summer listings" actually want tenants for the long haul, so search carefully. The helpful staff gives free advice on the intricacies of London flatting, from tenant/landlord responsibilities to inventories and deposits. Student ID required. Open M-F 9:30am-5:30pm.

Outlet, 32 Old Compton St. (☎ 7287 4244; fax 7734 2249; homes@outlet.co.uk; www.outlet.co.uk). Tube: Tottenham Court Rd. or Leicester Sq.) finds flats or rooms throughout London (no commission) for gays and lesbians.

Universal Aunts, P.O. Box 304, SW4 (☎ 7738 8937; fax 7622 1914), has central locations for about £75-150 plus a service charge.

BANKS

If you're going to be living and/or working in London for a long time, opening a sterling bank account will make managing funds convenient, especially because many employers offer direct deposit as an option. Decisions concerning opening accounts and extended credit privilges are ultimately at the discretion of the branch manager. In all cases you should contact your home bank a few months before you go and obtain a letter of introduction saying you're a customer in good standing. Check whether your bank can arrange in advance for an account to be opened at a UK bank so that it is available upon your arrival. When opening an acount, you must show your passport and your bank's letter of introduction, a letter from an employer confirming the tenure of employment in Britain and a regular salary or a letter from your university (in Britain) confirming your status as a full-time student, or a proof of residence such as a phone bill or lease.

While proof of employment or enrollment in a UK-based degree course almost always guarantees an account, study-abroad students are screened rigorously. Students of American colleges studying abroad should contact their home school's bursar's office, which may have a special arrangement with customers who are registered as Not Ordinarily Resident in the UK. To inquire visit the branch at 1 Waterloo Place Pall Mall or phone for an appointment (☎ 0845 730 1996).

The head branches of the big five UK banks are:

Barclays, 54 Lombard St., EC3 (☎ 7699 5000; www.barclays.com).

Lloyds TSB, 71 Lombard St., EC3 (☎ 7626 1500; www.llyodstsb.com).

HSBC, 27-32 Poultry, EC2 (☎ 7260 8000; www.hsbc.com).

National Westminster, 41 Lothbury, EC2 (☎ (0800) 50 50 50; www.natwest.com).

Abbey National, 201 Grafton Gate East, Milton Keynes (☎ (0800) 731 7774; www.abbeynational.co.uk).

BANK HOLIDAYS

During Bank holidays, schools, businesses, and restaurants are closed; however, many museums and attractions stay open to accommodate the those who have a day off. The following are the 2001 Bank Holidays for England and Wales.

DATE	HOLIDAY	DATE	HOLIDAYS
January 1	New Year's Day; London Parade	May 28	Spring
April 13	Good Friday	August 27	August
April 16	Easter Monday	December 25	Christmas
May 7	May Day	December 26	Boxing Day

MEDICAL CARE

In Britain, the state-run **National Health Service (NHS)** encompasses the majority of health-care center. Brits are strongly attached to the NHS—after all, it gives them something to complain about. While it's true that waiting lists are longer and comfort levels lower than in pricey private hospitals, going private doesn't mean better doctors; almost all of Britain's top doctors do both NHS and private work. If you are a member of an **EU** or certain **Commonwealth** countries, you can receive free treatment at any NHS clinic or hospitals. If you're working legally or a full-time student at a UK university, you will also be entitled to free NHS coverage. If not, you may be expected to pay upon receiving treatment; note that **opticians** and **dental care** are not covered by the NHS. US citizens should check with their insurance providers to see what it does and does not cover while abroad; note that although most US insurance plans (excluding Medicare) cover medical emergencies during short trips abroad, will probably not be covered for stays over a certain length of time. If you're ineligible for NHS treatment, **BUPA,** Cedar House, Chertsey Lane, Staines TW18 3DY (☎0345 553311; membership@bupa.com; www.bupa.co.uk) is the UK's largest private medical insurance provider.

For primary care, register with a local **General Practitioner** (GP). Most GPs are employed by the NHS, though many will also treat private patients. To register for NHS service, you will be asked to supply your NHS membership number; if you don't have one yet, you'll need to supply proof of eligibility; proof of residence in the local area is also required. Chemists and local community centers can supply you with a list of local doctors, but word-of-mouth is the best way to find a reliable physician. Most London doctors keep a few **surgery hours** per week, during which they offer walk-in service (well, more often walk-in-sit-down-wait-two-hours); at other times, you'll need to make an appointment. If you are too ill to go to the surgery, your most GPs will also make **home visits.** For more serious problems, your GP will refer you to a hospital specialist; you cannot make a hospital appointment without a prior referral. The NHS has a flat-fee system of **prescriptions;** all drugs prescribed by NHS physicians cost £5.80 (free for seniors, children under 16 or under 18 in full-time education, and the unemployed). For many generic drugs this fee is higher than the ordinary cost of the drug; in this case, you can ask your doctor to write you a private prescription (though they may refuse).

In case of urgent but non-life-threatening problems and injuries, you should go to the nearest **Accident & Emergency** or **Casualty** department, found in most large hospitals (for details see **Emergency rooms,** see p. 273). In case of an **emergency,** call 999 free from any phone and request an ambulance. For **Medical help lines,** see p. 274.

FITNESS

London is blessed with over 200 public sports and fitness centers; consult the yellow pages under "Leisure Centers" for more exhaustive listings or call the local borough council for a list of centers near you.

Barbican YMCA, 2 Fann St., EC2 (☎7628 0697; fax 7638 2420). Tube: Barbican. Spacious fitness center with weights, Nautilus machines, treadmills and bikes. Membership £55 per year, £27 for 3 months. Additional fee £3.50 per use, £35 unlimited use per month. Members only.

Jubilee Hall Recreation Centre, 30 The Piazza, WC2 (☎ 7836 4835), on the south side of Covent Garden. Tube: Covent Garden. Regular classes and activities include weight lifting, yoga, martial arts, gymnastics, dance, badminton, and aerobics. Special facilities include a sauna, solarium, and an alternative sports medicine clinic. Crowded with West End office workers at lunchtime. Membership (£51 month, direct-debit £45) includes unlimited use of all facilities. Non-members can purchase a day membership (£10), or shell out £6.90 per gym visit, £6 per class. Open M-F 7am-10pm, Sa 10am-6pm, Su 10am-5pm. AmEx, V, MC.

Queen Mother Sports Centre, 223 Vauxhall Bridge Rd., SW1 (☎ 7630 5522). Tube: Victoria. Over 14 sports and activities. Equipment rental. Activities and classes (£4.20-6.30 per hour) and full use of facilities on a pay-per-use basis are open to non-members. Use of weight gym (non-members £6.30 per use) requires completion of a 1-hr. induction course (non-members £28). Pool open M-Tu 6:30am-8pm, W-F 6:30am-7:30pm, Sa-Su 8am-5:30pm; non-members £2.25 per use, members £1.70. Membership £39 per year. Open M-F 6:30am-10pm, Sa 8am-8pm.

MEASUREMENTS

1 inch (in.) = 25.4 millimeters (mm)	1 millimeter (mm) = 0.039 in.
1 foot (ft.) = 0.30 m	1 meter (m) = 3.28 ft.
1 yard (yd.) = 0.914m	1 meter (m) = 1.09 yd.
1 mile = 1.61km	1 kilometer (km) = 0.62 mi.
1 ounce (oz.) = 28.35g	1 gram (g) = 0.035 oz.
1 pound (lb.) = 0.454kg	1 kilogram (kg) = 2.202 lb.
1 gallon (gal.) = 3.785L	1 liter (L) = 0.264 gal.
1 square mile (sq. mi.) = 2.59km^2	1 square kilometer (km^2) = 0.386 sq. mi.

SPEAKING BRITISH

Please see the running American-British glossary on p. 262–p. 266.

Service Directory

ACCOMMODATIONS AGENCIES

For full listings of the agencies below, see **Living in London,** p. 266.

■ **Jenny Jones Accommodations Agency,** 40 South Molton St., W1 (☎ 7493 4801). Tube: Bond St. Open M-F 10am-5:30pm.

Outlet, 32 Old Compton St. (☎ 7287 4244; fax 7734 2249; homes@outlet.co.uk; www.outlet.co.uk). Tube: Tottenham Court Rd. or Leicester Sq. Finds flats or rooms throughout London for gays and lesbians. No commission.

Universal Aunts, P.O. Box 304, SW4 (☎ 7738 8937; fax 7622 1914).

University of London Accommodations Office, University of London Senate House, Room B, Malet St., WC1 (☎ 7862 8880; fax 7862 8084; ulao@accom.lon.ac.uk; www.lon.ac.uk/accom). Tube: Russell Sq. Student ID required. Open M-F 9:30am-5:30pm.

BANKS

For info on opening accounts, see **Living in London,** p. 267. **Head offices** include:

Barclays, 54 Lombard St., EC3 (☎ 7699 5000; www.barclays.com).

Lloyds TSB, 71 Lombard St., EC3 (☎ 7626 1500; www.llyodstsb.com).

HSBC, 27-32 Poultry, EC2 (☎7260 8000; www.hsbc.com).

National Westminster, 41 Lothbury, EC2 (☎(0800) 50 50 50; www.natwest.com).

Abbey National, 201 Grafton Gate East, Milton Keynes (☎(0800) 731 7774; www.abbeyna-tional.co.uk).

BUDGET TRAVEL AGENCIES

Campus/Usit Youth and Student Travel, 52 Grovesner Gardens, SW1W (☎(0870) 240 1010; www.usitcampus.co.uk).

Council Travel, 28A Poland St., W1V (☎7287 3337). Tube: Oxford Circus.

CTS Travel, 44 Goodge St., W1 (☎7636 0031; fax 7637 5328; ctsinfo@ctstravel.co.uk; www.ctstravel.co.uk). Tube: Goodge St.

STA Travel, 6 Wrights Ln., W8 (☎7938 4711; www.sta-travel.com). Tube: High St. St. Kensington.

Travel CUTS 295A Regent St., W1R (☎7255 1944). Tube: Oxford Circus.

CAR RENTAL

To rent a car, you must have had a licence for at least a year. Overseas liscences are valid for a year in Britain, after which you must take a British driving test. All major agencies have offices in London, including:

Budget, 49 Woburn Pl. (☎(0845) 606 6669). Tube: Russell Sq. Must be 21. £10 per day fee for under 25. Open M-Sa 8am-10pm. Major credit cards.

Europcar BCR, 30 Woburn Pl. (☎7255 2339). Tube: Russell Sq. M-F 8am-6pm, Sa 8am-1pm. Must be 23. Major credit cards.

Wheelchair Travel. See **Disabled Resources,** below.

CURRENCY EXCHANGE

American Express (www.americanex-press.com). 15 locations in London including: **Victoria:** 7 Wilton Rd., SW1 (☎7630 6365; open M-Sa 9am-5:30pm, Su 10am-3pm); **Knightsbridge:** 78 Brompton Rd., SW3 (☎7761 7905; open M, Tu, and Th-F 9am-5:30pm, W 9:30am-5:30pm, Sa 9am-4pm); and **Piccadilly:** 30-31 Haymarket, SW1 (☎7484 9610; open M-F 9am-5:30pm, Sa 9am-4pm, Su 10am-1pm and 2pm-4pm).

Chequepoint (www.chequpointinc.com). Branches on virtually every street corner in cen-tral London offering commission-free exchange—but check the rates first.

Thomas Cook (☎08705 666 222, 24hr.; www.thomascookholdings.com). 44 London locations; call to locate one. Sells and cashes traveler's checks and offers a full range of travel services. For **Traveler's Check refunds,** call ☎0800 622 101.

CYBERCAFES

easyEverything, 9-13 Wilson Rd., W1 (☎7482 9502; www.easyeverything.com). Tube: Victoria. Also at numerous other branches.

The Buzz Bar, 95 Portobello Rd., W11 (☎7460 4906; www.portobellogold.com). Tube: Notting Hill Gate or Ladbroke Grove. AOL, telnet, Netscape and Hotmail at 10p per minute. Open M-Sa 10am-7pm. MC, V.

Internet Exchange, 37 The Market, Covent Garden, WC2 (☎7836 8636). 3p per minute, minimum charge £1. Open daily 10am-10pm.

Cyberia, 39 Whitfield St., W1 (☎7681 4200; www.cyberiacafe.net). Tube: Goodge St. £3 for 30 min., students £2.40. Open M-F 9am-9pm, Sa 11am-7pm, Su 11am-6pm. MC, V.

Webshack, 15 Dean St., W1 (☎7439 8000; www.webshack-cafe.com). Tube: Leicester Sq. or Tottenham Ct. Rd. Telnet, AOL, IRC, Netscape, fax, download to disk, and guest email send. £3 for 30min., £5 per hr., 10% student discount. Open M-F 9am-11pm, Sa 10am-11pm, Su 1-8pm. AmEx, MC, V.

DENTAL CARE

Dental Emergency Care Service (☎7955 2186). Refers callers to the nearest dental surgery. Open M-F 8:45am-3:30pm.

Eastman Dental Hospital, 256 Gray's Inn Rd., WCI (☎7915 100; fax 7915 1012). Tube: Chancery Ln. or King's Cross. Phone for emergency treatment availibility and times.

DISABLED RESOURCES

Wheelchair Travel, 1 Johnston Green, Guildford GU2 6XS, Surrey (☎(01483) 233 640; info@wheelchair-travel.co.uk; www.wheelchair-travel.co.uk), rents hand-controlled cars. and will deliver them to London.

DIPLOMATIC SERVICES

Australian High Commission, Australia House, The Strand, WC2 (☎7379 4334; www.austra-lia.org.uk). Tube: Temple. Open M-F 9:30am-3:30pm.

Canadian High Commission, MacDonald House, 1 Grosvenor Sq., W1 (☎7258 6600). Tube: Bond St. or Oxford Circus.

Irish Embassy, 17 Grosvenor Pl., SW1 (☎7235 2171). Tube: Hyde Park Corner. Consular services at **Montpelier House,** 106 Brompton Rd., Knightsbridge (☎7225 7700). Open M-F 9:30am-4:30pm.

New Zealand High Commission, New Zealand House, 80 Haymarket, SW1 (☎7930 8422). Tube: Charing Cross. Open M-F 10am-noon and 2-4pm.

South African High Commission, South Africa House, Trafalgar Sq., WC2 (☎7451 7299). Tube: Charing Cross. Consular services M-F 8:45am-12:45pm.

United States Embassy, 24 Grosvenor Sq., W1 (☎7499 9900). Tube: Bond St. Phones answered 24hr.

EMERGENCY ROOMS

Most major London hospitals offer **Accident and Emergency** or **Casualty.** If a condition requires urgent attention, call an **ambulance** by dialling 999 from any phone.

Charing Cross, Fulham Palace Rd., entrance on St. Dunstan's Rd., W6 (☎8846 1234). Tube: Baron's Court or Hammersmith.

Chelsea and Westminster, 369 Fulham Rd., SW 10 (☎8746 8000). Tube: Fulham Broadway then #14 or #211 bus.

Royal London Hospital Whitechapel, Whitechapel Rd., E1 (☎7377 7000).

Royal Free, Pond St., NW3 (☎7377 7000). Tube: Belsize Park.

St. Mary's, Praed St., W2 (☎7886 6666). Tube: Paddington

St. Thomas's, Lambeth Palace Rd., SE1 (☎7928 9292). Tube: Waterloo.

University College Hospital (UCH), Grafton Way, WC1 (☎7387 9300). Tube: Warren St.

Whittington, Highgate Hill, N19 (☎7272 3070). Tube: Archway.

FAMILY PLANNING

Those qualifying for NHS treatment, as well as all women staying in the UK longer than 6 months, can obtain contraceptives, including **condoms,** the **Pill,** and the **morning-after pill,** free from government-run family planning clinics and most doctors' surgeries. **Abortion** is also available free of charge through the NHS.

Family Planning Association: 2-12 Pentonville Rd., N1 (Helpline ☎7837 4044; staffed M-F 9am-7pm). Tube: Angel. Informational services: contraception, pregnancy test, and abortion referral.

FITNESS CENTERS

For details, see **Living in London,** p. 268.

Barbican YMCA, 2 Fann St., EC2 (☎7628 0697; fax 7638 2420). Tube: Barbican. Membership £55 per year, £27 for 3 months. Additional fee £3.50 per use, £35 unlimited use per month. Members only.

Jubilee Hall Recreation Centre, 30 The Piazza, WC2 (☎7836 4835). Tube: Covent Garden. Membership £51 per month (direct-debit £45), £10 per day. Non-members £6.90 per gym visit, £6 per class. Open M-F 7am-10pm, Sa 10am-6pm, Su 10am-5pm. AmEx, V, MC.

Queen Mother Sports Centre, 223 Vauxhall Bridge Rd. (☎7630 5522). Tube: Victoria. Pool £1.70 per use, non-members £2.25; open M-Tu 6:30am-8pm, W-F 6:30am-7:30pm, Sa-Su 8am-5:30pm. Membership £39 per year. Open M-F 6:30am-10pm, Sa 8am-8pm.

GAY AND LESBIAN

Gay's the Word. The largest gay and lesbian bookshop in the UK. See **Bookstores,** p. 136.

Silver Moon Women's Bookstore has Britain's largest selection of lesbian titles. See **Bookstores,** p. 136.

Outlet. Finds accommodations for gays and lesbians. See **Accommodations agencies.**

HELPLINES

See also **Women's Concerns: Crisis lines** and **Medical helplines.**

SUPPORT

Alcoholics Anonymous: London Helpline (☎7352 3001) answered daily 10am-10pm; answering machine from 10pm-10am.

Narcotics Anonymous: Call ☎7730 0009. Hotline answered daily 10am-10pm.

Samaritans: (☎7734 2800; 0345 909090). Highly respected 24hr. crisis line provides listening (rather than advice) for suicidal depression and other problems.

Victim Support National: Cranmer House, 39 Brixton Rd., SW9 (☎7735 9166; helpline ☎0845 303 0900). Tube: Oval. Trained volunteers offer support, information, and help to victims of crime. Open M-F 9am-5:30pm; helpline M-F 9am-9pm, Sa-Su 9am-7pm.

LEGAL ADVICE

Release, 388 Old St., EC1 (☎7729 9904; emergencies 7603 8654 24hr.). Tube: Liverpool St. or Old St. Specializes in criminal law and drug charges. By appointment only.

Legal Aid Board, 29-37 Red Lion St., WC1 (☎7813 5300). Tube: Holborn. Provides representation (upon a solicitor's referral) for minimal fees. Open M-F 9am-5pm.

Police Complaints: If the problem is the police, contact the **Police Complaint Authority,** 10 Great George St., SW1 (☎7273 6450). Be sure to note the offending officer's number (worn on the shoulder).

HOSPITALS

See **Emergency Rooms,** above.

KIDS

Kidsline (☎7222 8070)

London Tourist Board's Children's Information (☎(0839) 123 404)

LONDON TRANSPORT

Information Offices (☎7222 1234, 24hr.). At: **Euston** (open M-Sa 7:15am-6pm, Su 8:30am-5pm); **Victoria** (open M-Sa 7:45am-9pm, Su 8:45am-9pm); **King's Cross** (open M-Sa 8am-6pm, Su 8:30am-5pm); **Liverpool St.** (Open M-Sa 8am-6pm, Su 8:45am-5:30pm); **Oxford Circus** (open M-Sa 8:45am-6pm); **Piccadilly** (open daily 8:45am-6pm); **St. James's Park** (open M-F 8am-5:30pm); **Hammersmith** (open M-F 7:15am-6pm, Sa 8:15am-6pm); and **Heathrow Central** (open M-Sa 6:30am-7pm, Su 7:15am-7pm); **Heathrow Terminal 1** (open daily 7:15am-10pm); **Terminal 2** (open M-Sa 7:15am-5pm, Su 8:15am-5pm); and **Terminal 4** (open M-Sa 6am-3pm, Su 7:15am-3pm).

MAIL SERVICES

Royal Mail (www.royalmail.co.uk). Delivers twice a day M-F, once Sa. Rates within the UK: 1st class letter (next business day) 27p, 2nd class letter (3 business days), 19p. Airmail letters 36p within Europe, 45p inter-continental.

FedEx (☎(0800) 123 800). 2-day service from New York to London from US$25.50; Sydney to London AUS$65.80.

MEDICAL HELP LINES

AIDS: National AIDS Helpline (☎0800 567 123). Toll-free 24hr.

British Diabetic Association: (☎7323 1531). Careline open M-F 9am-5pm.

Sexual Abuse and Rape: London Women's Aid (☎7392 2092) offers 24-hour support for victims of violence. **Rape Crisis Center,** PO Box 69, WC1 (☎7837 1600). Hotline Mon-Fri 6am-10pm, Sat-Sun 10am-10pm.

Sexual Health: Jefferies Wing Centre for Sexual Health, St. Mary's Hospital, Praed St., W2 (tel. 725 6619). Tube: Paddington. Free and confidential sexual health services. Drop-in for free condoms and dental dams, and STD and HIV tests and counseling. Open M 8:45am-7pm, Tu and F 8:45am-6pm, W 10:45am-6pm, Th 8am-1pm, Sa 10am-noon.

MINORITY RESOURCES

Africa Centre. See **Nightlife,** p. 182.

Commission for Racial Equality, Elliot House, 10-12 Allington St., SW1E 5EH (☎7828 7022; www.cre.gov.uk).

National Council for Civil Liberties, 21 Tabard St., SE1. Tube: Borough. Advice on dealing with discrimination, excluding education and housing issues, by letter only.

Souls of Black Folks, 407 Coldharbour Ln. (☎7738 4141). Tube: Brixton. See **Bookstores,** p. 136. Open M-Th 11am-10pm, F 11am-3am, Sa 11am-1am, Su 10am-8pm.

RELIGIOUS WORSHIP

BUDDHIST

Buddhapadipa Temple, Calonne Rd., Wimbledon Parkside (☎8946 1357). Tube: Wimbledon Park, or train: Wimbledon. The first Buddhist temple in the UK, since 1965.

CHURCH OF ENGLAND

Churches of historical interest are covered in **Sights;** since admission to fee-charging churches is free during services, you can please both God and Mammon.

St. Paul's Cathedral (see p. 53). Services M-Sa 7:30am, 12:30pm, 5:00pm; Su 8am, 11:30am, 6pm.

Westminster Abbey (see p. 67). Services Tu-F 7:30am, 12:30om, 5pm.

GREEK ORTHODOX

Cathedral of All Saints, Pratt St., NW1 (☎ 7485 2149). Tube: Camden Town.
Cathedral of Dormition, Trinity Rd., N22 (☎ 8888 2295). Tube: Wood Green.

HINDU

Shri Swaminarayan Mandir, 105-119 Brentfield Rd., Neasden NW10 (☎ 8965 2651). Tube: Stonebridge Park or Neasden. A stunning temple carved out of 5,000 tons of imported marble and limestone. Viewing of the icons that form the centerpiece of the temple daily 7:15am-noon and 4pm-7:30pm.

ISLAMIC

London Central Mosque, 146 Park Rd., NW8 (☎ 7724 3363). Tube: Baker St. Also houses the **Islamic cultural centre,** offering advice on matters of Islamic law and custom.

JUDAISM

Central Synagogue, 120 Great Portland St., W1 (☎ 7580 1355). Tube: Great Portland St.
The Liberal Jewish Synagogue, St. John's Wood Rd., London NW8 (☎ 7286 5181).
West London Reform Synagogue, Upper Berkeley St., London Wl. (☎ 7723 4404).

ROMAN CATHOLIC

Westminster Cathedral (see p. 73). The seat of the Roman Catholic Church in Britain.
St. Mary of the Angels, Moorhouse Rd., W2 (☎ 7229 0487). Tube: Bayswater.
St. Mary's, Cadogan St., SW3 (☎ 7589 5487). Tube: Sloane Sq.
St. James's Spanish Place, 22 George St., W1 (☎ 7935 0943). Tube: Baker St.

TOURIST INFORMATION

British Travel Centre, 12 Regent St. (☎ 8846 9000). Tube: Piccadilly Circus. Run by the British Tourist Authority and ideal for travelers bound for destinations outside of London. £5 surcharge for accommodations booking and a required deposit (1 night or 15% of the total stay; does not book for hostels). Open M-F 9am-6:30pm, Sa-Su 10am-4pm.

London Tourist Board Information Centre, Victoria Station Forecourt, SW1 (recorded message ☎ (0839) 123 432; 39-49p per min.). Tube: Victoria. Offers information on London and England and an accommodations service (☎ 7932 2020, fax 7932 2021; £5 booking fee, plus 15% refundable deposit; MC, V). Open Apr.-Nov. daily 8am-7pm; Dec.-Mar. M-Sa 8am-7pm, Su 8am-5pm. Additional tourist offices located at: **Heathrow Airport** (open daily Apr.-Nov. 9am-6pm; Dec.-Mar. 9am-5pm); **Liverpool St. Underground Station** (open M 8:15am-7pm, Tu-Sa 8:15am-6pm, Su 8:30am-4:45pm); and **Selfridges** (open during store hours; see Department Stores, p. 128).

WOMEN'S CONCERNS

WOMAN'S CLINICS

See also **Women's Health,** p. 223.

Audre Lorde Clinic, at the Ambrose King Centre, Royal London Hospital, E1 (☎ 7377 7312; Tube: Whitechapel. Open F 10am-5pm

Bernhard Clinic, West London Centre for Sexual Health, Charing Cross Hospital, Fulham Palace Rd., W6 (☎ 8846 1576). Tube: Baron's Court or Hammersmith. Open W 2-4:30pm, and 5:30-6.30pm; call for appointments M-F.

CRISIS LINES

Women's Aid, 52-54 Featherstone St., EC1 (☎ 7392 2092). 24hr. helpline provides aid, advice, and emergency shelter for victims of domestic and sexual abuse.

Rape and Sexual Abuse Support Center (☎ 8239 1122). Hotline answered M-F noon-2:30pm and 7-9:30pm, Sa-Su and bank holidays 2:30-5pm.

London Rape Crisis Centre Hotline, (☎ 7837 1600). Legal and medical advice and referrals. They'll send someone to accompany you to the police, doctor, clinic, and court upon request. Staffed Tu 6:30-8:30pm Th 6-8pm; at other times a recording directs you to other appropriate numbers.

Rape Crisis Center, PO Box 69, WC1 (☎ 7837 1600). Hotline answered M-F 6am-10pm, Sa-Su 10am-10pm.

Liberty, Justice,
and Globe-trotting
for all.

Sip espresso in Paris. Cheer the bulls in Barcelona. Learn the waltz in Saltzburg. 85 years after the Wright brothers discovered flying was easier than walking, wings are available to all. When you Name Your Own Price℠ on airline tickets at priceline.com, the world becomes your playground, the skies your road-less-traveled. You can save up to 40% or more, and you'll fly on top-quality, time-trusted airlines to the destinations of your dreams. You no longer need a trust fund to travel the globe, just a passion for adventure! So next time you need an escape, log onto priceline.com for your passport to the skies.

priceline.com℠
Name Your Own Price℠

Index

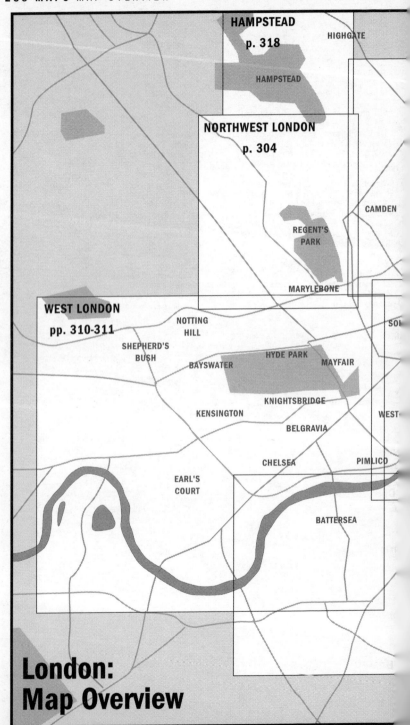

HAMPSTEAD

p. 318

HIGHGATE

HAMPSTEAD

NORTHWEST LONDON

p. 304

CAMDEN

REGENT'S
PARK

MARYLEBONE

WEST LONDON

pp. 310-311

NOTTING
HILL

SO

SHEPHERD'S
BUSH

BAYSWATER

HYDE PARK

MAYFAIR

KNIGHTSBRIDGE

WEST

KENSINGTON

BELGRAVIA

CHELSEA

PIMLICO

EARL'S
COURT

BATTERSEA

**London:
Map Overview**

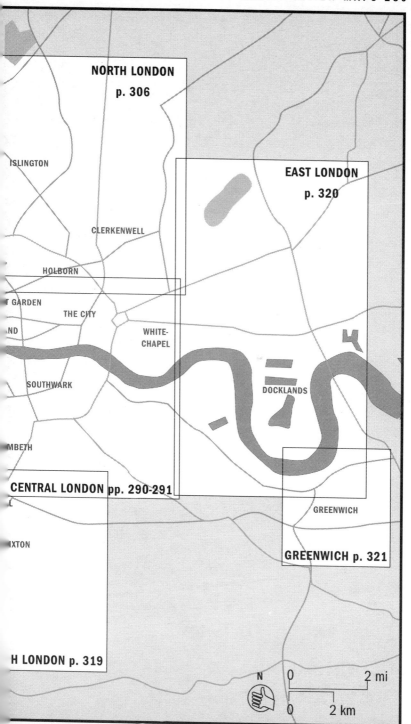

NORTH LONDON
p. 306

EAST LONDON
p. 320

ISLINGTON

CLERKENWELL

HOLBORN

T GARDEN

THE CITY

ND

WHITE-
CHAPEL

SOUTHWARK

DOCKLANDS

MBETH

CENTRAL LONDON pp. 290-291

L

GREENWICH

XTON

GREENWICH p. 321

H LONDON p. 319

N   0   2 mi

0   2 km

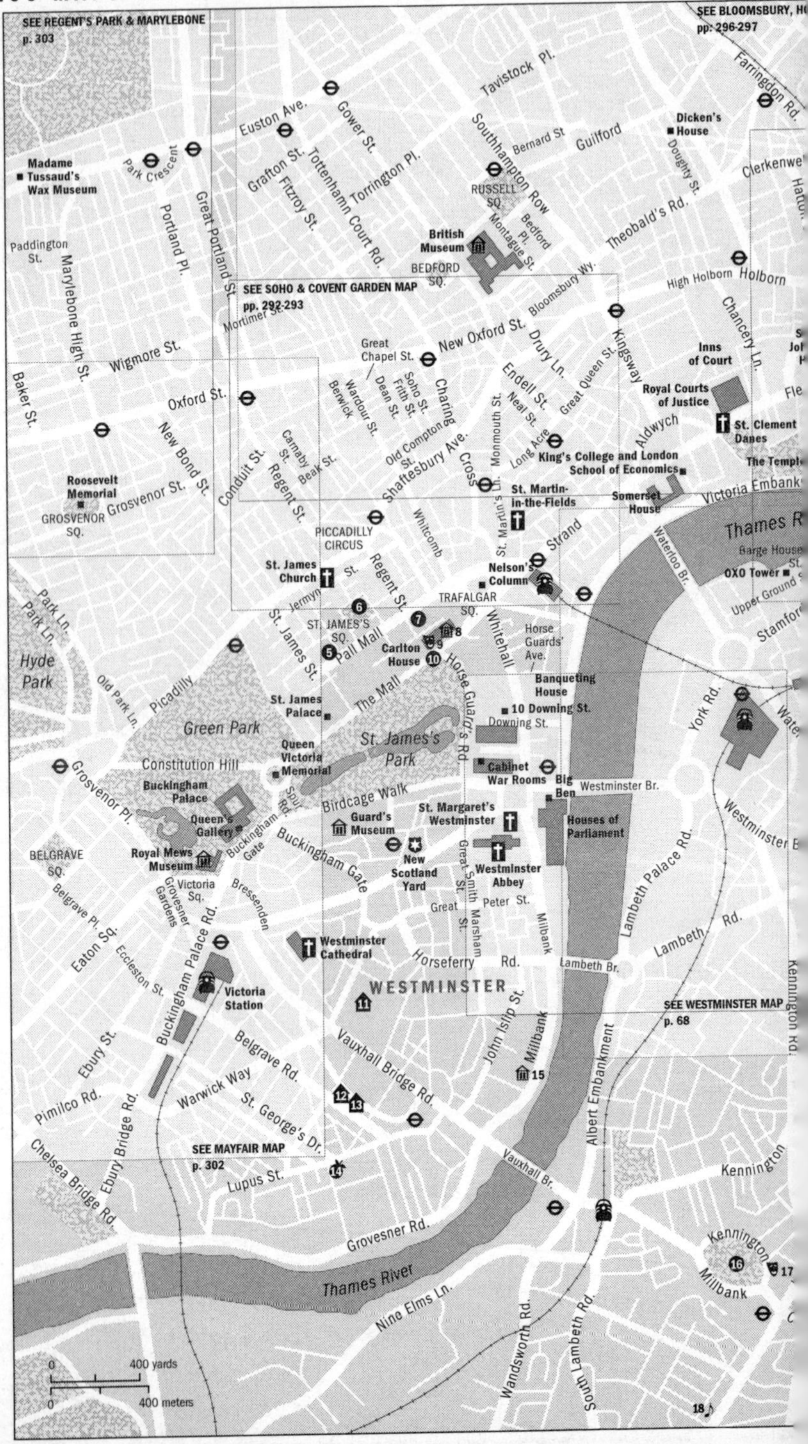
SEE REGENT'S PARK & MARYLEBONE p. 303
SEE BLOOMSBURY, HO
pp: 296-297
Tavistock Pl.
Farringdon Rd.
Euston Ave.
Gower St.
Southhampton Row
Bernard St
Guilford
Dicken's House
Doughty St.
Madame Tussaud's Wax Museum
Park Crescent
Grafton St.
Tottenhamn Court Rd.
Torrington Pl.
RUSSELL SQ.
Clerkenwel
Great Portland St.
Portland Pl.
Fitzroy St.
British Museum
Montague St.
Bedford Pl.
Theobald's Rd.
Paddington St.
Marylebone High St.
BEDFORD SQ.
SEE SOHO & COVENT GARDEN MAP pp. 292-293
Mortimer St.
Bloomsbury Wy.
High Holborn
Holborn
Chancery Ln.
Kingsway
Great Chapel St.
New Oxford St.
Drury Ln.
Inns of Court
Wigmore St.
Baker St.
Oxford St.
Berwick
Wardour St.
Dean St.
Soho St.
Frith St.
Charing
Endell St.
Great Queen St.
Royal Courts of Justice
Neal St.
Monmouth St.
St. Clement Danes
New Bond St.
Carnaby St.
Old Compton St.
Shaftesbury Ave.
Long Acre
Aldwych
King's College and London School of Economics
The Templ
Conduit St.
Regent St.
Beak St.
Cross
Roosevelt Memorial
GROSVENOR SQ.
Grosvenor St.
St. Martin-in-the-Fields
Somerset House
Victoria Embank
PICCADILLY CIRCUS
Whitcomb
St. Martin's Ln.
Strand
Waterloo Br.
Thames R
Barge House St.
St. James Church
Nelson's Column
OXO Tower
Upper Ground
Park Ln.
Jermyn St.
TRAFALGAR SQ.
ST. JAMES'S SQ.
Pall Mall
Carlton House
Horse Guards' Ave.
Whitehall
Stamford
Hyde Park
St. James St.
Old Park Ln.
Piccadilly
Horse Guard's Rd.
Banqueting House
St. James Palace
The Mall
10 Downing St.
Downing St.
York Rd.
Green Park
St. James's Park
Queen Victoria Memorial
Constitution Hill
Cabinet War Rooms
Big Ben
Westminster Br.
Buckingham Palace
Birdcage Walk
Spur Rd.
Grosvenor Pl.
Queen's Gallery
Guard's Museum
St. Margaret's Westminster
Houses of Parliament
Westminster B
Buckingham Gate
BELGRAVE SQ.
Royal Mews Museum
New Scotland Yard
Westminster Abbey
Great Smith St.
Victoria Sq.
Grovesner Gardens
Bressenden
Peter St.
Lambeth Palace Rd.
Belgrave Pl.
Great
Marsham
Millbank
Lambeth Rd.
Eaton Sq.
Buckingham Palace Rd.
Westminster Cathedral
Eccleston St.
Horseferry Rd.
Lambeth Br.
Victoria Station
WESTMINSTER
John Islip St.
SEE WESTMINSTER MAP p. 68
Kennington Rd.
Ebury St.
Belgrave Rd.
Vauxhall Bridge Rd.
Albert Embankment
Warwick Way
Pimilco Rd.
St. George's Dr.
Ebury Bridge Rd.
SEE MAYFAIR MAP p. 302
Chelsea Bridge Rd.
Lupus St.
Vauxhall Br.
Kennington
Grovesner Rd.
Thames River
Kennington
Millbank
Nine Elms Ln.
Wandsworth Rd.
South Lambeth Rd.
0 400 yards
0 400 meters

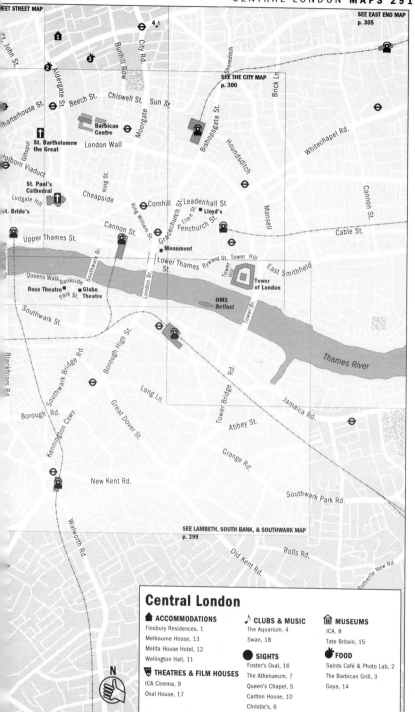

EET STREET MAP

SEE EAST END MAP
p. 305

SEE THE CITY MAP
p. 300

St. John St.

Aldergate St.

Bunhill Row

City Rd.

Shoreditch

Brick Ln.

Charterhouse St.

Beech St.

Chiswell St.

Sun St.

Whitechapel Rd.

Barbican
Centre

Moorgate

Bishopsgate St.

Houndsditch

Cannon St.

St. Bartholomew
the Great

London Wall

olborn Viaduct

St. Paul's
Cathedral

King St.

Cheapside

Cornhill

Leadenhall St.

Mansell

Cable St.

Ludgate Hill

King William St.

Gracechurch St.

Lime St.

Lloyd's

St. Bride's

Cannon St.

Fenchurch St.

Upper Thames St.

Southwark Br.

Monument

Lower Thames
St.

Byward St.

Tower Hill

Tower Hill

East Smithfield

Queens Walk

Bankside

Park St.

London Br.

Rose Theatre

Globe
Theatre

Tower of London

Tower Br.

HMS
Belfast

Southwark St.

Borough High St.

Thames River

Blackfriars Rd.

Southwark Bridge Rd.

Long Ln.

Tower Bridge Rd.

Jamaica Rd.

Borough Rd.

Kennington Cswy.

Great Dover St.

Abbey St.

Grange Rd.

New Kent Rd.

Southwark Park Rd.

Walworth Rd.

SEE LAMBETH, SOUTH BANK, & SOUTHWARK MAP
p. 299

Old Kent Rd.

Rolls Rd.

Rotherithe New Rd.

Central London

N

ACCOMMODATIONS
Finsbury Residences, 1
Melbourne House, 13
Melita House Hotel, 12
Wellington Hall, 11

THEATRES & FILM HOUSES
ICA Cinema, 9
Oval House, 17

CLUBS & MUSIC
The Aquarium, 4
Swan, 18

SIGHTS
Foster's Oval, 16
The Athenaeum, 7
Queen's Chapel, 5
Carlton House, 10
Christie's, 6

MUSEUMS
ICA, 8
Tate Britain, 15

FOOD
Saints Café & Photo Lab, 2
The Barbican Grill, 3
Goya, 14

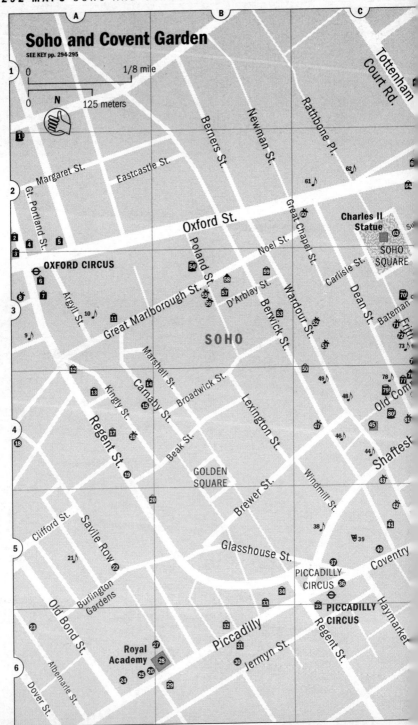

Soho and Covent Garden

SEE KEY pp. 294-295

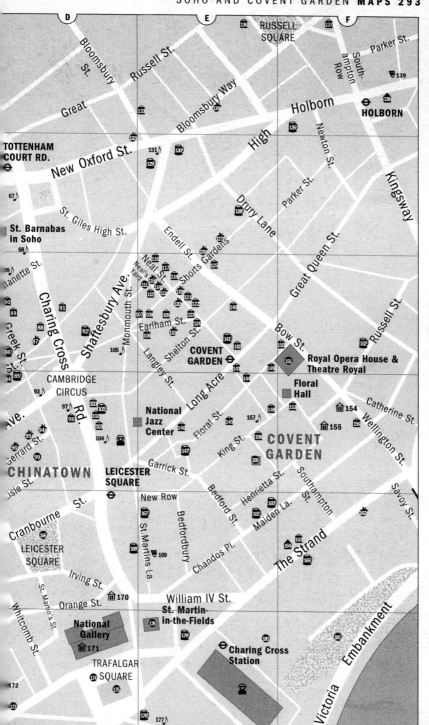

Soho & Covent Garden SEE MAP pp. 292-293

⬤ SHOPPING

Accessorize, 148	E4
American Retro, 84	D4
Bell, Book, & Radmall, 90	D3
Big Apple, 116	E3
Black Market, 57	B3
Blackout II, 140	E3
Blackwells, 91	D3
Buffalo, 121	E3
Clone Zone, 77	C4
Cyberdog, 108	E1
Daddy Kool, 50	C4
David Drummond, 89	D3
Diesel, 124	E3
Dr. Marten's Dept. Store Ltd., 158	E4
Duffer of St. George, 125	E3
Eternity, 64	C2
Fortnum & Mason, 29	B6
Foyles, 88	D3
French Connection (fcuk), 142	E3
G. Smith & Sons Snuff Shop, 102	D4
Gay's the Word, 136	E1
Grant and Cutler, 11	A3
H&M, 4	A4
Hamley's, 17	A4
Hatchards, 31	B6
Karen Miller, 144	E4
Laura Ashley, 7	A3
Levi's, 2	A4
Liberty's of London, 12	A3
Lillywhite's, 35	C6

⬤ ACCOMMODATIONS

High Holborn Residence, 138	F1
Hotel Strand Continental, 164	F5
Outlet, 76	C4
YHA Oxford St., 58	B3

♪ CLUBS & MUSIC

100 Club, 61	C2
79 CXR, 104	D4
Bar Rumba, 38	C5
Borderline, 69	D3
Freedom, 48	C4
Heaven, 177	E6
Legends, 21	A5
Limelight, 93	D4
London Palladium, 10	A3
Pizza Express Jazz Club, 78	C4
Rock Garden, 157	E4
Ronnie Scott's, 73	C3
Rupert St., 46	C4
Salsa!, 97	D4
The Astoria, 67	D2
The Box, 105	D3
The End, 131	E2
The Hanover Grand, 9	A3
The Office, 62	C2
The Village Soho, 49	C4
The Wag Club, 44	C4
Velvet Room, 68	D3

🏛 MUSEUMS

London Transport Museum, 155	F4

🍴 FOOD

1997 Special Zone Restaurant, 42	C5
Belgo Centraal, 110	E3
Busaba Eathai, 52	C3
Café Emm, 81	C4
Café Roma, 47	C4
Don Zoko, 16	A4
Est, 71	C3
Food for Thought, 120	E3
Frank's Café, 119	E3
Kowloon Restaurant, 96	D4
Lok Ho Fook, 94	D4
Mandeer, 134	E1
Mezzo, 51	C3
Neal's Yard Bakery & Tearoom, 114	E3
Neal's Yard Dairy, 127	E2
Neal's Yard Salad Bar, 113	E3
Nusa Dua, 74	C3
Old Compton Café, 75	C4
Patisserie Valerie, 83	C4
Pizza Express, 82	C4
Saigon, 72	C3
Schnecke, 55	B3
Square, 8	A3
The Dragon Inn, 95	D4
The Rock and Soul Plaice, 126	E2
The Savoy, 162	F5
The Star Café and Bar, 60	C2
Wagamama, 132	D2
West End Tandoori, 87	D3
Wong Kei, 43	C4
World Food Café, 115	E3

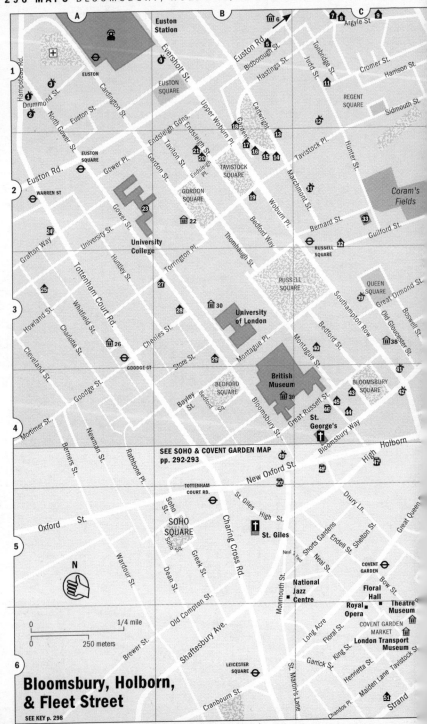

Euston Station

EUSTON

EUSTON SQUARE

WARREN ST

EUSTON SQUARE

University College

GOODGE ST

Euston Rd.

Euston Rd.

REGENT SQUARE

TAVISTOCK SQUARE

GORDON SQUARE

Coram's Fields

University of London

RUSSELL SQUARE

QUEEN SQUARE

RUSSELL SQUARE

British Museum

BLOOMSBURY SQUARE

St. George's

BEDFORD SQUARE

Holborn

SEE SOHO & COVENT GARDEN MAP pp. 292-293

New Oxford St.

High Holborn

TOTTENHAM COURT RD.

SOHO SQUARE

St. Giles

Oxford St.

St. Giles

COVENT GARDEN

National Jazz Centre

Floral Hall

Royal Opera

Theatre Museum

COVENT GARDEN MARKET

London Transport Museum

N

0   1/4 mile

0   250 meters

LEICESTER SQUARE

Strand

Bloomsbury, Holborn, & Fleet Street

SEE KEY p. 298

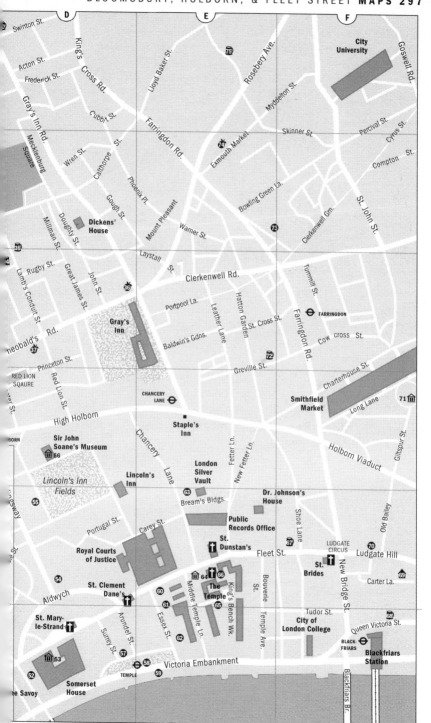

Bloomsbury, Holborn, & Fleet Street SEE MAP pp. 296-297

SIGHTS
House of Detention, 60	E2
Inner Temple Gardens, 65	E6
Inns of Court, 57	D6
King's College, 52	D6
London School of Economics, 54	D5
Middle Temple Gardens, 62	E6
Middle Temple Hall, 61	E5
New Hall, 5	D5
Old Hall, 63	E5
Royal Courts of Justice, 49	E5
St. George's, Bloomsbury, 40	C4
St. Martin Ludgate, 70	F5
Temple church of St Mary, 66	E5
Temple of Mithras, 68	F6
Temple, 51	E5
Thomas Coram Foundation for Children, 33	C2
University College London, 23	A2
Victoria Embankment Gardens, 56	E6
Wig and Pen Club, 60	E5

MUSEUMS
British Library, 6	B1
British Museum, 39	B4
Brunei Gallery, 30	B3
Courtauld Gallery, 53	D6
Museum of St. Bartholomew's Hospital, 71	F4
October Gallery, 38	C3
Percival David Foundation of Chinese Art, 22	B2
Pollock's Toy Museum, 26	A3
Prince Henry's Room, 64	E5

PUBS
Black Friar, 68	F6
Bleeding Heart Bistro, 72	E3
Filthy MacNasty's Whiskey Café, 75	E1
Grafton Arms, 24	A2
Museum Tavern, 46	C4
Old Crown, 48	C4
Point 101, 50	B4
Princess Louise, 47	C4
The Lamb, 25	D2
Vats, 34	D3
Water Rats, 10	D1
Ye Olde Cheshire Cheese, 67	F5

FOOD
Alara Wholefoods, 31	C2
Al's Cafe Bar, 74	E2
Buon Appetito, 42	C4
Chutney's, 1	A1
Cosmoba, 41	C4
Diwana Bhel Poori House, 2	A1
Great Nepalese Restaurant, 4	B1
Gupta Sweet Centre, 3	A1
Leigh St Café, 12	C1
Mille Pini Restaurant, 39	C3
The Fryer's Delight, 37	D3
Wagamama, 49	B4
Woolley's Salad Shop and Sandwich Bar, 36	D3

ACCOMMODATIONS
Afrosa Hotel, 27	B3
Alhambra Hotel, 7	C1
Astor's Museum Inn, 44	C4
Carr-Saunders Hall, 25	A3
Celtic Hotel, 32	C2
Central University of Iowa Hostel, 45	C4
Commonwealth Hall, 13	B2
Connaught Hall, 19	B2
Cosmo/Bedford House Hotel, 43	C4
Crescent Hotel, 12	B2
Euro Hotel, 16	B2
George Hotel, 14	B2
Hotel Apollo, 9	C1
Hotel Strand Continental, 51	C6
Jenkins Hotel, 18	B1
Jesmond Dene Hotel, 8	C1
John Adams Hall, 21	B2
King's Cross/St. Pancras, 5	B1
Mentone Hotel, 15	B2
Passfield Hall, 20	B2
Ridgemount Hotel, 28	B3
Ruskin Hotel, 40	C3
The Langland Hotel, 29	B3
Tonbridge Club, 11	C1
YHA Oxford Street, 69	A5

Lambeth, South Bank, & Southwark

SIGHTS
Golden Hinde, 23	D1
HMS Belfast, 35	F1
Lambeth Palace, 2	A4
Liberty of the Clink (aka Clink Prison Museum), 29	E1
London Aquarium, 3	A2
Millenium Wheel, 4	A2
Museum of Garden History, 1	A4
Old Operating Theatre and Herb Garret, 31	E2
Oxo Tower, 19	C1
Southwark Cathedral, 30	E1
The Globe, 24	D1
The Millenium Bridge, 22	D1

ACCOMMODATIONS
King's Campus Vacation Bureau, 12	B1

CLUBS & MUSIC
Royal Festival Hall, 5	A1
Queen Elizabeth Hall, 8	B1
Bug Bar, 28	D4
Mass, 27	D4
Ministry of Sound, 26	D3

MUSEUMS
Tate Modern, 22	D1
Tower Bridge Museum, 36	G2
London Dungeon, 33	F1
Winston Churchill's Britain at War, 34	F1
Bramah Tea & Coffee Museum, 37	G2
Bankside Gallery, 20	C1
Jerwood Space, 25	D2
Royal Festival Hall Galleries, 6	B1
Haywood Gallery, 5	B1
Imperial War Museum 15	B4

THEATRES & FILM HOUSES
National Film Theatre, 10	B1
Royal National Theatre, 9	B1
Old Vic, 16	C2
Young Vic, 18	C2

PUBS
The Fire Station, 11	B2
Tas, 17	B2
Cubana, 14	B2
Vinopolis, City of Wine, 32	F1

SHOPPING
Honour, 13	2B

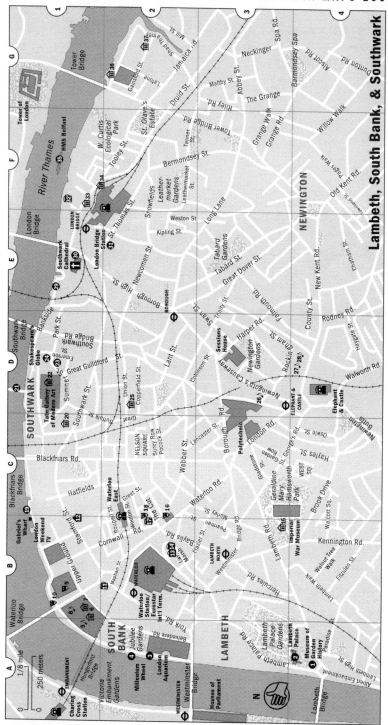

Lambeth, South Bank, & Southwark

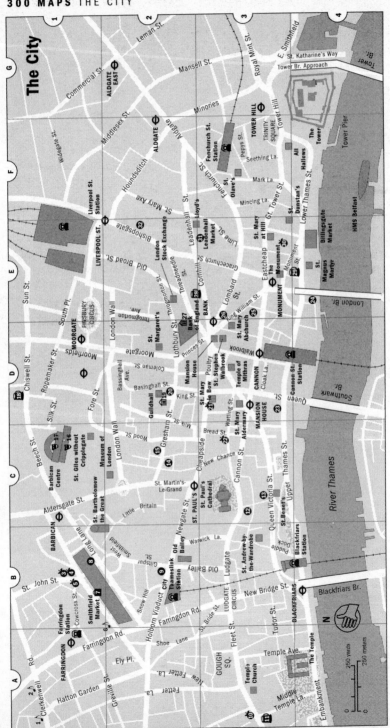

The City

The City

● SIGHTS

Fishmongers, 24	E4
Goldsmiths', 14	C2
Mansion House, 31	E3
National Westminster Tower, 32	E2
St. Sepulchre-without-Newgate, 9	B2
St. James Garlickhythe, 23	D3
St. Lawrence Jewry, 20	D2
St. Mary Woolnoth, 26	E3
Ther Charterhouse, 8	B1
The City of London Information Centre, 12	C3
The College of Arms, 13	C3
The London Sotone, 25	E3
Wax Chandlers, 15	C2

🍺 PUBS

Fuego Bar y Tapas, 29	E4
Simpson's, 28	E2
The King's Head, 18	D1
The Punch Tavern, 11	A3

♪ CLUBS & MUSIC

Dust, 1	A1
Fabric, 6	B2
Turnmills, 2	A1

🏛 MUSEUMS

Bank of England Museum, 27	E2
Guildhall Clock Museum, 19	D2

🍎 FOOD

Field's Sandwiches, 5	B1
Futures!, 30	E3
New Covent Garden Soup Company, 10	A3
Noto, 22	C3
St. John, 4	B1
The Place Below, 21	D3
Tinseltown 24-Hour Diner, 3	B1

🛍 SHOPPING

Smithfield, 7	B1

🎭 THEATRES & FILM HOUSES

Barbican Hall, 90	C1
Royal Shakespeare Company, 113	C1

Mayfair SEE MAP p. 302

● SIGHTS

Buckingham Palace, 18	D5
Green Park, 17	C4
Grovsenor Square, 2	B2
New Bond Street, 4	C1
Shepherd Market, 13	C3
Sotheby's 5	C1
St. James's Palace, 16	D4
The Carlton, 10	D3

♪ CLUBS & MUSIC

The Africa Centre, 15	D3

🛏 ACCOMMODATIONS

Alexander Hotel, 21	D7
Dover Hotel, 23	D7
Georgian House Hotel, 25	D7
Luna and Simone Hotel, 27	D7
Oxford House, 26	D7
Stanley House Hotel, 22	D7
Surtees Hotel, 24	D7

🍺 PUBS

The Coach and Horses, 6	C2
Ye Grapes, 12	C3

🏛 MUSEUMS

Marlborough Fine Arts, 8	D2
Royal Academy, 9	D2

🍎 FOOD

Ask!, 1	A1
Al-Fresco, 19	C6
Sofra, 14	C3
Claridges, 3	C1
The Ritz, 11	D3

🛍 SHOPPING

Honour, 13	2B

Regent's Park & Marylebone SEE MAP p. 303

● SIGHTS

221B Baker St., 9	B4
Boating Lake, 3	B3
Claridge's Hotel, 25	D7
London Central Mosque, 2	A3
Queen Mary's Gardens, 6	C3
Regent's Park, 4	C2
St. John's Lodge, 1	A2
The BBC Experience, 13	D5

🛏 ACCOMMODATIONS

Edward Lear Hotel, 19	B6
Glynne Court Hotel, 17	B6
International Studen House, 12	D4
Redland House Hotel, 16	A6

🎭 THEATRES & FILM HOUSES

Open Air Theatre, 5	C3

🛍 SHOPPING

HMV, 27	D6
Marks & Spencer, 20	C6
Miss Selfridge, 21	C6
Micole Farhi, 30	D7
Paul Smith Sale Shop, 26	D7
Selfridges, 22	C6
South Molton Drug Store, 28	D6
Vivienne Westwood, 24	D6

🏛 MUSEUMS

London Planetarium, 10	C4
Madame Tussauds, 11	C4
Sherlock Holmes Museum, 8	B4
Wallace Collection, 14	C6

🍎 FOOD

Ask!, 1	A1
Al-Fresco, 19	C6
Sofra, 14	C3
Claridges, 3	C1
The Ritz, 11	D3

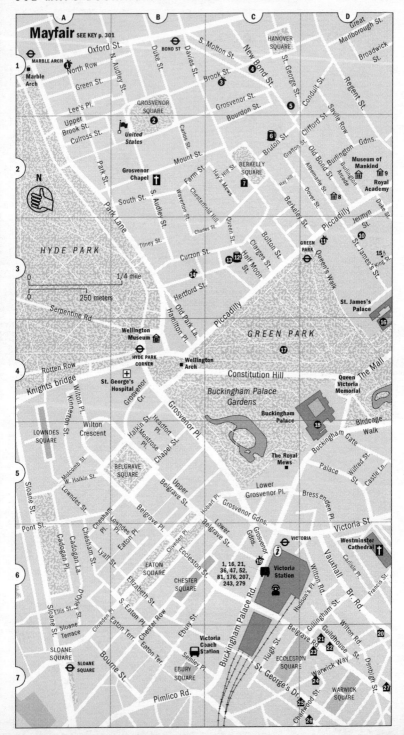

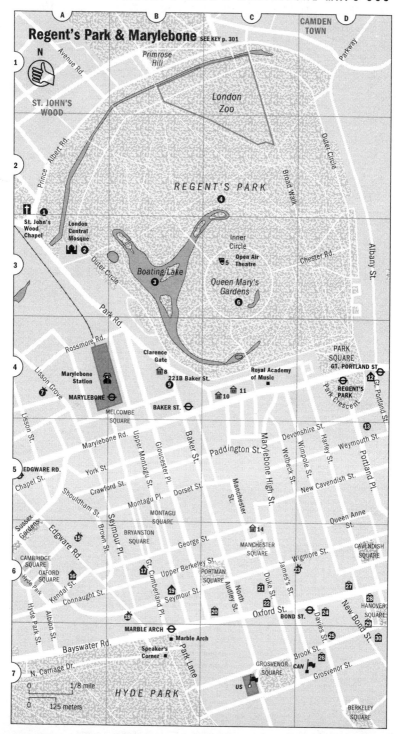

Regent's Park & Marylebone SEE KEY p. 301

N

CAMDEN TOWN

Parkway

Avenue Rd.

Primrose Hill

London Zoo

ST. JOHN'S WOOD

Prince Albert Rd.

Outer Circle

REGENT'S PARK

Broad Walk

❹

St. John's Wood Chapel ❶

London Central Mosque ❷

Outer Circle

Inner Circle

Chester Rd.

Albany St.

Boating Lake ❸

Open Air Theatre ❺

Queen Mary's Gardens ❻

Park Rd.

Rossmore Rd.

Clarence Gate

PARK SQUARE

GT. PORTLAND ST.

Lisson Grove

Marylebone Station

❽
221B Baker St.
❾

Royal Academy of Music

REGENT'S PARK ❿②

Park Crescent

Gt. Portland St.

MARYLEBONE

❼

MELCOMBE SQUARE

BAKER ST.

❿ ⑪

⑬

Lisson St.

Chapel St.

EDGWARE RD.

Marylebone Rd.

York St.

Crawford St.

Shouldham St.

Upper Montagu St.

Gloucester Pl.

Montagu Pl.

Dorset St.

Baker St.

Paddington St.

Manchester St.

Marylebone High St.

Devonshire St.

Welbeck St.

Wimpole St.

Harley St.

Weymouth St.

New Cavendish St.

Portland Pl.

MONTAGU SQUARE

⑭

Queen Anne St.

Sussex Gardens

Edgware Rd.

Brown St.

Seymour Pl.

BRYANSTON SQUARE

George St.

MANCHESTER SQUARE

CAVENDISH SQUARE

⑮

CAMBRIDGE SQUARE

OXFORD SQUARE

⑯

Kendal St.

Connaught St.

⑰

Gt. Cumberland Pl.

Upper Berkeley St.

Seymour St.

⑲

PORTMAN SQUARE

North Audley St.

Duke St.

⑳

Oxford St.

㉑

James's St.

Wigmore St.

㉓

㉒

BOND ST.

㉔

Davies St.

㉗

New Bond St.

㉘

HANOVER SQUARE

㉙

㉚

Hyde Park St.

Albion St.

⑱

MARBLE ARCH

Marble Arch

Bayswater Rd.

Speaker's Corner

Park Lane

GROSVENOR SQUARE

CAN ㉖

US

㉕

Brook St.

Grosvenor St.

N. Carriage Dr.

0   1/8 mile

0   125 meters

HYDE PARK

BERKELEY SQUARE

Northwest London

♪ **CLUBS & MUSIC**
Cube Bar, 2

🍎 **FOOD**
Oporto Patisserie, 6
Lisboa Patisserie, 7
Little Bay, 3

🏛 **MUSEUMS**
Saatchi Gallery, 4
Freud Museum, 1

● **SIGHTS**
Lord's, 5

The East End

🍎 **FOOD**

Aladin Balti House, 10	B4
Arkansas Café, 16	A4
Brick Lane Beigel Bake, 8	B4
Nazrul, 9	B4
Shampan, 13	B4
Spitz, 17	A4

🛏 **ACCOMMODATIONS**

Tent City, Hackney, 1	D1
YHA Rotherite, 31	D6

🎭 **THEATRES & FILM HOUSES**

Hackney Empire, 2	C1
Jongleurs at Bow Wharf, 19	D4

● **SIGHTS**

Bevis Marks Synagogue, 26	A5
Brick Lane, 11	B4
Christ Church, 23	B5
East London Mosque, 22	B5
Peticoat Lane, 25	A5
Spitalfields Market, 15	A4
St. George-in-the-East, 28	C5

🏛 **MUSEUMS**

Bethnal Green Museum of Childhood, 18	C3
Geffrye Museum, 3	A3
Whitechapel Art Gallery, 24	B5

🍺 **PUBS**

Cantaloupe, 7	A4
Prospect of Whitby, 29	C6
Shoreditch Electricity Showrooms, 6	A3
The Blind Beggar, 21	B5
The Dickens Inn, 27	B6
The Vibe Bar, 14	B4

🐄 **CITY FARMS**

Hackney, 4	B3
Stepping Stones, 20	D5
Surrey Docks, 30	C7

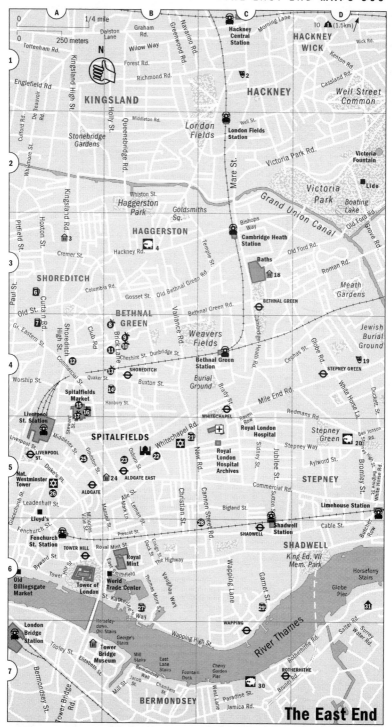

The East End

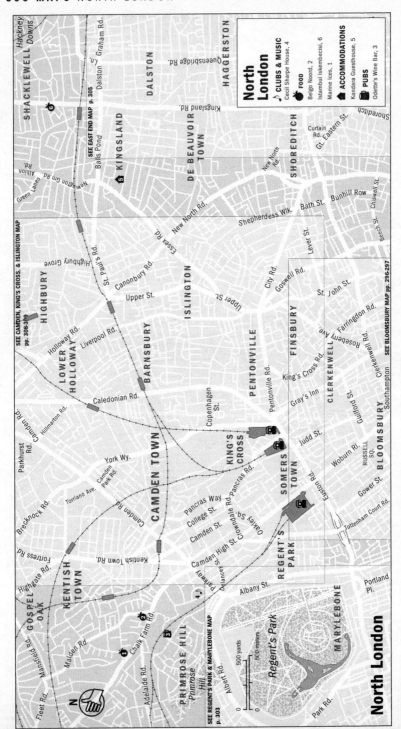

North London

♪ **CLUBS & MUSIC**
Cecil Sharpe House, 4

🍴 **FOOD**
Belgo Noord, 2
Istambul Iskembecisi, 6
Marine Ices, 1

🏠 **ACCOMMODATIONS**
Kandara Guesthouse, 5

🍺 **PUBS**
Odette's Wine Bar, 3

SEE EAST END MAP p. 305

SEE CAMDEN, KING'S CROSS, & ISLINGTON MAP pp. 308-309

SEE BLOOMSBURY MAP pp. 296-297

SEE REGENT'S PARK & MARYLEBONE MAP p. 303

North London

SHACKLEWELL

Hackney Downs

Graham Rd.

Dalston

DALSTON

Queensbridge Rd.

HAGGERSTON

Kingsland Rd.

Newington Grn. Rd.

Balls Pond

KINGSLAND

DE BEAUVOIR TOWN

SHOREDITCH

Shoreditch

Albion Rd.

Green Lanes

Newington Grn. Rd.

New North Rd.

New North Rd.

New North

Curtain Rd.

Gt. Eastern St.

Shepherdess Wlk.

Bath St.

Bunhill Row

Chiswell St.

Beech St.

Highbury Grove

St. Paul's Rd.

Canonbury Rd.

Upper St.

HIGHBURY

ISLINGTON

Essex Rd.

Upper St.

City Rd.

Lever St.

Goswell Rd.

St. John St.

FINSBURY

Holloway Rd.

Liverpool Rd.

LOWER HOLLOWAY

BARNSBURY

PENTONVILLE

Pentonville Rd.

CLERKENWELL

Rosebery Ave.

Farringdon Rd.

Clerkenwell Rd.

Camden Rd.

Hillmarton Rd.

Caledonian Rd.

Copenhagen St.

King's Cross Rd.

Gray's Inn

Guilford St.

Parkhurst Rd.

York Wy.

KING'S CROSS

Southampton

BLOOMSBURY

Judd St.

Breaknock Rd.

Camden Park Rd.

Torriano Ave.

CAMDEN TOWN

Camden Rd.

Pancras Way

College St.

Pancras Rd.

Crowndale Rd.

Oakley Sq.

SOMERS TOWN

RUSSELL SQ.

Woburn Pl.

Euston Rd.

Gower St.

Fortress Rd.

Kentish Town Rd.

Camden St.

Camden High St.

Delancey St.

REGENT'S PARK

Tottenham Court Rd.

Highgate Rd.

KENTISH TOWN

GOSPEL OAK

Parkway

Albany St.

Portland Pl.

MARYLEBONE

Fleet Rd.

Mansfield Rd.

Malden Rd.

Chalk Farm Rd.

Adelaide Rd.

PRIMROSE HILL

Primrose Hill

Albert Rd.

Regent's Park

Park Rd.

N

500 yards

500 meters

0

Camden Town, King's Cross, & Islington

SEE MAP pp. 308-309

🏠 ACCOMMODATIONS

Ashlee House, 30	C6
Five Kings Guesthouse, 1	B1
Jurys Inn, 31	D5
Roseberry Hall, 35	E6
University College London	
Residential Services, 24	C6
Walter Sickert Hall, 38	F5

🍎 FOOD

Afghan Kitchen, 46	E4
Angel Mangal, 55	E3
Bar Gansa, 5	A4
La Piragua, 57	E3
Le Mercury, 56	E3
Pasha, 61	E2
Ruby in the Dust, 15	A4
Tartuf, 47	E4
The New Culture Revolution, 14	A4

🛍 SHOPPING

Camden Markets, 7	A4
Camden Passage, 42	E5
Chapel Market, 32	D5
Compendium, 17	A4
Into You, 39	E5
Out on the Floor, 12	A4
Reckless Records, 41	E5

🍺 PUBS

Bierodrome, 59	E3
Dublin Castle, 13	A4
Duke of Cambridge, 44	F5
Liberty's, 18	A4
Nu Bar, 49	F4
The Camden Head, 45	E4
The King's Head, 52	E4
The Marquess, 54	F3
The Mitre, 58	E3

🐄 CITY FARMS

Kentish Town, 2	A2
Freightliners, 63	E2

♪ CLUBS & MUSIC

Bagleys, 28	C5
Camden Palace, 20	A5
Electric Ballroom, 9	A4
Jazz Café, 6	A4
Nu Bar, 49	F4
Postarz Liquid Lounge, 29	C5
The Black Cap, 11	A4
The Garage, 62	E2
The Water Rats, 48	D6
WKD, 8	A4

🏛 MUSEUMS

Jewish Museum Camden, 16	A4
Two10 Gallery, 22	B6
Crafts Council, 33	E5
The Estorick, 60	F2

⬤ SIGHTS

141 Bayham Street, 10	A4
British Library, 23	C5
Camden Locks & Canals, 3	A3
Camden Tourist	
Information Centre, 26	C6
Chapel Market, 40	E5
Little Angel Theatre, 53	F4
Regent's Canal, 43	F5
Sadler's Well Theatre, 34	E6
King's Cross/	
St. Pancras Station, 25	
St. Pancras, 21	B5

🎭 THEATRES & FILM HOUSES

Etcetera, 19	A4
Jongleurs at Camden Lock, 4	A3
Sadler's Well, 36	E6
The Almeida, 51	E4
The King's Head, 50	E4
The Old Red Lion, 37	E5

TO
(200m)

300 yards
300 meters

KENTISH
TOWN

LOWER
HOLLOWAY

Fortress Rd.
Leverton St.
Falkland Rd.
Lady Margaret Rd.
Monpelier Gr.
Leighton Grove
Fortriano Ave.
Brecknock Rd.
Hilldrop Rd.
Hilldrop Cres.
Hilldrop La.
Dalmeny Ave.
Hillmarton Rd.
Penn Rd.
Freegrove Rd.
Carl

Leighton Rd.

Kentish Town
Station

KENTISH TOWN

Holmes Rd.
Islip St.
Caversham Rd.

Oseney Cres.
Busby Pl.
Camden Park Rd.
Cliff Rd.
Hungerford Rd.
North Rd.
Hartham Rd.

CALEDONIAN
PARK

Willes Rd.
Anglers La.
Gaisford St.
Patshull Rd.
Lawford Rd.
Bartholomew Rd.

Prince of Wales Rd.

Kelly St.

Castle
Rd.
Rd.
Castlehaven Rd.
Rochester Rd.
Rochester Ter.
Camden Mews

CAMDEN
SQUARE
Murray St.

N. Villas
S. Villas
St. Augustine's Rd.
St. Paul's Cres.
Cantelowes Rd.
Marquis Rd.

BARNSBURY

Market Rd.
Brewery Rd.

Hawley Rd.
Camden
Road Station
Camden
Town Rd.
Kentish

Agar Gr.
Blundell Rd.
York Way

Chalk Farm Road

Kentish

Lyme St.
Camden Rd.
Georgiana St.
St. Pancras Way
Grand Union Canal
Camley St.
Randell's Rd.
Havelock St.

CAMDEN TOWN
Bayham St.
Royal College St.

CAMDEN
TOWN
Arlington Rd.
Gloucester
Parkway
Albert St.
Pratt St.
Camden St.
Camden High St.
Plender St.
College Pl.
Delancey St.

KING'S
CROSS

Wharf Rd.

ST.
PANCRAS
GARDENS

Crowndale Rd.
Mary Tc.
Mornington Cres.
OAKLEY
SQUARE
Chalton St.
St. Pancras
Goldington
Good's Way

Wharfd

MORNINGTON
CRESCENT
Mornington St.
Mornington Tc.
Stanhope St.
Harrington St.
Charrington St.
Purchese St.

KING'S CR
ST. PANCR

Regent's
Park
Barracks
Mary St.
Redhill St.
Augustus St.
Varndell Rd.
Everholt St.
Aldenham St.
SOMERSTOWN
Midland Rd.
British Library
St. Pancras
Station
King
Cross
Stati

Euston Station
Phoenix Rd.
Ossulston St.
Pancras Rd.

REGENT'S
PARK
Outer Circle
Cumberland
Market
Hampstead Rd.
Robert St.
Drummond Cres.
Chalton St.
Churchway

Euston Rd.
Cartwright Gdns.
Hastings St.
Judd St.
Tonbridge St.

Cromer
Harri

Euston
Square
Upper
Woburn Pl.

EUSTON

Euston Station
Colonnade
Euston Rd.

Sidmo

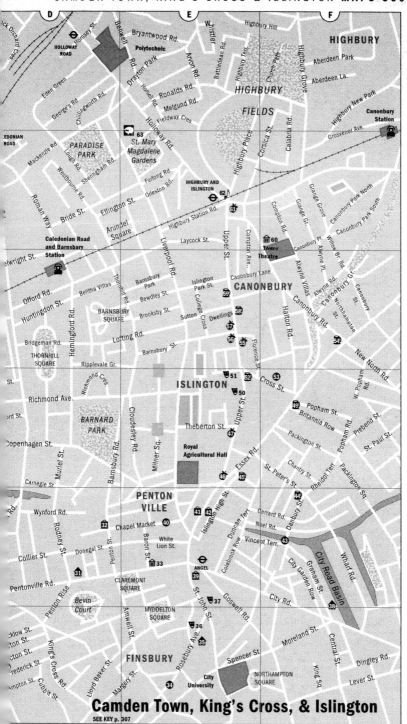

Camden Town, King's Cross, & Islington

SEE KEY p. 307

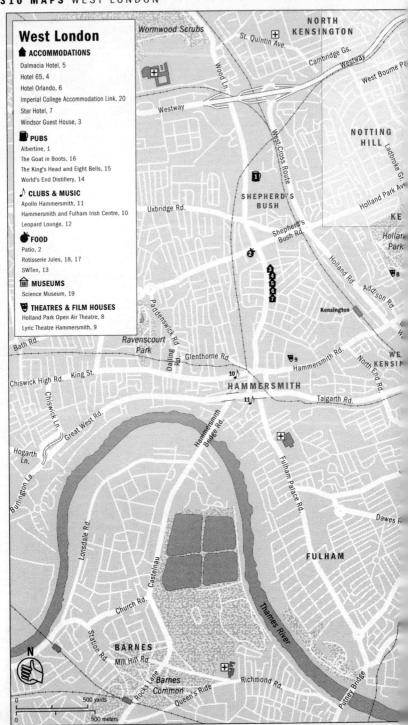

West London

⌂ ACCOMMODATIONS

Dalmacia Hotel, 5
Hotel 65, 4
Hotel Orlando, 6
Imperial College Accommodation Link, 20
Star Hotel, 7
Windsor Guest House, 3

🍺 PUBS

Albertine, 1
The Goat in Boots, 16
The King's Head and Eight Bells, 15
World's End Distillery, 14

♪ CLUBS & MUSIC

Apollo Hammersmith, 11
Hammersmith and Fulham Irish Centre, 10
Leopard Lounge, 12

🍅 FOOD

Patio, 2
Rotisserie Jules, 18, 17
SWTen, 13

🏛 MUSEUMS

Science Museum, 19

🎭 THEATRES & FILM HOUSES

Holland Park Open Air Theatre, 8
Lyric Theatre Hammersmith, 9

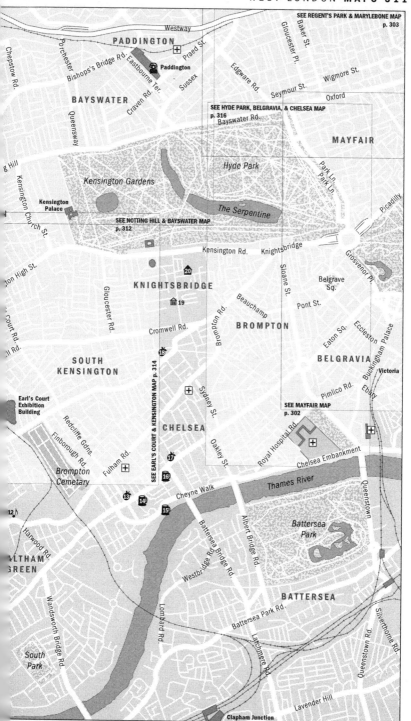

SEE REGENT'S PARK & MARYLEBONE MAP p. 303

Westway

PADDINGTON

Porchester Rd.

Bishops's Bridge Rd.

Eastbourne Ter.

Praed St.

Paddington

Sussex

Craven Rd.

Chepstow Rd.

Edgware Rd.

Baker St.

Gloucester Pl.

Seymour St.

Wigmore St.

Oxford

BAYSWATER

Queensway

SEE HYDE PARK, BELGRAVIA, & CHELSEA MAP p. 316

Bayswater Rd.

MAYFAIR

g Hill

Kensington Church St.

Kensington Gardens

Hyde Park

Park Ln.

Park Ln.

Piccadilly

Kensington Palace

The Serpentine

SEE NOTTING HILL & BAYSWATER MAP p. 312

Kensington Rd.

Knightsbridge

Grosvenor Pl.

ton High St.

Court Rd.

ll Rd.

Gloucester Rd.

KNIGHTSBRIDGE

20

19

Cromwell Rd.

Brompton Rd.

Beauchamp

Sloane St.

Belgrave Sq.

Pont St.

BROMPTON

Eaton Sq.

Eccleston

BELGRAVIA

Buckingham Palace

Victoria

SOUTH KENSINGTON

18

Sydney St.

CHELSEA

Pimlico Rd.

Ebury

SEE MAYFAIR MAP p. 302

Earl's Court Exhibition Building

Redcliffe Gdns.

Finborough Rd.

Fulham Rd.

17

16

Oakley St.

Royal Hospital Rd.

Chelsea Embankment

Brompton Cemetery

13

14

Cheyne Walk

Thames River

Queenstown

15

12

Harwood Rd.

Albert Bridge Rd.

Battersea Park

ALTHAM GREEN

Wandsworth Bridge Rd.

Westbridge Bridge Rd.

Battersea Bridge Rd.

South Park

Lombard Rd.

BATTERSEA

Battersea Park Rd.

Silverthorne Rd.

Lakchmere Rd.

Queenstown Rd.

Lavender Hill

Clapham Junction

SEE EARL'S COURT & KENSINGTON MAP p. 314

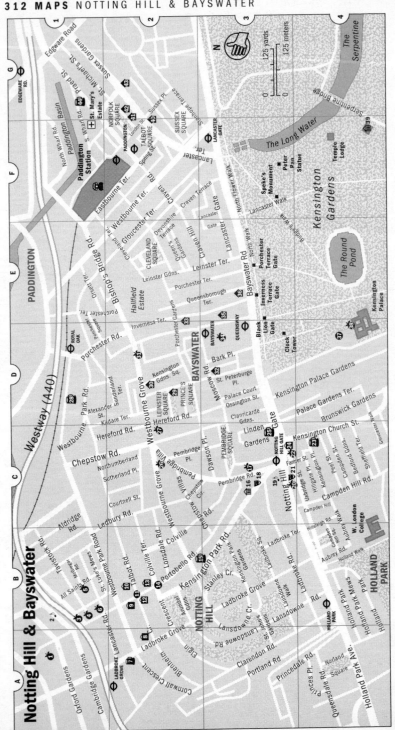

Notting Hill & Bayswater

Notting Hill & Bayswater

ACCOMMODATIONS

Barry House Hotel, 40	F2
Compton Hotel, 42	G2
Dean Court Hotel, 33	D2
Garden Court Hotel, 30	D2
Hyde Park Hostel, 35	E3
Hyde Park House, 32	D3
Hyde Park Rooms Hotel, 43	G2
Lords Hotel, 29	D2
Milliard's Hotel, 42	G2
Quest Hotel, 36	E3
Ruddimans Hotel, 41	G2
Tyburn Hotel, 42	G2

CLUBS & MUSIC

Notting Hill Arts Club, 19	C3
Subterania, 2	B1

MUSEUMS

Serpentine Gallery, 39	F4
Special Photographer Company, 16	C3

SHOPPING

Books for Cooks, 8	A2
Honest Jon's, 13	B2
Intoxica, 9	B2
Music and Video Exchange, 24	C3
Rough Trade, 10	B2
The Travel Bookshop, 12	B2

PUBS

192, 15	B2
Fountain's Abbey, 44	G1
Ion, 7	A2
Pharmacy, 25	C3
The Churchill Arms, 23	C4
The Westbourne, 28	D1

THEATRES & FILM HOUSES

Gate Cinema, 21	C3
The Gate, 18	C3

FOOD

Cockney's, 3	B1
Coconut Grove, 5	B1
Geale's, 22	C3
Jewel of Siam, 27	C2
Khan's, 31	D2
Makan, 4	B1
Mandola Café and Restaurant, 26	C2
Manzara, 17	C3
Rotisserie Jules, 20	C3
Royal China, 34	D4
The Grain Shop, 6	B1
The Orangery Tea Room, 38	D4

SIGHTS

Diana Fountain, 37	D4
Portobello Market, 11	B2

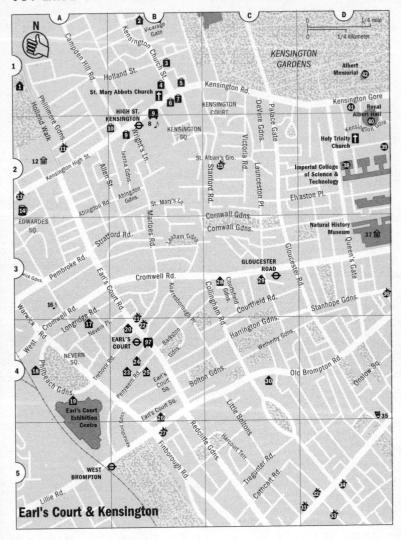

Earl's Court & Kensington

Earl's Court & Kensington

🏠 ACCOMMODATIONS

Abbey House Hotel, 2	B1
Ashburn Hotel, 29	C3
Ayers Rock Hotel, 17	A4
Beaver Hotel, 18	A4
Court Hotel, 20	B4
Half Moon Hotel, 26	B4
Hotel Europe, 28	C4
Lord Jim Hotel, 25	B4
Mowbray Court Hotel, 23	B4
Oxford Hotel, 24	B4
Philbeach Hotel, 19	A4
Queen Alexandra's House, 20	B4
Swiss Hotel, 30	C4
Vicarage Hotel, 2	B1
YHA Holland House, 1	A1

🎭 THEATRES & FILM HOUSES

Ciné Lumière, 35	D4

🍎 FOOD

Apadana, 13	A2
Café Floris, 36	D3
Chelsea Bun Dinner, 33	D5
Lomo, 31	D5
Perry's Bakery, 22	B4
Saffron, 32	D5
Sticky Fingers Café, 11	A2
Troubadour Coffee House, 26	B5
Vingt-Quatre, 34	D5
Wódka, 15	C2

🏛 MUSEUMS

Commonwealth Institute, 12	A2
Natural History Museum, 37	D3

🎵 CLUBS & MUSIC

606 Club, 16	A3
Roof Gardens, 8	B2

🛍 SHOPPING

Amazon, 4	B1
Big Apple, 9	B2
Hope and Glory, 3	B1
Hype Designer Forum, 5	B1
Next, 10	B2
Office, 6	B1
Urban Outfitters, 7	B1

🔴 SIGHTS

Albert Memorial, 42	D1
Imperial College of Science, 38	D2
Royal Albert Hall, 40	D2
Royal College of Art, 41	D1
Royal College of Music, 39	D2

🍺 PUBS

The Scarsdale, 14	A2

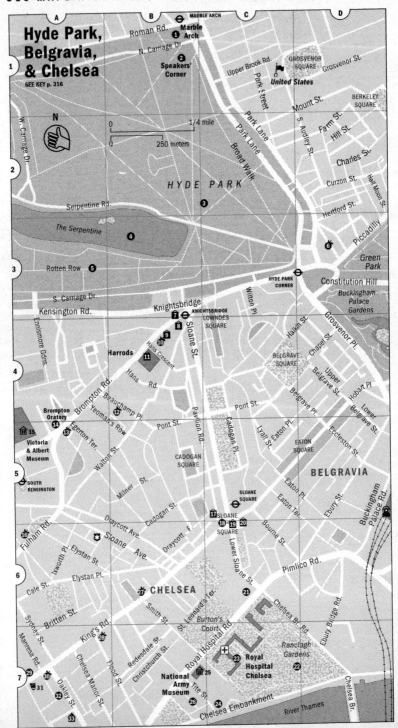

Hyde Park, Belgravia, & Chelsea

SEE KEY p. 316

Hyde Park, Belgravia, & Chelsea

● SIGHTS

Brompton Oratory, 14	A5
Carlyle's House, 32	A7
Chelsea Old Church, 24	C7
Chelsea Psysic Garden, 21	C6
Cheyne Walk, Cheyne Row, and Tite Street, 26	B7
Hyde Park, 3	C2
Marble Arch, 1	B1
Ranleigh Gardens, 22	C7
Rotten Row, 5	A3
Royal Hospital, 23	C7
Serpentine Lake, 4	B4
Sloane Square, 18	C6
Speakers' Corner, 2	B1
World's End, 29	A7

■ SHOPPING

Harrod's, 11	B4
Harvey Nichols, 7	B3
Jigsaw, 9	B4
King's Road, 20	C6
Kookai, 8	B4
Patrick Cox, 17	C5
Peter Jones, 19	C5

● FOOD

Arco Bars, 10	B4
Beverly Hills Bakery, 13	A5
Borshich 'N' Tears, 12	B4
Borshtch 'N' Cheers, 28	A7
Chelsea Kitchen, 27	B6
My Old Dutch Pancake House, 30	A7

● THEATRES & FILM HOUSES

Man in the Moon, 31	A7

▥ MUSEUMS

National Army Museum, 25	B7
Victoria & Albert, 15	A5

Hampstead

● SIGHTS

Admiral House, 3
Burgh House, 4
Church Row, 8
Fenton House, 2
Golders Green Crematorium, 1
Golders Hill Park, 7
Hampstead Heath, 19
Highgate Cemetary, 21
Keats House, 15
The Grove, 22
Two Willow Road, 12
Vale of Heath, 18

● FOOD

Al's Deli, 10
Bar Room Bar, 13
Giraffe, 14
Le Crèperie de Hampstead, 11
Polly's Café/Tea Room, 16

▤ PUBS

The Holly Bush, 5

▥ MUSEUMS

Fread Museum, 9
Iveagh Bequest, 20

● THEATRES & FILM HOUSES

New End Theatre, 6

♪ CLUBS & MUSIC

Forum, 17

● ACCOMMODATIONS

Hampstead Heath Hostel, 2

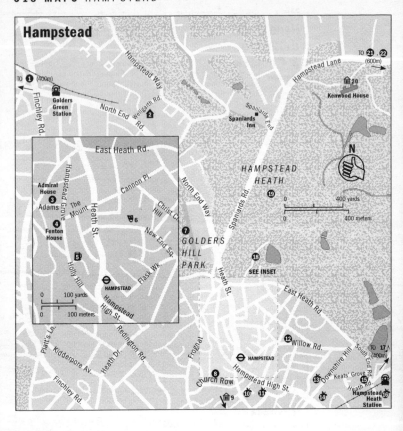

Hampstead

Hampstead Way

TO ① (400m)

Finchley Rd.

Golders
Green
Station

North End Rd.

Wellgarth Rd.

②

Spaniards End

Spaniards
Inn

Hampstead Lane

TO ㉑ , ㉒
(600m)

🏛 20

Kenwood House

East Heath Rd.

*HAMPSTEAD
HEATH*

N

Admiral
House
③

Adams

Hampstead Grove

The Mount

Heath St.

Cannon Pl.

Christ Ch. Hill

🍴 6

New End Sq.

North End Way

⑦

*GOLDERS
HILL
PARK*

19

0   400 yards

0   400 meters

④
Fenton
House

⑤

Holly Hill

🚇 HAMPSTEAD

Flask Wk.

Spaniards Rd.

Heath St.

18

SEE INSET

0   100 yards

0   100 meters

Platt's Ln.

Kidderpore Av.

Heath Dr.

Redington Rd.

Hampstead High St.

Frognal

East Heath Rd.

12 Willow Rd.

Finchley Rd.

Church Row

Hampstead High St.

🚇 HAMPSTEAD

⑧

🏛 9

10

11

Downshire Hill

South End Rd.

Keats' Grove

13

TO 17
(400m)

15

14

Heath Rd.

🏨 Hampstead
Heath
Station

16

Hampstead

⚫ **SIGHTS**

Admiral House, 3
Burgh House, 4
Church Row, 8
Fenton House, 2
Golders Green Crematorium, 1
Golders Hill Park, 7
Hampstead Heath, 19
Highgate Cemetary, 21
Keats House, 15
The Grove, 22
Two Willow Road, 12
Vale of Heath, 18

🍎 **FOOD**

Al's Deli, 10
Bar Room Bar, 13
Giraffe, 14
Le Crèperie de Hampstead, 11
Polly's Café/Tea Room, 16

🍺 **PUBS**

The Holly Bush, 5

🏛 **MUSEUMS**

Fread Museum, 9
Iveagh Bequest, 20

🎭 **THEATRES & FILM HOUSES**

New End Theatre, 6

🎵 **CLUBS & MUSIC**

Forum, 17

🏠 **ACCOMMODATIONS**

Hampstead Heath Hostel, 2

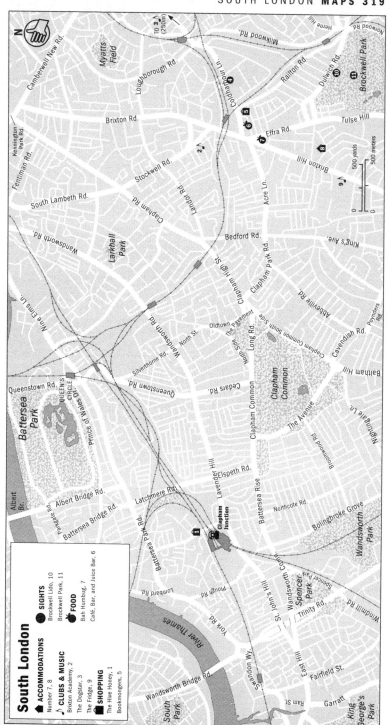

South London

♦ **ACCOMMODATIONS**
Number 7, 8

♪ **CLUBS & MUSIC**
Brixton Academy, 2
The Dogstar, 3
The Fridge, 9

■ **SHOPPING**
The Hive Honey, 1
Bookmongers, 5

● **SIGHTS**
Brockwell Lido, 10
Brockwell Park, 11

● **FOOD**
Bah Humbug, 7
Café, Bar, and Juice Bar, 6

Camberwell New Rd.
Myatts Field
Loughborough Rd.
Brixton Rd.
Kennington Park Rd.
Fentiman Rd.
South Lambeth Rd.
Wandsworth Rd.
Stockwell Rd.
Clapham Rd.
Landor Rd.
Larkhall Park
Coldharbour Ln.
Milkwood Rd.
Heme Hill
Norwood Rd.
Railton Rd.
Dulwich Rd.
Brockwell Park
Effra Rd.
Tulse Hill
Brixton Hill
Acre Ln.
Bedford Rd.
King's Ave.
Clapham Park Rd.
Abbeville Rd.
Cavendish Rd.
Balham Hill
Nightingale Ln.
Powders Rd.
Clapham High St.
Oldtown
The Pavement
North Side
North St.
Long Rd.
Clapham Common South Side
Clapham Common
The Avenue
Bromwood Rd.
Cedars Rd.
Nine Elms Ln.
Queenstown Rd.
QUEEN'S CIRCLE
Prince of Wales Dr.
Battersea Park
Albert Br.
Pakgate Rd.
Albert Bridge Rd.
Battersea Bridge Rd.
Wandsworth Rd.
Silverthorne Rd.
North St.
Latchmere Rd.
Battersea Park Rd.
Lavender Hill
Clapham Junction
Elspeth Rd.
Battersea Rise
Northcote Rd.
Bolingbroke Grove
Wandsworth Park
Lombard Rd.
Plough Rd.
York Rd.
Wandsworth Bridge Rd.
River Thames
South Park
Swandon Wy.
St. John's Hill
Wandsworth Comm.
Spencer Park
Spencer Park
Trinity Rd.
Windmill Rd.
East Hill
Fairfield St.
Ram St.
Garratt
King George's Park

TO 3 (250m)

500 yards 500
500 meters 500
0 0

N

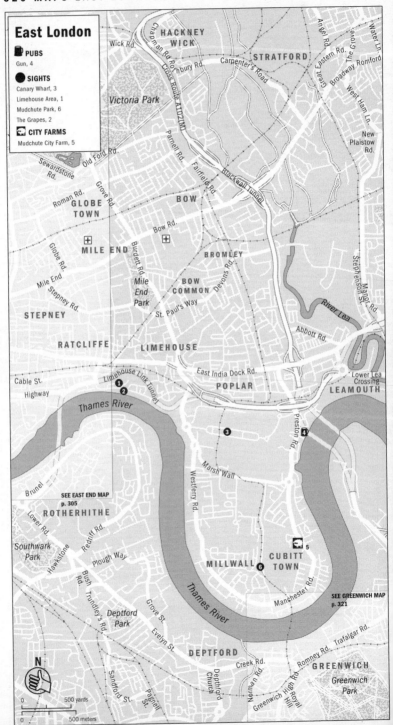

East London

🍺 **PUBS**
Gun, 4

⚫ **SIGHTS**
Canary Wharf, 3
Limehouse Area, 1
Mudchute Park, 6
The Grapes, 2

🏠 **CITY FARMS**
Mudchute City Farm, 5

Wick Rd.

HACKNEY WICK

STRATFORD

Chapman Rd. Rothbury Rd.

Carpenter's Road

Cross Route A102(M)

Great Eastern Rd.

Broadway The Grove Romford

Angel Rd.

Water Ln.

West Ham Ln.

New Plaistow Rd.

Victoria Park

Old Ford Rd.

Sewardstone Rd.

Roman Rd.

Parnell Rd.

Fairfield Rd.

Blackwall Tunnel

GLOBE TOWN

Grove Rd.

BOW

Bow Rd.

Globe Rd.

MILE END

Burdett Rd.

BROMLEY

Devons Rd.

River Lea

Mile End Rd.

Stepney Rd.

Mile End Park

BOW COMMON

St. Paul's Way

Abbott Rd.

Stephenson St.

Mary St.

STEPNEY

RATCLIFFE

LIMEHOUSE

East India Dock Rd.

POPLAR

Lower Lea Crossing

LEAMOUTH

Cable St.

Highway

Limehouse Link Tunnel

❶❷

Thames River

Preston Rd.

❹

Brunel

SEE EAST END MAP
p. 305

ROTHERHITHE

Lower Rd.

Rediff Rd.

❸

Marsh Wall

Westferry Rd.

Southwark Park

Hawkstone

Plough Way

Bush Rd.

Trundley's Rd.

Deptford Park

Grove St.

Evelyn St.

MILLWALL

CUBITT TOWN

🏠 5

❻

Manchester Rd.

SEE GREENWICH MAP
p. 321

Thames River

Creek Rd.

Deptford Church

Norman Rd.

Romney Rd.

Trafalgar Rd.

DEPTFORD

Sandford St.

Pagnall St.

Greenwich High Rd.

Royal Hill

GREENWICH

Greenwich Park

N

0 ___ 500 yards

0 ___ 500 meters

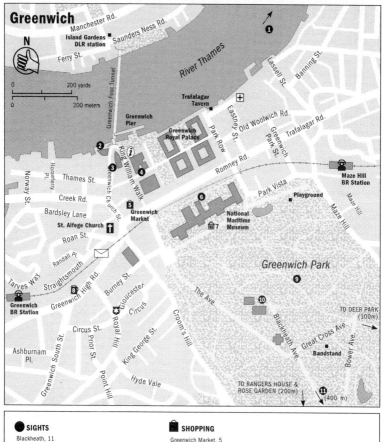

Greenwich

N

0 200 yards
0 200 meters

Manchester Rd.
Island Gardens
DLR station
Saunders Ness Rd.
Ferry St.

River Thames

Lassell St.
Banning St.

Greenwich Foot Tunnel

Trafalagar
Tavern

Old Woolwich Rd.

Greenwich
Pier

Eastney St.
Park Row

Greenwich Park St.
Trafalagar Rd.

Greenwich
Royal Palace

Romney Rd.

Maze Hill
BR Station

Norway St.

Horseferry Pl.

Thames St.

Greenwich Church St.

King William Walk

Park Vista

Maze Hill

Creek Rd.

Bardsley Lane

Greenwich
Market

Playground

St. Alfege Church

Roan St.

National
Maritime
Museum

Randall Pl.

Straightsmouth

Tarves Way

Greenwich High Rd.

Burney St.

Gloucester
Circus

Greenwich Park

Greenwich
BR Station

Circus St.

Royal Hill

King George St.

Point Hill

Prior St.

Croom's Hill

The Ave.

Blackheath Ave.

TO DEER PARK
(100m)

Ashburnam
Pl.

Greenwich South St.

Hyde Vale

Great Cross Ave.

Bandstand

Bower Ave.

TO RANGERS HOUSE &
ROSE GARDEN (200m)

(400 m)

SIGHTS
Blackheath, 11
Cutty Sark, 3
Gipsy Moth, 2
Greenwich Park, 9
Queen's House, 6
Royal Naval College, 4
Royal Observatory, 10
Thames barrier, 1

SHOPPING
Greenwich Market, 5

PUBS
North Pole, 8

MUSEUMS
National Maritime Museum, 7

ABOUT LET'S GO

FORTY YEARS OF WISDOM

As a new millennium arrives, *Let's Go: Europe*, now in its 41st edition and translated into seven languages, reigns as the world's bestselling international travel guide. For over four decades, travelers criss-crossing the Continent have relied on *Let's Go* for inside information on the hippest backstreet cafes, the most pristine secluded beaches, and the best routes from border to border. In the last 20 years, our rugged researchers have stretched the frontiers of backpacking and expanded our coverage into Asia, Africa, Australia, and the Americas. This year, we've introduced a new city guide series with titles to San Francisco and our hometown, Boston. Now, our seven city guides feature sharp photos, more maps, and an overall more user-friendly design. We've also returned to our roots with the inaugural edition of *Let's Go: Western Europe*.

It all started in 1960 when a handful of well-traveled students at Harvard University handed out a 20-page mimeographed pamphlet offering a collection of their tips on budget travel to passengers on student charter flights to Europe. The following year, in response to the instant popularity of the first volume, students traveling to Europe researched the first full-fledged edition of *Let's Go: Europe*, a pocket-sized book featuring honest, practical advice, witty writing, and a decidedly youthful slant on the world. Throughout the 60s and 70s, our guides reflected the times. In 1969 we taught travelers how to get from Paris to Prague on "no dollars a day" by singing in the street. In the 80s and 90s, we looked beyond Europe and North America and set off to all corners of the earth. Meanwhile, we focused in on the world's most exciting urban areas to produce in-depth, fold-out map guides. Our new guides bring the total number of titles to 51, each infused with the spirit of adventure and voice of opinion that travelers around the world have come to count on. But some things never change: our guides are still researched, written, and produced entirely by students who know first-hand how to see the world on the cheap.

HOW WE DO IT

Each guide is completely revised and thoroughly updated every year by a well-traveled set of nearly 300 students. Every spring, we recruit over 200 researchers and 90 editors to overhaul every book. After several months of training, researcher-writers hit the road for seven weeks of exploration, from Anchorage to Adelaide, Estonia to El Salvador, Iceland to Indonesia. Hired for their rare combination of budget travel sense, writing ability, stamina, and courage, these adventurous travelers know that train strikes, stolen luggage, food poisoning, and marriage proposals are all part of a day's work. Back at our offices, editors work from spring to fall, massaging copy written on Himalayan bus rides into witty, informative prose. A student staff of typesetters, cartographers, publicists, and managers keeps our lively team together. In September, the collected efforts of the summer are delivered to our printer, who turns them into books in record time, so that you have the most up-to-date information available for your vacation. Even as you read this, work on next year's editions is well underway.

WHY WE DO IT

We don't think of budget travel as the last recourse of the destitute; we believe that it's the only way to travel. Living cheaply and simply brings you closer to the people and places you've been saving up to visit. Our books will ease your anxieties and answer your questions about the basics—so you can get off the beaten track and explore. Once you learn the ropes, we encourage you to put *Let's Go* down now and then to strike out on your own. You know as well as we that the best discoveries are often those you make yourself. When you find something worth sharing, please drop us a line. We're Let's Go Publications, 67 Mount Auburn St., Cambridge, MA 02138, USA (email: feedback@letsgo.com). For more info, visit our website, www.letsgo.com.

Find Yourself. Somewhere Else.

Don't just land there, do something. Away.com is the Internet's preferred address for those who like their travel with a little something extra. Our team of travel enthusiasts and experts can help you design your ultimate adventure, nature or cultural escape. Make Away.com your destination for extraordinary travel. Then find yourself. Somewhere else.

Will you have enough stories to tell your grandchildren?

Yahoo! Travel

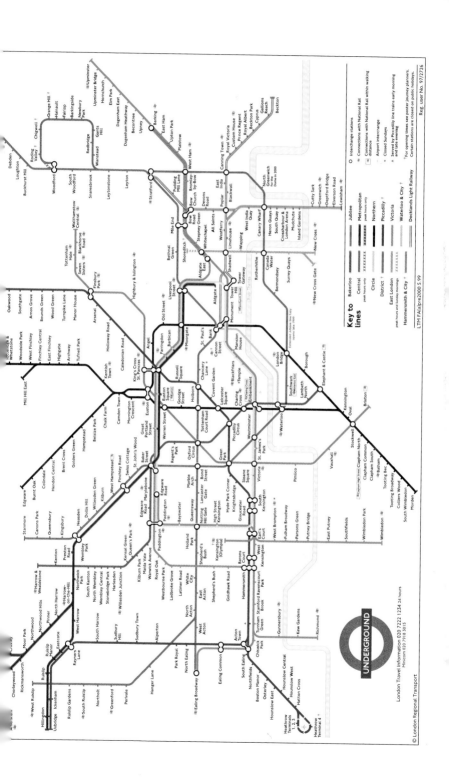

London

King's Cross Station

Pentonville Rd.

City Rd.

St. Pancras Station

King's Cross Rd.

Gray's Inn Rd.

Judd St.

Coram's Fields

Guilford St.

Woburn Pl.

Southampton Row

Roseberry Ave.

St. John's St.

Goswell Rd.

Lever St.

Bath St.

East Road

Hoxton St.

Old St.

City Rd.

Kingsland Rd.

Gt. Eastern St.

Shoreditch High St.

Commercial St.

Theobalds Rd.

Clerkenwell Rd.

Farringdon Rd.

Aldersgate

Barbican Centre

Liverpool St. Station

Holborn

New Oxford St.

High

Kingsway

Chancery La.

Charterhouse St.

Smithfield Market

London Wall

Moorgate

Bishopsgate

Houndsditch

Drury La.

Aldwych

Fetter La.

Holborn Viaduct

Newgate St.

Old Bailey

St. Paul's

Bank of England

Cheapside

Cornhill

Leadenhall St.

Fenchurch St.

Law Courts

Fleet St.

Queen Victoria St.

Cannon St.

Gracechurch St.

St. Eastcheap

National Gallery

Strand

Victoria Embankment

Blackfriars Br.

Blackfriars Station

Cannon St. Station

Upper Thames St.

The Tower

Tower Hill

Charing Cross Stn.

National Theatre

Southwark Br.

London Br.

Tower Br.

Whitehall

Waterloo Br.

Stamford St.

Southwark St.

River Thames

Todley St.

Royal Festival Hall

York Rd.

Waterloo Rd.

The Cut

Blackfriars Rd.

Union St.

St. Thomas St.

London Bridge Station

Westminster Br.

Waterloo Station

Long La.

Bridge Rd.

Abbey St.

Houses of Parliament

Lambeth Palace Rd.

Westminster Br. Rd.

Borough Rd.

London Rd.

Borough High St.

Great Dover St.

Harper Rd.

Tabard St.

Tower Bridge Rd.

Millbank

Lambeth Rd.

Kennington Rd.

Imperial War Museum

New Kent Rd.

Willow Walk

Lambeth Br.

rry Rd.

Albert Embankment

Black Prince Rd.

Kennington Park Rd.

Crampton St.

Manor Pl.

Rodney Pl.

Flint St.

East St.

Old Kent Rd.

Walworth Rd.

Thurlow St.

Portland St.

Albany Rd.

Kennington La.

Braganza St.

Vauxhall Station

Vauxhall Br.

Kennington Oval

N

0 ——— 1/2 mile

0 ——— 1/2 kilometer

Westminster and Whitehall

Piccadilly

Jermyn St.

ST. JAMES'S SQUARE

Lower Regent St.

Waterloo Place

National Gallery

Nelson's Column

CHARING CROSS STATION

Craven St.

TRAFALGAR SQUARE

Northumberland Ave.

St. James's St.

King St.

GREEN PARK

Pall Mall

Carlton House Tr.

Admiralty Arch

Whitehall

Gt. Scotland Yard

Whitehall Pl.

Old War Office

Marlborough House

Carlton House

The Mall

Admiralty

Banqueting House

Horse Guards Parade

Defence

Victoria Embankment

St. James's Palace

St. James's Park

Clarence House

Horse Guards Rd.

Treasury

Lancaster House

Downing St.

Foreign Office

King Charles St.

WEST-MINSTER

Queen Victoria Memorial

Cabinet War Rooms

Parliament St.

Westminster Br.

Buckingham Palace

Birdcage Walk

Anne's Gate

Old Queen St.

Great George St.

Margaret St.

Wellington Barracks

ST. JAMES'S PARK

Queen

Dartmouth St.

PARLIAMENT SQUARE

Houses of Parliament

Gate

Petty France

Broadway

Tothill St.

Westminster Abbey

Abingdon St.

Palace St.

Buckingham Gate

Castle Lane

Caxton St.

Victoria St.

Great Smith St.

Victoria Tower Gardens

Victoria St.

Thirleby Rd.

Strutton Ground

Great Peter St.

Carlisle Pl.

Westminster Cathedral

Rochester Row

Horseferry Rd.

Marsham St.

SMITH SQUARE

Lambeth Br.

Francis St.

VINCENT SQUARE

Regency St.

Page St.

Thames House

Wilton Rd.

Vincent St.

John Islip St.

Warwick Way

Tachbrook St.

Vauxhall Bridge Rd.

Erasmus St.

Tate Gallery

Belgrave Rd.

Denbigh St.

Caxton St.

Millbank

River Thames

St. George's Dr.

PIMLICO

Lupus St.

Claverton St.

Vauxhall Bridge

Albert Embankment

N

0   1/8 mile

0   125 meters

Soho and Covent Garden

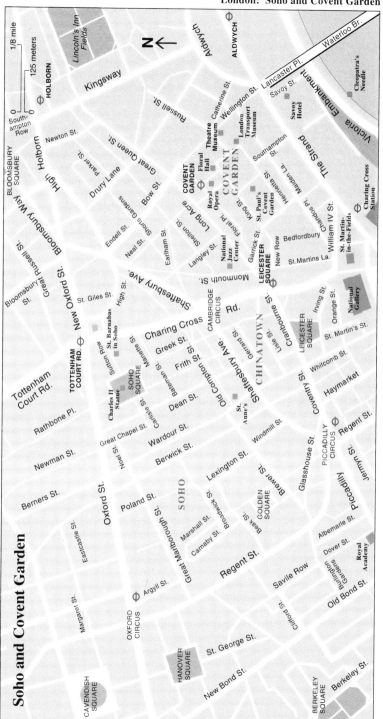

London: Soho and Covent Garden

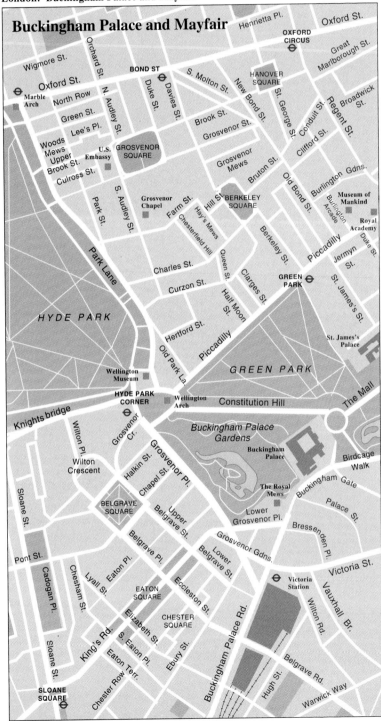

Buckingham Palace and Mayfair

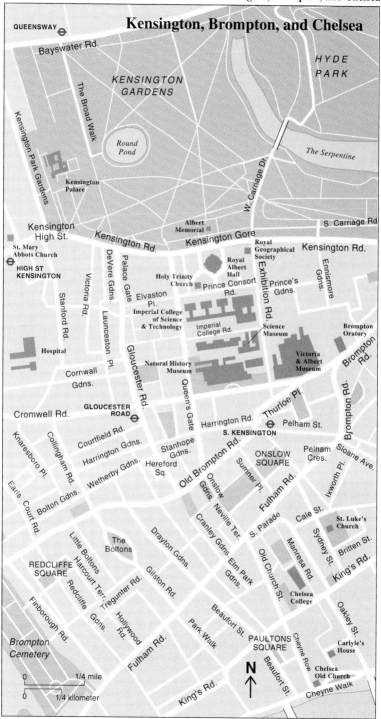

Kensington, Brompton, and Chelsea

London: City of London

The City

Leman St.

Commercial St.

Mansell St.

ALDGATE EAST

Widegate St.

Middlesex St.

Minories

Royal Mint St.

E. Smithfield

St. Katharine's Way

Tower Br. Approach

Tower Br.

ALDGATE

Aldgate

Houndsditch

Fenchurch St. Station

Pepys St.

TOWER HILL

TRINITY SQUARE

Tower Hill

Liverpool St. Station

St. Mary Axe

Fenchurch St.

Seething La.

All Hallows

The Tower

Tower Pier

Bishopsgate

Old Broad St.

London Stock Exchange

Leadenhall St.

Lloyd's

Leadenhall Market

Mark La.

Mincing La.

St. Olave's

St. Dunstan's

Gt. Tower St.

Lower Thames St.

Billingsgate Market

HMS Belfast

Sun St.

South Pl.

Threadneedle St.

Gracechurch St.

Lime St.

St. Mary at Hill

The Monument

St. Mary Axe

Throgmorton Ave.

Bank of England

Cornhill

Lombard St.

Eastcheap

Monument

St. Magnus Martyr

Chiswell St.

Ropemaker St.

MOORGATE

FINSBURY CIRCUS

London Wall

Moorfields

St. Margaret's

Lothbury

BANK

Princes St.

King William St.

St. Mary Abchurch

MONUMENT

London Br.

Silk St.

Fore St.

Moorgate

Coleman St.

Bassinghall Ave.

Basinghall St.

Poultry

St. Stephen Walbrook

Walbrook

Temple of Mithras

CANNON

Cannon St. Station

Southwark Br.

Beech St.

Barbican Centre

St. Giles without Cripplegate

Museum of London

Guildhall

Gresham St.

King St.

Mansion House

Queen St.

Cloak La.

Cannon St.

Aldersgate St.

London Wall

Wood St.

Milk St.

St. Mary le Bow

Watling St.

Bread St.

MANSION HOUSE

St. Mary Aldermary

Cannon St.

River Thames

BARBICAN

St. Bartholomew the Great

Little Britain

Cheapside

New Chance

St. Martin's-Le-Grand

Newgate St.

ST. PAUL'S

St. Paul's Cathedral

St. Andrew-by-the-Wardrobe

Queen Victoria St.

Upper Thames St.

FARRINGDON

Smithfield Market

Long Lane

West Smithfield

Giltspur St.

Holborn Viaduct Station

Warwick La.

Old Bailey

St. Mary

St. Benet's

Puddle Dock

Blackfriars Station

St. John St.

Snow Hill

Holborn Viaduct

Old Bailey

Fleet La.

LUDGATE CIRCUS

Ludgate Hill

New Bridge St.

BLACKFRIARS

Blackfriars Br.

Cowcross St.

Farringdon Rd.

St. Bride St.

Fleet St.

GOUGH SQ.

Tudor St.

Temple Ave.

Clerkenwell Rd.

Ely Pl

Shoe Lane

Temple Church

Victoria Embankment

Hatton Garden

Greville St.

New Fetter La.

Fetter La.

Middle Temple La.

The Temple

N

1/4 mile

1/4 km

0